Lecture Notes in Computer Science   9300

Commenced Publication in 1973
Founding and Former Series Editors:
Gerhard Goos, Juris Hartmanis, and Jan van Leeuwen

More information about this series at http://www.springer.com/series/7408

Lev D. Beklemishev · Andreas Blass
Nachum Dershowitz · Bernd Finkbeiner
Wolfram Schulte (Eds.)

Fields of Logic
and Computation II

Essays Dedicated to Yuri Gurevich
on the Occasion of His 75th Birthday

 Springer

Editors

Lev D. Beklemishev
Steklov Mathematical Institute
Moscow
Russia

Andreas Blass
University of Michigan
Ann Arbor, MI
USA

Nachum Dershowitz
Tel Aviv University
Tel Aviv
Israel

Bernd Finkbeiner
Universität des Saarlandes
Saarbrücken
Germany

Wolfram Schulte
Microsoft Research
Redmond, WA
USA

Cover illustration: The cover illustration is a "Boaz" Plate created by Maurice Ascalon's Pal-Bell Company circa 1948. Image and artwork copyright Prof. Shalom Sabar, Jerusalem. Used by permission. The Hebrew legend is from the Book of Psalms 126:5: "They that sow in tears shall reap in joy."

ISSN 0302-9743   ISSN 1611-3349   (electronic)
Lecture Notes in Computer Science
ISBN 978-3-319-23533-2   ISBN 978-3-319-23534-9   (eBook)
DOI 10.1007/978-3-319-23534-9

Library of Congress Control Number: 2015947108

LNCS Sublibrary: SL2 – Programming and Software Engineering

Printed on acid-free paper

Springer International Publishing AG Switzerland is part of Springer Science+Business Media
(www.springer.com)

Yuri Gurevich (June 2004 in Kraków, Poland)
Photograph taken by Adam Walanus.

Preface

This Festschrift is published in honor of Yuri Gurevich, on the occasion of his 75th birthday. Yuri Gurevich has made fundamental contributions to the broad spectrum of logic and computer science, including decision procedures, the monadic theory of order, abstract state machines, formal methods, foundations of computer science, security, and much more. Many of these areas are reflected in the articles in this Festschrift and in the presentations at the "Yurifest" symposium, which was held in Berlin, Germany, on September 11 and 12, 2015.

Yuri has spent his life in three different countries—the Soviet Union, Israel, and the USA—and has worked in at least as many scientific fields: on the interface between algebra and logic in the Soviet Union, on the monadic theory of order in Israel, and on logic and computer science in the USA. As Yuri would point out, with characteristic understatement, he has "always had a taste for foundational questions."[1]

The best known work of Yuri's Soviet period is on the decision problem for the ordered abelian groups. His 1964 thesis proved the decidability of the first-order theory of these groups; later, he showed the decidability of the richer theory that includes quantification over convex subgroups. Yuri also worked on the decision problem for first-order logic, completing in particular the decision problem for the prefix-vocabulary fragments of pure logic of predicates and functions. In Israel, Yuri worked with Saharon Shelah on the monadic theory of linear orders. The Forgetful Determinacy Theorem of Gurevich and Harrington is from this period as well. The theorem asserts the existence of a special kind of winning strategy in a class of infinite games, and has lead to a greatly simplified proof of Michael Rabin's result that the monadic theory of two successors is decidable.

In 1982, the University of Michigan hired Yuri as a professor of computer science on the promise that the algebraist and logician would become a computer scientist. And, indeed, Yuri immediately began making deep contributions to his new field. There are numerous results in complexity theory, in particular on average-case complexity. Yuri also worked on many questions on the interface between logic and computer science, including the introduction, together with Erich Grädel, of metafinite model theory, and the formulation of the conjecture that there is no logic that captures polynomial time computability on unordered structures.

Yuri felt that, while many foundational questions in mathematical logic had been settled, the foundational questions about computer science and the nature of computation were still wide open. To answer some of these questions, Yuri invented abstract state machines (ASMs). Unlike most other formal methods at the time, ASMs are operational, rather than declarative. Yuri's "ASM thesis" states that every algorithm can be faithfully represented as an ASM. In 1998, Jim Kajiya at Microsoft Research

---

[1] Yuri Gurevich. *Logician in the land of OS: Abstract State Machines in Microsoft.* Invited talk at LICS 2001.

realized the potential of ASMs and invited Yuri to start a new group, the Foundations of Software Engineering (FSE) group. At Microsoft, Yuri made many contributions involving ASMs, including the notion of "choiceless polynomial time" computation, and also many other contributions to computer science topics not directly related to ASMs, such as efficient file transfer, software testing, security, and authorization.

To a great number of researchers in algebra, logic, and computer science, Yuri Gurevich is a unique integrating figure, a cherished colleague, and a dear friend. In 2010, on the occasion of Yuri's 70th birthday, a symposium took place in Brno, the Czech Republic, that brought together many of Yuri's collaborators. Now, five years later, we have again asked Yuri's colleagues to come together for a symposium and to contribute to a volume in his honor. This Festschrift is the result of this effort. The articles cover a wide range of topics and still merely give a glimpse of the scope and depth of Yuri's many areas of interest.

The Yurifest symposium was co-located with the 24th EACSL Annual Conference on Computer Science Logic (CSL 2015). The editors would like to thank the organizers of CSL for their help with many practical issues. The symposium received generous support from the German Research Foundation (DFG) and from Microsoft Research. Thanks are also due to the anonymous referees of the contributions to this volume, and, last but not least, to the contributors for their immediate and enthusiastic commitment to participating in the second Yurifest.

To Yuri Gurevich, the great logician in the land of OS, with deep admiration, gratitude, and affection. Happy birthday!

July 2015

Lev D. Beklemishev
Andreas Blass
Nachum Dershowitz
Bernd Finkbeiner
Wolfram Schulte

Contents

K-trivial, K-low and *MLR*-low Sequences: A Tutorial

Laurent Bienvenu[1]($^{(\boxtimes)}$) and Alexander Shen[2]

[1] LIAFA, CNRS, University Paris Diderot – Paris 7, Paris, France
laurent.bienvenu@computability.fr
[2] University of Montpellier, CNRS, on Leave from IITP RAS, Montpellier, France
alexander.shen@lirmm.fr

Abstract. A remarkable achievement in algorithmic randomness and algorithmic information theory was the discovery of the notions of K-trivial, K-low and Martin-Löf-random-low sets: three different definitions turn out to be equivalent for very non-trivial reasons [1,3,5]. This survey, based on the course taught by one of the authors (L.B.) in Poncelet laboratory (CNRS, Moscow) in 2014, provides an exposition of the proof of this equivalence and some related results.

We assume that the reader is familiar with basic notions of algorithmic information theory (see, e.g., [7] for introduction and [8] for more detailed exposition). More information about the subject and its history can be found in [2,6].

1 Notation

We consider the Cantor space $\mathbb{B}^{\mathbb{N}}$ of infinite binary sequences $a_0 a_1 \ldots$; points in this space are idendified with sets (each sequence is considered as a characteristic sequence of a set of natural numbers) or paths in the full binary tree (nodes are elements of $\mathbb{B}^*$, i.e., binary strings; a sequence a is a path going through its prefixes $(a)_n = a_0 a_1 \ldots a_{n-1}$). We denote plain Kolmogorov complexity by $C(x)$; we use $C(x, y)$ to denote complexity of pairs and $C(x \mid y)$ for conditional complexity. The arguments x, y here are binary strings, natural numbers (that are often identified with binary strings using a standard bijection) or some other finite objects. Similar notation with K instead of C is used for prefix complexity.

By $\mathbf{m}(x)$ we denote the discrete a priori probability of x, the largest lower semicomputable semimeasure on $\mathbb{N}$; it is equal to $2^{-K(x)}$ up to a $\Theta(1)$-factor. The same notation is used when x is a binary string (identified with the corresponding natural number) or some other finite object.

2 K-trivial Sets: Definition and Existence

Consider an infinite bit sequence and complexities of its prefixes. If they are small, the sequence is computable or almost computable; if they are big, the sequence looks random. This idea goes back to 1960 s and appears in algorithmic

© Springer International Publishing Switzerland 2015
L.D. Beklemishev et al. (Eds.): Gurevich Festschrift II 2015, LNCS 9300, pp. 1–23, 2015.
DOI: 10.1007/978-3-319-23534-9_1

information theory in different forms (Schnorr–Levin criterion of randomness in terms of complexities of prefixes, the notion of algorithmic Hausdorff dimension). The notion of K-triviality is on the low end of this spectrum; here we consider sequences that have prefixes of minimal possible prefix complexity:

Definition 1. *An infinite binary sequence* $a_0 a_1 a_2 \ldots$, *is called K-trivial if its prefixes have minimal possible (up to a constant) prefix complexity, i.e., if*

$$K(a_0 a_1 \ldots a_{n-1}) = K(n) + O(1).$$

Note that n can be reconstructed from $a_0 \ldots a_{n-1}$, so $K(a_0 \ldots a_{n-1})$ cannot be smaller than $K(n) - O(1)$. Note also that every computable sequence is K-trivial, since $a_0 \ldots a_{n-1}$ can be computed given n. These two remarks together show that a K-trivial sequence is very close to being computable. And indeed, if we were to replace prefix complexity by plain complexity C in the definition, the resulting notion, call it C-triviality, would be equivalent to being computable (it is in fact enough to have $C(a_0 a_1 \ldots a_{n-1}) \leqslant \log n + O(1)$ to ensure that $a_0 a_1 a_2 \ldots$ is computable, see for example [8, problems 48 and 49]). Nonetheless, we shall see below that non-computable K-trivial sequences do exist. But before that, let us prove the following result, due to Chaitin.

Theorem 1. *Every K-trivial sequence is $\mathbf{0}'$-computable.*

Here $\mathbf{0}'$ is the oracle for the halting problem.

Proof. Assume that the complexity of the n-bit prefix $(a)_n = a_0 a_1 \ldots a_{n-1}$ is $K(n) + O(1)$. Recall that $(a)_n$ has the same information content as $(n, (a)_n)$, and use the formula for the complexity of a pair:

$$K((a)_n) = K(n, (a)_n) + O(1) = K(n) + K((a)_n \mid n, K(n)) + O(1);$$

This means that

$$K((a)_n \mid n, K(n)) = O(1).$$

So $(a)_n$ belongs to a $\mathbf{0}'$-computable (given n) list of n-bit strings that has size $O(1)$. Therefore, a is a path in a $\mathbf{0}'$-computable tree of bounded width and is $\mathbf{0}'$-computable. Indeed, assume that the tree has k infinite paths that all diverge before some level N. At levels after N we can identify all the paths, since all other nodes have finite subtrees above them, and we may wait until only k candidates remain. $\qquad\square$

The existence of non-computable K-trivial sets is not obvious, but not very difficult to establish, even if we additionally require the set to be enumerable. Here we identify a set A with its characteristic sequence $a_0 a_1 a_2 \ldots$ (where $a_i = 1$ if and only if $i \in A$).

Theorem 2. *There exists an enumerable undecidable K-trivial set.*

This result was proven by Solovay in the 1970s.

Let us make some preparations for this proof which will be useful in the rest of the paper. First, to deal with K-triviality, it is easier to use a priori discrete probability $\mathbf{m}$ instead of K (see, e.g., [7] or [8] for more background on $\mathbf{m}$ and its relation to prefix complexity; recall that $\mathbf{m}(x)$ coincides with $2^{-K(x)}$ up to a $\Theta(1)$-factor). In this setting, a sequence $a_0 a_1 \ldots$ is K-trivial if and only if

$$\mathbf{m}(a_0 a_1 \ldots a_{n-1}) \geq \mathbf{m}(n)/O(1)$$

Since $\mathbf{m}$ is multiplicatively maximal among all lower semicomputable semimeasures, the statement of Theorem 2 can be rephrased as follows:

for every lower semicomputable semimeasure μ, there exist an enumerable set A with its characteristic sequence $a = a_0 a_1 a_2 \ldots$ and a lower semicomputable semimeasure ν such that

$$\nu(a_0 a_1 \ldots a_{n-1}) \geq \mu(n)/O(1).$$

In fact, we need this only for $\mu = \mathbf{m}$, but the argument works for any lower semicomputable semimeasure μ (and in any case the statement for $\mu = \mathbf{m}$ is stronger and implies the same inequality for every μ, though with a different constant in $O(1)$-notation).

Proof. To prove Theorem 2, let us assume that μ is a lower semicomputable semimeasure. We want to build an enumerable set A that corresponds to a sequence $a_0 a_1 a_2 \ldots$, together with a lower semicomputable semimeasure ν such that $\nu(a_0 a_1 \ldots a_{n-1})$ matches $\mu(n)$ up to a multiplicative constant for all n. When we see that μ increases the weight of some n, we should respond by increasing the ν-weight of some node (=string) of length n, achieving the same weight (up to $O(1)$-factor). Moreover, all these nodes should lie on the tree path that corresponds to some enumerable set A.

Doing this would be trivial for a computable sequence a: constructing ν, we just place at $a_0 a_1 \ldots a_{n-1}$ the same weight as the current value of μ at n. This (evidently) gives a semimeasure since the sum of the weights is the same for μ and ν.

But we want A to be non-computable. To achieve this, we will ensure that A is simple in Post's sense. Recall that a simple set is an enumerable set A with infinite complement such that A has non-empty intersection with every W_n that is infinite. Here by W_n we denote the n-th enumerable set in some natural numbering of all (computably) enumerable sets. As in Post's cllassical construction, we want for every n to add some element of W_n greater than $2n$ into A, and then forget about W_n. The bound $2n$ guarantees that A has infinite complement. In Post's construction the elements are added without reservations: as soon as some element that is greater than $2n$ is discovered in W_n, it is added to A. But now, when adding such an element to A, we have to pay something for this action. Indeed, when we add some number u to A, the path in the Cantor space corresponding to it (i.e., A's characteristic sequence) changes.

The ν-weights put on the node $a_0 a_1 \ldots a_{u-1}$ and all its extensions are lost, and should be recreated along the new path (starting from length u). All this lost amount can be called the *cost* of the action.

Now we can explain the construction. Initially our set A is empty, and the corresponding path a in Cantor space is all zeros. Observing the growth of the semimeasure μ, we replicate the corresponding values along a. We also enumerate all W_n in parallel. When a new element u is enumerated into W_n, we add this element to A if the following two conditions are satisfied:

- $u > 2n$;
- the cost of adding u is small, say, less than 2^{-n}, so the total cost for all n is bounded.

Here the *cost of the action* is the total ν-weight we had placed on the nodes along the current path a starting from level u: this weight is lost and needs to be replicated along the new path. In this way the total ν-weight is bounded. Indeed, the lost weight is bounded by $\sum_n 2^{-n}$ (recall that we take care of each W_n at most once), and the replicated weight is bounded by $\sum \mu(n)$.

If W_n is infinite, it contains arbitrarily large elements, and the cost of adding u is bounded by

$$\mu(u) + \mu(u+1) + \mu(u+2) + \ldots,$$

which is guaranteed to go below the 2^{-n} threshold for large u. So for every infinite W_n, some element u of W_n will be added to A at some stage of the construction. As we have seen, the total ν-weight is bounded by $\sum_n \mu(n) + \sum_n 2^{-n}$. By construction, we have $\nu(a_0 a_1 \ldots a_{n-1}) \geq \mu(n)$ for all n. It remains to divide ν by some constant to make the total weight bounded by 1. $\quad\square$

This proof can be represented in a game form. In such a simple case this looks like an overkill, but the same technique is useful in more complicated cases, so it is instructive to look at this version of the proof. The game field consists of the set of the natural numbers (*lengths*), the full binary tree, and sets $W_1, W_2, \ldots$ (of natural numbers). The opponent increases the weights assigned to lengths: each length has some weight that is initially zero and can be increased by the opponent at any moment by any non-negative rational number; the only restriction is that the total weight of all lengths should not exceed 1. Also the opponent may add new elements to any of the sets W_i; initially they are empty. We construct a path a in the binary tree that is a characteristic sequence of some set A, initially empty, by adding elements to A; we also increase the weights of nodes of the binary tree in the same way as the opponent does for lengths; our total weight should not exceed 2.

One should also specify when the players can make moves. It is not important, since the rules of the game always allow each player to postpone moves. Let us agree that the players make their moves in turns and every move is finite: finitely many weights of lengths and nodes are increased by some rational numbers, and finitely many new elements are added to W_i and A. This is the game with full information, the moves of one player are visible to the other one.

The game is infinite, and the winner is determined in the limit, assuming that both players obey the weight restrictions. Namely, we win if

- for the limit path a our weight of $(a)_n$ is not less than the opponent's weight of n;
- for each n, if W_n is infinite, then W_n has a common element with A.

The winning strategy is as described: we match the opponent's weight along the current path, and also we add some u to A and change the path, matching the opponent's weights along the new path, if u belongs to W_n, is greater than $2n$ and the cost of the action, i.e., our total weight along the current path above u, does not exceed 2^{-n}.

This is a computable winning strategy. Indeed, the limit weights of all lengths form a converging series, so if W_n is infinite, it has some element that is greater than $2n$ and for which the loss, bounded by the tail of this series, is less than 2^{-n}.

Imagine now that we use this computable winning strategy against the "blind" computable opponent that ignores our moves and just enumerates from below the a priori probability (as lengths' weights) and the sets W_i (the list contains all enumerable sets). Then the game is computable, our limit A is an enumerable simple set, and our weights for the prefixes of a (and therefore $\mathbf{m}((a)_n)$, since the limit weights form a lower semicomputable semimeasure) match $\mathbf{m}(n)$ up to $O(1)$-factor.

3 K-trivial and K-low Sequences

Now we know that non-computable K-trivial sequences do exist. Our next big goal is to show that they are computationally weak. Namely, they are K-low in the sense of the following definition.

Consider a bit sequence a; one can relativize the definition of prefix complexity using a as an oracle (i.e., the decompressor algorithm used in the definition of complexity may use the values of a_i in its computation). For every oracle this relativized complexity K^a does not exceed (up to an $O(1)$ additive term) the non-relativized prefix complexity, since the decompressor may ignore the oracle. But it can be smaller or not, depending on a.

Definition 2. *A sequence a is K-low if $K^a(x) = K(x) + O(1)$.*

In other words, K-low oracles are useless for compression (or, more precisely, decompression) purposes.

Obviously, computable oracles are low; the question is whether there exist non-computable low oracles. Note that *"classical" undecidable sets, like the halting problem, are not K-low*: with oracle $\mathbf{0}'$ the table of complexities of all n-bit strings has complexity $O(\log n)$, but its non-relativized complexity is $n - O(1)$. One can also consider the relativized and non-relativized complexities of the prefixes of Chaitin's Ω-numbers: the n-bit prefix has complexity about n but its $\mathbf{0}'$-relativized complexity is about $\log n$, since Ω-numbers are $\mathbf{0}'$-computable.

Note also that *K-low oracles are K-trivial,* since $K^a((a)_n) = K^a(n) + O(1)$: the sequence a is computable in the presence of oracle a.

It turns out that the reverse implication is true, and all K-trivial sequences are K-low. This is quite surprising. For example, one may note that *the notion of a K-low sequence is Turing-invariant,* i.e., depends only on the computational power of the sequence, but for K-triviality there are no reasons to expect this, since the definition deals with prefixes.

On the other hand, it is easy to see that *if a and b are two K-trivial sequences, then their join* (the sequence $a_0 b_0 a_1 b_1 a_2 b_2 \ldots$) *is also K-trivial.* Indeed, as we have mentioned, the K-triviality of a sequence a means that $K((a)_n \mid n, K(n)) = O(1)$. If at the same time $K((b)_n \mid n, K(n)) = O(1)$, then the naïve bound for the complexity of a pair guarantees that

$$K((a)_n, (b)_n \mid n, K(n)) = O(1),$$

so

$$K(a_0 b_0 a_1 b_1 \ldots a_{n-1} b_{n-1} \mid n, K(n)) = O(1),$$

and therefore

$$K(a_0 b_0 a_1 b_1 \ldots a_{n-1} b_{n-1}) = K(n) + O(1).$$

It remains to note that $K(n) = K(2n) + O(1)$ and that we can extend the equality to sequences of odd length, since adding one bit changes the complexity of the sequence and its length only by $O(1)$. The analogue result for K-low sequences is not obvious: if each of the sequences a and b separately do not change the complexity function, why should their join be equally powerless in that regard? The usual proof of this result uses the equivalence between triviality and lowness.

The proof of the equivalence (every K-trivial sequence is K-low) requires a rather complicated combinatorial construction. It may be easier to start with a weaker statement: *no K-trivial sequence* (used as an oracle) *computes the halting problem.* This statement is indeed a corollary of the equivalence result, since $\mathbf{0}'$ (the halting set) is not K-low, as we have seen, and every sequence computable with a K-low oracle is obviously K-low. The proof of this weaker statement is given in the next section. On the other hand, the full proof (hopefully) can be understood without the training offered in the next section, so the reader may also skip it and go directly to Sect. 5.

4   *K*-trivial Sequences Cannot Compute 0′

In this section we prove that a K-trivial sequence cannot compute $\mathbf{0}'$, in the following equivalent version:

Theorem 3. *No K-trivial sequence can compute all enumerable sets.*

Note that, together with the existence result proved above (Theorem 2), this theorem provides an answer to classical *Post's problem,* the question whether non-complete enumerable undecidable sets exist.

The rest of the section is devoted to the proof of Theorem 3.

The Game Template. To make the proof of this theorem more intuitive, we first reformulate it in terms of a two-player game. Imagine that we want to prove that all K-trivial sequences have some property P, and our opponent wants to show that we are wrong, i.e., to construct a K-trivial sequence a that does not have the property P. We already know that all K-trivials are $\mathbf{0}'$-computable, so we may assume that our opponent presents a $\mathbf{0}'$-computable sequence a as a computable pointwise approximation (using Shoenfield's limit lemma). At every moment of the game the opponent chooses some values a_i; they may be changed during the game, but for each i the number of changes in a_i during the game should be finite, otherwise the opponent loses.

We want to show that the sequence constructed by the opponent is either not K-trivial or has property P. For that we challenge the opponent by building a semimeasure μ on integers by gradually increasing the weights of each integer. Recall the proof of Theorem 2; now the opponent tries to certify that a is K-trivial and is therefore in the same position in which we were in that proof. In other words, he is obliged to match our increases along the path a, i.e., he must construct a semimeasure ν on strings such that $\nu((a)_n) \geq \mu(n)/O(1)$ for the limit sequence a. At the same time the opponent needs to ensure that the limit sequence does not have the property P. In other terms, the opponent wins if (1) the limit sequence exists and does not have the property P; (2) ν is a semimeasure (the sum of all weight increases is bounded by 1); (3) $\nu((a)_n) \geq \mu(n)/O(1)$.

If we have a computable winning strategy in this game, then every K-trivial sequence a has property P. Indeed, assume that there exists some K-trivial sequence that does not have this property. Then, by Theorem 1, the opponent can present this sequence as a computable pointwise approximation, and also use increasing approximations to $\mathbf{m}$ (on strings) for ν. Our computable strategy will then generate some lower semicomputable semimeasure μ, and the inequality $\nu((a)_n) \geq \mu(n)/O(1)$ is guaranteed by the maximality of $\mathbf{m}$ and the triviality of a, so the opponent wins against our winning strategy—a contradiction.

Remark 1. One may also note that if the opponent has a computable winning strategy in the game, then there exists a K-trivial sequence a that does not have the property P. Indeed, let this strategy play and win against $\mathbf{m}$ (as μ); the resulting sequence will be K-trivial and will not have the property P. So the question whether all K-trivial sequences have property P or not can be resolved by providing a computable winning strategy for one of the players.

The Game for Theorem 3. We follow this scheme (in slightly modified form) and consider the following game. The opponent approximates some sequence a by changing the values of Boolean variables $a_0, a_1, a_2, \ldots$, so $a(i)$ is the limit value of a_i. (For the ith bit of a we use the notation $a(i)$ instead of usual a_i, since a_i is used as the name of ith variable.) He also assigns increasing weights to strings; the total weight should not exceed 1. We assume that initially all weights are zeros. We also assume that the initial values of the a_i's are zeros (just to be specific).

We assign increasing weights to integers (*lengths*); the sum of our weights is also bounded by 1. Since the property P says that a computes all enumerable sets, we also challenge this property and construct some set W by irreversibly adding elements to it.

The opponent wins the game if

- each variable a_i is changed only finitely many times (so some limit sequence a appears);
- the (opponent's) limit weight of $(a)_i$, the i-bit prefix of a, is greater than our limit weight of i, up to some multiplicative constant;
- the set W is Turing-reducible to a.

Again, it is enough to show that we can win this game using a computable winning strategy. Indeed, assume that some K-trivial a computes $\mathbf{0}'$. We know that a is limit computable, so the opponent can computably approximate it, and at the same time approximate from below the a priori probabilities $\mathbf{m}(s)$ for all strings s (ignoring our moves). Our strategy will then behave computably, generating some lower semicomputable semimeasure on lengths, and some enumerable set W. Then, according to the definition of the game, either this semimeasure is not matched by $\mathbf{m}((a)_i)$, or W is not Turing-reducible to a. In the first case a is not K-trivial; in the second case a is not Turing-complete.

Reduction to a Game with Fixed Machine and Constant. How can we computably win this game? First we consider a simpler game where the opponent has to declare in advance some constant c that relates the semimeasures constructed by the two players, and the machine Γ that reduces W to a. Imagine that we can win this game: assume that for each c and Γ we have a uniformly computable strategy that wins in this c-Γ-game, defined in a natural way. Since the constant c in the definition of the c-Γ-game is arbitrary, we may use c^2 instead of c and assume by scaling that we can force the opponent to spend more than 1 while using only $1/c$ total weight and allowing him to match our moves up to factor c.

Now we mix the strategies for different c and Γ into one strategy. Note that two strategies that simultaneously increase weights of some lengths can only help each other, so we only need to ensure that the sum of the increases made by all strategies is bounded by 1. More care is needed for the other condition related to the set W. Each of the strategies constructs its own W, so we should isolate them. For example, to mix two strategies, we split $\mathbb{N}$ into two parts N_1 and N_2, say, odd and even numbers, and let the first and second strategy construct a subset of N_1 and N_2, respectively. Of course, then each strategy is not required to beat the machine Γ; it should beat its restriction to N_i (the composition of Γ and the embedding of N_i into $\mathbb{N}$). In a similar way we can mix countably many strategies (splitting $\mathbb{N}$ into countably many infinite sets in a computable way).

It remains to consider some computable sequence $c_i > 0$ such that $\sum 1/c_i \leqslant 1$ and a computable sequence Γ_i that includes every machine Γ infinitely many times. (The latter is needed because we want every Γ to be beaten with arbitrarily large constant c.) Combining the strategies for these games as described, we get a computable winning strategy for the full game.

When constructing a wnning strategy for the c-Γ-game, it is convenient to scale this game and require the opponent to match our weights exactly (without any factor) but allow him to use total weight c instead of 1. We will prove the existence of the winning strategy by induction: assuming that a strategy for some c is given, we construct a strategy for a bigger c'. Let us first construct the strategy for $c < 2$.

Winning a Game with $c < 2$: Strong Strings. This winning strategy deals with some fixed machine Γ and ensures $\Gamma^a \neq W$ at one fixed point, say, 0 (i.e., the strategy ensures that $0 \in \Gamma^a \not\Leftrightarrow 0 \in A$); the other points are not used. Informally, we wait until the opponent puts a lot of weight on strings that imply $0 \notin \Gamma^a$. If this never happens, we win in one way; if it happens, we then add 0 to W and win in a different way.

Let us explain this more formally. We say that a string u is *strong* if it (as a prefix of a) enforces that $\Gamma^a(0)$ is equal to 0, i.e., Γ outputs 0 on input 0 using only oracle answers in u. Simulating the behavior of Γ for different oracles, we can enumerate all strong strings. During the game we look at the following quantity:

the total weight that our opponent has put on all known strong strings.

This quantity may increase because the opponent distributes more weight or because we discover new strong strings, but it never decreases. We try to force the opponent to increase this quantity (see below how). As we shall see, if he refuses, he loses the game, and the element 0 remains outside W. If the quantity comes close to 1, we change our mind and add 1 into W. After that all the weight put on strong strings is lost for the opponent: they cannot be the prefixes of a such that $\Gamma^a = W$, if $1 \in W$. So we can make our total weight equal to 1 in an arbitrary way (adding weight somewhere if the total weight was smaller than 1), and to counter this the opponent needs to use additional weight 1 along some final a that avoids all strong strings, therefore his weight comes close to 2.

Winning a Game with $c < 2$: Gradual Increase. So our goal is to force the opponent to increase the total weight of strong strings (or nodes, since we identify strings with nodes in the full binary tree). Let us describe our strategy as a set of substrategies (processes) that run in parallel. For each strong node x there is a process P_x; we start it when we discover that x is strong. This process tries to force the opponent to increase the weight of some extension of x, i.e., some node above x (this node is automatically strong); we want to make the lengths of these strings different, so for every string x we fix some number l_x that is greater than $|x|$, the length of x.

The process P_x is activated when the current path (i.e., the characteristic function of the current approximation to a) goes through node x. Otherwise P_x sleeps; it may happen that some P_x never becomes active. When awake, P_x always sees that the current path goes through x. The process P_x gradually increases the weight of length l_x: it adds some small δ_x to the weight of l_x and waits until the opponent matches[1] this weight along the current path (whatever this path is), then increases the weight again by δ_x, etc. The value of δ_x is fixed for each x in such a way that $\sum_x \delta_x$ is small (formally: we need it to be smaller than $1 - c/2$). The process repeats this increase by δ_x until it gets a termination signal from the supervisor (see below for the conditions when this happens). Note that at any moment the current path may change in such a way that x is not an initial segment of it anymore. Then P_x is suspended and wakes up only when, due to a later change of the current path, x lies on it again (and this may never happen).

The supervisor sends the termination signal to all the processes when (and if) the total weight they have distributed goes above a fixed threshold close to 1 (formally, we need this threshold to be greater than $c/2$). After that the strategy adds 0 to W, as explained above.

Let us show that this is indeed a winning strategy. Consider a game where it is used. By construction, we do not violate the weight restriction. If the opponent has no limit path, he loses, so we can assume that some limit path a exists. There are two possible cases:

- Case 1: The processes P_x never reach the threshold for the total weight used, and no termination signal is ever sent (thus 0 never enters W). This can be because of two reasons:
  - There is no strong node on the limit path a. In this case, the opponent loses because $\Gamma^a(0) \neq 0$ while $0 \notin W$, so $\Gamma^a \neq W$.
  - There exists a strong node x on the limit path a, and its associated process P_x remains active from some point onward, but the opponent refuses to match our weight at length l_x. In this case the opponent fails to match our weight on some prefix of a, and thus loses.
- Case 2: The processes P_x do reach the fixed total threshold, the termination signal is sent, and 0 is added to W. As we observed, all the weight we put on lengths was matched by our opponent on strong nodes, except for some small amount (at most $\sum_x \delta_x$). Now all the opponent's weight is lost since he must change the path and the limit path does not have strong prefixes. Then we distribute the remaining weight arbitrarily and win.

This finishes the explanation on how to win the c-Γ-game for $c < 2$.

Induction Statement. The idea of the induction step is simple: instead of forcing the weight increase for some extension of a strong node u directly, we recursively call the described strategy at the subtree rooted at u, adding or not adding some other element to W instead of 0. This cuts our costs almost in half, since we know how to win the game with c close to 2. In this way we can win the game for arbitrary $c < 3$, and so on.

---

[1] A technical remark: note that in our description of the game we have required that the opponent's weight along the path is strictly greater than our weight: if this is true in the limit, it happens at some finite stage.

To be more formal, we consider a recursively defined process $P(k, x, \alpha, L, M)$ with the following parameters:

- $k > 0$ is a rational number, the required coefficient of weight increase;
- x is the root of the subtree where the process operates;
- $\alpha > 0$ is also a rational number, our "budget" (how much weight we are allowed to use);
- L is an infinite set of integers (lengths where our process may increase weight);[2]
- M is an infinite set of integers (numbers that our process is allowed to add to W).

The process can be started or resumed only when x is a prefix of the current path a, and is suspended when a changes and this is no more true. The process then sleeps until x is an initial segment of the current path again. It is guaranteed that P never violates the rules (about α, L, and M). Running in parallel with other processes (as part of the game strategy) and assuming that other processes do not touch lengths in L and numbers in M, the process $P(k, x, \alpha, L, M)$ guarantees, if not suspended forever or terminated externally, that one of the following possibilities is realized:

- the limit path a does not exist;
- $W \neq \Gamma^a$ for limit a;
- the opponent never matches some weight put on some length in L;
- the opponent spends more than $k\alpha$ weight on nodes above x with lengths in L.

Base Case: $k < 2$. Now we can adapt the construction of the previous section and construct a process $P(k, x, \alpha, L, M)$ with these properties for arbitrary $k < 2$. For each y above x we select some $l_y \in L$ greater than the length of y, different for different y, and also select some positive δ_y such that $\sum \delta_y$ is small compared to the budget α. We choose some $m \in M$ and consider y (a node above x) as *strong* if it guarantees that $\Gamma^a(m) = 0$. Then for all strong y we start the process P_y that is activated when y is in the current path and increases the weight of l_y in δ_y-steps waiting until the opponent matches it. We terminate all the processes when (and if) the total weight used becomes close to α, and then add m to W, thus rendering useless all the weight placed by the opponent on strong nodes.

The restrictions are satisfied by the construction. Let us check that the declared goals are achieved. If there is no limit path, there is nothing to check. If the limit path a does not go through x, we have no obligations (the process is suspended forever). So we assume that the limit path goes through x.

Assume first that the total weight used by all P_y did not come close to α, so the termination signal was not sent. In this case $m \notin W$. If there is no strong node on the limit path a, then $\Gamma^a(m)$ is not 0, so $W \neq \Gamma^a$. If there is a strong

---

[2] To use infinite sets as parameters, we should restrict ourselves to some class of infinite sets. For example, we may consider infinite decidable sets and represent them by programs enumerating their elements in increasing order.

node y on the limit path, then the process P_y was started and worked without interruptions, starting from some moment. So either some of the δ_y-increases was not matched (third possibility) or the termination signal was sent (so there are no obligations).

It remains to consider the case when m was added to W and termination signal was sent to all P_y. In this case the total weight used is close to α, and after adding m to W it is lost, so either our weight is not matched or almost 2α is spent by the opponent on nodes above x (recall that all processes are active only when the current path goes through x).

Induction Step. The induction step is similar: we construct the process

$$P(k, x, \alpha, L, M)$$

in the same way as for the induction base. The difference is that instead of δ_y-increasing the weight of l_y the process P_y now recursively calls

$$P(k', y, \delta_y, L', M')$$

with some smaller k', say, $k' = k - 0.5$, the budget δ_y, and some $L' \subset L$ and $M' \subset M$. If the started process forces the opponent to spend more than $k'\delta_y$ on the nodes above y with lengths in L' and terminates, then a new process

$$P(k', y, \delta_y, L'', M'')$$

is started for some other $L'' \subset L$ and $M'' \subset M$, etc. All the subsets $L', L'', \dots$ should be disjoint, and also disjoint for different y, as well as $M', M'', \dots$. So we should first of all split L into a sum of disjoint infinite subsets L_y parametrized by y and then split each L_y into $L'_y + L''_y + \dots$ (for the first, second, etc. recursive calls). The same is done for M, but here, in addition to the sets M_y, we select some m outside all M_y. We add this m to A when our budget is exhausted (thus forcing the opponent to spend more weight). As before, strong nodes are defined as those that guarantee $\Gamma^a(m) = 0$.

We start the processes P_y as described above: each of them makes a potentially infinite sequence of recursive calls with the same $k' = k - 0.5$ and budget δ_y. The process P_y is created for each discovered strong node y, but is sleeping while y is not on the current path. We take note of the total weight used by all P_y (for all y) and send a termination signal to all P_y when this weight comes close to the threshold α, so it never crosses this threshold.

Let us show that we achieve the declared goal, assuming that the recursive calls fulfill their obligations. First, the restrictions about L, M and α are guaranteed by the construction. If there is no limit path, we have no other obligations. If the limit path exists but does not go through x, our process will be suspended externally, and again we have no obligations. So we may assume that the limit path goes through x, and that our process is not terminated externally. If the weight used by all P_y did not cross the threshold, and the limit path does not go through any strong node (defined using m), then $W \neq \Gamma^a$ for the limit path A, since $m \notin W$ and $\Gamma^a(m)$ does not output 0. If the limit path goes through some strong y, the process P_y will be active starting from some point onward, and makes recursive calls $P(k', y, \delta_y, L', M')$, $P(k', y, \delta_y, L'', M'')$, etc. Now we use the inductive assumption and assume that these calls achieve their declared goals. Consider the first call. If it succeeds by achieving one of three first alternatives (among the four alternatives listed above), then we are done. If it succeeds by achieving the fourth alternative, i.e., by forcing the opponent to spend more than $k'\delta_y$ on the weights from L', then the second call is made, and again either we are done or the opponent spends more than $k'\delta_y$ on the weights from L''. And so on: at some point we either succeed globally, or exhaust the budget and our main process sends the termination signal to all P_y. So it remains to consider the latter case. Then all the weight spent, except for the δ_y's for the last call at each node, is matched by the opponent with factor k', and on the final path the opponent has to match it with factor 1, so we are done (assuming that $k < k'+1$ and $\sum_y \delta_y$ is small enough).

This finishes the induction step, so we can win every c-Γ-game by calling the recursive process at the root. As we have explained, this implies that K-trivial sets do not compute $\mathbf{0}'$.

5 K-trivial Sequences Are K-low

Now we want to prove the promised stronger result [5]:

Theorem 4. *All K-trivial sequences are K-low.*

Proof. In this theorem the property P that we want to establish for an arbitrary K-trivial sequence a says that $K^a(x) \geqslant K(x) - O(1)$ for all $x \in \mathbb{B}^*$, or that

$$\mathbf{m}^a(x) \leqslant \mathbf{m}(x) \cdot O(1) \text{ for all } x \in \mathbb{B}^*.$$

Let us represent $\mathbf{m}^a(\cdot)$ in the following convenient way. The sequence a is a path in a full binary tree. Imagine that at every node of the tree there is a label of the form (i, η) where i is an integer, and η is a non-negative rational number. This label is read as "please add η to the weight of i". We assume that the labelling is computable. We also require that for every path in the tree the sum of all rational numbers along the path does not exceed 1. Having such a labelling, and a path a, we can obey all the labels along the path, and obtain a semimeasure on integers. This semimeasure is semicomputable with oracle a.

This construction is general in the following sense. Consider a machine M that generates a lower semicomputable discrete semimeasure $\mathbf{m}^a$ when given access to an oracle a. We can find a computable labelling that gives the same semimeasure $\mathbf{m}^a$ (in the way described) for every oracle a. (Note that, according to our claim, the labelling does *not* depend on the oracle.) Indeed, we may simulate the behavior of M for different oracles a, and look at the part of a that has been read when some increase in the output semimeasure happens. This can be used to create a label (i, η) at some tree node u: the number i is where the increase happened, η is the size of the increase, and u is the node that guarantees all the oracle answers used before the increase happened. We need to make the labelling computable; also, according to our assumption, each node has only one label (adds weight only to one object). Both requirements can be easily fulfilled by postponing the weight increase: we push the queue of postponed requests up the tree. If the sum of the increase requests along some path a becomes greater than 1, this means that for this path a we do not obtain a semimeasure. As usual, we can trim the requests and guarantee that we obtain semimeasures along all paths, without changing the existing valid semimeasures.

We may assume now that some computable labelling is fixed that corresponds to the universal machine: for every path a the semimeasure resulting from fulfilling all requests along a, equals $\mathbf{m}^a$.

Game Description. As in the previous section, we prove the theorem by showing the existence of a winning strategy in some game, which follows the same template.

As before, the opponent approximates some sequence a by changing the values of Boolean variables $a_0, a_1, a_2, \ldots$ and assigns increasing weights to strings; the total weight should not exceed 1 (we again assume that initially all weights and the values of the a_i's are zeros) while we assign increasing weights to integers (*lengths*); the sum of our weights is also bounded by 1.

Moreover (this is the part of the game tailored for the theorem to be proven), throughout the game we also assign increasing weights to another type of integers, called *objects*: on these we compare our semimeasure with the semimeasure $\mathbf{m}^a$ determined by the opponent's limit path a.[3]

The opponent wins the game if all of the following three conditions are satisfied:

- the limit sequence a exists;
- the opponent's semimeasure along the path exceeds our semimeasure on lengths up to some constant factor, i.e., there exists some $c > 0$ such that for all i the opponent's weight of the prefix $(a)_i$ is greater than our weight of i divided by c; for brevity we say in this case that the opponent's semimeasure *-exceeds* our semimeasure.
- our semimeasure on objects does not *-exceed $\mathbf{m}^a$.

Once again it is enough to construct a computable winning strategy in this game. Also, as in the previous section, we can consider an easier (for us) version of the game where the opponent starts the game by declaring some constant c that he plans to achieve for the second condition, and we need to beat only this c. If we can win this game for any $c = 2^{2k}$ declared in advance, then by scaling we can win the 2^k-game using only 2^{-k} of our capital, and it then suffices to combine all the corresponding strategies (we also assume that the total weight on

---

[3] Formally speaking, we construct two semimeasures on integers; to avoid confusion, it is convenient to call their arguments "lengths" and "objects".

objects for the kth strategy is bounded by 2^{-k}, but this is for free, since we only need to $*$-exceed $\mathbf{m}^a$ without any restrictions on the constant). So it remains to win the game for each c. And again, it is convenient to scale that game and assume that the opponent needs to match our weights on lengths exactly (not up to $1/c$-factor) while his total weight is bounded by c (not 1).

Winning the Game for $c < 2$. For $c = 1$ the game is trivial, since we require that the opponent's weight along the path is strictly greater than our weight on lengths, so it is enough to assign weight 1 to some length. We start our proof by explaining the strategy for the case $c < 2$.

The idea can be explained as follows. The naïve strategy is to assume all the time that the current path a is final, and to just assign the weights to objects according to $\mathbf{m}^a$, computed based on the current path a. (In fact, at each moment we look at some finite prefix of a and follow the labels that appear on this prefix.) If indeed a never changes, this is a valid strategy: we achieve $\mathbf{m}^a$, and never exceed the total weight 1 due to the assumption about the labels. But if the path suddenly changes, then all the weight placed because of nodes on the old path which are now outside the new path, is lost. If we now follow all the labels on the new path, then our total weight on objects may exceed 1 (the total weight was bounded only along every path individually, but now we have placed weight according to labels both on the old path and on the new path).

There is some partial remedy: we may match the weights only up to some constant, say, use only 1 % of what the labels ask. This is possible since the game allows us to match the measure with arbitrary constant factor. This way we can tolerate up to 100 changes in the path (each new path generates new weight of at most 0.01). However, this does not really help since the number of changes is (of course) unbounded. In fact, the strategy described so far *must* fail, as otherwise it would prove that all $\mathbf{0}'$-computable sets are K-low, which is certainly not the case. For a successfull proof we must take advantage of the fact that a is K-trivial.

How can we discourage the opponent from changing the path? Like in the previous proof we may assign a non-zero weight to some length and wait until the opponent matches this weight along the current path. This provides an incentive for the opponent not to leave a node where he has already put weight: if he does, this weight would be wasted, and he would be forced to put the same weight along the final path a second time. After that we may act as if the final path goes through this node and follow the labels (as described). Doing this, we know at least that if later the path changes and we lose some weight, the opponent loses some weight, too. This helps if we are careful enough.

Let us explain the details. It would be convenient to represent the strategy as a set of parallel processes: for each node x we have a process P_x that is awake when x is a prefix of the current path, and sleeps when x is not. When awake, the process P_x tries to create the incentive for the opponent not to leave x, by forcing him to increase the weight of some node above x. To make the processes more independent and to simplify the analysis, let us assume that for every node

x some length $l_x \geqslant |x|$ is chosen, lengths assigned to different nodes are different, and P_x increases only the weight of l_x.

Now we are ready to describe the process P_x. Assume that node x has label (i, η) that asks to add η to the weight of object i. The process P_x increases the weight of l_x, adding small portions to it and waiting after each portion until the opponent matches this increase along the current path (i.e., in the l_x-bit prefix of the current path). If and when the weight of l_x reaches $\varepsilon\eta$ (where ε is some small positive constant; the choice of ε depends on c, see below), the process increases the weight of object i by $\varepsilon\eta$ as well and terminates.

The processes P_x for different nodes x run in parallel independently, except for one thing: just before the total weight spent by all processes together would exceed 1, we terminate them, blocking the final weight increase that would have brought the total weight above 1. After that our strategy stops working and hopes that the opponent would be unable to match already existing weights not crossing the threshold c.

Concerning the small portions of weight increases mentioned above: for each node x we choose in advance the size δ_x of the portions used by P_x, in such a way that $\sum_x \delta_x < \varepsilon$. Note that here we use the same small ε as above. In this way we guarantee that the total loss (caused by last portions that were not matched because the opponent changes the path instead and does not return, so the process is not resumed) is bounded by ε.

It remains to prove that this strategy wins the c-game for c close to 2, assuming that ε is small enough. First note two properties that are true by construction:

- the sum of our weights for all lengths does not exceed 1;
- at every moment the sum of (our) weights for all objects does not exceed the sum of (our) weights for all lengths.

Indeed, we stop the strategy just before violating the first requirement, and the second is guaranteed for each x-process and therefore for the entire strategy.

If there is no limit path, the strategy wins the game by definition. So assume that a limit path a exists. Now we count separately the weights used by processes P_x for x's on the limit path a, and for others (incomparable with a). Since the weights for x are limited by $\varepsilon \cdot$ (the request in x), and the sum of all requests along a is at most 1, the sum of the weights along a is bounded by ε. Now there are two possibilities: either the strategy was stopped when trying to cross the threshold, or it runs indefinitely.

In the first case the total weight is close to 1: it is at least $1 - \varepsilon$, since the next increase will cross 1, and all the portions δ_x are less than ε. So the weight used by processes outside a is at least $1 - 2\varepsilon$, and if we do not count the last (unmatched) portions, we get at least $1 - 3\varepsilon$ of weight that the opponent needs to match twice: it was matched above x for P_x, and then should be matched again along the limit path (that does not go through x; recall that we consider the nodes outside the limit path). So the opponent needs to spend at least $2 - 6\varepsilon$, otherwise he loses.

In the second case each process P_x for x on the limit path is awake starting from some point onward, and is never stopped, so it reaches its target value $\varepsilon\eta$

and adds $\varepsilon\eta$ to the object i, if (i, ε) is the request in node x. So our weights on the objects match $\mathbf{m}^a$ for limit path a up to factor ε, and the opponent loses. We know also that the total weight on objects does not exceed 1, since it is bounded by the total weight on lengths.

We therefore have constructed a winning strategy for the $2 - 6\varepsilon$ game, and by choosing a small ε we can win the c-game for any given $c < 2$.

Using This Strategy on a Subtree. To prepare ourselves for the induction, let us look at the strategy previously described and modify it for use inside a subtree rooted at some node x. We also scale the game and assume that we have some budget α that we are allowed to use (instead of total weight 1). To guarantee that the strategy does not interfere with other actions outside the subtree rooted at x, we agree that it uses lengths only from some infinite set L of length and nobody else touches these lengths. Then we can assign $l_y \in L$ for every y in the subtree and use them as before.

Let us describe the strategy in more details. It is composed of processes P_y for all y above x. When x is not on the actual path, all these processes sleep, and the strategy is sleeping. But when the path goes through x, some processes P_y (for y on the path) become active and start increasing the weight of length l_y by small portions δ_y (the sum of all δ_y now is bounded by $\alpha\varepsilon$, since we scaled everything by α). A supervisor controls the total weight used by all P_y, and as soon as it reaches α, terminates all P_y. When the process P_y reaches the weight $\alpha\varepsilon\eta$, it increases the weight of object i by $\alpha\varepsilon\eta$ (here (i, η) is the request at node y). So everything is as before, but scaled by α and restricted to the subtree rooted at x.

What does this strategy guarantee?

- The total weight on lengths used by it is at most α.
- The total weight on objects does not exceed the total weight on lengths.
- If the limit path a exists and goes through x, then either
  - the strategy halts and the opponent either fails to match all the weights or spends more than $c\alpha$ on the subtree rooted at x; or
  - the strategy does not halt, and the semimeasure on objects generated by this strategy $*$-exceeds $\mathbf{m}^a$, if we omit from $\mathbf{m}^a$ all the requests on the path to x.

The argument is the same as for the full tree: if the limit path exists and the strategy does not halt, then all the requests along the limit path (except for finitely many of them below x) are fulfilled with coefficient $\alpha\varepsilon$. If the strategy halts, the weight used along the limit path does not exceed $\alpha\varepsilon$ (since the sum of requests along each path is bounded by 1). The weight used in the other nodes of the x-subtree is at least $\alpha(1 - 2\varepsilon)$, including at least $\alpha(1 - 3\varepsilon)$ matched weight that should be doubled along the limit path, and we achieve the desired goal for $c = 2 - 6\varepsilon$.

Remark 2. In the statement above we have to change $\mathbf{m}^a$ by deleting the requests on the path to x. We can change the construction by moving requests up the tree when processing node x to get rid of this problem. One may also note that omitted requests deal only with finitely many objects, so one can average the resulting semimeasure with some semimeasure that is positive everywhere. So we may ignore this problem in the sequel.

How to Win the Game for $c < 3$. Now we make the crucial step: we show how one can increase c by recursively using our strategies. Recall our strategy for $c < 2$, and change it in the following ways:

- Instead of assigning some length l_x for each node x, let us assign an infinite (decidable uniformly in x) set L_x of integers; all elements should be greater than $|x|$ (the length of x) and for different x these sets should be disjoint (this is easy to achieve).
- We agree that process P_x (to be defined) uses only lengths from L_x.
- As before P_x is active when x is on the current path, and sleeps otherwise.
- Previously P_x increased the weight of l_x in small portions, and after each small increase waited until the opponent matched this increase along the current path. Now, instead of that, P_x calls the x-strategy described in the previous section, with small $\alpha = \delta_x$, waits until this strategy terminates forcing the opponent to spend almost $2\delta_x$, then calls another instance of the x-strategy, waits until it terminates, and so on. For this, P_x divides L_x into infinite subsets $L_x^1 + L_x^2 + \ldots$, using L_x^s for the sth call of an x-strategy, and using δ_x as the budget for each call.

There are several possibilities for the behavior of an x-strategy called recursively. It may happen that it runs indefinitely. This happens when x is an initial segment of the limit path, the x-strategy never exceeds its budget δ_x, and the global strategy does not come close to 1 in its total spending. It this case we win the game, since the part of the semimeasure on objects built by the x-strategy is enough to $*$-exceed $\mathbf{m}^a$. This case is called "the golden run" in the original exposition of the proof.

If x is not on the limit path, the execution of the x-strategy may be interrupted; in this case we only know that it spent not more than its budget, and that the weight used for objects does not exceed the weight used for lengths. This is similar to the case when an increase at l_x was not matched because the path changed.

The x-strategy may also terminate. In this case we know that the opponent used almost twice the budget (δ_x) on the extensions of x, and a new call of the x-strategy is made for another set of lengths. This is similar to the case when the increase at l_x was matched; the advantage is that now the opponent used almost twice our weight.

Finally, the strategy may be interrupted because the total weight used by x-processes for all x came close to 1. After that everything stops, and we just wait until the opponent will be unable to match all the existing weights or forced to use total weight close to 3. Indeed, most of our weight, except for $O(\varepsilon)$, was used not on the limit path and already matched with factor close to 2 there — so matching it again on the limit path makes the total weight close to 3.

Induction Step. Now it is clear how one can continue this reasoning and construct a winning strategy for arbitrary c. To get a strategy for some c, we follow the described scheme, and the process P_x makes sequential recursive calls of c'-strategies for smaller c'. We need $c - c' < 1$, so let us use $c' = c - 0.5$. More formally, we recursively define a process $S(c, x, \alpha, L)$ where c is the desired amplification, x is a node, α is a positive rational number (the budget), and L is an infinite set of integers greater than $|x|$.[4] The requirements for $S(c, x, \alpha, L)$:

– It increases only weights of lengths in L.
– The total weight used for lengths does not exceed α.
– At each step the total weight used for objects does not exceed the total weight used for lengths.
– Assuming that the process is not terminated externally (this means that x belongs to the current path, starting from some moment), it may halt or not, and:
  • If the process halts, the opponent uses more that $c\alpha$ on strings that have length in L and are above x.
  • If the process does not halt and the limit path a exists, the part of the semimeasure on objects generated by this process alone is enough to $*$-exceed $\mathbf{m}^a$.

The implementation of $S(c, x, \alpha, L)$ uses recursive calls of $S(c - 0.5, y, \beta, L')$; for each y above x a sequence of those calls is made with $\beta = \delta_y$ and sets L' that are disjoint subsets of L (for different y these L' are also disjoint), similar to what we have described above for the case $c < 3$.   □

6 *K*-low and *MLR*-low Oracles

In this section we present one more characterization of K-low (or K-trivial) sequences: this class coincides with the class of sequences that (being used as oracles) do not change the notion of Martin-Löf randomness. As almost all notions of computability theory, the notion of Martin-Löf randomness can be relativized to an oracle a; this means that the algorithms that enumerate Martin-Löf tests now may use the oracle a. In this way we get (in general) a wider class of effectively null sets, and therefore fewer but more pronouncedly random sequences. However, for some a, relativizing to a leaves the class of Martin-Löf random sequences unchanged.

Definition 3. *A sequence a is MLR-low if every Martin-Löf random sequence is Martin-Löf random relative to the oracle a.*

---

[4] The pedantic reader may complain that the parameter is an infinite set. It is in fact enough to consider infinite sets from some class, say, decidable sets (as we noted in the previous section), or just arithmetic progressions. Such sets are enough for our purposes and have finite representation. Indeed, an arithmetic progression can be split into countably many arithmetic progressions. For example, $1, 2, 3, 4, \ldots$ can be split into $1, 3, 5, 7, \ldots$ (odd numbers), $2, 6, 10, 14 \ldots$ (odd numbers times 2), $4, 12, 20, 28, \ldots$ (odd numbers times 4), etc.

The Schnorr–Levin criterion of randomness in terms of prefix complexity shows that if a is K-low, then a is also *MLR*-low. The other implication is also true but more difficult to prove.

Theorem 5. *Every MLR-low sequence is K-low.*

We will prove a more general result, but first let us give the definitions.

Definition 4. *Let a and b be two sequences, considered as oracles. We say that $a \leqslant_{LK} b$ if*
$$K^b(x) \leqslant K^a(x) + O(1).$$
We say that $a \leqslant_{LR} b$ if every sequence that is Martin-Löf random relative to b is also Martin-Löf random relative to a.

If one oracle b is stronger in the Turing sense than another oracle a, then b allows to generate a larger class of effectively null sets, and the set of random sequences relative to b is smaller that the set of random sequences relative a; the Kolmogorov complexity function relative to b is also smaller than Kolmogorov complexity function relative to a. Therefore, we have $a \leqslant_{LR} b$ and $a \leqslant_{LK} b$. So both orderings are coarser than the Turing degree ordering.

We can now reformulate the definitions of K-lowness and *MLR*-lowness: a sequence a is K-low if $a \leqslant_{LK} 0$ and is *MLR*-low if $a \leqslant_{LR} 0$. So to prove Theorem 5 it is enough to prove the following result [4]:

Theorem 6. *The conditions $a \leqslant_{LK} b$ and $a \leqslant_{LR} b$ are equivalent.*

Proof. The left-to-right direction once again follows directly from the Schnorr–Levin randomness criterion. The proof in the other direction is more difficult[5], and will be split in several steps.

Recall that the set of non-random sequences (in the Martin-Löf sense; we do not use other notions of randomness here) can be described using a universal Martin-Löf test, that is, represented as the intersection of effectively open sets
$$U_1 \supset U_2 \supset U_3 \supset \ldots$$
where U_i has measure at most 2^{-i} for all i. The following observation goes back to Kučera and says that the first layer of this test, the set U_1, is enough to characterize all non-random sequences.

Lemma 1. *Let U be an effectively open set of measure less than 1 that contains all non-random sequences. Then a sequence $x = x_0 x_1 x_2 \ldots$ is non-random if and only if all its tails $x_k x_{k+1} x_{k+2} \ldots$ belong to U.*

---

[5] This was to be expected. The relation $a \leqslant_{LK} b$ is quantitative: it states that two functions coincide with $O(1)$-precision; whether the relation $a \leqslant_{LR} b$ holds, on the other hand, is a qualitative yes/no question. One can also consider the quantitative version, with randomness deficiencies, but this is unnecessary: the relation $\leqslant_{LR}$ is already strong enough to obtain an equivalence.

Proof. If x is non-random, then all its tails are non-random and therefore belong to U. For the other direction we represent U as the union of disjoint intervals $[u_0], [u_1], \ldots$ (by $[v]$ we denote the set of all sequences that have prefix v). Their total measure $\rho = \sum 2^{-|u_i|}$ is less than 1. If all tails of x, including x itself, belong to U, then x starts with some u_i. The rest is a tail that starts with some u_j, etc., so x can be split into pieces that belong to $\{u_0, u_1, \ldots\}$. The set of sequences of the form "some u_i, then something" has measure ρ, the set of sequences of the form "some u_i, some u_j, then something" has measure ρ^2, etc. These sets are effectively open and their measures ρ^n effectively converge to 0. So their intersection is an effectively null set and x is non-random.   □

The argument gives also the following:

Corollary 1. *A sequence x is non-random if there exists an effectively open set U of measure less than 1 such that all tails of x belong to U.*

This corollary can be relativized, so randomness with oracle a can be characterized in terms of a-effectively open sets of measure less that 1: *a sequence x is a-nonrandom if there exists an a-effectively open set U of measure less than 1 such that all tails of x belong to U.* This gives one implication in the following equivalence (here we denote the oracles by capitals letter to distinguish them from sequences):

Lemma 2. *Let A and B be two oracles. Then $A \leqslant_{LR} B$ if and only if every A-effectively open set of measure less than 1 can be covered by some B-effectively open set of measure less than 1.*

Proof. The "if" direction ($\Leftarrow$) follows from the above discussion: if x is not A-random, its tails can be covered by some A-effectively open set of measure less than 1 and therefore by some B-effectively open set of measure less than 1, so x is not B-random.

In the other direction: assume that U is an A-effectively open set of measure less than 1 that cannot be covered by any B-effectively open set of measure less than 1. The set U is the union of an A-enumerable sequence of disjoint intervals $[u_1], [u_2], [u_3]$, etc. Consider a set V that is B-effectively open, contains all B-non-random sequences and has measure less than 1 (e.g., the first level of the universal B-Martin-Löf test). By assumption U is not covered by V, so some interval $[u_i]$ of U is not entirely covered by V.

The set V has the following special property: if it does not contain *all* points of some interval, then it cannot contain *almost all* points of this interval, i.e., the uncovered part must have some positive measure. Indeed, the uncovered part is a B-effectively closed set, and if it has measure zero, it has B-effectively measure zero, so all non-covered sequences are B-non-random, and therefore should be covered by V.

So we found an interval $[u_i]$ in U such that $[u_i] \setminus V$ has positive measure. Then consider the set $V_1 = V/u_i$, i.e., the set of infinite sequences α such that $u_i \alpha \in V$. This is a B-effectively open set of measure less than 1, so it does not cover U (again by our assumption). So there exists some interval $[u_j]$ not covered by V/u_i. This means that $[u_i u_j]$ is not covered by V. We repeat the argument and conclude that the uncovered part has positive measure, so $V/u_i u_j$ is a B-effectively open set of measure less than 1, so it does not cover some $[u_k]$, etc. In the limit we obtain a sequence $u_i u_j u_k \ldots$ whose prefixes define intervals not covered fully by V. Since V is open, this sequence does not belong to V, so it is B-random. On the other hand, it is not A-random, as the argument from the proof of Lemma 1 shows.   □

Let us summarize how far we have come so far. Assuming that $A \leqslant_{\mathrm{LR}} B$, we have shown that every A-effectively open set of measure less than 1 can be covered by some B-effectively open set of measure less than 1. What we need to show is that $A \leqslant_{\mathrm{LK}} B$, i.e., $K^B \leqslant K^A$ (up to an additive constant), or $\mathbf{m}^A \leqslant \mathbf{m}^B$ (up to a constant factor). This can be reformulated as follows: *for every lower A-semicomputable converging series $\sum a_n$ of reals there exists a converging lower B-semicomputable series $\sum b_n$ of reals such that $a_n \leqslant b_n$ for every n.*

So to connect our assumption and our goal, we need to find a way to convert a converging lower semicomputable series into an effectively open set of measure less than 1 and vice versa. We may assume without loss of generality that all a_i are strictly less than 1. Then $\sum a_n < \infty$ is equivalent to

$$(1 - a_0)(1 - a_1)(1 - a_2)\ldots > 0.$$

This product is a measure of an A-effectively closed set

$$[a_0, 1] \times [a_1, 1] \times [a_2, 1] \times \ldots$$

whose complement

$$U = \{(x_0, x_1, \ldots) \mid (x_0 < a_0) \vee (x_1 < a_1) \vee \ldots\}$$

is an A-effectively open set of measure less than 1. (Here we split Cantor space into a countable product of Cantor spaces and identify each of them with $[0, 1]$ equipped with the standard uniform measure on the unit interval.) We are finally ready to apply our assumption and find some B-effectively open set V that contains U.

Let us define b_0 as the supremum of all z such that

$$[0, z] \times [0, 1] \times [0, 1] \times \ldots \subset V$$

This product is compact for every z, and V is B-effectively open, so we can B-enumerate all rational z with this property, and their supremum b_0 is lower B-semicomputable. Note that all $z < a_0$ have this property (the set $[0, a_0) \times [0, 1] \times [0, 1] \times \ldots$ is covered by U), so $a_0 \leqslant b_0$. In a similar way we define all b_i and get a lower B-semicomputable series b_i such that $a_i \leqslant b_i$. It remains to show that $\sum b_i$ is finite. Indeed, the set

$$\{(x_0, x_1, \ldots) \mid (x_0 < b_0) \vee (x_1 < b_1) \vee \ldots\}$$

is a part of V, and therefore has measure less than 1; its complement

$$[b_0, 1] \times [b_1, 1] \times [b_2, 1] \times \ldots$$

has measure $(1 - b_0)(1 - b_1)(1 - b_2) \ldots$, therefore this product is positive and the series $\sum b_i$ converges. This finishes the proof. $\square$

Acknowledgments. This exposition was finished while one of the authors (A.S.) was invited to the National University of Singapore IMS's *Algorithmic Randomness* program. The authors thank the IMS for the support and for the possibility to discuss several topics (including this exposition) with the other participants (special thanks to Rupert Hölzl and Nikolai Vereshchagin; R.H. also kindly looked at the final version and corrected many errors there). We also thank André Nies for the suggestion to write down this exposition for the Logic Blog and for his comments. We have very useful discussions with the participants of the course taught by L.B. at the Laboratoire Poncelet (CNRS, Moscow), especially Misha Andreev and Gleb Novikov. Last but not least, we are grateful to Joe Miller who presented the proof of the equivalence between $\leqslant_{LK}$ and $\leqslant_{LR}$ while visiting the LIRMM several years ago.

References

1. Downey, R., Hirschfeldt, D., Nies, A., Stephan, F.: Trivial reals. In: Downey, R., Decheng, D., Ping, T.S., Hui, Q.Y., Yasugi, M. (eds.) Proceedings of the 7th and 8th Asian Logic Conferences, pp. 103–131. Singapore University Press and World Scientific, Singapore (2003)
2. Downey, R., Hirschfeldt, D.: Algorithmic Randomness and Complexity. Springer, New York (2010)
3. Hirshfeldt, D., Nies, A., Stephan, F.: Using random sets as oracles. J. Lond. Math. Soc. **75**, 610–622 (2007)
4. Kjos-Hanssen, B., Miller, J., Solomon, R.: Lowness notions, measure and domination. J. Lond. Math. Soc. **85**(3), 869–888 (2012)
5. Nies, A.: Lowness properties and randomness. Adv. Math. **197**, 274–305 (2005)
6. Nies, A.: Computability and Randomness. Oxford University Press, Oxford (2009)
7. Shen, A.: Algorithmic information theory and Kolmogorov complexity, lecture notes, Uppsala University Technical report TR2000-034. http://www.it.uu.se/research/publications/reports/2000-034/2000-034-nc.ps.gz
8. Shen, A., Uspensky, V., Vereshchagin, N.: Kolmogorov complexity and algorithmic randomness. MCCME (2012) (Russian). Draft translation: www.lirmm.fr/ashen/kolmbook-eng.pdf

Horn Clause Solvers for Program Verification

Nikolaj Bjørner[1]([⊠]), Arie Gurfinkel[2],
Ken McMillan[1], and Andrey Rybalchenko[3]

[1] Microsoft Research, Redmond, USA
nbjorner@microsoft.com
[2] Software Engineering Institute, Pittsburgh, USA
[3] Microsoft Research, Cambridge, UK

Abstract. Automatic program verification and symbolic model checking tools interface with theorem proving technologies that check satisfiability of formulas. A theme pursued in the past years by the authors of this paper has been to encode symbolic model problems directly as Horn clauses and develop dedicated solvers for Horn clauses. Our solvers are called Duality, HSF, SeaHorn, and μZ and we have devoted considerable attention in recent papers to algorithms for solving Horn clauses. This paper complements these strides as we summarize main useful properties of Horn clauses, illustrate encodings of procedural program verification into Horn clauses and then highlight a number of useful simplification strategies at the level of Horn clauses. Solving Horn clauses amounts to establishing Existential positive Fixed-point Logic formulas, a perspective that was promoted by Blass and Gurevich.

1 Introduction

We make the overall claim that *Constrained Horn Clauses* provide a suitable basis for automatic program verification, that is, symbolic model checking. To substantiate this claim, this paper provides a self-contained, but narrowly selected, account for the use of Horn clauses in symbolic model checking. It is based on experiences the authors had while building tools for solving Horn clauses. At the practical level, we have been advocating the use of uniform formats, such as the SMT-LIB [6] standard as a format for representing and exchanging symbolic model checking problems as Horn clauses. The authors and many of our colleagues have developed several tools over the past years that solve Horn clauses in this format. We illustrate three approaches, taken from Duality, SeaHorn and HSF, for translating procedural programs into Horn clauses. At the conceptual level, Horn clause solving provides a uniform setting where we can discuss algorithms for symbolic model checking. This uniform setting allows us to consider integration of separate algorithms that operate as transformations of Horn clauses. We illustrate three transformations based on recent symbolic model checking literature and analyze them with respect to how they simplify the task of fully solving clauses. As a common feature, we show how solutions to the simplified clauses can be translated back to original clauses by means of Craig interpolation [22].

L.D. Beklemishev et al. (Eds.): Gurevich Festschrift II 2015, LNCS 9300, pp. 24–51, 2015.
DOI: 10.1007/978-3-319-23534-9_2

1.1 Program Logics and Horn Clauses

Blass and Gurevich [15] made the case that Existential positive Least Fixed-point Logic (E+LFP) provides a logical match for Hoare logic: Partial correctness of simple procedural imperative programs correspond to satisfiability in E+LFP. We can take this result as a starting point for our focus on Horn clauses. As we show in Sect. 2.1, the negation of an E+LFP formula can be written as set of Horn clauses, such that the negation of an E+LFP formula is false if and only if the corresponding Horn clauses are satisfiable.

The connections between Constrained Horn Clauses and program logics originates with Floyd-Hoare logic [29,37,53]. Cook's [21] result on relative completeness with respect to Peano arithmetic established that Hoare's axioms were complete for safety properties relative to arithmetic. Clarke [20] established boundaries for relative completeness. Cook's result was refined by Blass and Gurevich.

In the world of constraint logic programming, CLP, expressing programs as Horn clauses and reasoning about Horn clauses has been pursued for several years, spearheaded by Joxan Jaffar and collaborators [41]. The uses of CLP for program analysis is extensive and we can only mention a few other uses of CLP for program analysis throughout the paper. Note that the more typical objective in constraint logic programming [2,42] is to use logic as a declarative programming language. It relies on an execution engine that finds a set of *answers*, that is a set of substitutions that are solutions to a query. In an top-down evaluation engine, each such substitution is extracted from a refutation proof.

In the world of deductive databases [19], bottom-up evaluation of Datalog programs has, in addition to top-down, been explored extensively. Bottom-up evaluation infers consequences from facts and project the consequences that intersect with a query. Each such intersection corresponds to a refutation proof of a statement of the form "query is unreachable". Note that if the intersection is empty, then the smallest set of consequences closed under a Datalog program is a least model of the program and negated query.

Rybalchenko demonstrated how standard proof rules from program verification readily correspond to Horn clauses [32], and we have since been promoting constrained Horn clauses as a basis for program analysis [12].

1.2 Paper Outline

Figure 1 summarizes a use of Horn clauses in a verification workflow. Sections 3 and 4 detail translation of programs into clauses and simplifying transformations on clauses, respectively. Section 2 treat Horn clause basics. It is beyond the scope of this paper to go into depth of any of the contemporary methods for solving clauses, although this is central to the overall picture.

In more detail, in Sect. 2, we recall the main styles of Horn clauses used in recent literature and tools. We also outline contemporary methods for solving clauses that use strategies based on combinations of top-down and bottom-up search. As the main objective of solving Horn clauses is to show *satisfiability*,

Fig. 1. Horn clause verification flow

in contrast to showing that there is a derivation of the empty clause, we introduce a notion of models definable modulo an assertion language. We call these
symbolic models. Many (but not all) tools for Horn clauses search for symbolic
models that can be represented in a decidable assertion language. Note that symbolic models are simply synonymous to loop invariants, and [16] demonstrated
that decidable assertion languages are insufficient for even a class of very simple
programs. Section 3 compares some of the main approaches use for converting
procedural programs into clauses. The approaches take different starting points
on how they encode procedure calls and program assertions and we discuss how
the resulting Horn clauses can be related. Section 4 summarizes three selected
approaches for transforming Horn clauses. Section 4.1 recounts a query-answer
transformation used by Gallagher and Kafle in recent work [30,46]. In Sect. 4.2
we recall the well-known fold-unfold transformation and use this setting to recast
K-induction [64] in the form of a Horn clause transformation. Section 4.3 dis-
cusses a recently proposed optimization for simplifying symbolic model checking
problems [49]. We show how the simplification amounts to a rewriting strategy
of Horn clauses. We examine each of the above transformation techniques under
the lens of symbolic models, and address how they influence the existence and
complexity of such models. The treatment reveals a common trait: the transformations we examine preserve symbolic models if the assertion language admits
interpolation.

2   Horn Clause Basics

Let us first describe constrained Horn clauses and their variants. We take the
overall perspective that constrained Horn clauses correspond to a fragment of
first-order formulas modulo background theories.

We will assume that the *constraints* in constrained Horn Clauses are formulated in an assertion language that we refer to as $\mathcal{A}$. In the terminology of
CLP, an assertion language is a constraint theory. In the terminology of SMT,
an assertion language is a logic [6]. The terminology *assertion language* is bor-
rowed from [52]. Typically, we let $\mathcal{A}$ be quantifier-free (integer) linear arithmetic.
Other examples of $\mathcal{A}$ include quantifier-free bit-vector formulas and quantifier-
free formulas over a combination of arrays, bit-vectors and linear arithmetic.
Interpretations of formulas over $\mathcal{A}$ are defined by *theories*. For example, integer linear arithmetic can be defined by the signature $\langle Z, +, \leq \rangle$, where Z is an
enumerable set of constants interpreted as the integers, $+$ is a binary function
and $\leq$ is a binary predicate over integers interpreted as addition and the linear
ordering on integers.

Schematic examples of constrained Horn clauses are

$$\forall x, y, z \; . \; q(y) \land r(z) \land \varphi(x, y, z) \rightarrow p(x, y)$$

and

$$\forall x, y, z \; . \; q(y) \land r(z) \land \varphi(x, y, z) \rightarrow \psi(z, x)$$

where p, q, r are predicate symbols of various arities applied to variables x, y, z and φ, ψ are formulas over an assertion language $\mathcal{A}$. More formally,

Definition 1 (CHC: Constrained Horn Clauses). *Constrained Horn clauses are constructed as follows:*

$$
\begin{aligned}
\Pi \quad &::= chc \land \Pi \mid \top \\
chc \quad &::= \forall var \; . \; chc \mid body \rightarrow head \\
pred \quad &::= upred \mid \varphi \\
head \quad &::= pred \\
body \quad &::= \top \mid pred \mid body \land body \mid \exists var \; . \; body \\
upred \quad &::= an \; uninterpreted \; predicate \; applied \; to \; terms \\
\varphi \quad &::= a \; formula \; whose \; terms \; and \; predicates \; are \; interpreted \; over \; \mathcal{A} \\
var \quad &::= a \; variable
\end{aligned}
$$

We use P, Q, R as uninterpreted atomic predicates and B, C as bodies. A clause where the head is a formula φ is called a query *or a* goal *clause. Conversely we use the terminology* fact *clause for a clause whose head is an uninterpreted predicate and body is a formula φ.*

Note that constrained Horn clauses correspond to clauses that have at most one positive occurrence of an uninterpreted predicate. We use Π for a conjunction of constrained Horn clauses and chc to refer to a single constrained Horn clause.

Convention 1. *In the spirit of logic programming, we write Horn clauses as rules and keep quantification over variables implicit. Thus, we use the two representations interchangeably:*

$$\forall x, y, z \; . \; q(y) \land r(z) \land \varphi(x, y, z) \rightarrow p(x) \qquad as \qquad p(x) \leftarrow q(y), r(z), \varphi(x, y, z)$$

Example 1. Partial correctness for a property of the McCarthy 91 function can be encoded using the clauses

$$
\begin{aligned}
mc(x, r) &\leftarrow x > 100, r = x - 10 \\
mc(x, r) &\leftarrow x \leq 100, y = x + 11, mc(y, z), mc(z, r) \\
r = 91 &\leftarrow mc(x, r), x \leq 101
\end{aligned}
$$

The first two clauses encode McCarthy 91 as a constraint logic program. The last clause encodes the integrity constraint stipulating that whenever the McCarthy 91 function is passed an argument no greater than 101, then the result is 91.

Some formulas that are not directly Horn can be transformed into Horn clauses using a satisfiability preserving Tseitin transformation. For example, we can convert[1]

$$p(x) \leftarrow (q(y) \vee r(z)), \varphi(x, y, z) \tag{1}$$

into

$$s(y, z) \leftarrow q(y) \qquad s(y, z) \leftarrow r(z) \qquad p(x) \leftarrow s(y, z), \varphi(x, y, z) \tag{2}$$

by introducing an auxiliary predicate $s(y, z)$.

A wider set of formulas that admit an equi-satisfiable transformation to constrained Horn clauses is given where the body can be brought into negation normal form, NNF, and the head is a predicate or, recursively, a conjunction of clauses. When we later in Sect. 3 translate programs into clauses, we will see that NNF Horn clauses fit as a direct target language. So let us define the class of NNF Horn clauses as follows:

Definition 2 (NNF Horn)

$$
\begin{aligned}
\Pi &::= chc \wedge \Pi \mid \top \\
chc &::= \forall var \,.\, chc \mid body \rightarrow \Pi \mid head \\
head &::= pred \\
body &::= body \vee body \mid body \wedge body \mid pred \mid \exists var \,.\, body
\end{aligned}
$$

The previous example suggests there is an overhead associated with converting into constrained Horn clauses.

Proposition 1. *NNF Horn clauses with n sub-formulas and m variables can be converted into $O(n)$ new Horn clauses each using $O(m)$ variables.*

Thus, the size of the new formulas is $O(n \cdot m)$ when converting NNF Horn clauses into Horn clauses. The asymptotic overhead can be avoided by introducing a theory of tupling with projection and instead pass a single variable to intermediary formulas. For the formula (1), we would create the clauses:

$$s(u) \leftarrow q(\pi_1(u)) \qquad s(u) \leftarrow r(\pi_2(u)) \qquad p(x) \leftarrow s(\langle y, z \rangle), \varphi(x, y, z) \tag{3}$$

where π_1, π_2 take the first and second projection from a tuple variable u, and the notation $\langle x, y \rangle$ is used to create a tuple out of x and y.

Several assertion languages used in practice have *canonical* models. For example, arithmetic without division has a unique standard model. On the other hand, if we include division, then division by 0 is typically left under-specified and there is not a unique model, but many models, for formulas such as $x/0 > 0$.

---

[1] Note that we don't need the clause $s(x, y) \rightarrow q(y) \vee r(z)$ to preserve satisfiability because the sub-formula that $s(x, y)$ summarizes is only used in negative scope.

Recall the notion of convexity [55], here adapted to Horn clauses. We will establish that Horn clauses and an extension called universal Horn clauses are convex. We show that a further extension, called existential Horn clauses, is not convex as an indication of the additional power offered by existential Horn clauses. Let Π be a set of Horn clauses, then Π is convex if for every pair of uninterpreted atomic predicates P, Q:

$$\Pi \models P \vee Q \quad \text{iff} \quad \Pi \models P \text{ or } \Pi \models Q$$

Proposition 2. *Suppose $\mathcal{A}$ has a canonical model $\mathcal{I}(\mathcal{A})$, then Horn clauses over $\mathcal{A}$, where each head is an uninterpreted predicate, are convex.*

The proposition is an easy consequence of

Proposition 3. *Constrained Horn clauses over assertion languages $\mathcal{A}$ that have canonical models have unique least models.*

This fact is a well known basis of Horn clauses [25,40,67]. It can be established by closure of models under intersection, or as we do here, by induction on derivations:

Proof. Let $\mathcal{I}(\mathcal{A})$ be the canonical model of $\mathcal{A}$. The initial model $\mathcal{I}$ of Π is defined inductively by taking $\mathcal{I}_0$ as $\emptyset$ and $\mathcal{I}_{i+1} := \{r(c) \mid (r(x) \leftarrow body(x)) \in \Pi, \mathcal{I}_i \models body(c), c \text{ is a constant in } \mathcal{I}(\mathcal{A})\}$. The initial model construction stabilizes at the first limit ordinal ω with an interpretation $\mathcal{I}_\omega$. This interpretation satisfies each clause in Π because suppose $(r(x) \leftarrow body(x)) \in \Pi$ and $\mathcal{I}_\omega \models body(c)$ for $c \in \mathcal{I}(\mathcal{A})$. Then, since the body has a finite set of predicates, for some ordinal $\alpha < \omega$ it is the case that $\mathcal{I}_\alpha \models body(c)$ as well, therefore $r(c)$ is added to $\mathcal{I}_{\alpha+1}$.

To see that Proposition 2 is a consequence of least unique models, consider a least unique model $\mathcal{I}$ of Horn clauses Π, then $\mathcal{I}$ implies either P or Q or both, so every extension of $\mathcal{I}$ implies the same atomic predicate.

While constrained Horn clauses suffice directly for Hoare logic, we applied two kinds of extensions for parametric program analysis and termination. We used universal Horn clauses to encode templates for verifying properties of array-based systems [14].

Definition 3 (UHC). *Universal Horn clauses extend Horn clauses by admitting universally quantifiers in bodies. Thus, the body of a universal Horn clause is given by:*

$$body ::= \top \mid body \wedge body \mid pred \mid \forall var \,.\, body \mid \exists var \,.\, body$$

Proposition 4. *Universal Horn clauses are convex.*

Proof. The proof is similar as constrained Horn clauses, but the construction of the initial model does not finish at ω, see for instance [14,15]. Instead, we treat universal quantifiers in bodies as infinitary conjunctions over elements in the domain of $\mathcal{I}(\mathcal{A})$ and as we follow the argument from Proposition 3, we add $r(c)$ to the least ordinal greater than the ordinals used to establish the predicates in the bodies.

Existential Horn clauses can be used for encoding reachability games [9].

Definition 4 (EHC). *Existential Horn clauses extend Horn clauses by admitting existential quantifications in the head:*

$$head ::= \exists var \, . \, head \mid pred$$

Game formalizations involve handling fixed-point formulas that alternate least and greatest fixed-points. This makes it quite difficult to express using formalisms, such as UHC, that are geared towards solving only least fixed-points. So, as we can expect, the class of EHC formulas is rather general:

Proposition 5. *EHC is expressively equivalent to general universally quantified formulas over $\mathcal{A}$.*

Proof. We provide a proof by example. The clause $\forall x, y \, . \, p(x, y) \lor q(x) \lor \neg r(y)$, can be encoded as three EHC clauses

$$(\exists z \in \{0, 1\} \, . \, s(x, y, z)) \leftarrow r(y) \quad p(x, y) \leftarrow s(x, y, 0) \quad q(x) \leftarrow s(x, y, 1)$$

We can also directly encode satisfiability of UHC using EHC by Skolemizing universal quantifiers in the body. The resulting Skolem functions can be converted into *Skolem relations* by creating relations with one additional argument for the return value of the function, and adding clauses that enforce that the relations encode total functions. For example, $p(x) \leftarrow \forall y \, . \, q(x, y)$ becomes $p(x) \leftarrow sk(x, y), q(x, y)$, and $(\exists y \, . \, sk(x, y)) \leftarrow q(x, y)$. Note that (by using standard polarity reasoning, similar to our Tseitin transformation of NNF clauses) clauses that enforce sk to be functional, e.g., $y = y' \leftarrow sk(x, y), sk(x, y')$ are redundant because sk is introduced for a negative sub-formula.

As an easy corollary of Proposition 5 we get

Corollary 1. *Existential Horn clauses are not convex.*

2.1 Existential Fixed-Point Logic and Horn Clauses

Blass and Gurevich [15] identified Existential Positive Fixed-point Logic (E+LFP) as a match for Hoare Logic. They established a set of fundamental model theoretic and complexity theoretic results for E+LFP. Let us here briefly recall E+LFP and the main connection to Horn clauses. For our purposes we will assume that least fixed-point formulas are *flat*, that is, they use the fixed-point operator at the top-level without any nesting. It is not difficult to convert formulas with arbitrary nestings into flat formulas, or even convert formulas with multiple simultaneous definitions into a single recursive definition for that matter. Thus, using the notation from [15], a flat E+LFP formula Θ is of the form:

$$\Theta : \mathbf{LET} \bigwedge_i p_i(x) \leftarrow \delta_i(x) \, \mathbf{THEN} \, \varphi$$

where p_i, δ_i range over mutually defined predicates and neither δ_i nor φ contain any LET constructs. Furthermore, each occurrence of p_i in δ_j, respectively φ is positive, and δ_j and φ only contain existential quantifiers under an even number of negations. Since every occurrence of the uninterpreted predicate symbols is positive we can convert the *negation* of a flat E+LFP formula to NNF-Horn clauses as follows:

$$\Theta' : \bigwedge_i \forall x(\delta_i(x) \to p_i(x)) \wedge (\varphi \to \bot)$$

Theorem 1. *Let Θ be a flat closed E+LFP formula. Then Θ is equivalent to false if and only if the associated Horn clauses Θ' are satisfiable.*

Proof. We rely on the equivalence:

$$\neg(\textbf{LET } \bigwedge_i p_i(x) \leftarrow \delta_i(x) \textbf{ THEN } \varphi) \equiv \exists p . (\bigwedge_i \forall x . \delta_i(x) \to p_i(x)) \wedge \neg\varphi[p]$$

where p is a vector of the predicate symbols p_i. Since all occurrences of p_i are negative, when some solution for p satisfies the fixed-point equations, and also satisfies $\neg\varphi[p]$, then the *least* solution to the fixed-point equations also satisfies $\neg\varphi[p]$.

Another way of establishing the correspondence is to invoke Theorem 5 from [15], which translates E+LFP formulas into $\forall_1^1$ formulas. The negation is an $\exists_1^1$ Horn formula.

Remark 1. The logic U+LFP, defined in [15], is similar to our UHC. The differences are mainly syntactic in that UHC allows alternating universal and existential quantifiers, but U+LFP does not.

2.2   Derivations and Interpretations

Horn clauses naturally encode the set of reachable states of sequential programs, so satisfiable Horn clauses are program properties that hold. In contrast, unsatisfiable Horn clauses correspond to violated program properties. As one would expect, it only requires a finite trace to show that a program property does *not* hold. The finite trace is justified by a sequence of resolution steps, and in particular for Horn clauses, it is sufficient to search for SLD [2] style proofs. We call these *top-down derivations*.

Definition 5 (Top-down Derivations). *A top-down derivation starts with a goal clause of the form $\varphi \leftarrow B$. It selects a predicate $p(x) \in B$ and resolves it with a clause $p(x) \leftarrow B' \in \Pi$, producing the clause $\varphi \leftarrow B \setminus p(x), B'$, modulo renaming of variables in B and B'. The derivation concludes when there are no predicates in the goal, and the clause is false modulo $\mathcal{A}$.*

That is, top-down inferences maintain a goal clause with only negative predicates and resolve a negative predicate in the goal with a clause in Π. Top-down methods based on infinite descent or cyclic induction close sub-goals when they are implied by parent sub-goals. Top-down methods can also use interpolants or inductive generalization, in the style of the IC3 algorithm [17], to close sub-goals. In contrast to top-down derivations, bottom-up derivations start with clauses that have no predicates in the bodies:

Definition 6 (Bottom-up Derivations). *A bottom-up derivation maintains a set of* fact *clauses of the form $p(x) \leftarrow \varphi$. It then applies hyper-resolution on clauses (head $\leftarrow B$) $\in \Pi$, resolving away all predicates in B using fact clauses. The clauses are inconsistent if it derives a contradictory fact clause (which has a formula from $\mathcal{A}$ in the head).*

Bottom-up derivations are useful when working with abstract domains that have join and widening operations. Join and widening are operations over an abstract domain (encoded as an assertion language $\mathcal{A}$) that take two formulas φ and φ' and create a consequence that is entailed by both.

For constrained Horn clauses we have

Proposition 6 (unsat is r.e.). *Let $\mathcal{A}$ be an assertion language where satisfiability is recursively enumerable. Then unsatisfiability for constrained Horn clauses over $\mathcal{A}$ is r.e.*

Proof. Recall the model construction from Proposition 3. Take the initial model of the subset of clauses that have uninterpreted predicates in the head. Checking membership in the initial model is r.e., because each member is justified at level $\mathcal{I}_i$ for some $i < \omega$. If the initial model also separates from $\bot$, then the clauses are satisfiable. So assuming the clauses are unsatisfiable there is a finite justification (corresponding to an SLD resolution derivation [2]), of $\bot$. The constraints from $\mathcal{A}$ along the SLD chain are satisfiable.

From the point of view of program analysis, refutation proof corresponds to a sequence of steps leading to a bad state, a bug. Program proving is much harder that finding bugs: satisfiability for Horn clauses is generally not r.e.

Definition 7 ($\mathcal{A}$-Definable Models). *Let $\mathcal{A}$ be an assertion language, an $\mathcal{A}$-definable model assigns to each predicate $p(x)$ a formula $\varphi(x)$ over the language of $\mathcal{A}$.*

Example 2. A linear arithmetic-definable model for the mc predicate in Example 1 is as follows:

$$mc(x, y) := y \geq 91 \land (y \leq 91 \lor y \leq x - 10)$$

We can verify that the symbolic model for mc satisfies the original three Horn clauses. For example, $x > 100 \land y = x - 10$ implies that $y > 100 - 10$, so $y \geq 91$ and $y \leq x - 10$. Thus, $mc(x, r) \leftarrow x > 10, r = x - 10$ is true.

Presburger arithmetic and additive real arithmetic are not expressive enough to define all models of recursive Horn clauses, for example one can define multiplication using Horn clauses and use this to define properties not expressible with addition alone [16,63]. When working with assertion languages, such as Presburger arithmetic we are interested in more refined notions of completeness:

Definition 8 ($\mathcal{A}$-Preservation). *A satisfiability preserving transformation of Horn clauses from Π to Π' is $\mathcal{A}$-preserving if Π has an $\mathcal{A}$-definable model if and only if Π' has an $\mathcal{A}$-definable model.*

We are also interested in algorithms that are complete relative to $\mathcal{A}$. That is, if there is an $\mathcal{A}$-definable model, they will find one. In [47] we identify a class of universal sentences in the Bernays Schoenfinkel class and an associated algorithm that is relatively complete for the fragment. In a different context Revesz identifies classes of vector addition systems that can be captured in Datalog [61]. In [11] we investigate completeness as a relative notion between search methods based on abstract interpretation and property directed reachability.

2.3   Loose Semantics and Horn Clauses

A formula φ is satisfiable modulo a background theory $\mathcal{T}$ means that there is an interpretation that satisfies the axioms of $\mathcal{T}$ and the formula φ (with free variables x). Thus, in Satisfiability Modulo Theories jargon, the queries are of the form

$$\exists f \, . \, \mathcal{A}x(f) \, \wedge \, \exists x \, . \, \varphi \tag{4}$$

where f are the functions defined for the theory $\mathcal{T}$ whose axioms are $\mathcal{A}x$. The second-order existential quantification over f is of course benign because the formula inside the quantifier is equi-satisfiable.

When the axioms have a canonical model, this condition is equivalent to

$$\forall f \, . \, \mathcal{A}x(f) \, \rightarrow \, \exists x \, . \, \varphi \tag{5}$$

In the context of Horn clause satisfiability, the format (5) captures the proper semantics. To see why, suppose *unk* is a global unknown array that is initialized by some procedure we can't model, and consider the following code snippet and let us determine whether it is safe.

$$\ell_0 : \mathbf{if} \ (unk[x] > 0) \ \mathbf{goto} : error$$

In this example, the interpretation of the array *unknown* is not fully specified. So there could be an interpretation of *unknown* where the error path is not taken. For example, if ℓ_0 is reached under a context where $unk[x]$ is known to always be non-positive, the program is safe. Consider one possible way to translate this snippet into Horn clauses that we denote by $Safe(\ell_0, unk)$:

$$\forall x \, . \, (\top \rightarrow \ell_0(x)) \wedge (\ell_0(x) \wedge unk[x] > 0 \rightarrow \bot).$$

These clauses are satisfiable. For example, we can interpret the uninterpreted predicates and functions as follows: $unk := const(0)$, $\ell_0(x) := \top$, where we use $const(0)$ for the array that constantly returns 0. This is probably not what we want. For all that we know, the program is not safe. Proper semantics is obtained by quantifying over all loose models. This amounts to checking satisfiability of:

$$\forall unk \exists \ell_0 . Safe(\ell_0, unk)$$

which is equi-satisfiable to:

$$\forall unk, x . ((\top \rightarrow \ell_0(unk, x)) \quad \wedge \quad (\ell_0(unk, x) \wedge unk[x] > 0 \rightarrow \bot)).$$

which is easily seen to be false by instantiating with $unk := const(1)$.

3   From Programs to Clauses

The are many different ways to transition from programs to clauses. This section surveys a few of approaches used in the literature and in tools. The conceptually simplest way to establish a link between checking a partial correctness property in a programming language and a formulation as Horn clauses is to formulate an operational semantics as an interpreter in a constraint logic program and then specialize the interpreter when given a program. This approach is used in the VeriMAP [24] tool an by [30]. The methods surveyed here bypass the interpreter and produce Horn clauses directly. Note that it is not just sequential programs that are amenable to an embedding into Horn clauses. One can for instance model a network of routers as Horn clauses [51].

3.1   State Machines

A state machine starts with an initial configuration of state variables $\boldsymbol{v}$ and transform these by a sequence of steps. When the initial states and steps are expressed as formulas $init(\boldsymbol{v})$ and $step(\boldsymbol{v}, \boldsymbol{v}')$, respectively, then we can check safety of a state machine relatively to a formula $safe(\boldsymbol{v})$ by finding an inductive invariant $inv(\boldsymbol{v})$ such that [52]:

$$inv(\boldsymbol{v}) \leftarrow init(\boldsymbol{v}) \quad inv(\boldsymbol{v}') \leftarrow inv(\boldsymbol{v}) \wedge step(\boldsymbol{v}, \boldsymbol{v}') \quad safe(\boldsymbol{v}) \leftarrow inv(\boldsymbol{v}) \quad (6)$$

3.2   Procedural Languages

Safety of programs with procedure calls can also be translated to Horn clauses. Let us here use a programming language substrate in the style of the Boogie [4] system:

$$
\begin{aligned}
program &::= decl^* \\
decl &::= \textbf{def } p(x) \ \{ \ \textbf{local } \boldsymbol{v}; S \ \} \\
S &::= x := E \ \mid \ S_1; S_2 \ \mid \ \textbf{if } E \textbf{ then } S_1 \textbf{ else } S_2 \ \mid \ S_1 \square S_2 \\
&\quad \mid \ \textbf{havoc } x \ \mid \ \textbf{assert } E \ \mid \ \textbf{assume } E \\
&\quad \mid \ \textbf{while } E \textbf{ do } S \ \mid \ y := p(E) \ \mid \ \textbf{goto } \ell \ \mid \ \ell : S \\
E &::= \text{arithmetic logical expression}
\end{aligned}
$$

```
def main(x) {                                                     
    assume init(x);      def p(x) {                               
    z := p(x);               z := q(x);                           
    y := p(z);               ret := q(z);        def q(x) {       
    assert φ₁(y);            assert φ₂(ret);         assume ψ(x, ret);
}                        }                        }               
```

Fig. 2. Sample program with procedure calls

In other words, a program is a set of procedure declarations. For simplicity of presentation, we restrict each procedure to a single argument x, local variables $\boldsymbol{v}$ and a single return variable ret. Most constructs are naturally found in standard procedural languages. The non-conventional **havoc**(x) command changes x to an arbitrary value, and the statement $S_1 \square S_2$ non-deterministically chooses run either S_1 or S_2. We use $\boldsymbol{w}$ for the set of all variables in the scope of a procedure. For brevity, we write procedure declarations as **def** $p(x)$ $\{S\}$ and leave the return and local variable declarations implicit. All methods generalize to procedures that modify global state and take and return multiple values, but we suppress handling this here. We assume there is a special procedure called $main$, for the main entry point of the program. Notice that assertions are included in the programming language.

Consider the program schema in Fig. 2. The behavior of procedure q is defined by the formula ψ, and other formulas $init, \varphi_1, \varphi_2$ are used for pre- and post-conditions.

Weakest Preconditions. If we apply Boogie directly we obtain a translation from programs to Horn logic using a weakest liberal pre-condition calculus [26]:

$$\mathsf{ToHorn}(program) := wlp(Main(), \top) \wedge \bigwedge_{decl \in program} \mathsf{ToHorn}(decl)$$

$$\mathsf{ToHorn}(\mathbf{def}\ p(x)\ \{S\}) := wlp \begin{pmatrix} \mathbf{havoc}\ x_0; \mathbf{assume}\ x_0 = x; \\ \mathbf{assume}\ p_{pre}(x); S, \qquad p(x_0, ret) \end{pmatrix}$$

$$wlp(x := E, Q) := \mathbf{let}\ x = E\ \mathbf{in}\ Q$$

$$wlp((\mathbf{if}\ E\ \mathbf{then}\ S_1\ \mathbf{else}\ S_2), Q) := wlp(((\mathbf{assume}\ E; S_1)\square(\mathbf{assume}\ \neg E; S_2)), Q)$$

$$wlp((S_1 \square S_2), Q) := wlp(S_1, Q) \wedge wlp(S_2, Q)$$

$$wlp(S_1; S_2, Q) := wlp(S_1, wlp(S_2, Q))$$

$$wlp(\mathbf{havoc}\ x, Q) := \forall x\ .\ Q$$

$$wlp(\mathbf{assert}\ \varphi, Q) := \varphi \wedge Q$$

$$wlp(\mathbf{assume}\ \varphi, Q) := \varphi \rightarrow Q$$

$$wlp((\mathbf{while}\ E\ \mathbf{do}\ S), Q) := inv(\boldsymbol{w}) \wedge$$
$$\forall \boldsymbol{w}\ .\ \begin{pmatrix} ((inv(\boldsymbol{w}) \wedge E) \rightarrow wlp(S, inv(\boldsymbol{w}))) \\ \wedge\ ((inv(\boldsymbol{w}) \wedge \neg E) \rightarrow Q) \end{pmatrix}$$

$$wlp(y := p(E), Q) := p_{pre}(E) \wedge (\forall r\ .\ p(E, r) \rightarrow Q[r/y])$$

$$wlp(\mathbf{goto}\ \ell, Q) := \ell(\boldsymbol{w}) \wedge Q$$

$$wlp(\ell : S, Q) := wlp(S, Q) \wedge (\forall \boldsymbol{w}\ .\ \ell(\boldsymbol{w}) \rightarrow wlp(S, Q))$$

The rule for $\square$ duplicates the formula Q, and when applied directly can cause the resulting formula to be exponentially larger than the original program. Efficient handling of join-points has been the attention of a substantial amount of research around *large block* encodings [10] and optimized verification condition generation [5,28,33,50]. The gist is to determine when to introduce auxiliary predicates for join-points to find a sweet spot between formula size and ease of solvability. Auxiliary predicates can be introduced as follows:

$$wlp((S_1 \square S_2), Q) := wlp(S_1, p(\boldsymbol{w})) \wedge wlp(S_2, p(\boldsymbol{w})) \wedge \forall \boldsymbol{w} \ . \ (p(\boldsymbol{w}) \rightarrow Q)$$

Procedures can be encoded as clauses in the following way: A procedure $p(x)$ is summarized as a relation $p(x, ret)$, where x is the value passed into the procedure and the return value is ret.

Proposition 7. *Let prog be a program. The formula* ToHorn(*prog*) *is NNF Horn.*

Proof. By induction on the definition of wlp.

Example 3. When we apply ToHorn to the program in Fig. 2 we obtain a set of Horn clauses:

$$main(x) \leftarrow \top$$
$$\varphi_1(y) \leftarrow main(x), init(x), p(x, z), p(z, y)$$
$$p_{pre}(x) \leftarrow main(x), init(x)$$
$$p_{pre}(z) \leftarrow main(x), init(x), p(x, z)$$
$$p(x, y) \wedge \varphi_2(y) \leftarrow p_{pre}(x), q(x, z), q(z, y)$$
$$q_{pre}(x) \leftarrow p_{pre}(x)$$
$$q_{pre}(z) \leftarrow p_{pre}(x), q(x, z)$$
$$q(x, y) \leftarrow q_{pre}(x), \psi(x, y)$$

Error Flag Propagation. The SeaHorn verification system [34] uses a special parameter to track errors. It takes as starting point programs where asserts have been replaced by procedure calls to a designated error handler *error*. That is, **assert** φ statements are replaced by **if** $\neg\varphi$ **then** *error*(). Furthermore, it assumes that each procedure is described by a set of *control-flow edges*, i.e., statements of the form $\ell_{in} : S; \textbf{goto } \ell_{out}$, where S is restricted to a sequential composition of assignments, assumptions, and function calls.

To translate procedure declarations of the form **def** $p(x)$ { S }, SeaHorn uses procedure summaries of the form

$$p(x, ret, e_i, e_o),$$

where ret is the return value, and the flags e_i, e_o track the error status at entry and the error status at exit. If e_i is true, then the error status is transferred. Thus, for every procedure, we have the fact:

$$p(x, ret, \top, \top) \leftarrow \top \ .$$

In addition, for the error procedure, we have:

$$error(e_i, e_o) \leftarrow e_o .$$

We will use wlp to give meaning to basic statements here as well, using the duality of wlp and pre-image. To translate procedure calls that now take additional arguments we require to change the definition of wlp as follows:

$$wlp(y := p(E), Q) := \forall r, err \ . \ p(E, r, e_i, err) \rightarrow Q[r/y, err/e_i].$$

where err is a new global variable that tracks the value of the error flag.

Procedures are translated one control flow edge at a time. Each label ℓ is associated with a predicate $\ell(x_0, \boldsymbol{w}, e_o)$. Additionally, the entry of a procedure p is labeled by the predicate $p_{init}(x_0, \boldsymbol{w}, e_o)$ and the exit of a procedure is labeled by a predicate $p_{exit}(x_0, ret, e_o)$. An edge links its entry $\ell_{in}(x_0, \boldsymbol{w}, e_o)$ with its exit $\ell_{out}(x_0, \boldsymbol{w}', e_o')$, which is an entry point into successor edges. The rules associated with the edges are formulated as follows:

$$
\begin{aligned}
&p_{init}(x_0, \boldsymbol{w}, \bot) \leftarrow x = x_0 &&\text{where } x \text{ occurs in } \boldsymbol{w} \\
&p_{exit}(x_0, ret, \top) \leftarrow \ell(x_0, \boldsymbol{w}, \top) &&\text{for each label } \ell, \text{ and } ret \text{ occurs in } \boldsymbol{w} \\
&p(x, ret, \bot, \bot) \leftarrow p_{exit}(x, ret, \bot) \\
&p(x, ret, \bot, \top) \leftarrow p_{exit}(x, ret, \top) \\
&\ell_{out}(x_0, \boldsymbol{w}', e_o) \leftarrow \ell_{in}(x_0, \boldsymbol{w}, e_i) \wedge \neg e_i \wedge \neg wlp(S, \neg(e_i = e_o \wedge \boldsymbol{w} = \boldsymbol{w}'))
\end{aligned}
$$

A program is safe if the clauses compiled from the program together with:

$$\bot \leftarrow Main_{exit}(x, ret, \top)$$

are satisfiable.

Example 4. When we create clauses directly from program in Fig. 2 we get the following set of clauses:

$$
\begin{aligned}
&\bot \leftarrow main(\bot, \top) \\
&main(e_i, e_o) \leftarrow init(x), p(x, z, e_i, e_o'), p(y, z, e_o', e_o''), \neg\varphi_1(y), error(e_o'', e_o) \\
&main(e_i, e_o) \leftarrow init(x), p(x, y, e_i, e_o'), p(y, z, e_o', e_o), \varphi_1(y) \\
&p(x, ret, e_i, e_o) \leftarrow q(x, z, e_i, e_o'), q(z, ret, e_o', e_o''), \neg\varphi_2(ret), error(e_o'', e_o) \\
&p(x, ret, e_i, e_o) \leftarrow q(x, z, e_i, e_o'), q(z, ret, e_o', e_o), \varphi_2(ret) \\
&q(x, ret, e_i, e_o) \leftarrow \psi(x, ret), e_i = e_o \\
&p(x, ret, \top, \top) \leftarrow \top \\
&q(x, ret, \top, \top) \leftarrow \top \\
&main(\top, \top) \leftarrow \top \\
&error(e_i, e_o) \leftarrow e_o
\end{aligned}
$$

Transition Summaries. The HSF tool [32] uses summary predicates that capture relations between the program variables at initial locations of procedures and their values at a program locations within the same calling context. Transition summaries are useful for establishing termination properties. Their encoding captures the well-known RHS (Reps-Horwitz-Sagiv) algorithm [3,60] that relies on top-down propagation with tabling (for use of tabling in logic programming, see for instance [68]). Thus, let w be the variables x, ret, local variables v and program location π for a procedure p. Then the translation into Horn clauses uses predicates of the form:

$$p(w, w').$$

To translate a procedure call $\ell : y := q(E); \ell'$ within a procedure p, create the clauses:

$$p(w_0, w_4) \leftarrow p(w_0, w_1), call(w_1, w_2), q(w_2, w_3), return(w_1, w_3, w_4)$$
$$q(w_2, w_2) \leftarrow p(w_0, w_1), call(w_1, w_2)$$
$$call(w, w') \leftarrow \pi = \ell, x' = E, \pi' = \ell_{q_{init}}$$
$$return(w, w', w'') \leftarrow \pi' = \ell_{q_{exit}}, w'' = w[ret'/y, \ell'/\pi]$$

The first clause establishes that a state w_4 is reachable from initial state w_0 if there is a state w_1 that reaches a procedure call to q and following the return of q the state variables have been updated to w_4. The second clause summarizes the starting points of procedure q. So, if p can start at state w_0 For assertion statements $\ell : \textbf{assert } \varphi; \ell'$, produce the clauses:

$$\varphi(w) \leftarrow p(w_0, w), \pi = \ell$$
$$p(w_0, w[\ell'/\pi]) \leftarrow p(w_0, w), \pi = \ell, \varphi(w)$$

Other statements are broken into basic blocks similar to the error flag encoding. For each basic block $\ell : S; \ell'$ in procedure p create the clause:

$$p(w_0, w'') \leftarrow p(w_0, w), \pi_0 = \ell, \pi'' = \ell', \neg wlp(S, (w \neq w''))$$

Finally, add the following clause for the initial states:

$$main(w, w) \leftarrow \pi = \ell_{main_{init}}.$$

Note that transition summaries are essentially the same as what we get from ToHorn. The main difference is that one encoding uses program labels as state variables, the other uses predicates. Otherwise, one can extract the precondition for a procedure from the states that satisfy $p(w, w)$, and similarly the post-condition as the states that satisfy $p(w, w') \wedge \pi' = \ell_{exit}$. Conversely, given solutions to p_{pre} and p, and the predicates summarizing intermediary locations within p one can define a summary predicate for p by introducing program locations.

3.3   Proof Rules

The translations from programs to Horn clauses can be used when the purpose is to to check assertions of sequential programs. This methodology, however is insufficient for dealing with concurrent programs with recursive procedures, and there are other scenarios where Horn clauses are a by-product of establishing program properties. The perspective laid out in [32] is that Horn clauses are really a way to write down search for intermediary assertions in proof rules as constraint satisfaction problems. For example, many proof rules for establishing termination, temporal properties, for refinement type checking, or for rely-guarantee reasoning can be encoded also as Horn clauses.

As an example, consider the rules (6) for establishing invariants of state machines. If we can establish that each reachable step is well-founded, we can also establish termination of the state machine. That is, we may ask to solve for the additional constraints:

$$round(v, v') \leftarrow inv(v) \wedge step(v, v'). \quad wellFounded(round). \tag{7}$$

The well-foundedness constraint on *round* can be enforced by restricting the search space of solutions for the predicate to only well-founded relations.

Note that in general a proof rule may not necessarily be complete for establishing a class of properties. This means that the Horn clauses that are created as a side-effect of translating proof rules to clauses may be unsatisfiable while the original property still holds.

4   Solving Horn Clauses

A number of sophisticated methods have recently been developed for solving Horn clauses. These are described in depth in several papers, including [11, 23, 24, 27, 32, 38, 43, 48, 54, 63]. We will not attempt any detailed survey of these methods here, but just mention that most methods can be classified according to some main criteria first mentioned in Sect. 2.2:

1. Top-down derivations. In the spirit of SLD resolution, start with a goal and resolve the goals with clauses. Derivations are cut off by using cyclic induction or interpolants. If the methods for cutting off all derivation attempts, one can extract models from the failed derivation attempts. Examples of tools based on top-down derivation are [38, 48, 54].
2. Bottom-up derivations start with clauses that don't have uninterpreted predicates in the bodies. They then derive consequences until sufficiently strong consequences have been established to satisfy the clauses. Examples of tools based on bottom-up derivation are [32].
3. Transformations change the set of clauses in various ways that are neither top-down nor bottom-up directed.

We devote our attention in this section to treat a few clausal transformation techniques. Transformation techniques are often sufficiently strong to solve clauses directly, but they can also be used as pre-processing or in-processing techniques in other methods. As pre-processing techniques, they can significantly simplify Horn clauses generated from tools [8] and they can be used to bring clauses into a useful form that enables inferring useful consequences [46].

4.1 Magic Sets

The query-answer transformation [30,46], a variant of the Magic-set transformation [68], takes a set of horn clauses Π and converts it into another set Π^{qa} such that bottom-up evaluation in Π^{qa} simulates top down evaluation of of Π. This can be an advantage in declarative data-bases as the bottom-up evaluation of the transformed program avoids filling intermediary tables with elements that are irrelevant to a given query. In the context of solving Horn clauses, the advantage of the transformation is that the transformation captures some of the calling context dependencies making bottom-up analysis more precise.

The transformation first replaces each clause of the form $\varphi \leftarrow B$ in Π by a clause $g \leftarrow B, \neg\varphi$, where g is a fresh uninterpreted *goal* predicate. It then adds the goal clauses $g^q \leftarrow \top$, $\bot \leftarrow g^a$ for each goal predicate g. We use the superscripts a and q in order to create two fresh symbols for each symbol. Finally, for $p(x) \leftarrow P_1, \ldots, P_n, \varphi$ in Π the transformation adds the following clauses in Π^{qa}:

- Answer clause: $p^a(x) \leftarrow p^q(x), P_1^a, \ldots, P_n^a, \varphi$
- Query clauses: $P_j^q \leftarrow p^q(x), P_1^a, \ldots, P_{j-1}^a, \varphi$ for $j = 1, \ldots, n$.

Where, by $P_1, \ldots, P_n$ are predicates $p_1, \ldots, p_n$ applied to their arguments. Given a set of clauses Π, we call the clauses that result from the transformation just described Π^{qa}.

A symbolic solution to the resulting set of clauses Π^{qa} can be converted into a symbolic solution for the original clause Π and conversely.

Proposition 8. *Given a symbolic solution* φ^q, φ^a, ψ_1^q, ψ_1^a, ..., ψ_n^q, ψ_n^a, *to the predicates* $p, p_1, \ldots, p_n$, *then* $p(x) := \varphi^q \to \varphi^a$, $P_1 := \psi_1^q \to \psi_1^a$, ..., $P_n := \psi_n^q \to \psi_n^a$ *solves* $p(x) \leftarrow P_1, \ldots, P_n, \varphi$. *Conversely, any solution to the original clauses can be converted into a solution of the Magic clauses by setting the query predicates to* $\top$ *and using the solution for the answer predicates.*

Note how the Magic set transformation essentially inserts pre-conditions into procedure calls very much in the same fashion that the ToHorn and the transition invariant translation incorporates pre-conditions to procedure calls.

Remark 2. Sect. 4.3 describes transformations that eliminate pre-conditions from procedure calls. In some way, the Magic set transformation acts inversely to eliminating pre-conditions.

4.2 Fold/Unfold

The fold/unfold transformation [18,65,66] is also actively used in systems that check satisfiability of Horn clauses [36,57] as well as in the partial evaluation literature [45].

The *unfold* transformation resolves each positive occurrence of a predicate with all negative occurrences. For example, it takes a system of the form

$$q(y) \leftarrow B_1 \qquad\qquad p(x) \leftarrow B_1, C$$
$$q(y) \leftarrow B_2 \qquad \text{into} \qquad p(x) \leftarrow B_2, C \qquad\qquad (8)$$
$$p(x) \leftarrow q(y), C$$

To define this transformation precisely, we will use the notation $\phi|_\iota$ to mean the sub-formula of ϕ at syntactic position ι and $\phi[\psi]_\iota$ to mean ϕ with ψ substituted at syntactic position ι. Now suppose we have two NNF clauses $C_1 = H_1 \leftarrow B_1$ and $C_2 = p(x) \leftarrow B_2$ such that for some syntactic position ι in B_1, $B_1|_\iota = p(t)$. Assume (without loss of generality) that the variables occurring in C_1 and C_2 are disjoint. The *resolvent* of C_1 and C_2 at position ι is $H_1 \leftarrow B_1[B_2\sigma]_\iota$, where σ maps x to t_i. We denote this $C_1\langle C_2\rangle_\iota$. The *unfolding* of C_2 in C_1 is $C_1\langle C_2\rangle_{\iota_1} \cdots \langle C_2\rangle_{\iota_k}$ where $\iota_1 \ldots \iota_K$ are the positions in B_1 of the form $p(t)$. That is, unfolding means simultaneously resolving all occurrences of p.

The *unfold transformation* on p replaces each clause C_1 with the set of clauses obtained by unfolding all the p-clauses in C_1. The unfold transformation is a very frequently used pre-processing rule and we will use it later on in Sect. 4.3. It simplifies the set of clauses but does not change the search space for symbolic models. As we will see in many cases, we can use the tool of *Craig interpolation* [22] to characterize model preservation.

Proposition 9. *The unfold transformation preserves $\mathcal{A}$-definable models if $\mathcal{A}$ admits interpolation.*

Proof. Take for instance a symbolic model that contains the definition $p(x) := \varphi$ and satisfies the clauses on the right of (8) together with other clauses. Assume that the symbolic model also contains definitions $r_1(x) := \psi_1, \ldots, r_m(x) := \psi_m$ corresponding to other uninterpreted predicate symbols in B_1, B_2, C and in other clauses. Then $((B_1 \vee B_2) \to (C \to p(x)))[\varphi/p, \psi_1/r_1, \ldots, \psi_m/r_m]$ is valid and we can assume the two sides of the implication only share the variable y. From our assumptions, there is an interpolant $q(y)$.

We can do a little better than this in the case where there is exactly one p-clause $C : p(x) \leftarrow B$. We say the *reinforced resolvent* of C with respect to clause $H \leftarrow B'$ at position ι (under the same conditions as above) is $H \leftarrow B'[p(t)\wedge B\sigma]_\iota$. Instead of *replacing* the predicate $p(t)$ with its definition, we *conjoin* it with the definition. This is valid when there is exactly one p-clause. In this case the original clauses and the reinforced clauses have the same initial models (which can be seen by unfolding once the corresponding recursive definition for p). Reinforced resolution induces a corresponding notion of reinforced unfolding. The reinforced unfold transformation on p applies only if there is exactly one p-clause. It replaces each clause C with the clause obtained by reinforced unfolding the unique p-clause in C. As an example:

$$p(y) \leftarrow B \qquad\qquad p(y) \leftarrow B$$
$$q(x) \leftarrow p(y), \phi \qquad \text{unfolds into} \qquad q(x) \leftarrow p(y), B, \phi \qquad\qquad (9)$$

Proposition 10. *The reinforced unfold transformation preserves $\mathcal{A}$-definable models if $\mathcal{A}$ admits interpolation.*

Proof. Consider the example of (9), and suppose we have a solution $\mathcal{I}$ for the unfolded system (the right-hand side). Let $p'(y)$ be an interpolant for the valid implication $B\mathcal{I} \rightarrow (p(y) \wedge \phi \rightarrow q(x))\mathcal{I}$. Taking the conjunction of p' with $\mathcal{I}(p)$, we obtain a solution for the original (left-hand side) system. This construction can be generalized to any number of reinforced resolutions on p by using the conjunction of all the interpolants (but only under the assumption that there is just one p-clause).

The *fold* transformation takes a rule $q(x) \leftarrow B$ and replaces B everywhere in other rules by $q(x)$. For example it takes a system of the form:

$$
\begin{array}{lll}
q(x) \leftarrow B & & q(x) \leftarrow B \\
p(x) \leftarrow B, C & \text{into} & p(x) \leftarrow q(x), C \\
r(x) \leftarrow B, C' & & r(x) \leftarrow q(x), C'
\end{array}
\tag{10}
$$

To create opportunities for the *fold* transformation, rules for simplification and creating new definitions should also be used. For example, the rule $q(x) \leftarrow B$ is introduced for a fresh predicate q when there are multiple occurrences of B in the existing Horn clauses.

Remark 3. The fold/unfold transformations do not refer to goal, sub-goals or fact clauses. Thus, they can be applied to simplify and solve Horn clauses independent of top-down and bottom-up strategies.

K-induction and Reinforced Unfold. K-induction [64] is a powerful technique to prove invariants. It exploits the fact that many invariants become inductive when they are checked across more than one step. To establish that an invariant *safe* is 2-inductive for a transition system with initial state *init* and transition *step* it suffices to show:

$$
\begin{array}{c}
init(\boldsymbol{v}) \rightarrow safe(\boldsymbol{v}) \\
init(\boldsymbol{v}) \wedge step(\boldsymbol{v}, \boldsymbol{v}') \rightarrow safe(\boldsymbol{v}') \\
safe(\boldsymbol{v}) \wedge step(\boldsymbol{v}, \boldsymbol{v}') \wedge safe(\boldsymbol{v}') \wedge step(\boldsymbol{v}', \boldsymbol{v}'') \rightarrow safe(\boldsymbol{v}'')
\end{array}
\tag{11}
$$

Formally, 2-induction can be seen as simply applying the reinforced unfold transformation on *safe*. That is, in NNF we have:

$$
safe(\boldsymbol{v}') \leftarrow init(\boldsymbol{v}') \vee (safe(\boldsymbol{v}) \wedge step(\boldsymbol{v}, \boldsymbol{v}'))
$$

which unfolds to:

$$
safe(\boldsymbol{v}'') \leftarrow init(\boldsymbol{v}'') \vee (safe(\boldsymbol{v}') \wedge (init(\boldsymbol{v}') \vee (safe(\boldsymbol{v}) \wedge step(\boldsymbol{v}, \boldsymbol{v}'))) \wedge step(\boldsymbol{v}', \boldsymbol{v}'')))
$$

which is equivalent to the clauses above. We can achieve K-induction for arbitrary K by simply unfolding the original definition of *safe* $K - 1$ times in itself.

Checking that any given predicate ϕ is K-inductive amounts to plugging it in for *safe* and checking validity. Interestingly, given a certificate π of K-induction of ϕ and feasible interpolation [58], the proof of Proposition 10 gives us a way to solve the original clause set. This gives us an ordinary safety invariant whose size is polynomial in π (though for propositional logic it may be exponential in the size of the original problem and ϕ).

4.3 A Program Transformation for Inlining Assertions

To improve the performance of software model checking tools Gurfinkel, Wei and Chechik [35] used a transformation called *mixed semantics* that eliminated call stacks from program locations with assertions. It is used also in Corral, as described by Lal and Qadeer [49], as a pre-processing technique that works with sequential and multi-threaded programs. The SeaHorn verification tool [34] uses this technique for transforming intermediary representations. In this way, the LLVM infrastructure can also leverage the transformed programs. The technique transforms a program into another program while preserving the set of assertions that are provable. We will here be giving a logical account for the transformation and recast it at the level of Horn clauses. We will use Horn clauses that are created from the ToHorn transformation and we will then use Horn clauses created from the error flag encoding. We show in both cases that call stacks around assertions can be eliminated, but the steps are different. They highlight a duality between the two translation techniques: Boogie inserts predicates to encode *safe pre-conditions* to procedures. SeaHorn generates predicates to encode *unsafe post-conditions* of procedures. Either transformation eliminates the safe pre-condition or the unsafe post-condition.

Optimizing ToHorn. Recall the Horn clauses from Example 3 that were extracted from Fig. 2. The clauses are satisfiable if and only if:

$$\varphi_2(y) \leftarrow init(x), \psi(x, z), \psi(z, y)$$
$$\varphi_1(y) \leftarrow init(x), \psi(x, z_1), \psi(z_1, z), \psi(z, z_2), \psi(z_2, y)$$

is true. There are two main issues with direct inlining: (1) the result of inlining can cause an exponential blowup, (2) generally, when a program uses recursion and loops, finite inlining is impossible.

As a sweet spot one can inline stacks down to assertions in order to create easier constraint systems. The transformation proposed in [35, 49] converts the original program into the program in Fig. 3.

It has the effect of replacing the original Horn clauses by the set

$$\varphi_1(y) \leftarrow init(x), p(x, z), p(z, y) \tag{12}$$
$$\varphi_2(z) \wedge p_{pre}(z) \leftarrow init(x), q(x, z_1), q(z_1, z)$$
$$\varphi_2(y) \leftarrow init(x), p(x, z), q(z, z_1), q(z_1, y)$$
$$p_{pre}(x) \leftarrow init(x)$$
$$p(x, y) \leftarrow p_{pre}(x), q(x, z), q(z, y), \varphi_2(y)$$
$$q(x, y) \leftarrow \psi(x, y)$$

```
def main(x) {
    assume init(x);
    z := p(x) □ goto p_e;
    y := p(z) □ x := z; goto p_e;        def p(x) {
    assert φ₁(y);                            z := q(x);
    assume ⊥;                                ret := q(z);
p_e:                                         assume φ₂(y);
    z := q(x) □ goto q_e;                }
    y := q(z) □ x := z; goto q_e;
    assert φ₂(y);                        def q(x) {
    assume ⊥;                                assume ψ(x, ret);
q_e:                                     }
    assume ψ(x, y);
    assume ⊥;
}
```

Fig. 3. Program with partially inlined procedures

Part of this transformation corresponds to simple inlining of the calling contexts, but the transformation has another effect that is not justified by resolution alone: The formula $\varphi_2(y)$ is used as an assumption in the second to last rule. The transformation that adds φ_2 as an assumption is justified by the following proposition:

Proposition 11. *The following clauses are equivalent:*

$$\begin{array}{ll} \varphi \leftarrow B & \varphi \leftarrow B \\ P \leftarrow B & P \leftarrow B, \varphi \end{array}$$

We could in fact have baked in this transformation already when generating Horn clauses by pretending that every **assert** is followed by a matching **assume**, or by defining:

$$wlp(\textbf{assert } \varphi, Q) := \varphi \wedge (\varphi \rightarrow Q)$$

Furthermore, the clauses from our running example are equi-satisfiable to:

$$\begin{aligned} \varphi_1(y) &\leftarrow init(x), p(x, z), p(z, y) & (13) \\ \varphi_2(z) &\leftarrow init(x), q(x, z_1), q(z_1, z) \\ \varphi_2(y) &\leftarrow init(x), p(x, z), q(z, z_1), q(z_1, y) \\ p(x, y) &\leftarrow q(x, z), q(z, y), \varphi_2(y) \\ q(x, y) &\leftarrow \psi(x, y) \end{aligned}$$

These clauses don't contain p_{pre}. The place where p_{pre} was used is in the rule that defines p. To justify this transformation let us refer to a general set of Horn clauses Π, and

- Let $\mathcal{P} : C_1, C_2, \ldots$ be the clauses where P occurs negatively at least once.
- Let $\mathcal{R} : Q \leftarrow D_1, Q \leftarrow D_2, \ldots$ be the clauses where Q occurs positively and assume Q does not occur negatively in these clauses.

Proposition 12. *Let $P \leftarrow Q \wedge B$ be a clause in Π. Then Π is equivalent to $\{P \leftarrow B\} \cup \Pi$ if the following condition holds: For every clause $C \in \mathcal{P}$ let C' be the result of resolving all occurrences of P with $P \leftarrow Q \wedge B$, then there exists a sequence of resolvents for Q from $\mathcal{R}$, such that each resolvent subsumes C'.*

The intuition is of course that each pre-condition can be discharged by considering the calling context. We skip the tedious proof and instead give an example tracing how the proposition applies.

Example 5. Consider the clause $q(x, y) \leftarrow q_{pre}(x), \psi(x, y)$ from (3). We wish to show that $q_{pre}(x)$ can be removed from the premise. Thus, take for example the clause $q_{pre}(z) \leftarrow p_{pre}(x), q(x, z)$ where q occurs negatively. Then resolving with q produces C': $q_{pre}(z) \leftarrow p_{pre}(x), q_{pre}(x), \psi(x, y)$. The pre-condition is removed by resolving with $q_{pre}(x) \leftarrow p_{pre}(x)$, producing the subsuming clause $q_{pre}(z) \leftarrow p_{pre}(x), p_{pre}(x), \psi(x, y)$. A somewhat more involved example is the clause $p(x, y) \leftarrow p_{pre}(x), q(x, z), q(z, y)$. We will have to resolve against q in both positions. For the first resolvent, we can eliminate q_{pre} as we did before. Resolving against the second occurrence of q produces

$$p(x, y) \leftarrow p_{pre}(x), q(x, z), q_{pre}(z), \psi(z, y).$$

This time resolve with the clause $q_{pre}(z) \leftarrow p_{pre}(x), q(x, z)$ producing

$$p(x, y) \leftarrow p_{pre}(x), q(x, z), q(x', z), p_{pre}(x'), \psi(z, y),$$

which is equivalent to $p(x, y) \leftarrow p_{pre}(x), q(x, z), \psi(z, y)$.

The resulting Horn clauses are *easier* to solve: the burden to solve for p_{pre} has been removed, and the clauses that constrain P have been weakened with an additional assumption. However, similar to other transformations, we claim we can retrieve a solution for p_{pre} if $\mathcal{A}$ admits interpolation.

Error Flag Specialization. We can arrive to the same result using *specialization* of the Horn clauses generated from Sect. 3.2 followed by inlining. The specialization step is to create fresh copies of clauses by grounding the values of the Booleans e_i and e_o.

Consider the clauses from Example 4. We *specialize* the clauses with respect to e_i, e_o by instantiating the clauses according to the four combinations of the e_i, e_o arguments. This reduction could potentially cause an exponential increase in number of clauses, but we can do much better: neither $p(x, y, \top, \bot)$ nor $q(x, y, \top, \bot)$ are derivable. This reduces the number of instantiations significantly from exponential to at most a linear overhead in the size of the largest clause.

To reduce clutter, let $p_{fail}(x, y)$ be shorthand for $p(x, y, \bot, \top)$ and $p_{ok}(x, y)$ be shorthand for $p(x, y, \bot, \bot)$.

$$\bot \leftarrow main_{fail} \qquad (14)$$
$$main_{fail} \leftarrow init(x), p_{fail}(x, y)$$
$$main_{fail} \leftarrow init(x), p_{ok}(x, y), p_{fail}(y, z)$$
$$main_{fail} \leftarrow init(x), p_{ok}(x, y), p_{ok}(y, z), \neg\varphi_1(y)$$
$$p_{fail}(x, ret) \leftarrow q_{fail}(x, z)$$
$$p_{fail}(x, ret) \leftarrow q_{ok}(x, z), q_{fail}(z, ret)$$
$$p_{fail}(x, ret) \leftarrow q_{ok}(x, z), q_{ok}(z, ret), \neg\varphi_2(ret)$$
$$p_{ok}(x, ret) \leftarrow q_{ok}(x, z), q_{ok}(z, ret), \varphi_2(ret)$$
$$q_{ok}(x, ret) \leftarrow \psi(x, ret)$$

In the end we get by unfolding the post-conditions for failure $main_{fail}$, p_{fail} and q_{fail}:

$$\bot \leftarrow init(x), q_{ok}(x, z), q_{ok}(z, y), \neg\varphi_2(y) \qquad (15)$$
$$\bot \leftarrow init(x), p_{ok}(x, y), q_{ok}(y, u), q_{ok}(u, z), \neg\varphi_2(z)$$
$$\bot \leftarrow init(x), p_{ok}(x, y), p_{ok}(y, z), \neg\varphi_1(y)$$
$$p_{ok}(x, ret) \leftarrow q_{ok}(x, z), q_{ok}(z, ret), \varphi_2(ret)$$
$$q_{ok}(x, ret) \leftarrow \psi(x, ret)$$

which are semantically the same clauses as (13).

5   Conclusions and Continuations

We have described a framework for checking properties of programs by checking satisfiability of (Horn) clauses. We described main approaches for mapping sequential programs into Horn clauses and some main techniques for transforming Horn clauses. We demonstrated how many concepts developed in symbolic model checking can be phrased in terms of Horn clause solving. There are many extensions we did not describe here, and some are the focus of active research. Let us briefly mention a few areas here.

Games. Winning strategies in infinite games use alternations between least and greatest fixed-points. Horn clauses are insufficient and instead [9] encodes games using EHC, which by Proposition 5 amounts to solving general universally quantified formulas.

Theories. We left the assertion language $\mathcal{A}$ mostly unspecified. Current Horn clause solvers are mainly tuned for real and linear integer arithmetic and Boolean domains, but several other domains are highly desirable, including strings, bit-vectors, arrays, algebraic data-types, theories with quantifiers (EPR, the Bernays

Schoenfinkel class). In general $\mathcal{A}$ can be defined over a set of templates or syntactically as formulas over a grammar for a limited language. For example, the sub-language of arithmetic where each inequality has two variables with coefficients ± 1 is amenable to specialized solving. Finally, one can also treat separation logic as a theory [56].

Consequences and Abstraction Interpretation In CLP. While the strongest set of consequences from a set of Horn clauses is a least fixed-point over $\mathcal{A}$, one can use abstract domains to over-approximate the set of consequences. Thus, given a set of Horn clauses Π over assertion language $\mathcal{A}$ compute the strongest consequences over assertion language $\mathcal{A}' \subseteq \mathcal{A}$.

Classification. There are several special cases of Horn clauses that can be solved using dedicated algorithms [63]. An example of "easier" clauses is *linear Horn clauses* that only contain at most one uninterpreted predicate in the bodies. Naturally, recursion-free Horn clauses can be solved whenever $\mathcal{A}$ is decidable. Horn clauses obtained from QBF problems with large blocks of quantified variables are solved more efficiently if one realizes that clauses can be rewritten corresponding to re-ordering variables.

Higher-Order Programs. The interpreter approach for assigning meanings to programs can be extended to closures in a straight-forward way. Closures encode function pointers and state and they can be encoded when $\mathcal{A}$ supports algebraic data-types [13]. This allows establishing properties of functional programs where all closures are defined within the program. The more general setting was given a custom proof system in [31], and modern approaches to proving properties of higher-order rewriting systems use a finite state abstraction as higher-order Boolean programs [59]. A different approach extracts Horn clauses from refinement based type systems for higher-order programs [44,62].

Beyond $\mathcal{A}$-definable Satisfiability. Our emphasis on $\mathcal{A}$-definable models is partially biased based on the methods developed by the authors, but note that methods based on superposition, infinite descent and fold/unfold can establish satisfiability of Horn clauses without producing a $\mathcal{A}$-definable model. Some other clausal transformation techniques we have not described are based on accelerating transitive relations [1,27,39].

Aggregates and Optimality. Suppose we would like to say that a program has at most a $2 \cdot n$ reachable states for a parameter n. We can capture and solve such constraints by introducing cardinality operators that summarize the number of reachable states. Note that upper bounds constraints on cardinalities preserve least fixed-points: If there is a solution not exceeding a bound, then any conjunction of solutions also will not exceed a bound. Lower-bound constraints, on the other hand, are more subtle to capture. Rybalchenko et al. use a symbolic version of Barvinok's algorithm [7] to solve cardinality constraints. Instead of proving bounds, we may also be interested in finding solutions that optimize objective functions.

We would like to thank Dejan Jovanovic and two peer reviewers for extensive feedback on an earlier version of the manuscript.

References

1. Alberti, F., Ghilardi, S., Sharygina, N.: Booster: an acceleration-based verification framework for array programs. In: Cassez, F., Raskin, J.-F. (eds.) ATVA 2014. LNCS, vol. 8837, pp. 18–23. Springer, Heidelberg (2014)
2. Apt, K.R.: Logic programming. In: Handbook of Theoretical Computer Science, Volume B: Formal Models and Sematics (B), pp. 493–574. Elsevier (1990)
3. Ball, T., Rajamani, S.K.: Bebop: a path-sensitive interprocedural dataflow engine. In: Proceedings of the 2001 ACM SIGPLAN-SIGSOFT Workshop on Program Analysis for Software Tools and Engineering, PASTE 2001, Snowbird, Utah, USA, 18–19 June 2001, pp. 97–103 (2001)
4. Barnett, M., Chang, B.-Y.E., DeLine, R., Jacobs, B., M. Leino, K.R.: Boogie: a modular reusable verifier for object-oriented programs. In: de Boer, F.S., Bonsangue, M.M., Graf, S., de Roever, W.-P. (eds.) FMCO 2005. LNCS, vol. 4111, pp. 364–387. Springer, Heidelberg (2006)
5. Barnett, M., Leino, K.R.M.: Weakest-precondition of unstructured programs. In: PASTE, pp. 82–87 (2005)
6. Barrett, C., Stump, A., Tinelli, C.: The Satisfiability Modulo Theories Library (SMT-LIB) (2010). www.SMT-LIB.org
7. Barvinok, A.I.: A polynomial time algorithm for counting integral points in polyhedra when the dimension is fixed. In: 34th Annual Symposium on Foundations of Computer Science, Palo Alto, California, USA, 3–5 November 1993, pp. 566–572 (1993)
8. Berdine, J., Bjørner, N., Ishtiaq, S., Kriener, J.E., Wintersteiger, C.M.: Resourceful reachability as HORN-LA. In: McMillan, K., Middeldorp, A., Voronkov, A. (eds.) LPAR-19 2013. LNCS, vol. 8312, pp. 137–146. Springer, Heidelberg (2013)
9. Beyene, T.A., Chaudhuri, S., Popeea, C., Rybalchenko, A.: A constraint-based approach to solving games on infinite graphs. In: POPL, pp. 221–234 (2014)
10. Beyer, D., Cimatti, A., Griggio, A., Erkan Keremoglu, M., Sebastiani, R.: Software model checking via large-block encoding. In: FMCAD, pp. 25–32 (2009)
11. Bjørner, N., Gurfinkel, A.: Property directed polyhedral abstraction. In: D'Souza, D., Lal, A., Larsen, K.G. (eds.) VMCAI 2015. LNCS, vol. 8931, pp. 263–281. Springer, Heidelberg (2015)
12. Bjørner, N., McMillan, K.L., Rybalchenko, A.: Program verification as satisfiability modulo theories. In: SMT at IJCAR, pp. 3–11 (2012)
13. Bjørner, N., McMillan, K.L., Rybalchenko, A.: Higher-order program verification as satisfiability modulo theories with algebraic data-types. CoRR, abs/1306.5264 (2013)
14. Bjørner, N., McMillan, K., Rybalchenko, A.: On solving universally quantified horn clauses. In: Logozzo, F., Fähndrich, M. (eds.) SAS 2013. LNCS, vol. 7935, pp. 105–125. Springer, Heidelberg (2013)

15. Blass, A., Gurevich, Y.: Existential fixed-point logic. In: Börger, E. (ed.) Computation Theory and Logic. LNCS, vol. 270, pp. 20–36. Springer, Heidelberg (1987)
16. Blass, A., Gurevich, Y.: Inadequacy of computable loop invariants. ACM Trans. Comput. Log. **2**(1), 1–11 (2001)
17. Bradley, A.R.: SAT-based model checking without unrolling. In: Jhala, R., Schmidt, D. (eds.) VMCAI 2011. LNCS, vol. 6538, pp. 70–87. Springer, Heidelberg (2011)
18. Burstall, R.M., Darlington, J.: A transformation system for developing recursive programs. JACM **24**, 44–67 (1977)
19. Ceri, S., Gottlob, G., Tanca, L.: Logic Programming and Databases. Springer, Heidelberg (1990)
20. Clarke, E.M.: Programming language constructs for which it is impossible to obtain good hoare axiom systems. J. ACM **26**(1), 129–147 (1979)
21. Cook, S.A.: Soundness and completeness of an axiom system for program verif. SIAM J. Comput. **7**(1), 70–90 (1978)
22. Craig, W.: Three uses of the herbrand-gentzen theorem in relating model theory and proof theory. J. Symb. Log. **22**(3), 269–285 (1957)
23. De Angelis, E., Fioravanti, F., Pettorossi, A., Proietti, M.: Program verification via iterated specialization. Sci. Comput. Program. **95**, 149–175 (2014)
24. De Angelis, E., Fioravanti, F., Pettorossi, A., Proietti, M.: VeriMAP: a tool for verifying programs through transformations. In: Ábrahám, E., Havelund, K. (eds.) TACAS 2014 (ETAPS). LNCS, vol. 8413, pp. 568–574. Springer, Heidelberg (2014)
25. Dellunde, P., Jansana, R.: Some characterization theorems for infinitary universal horn logic without equality. J. Symb. Log. **61**(4), 1242–1260 (1996)
26. Dijkstra, E.W.: A Discipline of Programming. Prentice-Hall, New Jersey (1976)
27. Fietzke, A., Weidenbach, C.: Superposition as a decision procedure for timed automata. Math. Comput. Sci. **6**(4), 409–425 (2012)
28. Flanagan, C., Leino, K.R.M., Lillibridge, M., Nelson, G., Saxe, J.B., Stata, R.: Extended static checking for java. In: PLDI, pp. 234–245 (2002)
29. Floyd, R.W.: Assigning meaning to programs. In: Proceedings of Symposium on Applied Mathematics, vol. 19, pp. 19–32. American Math. Soc. (1967)
30. Gallagher, J.P., Kafle, B.: Analysis and transformation tools for constrained horn clause verification. CoRR, abs/1405.3883 (2014)
31. German, S.M., Clarke, E.M., Halpern, J.Y.: Reasoning about procedures as parameters in the language L4. Inf. Comput. **83**(3), 265–359 (1989)
32. Grebenshchikov, S., Lopes, N.P., Popeea, C., Rybalchenko, A.: Synthesizing software verifiers from proof rules. In: PLDI (2012)
33. Gurfinkel, A., Chaki, S., Sapra, S.: Efficient Predicate Abstraction of Program Summaries. In: Bobaru, M., Havelund, K., Holzmann, G.J., Joshi, R. (eds.) NFM 2011. LNCS, vol. 6617, pp. 131–145. Springer, Heidelberg (2011)
34. Gurfinkel, A., Kahsai, T., Komuravelli, A., Navas, J.A.: The seahorn verification framework. In: Kroening, D., Pǎsǎreanu, C.S. (eds.) CAV 2015. LNCS, vol. 9206, pp. 343–361. Springer, Heidelberg (2015)
35. Gurfinkel, A., Wei, O., Chechik, M.: Model checking recursive programs with exact predicate abstraction. In: Cha, S.S., Choi, J.-Y., Kim, M., Lee, I., Viswanathan, M. (eds.) ATVA 2008. LNCS, vol. 5311, pp. 95–110. Springer, Heidelberg (2008)
36. Hermenegildo, M.V., Bueno, F., Carro, M., Lopez-Garcia, P., Mera, E., Morales, J.F., Puebla, G.: An overview of ciao and its design philosophy. TPLP **12**(1–2), 219–252 (2012)
37. Hoare, C.A.R.: An axiomatic basis for computer programming. Commun. ACM **12**(10), 576–580 (1969)

38. Hoder, K., Bjørner, N.: Generalized property directed reachability. In: Cimatti, A., Sebastiani, R. (eds.) SAT 2012. LNCS, vol. 7317, pp. 157–171. Springer, Heidelberg (2012)

39. Hojjat, H., Iosif, R., Konečný, F., Kuncak, V., Rümmer, P.: Accelerating interpolants. In: Chakraborty, S., Mukund, M. (eds.) ATVA 2012. LNCS, vol. 7561, pp. 187–202. Springer, Heidelberg (2012)

40. Horn, A.: On sentences which are true of direct unions of algebras. J. Symb. Log. **16**(1), 14–21 (1951)

41. Jaffar, J.: A CLP approach to modelling systems. In: Davies, J., Schulte, W., Barnett, M. (eds.) ICFEM 2004. LNCS, vol. 3308, p. 14. Springer, Heidelberg (2004)

42. Jaffar, J., Maher, M.J.: Constraint logic programming: a survey. J. Log. Program. **19**(20), 503–581 (1994)

43. Jaffar, J., Santosa, A.E., Voicu, R.: An interpolation method for CLP traversal. In: Gent, I.P. (ed.) CP 2009. LNCS, vol. 5732, pp. 454–469. Springer, Heidelberg (2009)

44. Jhala, R., Majumdar, R., Rybalchenko, A.: HMC: verifying functional programs using abstract interpreters. In: Gopalakrishnan, G., Qadeer, S. (eds.) CAV 2011. LNCS, vol. 6806, pp. 470–485. Springer, Heidelberg (2011)

45. Jones, N.D., Gomard, C.K., Sestoft, P.: Partial Evaluation and Automatic Program Generation. Prentice Hall international series in computer science. Prentice Hall, Englewood Cliff (1993)

46. Kafle, B., Gallagher, J.P.: Constraint specialisation in horn clause verification. In: PEPM, pp. 85–90 (2015)

47. Karbyshev, A., Bjørner, N., Itzhaky, S., Rinetzky, N., Shoham, S.: Property-directed inference of universal invariants or proving their absence (2015)

48. Komuravelli, A., Gurfinkel, A., Chaki, S.: SMT-based model checking for recursive programs. In: Biere, A., Bloem, R. (eds.) CAV 2014. LNCS, vol. 8559, pp. 17–34. Springer, Heidelberg (2014)

49. Lal, A., Qadeer, S.: A program transformation for faster goal-directed search. In: Formal Methods in Computer-Aided Design, FMCAD 2014, Lausanne, Switzerland, 21–24 October 2014, pp. 147–154 (2014)

50. Rustan, K., Leino, M.: Efficient weakest preconditions. Inf. Process. Lett. **93**(6), 281–288 (2005)

51. Lopes, N.P., Bjørner, N., Godefroid, P., Jayaraman, K., Varghese, G.: Checking beliefs in dynamic networks. In: NSDI, May 2015

52. Manna, Z., Pnueli, A.: Temporal Verification of Reactive Systems: Safety. Springer, Berlin (1995)

53. McCarthy, J.: Towards a mathematical science of computation. In: IFIP Congress, pp. 21–28 (1962)

54. McMillan, K.L.: Lazy annotation revisited. In: Biere, A., Bloem, R. (eds.) CAV 2014. LNCS, vol. 8559, pp. 243–259. Springer, Heidelberg (2014)

55. Oppen, D.C.: Complexity, convexity and combinations of theories. Theor. Comput. Sci. **12**, 291–302 (1980)

56. Navarro Pérez, J.A., Rybalchenko, A.: Separation logic modulo theories. In: Shan, C. (ed.) APLAS 2013. LNCS, vol. 8301, pp. 90–106. Springer, Heidelberg (2013)

57. Pettorossi, A., Proietti, M.: Synthesis and transformation of logic programs using unfold/fold proofs. Technical report 457, Universitá di Roma Tor Vergata (1997)

58. Pudl'ak, P.: Lower bounds for resolution and cutting planes proofs and monotone computations. J. Symbolic Logic **62**(3), 981–998 (1995)

59. Ramsay, S.J., Neatherway, R.P., Luke Ong, C.-H.: A type-directed abstraction refinement approach to higher-order model checking. In: POPL, pp. 61–72 (2014)
60. Reps, T.W., Horwitz, S., Sagiv, S.: Precise interprocedural dataflow analysis via graph reachability. In: POPL, pp. 49–61 (1995)
61. Revesz, P.Z.: Safe datalog queries with linear constraints. In: Maher, M.J., Puget, J.-F. (eds.) CP 1998. LNCS, vol. 1520, pp. 355–369. Springer, Heidelberg (1998)
62. Rondon, P.M., Kawaguchi, M., Jhala, R.: Liquid types. In: PLDI, pp. 159–169 (2008)
63. Rümmer, P., Hojjat, H., Kuncak, V.: Disjunctive interpolants for horn-clause verification. In: Sharygina, N., Veith, H. (eds.) CAV 2013. LNCS, vol. 8044, pp. 347–363. Springer, Heidelberg (2013)
64. Sheeran, M., Singh, S., Stålmarck, G.: Checking safety properties using induction and a SAT-solver. In: Johnson, S.D., Hunt Jr., W.A. (eds.) FMCAD 2000. LNCS, vol. 1954, pp. 108–125. Springer, Heidelberg (2000)
65. Tamaki, H., Sato, T.: Unfold/fold transformation of logic programs. In: Proceedings of the Second International Conference on Logic Programming (1984)
66. Turchin, V.F.: The concept of a supercompiler. ACM TOPLAS 8(3), 292–325 (1986)
67. van Emden, M.H., Kowalski, R.A.: The semantics of predicate logic as a programming language. J. ACM 23(4), 733–742 (1976)
68. Warren, D.S.: Memoing for logic programs. Commun. ACM 35(3), 93 111 (1992)

Existential Fixed-Point Logic as a Fragment of Second-Order Logic

Andreas Blass

Mathematics Department, University of Michigan,
Ann Arbor, MI 48109–1043, USA
ablass@umich.edu

To Yuri Gurevich, on the occasion of his 75th birthday.

Abstract. The standard translation of existential fixed-point formulas into second-order logic produces strict universal formulas, that is, formulas consisting of universal quantifiers on relations (not functions) followed by an existential first-order formula. This form implies many of the pleasant properties of existential fixed-point logic, but not all. In particular, strict universal sentences can express some co-NP-complete properties of structures, whereas properties expressible by existential fixed-point formulas are always in P. We therefore investigate what additional syntactic properties, beyond strict universality, are enjoyed by the second-order translations of existential fixed-point formulas. In particular, do such syntactic properties account for polynomial-time model-checking?

1 Introduction

In [3], Yuri Gurevich and I pointed out numerous pleasant properties of existential fixed-point logic ($\exists$FPL), the logic roughly described as first-order logic, minus universal quantification, plus the least-fixed-point operator for positive inductive definitions. (This and other concepts used in this introduction are explained in more detail in Sect. 2.) In that paper, we also showed that formulas of existential fixed-point logic can be translated into equivalent formulas in a fragment of second-order logic called "strict $\forall_1^1$". Many, but not all of the pleasant properties of $\exists$FPL formulas are consequences of this translation; that is, they are enjoyed not only by $\exists$FPL formulas but by all strict $\forall_1^1$ formulas. The "not all" here refers particularly to PTime model-checking for all $\exists$FPL formulas; strict $\forall_1^1$ formulas do not all enjoy this property unless P=NP.

This situation suggests that perhaps the second-order translations of $\exists$FPL formulas actually lie in a smaller fragment of second-order logic, a subset of the strict $\forall_1^1$ fragment, such that the subset enjoys PTime model-checking. Of course, one could trivially define such a subset, namely the set of formulas that result from the standard translation procedure applied to $\exists$FPL formulas.

Partially supported by NSF grant DMS-0653696

L.D. Beklemishev et al. (Eds.): Gurevich Festschrift II 2015, LNCS 9300, pp. 52–68, 2015.
DOI: 10.1007/978-3-319-23534-9_3

The purpose of this paper[1] is to give a more detailed description of a subset with the desired properties.

We first show, in Sect. 3, that the model-checking problem for any $\exists$FPL sentence reduces to the propositional satisfiability problem for instances of a corresponding quantifier-free first-order formula. We describe the structure of these quantifier-free formulas and exploit that structure to transform these formulas, in Sects. 4 and 6, in a way that, on the one hand, does not alter the satisfiability of their instances but, on the other hand, ultimately leads to Horn formulas, so that satisfiability can be decided in polynomial time.

Along the way, the material in Sect. 5 presents an apparently new satisfiability-preserving transformation of propositional formulas in conjunctive normal form.

2   Preliminaries

2.1   Existential Fixed-Point Logic

In this subsection, we review the syntax and semantics of existential fixed-point logic.

A *vocabulary* for existential fixed-point logic ($\exists$FPL) consists of a vocabulary in the usual sense for first-order logic (predicate symbols and function symbols with specified natural numbers as arities) plus a specification, for each predicate symbol, whether it is *positive* or *negatable*. Terms and atomic formulas are defined as in first-order logic (without equality, for simplicity). Then $\exists$FPL formulas of a vocabulary L are defined by the following recursion, in which we omit some parentheses to improve readability.

- Atomic formulas of L are L-formulas.
- If φ is an atomic L-formula whose predicate symbol is negatable, then $\neg\varphi$ is an L-formula.
- If φ and ψ are L-formulas, then so are $\varphi \wedge \psi$ and $\varphi \vee \psi$.
- If φ is an L-formula and x is a variable, then $\exists x\, \varphi$ is an L-formula.
- Let $L' = L \cup \{P_1, \ldots, P_k\}$ be a language obtained by adding to L some k new (i.e., not already in L) positive predicate symbols P_i, say of arities r_i. Let $\mathbf{x}_1, \ldots, \mathbf{x}_k$ be lists of distinct variables of lengths r_i, respectively. Let $\delta_1, \ldots, \delta_k$ and φ be L'-formulas. Then

$$\text{Let } P_1(\mathbf{x}_1) \leftarrow \delta_1, \ldots, P_k(\mathbf{x}_k) \leftarrow \delta_k \text{ then } \varphi$$

is an L-formula. Formulas of this form are called *fixed-point formulas*, the predicate symbols P_i are called the *recursion variables*, the δ_i's are called their *defining formulas*, and φ is called the *conclusion*.

---

[1] My talk at Yuri Gurevich's 70th birthday conference in Brno contained much of the present paper's material, but I had overlooked what I now call the conjunction problem in Sect. 3. The solution of that problem given here in Sect. 4 is new. This paper is, except for preliminary material, disjoint from my written contribution [2] to Yuri's 70th birthday celebration.

Free variables of a formula are defined as in first-order logic with the additional clause that a variable is free in the fixed-point formula

$$\text{Let } P_1(\mathbf{x}_1) \leftarrow \delta_1, \dots, P_k(\mathbf{x}_k) \leftarrow \delta_k \text{ then } \varphi$$

if either it is free in some δ_i and is not in the list $\mathbf{x}_i$ or it is free in φ.

The semantics of ∃FPL is defined like that of first-order logic, with the following additional clause for fixed-point formulas. Let θ be the fixed-point formula displayed above. Let $\mathfrak{A}$ be an L-structure with underlying set A, and let values in A for the free variables of θ be given. Consider any k-tuple $(R_1, \dots, R_k)$ of relations on A, where each R_i is r_i-ary. Let $(\mathfrak{A}, R_1, \dots, R_k)$ be the L'-structure that agrees with $\mathfrak{A}$ as an L-structure and interprets the additional predicate symbols P_i as the corresponding R_i. Each of the L'-formulas δ_j defines, in $(\mathfrak{A}, R_1, \dots, R_k)$, an r_j-ary relation S_j on A. In detail, an r_j-tuple $\mathbf{a}$ of elements of A is in S_j if δ_j is true in $(\mathfrak{A}, R_1, \dots, R_k)$ when the variables $\mathbf{x}_j$ are interpreted as $\mathbf{a}$ and the other free variables have their originally given interpretations. This construction $\mathbf{\Delta}$ sending k-tuples $(R_1, \dots, R_k)$ to k-tuples $(S_1, \dots, S_k)$ is a monotone operator on k-tuples of relations of arities r_i on A. (Monotonicity is with respect to componentwise set-thoretic inclusion; it follows from the requirement that the P_i's are positive in the δ_j's.) Let $\mathbf{\Delta}^\infty$ be the least fixed-point of this monotone operator. Then the interpretation of θ in $\mathfrak{A}$ is defined to be the interpretation of the conclusion φ in $(\mathfrak{A}, \mathbf{\Delta}^\infty)$.

Less formally, the "Let ... then ..." construction produces the least fixed-point of any definable positive operator on (tuples of) relations, and then uses that fixed-point in a further formula φ.

The absence of the universal quantifier would be meaningless if we allowed negation of arbitrary formulas, as one can simulate $\forall x$ with $\neg \exists x \neg$. This is why negation is allowed only on atomic formulas. The distinction between positive and negatable predicate symbols and the prohibition of negation on positive atomic formulas serve to ensure that the δ_i in the fixed-point formula θ above contain only positive occurrences of the recursion variables P_j and thus define a monotone operator $\mathbf{\Delta}$. They also serve to ensure that the conclusion φ in θ contains only positive occurrences of the predicates P_j; without such a restriction, we could surreptitiously introduce the negation of a positive predicate Q by writing $\text{Let } P(x) \leftarrow Q(x) \text{ then } \neg P(x)$, which would be equivalent to $\neg Q(x)$.

The definition of ∃FPL formulas is a recursion involving all vocabularies simultaneously, because fixed-point formulas of one vocabulary L can have subformulas, like the δ_i's and φ above, from a larger vocabulary L'. In effect, the additional symbols P_i of L' play the role of bound second-order variables. This connection with second-order logic will be clarified in the next subsection.

2.2   Translation to Second-Order Logic

In this subsection, we review the standard translation from ∃FPL formulas to strict $\forall_1^1$ formulas of second-order logic. As mentioned in the introduction, these are formulas obtained from existential formulas of first-oder logic by prefixing them with a string (possibly an empty string) of universal second-order quantifiers over predicate symbols.[2]

Note that there is a symbiosis between the two requirements (1) that the second-order quantifiers apply to predicate symbols and not function symbols and (2) that the first-order part of the formula be purely existential. Each of these requirements alone would be meaningless. Specifically, if we imposed only requirement (1) but allowed arbitrary first-order parts, then we could use the first-order part to say that the universally quantified predicates are the graphs of functions, thereby making (1) pointless. If, on the other hand, we imposed only requirement (2) but allowed universal quantification of functions rather than predicates, then arbitrary first-order parts could be simulated by converting them to Herbrand normal form (the dual of Skolem normal form).

We now check, by induction on ∃FPL formulas φ, that they are equivalent to strict $\forall_1^1$ formulas. This is obvious in the case of atomic or negated atomic formulas.

In the case of conjunctions and disjunctions, we write the conjuncts or disjuncts in strict $\forall_1^1$ form using different bound second-order variables, combine them with $\land$ or $\lor$, and pull the second-order quantifiers out as a prefix using the usual prenexing rules.

In the case of existential quantification, we pull the second-order universal quantifiers out of the scope of the new existential first-order quantifier using the logical equivalence

$$(\exists x)(\forall P)\,\varphi(P(\dots)) \iff (\forall P')(\exists x)\,\varphi(P'(x,\dots)).$$

Here the arity of P' exceeds that of P by one, and every occurrence of P in the body of the formula is changed to an occurrence of P' with the additional argument x.

Finally, in the case of fixed-point formulas, we use the fact that

$$\textbf{Let } P_1(\mathbf{x}_1) \leftarrow \delta_1, \dots, P_k(\mathbf{x}_k) \leftarrow \delta_k \textbf{ then } \varphi$$

is equivalent to

$$(\forall P_1)\dots(\forall P_k)\left[\left(\bigwedge_{i=1}^{k}(\forall \mathbf{x}_i)\,(\delta_i \implies P_i(\mathbf{x}))\right) \implies \varphi\right].$$

To see the equivalence, note that, since the P_i's occur only positively in φ, if φ holds for the intended interpretation $\mathbf{\Delta}^\infty$ of the P_i's, then it also holds for all larger relations, and, in particular, for all relations closed under the operator $\mathbf{\Delta}$. And this is precisely what the second-order formula above says: φ holds whenever the (interpretations of the) P_i are closed under the operator $\mathbf{\Delta}$ given by the defining formulas δ_i.

---

[2] The terminology "strict $\forall_1^1$" was chosen in analogy with "strict Π_1^1" in [1, Sect. 8.2]. The difference is that "strict Π_1^1" is used in a set-theoretic context and allows not only existential quantifiers but also bounded universal quantifiers ($\forall x \in y$) in the first-order part of the formula.

Now if we insert into this equivalent formula some strict $\forall_1^1$ forms of the δ_i's and φ and then apply standard prenex operations, the result is in strict $\forall_1^1$ form, as desired. Note, in particular, that the universal first-order quantifiers $\forall \mathbf{x}_i$ are in the antecedent of an implication so the first-order part is existential.

The preceding proof, showing that $\exists$FPL formulas can be translated to equivalent strict $\forall_1^1$ formulas, would become an algorithm for carrying out the translation if we added some unimportant details, such as the choice of bound variables and the order in which similar quantifiers are pulled out during prenex operations. We assume henceforth that these details have been supplied, and we refer to the resulting algorithm as the *standard translation* from $\exists$FPL to strict $\forall_1^1$.

In [3] some semantic properties of $\exists$FPL formulas were established by showing that they actually hold for all strict $\forall_1^1$ formulas. These properties include the facts that

- The set of valid $\exists$FPL sentences is a complete computably enumerable set.
- The set of satisfiable $\exists$FPL sentences is a complete computably enumerable set.[3]
- If a formula is satisfied by some elements in a structure, then this fact depends only on a finite part of the structure.

But at least one important property of $\exists$FPL formulas, namely PTime model-checking, does not (unless P=NP) hold for arbitrary strict $\forall_1^1$ formulas. Specifically, on undirected graphs, regarded as structures with a single binary relation E of adjacency, the strict $\forall_1^1$ formula

$$(\forall P_1)(\forall P_2)(\forall P_3)(\exists x)(\exists y)\left[\bigwedge_{i=1}^{3} \neg P_i(x) \vee \bigvee_{i=1}^{3}(E(x,y) \wedge P_i(x) \wedge P_i(y))\right]$$

expresses that the graph is not 3-colorable, a co-NP-complete property.

This situation suggests that perhaps the second-order translations of $\exists$FPL formulas are not merely strict $\forall_1^1$ but have some additional syntactic property that ensures their PTime decidability. The main purpose of this paper is to establish such an additional property.

3   Model-Checking

In this section, we discuss model-checking for strict $\forall_1^1$ sentences. That is, we consider, for any fixed strict $\forall_1^1$ sentence φ in vocabulary L, the following decision problem:[4] An instance is a finite L-structure $\mathfrak{A}$ and the question is whether $\mathfrak{A} \models \varphi$.

---

[3] The expected duality between validity and satisfiability is not available for logics, like $\exists$FPL, that are not closed under negation.

[4] We are dealing here with what is often called data complexity of the model-checking problem. That is, we regard the "data" $\mathfrak{A}$ as the input, and we measure resource usage relative to the size of $\mathfrak{A}$, while the "query" φ is held fixed.

It is convenient to address this problem by considering the negation of φ instead. It has a standard translation to a strict $\exists_1^1$ sentence; that is, $\neg\varphi$ can be put into the form

$$(\exists R_1)\ldots(\exists R_m)\,\psi$$

where the R_i are predicate symbols and where ψ is a universal first-order sentence of the vocabulary $L' = L \cup \{R_1, \ldots, R_m\}$. This strict $\exists_1^1$ sentence is true in $\mathfrak{A}$ if and only if there are relations[5] R_i on the underlying set A such that all instances of ψ are true for this interpretation of the existentially quantified predicate variables in $\neg\varphi$. Here "instances of ψ" refers to all the formulas obtained by replacing the (universally) quantified first-order variables in ψ by arbitrary elements of A.

This criterion for $\mathfrak{A} \models \neg\varphi$ is essentially a question of propositional satisfiability. Indeed, consider the set Σ of all instances of ψ. These are quantifier-free $L'(A)$-sentences, where $L'(A)$ is the language obtained from $L' = L \cup \{R_1, \ldots, R_m\}$ by adding (names for) all the elements of A as constant symbols. In these sentences, replace each atomic sentence that uses an L-predicate symbol (i.e., any predicate symbol other than the R_i's) by its truth value in $\mathfrak{A}$. What remains is a set Σ' of sentences that are Boolean combinations of instances of the R_i's. Regard all these instances of R_i's as propositional variables. Any truth assignment to these propositional variables amounts to a choice of relations R_i; the truth assignment satisfies Σ' if and only if the R_i relations satisfy ψ. Therefore $\neg\varphi$ is true in $\mathfrak{A}$ if and only if Σ' is (truth-functionally) satisfiable.

The process leading from φ and $\mathfrak{A}$ to Σ' can be summarized as follows.

1. Perform the standard translation of φ to strict $\forall_1^1$ form.
2. Negate the result and push the negation in past quantifiers and connectives, until only atomic formulas are negated; the result is the standard strict $\exists_1^1$ form of $\neg\varphi$.
3. Delete all quantifiers, but remember which predicate symbols were bound second-order variables.
4. Form all instances of the resulting formula, replacing the first-order variables by (names of) elements of $\mathfrak{A}$ in all possible ways.
5. In the resulting formulas, replace the atomic subformulas whose predicate symbols are in the vocabulary of $\mathfrak{A}$ (as opposed to the predicate symbols that were quantified second-order variables before step 3) by their truth values in $\mathfrak{A}$.

The resulting set of formulas is the propositional translation Σ' of $\neg\varphi$. Its propositional variables are of the form $R(\mathbf{a})$, where R was a bound second-order variable before step 3, and $\mathbf{a}$ is a tuple of elements of $\mathfrak{A}$.

Note that we have arranged the steps so that the input $\mathfrak{A}$ of our model-checking problem enters the process only at step 4.

The propositional translation has two key properties. First, $\mathfrak{A} \models \varphi$ if and only if the propositional translation of $\neg\varphi$ is not satisfiable. Second, the propositional

---

[5] To avoid excessive notation, we use the same symbols for these relations as for the corresponding symbols in our strict $\exists_1^1$ sentence.

translation is, for fixed φ, computable in polynomial time from $\mathfrak{A}$. In particular, the size of the propositional translation of $\neg\varphi$ is bounded by the product of

- $|A|^d$, where d is the number of universally quantified, first-order variables in the strict $\forall_1^1$ translation of φ, because these are the variables that must be replaced, in all possible ways, by elements of A,
- $\log|A|$ to account for the length in bits of the names of the elements of A, and
- a constant, namely the length of the formula obtained in step 3 above, before $\mathfrak{A}$ entered the process.

Thus, we have a PTime reduction of the model-checking problem for a (fixed) $\exists$FPL sentence φ to a propositional satisfiability problem. Our goal is to detect the special properties of the propositional translations of $\exists$FPL sentences that make their satisfiability decidable in PTime. For example, if the propositional translations always consisted of Horn formulas, then that would provide a PTime solution of the model-checking problem. We therefore turn our attention to the structure of the formulas that arise in the propositional translations of $\exists$FPL sentences.

Let us begin by disposing of a tempting error. When we translated $\exists$FPL formulas θ into second-order logic, the second-order variables originated from the recursion variables P_i in the $P_i(\mathbf{x}) \leftarrow \delta_i(\mathbf{x})$ parts of fixed-point formulas. Those P_i's are positive predicate symbols. So they occur only positively in the strict $\forall_1^1$ form of θ, and therefore the resulting propositional variables occur only negatively in the propositional translation of $\neg\varphi$. It is, of course, trivial to decide satisfiability of propositional formulas in which all the variables occur only negatively; just give them all the value "false" and see whether the formulas become true.

The error in the preceding paragraph is that, although the P_i are positive predicate symbols and therefore occur only positively in the defining formulas δ_i and in the conclusion φ, they nevertheless acquire negative occurrences in the strict $\forall_1^1$ translation. Specifically, the underlined occurrences in the translation

$$(\forall P_1)\dots(\forall P_k)\left[\left(\bigwedge_{i=1}^{k}(\forall \mathbf{x}_i)\,(\delta_i \implies \underline{P_i(\mathbf{x})})\right) \implies \varphi\right]$$

of a fixed-point formula are negative. So the situation is not so trivial as the preceding paragraph would suggest.

A better, but still incorrect approach involves rewriting the translation of a fixed-point formula exhibited above in the logically equivalent form

$$(\forall P_1)\dots(\forall P_k)\left[\varphi \vee \bigvee_{i=1}^{k} \exists \mathbf{x}_i(\neg P_i(\mathbf{x}_i) \wedge \delta_i)\right].$$

The negation, in strict $\exists_1^1$ form, then looks like

$$(\exists P_1)\dots(\exists P_k)\left[\neg\varphi \wedge \bigwedge_{i=1}^{k}(\forall \mathbf{x}_i)\,(P_i(\mathbf{x}_i) \vee \neg\delta_i)\right].$$

The first-order body of this formula is a conjunction of $k+1$ subformulas, each of which contains at most one positive occurrence of a P_i. When we form instances of this body, we get at most one positive literal in each conjunct. That is, we get only Horn clauses, and it is well-known that satisfiability of sets of Horn clauses is decidable in PTime.

There are two errors in this approach. The first is that ∃FPL formulas are not simply fixed-point formulas like the one under consideration here. In particular, we might have the conjunction of two (or more) such formulas. Then the propositional translation of the negation will be a disjunction of formulas like those here, and, when put into conjunctive normal form, will have two (or more) positive literals in some of its clauses. We shall address this *conjunction problem* in Sect. 4.

The second error in the argument above is that a conjunct $P_i(\mathbf{x}) \vee \neg \delta_i$ can have more positive occurrences of literals than just the visible $P_i(\mathbf{x})$. If the formula δ_i contains some fixed-point formulas as subformulas, then the second-order variables arising from those subformulas will have negative occurrences (analogous to the underlined P_i's above) in δ_i and therefore positive occurrences in the conjunct $P_i(\mathbf{x}) \vee \neg \delta_i$ under consideration. So the conjunctive normal forms of our propositional translations need not be Horn formulas.

Notice that this error is relevant only when recursions are nested, that is, when the defining formula δ_i in a recursive clause $P_i(\mathbf{x}_i) \leftarrow \delta_i$ contains further fixed-point formulas. Accordingly, we call this the *nesting problem*; we shall address it in Sects. 5 and 6.

It is known that nesting of recursions is never really needed in ∃FPL. For example, the nested recursion

Let $P(x) \leftarrow$ [Let $Q(y) \leftarrow \delta(P, Q, x, y)$ then $\theta(P, Q, x)$] then $\varphi(P)$

(where we have indicated which predicate symbols and bound variables are available in the subformulas) is equivalent to

Let $P(x) \leftarrow \theta(P, Q'_x, x)$, $Q'(x, y) \leftarrow \delta(P, Q'_x, x, y)$ then $\varphi(P)$,

where Q'_x means the binary predicate symbol Q' with x inserted as its first argument. For the general proof that unnested recursions suffice, see, for example, [5, Sect. 1.C].

One can similarly circumvent the conjunction problem, because conjunctions in ∃FPL formulas can be pushed inward to apply only to atomic and negated atomic formulas. For example, the conjunction

(Let $P(x) \leftarrow \delta(x)$ then φ) $\wedge$ (Let $P'(y) \leftarrow \delta'(y)$ then φ')

is equivalent to

Let $P(x) \leftarrow \delta(x), P'(y) \leftarrow \delta'(y)$ then $\varphi \wedge \varphi'$

(where we assume that bound variables have been renamed if necessary to avoid clashes).

In a sense, these observations explain, via the strict $\forall_1^1$ translation, why $\exists$FPL has PTime model-checking. Explicitly: Given an $\exists$FPL sentence, rewrite it to avoid nested recursions and to avoid conjunctions of compound formulas. Then produce the propositional translation of the negation of the new $\exists$FPL sentence, using a conjunctive normal form of its matrix. The result consists of Horn clauses, for which satisfiability is decidable in PTime. (The use of the conjunctive normal form can exponentially increase the size of the formula, but this doesn't matter as we are considering a single formula at a time and measuring complexity relative to the structure $\mathfrak{A}$.)

Unfortunately, this does not quite answer our original question, which concerned the direct translation of arbitrary $\exists$FPL formulas to strict $\forall_1^1$ form, without pre-processing to eliminate nested recursions and non-trivial conjunctions.

Fortunately, the satisfiability problem for the sets of formulas that actually arise can be transformed, on the level of propositional logic, to an equivalent satisfiability problem for Horn formulas. In the following sections, we shall carry out this transformation. In Sect. 4, we show how to convert the formulas that actually arise to formulas that avoid the conjunction problem; the conversion preserves satisfiability. In Sects. 5 and 6, we do the same for the nesting problem. Section 5 isolates the relevant construction in general, not just for the formulas obtained by translating $\exists$FPL formulas; this general, satisfiability-preserving transformation seems to be of independent interest. The application of the general transformation to the nesting problem for translated $\exists$FPL formulas is described in Sect. 6.

Remark 1. The general theme of this paper is that model-checking for a certain class of second-order formulas is in polynomial time because it can be reduced to the propositional satisfiability problem for Horn formulas. The same theme occurs in a paper [4] of Erich Grädel. The class of second-order formulas considered there, called SO-HORN, is, however, quite different from the class arising here from $\exists$FPL. The appropriate comparison would be between SO-HORN and the strict $\exists_1^1$ formulas arising from the negations of $\exists$FPL formulas. In both cases, the second-order quantifiers range only over relation variables, and in both cases the first-order matrix is required to be a universal formula, but the smiilarity ends there. SO-HORN allows both universal and existential second-order quantifiers, whereas strict $\exists_1^1$ requires the second-order quantifiers to be existential. On the other hand, the quantifier-free parts of SO-HORN formulas are required to already be in Horn form (at least with regard to the quantified predicate symbols), whereas, as we have seen above, we must deal with non-Horn formulas. Indeed, the following sections are primarily devoted to the problem of converting our formulas to Horn form without altering the satisfiability of their instances.

4   Conjunctions

To avoid annoying distractions during our manipulations of formulas, we assume from now on that there are no clashes of variables in our $\exists$FPL formulas. That is, no (first-order) variable has both free and bound occurrences, nor is any such variable bound twice (by $\exists$ or by the fixed-point construction); also no predicate symbol occurs more than once as a recursion variable. This simplification can, of course, be achieved by renaming bound variables and recursion variables as necessary. We shall refer to this convention as the "no clashes" assumption.

We point out, for future reference, a consequence of the no clashes assumption. Suppose that, in some $\exists$FPL sentence φ, a certain variable x occurs in two or more fixed-point subformulas, say with recursion variables P and Q. Then the scope of that x must include both of those fixed-point subformulas. As a result, when one converts φ to strict $\forall_1^1$ form, the second-order quantifiers $\forall P$ and $\forall Q$ will be pulled out of the scope of an $\exists x$, and so the predicate symbols P and Q will have their arities increased and will have x inserted as an additional argument. Thus, if x occurs in two or more fixed-point subformulas of φ, then the recursion variables of those subformulas will, in the strict $\forall_1^1$ translation of φ, have x among their arguments. We shall refer to this observation as "argument joining".

As a first step in the solution of the conjunction problem, we describe carefully the class of formulas that arise from steps 1 to 3 in the process described above for obtaining Σ' from φ and $\mathfrak{A}$. As remarked there, these three steps do not involve $\mathfrak{A}$, which enters only at steps 4 and 5. So we are working with just an $\exists$FPL formula φ. We first produce the standard strict $\exists_1^1$ form of $\neg\varphi$, and then we delete all the quantifiers, obtaining a quantifier-free first-order formula in the vocabulary consisting of the vocabulary of φ plus amplified recursion variables from φ. Here "amplified" refers to the extra argument places that recursion variables acquire when, in the production of the strict $\forall_1^1$ form, they are pulled out of the scope of first-order existential quantifiers. By inspection of the definitions of $\exists$FPL formulas and of their standard translations to strict $\forall_1^1$ form, we see that the quantifier-free formulas obtained by this process are among the primary formulas defined as follows.

Definition 2. The *primary* formulas of a vocabulary L form the smallest class such that

- atomic formulas whose predicate symbol is negatable are primary,
- negations of arbitrary atomic formulas are primary,
- conjunctions of primary formulas are primary,
- disjunctions of primary formulas are primary, and
- if α and $\delta_1, \ldots, \delta_k$ are primary formulas for the vocabulary $L \cup \{P_1, \ldots, P_k\}$, where the P_i are new positive predicate symbols, then

$$\alpha \wedge \bigwedge_{i=1}^{k} (P_i(\mathbf{x}_i) \vee \delta_i)$$

is primary.

We refer to the last item in this list of constructors as the *mix constructor*, because it mixes conjunction and disjunction. Each P_i occurring there will be called a *key* predicate, and $\mathbf{x}_i$ and δ_i will be called its *associated* variables and formula, respectively.

Note that the primary formulas include all negated atomic formulas, but they include the unnegated ones only when the predicate symbol is negatable. This strange-sounding situation — the predicate must be negatable in order to appear unnegated — arises from the fact that we are working with the translations not of ∃FPL formulas themselves but of their negations. Note further that a positive predicate can have at most one positive occurrence in a primary formula, namely an occurrence as the key predicate of a mix construction. Here the "at most one" claim follows from our no clashes assumption.

In this new context, argument joining becomes the fact that, if α is a primary formula and if a variable occurs in two or more subformulas of α obtained by the mix construction, then that variable is among the arguments of the key predicates of those mix subformulas.

The next definition describes a subclass of the primary formulas for which the conjunction problem does not arise. In fact, formulas in this subclass have an especially useful structure, which we describe, in terms of their parse trees, after the definition.

Definition 3. The *basic secondary* formulas of a vocabulary L form the smallest class such that

- atomic formulas whose predicate symbol is negatable are basic secondary,
- negations of arbitrary atomic formulas are basic secondary,
- conjunctions of basic secondary formulas are basic secondary, and
- disjunctions of basic secondary formulas are basic secondary.

The *secondary* formulas of a vocabulary L form the smallest class such that

- all basic secondary formulas are secondary, and
- if α and $\delta_1, \ldots, \delta_k$ are secondary formulas for the vocabulary $L \cup \{P_1, \ldots, P_k\}$, where the P_i are new positive predicate symbols, then the result of the mix construction,

$$\alpha \wedge \bigwedge_{i=1}^{k} (P_i(\mathbf{x}_i) \vee \delta_i),$$

is secondary.

Thus, secondary formulas are built by the same constructors as primary formulas but, in a secondary formula, the mix constructors must be applied after all the others, not intermingled with the others.

It is useful to consider parse trees showing how secondary formulas are built from basic secondary ones. The internal nodes of such a tree correspond to the mix construction $\alpha \wedge \bigwedge_{i=1}^{k}(P_i(\mathbf{x}_i) \vee \delta_i)$; such a node has $2k+1$ children, one for α, k for the key predicate subformulas $P_i(\mathbf{x}_i)$, and k corresponding to the associated δ_i's. Of these, the k corresponding to $P_i(\mathbf{x}_i)$ are leaves of the parse tree; the other $k+1$ might be leaves or internal nodes. All the leaves of the parse tree are either of the $P_i(\mathbf{x}_i)$ form just mentioned or basic secondary formulas. Notice that the leaves of the $P_i(\mathbf{x}_i)$ sort are the only place where positive predicate symbols have positive occurrences.

The main result in this section will say that every primary formula can be transformed into a secondary one while preserving the essential property relevant for ∃FPL. That essential property is, in view of the results of Sect. 3, instance-equisatisfiability, defined as follows.

Definition 4. Two sets of quantifier-free formulas Σ_1 and Σ_2 (in a first-order language that extends L) are *equisatisfiable* if, whenever there exists a truth assignment satisfying one of them, there also exists a (possibly different) truth assignment satisfying the other. They are *instance-equisatisfiable* if, for every L-structure $\mathfrak{A}$, $\Sigma_1(\mathfrak{A})$ and $\Sigma_2(\mathfrak{A})$ are equisatisfiable, where $\Sigma_i(\mathfrak{A})$ is obtained from Σ_i by replacing the variables by elements of $\mathfrak{A}$ in all possible ways and then replacing all atomic subformulas whose predicate is in L by their truth values in $\mathfrak{A}$.

Notice that the construction of $\Sigma_i(\mathfrak{A})$ from Σ_i described in this definition is exactly the last two steps, 4 and 5, in the construction of Σ' in Sect. 3. Thus, for the purpose of model-checking ∃FPL formulas, the Σ' there, which consists of primary formulas, can safely be replaced by any instance-equisatisfiable set of formulas. That is how we shall use the following proposition and its corollary.

Proposition 5. *The conjunction and disjunction of two secondary formulas are each instance-equisatisfiable with a secondary formula.*

Proof. We proceed by induction on the two given secondary formulas, and we treat the most difficult case, namely where both of them arise from the mix construction. (If both of the given formulas are basic, then the result is trivial. If one arises from mix and the other is basic, then the proof is easier, or one can regard the basic formula as resulting from a mix in which the number of key predicates happens to be zero.) Suppose, therefore, that the given formulas are

$$\gamma = \alpha \wedge \bigwedge_{i=1}^{k}(P_i(\mathbf{x}_i) \vee \delta_i) \quad \text{and} \quad \gamma' = \alpha' \wedge \bigwedge_{i=1}^{k'}(P_i'(\mathbf{x}_i') \vee \delta_i').$$

Their conjunction $\gamma \wedge \gamma'$ is not merely instance-equisatisfiable but tautologically equivalent with

$$(\alpha \wedge \alpha') \wedge \bigwedge_{i=1}^{k}(P_i(\mathbf{x}_i) \vee \delta_i) \wedge \bigwedge_{i=1}^{k'}(P_i'(\mathbf{x}_i') \vee \delta_i'),$$

which is a secondary formula with $k+k'$ key predicates, because, by the induction hypothesis, $\alpha \wedge \alpha'$ is a secondary formula.

For the disjunction, we use

$$\theta = (\alpha \vee \alpha') \wedge \bigwedge_{i=1}^{k}(P_i(\mathbf{x}_i) \vee \delta_i) \wedge \bigwedge_{i=1}^{k'}(P_i'(\mathbf{x}_i') \vee \delta_i'),$$

which is a secondary formula, as above, because $\alpha \vee \alpha'$ is secondary by induction hypothesis. It is easy to see that θ tautologically implies $\gamma \vee \gamma'$. The converse, however, is not generally correct; we do not get equivalence but only instance-equisatisfiability.

To prove the non-trivial direction of instance-equisatisfiability, suppose we have an L-structure $\mathfrak{A}$ and truth assignment v satisfying all the instances of $\gamma \vee \gamma'$, where by "instance" we understand, as in the definition of instance-equisatisfiability, the result of substituting elements of $\mathfrak{A}$ for variables and then replacing all atomic formulas involving L-symbols by their truth values in $\mathfrak{A}$. Notice that the predicate symbols in γ and γ' are all either L-symbols or key predicates of mix constructions.

To emphasize the essential idea of the proof, we first consider the special case where γ and γ' have no (first-order) variables in common. In this case, we claim that v either satisfies all instances of γ or satisfies all instances of γ' (not merely some instances of the one and the remaining instances of the other). Suppose the claim were false, so some instance of γ, and some other instance of γ' were falsified by v. Then we could form a third instance, giving the variables in γ the same values as in the first instance (thus making γ false under v) and giving the variables in γ' the same values as in the second instance (thus making γ' false under v). But then this third instance would make $\gamma \vee \gamma'$ false under v, contrary to our choice of v.

Thus, we may suppose without loss of generality, that v satisfies all instances of γ. Now we can produce a truth assignment v^* satisfying θ as follows. Let v^* assign the value "true" to all those atomic formulas whose predicate symbol is one of the key predicates P_i' of γ', and let v^* agree with v on all other atomic formulas. The difference between v and v^*, affecting only the P_i', will not affect γ, because the P_i' don't occur in γ (thanks to the no clashes assumption). Thus v^* satisfies γ and therefore satisfies the part $(\alpha \vee \alpha') \wedge \bigwedge_{i=1}^{k}(P_i(\mathbf{x}_i) \vee \delta_i)$ of θ. But it also satisfies the remaining conjunct, $\bigwedge_{i=1}^{k'}(P_i'(\mathbf{x}_i') \vee \delta_i')$ of θ. So v^* satisfies θ as required.

The preceding argument used the assumption that γ and γ' have no common variables. We now indicate how to modify it to accommodate common variables, say the list $\mathbf{y}$ of variables. We no longer claim that v satisfies all instantiations of γ or all instantiations of γ'; instead, we claim that, for any fixed instantiation of $\mathbf{y}$, v satisfies all its extensions to instantiations of γ or all its extensions to instantiations of γ'. In other words, whether γ or γ' is satisfied (by v) may depend on the instantiation but only via the values assigned to the common variables $\mathbf{y}$. The proof of this modified claim is exactly as in the easier argument given above; once we fix the values of $\mathbf{y}$, the remaining variables, occurring in only one of γ and γ', can be treated as before.

In the easier argument, we obtained v^* by modifying the truth values assigned by v to the key predicates of γ', under the assumption that v satisfied all instances of γ. Of course, if v had satisfied all instances of γ', then we would have modified the truth values assigned to the key predicates of γ. Now in the present, more complicated situation, the decision as to which predicates should get new truth values may depend on the values assigned to **y**. Thanks to argument joining, this is no problem. The variables **y** occur as arguments of all the key predicates in γ and in γ'. So we can modify the values assigned to instances of P_i with certain values for the **y** arguments and modify the values assigned to instances of P_i' with other values for the **y** arguments. What we do with one instantiation of **y** has no effect on what happens with other instantiations. (Another way to view this argument is that we treat the variables **y** as new constant symbols and consider separately all the expansions of $\mathfrak{A}$ giving values to these new constants. That reduces the problem to the easier case already treated.)

This completes the proof of the proposition.

Corollary 6. *Every primary formula is instance-equisatisfiable with a secondary formula.*

Proof. Induction on primary formulas, using Proposition 5 for the only nontrivial cases.

The proofs of the proposition and corollary provide an explicit algorithm for converting a primary formula to an instance-equisatisfiable secondary one.

5 Satisfiability and Trimming

This section is entirely about propositional logic, specifically about satisfiability of sets of clauses. Here "clause" means, as usual, a disjunction of literals, i.e., of propositional variables and negations of propositional variables. So a set of clauses is semantically equivalent to a conjunctive normal form, namely the conjunction of its clauses.

Theorem 7. *Let Γ be a set of clauses, let p be a propositional variable, and let Q be a set of propositional variables other than p. Suppose that, whenever a clause in Γ contains a negative occurrence of a variable from Q, it also contains a positive occurrence of p or of some variable from Q. Obtain Γ' from Γ by deleting positive occurrences of p from those clauses that also contain positive occurrences of at least one variable from Q. Then Γ is satisfiable if and only if Γ' is.*

Proof. One direction is trivial, because any truth assignment that satisfies all the clauses in Γ' will certainly satisfy the corresponding clauses in Γ, since the latter differ from the former at most by having additional disjuncts.

Suppose, therefore, that we have a truth assignment v that satisfies all the clauses in Γ. If it makes p false, then it also satisfies all the clauses in Γ', because the positive occurrences of p that were removed when we produced Γ' were not satisfied by v and so some other disjuncts in those clauses must have been satisfied.

So we may assume that v makes p true. In this situation, v need not satisfy Γ', but we can find another truth assignment v' that will satisfy Γ'. Let v' make all the variables in Q true, and let it agree with v on all the other variables. To show that v' satisfies every clause γ in Γ', we consider three cases.

First, suppose γ is one of the clauses that was altered, by removing the positive disjunct p, when we transformed Γ to Γ'. Recall that we undertook such a removal only when the clause in Γ contained, along with p, a positive occurrence of some variable from Q. Such variables are true under v', and therefore our clause γ is also true under v'.

It remains to consider those clauses γ that were not changed in the transition from Γ to Γ'. These were true under v, but we need that they are true under v'. That is very easy to check for those clauses γ in which variables from Q occur only positively. Since, in going from v to v', the only changes were that variables in Q, which might have been false under v, became true under v', any clause containing them only positively cannot change from true under v to false under v'.

There remain those clauses γ that are the same in Γ and in Γ' but have negative occurrences of some variable(s) from Q. By the hypothesis of the theorem, every such γ also has positive occurrences of p or of some variable from Q. Since p and all variables from Q are true under v', it follows that v' satisfies all such clauses γ.

Definition 8. The transformation from Γ to Γ' described in the theorem is called *trimming* Γ or, in more detail, trimming p using Q.

6 Trimming to Horn Form

In this section, we complete the reduction of the model-checking problem for any ∃FPL sentence to a decidable case of the propositional satisfiability problem, namely the satisfiability of sets of Horn clauses.

Given an ∃FPL sentence φ, we saw in Sect. 3 how to reduce the problem "Given $\mathfrak{A}$, decide whether φ is true in $\mathfrak{A}$" to the problem of satisfiability of the set of all $\mathfrak{A}$-instances of a certain formula constructed from φ. That formula is primary, in the sense defined in Sect. 4 and, as proved there, instance-equisatisfiable with a certain secondary formula. So the model-checking problem for φ is reduced to determining the satisfiability of the instances of this secondary formula.

The next step is to convert this secondary formula, say ψ, into conjunctive normal form. (As mentioned earlier, the possible exponential increase in the formula's size caused by this conversion is not a problem, because we are considering the model-checking problem for a fixed formula, with only the structure $\mathfrak{A}$ as input. The set of all $\mathfrak{A}$-instances still has size polynomial in the size of $\mathfrak{A}$.) We now look into the structure of this conjunctive normal form and its $\mathfrak{A}$-instances (for arbitrary $\mathfrak{A}$).

Recall that, when forming $\mathfrak{A}$-instances of ψ, we replace any atomic subformulas that use predicates from L by their truth values in $\mathfrak{A}$. The atomic subformulas of an instance therefore use only the predicates not in L, which are the recursion variables of φ and the key predicates of the primary and secondary formulas derived from φ. We shall use the letters P and Q to stand for such predicates in the following discussion.

Let us consider the conjunctive normal form of a secondary formula ψ, paying particular attention to the positive occurrences of atomic subformulas using the P, Q predicates. Basic secondary formulas are built using $\wedge$ and $\vee$ from atomic subformulas, subject to the condition that positive predicates — which include the P, Q predicates — occur only negatively. So there are not yet any positive occurrences of P's and Q's at this basic stage. That situation changes when we apply the mix construction to produce secondary formulas of the form

$$\alpha \wedge \bigwedge_{i=1}^{k} (P_i(\mathbf{x}_i) \vee \delta_i).$$

Now each P_i has a positive occurrence, and, in addition, other P's and Q's may have positive occurrences in α and in the δ_i's. To convert $\alpha \wedge \bigwedge_{i=1}^{k}(P_i(\mathbf{x}_i) \vee \delta_i)$ to conjunctive normal form, we would first convert α and the δ_i's to conjunctive normal form and then, for each i, distribute $P_i(\mathbf{x}_i) \vee -$ across the conjunctive normal form of δ_i. Thus, each conjunct of that conjunctive form acquires $P_i(\mathbf{x}_i)$ as a new literal. Note that such a conjunct may already have other positive occurrences of other P's and Q's, but only when these are the key predicates of subformulas of δ_i. Thus, those other P's and Q's come from mix subformulas that are descendants of the current mix formula $\alpha \wedge \bigwedge_{i=1}^{k}(P_i(\mathbf{x}_i) \vee \delta_i)$ in the parse tree of ψ. We emphasize that, in this conjunct, the new positive P and previously present Q are key predicates of comparable mix nodes of the parse tree.

Repeating this process for every application of the mix constructor in ψ, we arrive at a conjunctive normal form θ in which every individual conjunct has, because of the comparability noted at the end of the preceding paragraph, the following crucial property: All the positive occurrences of P's and Q's in it originated from mix nodes in a single branch of the parse tree of ψ.

From now on, to make contact with the terminology of Sect. 5, we shall identify the conjunction θ with the set of its conjuncts, which may thus be called clauses.

Consider a P and a Q such that the mix node with key P is an ancestor of the mix node with key Q in the parse tree of ψ. So P is some P_i in a mix formula $\alpha \wedge \bigwedge_{i=1}^{k}(P_i(\mathbf{x}_i) \vee \delta_i)$, while Q is the key of a mix subformula of δ_i. That mix subformula contains all the occurrences of Q in ψ, because of our no clash assumption. As a result, in the conjunctive normal form θ, every clause with an occurrence of Q also has a positive occurrence of $P(\mathbf{x}_i)$. (We need this information only for the negative occurrences of Q, but it is true for all occurrences of Q.)

Recall that, in this situation, when we formed the strict $\forall_1^1$ form of φ (as the first step toward ψ and θ), the variables $\mathbf{x}_i$ associated to P_i became additional arguments of Q. Because of that, when we now form instances of θ, all clauses containing negative occurrences of any particular instance of Q will also contain a positive occurrence of the corresponding instance of $P_i(\mathbf{x}_i)$. This means, by

Theorem 7, that we can delete positive occurrences of any instance of P from any clause that also contains a positive occurrence of a corresponding instance Q.

These deletions can be uniformly summarized as follows, in terms of θ itself rather than its instances: In any clause containing positive occurrences of P and Q, where Q originated in a descendant of the mix formula of P, one can delete the occurrence of P. But, in every conjunct of θ, the positively occurring P's and Q's originated along a branch, and so one can delete all the positive P's and Q's except the one farthest from the root of the parse tree of ψ.

That leaves at most one positive P in any clause; all instances then have at most one positive literal. That is, we have only Horn clauses in the trimmed conjunctive normal form.

7 Summary

The strict $\forall_1^1$ translation of any $\exists$FPL sentence has a special syntactic form. Its quantifier-free matrix is the negation of what we called a primary formula in Sect. 4, and the occurrences of variables are constrained by the no clash assumption and the argument joining property. This special form ensures polynomial-time model-checking, because this special syntactic form allows, first, reduction to a secondary formula (still subject to no clashes and argument joining) and, second, trimming to Horn form. Then the original $\exists$FPL sentence holds in $\mathfrak{A}$ if and only if the set of all $\mathfrak{A}$-instances of this Horn form is not satisfiable.

Acknowledgement. Because of the last-minute discovery of the conjunction problem, this paper was submitted after the official deadline, leaving less than the normal time for refereeing. Nevertheless, the referee provided a very useful report. I thank him or her for the report, in particular for informing me about the existence and relevance of [4].

References

1. Barwise, J.: Admissible Sets and Structures: An Approach to Definability Theory. Perspectives in Mathematical Logic. Springer-Verlag, Berlin (1975)
2. Blass, A.: Existential fixed-point logic, universal quantifiers, and topoi. In: Blass, A., Dershowitz, N., Reisig, W. (eds.) Fields of Logic and Computation. LNCS, vol. 6300, pp. 108–134. Springer, Heidelberg (2010)
3. Blass, A., Gurevich, Y.: Existential fixed-point logic. In: Börger, E. (ed.) Computation Theory and Logic. LNCS, vol. 270, pp. 20–36. Springer, Heidelberg (1987)
4. Grädel, E.: Capturing complexity classes by fragments of second-order logic. Theoret. Computer Sci. **101**, 35–57 (1992)
5. Moschovakis, Y.N.: Elementary Induction on Abstract Structures. Studies in Logic and the Foundations of Mathematics. North-Holland, New York (1974)

On the Unpredictability of Individual Quantum Measurement Outcomes

Alastair A. Abbott[1,2], Cristian S. Calude[1(✉)], and Karl Svozil[3]

[1] Department of Computer Science, University of Auckland,
Private Bag, 92019 Auckland, New Zealand
{a.abbott,c.calude}@auckland.ac.nz
[2] Centre Cavaillès, CIRPHLES, École Normale Supérieure,
29 rue d'Ulm, 75005 Paris, France
[3] Institute for Theoretical Physics, Vienna University of Technology,
Wiedner Hauptstrasse 8-10/136, 1040 Vienna, Austria
svozil@tuwien.ac.at

Abstract. We develop a general, non-probabilistic model of prediction which is suitable for assessing the (un)predictability of individual physical events. We use this model to provide, for the first time, a rigorous proof of the unpredictability of a class of individual quantum measurement outcomes, a well-known quantum attribute postulated or claimed for a long time.

We prove that quantum indeterminism—formally modelled as value indefiniteness—is incompatible with the supposition of predictability: *measurements of value indefinite observables are unpredictable.* The proof makes essential use of a strengthened form of the Kochen-Specker theorem proven previously to identify value indefinite observables. This form of quantum unpredictability, like the Kochen-Specker theorem, relies on three assumptions: compatibility with quantum mechanical predictions, non-contextuality, and the value definiteness of observables corresponding to the preparation basis of a quantum state.

We explore the relation between unpredictability and incomputability and show that the unpredictability of individual measurements of a value indefinite quantum observable complements, and is independent of, the global strong incomputability of any sequence of outcomes of this particular quantum experiment.

Finally, we discuss a real model of hypercomputation whose computational power has yet to be determined, as well as further open problems.

1 Introduction

The outcomes of measurements on a quantum systems are often regarded to be fundamentally unpredictable [33]. However, such claims are based on intuition and experimental evidence, rather than precise mathematical reasoning. In order to investigate this view more precisely, both the notion of unpredictability and the status of quantum measurements relative to such a notion need to be carefully studied.

© Springer International Publishing Switzerland 2015
L.D. Beklemishev et al. (Eds.): Gurevich Festschrift II 2015, LNCS 9300, pp. 69–86, 2015.
DOI: 10.1007/978-3-319-23534-9_4

Unpredictability is difficult to formalise not just in the setting of quantum mechanics, but that of classical mechanics too. Various physical processes from classical chaotic systems to quantum measurement outcomes are often considered unpredictable, and various definitions, both domain specific [30] or more general [13], and of varying formality, have been proposed. For precise claims to be made, the appropriate definitions need to be scrutinised and the results proven relative to specific definitions.

Quantum indeterminism has been progressively formalised via the notion of value indefiniteness in the development of the theorems of Bell [5] and, particularly, Kochen and Specker [16]. These theorems, which have also been experimentally tested via the violation of various inequalities [29], express the impossibility of certain classes of deterministic theories. The conclusion of value indefiniteness from these no-go theorems rests on various assumptions, amounting to the refusal to accept non-classical alternatives such as non-locality and contextual determinism. And if value indefiniteness is, as often stated, related to unpredictability, any claims of unpredictability need to be similarly evaluated with respect to, and seen to be contingent on such assumptions.

In this paper we address these issues in turn. We first discuss various existing notions of predictability and their applicability to physical events. We propose a new formal model of prediction which is non-probabilistic and, we argue, captures the notion that an arbitrary single physical event (be it classical, quantum, or otherwise) or sequence thereof is 'in principle' predictable. We review the formalism of value indefiniteness and the assumptions of the Kochen-Specker theorems (classical and stronger forms), and show that the outcomes of measurements of value indefinite properties are indeed unpredictable with respect to our model. Thus, in this framework unpredictability rests on the same assumptions as quantum value indefiniteness. Finally, we discuss the relationship between quantum randomness and unpredictability, and show that unpredictability does not, in general, imply the incomputability of sequences generated by repeating the experiment *ad infinitum*. Thus, the strong incomputability of sequences of quantum measurement outcomes appears to rest independently on the assumption of value indefiniteness.

2   Models of Prediction

To predict—in Latin prædicere, "to say before"—means *to forecast what will happen under specific conditions before the phenomenon happens*. Various definitions of predictability proposed by different authors will be discussed regarding their suitability for capturing the notion of predictability of individual physical events or sequences thereof in the most general sense. While some papers, particularly in physics and cryptographic fields, seem to adopt the view that probabilities mean unpredictability [4,33], this is insufficient to describe unpredictable physical processes. Probabilities are a formal description given by a particular theory, but do not entail that a physical process is fundamentally, that is, ontologically, indeterministic nor unpredictable, and can (often very reasonably) represent simply an epistemic lack of knowledge or underdetermination of the theory. Instead, a more robust way to formulate prediction seems to be in terms of a 'predicting agent' of some form. This is indeed the approach taken by some definitions, and that we also will follow.

In the theory of dynamical systems, unpredictability has long been linked to chaos and has often been identified as the inability to calculate with any reasonable precision the state of a system given a particular observable initial condition [30]. The observability is critical, since although a system may presumably have a well-defined initial state (a point in phase-space), any observation yields an interval of positive measure (a region of phase space). This certainly seems the correct path to follow in formalising predictability, but more generality and formalism is needed to provide a definition for arbitrary physical processes.

Popper, in arguing that unpredictability *is* indeterminism, defines prediction in terms of "physical predicting machines" [21]. He considers these as real machines that can take measurements of the world around them, compute via physical means, and output (via some display or tape, for example) predictions of the future state of the system. He then studies experiments which must be predicted with a certain accuracy and considers these to be predictable if it is *physically* possible to construct a predictor for them.

Wolpert [31] formalised this notion much further in developing a general abstract model of physical inference. Like Popper, Wolpert was interested in investigating the limits of inference, including prediction, arising from the simple fact that any inference device must itself be a physical device, hence an object whose behaviour we can try to predict. While Wolpert's aim was not so focused on the predictability arising from the nature of specific physical theories, he identified and formalised the need for an experimenter to develop prediction techniques and initialise them by interacting with the environment via measurements.

A more modern and technical definition of unpredictability was given by Eagle [13] in defining randomness as maximal unpredictability. While we will return to the issue of randomness later, Eagle's definition of unpredictability deserves further attention. He defined prediction relative to a particular theory and for a particular predicting agent, an approach thus with some similarity to that of Wolpert. Specifically, a prediction function is defined as a function mapping the state of the system described by the theory and specified epistemically (and thus finitely) by the agent to a probability distribution of states at some time. This definition formalises more clearly prediction as the output of a function operating on information extracted about the physical system by an agent.

Popper's and Wolpert's notions of predictability perhaps lack generality by requiring the predictor to be embedded, that is, physically present, in its environment [28], and are not so suited to investigating the predictability of particular physical processes, but rather of the physical world as a whole. Similarly, Eagle's definition renders predictability relative to a particular physical theory.

In order to relate the intrinsic indeterminism of a system to unpredictability, it would be more appropriate to have a definition of events as unpredictable *in principle*. Thus, the predictor's ignorance of a better theory might change their associated epistemic ability to know if an event is predictable or not, but would not change the fact that an event may or may not be, in principle, predictable.

Last but not least, it is important to restrict the class of prediction functions by imposing some effectivity (i.e. computability) constraints. Indeed, we suggest that "to predict" is to say in advance in some effective/constructive/computable way what physical event or outcome will happen. Thus, motivated by the Church-Turing Thesis, we choose here Turing computability. Any predicting agent operating with incomputable means—incomputable/infinite inputs or procedures that can go beyond the power of algorithms (for example, by executing infinitely many operations in a finite amount of time)—seems to be physically highly speculative if not impossible. Technically, "controlled incomputability" could be easily incorporated in the model, if necessary.

Taking these points into account, we propose a definition—similar in some aspects to Wolerpt's and Eagle's definitions—based on the ability of some computably operating agent to correctly predict using finite information extracted from the system of the specified experiment. For simplicity we will consider experiments with binary observable values (0 or 1), but the extension to finitely or countable many (i.e. finitely specified) output values is straightforward. Further, unlike Eagle [13], we consider only prediction with certainty, rather than with probability. While it is not difficult nor unreasonable to extend our definition to the more general scenario, this is not needed for our application to quantum measurements; moreover, in doing so we avoid any potential pitfalls related to probability 1 or 0 events [32].

Our main aim is to define the (correct) prediction of individual events [13], which can be easily extended to an infinite sequence of events. An individual event can be correctly predicted simply by chance, and a robust definition of predictability clearly has to avoid this possibility. Popper succinctly summarises this predicament in Ref. [21, 117–118]:

> "If we assert of an observable event that it is unpredictable we do not mean, of course, that it is logically or physically impossible for anybody to give a correct description of the event in question before it has occurred; for it is clearly not impossible that somebody may hit upon such a description accidentally. What is asserted is that certain rational methods of prediction break down in certain cases—the methods of prediction which are practised in physical science."

One possibility is then to demand a proof that the prediction is correct, thus formalising the "rational methods of prediction" that Popper refers to. However, this is notoriously difficult and must be made relative to the physical theory considered, which generally is not well axiomatised and can change over time. Instead we demand that such predictions be *repeatable*, and not merely one-off events. This point of view is consistent with Popper's own framework of empirical falsification [20, 22]: an empirical theory (in our case, the prediction) can never be proven correct, but it can be falsified through decisive experiments pointing to incorrect predictions. Specifically, we require that the *predictions remain correct in any arbitrarily long (but finite) set of repetitions of the experiment*.

3   A Model for Prediction of Individual Physical Events

In order to formalise our non-probabilistic model of prediction we consider a hypothetical experiment E specified effectively by an experimenter. We formalise the notion of a predictor as an effective (i.e. computational) method of uniformly producing the outcome of an experiment using finite information extracted (again, uniformly) from the experimental conditions along with the specification of the experiment, but *independent* of the results of the experiments. An experiment will be predictable if any potential sequence of repetitions (of unbounded, but finite, length) of it can always be predicted correctly by such a predictor.

In detail, we consider a finitely specified physical experiment E producing a single bit $x \in \{0,1\}$ (which, as we previously noted, can readily be generalised). Such an experiment could, for example, be the measurement of a photon's polarisation after it has passed through a 50-50 polarising beam splitter, or simply the toss of a physical coin with initial conditions and experimental parameters specified finitely. Further, with a particular instantiation or trial of E we associate the parameter λ which fully describes the trial. While λ is not in its entirety an obtainable quantity, it contains any information that may be pertinent to prediction and any predictor can have practical access to a finite amount of this information. In particular this information may be directly associated with the particular trial of E (e.g. initial conditions or hidden variables) and/or relevant external factors (e.g. the time, results of previous trials of E). We can view λ as a resource that one can extract finite information from in order to predict the outcome of the experiment E. Any such external factors should, however, be local in the sense of special relativity, as (even if we admit quantum non-locality) any other information cannot be utilised for the purpose of prediction [17]. We formalise this in the following.

An *extractor* is a physical device selecting a finite amount of information included in λ without altering the experiment E. It can be used by a predicting agent to examine the experiment and make predictions when the experiment is performed with parameter λ. Mathematically, an extractor is represented by a (deterministic) function $\lambda \mapsto \xi(\lambda) \in \{0,1\}^*$ where $\xi(\lambda)$ is a finite string of bits. For example, $\xi(\lambda)$ may be an encoding of the result of the previous instantiation of E, or the time of day the experiment is performed. As usual, the formal model is significantly weaker: here, an extractor is a deterministic function which can be physically implemented without affecting the experimental run of E.

A predictor for E is an algorithm (computable function) P_E which *halts* on every input and *outputs* either 0, 1 (cases in which P_E has made a prediction), or "prediction withheld". We interpret the last form of output as a refrain from making a prediction. The predictor P_E can utilise as input the information $\xi(\lambda)$ selected by an extractor encoding relevant information for a particular instantiation of E, but must not disturb or interact with E in any way; that is, it must be *passive*.

As we noted earlier, a certain predictor may give the correct output for a trial of E simply by chance. This may be due not only to a lucky choice of predictor, but also to the input being chosen by chance to produce the correct output. Thus, we rather consider the performance of a predictor P_E using, as input, information extracted by a particular fixed extractor. This way we ensure that P_E utilises in ernest information extracted from λ, and we avoid the complication of deciding under what input we should consider P_E's correctness.

A predictor P_E provides a *correct prediction* using the extractor ξ for an instantiation of E with parameter λ if, when taking as input $\xi(\lambda)$, it outputs 0 or 1 (i.e. it does not refrain from making a prediction) and this output is equal to x, the result of the experiment.

Let us fix an extractor ξ. The predictor P_E is k *correct for* ξ if there exists an $n \geq k$ such that when E is repeated n times with associated parameters $\lambda_1, \ldots, \lambda_n$ producing the outputs $x_1, x_2, \ldots, x_n$, P_E outputs the sequence $P_E(\xi(\lambda_1)), P_E(\xi(\lambda_2)), \ldots, P_E(\xi(\lambda_n))$ with the following two properties:

1. no prediction in the sequence is incorrect, and
2. in the sequence there are k correct predictions.

The repetition of E must follow an algorithmic procedure for resetting and repeating the experiment; generally this will consist of a succession of events of the form "E is prepared, performed, the result (if any) recorded, E is reset".

If P_E is k-correct for ξ we can bound the probability that P_E is in fact operating by chance and may not continue to give correct predictions, and thus give a measure of our confidence in the predictions of P_E. Specifically, the sequence of n predictions made by P_E can be represented as a string of length n over the alphabet $\{T, F, W\}$, where T represents a correct prediction, F an incorrect prediction, and W a withheld prediction. Then, for a predictor that is k-correct for ξ there exists an $n \geq k$ such that the sequence of predictions contains k T's and $(n - k)$ W's. There are $\binom{n}{k}$ such possible prediction sequences out of 3^n possible strings of length n. Thus, the probability that such a correct sequence would be produced by chance tends to zero when k goes to infinity because

$$\frac{\binom{n}{k}}{3^n} < \frac{2^n}{3^n} \leq \left(\frac{2}{3}\right)^k.$$

Clearly the confidence we have in a k-correct predictor increases as $k \to \infty$. If P_E is k-correct for ξ for all k, then P_E never makes an incorrect prediction and the number of correct predictions can be made arbitrarily large by repeating E enough times. In this case, we simply say that P_E *is correct for* ξ. The infinity used in the above definition is *potential* not actual: its role is to guarantee arbitrarily many correct predictions.

This definition of correctness allows P_E to refrain from predicting when it is unable to. A predictor P_E which is correct for ξ is, when using the extracted information $\xi(\lambda)$, guaranteed to always be capable of providing more correct predictions for E, so it will not output "prediction withheld" indefinitely. Furthermore, although P_E is technically used only a finite, but arbitrarily large, number of times, the definition guarantees that, in the hypothetical scenario where it is executed infinitely many times, P_E will provide infinitely many correct predictions and not a single incorrect one.

While a predictor's correctness is based on its performance in repeated trials, we can use the predictor to define the prediction of single bits produced by the experiment E. If P_E is not correct for ξ then we cannot exclude the possibility that any correct prediction P_E makes is simply due to chance. Hence, we propose the following definition:

> the outcome x of a single trial of the experiment E performed with parameter λ is predictable (with certainty) if there exist an extractor ξ and a predictor P_E which is correct for ξ, and $P_E(\xi(\lambda)) = x$.

Accordingly, P_E correctly predicts the outcome x, never makes an incorrect prediction, and can produce arbitrarily many correct predictions.

4 Computability Theoretic Notions of Unpredictability

The notion of unpredictability defined in the previous section has both physical components (in extracting information from the system for prediction via ξ) and computability theoretic ones (in predicting via an effective procedure, P_E). Both these components are indispensable for a good model of prediction for physical systems, but it is nonetheless important to discuss their relation to pure computability theoretic notions of prediction, since these place unpredictability in a context where the intuition is stripped to its abstract basics.

The algorithmic notions of bi-immunity (a strong form of incomputability) and Martin-Löf randomness describe some forms of unpredictability for infinite sequences of bits [9]. A sequence is *bi-immune* if it contains no infinite computable subsequence (i.e., both the bits of the subsequence and their positions in the original sequence must be computable). A sequence is *Martin-Löf random* if all prefixes of the sequence cannot be compressed by more than an additive constant by a universal prefix-free Turing machine (see [9,12] for more details). Thus, for a bi-immune sequence, we cannot effectively compute the value of any bit in advance and only finitely many bit-values can be correctly "guessed", while a Martin-Löf random sequence contains no "algorithmic" patterns than can be used to effectively compress it.

However, the notions of predictability presented by Tadaki [27] are perhaps the most relevant for this discussion. *An infinite sequence of bits* $\mathbf{x} = x_1 x_2 \ldots$ is Tadaki totally predictable *if there exists a Turing machine* $F : \{0,1\}^* \to \{0,1,W\}$ *that halts on every input, and satisfies the following two conditions: (i) for every n, either $F(x_1 \ldots x_n) = x_{n+1}$ or $F(x_1 \ldots x_n) = W$; and (ii) the set $\{n \in \mathbb{N}^+ \mid F(x_1 \ldots x_n) \neq W\}$ is infinite; F is called a total predictor for $\mathbf{x}$.*

A similar notion, called *Tadaki predictability*, requires only that F halts on all input $x_1 \ldots x_n$, and thus may be a partially computable function instead of a computable one. This emphasises that, as we mentioned earlier, the notion of predictability can be strengthened or weakened by endowing the predictor with varying computational powers.

Tadaki predictability can be related to various other algorithmic notions of randomness. For example, *no Martin-Löf random sequence is Tadaki (totally) predictable* [27, Theorem 4], while *all non-bi-immune sequences are Tadaki totally predictable*. This last fact can be readily proven by noting that a non-bi-immune sequence **x** must contain a computable subsequence $(k_1, x_{k_1}), (k_2, x_{k_2}), \ldots$. Equivalently, there is an infinite computable set $K \subset \mathbb{N}$ and a computable function $f : K \to \{0,1\}$ such that for all $k \in K$, $f(k) = x_k$. Hence, for a string $\sigma \in \{0,1\}^*$ the function

$$F(\sigma) = \begin{cases} f(|\sigma| + 1), & \text{if } |\sigma| + 1 \in K, \\ W, & \text{otherwise,} \end{cases}$$

is a Tadaki total predictor for **x** ($|\sigma|$ is the length of σ).

Furthermore, the notion of *Tadaki total unpredictability is strictly stronger than bi-immunity*, since there exist bi-immune, totally predictable sequences. For example, let $\mathbf{x} = x_1 x_2 \ldots$ be a Martin-Löf random sequence (and hence bi-immune [9]). It is not difficult to show that $\mathbf{y} = y_1 y_2 \cdots = x_1 x_1 x_2 x_2 \ldots$ created by doubling the bits of **x** is bi-immune. However, **y** has a Tadaki total predictor F defined as

$$F(\sigma_1 \ldots \sigma_n) = \begin{cases} \sigma_n, & \text{if } n \text{ is odd}, \\ W, & \text{if } n \text{ is even}, \end{cases}$$

since this correctly predicts the value of every bit at an even position in **y**.

This notion of predictability can be physically interpreted in the following way. Consider a black-box $B(\mathbf{x})$ with a button that, when pressed, gives the next digit of **x**; by repeating this operation one can slowly learn, in order, the bits of **x**. A sequence is Tadaki predictable if there is a uniform way to compute infinitely often x_{n+1} having learnt the initial segment $x_1 \ldots x_n$, with the proviso that we must know *in advance* when—that is, the times at which—we will be able to do so.

When viewed from the physical point of view described above, there is a clear relation to our notion of predictability. In particular, we can consider a deterministic experiment $E_\mathbf{x}$ that consists of generating a bit from the black-box $B(\mathbf{x})$, and asking if $E_\mathbf{x}$ is predictable for the 'prefix' extractor $\xi_p(\lambda_i) = x_1 \ldots x_{i-1}$ for the trial of $E_\mathbf{x}$ producing x_i—that is, using just the results of the previous repetitions of $E_\mathbf{x}$. It is not too difficult to see that $E_\mathbf{x}$ *is predictable if and only if* **x** *is Tadaki totally predictable*. Indeed, equate the function F from Tadaki's definition and the predictor P_E, as well as the outputs 'W' and "prediction withheld".

In general, algorithmic information theoretical properties of sequences could be explored using our model of prediction via such an approach. However, the relation between these notions exists only when one considers particular, abstract, extractors such as ξ_p. The generality of our model originates in the importance it affords to physical properties of systems, *via* extractors, which are essential for prediction in real systems. Depending on the physical scenario investigated, then, physical devices might allow us to extract information allowing to predict an experiment, regardless of the algorithmic content of this information, as long as finite information suffices for a single prediction.

5 Quantum Unpredictability

We now apply the notion developed above to formally justify the well-known claim that quantum events are completely unpredictable.

5.1 The Intuition of Quantum Indeterminism and Unpredictability

Intuitively, it would seem that quantum indeterminism corresponds to the *absence of physical reality*; if no unique element of physical reality corresponding to a particular physical quantity exists, this is reflected by the physical quantity being indeterminate. That is, for such an observable none of the possible exclusive measurement outcomes are certain to occur and therefore we should conclude that any kind of prediction of the outcome with certainty cannot exist, and the outcome of this individual measurement must thus be unpredictable. For example, an agent trying to predict the outcome of a measurement of a projection observable in a basis unbiased with respect to the preparation basis (i.e. if there is a "maximal mismatch" between preparation and measurement) could do no better than blindly guess the outcome of the measurement.

However, such an argument is too informal. To apply our model of unpredictability the notion of indeterminism needs to be specified much more rigorously: this implies developing a formalism for quantum indeterminism, as well as a careful discussion of the assumptions which indeterminism is reliant on.

5.2 A Formal Basis for Quantum Indeterminism

The phenomenon of quantum indeterminism cannot be deduced from the Hilbert space formalism of quantum mechanics alone, as this specifies only the probability distribution for a given measurement which in itself need not indicate intrinsic indeterminism. Indeterminism has had a role at the heart of quantum mechanics since Born postulated that the modulus-squared of the wave function should be interpreted as a probability density that, unlike in classical statistical physics [18], expresses fundamental, irreducible indeterminism [7]. In Born's own words, "*I myself am inclined to give up determinism in the world of atoms.*" The nature of individual measurement outcomes in quantum mechanics was, for a period, a subject of much debate. Einstein famously dissented, stating his belief that [8, p. 204] "*He does not throw dice.*" Nonetheless, over time the conjecture that measurement outcomes are themselves fundamentally indeterministic became the quantum orthodoxy [33].

Beyond the blind belief originating with Born, the Kochen-Specker theorem, along with Bell's theorem, are among the primary reasons for the general acceptance of quantum indeterminism. The belief in quantum indeterminism thus rests largely on the same assumptions as these theorems. In the development of the Kochen-Specker theorem, quantum indeterminism has been formalised as the notion of value indefiniteness [1], which allows us to discuss indeterminism in a more general formal setting rather than restricting ourselves to any particular interpretation. Here we will review this formalism, as well as a stronger form of the Kochen-Specker theorem and its assumptions which are important for the discussion of unpredictability.

For a given quantum system in a particular state, we say that an observable is *value definite* if the measurement of that observable is predetermined to take a (potentially hidden) value. If no such predetermined value exists, the observable is *value indefinite*. Formally, this notion can be represented by a *(partial) value assignment function* (see [1] for the complete formalism).

In addressing the question of when we should conclude that a physical quantity is value definite, Einstein, Podolsky and Rosen (EPR) give *a sufficient criterion of physical reality* in terms of certainty and predictability in [14, p. 777]. Based on this accepted *sufficient* condition for the existence of an element of physical reality, we allow ourselves to be guided by the following "EPR principle":[1]

> *EPR principle*: If, without in any way disturbing a system, we can predict with certainty the value of a physical quantity, then there exists a *definite value* prior to observation corresponding to this physical quantity.

As we discussed earlier, the notion of prediction the EPR principle refers to needs to be effective; further, we note that the constraint that prediction acts "without in any way disturbing a system" is perhaps non-trivial [17], but is equally required by our model of prediction.

The EPR principle justifies the subtle but often overlooked

> *Eigenstate principle*: If a quantum system is prepared in a state $|\psi\rangle$, then the projection observable $P_\psi = |\psi\rangle\langle\psi|$ is value definite.

This principle is necessary in order to use the strong Kochen-Specker theorem to single-out value indefinite observables, and is similar to, although weaker, than the eigenstate-eigenvalue link (as only one direction of the implication is asserted) [25].

A further requirement called *admissibility* is used to avoid outcomes impossible to obtain according to quantum predictions. Formally, admissibility states that an observable in a context—that is, a set of mutually commuting (i.e. compatible) observables—cannot be value indefinite if all but one of the possible measurement outcomes would contradict quantum mechanical identities given the values of other, value definite observables in the same context. In such a case, the observable must have the definite value of that sole 'consistent' measurement outcome.

---

[1] They continue: "It seems to us that this criterion, while far from exhausting all possible ways of recognizing a physical reality, at least provides us with one such way, whenever the conditions set down in it occur."

Here is an example: given a context $\{P_1, \ldots, P_n\}$ of commuting projection observables, if P_1 were to have the definite value 1, all other observables in this context must have the value 0. Were this not the case, there would be a possibility to obtain the value 1 for more than one compatible projection observable, a direct contradiction of the quantum prediction that one and only one projector in a context give the value 1 on measurement. Note that we require this to hold only when any indeterminism (which implies multiple possible outcomes) would allow quantum mechanical predictions to be broken: were P_1 to have the value 0, admissibility would not require anything of the other observables if the rest were value indefinite, as neither a measurement outcome of 0 or 1 for $P_2 \ldots P_n$ would lead to a contradiction.

The Kochen-Specker theorem [16] shows that no value assignment function can consistently make *all* observables value definite while maintaining the requirement that the values are assigned non-contextually—that is, the value of an observable is the same in each context it is in. This is a global property: non-contextuality is incompatible with *all* observables being value definite. However, it is possible to go deeper and localise value indefiniteness to prove that even the existence of two non-compatible value definite observables is in contradiction with admissibility and the requirement that any value definite observables behave non-contextually, without requiring that all observables be value definite. Thus, any mismatch between preparation and measurement context leads to the measurement of a value indefinite observable: this is stated formally in the following strong version of the Kochen-Specker theorem.

Theorem 1 (From [1,3]). *Let there be a quantum system prepared in the state $|\psi\rangle$ in dimension $n \geq 3$ Hilbert space $\mathbb{C}^n$, and let $|\phi\rangle$ be any state neither orthogonal nor parallel to $|\psi\rangle$, i.e. $0 < |\langle\psi|\phi\rangle| < 1$. Then the projection observable $P_\phi = |\phi\rangle\langle\phi|$ is value indefinite under any non-contextual, admissible value assignment.*

Hence, accepting that definite values, *should they exist* for certain observables, behave non-contextually is in fact enough to derive rather than postulate quantum value indefiniteness.

5.3 Contextual Alternatives

It is worth keeping in mind that, while indeterminism is often treated as an assumption or aspect of the orthodox viewpoint [7,33], this usually rests implicitly on the deeper assumptions (mentioned in Sect. 5.2) that the Kochen-Specker theorem relies on. If these assumptions are violated, deterministic theories could not be excluded, and the status of value indefiniteness and unpredictability would need to be carefully revisited.

If this were the case, perhaps the simplest alternative would be the explicit assumption of (albeit non-local) context dependant predetermined values. Many attempts to interpret quantum mechanics deterministically, such as Bohmian mechanics [6], can be expressed in this framework. Since such a theory would no longer be indeterministic, the intuitive argument for unpredictability would break down, and the theory could in fact be totally predictable. However, predictability is still not an immediate consequence, as such hidden variables could potentially be "assigned" by a demon operating beyond the limits of any predicting agent (e.g. incomputably).

Another possibility would be to consider the case that any predetermined outcomes may in fact not be determined by the observable alone, but rather by *"the complete disposition of the apparatus"* [5, Sect. 5]. In this viewpoint, even when the macroscopic measurement apparatuses are still idealised as being perfect, their many degrees of freedom (which may by far exceed Avogadro's or Loschmidt's constants) contribute to any measurement of the single quantum. Most of these degrees of freedom might be totally uncontrollable by the experimenter, and may result in an *epistemic unpredictability* which is dominated by the combined complexities of interactions between the single quantum measured and the (macroscopic) measurement device producing the outcome.

In such a measurement, the pure single quantum and the apparatus would become entangled. In the absence of one-to-one uniqueness between the macroscopic states of the measurement apparatus and the quantum, any measurement would amount to a partial trace resulting in a mixed state of the apparatus, and thus to uncertainty and unpredictability of the readout. In this case, just as for irreversibility in classical statistical mechanics [18], the unpredictability of single quantum measurements might not be irreducible at all, but an expression of, and relative to, the limited means available to analyse the situation.

5.4   Unpredictability of Individual Quantum Measurements

With the notion of value indefiniteness presented, let us now turn our attention to applying our formalism of unpredictability to quantum measurement outcomes of the type discussed in Sect. 5.2.

Throughout this section we will consider an experiment E performed in dimension $n \geq 3$ Hilbert space in which a quantum system is prepared in a state $|\psi\rangle$ and a value indefinite observable P_ϕ is measured producing a single bit x. By Theorem 1 such an observable is guaranteed to exist, and to identify one we need only a mismatch between preparation and observation contexts. The nature of the physical system in which this state is prepared and the experiment performed is not important, whether it be photons passing through generalised beam splitters [23], ions in an atomic trap, or any other quantum system in dimension $n \geq 3$ Hilbert space.

We first show that experiments utilising quantum value indefinite observers cannot have a predictor which is correct for some ξ. More precisely:

Theorem 2. *If E is an experiment measuring a quantum value indefinite observable, then for every predictor P_E using any extractor ξ, P_E is not correct for ξ.*

Let us fix an extractor ξ, and assume for the sake of contradiction that there exists a predictor P_E for E which is correct for ξ. Consider the case when the experiment E is repeatedly initialised, performed and reset an arbitrarily large but finite, number of times in an algorithmic "ritual" generating a finite sequence of bits $x_1 x_2 \ldots x_n$.

Since P_E *never* makes an incorrect prediction, each of its predictions is correct with certainty. Then, according to the EPR principle we must conclude that each such prediction corresponds to a value definite property of the system measured in E. However, we chose E such that this *is not* the case: each x_i is the result of the measurement of a value indefinite observable, and thus we obtain a contradiction and conclude no such predictor P_E can exist.

Moreover, since there does not exist a predictor P_E which is correct for some ξ, for such a quantum experiment E, no single outcome is predictable with certainty.

Theorem 3. *If the experiment E described above is repeated a) an arbitrarily large, but finite number of times producing the finite sequence $x_1 x_2 \ldots \mathbf{x}_n$, or b) hypothetically, ad infinitum, generating the infinite sequence $\mathbf{x} = x_1 x_2 \ldots$, then no single bit x_i can be predicted with certainty.*

6   Incomputability, Unpredictability, and Quantum Randomness

While there is a clear intuitive link between unpredictability and randomness, it is an important point that the unpredictability of quantum measurement outcomes should not be understood to mean that quantum randomness is "truly random". Indeed, the subject of randomness is a delicate one: randomness can come in many flavours [12], from statistical properties to computability theoretic properties of outcome sequences. For physical systems, the randomness of a process also needs to be differentiated from that of its outcome.

As mentioned earlier, Eagle has argued that a physical process is random if it is "maximally unpredictable" [13]. In this light it may be reasonable to consider quantum measurements as random events, giving a more formal meaning to the notion of "quantum randomness". However, given the intricacies of randomness, it should be clear that this refers to the measurement *process*, and does not entail that quantum measurement outcomes are maximally random. In fact, maximal randomness in the sense that no correlations exist between successive measurement results is mathematically impossible [9,15]: there exist only degrees of randomness with no upper limit. As a result, any claims regarding the quality of quantum randomness need to be analysed carefully.

Indeed, in many applications of quantum randomness stronger computability theoretic notions of randomness, such as Martin-Löf randomness [9], which apply to sequences of outcomes would be desirable. *It is not known if quantum outcomes are indeed random in this respect.* However, it was shown previously [1,10] that *a sequence $\mathbf{x}$ produced by repeated outcomes of a value indefinite observable must be bi-immune.*[2] This result was proved using a further physical

---

[2] See Sect. 4 for definitions.

assumption, related to and motivated by the EPR principle, called the *e.p.r.* *assumption.*[3] This assumption states that, *if a repetition of measurements of an observable generates a computable sequence, then this implies these observables were value definite prior to measurement.* In other words, it specifies a particular sufficient condition for value definiteness.

Given the relation between unpredictability and Tadaki total unpredictability (which implies bi-immunity) discussed in Sect. 4, it is natural to ask whether the bi-immunity of sequences generated by measuring repeatedly a value indefinite observable is a general consequence of its unpredictability, or if it is an independent consequence of value indefiniteness.

The links between unpredictability and Tadaki total unpredictability we explored earlier are relative to the use of specific extractors—such as ξ_p—and, as we discussed, need not hold when other more physically relevant extractors are considered. Furthermore, for the unpredictability of an experiment E to guarantee that *any* outcome of an infinite repetition of E be incomputable—a much weaker statement than bi-immunity—it would have to be the case that (taking the contrapositive) if even a single infinite repetition $\lambda_1, \lambda_2, \ldots$ of E could generate a computable sequence this would imply that E is predictable. However, the definition of a predictor P_E for E requires that P_E gives correct predictions for *all* repetitions. Hence, we will elaborate a simple example of an unpredictable experiment E that can produce *both* computable and incomputable sequences, showing that unpredictability does not imply incomputability (let alone bi-immunity).

Let d be the dyadic map; that is, the operation on infinite sequences of bits defined by $d(x_1 x_2 x_3 \ldots) = x_2 x_3 \ldots$. This operation is well known to be chaotic and equivalent (more precisely, topologically conjugate) to many others, e.g. the logistic map with $r = 4$ [11]. Let us consider an experiment E_d which involves iterating the dyadic map $k \geq 2$ times on a 'seed' $\mathbf{x} = 0 x_2 x_3 \ldots$ until $x_{k+1} = 0$. In other words, given $\mathbf{x}$ we look for the smallest integer $k \geq 2$ such that $x_{k+1} = 0$, hence $d^k(\mathbf{x}) = 0 x_{k+2} x_{k+3} \ldots$. *If such a k exists, then the outcome of the experiment is $x_{k+2} \in \{0, 1\}$. We assume that such an E_d (ideally) is physically implementable.* We have chosen this example for simplicity; a more 'physically natural' example might be the evolution of a chaotic double pendulum from some set initial condition (up to finite accuracy) for which the outcome is read off once the pendulum returns sufficiently close to its initial conditions.

This experiment can, of course, be repeated in many different ways to generate an infinite sequence, but it suffices to consider the simplest case where the transformed seed $\mathbf{x}^{(1)} = d^k(\mathbf{x})$ after one iteration is taken as the seed for the next step; note that this, by design, satisfies the requirement that the first bit of $\mathbf{x}^{(1)}$ is 0 (i.e., $x_1^{(1)} = 0$), provided k exists. *Let us assume further that any sequence $\mathbf{x} = x_1 x_2 \ldots$ such that $x_1 = 0$ is a valid physical seed.* For the case of a

---

[3] Here, e.p.r. stands for 'elements of physical reality', not 'Einstein, Podolsky and Rosen' as in the EPR principle.'

double pendulum this is akin to assuming that the position of a pendulum can take any value in the continuum—not an unreasonable, if nonetheless important, assumption.

Let $\mathbf{y} = y_1 y_2 \ldots$ be an arbitrary infinite sequence, and consider the sequence $\mathbf{x} = 010 y_1 0 y_2 0 y_3 \ldots$. For any such sequence $\mathbf{x}$ of this form, $d^2(\mathbf{x}) = 0 y_1 0 y_2 \ldots$, so the outcome of E_d with seed $\mathbf{x}$ is precisely y_1, and the new seed $\mathbf{x}^{(1)} = d^2(\mathbf{x}) = 0 y_1 0 y_2 \ldots$. Similarly, for all i, starting with the seed $\mathbf{x}^{(0)} = \mathbf{x}$, the outcome of the ith repetition is precisely y_i, since a minimum number of $k = 2$ applications of d suffices for the first bit of $d^2(\mathbf{x}^{(i-1)})$ to be 0, and the seed after this repetition is precisely $\mathbf{x}^{(i)} = 0 y_i 0 y_{i+1} \ldots$. Hence, starting with the seed $\mathbf{x}$ one obtains the infinite sequence $\mathbf{y}$ by repeating E_d to infinity. In particular, since $\mathbf{y}$ can be any sequence at all, one can obtain both computable and incomputable sequences by repeating E_d.

Let us show also that E_d is unpredictable. Let us assume, for the sake of contradiction, that there exists a predictor P_{E_d} and extractor ξ_d such that P_{E_d} is correct for ξ_d. Then P_{E_d} must give infinitely many correct predictions using ξ_d for any two runs $\lambda_1 \lambda_2 \ldots$ and $\lambda_1' \lambda_2' \ldots$ which differ only in their seeds $\mathbf{x}$ and $\mathbf{x}'$. In particular, this is true if $\mathbf{x}, \mathbf{x}'$ are sequences of the form $0 a_1 a_2 \ldots$ where $a_i \in \{1^t 00, 1^t 01\}$ for all i, and $t \geq 1$ is fixed, since these are possible seeds for E_d. For such seeds $\mathbf{x}, \mathbf{x}'$ the minimum $k \geq 2$ such that the first bit of $d^k(\mathbf{x})$ is 0 is precisely $k = t + 1$. Furthermore, if we let $\mathbf{x}^{(0)} = \mathbf{x}$ and $\mathbf{x}^{(i)} = d^{k_i}(\mathbf{x}^{(i-1)})$ be the seed for the ith repetition of E_d, then $k_i = t + 1$ for all i; that is, each iteration of E_d shifts the seed precisely $t + 1$ bits. Thus, to make infinitely many predictions for E_d starting with seeds $\mathbf{x}$ and $\mathbf{x}'$ correctly, P_E must have access, via ξ_d, to more than $t + 3$ bits of the current seed, since the first $t + 2$ bits of $\mathbf{x}^{(i)}$ and $\mathbf{x}'^{(i)}$ are the same for all i. However, since t is arbitrary, and the same extractor ξ_d must be used for all repetitions regardless of the seed, this implies that ξ_d is *arbitrarily accurate*, which it is, again, not unreasonable *to assume to be physically impossible*. Consequently, E_d must be unpredictable.

The construction of E_d may be slightly artificial and its unpredictability relies, of course, on certain physical assumptions about the possibility of certain extractors. However, this concrete example shows that there is no mathematical obstacle to an unpredictable experiment producing both computable and incomputable outcomes when repeated, and is, at the very least, physically conceivable.

Any link between the unpredictability of an experiment and computability theoretic properties of its output thus relies critically on physical properties— and assumptions—of the particular experiment. Indeed, this careful dependance on the particular physical description of E is one of the strengths of this general model. This gives the model more physical relevance as a notion of (un)predictability than purely algorithmic proposals.

The bi-immunity of quantum randomness is a crucial illustration of this fact. Using a slightly a stronger additional hypothesis on the nature of value (in)definiteness, bi-immunity can be guaranteed for every sequence of quantum random bits obtained by measuring a value indefinite observable [1]. For this particular quantum experiment bi-immunity complements, and is independent of, unpredictability.[4]

7   Summary

In this paper, we addressed two specific points relating to physical unpredictability. Firstly, we developed a generalised model of prediction for both individual physical events, and (by extension) infinite repetitions thereof. This model formalises the notion of an effective prediction agent being able to predict 'in principle' the outcome of an effectively specified physical experiment. This model can be applied to classical or quantum systems of any kind to assess their (un)predictability, and doing so to various systems, particularly classical, could be an interesting direction of research for the future.

Secondly, we applied this model to quantum measurement events. Our goal was to formally deduce the unpredictability of single quantum measurement events, via the strong Kochen-Specker theorem and value indefiniteness, rather than rely on the *ad hoc* postulation of these properties.

More specifically, suppose that we prepare a quantum in a pure state corresponding to a unit vector in Hilbert space of dimension at least three. Then any complementary observable property of this quantum—corresponding to some projector whose respective linear subspace is neither collinear nor orthogonal with respect to the pure state vector—is value indefinite. Furthermore, the outcome of a measurement of such a property is unpredictable with respect to our model of prediction.

Quantum value indefiniteness is key for the proof of unpredictability. In this framework, the bit resulting from the measurement of such an observable property is "created from nowhere" (*creatio ex nihilo*), and cannot be causally connected to any physical entity, whether it be knowable in practice or hidden. While quantum indeterminism is often informally treated as an assumption in and of itself, it is better seen as a formal consequence of Kochen-Specker theorems in the form of value indefiniteness. (Indeed, without these theorems such an assumption would appear weakly grounded.) Yet this derivation of value indefiniteness rests on the three assumptions: admissibility, non-contextuality, and the eigenstate principle. As we discussed in Sect. 5.3, models in which some of these assumptions are not satisfied exist.

The single-bit unpredictability of the output obtained by measuring a value indefinite quantum observable complements the fact—proven in [1] with an additional hypothesis—that such an experiment generates, in the limit, a strongly incomputable sequence. We show that this additional hypothesis is necessary in the sense that unpredictable experiments are, in general, capable of generating both incomputable and computable infinite sequences.

The unpredictability and strong incomputability of these quantum measurements "certify" the use of the corresponding quantum random number generator

---

[4] Recall that bi-immunity need not imply unpredictability either.

for various computational tasks in cryptography and elsewhere [19,24,26]. As a consequence, this quantum random number generator can be seen and used as an *incomputable oracle*, thus justifying a form of *hypercomputation*. Indeed, no universal Turing machine can ever produce in the limit an output that is identical with the sequence of bits generated by this quantum oracle [2]. More than that—no single bit of such sequences can ever be predicted. Evaluating the computational power of a (universal) Turing machine provided with a quantum random oracle certified by maximum unpredictability is a challenging, both theoretical and practical, *open problem*.

In this context incomputability appears *maximally* in two forms: *individualised*—no single bit can be predicted with certainty (Theorem 3); that is, an algorithmic computation of a single bit, even if correct, cannot be formally certified; and, relative to slightly stronger hypotheses, *asymptotic* via bi-immunity—only finitely many bits can be correctly predicted via an algorithmic computation.

Finally, we emphasise that the indeterminism and unpredictability of quantum measurement outcomes proved in this paper are based on the strong form of the Kochen-Specker, and hence require at minimum three-dimensional Hilbert space. The question of whether this result can also be proven for two-dimensional Hilbert space without simply assuming value indefiniteness is an *open problem*; this question is important not only theoretically, but also practically, because many current quantum random generators are based on two-dimensional measurements.

Acknowledgement. Abbott thanks Thierry Paul for discussions on the assumptions needed to deduce quantum incomputability. Calude thanks Giuseppe Longo for raising the question of the randomness of individual bits (September 2008). This work was supported in part by Marie Curie FP7-PEOPLE-2010-IRSES Grant RANPHYS.

References

1. Abbott, A.A., Calude, C.S., Conder, J., Svozil, K.: Strong Kochen-Specker theorem and incomputability of quantum randomness. Phys. Rev. A **86**, 062109 (2012)
2. Abbott, A.A., Calude, C.S., Svozil, K.: A quantum random oracle. In: Cooper, S.B., van Leeuwen, J. (eds.) Alan Turing: His Work and Impact, pp. 206–209. Elsevier Science (2013)
3. Abbott, A.A., Calude, C.S., Svozil, K.: Value-indefinite observables are almost everywhere. Phys. Rev. A **89**, 032109 (2014)
4. Acín, A.: True quantum randomness. In: Suarez, A., Adams, P. (eds.) Is Science Compatible with Free Will?: Exploring Free Will and Consciousness in the Light of Quantum Physics and Neuroscience, Chap. 2, pp. 7–22. Springer, Heidelberg (2013)
5. Bell, J.S.: On the problem of hidden variables in quantum mechanics. Rev. Mod. Phys. **38**, 447–452 (1966)
6. Bohm, D.: A suggested interpretation of the quantum theory in terms of "hidden" variables. I, II. Phys. Rev. **85**(2), 166–193 (1952)
7. Born, M.: Zur Quantenmechanik der Stoßvorgänge. Zeitschrift für Physik **37**, 863–867 (1926)
8. Born, M.: Physics in My Generation, 2nd edn. Springer, New York (1969)

9. Calude, C.: Information and Randomness–An Algorithmic Perspective, 2nd edn. Springer, Heidelberg (2002)
10. Calude, C.S., Svozil, K.: Quantum randomness and value indefiniteness. Adv. Sci. Lett. **1**(2), 165–168 (2008)
11. Devaney, R.L.: An Introduction to Chaotic Dynamical Systems, 2nd edn. Addison-Wesley, Redwood City (1989)
12. Downey, R., Hirschfeldt, D.: Algorithmic Randomness and Complexity. Springer, Heidelberg (2007)
13. Eagle, A.: Randomness is unpredictability. Br. J. Philos. Sci. **56**(4), 749–790 (2005)
14. Einstein, A., Podolsky, B., Rosen, N.: Can quantum-mechanical description of physical reality be considered complete? Phys. Rev. **47**(10), 777–780 (1935)
15. Graham, R., Spencer, J.H.: Ramsey theory. Sci. Am. **262**, 112–117 (1990)
16. Kochen, S., Specker, E.P.: The problem of hidden variables in quantum mechanics. J. Math. Mech. **17**(1), 59–87 (1967). (now Indiana University Mathematics Journal)
17. Laloë, F.: Do We Really Understand Quantum Mechanics?. Cambridge University Press, Cambridge (2012)
18. Myrvold, W.C.: Statistical mechanics and thermodynamics: a Maxwellian view. Stud. Hist. Philos. Sci. Part B Stud. Hist. Philos. Mod. Phys. **42**(4), 237–243 (2011)
19. Pironio, S., Acín, A., Massar, S., de la Giroday, B.A., Matsukevich, D.N., Maunz, P., Olmschenk, S., Hayes, D., Luo, L., Manning, T.A., Monroe, C.: Random numbers certified by Bell's theorem. Nature **464**, 1021–1024 (2010)
20. Popper, K.R.: Logik der Forschung. Springer, Heidelberg (1934)
21. Popper, K.R.: Indeterminism in quantum physics and in classical physics I. Br. J. Philos. Sci. **1**, 117–133 (1950)
22. Popper, K.R.: The Logic of Scientific Discovery. Basic Books, New York (1959)
23. Reck, M., Zeilinger, A., Bernstein, H.J., Bertani, P.: Experimental realization of any discrete unitary operator. Phys. Rev. Lett. **73**, 58–61 (1994)
24. Stefanov, A., Gisin, N., Guinnard, O., Guinnard, L., Zbinden, H.: Optical quantum random number generator. J. Mod. Optics **47**, 595–598 (2000)
25. Suárez, M.: Quantum selections, propensities and the problem of measurement. Br. J. Philos. Sci. **55**(2), 219–255 (2004)
26. Svozil, K.: The quantum coin toss–testing microphysical undecidability. Phys. Lett. A **143**, 433–437 (1990)
27. Tadaki, K.: Phase transition and strong predictability. In: Ibarra, O.H., Kari, L., Kopecki, S. (eds.) UCNC 2014. LNCS, vol. 8553, pp. 340–352. Springer, Heidelberg (2014)
28. Toffoli, T.: The role of the observer in uniform systems. In: Klir, G.J. (ed.) Applied General Systems Research, Recent Developments and Trends, pp. 395–400. Plenum Press, New York (1978)
29. Weihs, G., Jennewein, T., Simon, C., Weinfurter, H., Zeilinger, A.: Violation of Bell's inequality under strict Einstein locality conditions. Phys. Rev. Lett. **81**, 5039–5043 (1998)
30. Werndl, C.: What are the new implications of chaos for unpredictability? Br. J. Philos. Sci. **60**(1), 195–220 (2009)
31. Wolpert, D.H.: Physical limits of inference. Phys. D **237**, 1257–1281 (2008)
32. Zaman, A.: On the impossibility of events of zero probability. Theory Decis. **23**, 157–159 (1987)
33. Zeilinger, A.: The message of the quantum. Nature **438**, 743 (2005)

The Ehrenfeucht-Fraïssé Method
and the Planted Clique Conjecture

Yijia Chen[1]([✉]) and Jörg Flum[2]

[1] Fudan University, Shanghai, China
yijiachen@fudan.edu.cn
[2] Albert-Ludwigs-Universität Freiburg, Freiburg im Breisgau, Germany

Abstract. The Ehrenfeucht-Fraïssé method for first-order logic and further logics relevant in descriptive complexity has been quite successful. However, for key problems such as P $\neq$ NP or NP $\neq$ co-NP no progress has been achieved using it. We show that for these problems we can not get the board for the corresponding Ehrenfeucht-Fraïssé game in polynomial output time, even if we allow probabilistic methods to obtain the board. In order to get this result in the probabilistic case, we need an additional hypothesis, namely that there is an algorithm, the verifier, verifying in a reasonable time that the two structures of the board satisfy the same properties expressible in a suitable fragment of the logic. The (non)existence of such a verifier is related to a logic version of the planted clique conjecture.

1 Introduction

In finite model theory and in descriptive complexity theory the Ehrenfeucht-Fraïssé method for first-order logic FO is mainly used to obtain *inexpressibility results* and *hierarchy results*. While Fraïssé [9] introduced this method in more algebraic terms, Ehrenfeucht [6] phrased it in an appealing game-theoretic form. Concerning generalizations, games were developed for further logics, mainly for logics relevant in descriptive complexity theory such as least fixed-point logic LFP, (monadic) existential second-order logic (monadic) Σ_1^1, and finite variable logics.

An inexpressibility result for a logic L shows that a given property is not definable (or expressible) in L. A hierarchy result states that a certain increasing sequence $H_1 \subseteq H_2 \subseteq \ldots$ of classes H_m of sentences of a given logic is strict; that is, that for every $m \in \mathbb{N}$ there is a property of finite structures expressible by some sentence of H_{m+1} but by no sentence of H_m. Often, to obtain such an inexpressibility result, Ehrenfeucht-Fraïssé games have been used. The finite variable hierarchy $(\mathrm{FO}^m)_{m \in \mathbb{N}}$ is an example of a strict hierarchy. Here FO^m consists of those FO-formulas which contain at most m variables.

Suppose we want to show, using the Ehrenfeucht-Fraïssé method, that for (finite) ordered graphs "eveness" of the cardinality of the vertex set is not expressible in FO, or equivalently, that for every $m \in \mathbb{N}$ "eveness" is not expressible by an FO_m-sentence. Here FO_m denotes the set of sentences of first-order logic of quantifier rank at most m. One chooses ordered graphs G_m and H_m that

© Springer International Publishing Switzerland 2015
L.D. Beklemishev et al. (Eds.): Gurevich Festschrift II 2015, LNCS 9300, pp. 87–108, 2015.
DOI: 10.1007/978-3-319-23534-9_5

are paths of length $2^m + 1$ and 2^m, respectively, and shows that $G_m \equiv_{FO_m} H_m$, that is, that G_m and H_m satisfy the same sentences of FO_m. The latter property is shown by playing, more precisely, by analyzing the Ehrenfeucht-Fraïssé game (for first-order logic) with board (G_m, H_m). It is not hard to show that the size of the board (G_m, H_m) must be exponential in m.

Let us mention some further results obtained by the Ehrenfeucht-Fraïssé method (or by a probabilistic generalization of it):

- Reachability in directed graphs is not expressible in monadic Σ_1^1 [1].
- For ordered graphs connectivity is not expressible in monadic Σ_1^1 [20].
- The finite variable hierarchy for FO on ordered structures is strict [12,18].
- The arity hierarchy is strict for LFP [10].
- For every $k \in \mathbb{N}$ the hierarchy whose mth member consists of formulas with at most m nested k-ary fixed-point operators is strict for LFP [15].

We know (see Theorem 1) that P $\neq$ NP if and only if for every m there are a 3-colorable ordered graph G_m and an ordered graph H_m, which is not 3-colorable, such that G_m and H_m are indistinguishable by sentences of LFP of "quantifier rank" or length at most m; this last property, denoted by $G_m \equiv_{LFP_m} H_m$, would be shown by the Ehrenfeucht-Fraïssé game for LFP. Let us call such a sequence $(G_m, H_m)_{m \in \mathbb{N}}$ a (3-COL, LFP)-sequence. Furthermore, NP $\neq$ co-NP if and only if there is a (3-COL, Σ_1^1)-sequence, where a (3-COL, Σ_1^1)-sequence is defined in a similar way. In [8], the authors remark:

> It is known that $\Sigma_1^1 \neq \Pi_1^1$ if and only if such a separation can be proven via second-order Ehrenfeucht-Fraïssé games. Unfortunately, "playing" second-order Ehrenfeucht-Fraïssé games is very difficult, and the above promise is still largely unfulfilled; for example, the equivalence between the NP = co-NP question and the $\Sigma_1^1 = \Pi_1^1$ question has not so far led to any progress on either of these questions.

And Kolaitis remarks in [7, page 56]:

> Although ... Ehrenfeucht-Fraïssé games yield a sound and complete method for studying ESO-definability [that is, Σ_1^1-definability] (and thus potentially leading to the separation of NP and co-NP), so far this approach has had rather limited success. The reason is that formidable combinatorial difficulties arise in implementing this method ... when dealing with ESO-formulas in which at least one of the existentially quantified second-order variables has an arity bigger than 1.

Definitely the authors are right with their observation that "playing" second-order Ehrenfeucht-Fraïssé games is very difficult. However, in order to derive the last two hierarchy results mentioned above, the corresponding authors successfully apply games for logics containing nonmonadic second-order quantifiers.

In the example of "eveness" we already observed that the size of a board (G_m, H_m) of ordered graphs has to be exponential in m. On the other hand, analyzing most of the successful applications of the Ehrenfeucht-Fraïssé method obtained so far, we realized that the boards $(G_m, H_m)_{m \in \mathbb{N}}$ could be constructed in polynomial output time, that is, in time $(|V(G_m)| + |V(H_m)|)^{O(1)}$. However, by a simple and standard diagonal argument we show:

(A) *No* (3-COL, LFP)-*sequence can be generated in polynomial output time.*

Even more, to the best of our knowledge, it is open whether we can get such a sequence of boards by an algorithm more efficient than brute force.

Mostly in successful applications of the Ehrenfeucht-Fraïssé method the main task consisted in constructing boards such that one can find an argument showing, via Ehrenfeucht-Fraïssé games for the given logic, that the corresponding structures are indistinguishable to a certain extent. As mentioned, for a proof of $P \neq NP$ via the Ehrenfeucht-Fraïssé method, already the presumably easier step of merely constructing the sequence of boards (and forgetting about the concrete verification of their indistinguishability) is hard. This makes our "negative" result even stronger with respect to the existence of positive applications of the Ehrenfeucht-Fraïssé method for sufficiently rich logics. It is an interesting challenge, though: how can we use the Ehrenfeucht-Fraïssé method to prove $P \neq NP$ if we must necessarily work with non-constructive boards?

What happens if we allow probabilistic algorithms[1] to yield the boards for the Ehrenfeucht-Fraïssé method? Such random constructions have been used for two of the applications mentioned above, namely to show that reachability in directed graphs is not definable in monadic second-order logic and in the proof of Rossman [18] that the finite variable hierarchy for first-order logic on ordered graphs is strict. It turns out that in order to derive a probabilistic generalization of (A) of the type "No (3-COL, LFP)-sequence can be generated by a probabilistic algorithm in polynomial output time" we need a further assumption,[2] namely that there is a *verifier*, that is, an algorithm that in a reasonable time verifies that with high probability the board (G_m, H_m) satisfies

$$G_m \in 3\text{-COL}, H_m \notin 3\text{-COL}, \text{ and } G_m \equiv_{\text{LFP}_m} H_m.$$

So we get:

(B) *Assume that there is a pseudorandom generator. No* (3-COL, LFP)-*sequence having a verifier can be generated by a probabilistic algorithm in polynomial output time.*

Is the assumption of the existence of a verifier necessary? The question is related to the *planted clique conjecture*. This conjecture claims that there is no polynomial time algorithm that detects a clique of size $4 \cdot \log n$, which has been planted

---

[1] At least here we should mention that there exist successful applications of the Ehrenfeucht-Fraïssé method, where the boards are not defined by a (probabilistic) *algorithm*; for example, in [21] random graphs with edge probability $n^{-\alpha}$ are considered, where n is the cardinality of the vertex set and α is *irrational*.

[2] Besides the assumption of the existence of a pseudorandom generator.

uniformly at random in a random graph with n vertices and edge probability $1/2$. In this article we introduce a stronger conjecture, a logic version LPCC of the planted clique conjecture. It is not hard to show:

(C) *If LPCC holds, then a* (3-COL, LFP)-*sequence can be generated by a probabilistic algorithm in polynomial output time.*

As already the planted clique conjecture implies P $\neq$ NP, so does LPCC. Can we refute LPCC? We show that this is the case for some strengthening of LPCC.

The content of the different sections is the following. After fixing some notation (in Sect. 2), we recall the Ehrenfeucht-Fraïssé method in Sect. 3. In Sect. 4, first we study the minimum size of the board (G_m, H_m) of a (3-COL, LFP)-sequence and then we prove statement (A). Section 5 is devoted to a proof of the probabilistic generalization of this result, stated as (B) above. In Sect. 6 we introduce the logic version LPCC of the planted clique conjecture and derive statement (C) in Sect. 7. In Sect. 8 we show that some strengthened versions of LPCC are refutable. Finally, in the last section we mention extensions of our results and some further results related to the topic of this article. Moreover, we state some conjectures and open questions.

2   Preliminaries

For a natural number n we set $[n] := \{1, \ldots, n\}$. For a graph G we denote by $V(G)$ and $E(G)$ its vertex set and its edge set, respectively. We speak of an *ordered graph* G if G comes with an ordering of its vertex set. As already mentioned, in this article graph always means finite graph. A *problem* (or, *property*) Q of ordered graphs is a class of ordered graphs closed under isomorphism.

We assume familiarity with basic notions of first-order logic FO and of least fixed-point logic LFP. Concerning LFP, till Sect. 8 essentially we only need the Immerman-Vardi Theorem, which we recall in the next section.

Let L be a logic. A property Q of ordered graphs is *definable in L* (or, *expressible in L*) if there is a sentence of L such that Q is its class of models.

3   The Ehrenfeucht-Fraïssé-method

Let us denote by FO_m the set of sentences of first-order logic of quantifier rank (= maximum number of nested quantifiers) at most m and by LFP_m the set of LFP-sentences φ of length $|\varphi| \leq m$. Here $|\varphi|$ denotes the number of *symbols* in φ (that is, the number of connectives, quantifiers, LFP-operators, variables, ...; however, two occurrences, say, of the same variable in φ count as two symbols).

Let L be one of the logics FO or LFP and denote by L_m the corresponding set FO_m or LFP_m. The Ehrenfeucht-Fraïssé method relies on the following result.

Theorem 1. *For $L \in \{FO, LFP\}$ and a problem Q of ordered graphs the following are equivalent:*

(i) For all $m \in \mathbb{N}$ there are ordered graphs G_m and H_m with

$$G_m \in Q, \quad H_m \notin Q, \quad \text{and} \quad G_m \equiv_{L_m} H_m. \tag{1}$$

(ii) Q is not definable in L.

So, in order to show that the problem Q is not definable in the logic $L \in \{\text{FO}, \text{LFP}\}$, it suffices to exhibit a (Q, L)-sequence in the sense of the following definition.

Definition 2. Assume $L \in \{\text{FO}, \text{LFP}\}$ and let Q be a problem of ordered graphs. A sequence $(G_m, H_m)_{m \in \mathbb{N}}$ of ordered graphs is a (Q, L)-sequence if for al $m \in \mathbb{N}$

$$G_m \in Q, \quad H_m \notin Q, \text{ and } G_m \equiv_{L_m} H_m.$$

In many concrete applications of Theorem 1, Ehrenfeucht-Fraïssé-games are applied to show that $G_m \equiv_{L_m} H_m$. We recall the Ehrenfeucht-Fraïssé-game for FO (see [4,10,15] for the Ehrenfeucht-Fraïssé-game for LFP and other extensions of FO by fixed-point operators). Let G and H be ordered graphs and $m \in \mathbb{N}$. The Ehrenfeucht-Fraïssé-game $G_m(G, H)$ (with *boards* G and H) is played by two players called Spoiler and Duplicator. The game consists of a sequence of m rounds. In round i of the game, first Spoiler picks a graph (either G or H) and a vertex of his choice in that graph. Duplicator then replies by picking a vertex of his choice in the other graph. Thus, after m rounds, vertices $u_1, \ldots, u_m$ in $V(G)$ and $v_1, \ldots, v_m$ in $V(H)$ have been selected, u_i and v_i being the vertices chosen in round i. Duplicator *wins* if the induced ordered subgraphs $G[\{u_1, \ldots, u_m\}]$ and $H[\{v_1, \ldots, v_m\}]$ (induced by G on $\{u_1, \ldots, u_m\}$ and by H on $\{v_1, \ldots, v_m\}$, respectively) are isomorphic via the mapping $f(u_i) := v_i$ for $i \in [m]$. It should be clear what it means that Duplicator has a winning strategy for the game $G_m(G, H)$.

Theorem 3 (Ehrenfeucht-Fraïssé-Theorem). *Let G and H be ordered graphs and $m \in \mathbb{N}$. Then Duplicator has a winning strategy for the game $G_m(G, H)$ if and only if $G \equiv_{FO_m} H$.*

The following simple application of the Ehrenfeucht-Fraïssé-game shows that the class EVEN of ordered graphs with vertex set of even cardinality is not definable in FO: For $m \in \mathbb{N}$ let the ordered graphs G_m and H_m be paths of length $2^m + 1$ and 2^m, respectively. Then Duplicator has a winning strategy for the game $G_m(G_m, H_m)$. In fact, in the ith round he picks his vertex, u_i or v_i, such that for all $j \in [i-1]$,

$$d^{G_m}(u_i, u_j) = d^{H_m}(v_i, v_j) \quad \text{or} \quad \left(d^{G_m}(u_i, u_j) > 2^{m-i} \text{ and } d^{H_m}(v_i, v_j) > 2^{m-i}\right).$$

Here $d^G(u, u')$ denotes the distance of the vertices u and u' in the graph G. Thus, $G_m \equiv_{FO_m} H_m$ and hence, $(G_m, H_m)_{m \in \mathbb{N}}$ is an (EVEN, FO)-sequence.

The graphs G_m and H_m just constructed have size exponential in m. We can't do it better: the sizes of the graphs of every (Q, FO)-sequence for any problem Q of ordered graphs must be exponential in m. This follows from the following result, which can easily been derived.

Proposition 4. *Let $m \in \mathbb{N}$. If G and H are nonisomorphic ordered graphs, then*

$$G \equiv_{\mathrm{FO}_{m+3}} H \text{ implies } |V(G)|, |V(H)| > 2^m.$$

4   A Logical Reformulation of P $\neq$ NP

Immerman and Vardi have proven that least fixed-point logic LFP captures the complexity class P in the following sense.

Theorem 5 (Immerman-Vardi Theorem). *A problem of ordered graphs is decidable in polynomial time if and only if it can be defined in least fixed-point logic LFP.*

As the problem 3-COL, the 3-colorability problem of ordered graphs, is NP-complete, we get:

Corollary 6. P $\neq$ NP *if and only if* 3-COL *is not definable in* LFP.

We defined φ an LFP_m-sentence with $|\varphi| \leq m$. The previous corollary together with Theorem 1 yield:

Corollary 7. P $\neq$ NP *if and only if there is a* (3-COL, LFP)-*sequence, that is, a sequence* $(G_m, H_m)_{m \in \mathbb{N}}$ *of ordered graphs such that for all* m,

$$G_m \in \text{3-COL}, \quad H_m \notin \text{3-COL}, \quad and \quad G_m \equiv_{\mathrm{LFP}_m} H_m.$$

Assume P $\neq$ NP. What can we say about the minimum size of the graphs of a (3-COL, LFP)-sequence and what about the running time of an algorithm generating a (3-COL, LFP)-sequence? We set

$$\text{SIZE(3-COL)}(m) := \min\{\max\{|V(G)|, |V(H)|\} \mid G \text{ and } H \text{ are ordered graphs with}$$
$$G \in \text{3-COL}, H \notin \text{3-COL}, \text{ and } G \equiv_{\mathrm{LFP}_m} H\}.$$

Recall that a problem Q has circuit size c, where $c : \mathbb{N} \to \mathbb{N}$, if for $n \in \mathbb{N}$, $c(n)$ is the least $d \in \mathbb{N}$ such there exists a (Boolean) circuit C with n input variables of size $\leq d$ such that for every x with $|x| = n$,

$$x \in Q \quad \Longleftrightarrow \quad C(x) = 1 \text{ (i.e., } C \text{ accepts } x).$$

In [5] we derived the following lower and upper bound for SIZE(3-COL)(m).

Proposition 8. *Assume* P $\neq$ NP. *Then:*

(a) There is an $\varepsilon > 0$ such that for all $m \in \mathbb{N}$ we have $2^{\varepsilon \cdot m} \leq \text{SIZE(3-COL)}(m)$.
(b) If the circuit size of 3-COL *is not in* $2^{o(n)}$, *then for all $\varepsilon > 0$ and infinitely many m,*

$$\text{SIZE(3-COL)}(m) \leq 2^{(1+\varepsilon) \cdot m \cdot \log m}.$$

Definition 9. *An algorithm* $\mathbb{A}$ *generates the sequence* $(G_m, H_m)_{m \in \mathbb{N}}$ *if* $\mathbb{A}$ *on input $m \in \mathbb{N}$ outputs* (G_m, H_m).

By systematically testing, for $\ell = 1, 2, \ldots$, all graphs G and H with vertex sets of cardinality $\leq \ell$ whether they satisfy

$$G \in 3\text{-}\mathrm{COL}, \quad H \notin 3\text{-}\mathrm{COL}, \quad \text{and} \quad G \equiv_{\mathrm{LFP}_m} H,$$

we obtain from the previous result an upper bound for the time needed to get the graphs of a $(3\text{-}\mathrm{COL}, \mathrm{LFP})$-sequence, even of a sequence with boards of minimum size:

Proposition 10 ([5]). *If* $\mathrm{P} \neq \mathrm{NP}$, *then there is an algorithm that generates a* $(3\text{-}\mathrm{COL}, \mathrm{LFP})$*-sequence in time* $2^{O(\mathrm{SIZE}(3\text{-}\mathrm{COL})(m)^2)}$. *The sequence* $(G_m, H_m)_{m \in \mathbb{N}}$ *generated by the algorithm satisfies* $\mathrm{SIZE}(3\text{-}\mathrm{COL})(m) = \max\{|V(G_m)|, |V(H_m)|\}$.

By Proposition 4, the boards of all (Q, FO)-sequences for any problem Q of ordered graphs must have size exponential in m. However we could construct the graphs G_m and H_m of an $(\mathrm{EVEN}, \mathrm{FO})$-sequence in *polynomial output time*, that is, in time $(|V(G_m)| + |V(H_m)|)^{O(1)}$. In fact, we realized that in most successful applications of the Ehrenfeucht-Fraïssé method showing that a property is not definable in a given logic, the boards for the corresponding game can be constructed in polynomial output time. So we ask, is it possible to construct a $(3\text{-}\mathrm{COL}, \mathrm{LFP})$-sequence in polynomial output time? By a standard diagonalization argument we show that this is not possible:

Theorem 11. *No* $(3\text{-}\mathrm{COL}, \mathrm{LFP})$*-sequence can be constructed in polynomial output time.*

Proof. We sketch the main steps of a proof (for more details see [5]). Assume for a contradiction that the algorithm $\mathbb{A}$ generates a $(3\text{-}\mathrm{COL}, \mathrm{LFP})$-sequence $(G_m, H_m)_{m \in \mathbb{N}}$ in polynomial output time. By passing to a suitable subsequence (cf. the proof of Lemma 16), we can assume that $(G_m, H_m)_{m \in \mathbb{N}}$ is *monotone*, that is, that it satisfies

$$\max\{|V(G_m)|, |V(H_m)|\} < \min\{|V(G_{m+1})|, |V(H_{m+1})|\}.$$

Furthermore, we can assume (again by passing to a suitable subsequence) that $|V(G_m)| \geq |V(H_m)|$ for all $m \in \mathbb{N}$ or that $|V(G_m)| \leq |V(H_m)|$ for all $m \in \mathbb{N}$. Then we can transform $\mathbb{A}$ into an algorithm $\mathbb{B}$ running in polynomial time such that for all $m \in \mathbb{N}$,

$$\mathbb{B} \text{ accepts } G_m \quad \text{and} \quad \mathbb{B} \text{ rejects } H_m.$$

By the Immerman-Vardi Theorem there is an LFP-sentence $\varphi_{\mathbb{B}}$, say $\varphi_{\mathbb{B}} \in \mathrm{LFP}_{m_0}$, such that for all ordered graphs G,

$$G \models \varphi_{\mathbb{B}} \iff \mathbb{B} \text{ accepts } G.$$

In particular, for all $m \in \mathbb{N}$,

$$G_m \models \varphi_{\mathbb{B}} \quad \text{and} \quad H_m \not\models \varphi_{\mathbb{B}}.$$

For $m \geq m_0$, this equivalence contradicts $G_m \equiv_{\mathrm{LFP}_m} H_m$. $\square$

The same proof works for every property Q of ordered graphs (instead of 3-COL), even more: By definition, an LFP-*sequence* is a sequence $(G_m, H_m)_{m \in \mathbb{N}}$ of ordered graphs G_m and H_m with

$$G_m \not\cong H_m \; (G_m \text{ and } H_m \text{ are not isomorphic}) \text{ and } G_m \equiv_{\text{LFP}_m} H_m.$$

Clearly every (Q, LFP)-sequence for any property Q of ordered graphs is an LFP-sequence. We state the following result, which can be derived similarly to Theorem 11.

Theorem 12 ([5]). *No LFP-sequence can be generated in polynomial output time.*

We should mention that also for first-order logic there are problems Q such that no (Q, FO)-sequence can be generated in polynomial output time:

Example 13. Let $B \subseteq \{0,1\}^*$ be a P-bi-immune set; that is, neither B nor $\{0,1\}^* \setminus B$ contains an infinite subset decidable in polynomial time. For $x \in B$, $x = x_1 \ldots x_s$ with $x_i \in \{0,1\}$, let $G(x)$ be the ordered graph with vertex set $[s+1]$, with the natural ordering on $[s+1]$, and with edge set $\{\{i, i+1\} \mid i \in [s] \text{ and } x_i = 1\}$. Let $Q(B)$ be the smallest class of ordered graphs containing all $G(x)$ with $x \in B$ and closed under isomorphism. No $(Q(B), \text{FO})$-sequence can be generated in polynomial output time. For a contradiction assume that $(G_m, H_m)_{m \in \mathbb{N}}$ is a $(Q(B), \text{FO})$-sequence generated in polynomial output time. As above we can assume that the sequence is monotone and that $|V(G_m)| \geq |V(H_m)|$ for all $m \in \mathbb{N}$ or that $|V(G_m)| \leq |V(H_m)|$ for all $m \in \mathbb{N}$. In the first case, B contains an infinite subset in P and in the second case $\{0,1\}^* \setminus B$.

5   On Random (3-COL,LFP)-Sequences

We have seen that we cannot construct a $(3\text{-COL}, \text{LFP})$-sequence in polynomial output time. What happens if we consider random sequences? There are successful applications of the Ehrenfeucht-Fraïssé-method where the graphs of the corresponding sequences are constructed randomly. For example, in this way it has been shown that reachability in directed graphs is not definable in monadic second-order logic (see [1]) and that the finite variable hierarchy for first-order logic on ordered graphs is strict (see [18]).

We aim at a result showing limitations of the probabilistic Ehrenfeucht-Fraïssé-method similar to Theorem 11. For this purpose we have to take into consideration a further property of such sequences $(G_m, H_m)_{m \in \mathbb{N}}$ satisfied in most successful applications of the Ehrenfeucht-Fraïssé-method obtained so far. For $(3\text{-COL}, \text{LFP})$-sequences $(G_m, H_m)_{m \in \mathbb{N}}$ this property ensures that we can verify that $G_m \in 3\text{-COL}$, $H_m \notin 3\text{-COL}$, and that $G_m \equiv_{\text{LFP}_m} H_m$ in a reasonable time. Condition (r2) of the following definition of random $(3\text{-COL}, \text{LFP})$-sequence contains the precise formulation.

Definition 14. A probabilistic algorithm $\mathbb{P}$ *generates a random* $(3\text{-COL}, \text{LFP})$-*sequence* $(G_m, H_m)_{m \in \mathbb{N}}$ if (r1) and (r2) are satisfied.

(r1) For every $m \in \mathbb{N}$ the algorithm $\mathbb{P}$, on input m, first *deterministically* computes the vertex sets $V(G_m)$ and $V(H_m)$, and then it constructs the ordered graphs G_m and H_m probabilistically.

(r2) There is an algorithm $\mathbb{V}$, the *verifier*, such that (a)–(c) hold.

    (a) For all ordered graphs G and H and all $m \in \mathbb{N}$,

$$\text{if } \mathbb{V} \text{ accepts } (G, H, m), \text{ then } G \equiv_{\text{LFP}_m} H, \quad G \in 3\text{-COL}, \text{ and } H \notin 3\text{-COL}.$$

    (b) For sufficiently large $m \in \mathbb{N}$ and all $m' \geq m$,

$$\Pr\left[\mathbb{V} \text{ accepts } (G_{m'}, H_{m'}, m)\right] \geq \frac{1}{\big(|V(G_{m'})| + |V(H_{m'})|\big)^{O(1)}}.$$

    (c) The running time of $\mathbb{V}$ on input (G, H, m) is bounded by $f(m) \cdot (|V(G)| + |V(H)|)^{O(1)}$ for some computable function $f : \mathbb{N} \to \mathbb{N}$.

In this section we show:

Theorem 15. *Assume that there is a $2^{\lceil \ell/c \rceil}$-pseudorandom generator[3] for some natural number $c \geq 1$. Then there is no probabilistic algorithm that generates a random $(3\text{-COL}, \text{LFP})$-sequence $(G_m, H_m)_{m \in \mathbb{N}}$ in polynomial output time.*

The following lemmas will finally yield a proof of Theorem 15 along the following lines: For a contradiction we assume that there exists a probabilistic algorithm $\mathbb{P}$ generating a random $(3\text{-COL}, \text{LFP})$-sequence in polynomial output time. Essentially we use the pseudorandom generator to derandomize the algorithm $\mathbb{P}$. In this way we obtain a deterministic algorithm which generates a $(3\text{-COL}, \text{LFP})$-sequence $(G_m, H_m)_{m \in \mathbb{N}}$ in polynomial output time. This contradicts Theorem 11.

As in the deterministic case we say that a probabilistic algorithm $\mathbb{P}$ generates a random *monotone* $(3\text{-COL}, \text{LFP})$-sequence if it generates a random $(3\text{-COL}, \text{LFP})$-sequence $(G_m, H_m)_{m \in \mathbb{N}}$, which in addition to (r1) and (r2) satisfies (r3), where

(r3) for all $m \in \mathbb{N}$, $\max\{|V(G_m)|, |V(H_m)|\} < \min\{|V(G_{m+1})|, |V(H_{m+1})|\}$.

If furthermore (r4) and (r5) hold, where

(r4) $\lceil \log (|V(G_m)| + |V(H_m)|) \rceil < \lceil \log (|V(G_{m+1})| + |V(H_{m+1})|) \rceil$

(r5) $f(m) \leq \max\{|V(G_m)|, |V(H_m)|\}$ (where f is the computable function of (r2)(c) used to bound the running time of the verifier $\mathbb{V}$),

then we speak of a *strongly monotone $(3\text{-COL}, \text{LFP})$-sequence*.

For our proof of Theorem 15 we need to show that we can restrict ourselves to strongly monotone $(3\text{-COL}, \text{LFP})$-sequences.

---

[3] We recall the notion of a pseudorandom generator in Definition 17.

Lemma 16. *If there is a probabilistic algorithm generating a random* (3-COL, LFP)-*sequence in polynomial output time, then there is a probabilistic algorithm that generates a strongly monotone random* (3-COL, LFP)-*sequence in polynomial output time.*

Proof. Similar to Proposition 4 one gets an increasing function $s : \mathbb{N} \to \mathbb{N}$ such that $s(m)$ is computable in space $O(\log m)$ and such that for all ordered graphs G and H and all $m \in \mathbb{N}$,

$$\text{if } G \equiv_{\text{LFP}_{s(m)}} H \text{ and } G \ncong H, \text{then} |V(G)|, |V(H)| > m.$$

Assume that the (3-COL, LFP)-sequence $(G_m, H_m)_{m\in\mathbb{N}}$ is generated by the probabilistic algorithm $\mathbb{P}$ in polynomial output time. Recall that the universes of G_m and H_m are obtained deterministically. We define a function $h : \mathbb{N} \to \mathbb{N}$ inductively by

$$h(m) := \begin{cases} s(0), & \text{if } m=0, \\ s\big(\max\{|V(G_{h(m-1)})|, |V(H_{h(m-1)})|\}\big), & \text{if } m > 0. \end{cases}$$

As $G_{h(m)} \equiv_{\text{LFP}_{h(m)}} H_{h(m)}$, that is, $G_{h(m)} \equiv_{\text{LFP}_{s\big(\max\{|V(G_{h(m-1)})|,|V(H_{h(m-1)})|\}\big)}} H_{h(m)}$, we have

$$|V(G_{h(m)})|, |V(H_{h(m)})| > \max\{|V(G_{h(m-1)})|, |V(H_{h(m-1)})|\}.$$

As $G_{h(m)} \equiv_{\text{LFP}_{h(m)}} H_{h(m)}$, we have $G_{h(m)} \equiv_{\text{LFP}_m} H_{h(m)}$. Therefore, it is routine to show that the probabilistic algorithm, which on input m first computes $h(m)$ and then simulates $\mathbb{P}$ on $h(m)$, generates a random monotone (3-COL, LFP)-sequence in polynomial in output time.

So we may assume that the (3-COL, LFP)-sequence $(G_m, H_m)_{m\in\mathbb{N}}$ generated by $\mathbb{P}$ is monotone. We will get the sequence satisfying (r4) and (r5) as a subsequence of $(G_m, H_m)_{m\in\mathbb{N}}$, therefore it will be itself monotone. We may assume that the function $f : \mathbb{N} \to \mathbb{N}$ mentioned in (r2) is time constructible. We define $g : \mathbb{N} \to \mathbb{N}$ by

$$g(k) := \begin{cases} \text{the least } m \text{ such that } f(0) \leq \max\{|V(G_m)|, |V(H_m)|\}, & \text{if } k = 0, \\ \text{the least } m \text{ such that } f(k) \leq \max\{|V(G_m)|, |V(H_m)|\} \text{ and} \\ \lceil \log\left(|V(G_{g(k-1)})| + |V(H_{g(k-1)})|\right) \rceil < \lceil \log\left(|V(G_m)| + |V(H_m)|\right) \rceil, & \text{if } k > 0. \end{cases}$$

Again it is routine to show that the probabilistic algorithm, which on input m first computes $g(m)$ and then simulates $\mathbb{P}$ on $g(m)$, generates a random and strongly monotone (3-COL, LFP)-sequence in polynomial output time.   □

Before turning to the main step of the proof of Theorem 15, for the reader's convenience we recall the definition of pseudorandom generator (following [3, Definition 20.2]).

Definition 17. Let $c \in \mathbb{N}$. An algorithm $\mathbb{G}$ is a $2^{\lceil \ell/c \rceil}$-pseudorandom generator if it satisfies (g1) and (g2).

(g1) On every input $s \in \{0,1\}^*$ the algorithm $\mathbb{G}$ computes a string $\mathbb{G}(s) \in \{0,1\}^*$ with $|\mathbb{G}(s)| = 2^{\lceil |s|/c \rceil}$ in time $2^{|s|}$.

(g2) For every $\ell \in \mathbb{N}$ and every circuit C of size at most t^3, where $t := 2^{\lceil \ell/c \rceil}$, we have

$$\left| \Pr_{s \in \{0,1\}^\ell} \left[C(\mathbb{G}(s)) = 1 \right] - \Pr_{r \in \{0,1\}^t} \left[C(r) = 1 \right] \right| < 1/10.$$

In the left term we consider the uniform probability space on $\{0,1\}^\ell$, in the right term the uniform probability space on $\{0,1\}^t$.

Lemma 18. *Assume*

- *there is a $2^{\lceil \ell/c \rceil}$-pseudorandom generator $\mathbb{G}$ for some $c \in \mathbb{N}$;*
- *there is a probabilistic algorithm $\mathbb{P}$ that generates a strongly monotone random (3-COL, LFP)-sequence $(G_m, H_m)_{m \in \mathbb{N}}$ in polynomial output time.*

Then there is a deterministic algorithm $\mathbb{A}$ such that for every $m \in \mathbb{N}$ the algorithm $\mathbb{A}$ on input m computes a sequence of pairs

$$(G_m^1, H_m^1), \ldots, (G_m^{t_m}, H_m^{t_m})$$

of ordered graphs, where all G_m^i have $V(G_m)$ as vertex set, and all H_m^i have $V(H_m)$ as vertex set (recall that $V(G_m)$ and $V(H_m)$ are the vertex sets deterministically computed by $\mathbb{P}$ on input m). Moreover, the following conditions (a1)–(a3) hold:

(a1) *The algorithm $\mathbb{A}$ runs in time $(|V(G_m)| + |V(H_m)|)^{O(1)}$; in particular, $t_m = (|V(G_m)| + |V(H_m)|)^{O(1)}$.*

(a2) *For sufficiently large $m \in \mathbb{N}$,*

$$\Pr_{p \in [t_m]} \left[G_m^p \equiv_{\mathrm{LFP}_m} H_m^p, \ G_m^p \in \text{3-COL} \ \text{and} \ H_m^p \notin \text{3-COL} \right]$$

$$\geq \Pr_{p \in [t_m]} \left[\mathbb{V} \text{ accepts } (G_m^p, H_m^p, m) \right] > 1/2,$$

where $\mathbb{V}$, the verifier, is the algorithm associated with $\mathbb{P}$ and mentioned in condition (r2) of Definition 14. Note that the first inequality holds by this condition.

(a3) *For every $m \in \mathbb{N}$ we have*

- *$\max\{|V(G_m)|, |V(H_m)|\} < \min\{|V(G_{m+1})|, |V(H_{m+1})|\}$*
- *$\lceil \log(|V(G_m)| + |V(H_m)|) \rceil < \lceil \log(|V(G_{m+1})| + |V(H_{m+1})|) \rceil$;*
- *$f(m) \leq \max\{|V(G_m)|, |V(H_m)|\}$ (where f is the function mentioned in (r2)(c)).*

Proof. For the probabilistic algorithm $\mathbb{P}$ we choose the verifier $\mathbb{V}$ according to (r2). By (r5) we know that $\mathbb{V}$ on input (G_m, H_m, m) runs in time polynomial in $(|V(G_m)| + |V(H_m)|)$. We can assume that $\mathbb{P}$ satisfies (r2)(b') instead of (r2)(b), where

(r2)(b') for sufficiently large $m \in \mathbb{N}$, $\Pr\left[\mathbb{V} \text{ accepts } (G_m, H_m, m)\right] \geq 4/5$.

This is achieved by the standard amplification method. More precisely, by repeating the algorithm $\mathbb{P}$, on input m, polynomial many times, that is, polynomial in $(|V(G_m)| + |V(H_m)|)$ many times, and each time checking whether $\mathbb{V}$ accepts (G_m, H_m, m), where (G_m, H_m) is the output of $\mathbb{P}$.

By the properties of $\mathbb{P}$, we know that for some $d \in \mathbb{N}$ with $d \geq 10$:

- The running time of $\mathbb{P}$ on m is bounded by $(|V(G_m)| + |V(H_m)|)^d$.
- The running time of the algorithms $\mathbb{V}$ on inputs (G, H, m) with $f(m) \leq \max\{|V(G)|, |V(H)|\}$ is bounded by $(|V(G)| + |V(H)|)^d$.

We let $\mathbb{A}$ be the following deterministic algorithm:

$\mathbb{A}$ // $m \in \mathbb{N}$ in unary

1. simulate the (deterministic) part of the computation of $\mathbb{P}$
2.   on input m yielding the universes $V(G_m)$ and $V(H_m)$
3. $n \leftarrow |V(G_m)| + |V(H_m)|$
4. $\ell \leftarrow c \cdot \lceil d \cdot \log n \rceil$
5. **for all** $s \in \{0,1\}^\ell$ **do**
6.   compute $\mathbb{G}(s)$
7.   simulate $\mathbb{P}$ on input m where in the simulation
8.   the internal coin tosses of $\mathbb{P}$ are replaced according to $\mathbb{G}(s)$
9.   output (G_m^s, H_m^s), the output of this simulation of $\mathbb{P}$.

Then (a1) holds as $2^\ell = (|V(G_m)| + |V(H_m)|)^{O(1)}$. Since $\mathbb{P}$ generates strongly monotone sequences, also (a3) holds. It remains to establish (a2). For a contradiction assume that

$$\text{for infinitely many } m \in \mathbb{N}: \Pr_{p \in [t_m]}\left[\mathbb{V} \text{ accepts } (G_m^p, H_m^p, m)\right] \leq 1/2. \qquad (2)$$

For every $m \in \mathbb{N}$ we let

$$n_m := |V(G_m)| + |V(H_m)|.$$

Clearly there is an algorithm that decides in time $O(n^{d+1})$ whether a given $n \in \mathbb{N}$ is equal to n_m for some $m \in \mathbb{N}$, and if so, outputs m (which is unique by (a3)). We consider the following algorithm $\mathbb{D}$:

$\mathbb{D}$ // $r \in \{0,1\}^*$

1. compute an m with $|r| = 2^{\lceil d \cdot \log n_m \rceil}$
2. **if** no such m exists **then** reject
3. compute the output (G_m, H_m) of $\mathbb{P}$ on input m if
4.   the internal coin tosses of $\mathbb{P}$ are replaced according to r
5. simulate $\mathbb{V}$ on (G_m, H_m, m)
6. **if** the simulation rejects **then** reject
7. accept.

By (r2)(b'), for sufficiently large $m \in \mathbb{N}$, and hence sufficiently large $n^* := 2^{\lceil d \cdot \log n_m \rceil}$,

$$\Pr_{r \in \{0,1\}^{n^*}} \big[\mathbb{D} \text{ accepts } r\big] = \Pr_{p \in [t_m]} \big[\mathbb{V} \text{ accepts } (G_m^p, H_m^p, m)\big] \geq 4/5. \tag{3}$$

Furthermore note that by (2),

$$\text{for infinitely many } m \text{ and } \ell := c \cdot \lceil d \cdot \log n_m \rceil : \quad \Pr_{s \in \{0,1\}^\ell} \big[\mathbb{D}(\mathbb{G}(s)) = 1\big] \leq 1/2. \tag{4}$$

Moreover, as $f(m) \leq \max\{|V(G_m)|, |V(H_m)|\}$ (by the strong monotonicity of the random $(\text{3-COL}, \text{LFP})$-sequence computed by $\mathbb{P}$), we see that the running time of $\mathbb{D}$ is bounded by $O(|r|^{1+1/d}) \leq O(|r|^{1.1})$. Using the Cook-Levin's reduction, from the algorithm $\mathbb{D}$ we can construct, for every $m \in \mathbb{N}$ and $n^* := 2^{\lceil d \cdot \log n_m \rceil}$, a circuit C_{n^*} such that for every $r \in \{0,1\}^{n^*}$,

$$C_{n^*}(r) = 1 \iff \mathbb{D} \text{ accepts r} \tag{5}$$

and such that for the size $|C_{n^*}|$ of the circuit C_{n^*} we have

$$|C_{n^*}| = O\big((n^*)^{2.2}\big). \tag{6}$$

By (3) and (5), for sufficiently large $m \in \mathbb{N}$, and hence sufficiently large $n^* = 2^{\lceil d \cdot \log n_m \rceil}$,

$$\Pr_{r \in \{0,1\}^{n^*}} \big[C_{n^*}(r) = 1\big] = \Pr_{p \in [t_m]} \big[\mathbb{V} \text{ accepts } (G_m^p, H_m^p, m)\big] \geq 4/5.$$

By (4) and (5), we know that for infinitely many $m \in \mathbb{N}$ and $\ell := c \cdot \lceil d \cdot \log n_m \rceil$ we have for $n^* = 2^{\lceil d \cdot \log n_m \rceil}$,

$$\Pr_{s \in \{0,1\}^\ell} \big[C_{n^*}(\mathbb{G}(s)) = 1\big] \leq 1/2.$$

Together with the previous inequality, for such an m and the corresponding ℓ and n^*,

$$\left| \Pr_{r \in \{0,1\}^{n^*}} \big[C_{n^*}(r) = 1\big] - \Pr_{s \in \{0,1\}^\ell} \big[C_{n^*}(\mathbb{G}(s)) = 1\big] \right| \geq 4/5 - 1/2 > 1/10,$$

which, by (6), contradicts (g2) in Definition 17.

$\square$

Proof of Theorem 15: Assume that there is a probabilistic algorithm that generates a random ordered (3-COL, LFP)-sequence in polynomial output time. We show that there is a deterministic algorithm which generates a (3-COL, LFP)-sequence in polynomial output time. This contradicts Theorem 11.

By Lemmas 16 and 18 there is an algorithm $\mathbb{A}$ with the properties stated in Lemma 18. We show that the following algorithm $\mathbb{S}$ generates a (3-COL, LFP)-sequence $(G'_m, H'_m)_{m \in \mathbb{N}}$ in polynomial output time.

$\mathbb{S}$ // $m \in \mathbb{N}$

1.   simulate $\mathbb{A}$ on input m to compute $(G_m^1, H_m^1), \dots, (G_m^{t_m}, H_m^{t_m})$
2.   **for all** $i \in [t_m]$ **do**
3.   simulate $\mathbb{V}$ on (G_m^i, H_m^i, m)
4.   **if** the simulation accepts **then** output (G_m^i, H_m^i) as (G'_m, H'_m)
     and halt

By (a2) of Lemma 18, the algorithm $\mathbb{S}$ will halt on input m and yield the desired (G'_m, H'_m). By (a3) of Lemma 18, the algorithm $\mathbb{V}$ is applied to inputs (G, H, m) with $f(m) \leq \max\{|V(G)|, |V(H)|\}$; on such inputs its running time is bounded by $(|V(G)| + |V(H)|)^{O(1)}$. Together with (a1), this shows that $\mathbb{S}$ runs in polynomial output time.   □

In contrast to deterministic algorithms generating "standard" (3-COL, LFP)-sequences we require of randomized (3-COL, LFP)-sequences $(G_m, H_m)_{m \in \mathbb{N}}$ that the property

$$G_m \equiv_{\text{LFP}_m} H_m, \quad G_m \in \text{3-COL, and } H_m \notin \text{3-COL}$$

can be checked in a reasonable time (the existence of the verifier, see property (r2) in Definition 14). What happens if we drop this requirement? The following sections address this problem.

6   The Planted Clique Conjecture

In the standard planted clique problem, we are given a graph G whose edges are generated by starting with a random graph with universe $[n]$, then "planting" (adding edges to make) a random clique on k vertices; the problem asks for efficient algorithms finding such a clique of size k. The problem was addressed in [2,13,16], the authors of the last paper mention that it was suggested by M. Saks. It has applications in cryptography [14], algorithmic game theory [11,17], and classical complexity [19]. Here we study some consequences for the Ehrenfeucht-Fraïssé method of a "logic reformulation" of the planted clique problem.

The Erdős-Rényi probability space $\text{ER}(n, 1/2)$ is obtained as follows. We start with the set $[n]$ of vertices. Then we choose every $e \in \binom{[n]}{2}$ $\left(:= \{X \subseteq [n] \mid |X| = 2\}\right)$ as an edge with probability $1/2$, independently of the choices of other edges.

For $G \in ER(n, 1/2)$ the expected size of a maximum clique is approximately $2 \cdot \log n$. Clearly, the probability that $G \in ER(n, 1/2)$ contains a clique of size k is bounded by

$$\binom{n}{k} \cdot 2^{-\binom{k}{2}}.$$

For $k = 4 \cdot \log n$ we have

$$\binom{n}{k} \cdot 2^{-\binom{k}{2}} \leq n^{4 \cdot \log n} \cdot 2^{-\binom{k}{2}} = 2^{4 \cdot \log^2 n} \cdot 2^{2 \cdot \log n - 8 \cdot \log^2 n} \leq 2^{-2 \cdot \log^2 n} = n^{-2 \cdot \log n}.$$

Thus

Proposition 19. $\Pr_{G \in ER(n,1/2)} \left[G \text{ contains a clique of size } 4 \cdot \log n \right] = \frac{1}{n^{\Omega(\log n)}}$.

For any graph G with vertex set $[n]$ and $A \subseteq [n]$ we denote by $G + K(A)$ the graph obtained from G by adding edges such that the subgraph induced on A is a clique. For $n \in \mathbb{N}$ and $k \in [n]$ we consider a second distribution $ER(n, 1/2, k)$: pick a random (ordered) graph $G \in ER(n, 1/2)$ and a uniformly random subset A of $[n]$ of size k and plant in a clique on A in G, thus getting $G + K(A)$.[4] We view G and $G + K(A)$ as *ordered* graphs equipped with the natural ordering on $[n]$.

The following decision version $PCC(\delta)$ of the planted clique conjecture states that no polynomial time algorithm distinguishes between the distributions $ER(n, 1/2)$ and $ER(n, 1/2, 4 \cdot \log n)$ more than $\delta(n)$.

Conjecture 20 (The Planted Clique Conjecture PCC (δ)). Let $\delta : \mathbb{N} \to \mathbb{R}$ with $0 < \delta(n) < 1$ for all $n \in \mathbb{N}$. For every polynomial time algorithm $\mathbb{A}$ there is an $n_0 \in \mathbb{N}$ such that for all $n \geq n_0$,

$$\left| \Pr_{G \in ER(n,1/2)} \left[\mathbb{A} \text{ accepts G} \right] - \Pr_{G + K(A) \in ER(n,1/2,\, 4 \cdot \log n)} \left[\mathbb{A} \text{ accepts } G + K(A) \right] \right| \leq \delta(n).$$

Clearly, if $\delta(n) \leq \delta'(n)$ for all $n \in \mathbb{N}$, then $PCC(\delta)$ implies $PCC(\delta')$. In [14] the assumption $PCC(1 - 1/q)$ for some $q \in \mathbb{N}[X]$, that is, for some polynomial q with natural numbers as coefficients, has been put to good use.

Proposition 21. For $q \in \mathbb{N}[X]$, the statement $PCC(1 - 1/q)$ implies $P \neq NP$.

Proof. By Proposition 19 we know that for sufficiently large n,

$$\Pr_{G \in ER(n,1/2)} \left[G \text{ contains a clique of size } 4 \cdot \log n \right] < 1/q(n). \tag{7}$$

If $P = NP$, then there is a (deterministic) polynomial time algorithm $\mathbb{A}$ deciding whether a graph contains a clique of size $4 \cdot \log n$. For such an $\mathbb{A}$ we have by (7),

$$\Pr_{G + K(A) \in ER(n,1/2,\, 4 \cdot \log n)} \left[\mathbb{A} \text{ accepts } G + K(A) \right] - \Pr_{G \in ER(n,1/2)} \left[\mathbb{A} \text{ accepts } G \right] > 1 - \frac{1}{q(n)}.$$

This contradicts to $PCC(1 - 1/q)$. $\qquad\qquad\square$

---

[4] In the following the notation $G + K(A) \in ER(n, 1/2, k)$ should give the information that the random graph was G and that the random subset of $[n]$ of size k was A.

By the Immerman-Vardi Theorem, on ordered graphs polynomial time algorithms correspond to LFP-sentences. Therefore, PCC(δ) just says that for every LFP-sentence φ and all sufficiently large n,

$$\left| \Pr_{G \in \mathrm{ER}(n,1/2)} \left[G \models \varphi \right] - \Pr_{G+K(A) \in \mathrm{ER}(n,1/2,\ 4 \cdot \log n)} \left[G + K(A) \models \varphi \right] \right| \le \delta(n).$$

This holds if

$$\Pr_{G+K(A) \in \mathrm{ER}(n,1/2,\ 4 \cdot \log n)} \left[G \models \varphi \iff G + K(A) \models \varphi \right] \ge 1 - \delta(n). \tag{8}$$

For our intended application to the Ehrenfeucht-Fraïssé-method we need an even stronger assumption, namely that for every $m \in \mathbb{N}$ and all sufficiently large n,

$$\Pr_{G+K(A) \in \mathrm{ER}(n,1/2,\ 4 \cdot \log n)} \left[\text{for all } \varphi \in \mathrm{LFP}_m : (G \models \varphi \iff G+K(A) \models \varphi) \right] \ge 1 - \delta(n),$$

or more succinctly,

$$\Pr_{G+K(A) \in \mathrm{ER}(n,1/2,\ 4 \cdot \log n)} \left[G \equiv_{\mathrm{LFP}_m} G + K(A)) \right] \ge 1 - \delta(n).$$

We shall need an effective bound for the rate of convergence. So we introduce the following logic version LPCC(ε) of the planted clique conjecture.

Conjecture 22 (LPCC (ε)). Let $\varepsilon : \mathbb{N} \to \mathbb{R}$ with $0 < \varepsilon(n) < 1$ for all $n \in \mathbb{N}$. There is a computable function $f : \mathbb{N} \to \mathbb{N}$ such that for every $m \in \mathbb{N}$ and all $n \ge f(m)$,

$$\Pr_{G+K(A) \in \mathrm{ER}(n,1/2,\ 4 \cdot \log n)} \left[G \equiv_{\mathrm{LFP}_m} G + K(A) \right] \ge \varepsilon(n).$$

The previous remarks show:

Proposition 23. Let $\varepsilon : \mathbb{N} \to \mathbb{R}$ with $0 < \varepsilon(n) < 1$ for all $n \in \mathbb{N}$. Then LPCC(ε) implies PCC($1 - \varepsilon$).

By this proposition and Proposition 21, we get

Corollary 24. For $q \in \mathbb{N}[X]$, LPCC($1/q$) implies P $\ne$ NP.

Assume that LPCC(ε) holds. By taking a natural number m such that LFP_m contains a sentence expressing that the number of edges is even, we see that $\lim_{n \in \mathbb{N}} \varepsilon(n) \le 1/2$. In Proposition 26 we generalize this and show that $\lim_{n \to \infty} \varepsilon(n)$ must be 0.

7   The Planted Clique Conjecture and (3-COL,LFP)-sequences

The following result shows that, assuming LPCC($1/q$), there is a probabilistic algorithm yielding a random sequence $(G_m, H_m)_{m \in \mathbb{N}}$ such that

$$G_m \equiv_{\mathrm{LFP}_m} H_m, \quad G_m \in 3\text{-COL}, \quad \text{and} \quad H_m \notin 3\text{-COL} \tag{9}$$

holds with high probability. By Theorem 15 we cannot have a verifier for this algorithm, that is an efficient algorithm that verifies the properties stated in (9) (assuming the existence of a pseudorandom generator).

Theorem 25. *Assume that* LPCC(1/q) *holds for some polynomial* $q \in \mathbb{N}[X]$. *Then there is a probabilistic algorithm* $\mathbb{P}$ *which on input* $m \in \mathbb{N}$ *generates a pair* (G_m, H_m) *of ordered graphs in time* $(|V(G_m)| + |V(H_m)|)^{O(1)}$ *such that*

$$\Pr\left[G_m \equiv_{\mathrm{LFP}_m} H_m, \ G_m \in 3\text{-}\mathrm{Col}, \ and \ H_m \notin 3\text{-}\mathrm{Col}\right] \geq \frac{1}{\left(|V(G_m)| + |V(H_m)|\right)^{O(1)}}.$$

Moreover, $\mathbb{P}$ *on input* $m \in \mathbb{N}$ *first deterministically computes the vertex sets of the graphs* G_m *and* H_m.

Proof. Consider the problem

CLIQUE($4 \cdot \log$)
    Instance: An $n \in \mathbb{N}$ and an ordered graph G with
        $|V(G)| = n$.
    Problem: Does G have a clique of size $4 \cdot \log n$?

The proof relies on the following two facts (we leave the details to the reader):

- "LPCC(1/q) for some $q \in \mathbb{N}[X]$" essentially states that there is a probabilistic algorithm $\mathbb{P}$ which generates a $\big(\mathrm{CLIQUE}(4 \cdot \log), \mathrm{LFP}\big)$-sequence $(G_m, H_m)_{m \in \mathbb{N}}$ of ordered graphs in polynomial output time such that

$$\Pr\left[G_m \equiv_{\mathrm{LFP}_m} H_m, \ G_m \in \mathrm{CLIQUE}(4 \cdot \log), \ and \ H_m \notin \mathrm{CLIQUE}(4 \cdot \log)\right]$$
$$\geq \frac{1}{\big(|V(G_m)| + |V(H_m)|\big)^{O(1)}}.$$

- As CLIQUE($4 \cdot \log$) is in NP and 3-COL is NP-complete and has a padding function, we can transform the $\big(\mathrm{CLIQUE}(4 \cdot \log), \mathrm{LFP}\big)$-sequence into a (3-COL, LFP)-sequence. □

8   Some Remarks on the Logic Version of the Planted Clique Conjecture

In this section we show (see Lemma 27) that with positive asymptotic probability we can distinguish the LFP_m-theory of the graphs G and $G + K(A)$ by modulo counting their edges (see Lemma 27 for the precise statement). Using this fact, we refute LPCC(ε) unless $\lim_{n \in \mathbb{N}} \varepsilon(n) = 0$.

Proposition 26. *Let* $\varepsilon : \mathbb{N} \to \mathbb{R}^+$. *If* LPCC($\varepsilon$) *holds, then* $\lim_{n \in \mathbb{N}} \varepsilon(n) = 0$

Proof. It suffices to show that for every positive $\delta \in \mathbb{R}$ there is an $m \in \mathbb{N}$ such that

$$\lim_{n \to \infty} \Pr_{G+K(A) \in ER(n,1/2, \; 4 \cdot \log n)} \left[G \equiv_{LFP_m} G + K(A) \right] \leq \delta.$$

This is an immediate consequence of the following lemma as there are LFP-sentences expressing in an ordered graph that the number of edges is congruent i modulo ℓ (for $\ell \in \mathbb{N}$ and $i \in \{0, \ldots, \ell - 1\}$). □

Lemma 27. *Let $\ell \in \mathbb{N}$ and $i \in \{0, \ldots, \ell-1\}$. Then for every nondecreasing and unbounded function $h : \mathbb{N} \to \mathbb{N}$,*

$$\lim_{n \to \infty} \Pr_{G+K(A) \in ER(n,1/2, \; h(n))} \left[\; |E(G + K(A))| - |E(G)| \equiv i \mod \ell \right] = \frac{1}{\ell}.$$

Proof. Let $n \in \mathbb{N}$ and $k \in [n]$. Then, for every graph G with vertex set $[n]$, every subset A of $[n]$ of size k, and every $i \in \{0, 1, \ldots, \ell - 1\}$, we have

$$|E(G+K(A))| - |E(G)| \equiv i \mod \ell \Longleftrightarrow |E(G) \cap E(K(A))| \equiv \binom{k}{2} - i \mod \ell. \quad (10)$$

Here, $E(K(A))$ denotes the set of edges of the clique on A. We set $s(k) := \binom{k}{2}$. Then $|E(K(A))| = s(k)$. For every $r \in \{0, 1, \ldots, \ell - 1\}$, we let $a_r(k)$ be the number of those subsets of $E(K(A))$, whose cardinality is equivalent to r modulo ℓ; thus

$$a_r(k) = \sum_{\substack{0 \leq j \leq s}}^{j \equiv r \mod \ell} \binom{s(k)}{j}.$$

Note that $a_r(k)$ does not depend on n (and in particular, not on the chosen subset A of $[n]$ of size k). By (10), we get for all $n \geq k$, all subsets A of $[n]$ of size k, and all $i \in \{0, 1, \ldots, \ell - 1\}$,

$$\Pr_{G \in ER(n,1/2)} \left[\; |E(G + K(A))| - |E(G)| \equiv i \mod \ell \right] = \frac{a_{s(k)-i}}{2^{s(k)}}. \quad (11)$$

Claim 1. Let $r \in \{0, 1, \ldots, \ell - 1\}$. Then (here $a_\ell(k) := a_0(k)$),

$$\lim_{k \to \infty} \frac{|a_{r+1}(k) - a_r(k)|}{2^{s(k)}} = 0.$$

Proof of Claim 1: First we show that there is a positive $\iota \in \mathbb{R}$ such for all sufficiently small positive $\delta \in \mathbb{R}$ and all $n \in \mathbb{N}$ with $(1/2 - \delta) \cdot n \in \mathbb{N}$,

$$\binom{n}{(1/2 - \delta) \cdot n} = O\left(\frac{2^{(1 - \iota \delta^2) \cdot n}}{\sqrt{n}} \right). \quad (12)$$

In fact, using Stirling's formula

$$\sqrt{2\pi n} \cdot \left(\frac{n}{e} \right)^n \leq n! \leq e \cdot \sqrt{n} \cdot \left(\frac{n}{e} \right)^n,$$

we get for $n \in \mathbb{N}$ and $\varepsilon \in \mathbb{R}$ with $\varepsilon \cdot n \in \mathbb{N}$,

$$\binom{n}{\varepsilon \cdot n} \leq \frac{e \cdot 2^{H(\varepsilon) \cdot n}}{2\pi \cdot \sqrt{\varepsilon \cdot (1 - \varepsilon) \cdot n}}. \tag{13}$$

Here $H : (0, 1) \to \mathbb{R}$ denotes the *binary entropy* function defined by

$$H(\varepsilon) = -\varepsilon \cdot \log \varepsilon - (1 - \varepsilon) \cdot \log (1 - \varepsilon).$$

Recall that H attains 1, its maximum value, at $\varepsilon = 1/2$. We want to bound the values of H in the neighborhood of $1/2$. Let $\delta \in \mathbb{R}$ with $0 \leq \delta < 1/2$. Then

$$H(1/2 - \delta) = -(1/2 - \delta) \cdot \log (1/2 - \delta) - (1/2 + \delta) \cdot \log (1/2 + \delta).$$

Using the Taylor series for $\log x$, we get from this equality that there is an $\iota \in \mathbb{R}$ with $\iota > 0$ such that for sufficiently small $\delta \in \mathbb{R}$ with $\delta \geq 0$,

$$H(1/2 - \delta) \leq 1 - \iota \cdot \delta^2. \tag{14}$$

Hence, assuming in addition that $\delta < 1/\sqrt{8}$ and $(1/2 - \delta) \cdot n \in \mathbb{N}$,

$$\binom{n}{(1/2 - \delta) \cdot n} \leq \frac{e \cdot 2^{(1 - \iota \cdot \delta^2) \cdot n}}{2\pi \cdot \sqrt{(1/4 - \delta^2) \cdot n}} \qquad \text{(by (13) and (14))}$$

$$= O\left(\frac{2^{(1 - \iota \cdot \delta^2) \cdot n}}{\sqrt{n}}\right) \qquad \text{(as } \delta^2 < 1/8\text{)},$$

which is the desired equality.

Now let $j, s \in \mathbb{N}$ satisfy $0 \leq j < s$. Note that

$$\binom{s}{j+1} - \binom{s}{j} = \frac{s - 2j - 1}{j + 1} \cdot \binom{s}{j}. \tag{15}$$

We distinguish two cases.

Case $j \leq s/2 - \sqrt[3]{s^2}$: Then $j \leq (1/2 - \delta) \cdot s$ for $\delta \in (s^{-2/3}, s^{-1/3})$. If $(1/2 - \delta) \cdot s \in \mathbb{N}$, we get by (12)

$$\binom{s}{j+1} - \binom{s}{j} \leq s \cdot \binom{s}{(1/2 - \delta) \cdot s} \leq s \cdot O\left(\frac{2^{(1 - \iota \cdot \delta^2) \cdot s}}{\sqrt{s}}\right) \qquad \text{(by (15) and (12))}$$

$$= O\left(\frac{s \cdot 2^s}{\sqrt{s} \cdot 2^{\iota \cdot \sqrt[3]{s}}}\right) = O\left(\frac{\sqrt{s} \cdot 2^s}{2^{\iota \cdot \sqrt[3]{s}}}\right).$$

Case $s/2 - \sqrt[3]{s^2} < j < s/2$: Then

$$\binom{s}{j+1} - \binom{s}{j} \leq \frac{2\sqrt[3]{s^2}}{s/2 - \sqrt[3]{s^2} + 1} \cdot \binom{s}{s/2} \qquad \text{(by (15)}$$

$$= O\left(\frac{2^s}{s^{-2/3+3/3+1/2}}\right) = O\left(\frac{2^s}{s^{5/6}}\right).$$

Putting all together we get the statement of Claim 1 as follows

$$a_{r+1}(k) - a_r(k) = \sum_{\substack{j \equiv r+1 \mod \ell \\ 0 \le j \le s(k)}}^{} \binom{s(k)}{j} - \sum_{\substack{j \equiv r \mod \ell \\ 0 \le j \le s(k)}}^{} \binom{s(k)}{j}$$

$$\le \sum_{\substack{j \equiv r \mod \ell \\ 0 \le j < s(k)/2}}^{} \left(\binom{s(k)}{j+1} - \binom{s(k)}{j} \right)$$

$$= \sum_{\substack{j \equiv r \mod \ell \\ 0 \le j \le s(k)/2 - \sqrt[3]{s(k)^2}}}^{} \left(\binom{s(k)}{j+1} - \binom{s(k)}{j} \right)$$

$$+ \sum_{\substack{j \equiv r \mod \ell \\ s(k)/2 - \sqrt[3]{s(k)^2} < j < s(k)/2}}^{} \left(\binom{s(k)}{j+1} - \binom{s(k)}{j} \right)$$

$$= O\left(\frac{s(k) \cdot \sqrt{s} \cdot 2^{s(k)}}{2^{\iota \cdot \sqrt[3]{s(k)}}} \right) + O\left(\frac{s(k)^{2/3} \cdot 2^{s(k)}}{s(k)^{5/6}} \right) \qquad \text{(by the equalities derived above)}$$

$$= o(2^{s(k)})$$

Similarly we can show $a_r(k) - a_{r+1}(k) = o(2^{s(k)})$. ⊣

Claim 2. Let $\delta > 0$. If k is sufficiently large, then for all $n \ge k$, all subsets A of $[n]$ of size k, and all $i \in \{0, 1, \dots, \ell - 1\}$, we have

$$\frac{1}{\ell} - \delta \le \Pr_{G \in ER(n,1/2)} \left[\, |E(G + K(A))| - |E(G)| \equiv i \mod \ell \right] \le \frac{1}{\ell} + \delta.$$

Proof of Claim 2: For every $i \in \{0, 1, \dots, \ell - 1\}$ let

$$p_i(k) := \frac{a_{s(k)-i}(k)}{2^{s(k)}}.$$

Claim 1 implies that for every $\iota > 0$ and all sufficiently large k,

$$\left| p_{i+1}(k) - p_i(k) \right| \le \iota.$$

Thus,

$$p_0(k) - i \cdot \iota \le p_i(k) \le p_0(k) + i \cdot \iota. \tag{16}$$

As $\sum_{j=0}^{\ell-1} j = \ell \cdot (\ell - 1)/2$, we obtain

$$\ell \cdot p_0(k) - \frac{\ell \cdot (\ell - 1)}{2} \cdot \iota \le \sum_{j=0}^{\ell-1} p_j(k) = 1 \le \ell \cdot p_0(k) + \frac{\ell \cdot (\ell - 1)}{2} \cdot \iota$$

Hence,

$$\frac{1}{\ell} - \frac{(\ell - 1)}{2} \cdot \iota \le p_0(k) \le \frac{1}{\ell} + \frac{(\ell - 1)}{2} \cdot \iota. \tag{17}$$

Choosing ι small enough, (16) and (17) imply for all sufficiently large k and every $i \in \{0, 1, \dots, \ell - 1\}$,

$$\frac{1}{\ell} - \delta \le p_i(k) \le \frac{1}{\ell} + \delta.$$

As for all $n \geq k$, all subsets A of $[n]$ of size k, and all $i \in \{0, 1, \ldots, \ell - 1\}$, we have (compare (11))

$$p_i(k) = \frac{a_{s(k)-i}}{2^{s(k)}} = \Pr_{G \in \text{ER}(n,1/2)} \left[\left| E(G + K(A)) \right| - \left| E(G) \right| \equiv i \mod \ell \right],$$

this yields our claim.   ⊣

Clearly, Claim 2 immediately implies the statement of Lemma 27.   □

9 Further Results and Open Questions

In Sect. 4 we have seen that for no problem Q of ordered graphs there exists a (Q, LFP)-sequence, which can be generated in polynomial output time. Recall that LFP captures polynomial time on ordered graphs. More generally, let L be a logic capturing one of the complexity classes LOGSPACE, P, or PSPACE on (ordered) graphs: Then, for no problem Q of (ordered) graphs we can generate a (Q, L)-sequence (G_m, H_m) by an algorithm which satisfies the resource bound in $|V(G_m)| + |V(H_m)|$ characteristic for the corresponding complexity class, e.g., not in space $O(\log(|V(G_m)| + |V(H_m)|))$ for LOGSPACE. Furthermore there are extensions of these results to "nondeterministic classes" such as NLOGSPACE and NP and extensions for so-called Ajtai-Fagin games adequate for (monadic) Σ_1^1 (see [5] for most of these results).

We are far from understanding when an efficiently computable (Q, L)-sequence exists. Even for first-order logic we have no simple and informative characterization of the problems Q with a (Q, FO)-sequence computable in polynomial output time. Besides the "negative" Example 13, we have a positive result: If Q is NP-hard under FO-reductions (a property shared by many natural NP-complete problems), then a (Q, FO)-sequence can be generated in polynomial output time.

In Sect. 5 we have mentioned that in most applications of the Ehrenfeucht-Fraïssé-method the verification that G_m and H_m satisfy the same sentences of the corresponding logic of "quantifier rank" or length $\leq m$ was done by an algorithm running in time $f(m) \cdot (|V(G_m)| + |V(H_m)|)^{O(1)}$ for some computable function f. In the Appendix of [5], we have shown this explicitly for two (nontrivial) applications of the method. However, this is not always the case; for example, not for the highly nontrivial application of the Ehrenfeucht-Fraïssé-method in [21].

We have seen in Sect. 6 that LPCC($1/q$) for some $q \in \mathbb{N}[X]$ implies P $\neq$ NP. Can one refute the statement "there is a $q \in \mathbb{N}[X]$ with LPCC($1/q$)?" or are there results or insights which make the statement plausible?

Furthermore, we ask: Is it true that for every single LFP-sentence φ we have

$$\lim_{n \to \infty} \Pr_{G + K(A) \in \text{ER}(n,1/2,\ 4 \cdot \log n)} \left[G \models \varphi \iff G + K(A) \models \varphi \right] \geq 1/2?$$

References

1. Ajtai, M., Fagin, R.: Reachability is harder for directed than for undirected finite graphs. J. Symb. Log. **55**(1), 113–150 (1990)

2. Alon, N., Krivelevich, M., Sudakov, B.: Finding a large hidden clique in a random graph. Random Struct. Algorithms **13**(3–4), 457–466 (1998)

3. Arora, S., Barak, B.: Computational Complexity - A Modern Approach. Cambridge University Press, New York (2009)

4. Bosse, U.: An "Ehrenfeucht-Fraïssé game" for fixpoint logic and stratified fixpoint logic. In: Martini, S., Börger, E., Kleine Büning, H., Jäger, G., Richter, M.M. (eds.) CSL 1992. LNCS, vol. 702. Springer, Heidelberg (1993)

5. Chen, Y., Flum, J.: On limitations of the Ehrenfeucht-Fraïssé-method in descriptive complexity. In: Electronic Colloquium on Computational Complexity (ECCC), 20:65 (2013)

6. Ehrenfeucht, A.: An application of games to the completeness problem for formalized theories. Fundam. Math. **49**, 129–141 (1961)

7. Grädel, E., et al.: Finite Model Theory and Its Applications. Texts in Theoretical Computer Science. An EATCS Series. Springer, Heidelberg (2006)

8. Fagin, R., Stockmeyer, L.J., Vardi, M.Y.: On monadic NP vs. monadic co-NP. Inf. Comput. **120**(1), 78–92 (1995)

9. Fraïssé, R.: Sur quelques classifications des systèmes de relations. Univ. Alger Publi. Sci. Sér. A **1**, 35–182 (1954)

10. Grohe, M.: Arity hierarchies. Ann. Pure Appl. Log. **82**(2), 103–163 (1996)

11. Hazan, E., Krauthgamer, R.: How hard is it to approximate the best Nash equilibrium? SIAM J. Comput. **40**(1), 79–91 (2011)

12. He, Y.: k variables are needed to define k-clique in first-order logic. In: CoRR, abs/1501.04572 (2015)

13. Jerrum, M.: Large cliques elude the metropolis process. Random Struct. Algorithms **3**(4), 347–360 (1992)

14. Juels, A., Peinado, M.: Hiding cliques for cryptographic security. Des. Codes Crypt. **20**(3), 269–280 (2000)

15. Kubierschky, M.: Yet another hierarchy theorem. J. Symb. Log. **65**(2), 627–640 (2000)

16. Kučera, L.: Expected complexity of graph partitioning problems. Discrete Appl. Math. **57**(2–3), 193–212 (1995)

17. Minder, L., Vilenchik, D.: Small clique detection and approximate nash equilibria. In: Dinur, I., Jansen, K., Naor, J., Rolim, J. (eds.) Approximation, Randomization, and Combinatorial Optimization. LNCS, vol. 5687, pp. 673–685. Springer, Heidelberg (2009)

18. Rossman, B.: Ehrenfeucht-Fraïssé games on random structures. In: Ono, H., Kanazawa, M., de Queiroz, R. (eds.) WoLLIC 2009. LNCS, vol. 5514, pp. 350–364. Springer, Heidelberg (2009)

19. Santhanam, R.: The complexity of explicit constructions. Theor. Comput. Syst. **51**(3), 297–312 (2012)

20. Schwentick, T.: Graph connectivity and monadic NP. In: Proceedings of the 35th Annual Symposium on Foundations of Computer Science (FOCS 1994), pp. 614–622. IEEE Computer Society (1994)

21. Shelah, S., Spencer, J.: Zero-one laws for sparse random graphs. J. Am. Math. Soc. **1**, 97–115 (1988)

Monadic Theory of a Linear Order Versus the Theory of Its Subsets with the Lifted Min/Max Operations

Christian Choffrut and Serge Grigorieff[✉]

LIAFA, CNRS UMR 7089, Université Paris 7 Denis Diderot, Paris, France
{cc,seg}@liafa.univ-paris-diderot.fr

Abstract. We compare the monadic second-order theory of an arbitrary linear ordering L with the theory of the family of subsets of L endowed with the operation on subsets obtained by lifting the max operation on L. We show that the two theories define the same relations. The same result holds when lifting the min operation or both max and min operations.

1 Introduction

We initiated a couple of years ago an investigation aiming at comparing the theory of a monadic second-order structure $S = \langle U, \mathcal{P}(U); =_U, \in, \omega_1, \ldots, \rangle$ and that of the associated first-order structure $T = \langle \mathcal{P}(U); =, \Omega_1, \ldots, \rangle$ where Ω_i is the operation ω_i lifted to subsets: $\Omega_i(X_1, \ldots,) = \{\omega_i(x_1, \ldots,) \mid x_1 \in X_1, \ldots\}$. The structure T can be viewed as follows: lift all operations to subsets and consider the sole formulas about S with no occurrence of an individual variable, whether free or bound. Let us stress that *the inclusion relation and the Boolean operations on sets are not given as primitives in T.* The structure T is clearly definable in S: the unique sort of T (namely $\mathcal{P}(U)$) is among the two sorts of S (which are U and $\mathcal{P}(U)$) and the lifted operations Ω_i's are definable in S. The general issue is: what can be known of S within T? More precisely,

(Q_1) Concerning relations on $\mathcal{P}(U)$, does definability in S implies definability in T? This question reduces to the following one: is it possible to define in T the class of singleton sets and the set-inclusion relation hence to define in T the most natural isomorphic copy of S.

(Q_2) In case question (Q_1) receives negative answer then
(*) which S-definable families of subsets of U are also T-definable?
(**) is it still possible to define in T an isomorphic copy of S?

In previous works we studied two particular cases: $S_1 = \langle \mathbb{N}; =_{\mathbb{N}}, \in, + \rangle$ and $S_2 = \langle \Sigma^*; =_{\Sigma^*}, \in, \cdot \rangle$, cf. [4,5]. We showed that in these two cases question (Q_1) has a negative answer but question (*) gets a positive solution: an isomorphic copy of S is definable in T. Let us give a brief account for S_1. Consider the maps

Partially supported by TARMAC ANR agreement 12 BS02 007 01.

L.D. Beklemishev et al. (Eds.): Gurevich Festschrift II 2015, LNCS 9300, pp. 109–128, 2015.
DOI: 10.1007/978-3-319-23534-9_6

$\sigma : \mathcal{P}(\mathbb{N}) \to \mathcal{P}(\mathbb{N})$ and $f : \mathbb{N} \to \mathcal{P}(\mathbb{N})$ such that $\sigma(X) = \{0\} \cup (1 + X)$ and $f(n) = \{0\} \cup (1 + n + \mathbb{N})$. We proved that the ranges of σ and f and the images under σ and f of membership and addition, namely, the four predicates

$$\sigma(\mathcal{P}(\mathbb{N})) \subseteq \mathcal{P}(\mathbb{N}) \qquad f(\mathbb{N}) \subseteq \mathcal{P}(\mathbb{N}) \qquad \{(f(x), \sigma(X)) \mid x \in X\} \subseteq \mathcal{P}\mathbb{N}) \times \mathcal{P}(\mathbb{N})$$
$$\{(f(x), f(y), f(z)) \mid x, y, z \in \mathbb{N}, z = x + y\} \subseteq \mathcal{P}(\mathbb{N}) \times \mathcal{P}(\mathbb{N}) \times \mathcal{P}(\mathbb{N})$$

are all definable in T with respective complexities Σ_1, Π_3, Δ_4 and Δ_5.

In this paper we consider an arbitrary linear order L with possibly minimum and maximum elements and show that its monadic second-order theory is equivalent to the first-order theory of its power set when the order relation is lifted by defining the predicate $\texttt{Max}(X, Y, Z)$ where $X = \{\max\{y, z\} \mid y \in Y, z \in Z\}$. The situation is much simpler than above since question (Q_1) gets a positive answer: we can express in T the predicates "X is a singleton" and "X is a subset of Y".

Let us recall that the monadic theory of a linear order has been intensively studied. As a prelude to the general monadic theory of linear orders, Gurevich 1964 [6] proved the decidability of the theory of linear orders with one-place predicates. Büchi 1960 [1] proved the decidability of the monadic theory of the order on $\mathbb{N}$. The result has been extended to all countable ordinals, Büchi 1973 [2], and then to all ordinals $< \omega_2$, Büchi and Zaiontz 1983 [3]. The decision problem for the monadic theory of the ordinal ω_2 happens to depend on axioms of set theory, Gurevich et al. 1983 [7], Lifsches and Shelah 1992 [12]. The monadic theory of the order on $\mathbb{R}$ is undecidable, Shelah 1975 [14], and in fact very complex, Gurevich 1979 [8], Gurevich and Shelah 1982–84 [9–11].

We now give a brief outline of the paper. Section 2 recalls the basics on linear orderings. It also introduces the two structures to be compared. In Sect. 3 we study for its own sake the structure obtained by lifting a linear ordering to subsets. We consider it both as a monoid and as a partial ordering of which we give a couple of alternative characterizations.

The expressibility of singletons is obtained in Sect. 4 by a careful study of the set of immediate predecessors of a given subset in the lifted ordering since the cardinal of this set discriminates the singletons among all subsets. The same is done for pairs.

Membership of an element to an arbitrary subset (more exactly, inclusion of a singleton set in a set) is the second ingredient to prove the equivalence of the two structures and it is considered in Sect. 5. Two different expressions are given according to whether or not the ordering possesses a zero. The two expressions have the same complexity Δ_4 but they are based on different approaches which we found interesting to keep.

The equivalence of different structures, mainly those introduced in paragraph 2.2 along with their natural variants is established in Sect. 6.

2   Preliminaries

2.1   Linear Orders

This section is meant to keep this paper self-contained. We recall the basic definitions on orderings, see e.g., [13]

Definition 1. *An element $a \in L$ is an* upper bound *of $X \subseteq L$ if $x \leq a$ for all $x \in X$. It is a* least upper bound *if it is an upper bound and for all upper bounds b it holds $a \leq b$. It is the* maximum element *of X and denoted $max(X)$ if furthermore it belongs to X. If L has a maximum element we denote it by 1.*

A final segment *is a subset which is* upward saturated, *i.e., $x \in X$ and $y \geq x$ implies $y \in X$. It is a* closed final segment *if it is of the form $\{x \mid x \geq a\}$ for some $a \in L$, else it is an* open final segment.

The notions of lower bound, *greatest lower bound* $glb(X)$ *and* minimum element $min(X)$ *of a set X are defined in the obvious similar way. So is the notion of minimum element 0.*

Definition 2. *Two elements a, b are* successive *if $a < b$ and the condition $a \leq c \leq b$ implies $c = a$ or $c = b$. We then say that a is an* immediate predecessor *of b and that b is an* immediate successor *of a.*

An element is a successor *if it admits an immediate predecessor, it is a* predecessor *if it admits an immediate successor.*

If $a \in L$ is not a successor and if it is not 0, it is a limit.

Notation 3. *The final segments canonically associated to a subset $X \subseteq L$ are denoted by*

$$X^{\geq} = \{y \mid \exists x \in X \ \ x \leq y\} \ (the \ smallest \ final \ segment \ containing \ X)$$
$$X^{>} = \{y \mid \exists x \in X \ \ x < y\}$$

and the set of strict lower bounds by

$$X^{<} = \{y \mid \forall x \in X \ \ y < x\}$$

Lemma 4. *Given two final segments $F, G \subseteq L$ we have*

$$F \subsetneq G \quad or \quad F = G \quad or \quad G \subsetneq F$$

Proof. Assume $F \neq G$, i.e., without loss of generality assume there exists $x \in F \setminus G$. Then for all $y \in G$ we have $x \not\geq y$ or equivalently $x < y$. But then $G \subseteq \{z \in L \mid x < z\} \subsetneq F$. □

Remark 5. The following elementary observation underlies many proofs of this paper. It helps having it in mind.

For all nonempty subsets $X \subseteq L$ exactly one of the following conditions holds.

- X has a minimum and $X^{<}$ is empty or has a maximum (e.g., in any finite linear order).
- X has a minimum and $X^{<}$ is nonempty and has no maximum (consider the order $A + B$ with $A = B = \mathbb{N}$ and take $X = B$).
- X has no minimum and $X^{<}$ is empty or has a maximum (consider the order $A + B$ with $A = B = -\mathbb{N}$ and take $X = B$).
- X has no minimum and $X^{<}$ is nonempty and has no maximum (consider the order $A + B$ with $A = \mathbb{N}, B = -\mathbb{N}$ and take $X = B$).

2.2   Logical Structures

Given an arbitrary linear order $\leq$ on a nonempty set L, we consider the struc-
ture $\langle L; =, \max\rangle$ or $\langle L; =, \max, 0, 1\rangle$ where max has the natural interpretation
$\max\{x, y\} = x$ if $x \leq y$ and y otherwise and 0 and 1 are respectively the minimum and maximum elements (in case they exist).

We consider the operation on $\mathcal{P}(L)$ obtained by lifting the max operation
on L.

Definition 6. *For $X, Y \subseteq L$, we set*

$$X \uparrow Y = \{\max\{x, y\} \mid x \in X, \ y \in Y\}$$

We compare the two associated structures dealing with sets:

$$S = \left\{ \begin{array}{l} \langle L, \mathcal{P}(L); =, \in, \max\rangle \\ \text{or } \langle L, \mathcal{P}(L); =, \in, \max, 0, 1\rangle \end{array}\right., \quad T = \langle \mathcal{P}(L); =, \uparrow\rangle \tag{1}$$

Now, we define precisely what question (Q_1) supra means for the two structures S and T. Question (Q_1) (slightly revisited) is as follows: given any second-
order formula ϕ for S with m first-order and n second-order variables, does there
exist some first-order formula ψ for T with $m + n$ first-order variables such that,
for all $a_1, \ldots, a_m \in L$ and $A_1, \ldots, A_n \in \mathcal{P}(L)$ the following equivalence holds

$$\langle L, \mathcal{P}(L); =, \in, \max\rangle \models \phi(a_1, \ldots, a_m, A_1, \ldots, A_n)$$
$$\Longleftrightarrow \tag{2}$$
$$\langle \mathcal{P}(L); =, \uparrow\rangle \models \psi(\{a_1\}, \ldots, \{a_m\}, A_1, \ldots, A_n)$$

An easy induction on formulas ϕ shows that it suffices to get such a formula
ψ for the two particular formulas ϕ expressing the predicates "$X = \{x\}$" and
"$\{x\} \subseteq X$".

Observe that the reverse question "given ψ get ϕ" is straightforward since
the lifting of operations from L to $\mathcal{P}(L)$ can be expressed in S.

In all cases, when showing that a predicate is expressible in the language we
give an estimate of its syntactic complexity. We recall that a predicate is Σ_n
(resp. Π_n) if it is defined by a formula that begins with some existential (resp.
universal) quantifiers and alternates $n - 1$ times between series of existential and
universal quantifiers. It is Δ_n if it is both Σ_n and Π_n. It is $\Sigma_n \wedge \Pi_n$ if it is
defined by a conjunction of a Σ_n formula and a Π_n formula.

3   Lifted Structure

Every linear ordering L is a lattice which allows one to view it as a universal
algebra equipped with binary operations of lower and upper bound of two elements. Here we show that the lifted binary operation of $\mathcal{P}(L)$ allows us to define
a partial ordering which makes it a join-semilattice. We investigate $\mathcal{P}(L)$ both
as an algebra and as a partially ordered set.

3.1   The Semigroup $\langle \mathcal{P}(L), \uparrow \rangle$

Here we are interested in the algebraic structure of the operation $\uparrow$ on the subsets of L.

Lemma 7. *1. The operation $\uparrow$ on $\mathcal{P}(L)$ is idempotent, commutative and associative and admits the empty set $\emptyset$ as an absorbing element.*
2. The operation $\uparrow$ has a neutral element if and only if $(L, \le)$ has a minimum element 0. In this case, $\{0\}$ is the neutral element of $\uparrow$.
3. The operation $\uparrow$ distributes over the set union.

Proof. Straightforward.

Corollary 8. *1. The predicate $X = \emptyset$ is Π_1 expressible in $\langle \mathcal{P}(L); =, \uparrow \rangle$.*
2. If L has a minimum element 0 then the predicate $X = \{0\}$ is Π_1.

Proof. 1. Since $\emptyset$ is absorbing in $\langle \mathcal{P}(L); =, \uparrow \rangle$ and there is at most one absorbing element, $X = \emptyset$ holds if and only if $\forall Y \; X \uparrow Y = X$.
2. Similarly, $\{0\}$ is the unique neutral element in $\langle \mathcal{P}(L); =, \uparrow \rangle$, hence $X = \{0\}$ holds if and only if $\forall Y \; X \uparrow Y = Y$. $\square$

3.2   A Characterization of the Operation $\uparrow$

Because of Lemma 4, for two given final segments one is included into the other. Therefore the following result exhausts all possible cases. Its purpose is to work as much as possible with subsets rather than applying the original Definition 6 which mixes subsets and elements.

Lemma 9. *For all $X, Y \subseteq X$ we have*

$$X \uparrow Y = (X \cup Y) \cap X^{\ge} \cap Y^{\ge} = \begin{cases} Y \cup (X \cap Y^{>}) = Y \cup (X \cap Y^{\ge}) & \text{if } Y^{\ge} \subseteq X^{\ge} \\ X \cup (X^{>} \cap Y) = X \cup (X^{\ge} \cap Y) & \text{if } X^{\ge} \subseteq Y^{\ge} \end{cases}$$

Proof. If $z \in X \uparrow Y$ then $z = x \vee y$ for some $x \in X$ and $y \in Y$. If $x \le y$ then $z = y \in X^{\ge} \cap Y$ and if $x \ge y$ then $z = x \in X \cap Y^{\ge}$. In both cases we have $z \in (X \cup Y) \cap X^{\ge} \cap Y^{\ge}$. Conversely, let $z \in (X \cup Y) \cap X^{\ge} \cap Y^{\ge}$. If $z \in X$ then $z \in X \cap Y^{\ge}$ hence $z \ge y$ for some $y \in Y$ and $z = z \vee y \in X \uparrow Y$. Similarly, if $z \in Y$ then z is also in $X \uparrow Y$. This proves equality $X \uparrow Y = (X \cup Y) \cap X^{\ge} \cap Y^{\ge}$. Since $X \subseteq X^{\ge}$ and $Y \subseteq Y^{\ge}$, the other stated equalities (under assumption $Y^{\ge} \subseteq X^{\ge}$ or $X^{\ge} \subseteq Y^{\ge}$) are derived by simple set computation. $\square$

3.3   The Partially Ordered Set $\langle \mathcal{P}(L), \preceq \rangle$

We consider the following binary relation on subsets which happens to be an ordering.

Definition 10. *For $X, Y \subseteq L$ we let $X \preceq Y \iff X \uparrow Y = Y$.*

E.g., if Y is the singleton $\{y\}$ then $X \preceq Y \iff \forall x \in X \; x \leq y$. In particular, if X, Y are the singletons $\{x\}, \{y\}$ then $\{x\} \preceq \{y\} \iff x \leq y$.

Proposition 11. *1. The relation $\preceq$ is a partial ordering on $\mathcal{P}(L)$ with $\emptyset$ as maximum element.*
2. The order $\preceq$ has a minimum element if and only if $(L, \leq)$ has a minimum element 0. In this case, $\{0\}$ is the minimum element of $\preceq$.
3. The order $\preceq$ restricted to $\mathcal{P}(L) \setminus \{\emptyset\}$ has a maximum element if and only if $(L, \leq)$ has a maximum element 1. In this case, $\{1\}$ is the maximum element of this restriction of $\preceq$.

Proof. 1. Reflexivity and antisymmetry are clear. We prove transitivity. Suppose $X \preceq Y \preceq Z$ then $X \uparrow Y = Y$ and $Y \uparrow Z = Z$ hence
$$X \uparrow Z = X \uparrow (Y \uparrow Z) = (X \uparrow Y) \uparrow Z = Y \uparrow Z = Z.$$
Since $\emptyset$ is absorbing for $\uparrow$ it is the maximum element of $(\mathcal{P}(L), \preceq)$.
Claims 2, 3 are straightforward. □

Lemma 12. *If $X \preceq Y$ then $Y \subseteq X^{\geq}$ hence $Y^{\geq} \subseteq X^{\geq}$.*

Proof. Apply equality $X \uparrow Y = Y$ and Lemma 9: $X \uparrow Y \subseteq X^{\geq}$. □

As usual, we denote by $X \prec Y$ the strict ordering defined by $X \preceq Y$ and $X \neq Y$.

Remark 13. It is a simple exercise to verify that $\langle \mathcal{P}(L), \preceq \rangle$ is a linear order if and only if L has at most two elements.

With a structure of linear ordering L is naturally associated a structure of lattice. We lifted the linear ordering to a partial ordering on the power set of L. This partial ordering is not associated with a structure of lattice, only with a structure of join semilattice.

Proposition 14. $\langle \mathcal{P}(L); \preceq \rangle$ *is a join semilattice: $X \uparrow Y$ is the join of X and Y.*

Proof. Since $(X \uparrow Y) \uparrow X = (X \uparrow Y) \uparrow Y = X \uparrow Y$ we have $X, Y \preceq X \uparrow Y$. Suppose $X, Y \preceq Z$. Then $(X \uparrow Y) \uparrow Z = (X \uparrow Z) \uparrow Y = Z \uparrow Y = Z$ hence $X \uparrow Y \preceq Z$. This proves that $X \uparrow Y$ is the join of X, Y. □

Remark 15. The $\preceq$ order may have no meet. For instance, consider the set $L = \omega^*$ of negative or null integers with the usual order and let $X = -2\mathbb{N}$ and $Y = -(2\mathbb{N}+1)$. Then $Z \preceq X$ if and only if Z is an infinite subset of X. Similarly with Y. Thus, X, Y have no common lower bound.
Considering the same sets as subsets of ω^* in the linear order $\omega + \omega^*$, $Z \preceq X$ if and only if $Z \subseteq \omega \cup X$ and $Z \cap \omega \neq \emptyset$ or $Z \cap \omega^*$ is infinite. Thus, X, Y have common lower bounds which are exactly the nonempty subsets of ω. However, any common lower bound Z is strictly upper bounded by another common lower bound T : if $z \in Z$ then let $T = \{t \in \omega \mid t > z\}$.

3.4 Final Segments

It is clear that final subsets play a special rôle. Indeed, the partial order restricted to the final segments is linear and more importantly the binary operation $\uparrow$ and the partial order $\preceq$ between arbitrary subsets use final segments in their alternative definitions, such as Lemmas 9 and 18.

Lemma 16. *If F is a final segment and $F \preceq Y$ then Y is a final segment.*

Proof. Suppose $y \in Y$ and $z \geq y$. Equality $F \uparrow Y = Y$ shows that $y \geq x$ for some $x \in F$. But then $z \geq x$ and since F is upwards closed we have $z \in F$ hence $z = \max\{z, y\} \in F \uparrow Y = Y$. Thus, Y is upwards closed. $\square$

Lemma 17. *If F, G are final segments then $F \uparrow G = F \cap G$. In particular, $F \preceq G$ if and only if $F \supseteq G$.*

Proof. Since F and G are final segments we have $F = F^{\geq}$ and $G = G^{\geq}$. By Lemma 9 we obtain $F \uparrow G = (F \cup G) \cap F^{\geq} \cap G^{\geq} = (F \cup G) \cap F \cap G = F \cap G$. $\square$

3.5 A Characterization of the Ordering $\preceq$

The following is an alternative definition of the relation $\preceq$ in set theoretical terms.

Lemma 18. *For all $X, Y \subseteq L$ we have $X \preceq Y$ if and only if*

$$X \cap Y^{\geq} \subseteq Y \subseteq X^{\geq}. \tag{3}$$

Note. Observe that the last occurrence of $X^{\geq}$ in the above expression cannot be replaced by $X^{>}$ (take $X = Y$ where X has a minimal element).

Proof. The statement follows from the next inclusions

$$\begin{cases} X \uparrow Y \subseteq Y \iff X \cap Y^{\geq} \subseteq Y \iff X \cap Y^{>} \subseteq Y \\ X \uparrow Y \supseteq Y \iff Y \subseteq X^{\geq} \end{cases}$$

Indeed, condition $X \uparrow Y \subseteq Y$ holds if and only if, for all $x \in X$ and $y \in Y$, $x > y \Rightarrow x \in Y$ (resp. $x \geq y \Rightarrow x \in Y$), which means $X \cap Y^{>} \subseteq Y$ (resp. $X \cap Y^{\geq} \subseteq Y$). Condition $X \uparrow Y \supseteq Y$ holds if and only if for all $y \in Y$ there exists $x \in X$ such that $x \leq y$, which means $Y \subseteq X^{\geq}$. $\square$

The following "constructive" characterization of the relation $\prec$ will help when determining the immediate $\preceq$-predecessors of a subset (cf. Sect. 4.1).

Lemma 19. *The condition $X \prec Y$ holds if and only if one of the following two conditions is satisfied:*

$$X^{\geq} = Y^{\geq} \text{ and } X \subsetneq Y \tag{4}$$
$$X \setminus Y^{\geq} \neq \emptyset \text{ and } X \cap Y^{\geq} \subseteq Y \tag{5}$$

Proof. ⇒. By Lemma 18 we know that $X \prec Y$ if and only if $X \neq Y$ and (3) above holds. The last inclusion $Y \subseteq X^{\geq}$ of (3) yields $Y^{\geq} \subseteq X^{\geq}$.

If $X^{\geq} = Y^{\geq}$ holds then $X = X \cap X^{\geq} = X \cap Y^{\geq} \subseteq Y$ by the first inclusion of (3) and thus $X \subsetneq Y$, showing that condition (4) is true. Otherwise $Y^{\geq} \subsetneq X^{\geq}$ hence $X \setminus Y^{\geq} \neq \emptyset$. Since we also have $X \cap Y^{\geq} \subseteq Y$ we see that condition (5) is true.

⇐. Conversely, suppose condition (4) is satisfied: $X^{\geq} = Y^{\geq}$ and $X \subsetneq Y$ holds. Then $X \cap Y^{\geq} \subseteq Y \cap Y^{\geq} = Y \subseteq Y^{\geq} = X^{\geq}$ and, by Lemma 18 $X \preceq Y$. Since $X \subsetneq Y$ we have $X \prec Y$.

Suppose condition (5) is satisfied. Then $X^{\geq} \setminus Y^{\geq} \neq \emptyset$ and Lemma 4 yields $Y^{\geq} \subseteq X^{\geq}$. Thus, using the assumption $X \cap Y^{\geq} \subseteq Y$, we get $X \cap Y^{\geq} \subseteq Y \subseteq Y^{\geq} \subseteq X^{\geq}$ hence $X \preceq Y$ (by Lemma 18). Now, $X \neq Y$ since $X \setminus Y^{\geq} \neq \emptyset$. Thus, $X \prec Y$. □

4   Defining Single Elements

As said in the introduction, the objective of this paper is to show that the two structures S and T (cf. (1) in Sect. 2.2) can be identified when properly encoded. This requires in particular to prove that individual variables can be recovered in the structure T. This is achieved in Theorem 26.

We illustrate our approach by means of examples. With $L = \mathbb{N}$, one can convince oneself that every singleton $\{a\}$ can be defined by the number of sub-sets X such that $X \prec \{a\}$ (e.g., with $a = 0$ there is no strict predecessor, with $a = 1$ there are exactly 2 strict predecessors, namely $\{0\}, \{0,1\}$, with $a = 2$ there are exactly 6 strict predecessors, namely $\{0\}, \{0,1\}, \{0,2\}, \{0,1,2\}, \{1\}, \{1,2\}$). This however cannot be extended to linear orders such as $\mathbb{Z}$ and worse it suggests a new formula must be designed for each singleton. Luckily, whatever the linear order, the fact of being a singleton is defined by a unique formula asserting how many *immediate* predecessors it has. E.g., in $\mathbb{Z}$ it is the case for the three values of a above that there is exactly one immediate predecessor. The definability of singletons in established in Theorem 26. As we make no assump-tion on L in the investigation of the possible immediate predecessors we are led to consider different cases according to whether or not the given subset of L has a minimum, a greatest lower bound, a lower bound or no lower bound (as observed in Remark 5).

4.1   Immediate Predecessors

The notion of immediate predecessors is as expected (cf. Definition 2).

Notation 20. *We denote by* $Suc(X, Y)$ *the* Π_1-*predicate asserting that* Y *is an immediate successor of* X *(or* X *is an immediate predecessor of* Y*), i.e.*

$$X \prec Y \ \wedge \ \forall Z \ (X \preceq Z \preceq Y \ \Longleftrightarrow \ (Z = X \ \vee \ Z = Y)) \tag{6}$$

We state the main result of this subsection.

Theorem 21. *X and Y are successive sets for $\preceq$ (i.e. $\mathsf{Suc}(X,Y)$ is true) if and only if one of the following conditions holds*

1. *$Y = X \cup \{a\}$ for some $a \in X^{\geq} \setminus X$ (in particular, a is not the minimum element of Y)*
2. *$X = Y \cup \{b\}$ where b is the maximum element of $\{z \mid \forall y \in Y \;\; z < y\}$*

We first inquire under which condition a subset X of Y is an immediate predecessor.

Lemma 22. *A subset $X \subsetneq Y$ is an immediate predecessor of Y if and only if $X = Y \setminus \{a\}$ where $a \in Y$ is not the minimum element in Y.*

Proof. $\Leftarrow$. Assume a is not minimum in Y. Then $Y^{\geq} = (Y \setminus \{a\})^{\geq}$. Because of $Y \setminus \{a\} \subsetneq Y$ Lemma 19 implies $Y \setminus \{a\} \prec Y$. Assume there exists Z such that $Y \setminus \{a\} \prec Z \prec Y$. Lemma 12 yields $Y^{\geq} \subseteq Z^{\geq} \subseteq (Y \setminus \{a\})^{\geq}$ which implies equalities $(Y \setminus \{a\})^{\geq} = Z^{\geq} = Y^{\geq}$ hence $Y \setminus \{a\} \subsetneq Z \subsetneq Y$ (by Lemma 19) which is impossible. This proves that $Y \setminus \{a\}$ is an immediate predecessor of Y.

$\Rightarrow$. Conversely, assume X is an immediate predecessor of Y and $X \subsetneq Y$. This last inclusion implies $X \setminus Y^{\geq} = \emptyset$ hence the first case of Lemma 19 applies: $X^{\geq} = Y^{\geq}$. If $Y \setminus X$ contains two elements $b, c \neq a$ then $X \subsetneq (X \cup \{b\}) \subsetneq Y$ and $X^{\geq} \subseteq (X \cup \{b\})^{\geq} \subseteq Y^{\geq}$ hence $X^{\geq} = (X \cup \{b\})^{\geq} = Y^{\geq}$ which, again by Lemma 19, implies $X \prec (X \cup \{b\}) \prec Y$, contradicting the assumption that X is an immediate predecesor of Y. We conclude that $Y \setminus X$ has exactly one element, i.e. $Y = X \cup \{a\}$ for some $a \notin X$. Since $X^{\geq} = Y^{\geq}$. this element a cannot be the minimum element of Y. $\qquad\square$

In the next lemma it is assumed that the set of strict lower bounds of Y has a maximum. This is for example the case if the linear order L is Noetherian (i.e. reverse of an ordinal) and the set Y is not coinitial in L.

Lemma 23. *Assume that the set $L \setminus Y^{\geq} = \{z \mid \forall y \in Y \;\; z < y\}$ has a maximum element b (i.e. either b is a predecessor of the minimum element of Y or Y has no minimum element but has a greatest lower bound which is b).*
Then $Y \cup \{b\}$ is an immediate predecessor of Y.

Proof. Since $b \in (Y \cup \{b\}) \setminus Y^{\geq}$ and $(Y \cup \{b\}) \cap Y^{\geq} = Y$ the second condition of Lemma 19 is satisfied hence $Y \cup \{b\} \prec Y$. Assume that Z satisfies

$$Y \cup \{b\} \prec Z \prec Y \tag{7}$$

By Lemma 12 we have

$$Y^{\geq} \subseteq Z^{\geq} \subseteq (Y \cup \{b\})^{\geq} = Y^{\geq} \cup \{b\}$$

hence $Z^{\geq} = (Y \cup \{b\})^{\geq}$ or $Z^{\geq} = Y^{\geq}$.

Assume first $Z^{\geq} = Y^{\geq}$. Applying Lemma 19 with inequality $Z \prec Y$, we get $Z \subsetneq Y$. Since condition $Z^{\geq} = Y^{\geq}$ implies $Z^{\geq} \subsetneq (Y \cup \{b\})^{\geq}$, applying Lemma 19 to inequality $Y \cup \{b\} \prec Z$ yields $(Y \cup \{b\}) \cap Z^{\geq} \subseteq Z$. Now, $(Y \cup \{b\}) \cap Z^{\geq} = (Y \cup \{b\}) \cap Y^{\geq} = Y$ hence $Y \subseteq Z$, contradicting the strict inclusion $Z \subsetneq Y$.

Assume now that $Z^{\geq} = (Y \cup \{b\})^{\geq}$. Then Lemma 19 applied to inequality $Y \cup \{b\} \prec Z$ yields $Y \cup \{b\} \subsetneq Z$. The same Lemma applied to inequality $Z \prec Y$ yields $Z \cap Y^{\geq} \subseteq Y$. Now, since $Z^{\geq} = (Y \cup \{b\})^{\geq} = Y^{\geq} \cup \{b\}$, we have $Y^{\geq} = Z^{\geq} \setminus \{b\}$ and inclusion $Z \cap Y^{\geq} \subseteq Y$ becomes $Z \setminus \{b\} \subseteq Y$ hence $Z \subseteq Y \cup \{b\}$ which contradicts the strict inclusion $Y \cup \{b\} \subsetneq Z$.   □

Proof of Theorem 21. It suffices to prove that there exist no other predecessor than those defined in the previous two lemmas.

Let X be an immediate predecessor of Y. Lemma 19 insures that the two following cases are exhaustive.

Case $X \setminus Y^{\geq} = \emptyset$ and $X \subsetneq Y$. We conclude by Lemma 22 that X is as claimed in the first item of Theorem 21.

Case $X \setminus Y^{\geq} \neq \emptyset$ and $X \cap Y^{\geq} \subseteq Y$. We distinguish three subcases.

Subcase $X \cap Y^{\geq} \subsetneq Y$. We show that this subcase is impossible. Since X is the disjoint union of $X \setminus Y^{\geq}$ and $X \cap Y^{\geq}$, we have $X \subsetneq (X \setminus Y^{\geq}) \cup Y$. Also,

$$
\begin{aligned}
X \uparrow ((X \setminus Y^{\geq}) \cup Y) &= \big(X \uparrow (X \setminus Y^{\geq})\big) \cup (X \uparrow Y) \\
&= \big(X \uparrow (X \setminus Y^{\geq})\big) \cup Y \\
&= \big((X \setminus Y^{\geq}) \uparrow (X \setminus Y^{\geq})\big) \cup \big((X \cap Y^{\geq}) \uparrow (X \setminus Y^{\geq})\big) \cup Y \\
&= (X \setminus Y^{\geq}) \cup (X \cap Y^{\geq}) \cup Y \\
&= (X \setminus Y^{\geq}) \cup Y \qquad \text{since } X \cap Y^{\geq} \subseteq X \uparrow Y = Y .
\end{aligned}
$$

Thus, $X \prec (X \setminus Y^{\geq}) \cup Y$. We also have $(X \setminus Y^{\geq}) \cup Y \prec Y$ since $(X \setminus Y^{\geq}) \cup Y \neq Y$ and $((X \setminus Y^{\geq}) \cup Y) \uparrow Y = ((X \setminus Y^{\geq}) \uparrow Y) \cup (Y \uparrow Y) = Y$. This contradicts the fact that X is an immediate predecessor of Y.

Subcase $X \cap Y^{\geq} = Y$ and $L \setminus Y^{\geq}$ has a maximum element b. Then $X \setminus Y^{\geq} \subseteq \{z \mid z \leq b\}$. Observe that $X \preceq (\{b\} \cup Y) \prec Y$ since $(\{b\} \cup Y) \uparrow Y = Y$ and

$$
X \uparrow (\{b\} \cup Y) = ((X \setminus Y^{\geq}) \cup Y) \uparrow (\{b\} \cup Y) = \{b\} \cup Y
$$

Since X is an immediate predecessor of Y this implies $X = Y \cup \{b\}$. This case is covered by Lemma 23 and gives the second item of Theorem 21.

Subcase $X \cap Y^{\geq} = Y$ and $L \setminus Y^{\geq}$ has no maximum element. We show that this subcase is impossible. Recall an assumption of the case (of which this is a subcase): $X \setminus Y^{\geq} \neq \emptyset$. Let $d \in X \setminus Y^{\geq} \subseteq L \setminus Y^{\geq}$. Since $L \setminus Y^{\geq}$ has no maximum element, there exists some $c \notin Y^{\geq}$ such that $d < c$. Pose $X_0 = \{z \notin Y^{\geq} \mid z \geq c\}$ and observe that $Y \uparrow X_0 = Y$ (since X_0 is disjoint from $Y^{\geq}$) and also $(X \setminus Y^{\geq}) \uparrow X_0 = X_0$ (inclusion: use the fact that X_0 is a final segment, containment: inequality $d < c$ implies $\{d\} \uparrow X_0 = X_0$, conclude with the fact that $d \in X$). Using the assumption equality $X \cap Y^{\geq} = Y$, we obtain $X = (X \setminus Y^{\geq}) \cup Y$ hence

$$
\begin{aligned}
X \uparrow (X_0 \cup Y) &= ((X \setminus Y^{\geq}) \cup Y) \uparrow X_0) \cup (X \uparrow Y) \\
&= ((X \setminus Y^{\geq}) \uparrow X_0) \cup (Y \uparrow X_0) \cup (X \uparrow Y) = X_0 \cup Y
\end{aligned}
$$

Since $X \neq X_0 \cup Y$ (witnessed by d) and $X_0 \cup Y \neq Y$ (witnessed by c) we get $X \prec X_0 \cup Y \prec Y$, which is a contradiction.   □

Corollary 24. *The set $\{a\}$ has an immediate predecessor in $\langle \mathcal{P}(L), \preceq \rangle$ if and only if a has a predecessor c (necessarily unique) in the linear order $\langle L, \leq \rangle$. In that case, $\{c, a\}$ is the unique immediate predecessor of $\{a\}$.*

4.2 Singleton Sets

With the help of the previous inquiry on the immediate predecessors of a given subset, the characterization of the singletons is obtained by a simple bookkeeping on the number of their immediate predecessors. We start with listing all possible numbers of immediate predecessors of a given subset.

Proposition 25. *Let X be a nonempty subset with cardinality $|X|$.*
1. If X is infinite then it has infinitely many immediate predecessors.
2. If X is finite and nonempty then
- if $\min(X)$ is 0 or a limit, then X has $|X| - 1$ immediate predecessors,
- otherwise (i.e., if $\min(X)$ is a successor) X has $|X|$ immediate predecessors.
The set of immediate predecessors is gathered in Table 1.

Table 1. Immediate predecessors of a nonempty finite set X

	$\mathrm{Min}(X)$ is 0 or limit in L	$\mathrm{Min}(X)$ is the successor of b in L
$X = \{x_1, \ldots, x_n\}$ with $x_1 < \ldots < x_n$	$X \setminus \{x_i\}$, $2 \leq i \leq n$	$X \setminus \{x_i\}$, $2 \leq i \leq n$ $\{b\} \cup X$
$X = \{x\}$	no immediate predec.	$\{b, x\}$

Proof. This is a direct consequence of Theorem 21.   □

Theorem 26. *The following families are definable with the stated complexity:*

$HasPred0(X)$	$\equiv$	X has no predecessor	Π_2
$HasPredn(X)$	$\equiv$	X has exactly n predecessors	$\Sigma_2 \wedge \Pi_2$
$SingLimit(X)$	$\equiv$	$X = \{x\}$ for some limit $x \in L$	Π_2
$SingSucc(X)$	$\equiv$	$X = \{x\}$ for some successor $x \in L$	$\Sigma_2 \wedge \Pi_2$
$Single(X)$	$\equiv$	$X = \{x\}$ for some $x \in L$	$\Sigma_2 \wedge \Pi_2$

Proof. Recall that $X = \emptyset$, $X = \{0\}$ and $\mathrm{Suc}(Z, X)$ are Π_1 (cf. Corollary 8 and Notation 20).

- For HasPred0(X) consider the Π_2 formula $\forall Z \ \neg\text{Suc}(Z, X)$.
- When $n \geq 1$, for HasPred$n(X)$ consider the $\Sigma_2 \wedge \Pi_2$ formula

$$\exists Z_1, \ldots, Z_n \ \left(\left(\bigwedge_{1 \leq i \leq n} \text{Suc}(Z_i, X) \right) \wedge \left(\bigwedge_{1 \leq i < j \leq n} Z_i \neq Z_j \right) \right)$$

$$\wedge \ \forall T_1, \ldots, T_{n+1} \ \left(\left(\bigwedge_{1 \leq i \leq n+1} \text{Suc}(T_i, X) \right) \Longrightarrow \bigvee_{1 \leq i < j \leq n+1} T_i = T_j \right)$$

Applying Proposition 25 and the above, we see that

- SingLimit(X) can be taken to be the Π_2 conjunction of HasPred0(X) with the formulas expressing that $X \neq \emptyset, \{0\}$.
- Observe that a set X has a unique predecessor in $\mathcal{P}(L)$ in only two cases:

(1) $X = \{u, v\}$ and $u < v$ and u is 0 or a limit element in L. Then in $\mathcal{P}(L)$ the unique predecessor of X is $\{u\}$ which itself has no predecessor in $\mathcal{P}(L)$.
(2) $X = \{x\}$ and x has a predecessor z in L. Then in $\mathcal{P}(L)$ the unique predecessor of X is $\{z, x\}$ which itself has a predecessor $\{z\}$ (it may also have another one, $\{v, z, x\}$ in case z has a predecessor v in L).

Thus, SingSucc(X) can be taken to be the $\Sigma_2 \wedge \Pi_2$ formula

$$X \neq \emptyset, \{0\} \ \wedge \ \text{HasPred1}(X) \ \wedge \ \exists Z, T \ (\text{Suc}(T, Z) \wedge \text{Suc}(Z, X))$$

- Single(X) is the formula $X = \{0\} \vee \text{SingLimit}(X) \vee \text{SingSucc}(X)$.   □

4.3   Recovering the Linear Order

We already observed that the relation $\leq$ is expressible with the relation $\preceq$ on the singletons. For future use (in Proposition 38), we give an estimate of the complexity of the formula.

Lemma 27. *The following relations are* $\Sigma_2 \wedge \Pi_2$:

$$\text{Leq} = \{(\{x\}, \{y\}) \mid x \leq y\} \qquad R = \{(\{x\}, \{y\}) \mid y \text{ is the successor of } x\}$$

Proof. Observe that $x \leq y$ if and only if $\{x\} \preceq \{y\}$. It suffices to define Leq(X, Y) via the formula Single$(X) \wedge \text{Single}(Y) \wedge X \preceq Y$ and $R(X, Y)$ via the formula Single$(X) \wedge \text{Single}(Y) \wedge \text{Suc}(X, Y)$.   □

4.4   Pairs

The operation $\uparrow$ is not appropriate to express that an element belongs to a subset. Indeed, $\{a\} \uparrow X = X$ holds if and only if a is a lower bound of X, i.e., if a is the minimum in which case it belongs to X or is a strict lower bound and then it does not belong to X. This ambiguity is lifted if instead of the singleton $\{a\}$ we use paris of the form $\{z, a\}$ as will be amply employed in Sect. 5. The following result is the key to the proof that the membership predicate is definable with complexity Δ_4.

Proposition 28. *The following predicates have the stated complexities:*

$$
\begin{array}{llr}
R(Z,P) & \equiv Z = \{z\}, \ P = \{z,a\} \ \textit{for some } z < a & \Sigma_2 \wedge \Pi_2 \\
K(P) & \equiv P = \{0,a\} \ \textit{for some } a \in L & \Delta_2 \\
\mathtt{Pair_0}(A,P) & \equiv A = \{a\}, P = \{0,a\} \ \textit{for some } a \in L & \Pi_3 \\
\mathtt{Pair}(Z,A,P) & \equiv Z = \{z\}, \ A = \{a\}, \ P = \{z,a\} \ \textit{for some } z < a & \Pi_3
\end{array}
$$

Proof. Observe (Theorem 21 and Table 1) that $\{z\}$ is the immediate predecessor of a set P if and only if P is of the form $\{z,a\}$ for some $a > z$. This shows that the above predicate R is defined by the $\Sigma_2 \wedge \Pi_2$ formula $\mathtt{Single}(Z) \wedge \mathtt{Suc}(Z,P)$ whereas K is defined by the Σ_2 formula $\exists Z \ (Z = \{0\} \wedge \mathtt{Suc}(Z,P))$ and the Π_2 formula $\forall Z \ (Z = \{0\} \Rightarrow \mathtt{Suc}(Z,P))$.

Also, for all u we have $\{z,a\} \preceq \{u\}$ if and only if $a \leq u$. Thus, a triple (Z,A,P) is in $\mathtt{Pair}$ if and only if $(Z,P) \in R$ and A is the smallest singleton set which dominates P. Considering the conjunction of the definition of $(Z,P) \in R$ with the formula $\forall U \ (\mathtt{Single}(U) \Rightarrow (P \preceq U \Leftrightarrow A \preceq U))$ shows that $\mathtt{Pair}$ is Π_3. Finally, $\mathtt{Pair_0}$ can be Π_3 expressed as $\forall Z \ (Z = \{0\} \Rightarrow \mathtt{Pair}(Z,A,P))$. $\qquad\square$

5   Defining Membership

In this section we solve the second ingredient of our proof, namely we show that the predicate $x \in X$ can be encoded in the structure T. More precisely we show that the membership predicate

$$
\{(A,X) \mid A = \{a\} \ \text{for some } a \in X\}
$$

is Δ_4.

Before proving the general case (cf. Theorem 37) we consider the case where L has a minimum element 0 since we then get a simpler proof (cf. Sect. 5.3 and Theorem 35).

We give an intuition of the way we proceed in this simpler case. Let $a \in L$ and $X \subseteq L$. The condition $\{0,a\} \uparrow X = X$ is equivalent to $\{a\} \uparrow X \subseteq X$. This last condition is itself equivalent to the fact that a is a strict lower bound of X or that a belongs to X. In order to rule out the former condition, it suffices to say that $a^{\geq} \subseteq X^{\geq}$. This is the reason why the definability of the final segments and the upward closure of a subset take so much place in this section.

5.1   Defining Final Segments

Lemma 29. *Consider the Π_1 predicate $\Phi(X)$ which expresses that any two $\preceq$-upper bounds of X are $\preceq$ comparable.*

$$
\Phi(X) \quad \equiv \quad \forall Y, Z \ \Big((X \preceq Y \ \wedge \ X \preceq Z) \Rightarrow (Y \preceq Z \vee Z \preceq Y) \Big)
$$

Then $\Phi(X)$ holds if and only if X is a final segment or $X = \{a\}^{\geq} \setminus \{a^+\}$ where a^+ is the immediate successor of a in L (in case there is some).

Proof. $\Leftarrow$, *1st case.* Assume X is a final segment. Conditions $X \preceq Y$ and $X \preceq Z$ imply that Y and Z are also final segments by Lemma 16 and these segments are $\preceq$-comparable by Lemma 4.

$\Leftarrow$, *2d case.* Assume now that a has an immediate successor a^+ and $X = \{a\}^{\geq} \setminus \{a^+\} = \{a\} \cup \{a^+\}^{>}$. Consider some $X \prec U$. Since $U = (\{a\} \cup \{a^+\}^{>}) \uparrow U$ we have $\{a\} \uparrow U \subseteq U$ hence

$$U \subseteq \{a\}^{\geq} \qquad\qquad (*)$$

Subcase $a \in U$. Then $X = X \uparrow \{a\} \subseteq X \uparrow U = U$. Since $U \subseteq \{a\}^{\geq} = X \cup \{a^+\}$ and $U \neq X$ we see that $U = \{a\}^{\geq}$ is a final segment.

Subcase $a \notin U$ and $a^+ \in U$. Then $U = X \uparrow U \supseteq (\{a\} \cup \{a^+\}^{>}) \uparrow \{a^+\} = \{a^+\}^{\geq}$. Using (*) and the case assumption, we see that $U = \{a^+\}^{\geq}$ is a final segment.

Subcase $a \notin U$ and $a^+ \notin U$. Then (*) yields $U \subseteq \{a^+\}^{>}$ and $U = X \uparrow U = (\{a\} \cup \{a^+\}^{>}) \uparrow U = \{a^+\}^{>} \uparrow U$ hence $U = \{a^+\}^{>} \uparrow U$, i.e. $\{a^+\}^{>} \preceq U$. As an upper bound of the final segment $\{a^+\}^{>}$, the set U is also a final segment (cf. Lemma 16).

Thus, in all cases the set U is a final segment. Since all upper bounds U of X are final segments they are pairwise $\preceq$-comparable (by Lemma 4 and Proposition 11). This proves that property $\Phi(X)$ is true.

$\Rightarrow$. We first show that condition $\Phi(X)$ implies that $X^{\geq} \setminus X$ has at most one element. By way of contradiction, assume there exist distinct $b, c \in X^{>} \setminus X$. Without loss of generality for some $a \in X$ we have $a < b < c$. Then $X \prec X \cup \{b\}$ and $X \prec X \cup \{c\}$ and b, c respectively witness that $(X \cup \{b\}) \uparrow (X \cup \{c\})$ is different from $X \cup \{b\}$ and $X \cup \{c\}$ which shows that $X \cup \{b\}$ and $X \cup \{c\}$ are incomparable, contradicting condition $\Phi(X)$.

At this point we know that if X is not a final segment but satisfies Φ then $X = X^{\geq} \setminus \{b\}$ where $b > a$ for some $a \in X$.

We claim that a is the minimum element of X. By way of contradiction, suppose $c \in X$ is such that $c < a$. Letting $U = X^{\geq} = X \cup \{b\}$ and $V = X \cap \{c\}^{\geq}$, we have $X \uparrow U = U$ and $X \uparrow V = V$ whereas $U \uparrow V = \{c\}^{\geq}$ is different from both U and V. Thus, U, V are incomparable upper bounds of X, contradicting $\Phi(X)$. We now know that $X = \{a\}^{\geq} \setminus \{b\}$ where $a < b$. We claim that b is the successor in L of this minimum element a of X. By way of contradiction, suppose c is such that $a < c < b$. Letting $U = \{a\}^{\geq}$ and $V = X \setminus \{a\} = \{a\}^{>} \setminus \{b\}$, we again have $X \uparrow U = U$ and $X \uparrow V = V$ whereas $U \uparrow V = \{a\}^{\geq} \uparrow (\{a\}^{>} \setminus \{b\}) = \{a\}^{>}$ because $b = b \vee c \in \{a\}^{\geq} \uparrow (\{a\}^{>} \setminus \{b\})$. Thus, $U \uparrow V$ is different from both U and V hence U, V are incomparable upper bounds of X, contradicting $\Phi(X)$. $\square$

Lemma 30. *The predicate X is a final segment is $\Sigma_2 \vee \Pi_2$. In case L has a minimum element it is Π_2.*

Proof. First, we consider the special case where L has a minimum element. The idea is to define the final segments X by saying: for all $\{0, a\}$, we have

$\{0, a\} \uparrow X = X$, a property which is expressible by the Π_2 formula

$$\forall Y, Z \; ((Z = \{0\} \wedge \operatorname{Suc}(Z, Y)) \Rightarrow Y \uparrow X = X).$$

Assume X is a final segment, i.e. $X = X^{\geq}$. We have $\{0, a\} \uparrow X = \{0, a\} \uparrow X^{\geq} = X \cup (\{a\} \uparrow X^{\geq})$. Now, if $a \in X$ then $\{a\} \uparrow X = X \cap \{a\}^{\geq} \subseteq X$ and if $a \notin X = X^{\geq}$ then all elements of X dominate a hence $\{a\} \uparrow X = X$. In both cases, we see that $\{0, a\} \uparrow X = X$. Assume X is not a final segment. Then there exists $a < b$ with $a \in X$, $b \notin X$. Since $b = b \uparrow a \in \{0, b\} \uparrow X$ we see that $\{0, b\} \uparrow X \neq X$.

We now make no assumption on whether or not L has a minimum element. Consider the Π_1 predicate $\Phi(X)$ from Lemma 30. Rephrasing this last Lemma, there are three different possibilities for the set X to satisfy Φ:

1. $X = L$
2. X is a final segment different from L
3. $X = \{a\}^{\geq} \setminus \{a^+\}$, where a^+ is the L-successor of a.

We discriminate case 3 from cases 1 and 2 as follows:

Case 1i: $X = L$ and there is no minimum element in L.
Then L has no immediate successor.
Case 1ii: $X = L$ and L has a minimum element 0 which admits a successor 0^+.
Then $L \setminus \{0^+\} = \{0\}^{\geq} \setminus \{0^+\}$ is a strict predecessor of X which satisfies Φ.
Case 1iii: $X = L$ and L has a minimum element 0 which is right limit.
Then L has an immediate successor $L \setminus \{0\}$ which has no immediate successor.
Case 2. X is a final segment different from L
Then L is a strict predecessor of X which satisfies Φ.
Case 3. $X = \{a\}^{\geq} \setminus \{a^+\}$, where a^+ is the L-successor of a. Then X satisfies the following two properties:

(α) X has an immediate successor (namely, $\{a\}^{\geq}$) which itself has an immediate successor (namely $\{a\}^{>}$), unlike Cases 1i and 1ii,

(β) X has no strict predecessor which satisfies Φ, unlike Cases 1ii and 2.

Indeed, concerning (β), every (not necessarily immediate) predecessor Y of X is of one of the following two forms:

i. $Y = X \setminus Z$ with $\emptyset \neq Z \subseteq \{a^+\}^{>}$.

ii. $Y = Z \cup T$ where $\emptyset \neq Z$ and $Z \cap X^{\geq} = \emptyset$ and $T \subseteq X$.

Consequently, Y is not a final segment and $Y^{\geq} \setminus Y$ contains two elements except if (case (ii)) Y is of the form $Y^{\geq} \setminus \{a^+\}$. In this last case either Y has no minimum or it has a minimum and a^+ is not its immediate successor in L.

This proves that the $\Sigma_2 \vee \Pi_2$ formula

$$\Phi(X) \;\wedge\; \neg\Big((\exists U, V \; (\operatorname{Suc}(X, U) \wedge \operatorname{Suc}(U, V)) \;\wedge\; \forall Y \prec X \; \neg\Phi(Y)\Big)$$

expresses that X is a final segment. $\square$

Corollary 31. *The predicate* $X = L$ *is* Π_3.

Proof. Lemma 17 insures that L is the $\preceq$-minimal final segment:

$$X \text{ is final } \wedge\ \forall Y\ (Y \text{ is final} \Rightarrow X \preceq Y)$$

Since the predicate "is final" is $\Sigma_2 \vee \Pi_2$ this formula is Π_3. $\square$

5.2 Upwards Closure

Given $X \subseteq L$ we recall that $X^{\geq} = \{x \in L \mid \exists y \in X, y \leq x\}$.

Lemma 32. *The relation* $\{(X,Y) \mid Y = X^{\geq}\}$ *is* Π_3.

Proof. Observe that $X^{\geq}$ is the $\preceq$-minimum final set Z such that $X \preceq Z$. Thus, $Y = X^{\geq}$ is Π_3 expressible:

$$Y \text{ is final} \wedge\ X \preceq Y\ \wedge\ \forall Z\ ((Z \text{ is final} \wedge X \preceq Z) \Rightarrow Y \preceq Z) \qquad \square$$

5.3 Membership When L has a Minimum Element 0

Lemma 33. *For all* $a \in L$ *and* $X \subseteq L$ *it holds*

$$a \notin X^{>} \iff \{a\} \uparrow X = X.$$

Proof. By Lemma 18 the condition $\{a\} \uparrow X = X$ implies $X \subseteq \{a\}^{\geq}$, i.e., $a \notin X^{>}$. Conversely, $a \notin X^{>}$ implies $\emptyset = \{a\} \cap X^{>} \subseteq X \subseteq \{a\}^{\geq}$ and we conclude by the same lemma. $\square$

Lemma 34. *For all* $a \in L$ *and* $X \subseteq L$ *we have*

$$a \in X \iff a \in X^{\geq}\ \wedge\ (\{0,a\} \uparrow X = X)$$

Proof. $\Rightarrow$. If $a \in X$ then $a \in X^{\geq}$ and $\{a\} \uparrow X \subseteq X$ hence $\{0,a\} \uparrow X = X \cup (\{a\} \uparrow X) = X$.
$\Leftarrow$. By contraposition it suffices to show that if $a \notin X$ and $a \in X^{\geq}$ then $\{0,a\} \uparrow X \neq X$. But this is clear since then $a \in \{a\} \uparrow X$ and a fortiori $a \in \{0,a\} \uparrow X$ whereas $a \notin X$. $\square$

Theorem 35. *Assume* L *has a minimum element* 0. *Then the following membership predicate is* Δ_4

$$\mathtt{IsIn}(A, X) \quad \equiv \quad A = \{a\} \text{ for some } a \in X$$

Proof. Let $\varphi(A, Z, U, X, Y)$ be the Π_3 conjunction of the formulas expressing that $A = \{a\}$ and $Z = \{0,a\}$ for some a (which is $\Sigma_2 \wedge \Pi_2$ by Proposition 28) and the formulas expressing that $U = A^{\geq}$ and $Y = X^{\geq}$ (which are Π_3 by Lemma 32). Observe that $a \in X^{\geq}$ if and only if $\{a\}^{\geq} \uparrow X^{\geq} = \{a\}^{\geq}$. Using Lemma 34, $\mathtt{IsIn}(A, X)$ can be expressed by the following Σ_4 and Π_4 formulas:

$$\exists Z, U, Y\ (\varphi(A, Z, U, X, Y) \wedge\ U \uparrow Y = U\ \wedge\ Z \uparrow X = X)$$
$$\forall Z, U, Y\ (\varphi(A, Z, U, X, Y) \Rightarrow (U \uparrow Y = U\ \wedge\ Z \uparrow X = X)) \qquad \square$$

5.4   Membership in the General Case

The definition of membership we are looking for is based on the following characterization.

Lemma 36. *Let $a \in L$ and $X \subseteq L$. The following three conditions are equivalent:*

1. $a \in X$
2. *either* $\left(\{a\}^{\geq} \subsetneq X^{\geq} \text{ and } \forall z \in (X^{\geq} \setminus \{a\}^{\geq})\ \ X \uparrow \{z\} = X \uparrow \{z, a\}\right)$
   or $\{a\}^{\geq} = X^{\geq}$
3. *either* $\left(\{a\}^{\geq} \subsetneq X^{\geq} \text{ and } \exists z \in (X^{\geq} \setminus \{a\}^{\geq})\ \ X \uparrow \{z\} = X \uparrow \{z, a\}\right)$
   or $\{a\}^{\geq} = X^{\geq}$

Proof. (1) $\Rightarrow$ (2). Assume $a \in X$. Then $\{a\} \subseteq X$ hence $\{a\}^{\geq} \subseteq X^{\geq}$. If $\{a\}^{\geq} = X^{\geq}$ then we are done so we assume $\{a\}^{\geq} \subsetneq X^{\geq}$. Let $z \notin \{a\}^{\geq}$, i.e. $z < a$. Since $a \in X$ we have equality $X \uparrow \{a\} = X \cap \{a\}^{\geq}$ and since $z < a$ we have $X \cap \{a\}^{\geq} \subseteq X \cap \{z\}^{\geq} \subseteq X \uparrow \{z\}$. Thus, $X \uparrow \{a\} \subseteq X \uparrow \{z\}$ and

$$X \uparrow \{z\} \subseteq X \uparrow \{z, a\} = (X \uparrow \{z\}) \cup (X \uparrow \{a\}) = X \uparrow \{z\}$$

which implies $X \uparrow \{z\} = X \uparrow \{z, a\}$. This proves the first disjunct in the expression of point 2 (even a little more since we do not need the constraint $z \in X^{\geq}$).

(2) $\Rightarrow$ (3). Trivial.

$\neg$(1) $\Rightarrow$ $\neg$(3). Assume $a \notin X$. Since $\{a\}^{\geq}$ and $X^{\geq}$ are final segments, Lemma 4 insures that $\{a\}^{\geq}$ and $X^{\geq}$ are comparable for inclusion.
Case $\{a\}^{\geq} = X^{\geq}$. Then a is the minimum element of X hence $a \in X$, contradiction.
Case $X^{\geq} \subsetneq \{a\}^{\geq}$. Then (3) trivially fails (as wanted).
Case $\{a\}^{\geq} \subsetneq X^{\geq}$. Let $z \in X^{\geq} \setminus \{a\}^{\geq}$. Then there exists $b \in X$ such that $b \leq z < a$. We have $a = \max\{b, a\} \in X \uparrow \{z, a\}$ whereas $a \notin X \uparrow \{z\}$ (since $a \notin X$ and $z < a$). Thus, $X \uparrow \{z, a\} \neq X \uparrow \{z\}$ and (3) fails.   □

Theorem 37. *The following membership predicate is Δ_4*

$$\texttt{IsIn}(A, X) \quad \equiv \quad A = \{a\} \text{ for some } a \in X$$

Proof. Let $\alpha(T, U)$ be a Π_3 formula expressing that $U = T^{\geq}$ (cf. Lemma 32). Recall that, for final segments F, G we have $F \subseteq G$ if and only if $G \preceq F$ (cf. Lemma 17). Also, $z \in F$ if and only if $\{z\}^{\geq} \subseteq F$ if and only if $F \preceq \{z\}^{\geq}$. Let $\theta^{\exists}(X, Y, A, U)$ and $\theta^{\forall}(X, Y, A, U)$ be the following Σ_4 and Π_4 formulas

$$\exists Z, V, P\ \left(\texttt{Single}(Z) \wedge \alpha(Z, V) \wedge Y \preceq Z \wedge U \npreceq Z \wedge \texttt{Pair}(Z, A, P)\right.$$
$$\left. \wedge X \uparrow Z = X \uparrow P\right)$$
$$\forall Z, V, P\ \left(\texttt{Single}(Z) \wedge \alpha(Z, V) \wedge Y \preceq Z \wedge U \npreceq Z \wedge \texttt{Pair}(Z, A, P)\right.$$
$$\left. \Longrightarrow X \uparrow Z = X \uparrow P\right)$$

Recall that
- if F is a final segment then $z \in F \iff \{z\}^{\geq} \subseteq F$,

- $\mathtt{Pair}(Z,A,P)$ means that $Z = \{z\}$, $A = \{a\}$ and $P = \{z,a\}$ for some $z < a$.
Let $\alpha(Z,V)$ be a Π_3 formula expressing that $V = Z^\geq$ (cf. Lemma 32) and let
$\theta^\exists(X,Y,A,U)$ and $\theta^\forall(X,Y,A,U)$ be the following Σ_4 and Π_4 formulas

$$\exists Z,V,P \; (\mathtt{Pair}(Z,A,P) \wedge \alpha(Z,V) \wedge \; Y \preceq Z \; \wedge \; U \npreceq Z \; \wedge \; X \uparrow Z = X \uparrow P)$$
$$\forall Z,V,P \; (\mathtt{Pair}(Z,A,P) \wedge \alpha(Z,V) \wedge \; Y \preceq Z \; \wedge \; U \npreceq Z) \Longrightarrow X \uparrow Z = X \uparrow P)$$

which, applied to $Y = X^\geq$, $A = \{a\}$ and $U = \{a\}^\geq$ express respectively

$$\exists z \in (X^\geq \setminus \{a\}^\geq) \;\; X \uparrow \{z\} = X \uparrow \{z,a\}$$
$$\forall z \in (X^\geq \setminus \{a\}^\geq) \;\; X \uparrow \{z\} = X \uparrow \{z,a\}$$

Let $\Phi(X,Y,A,U)$ be the Π_3 conjunction of $\alpha(X,Y)$ and $\alpha(A,U)$. Using the
$\Sigma_2 \wedge \Pi_2$ predicate $\mathtt{Single}$ from Theorem 26, consider the Σ_4 and Π_4 formulas

$$\mathtt{Single}(A) \wedge \; \exists Y,U \; \big(\Phi(X,Y,A,U) \wedge ((Y \prec U \; \wedge \theta^\exists(X,Y,A,U))) \; \vee \; U = Y\big)$$
$$\mathtt{Single}(A) \wedge \; \forall Y,U \; \big(\Phi(X,Y,A,U) \Rightarrow ((Y \prec U \; \wedge \theta^\forall(X,Y,A,U))) \; \vee \; U = Y\big)$$

Conditions (2) and (3) of Lemma 36 show that these formulas define the predicate
$\mathtt{IsIn}$. □

6   Final Proofs

6.1   Defining the Downarrow Operation with Uparrow

Proposition 38. *The predicate* $X \downarrow Y = Z$ *is* Π_5.

Proof. Recall the $\Sigma_2 \wedge \Pi_2$ predicate $\mathtt{Leq} = \{(\{a\},\{b\}) \mid a \leq b\}$ (cf. Lemma 27).
Let $\theta(A,B,C)$ be the $\Sigma_2 \vee \Pi_2$ formula expressing that $A = \{a\}$, $B = \{b\}$ and
$C = \{\min(a,b)\}$, for some $a,b \in L$:

$$(\mathtt{Leq}(A,B) \Rightarrow C = A) \wedge (\mathtt{Leq}(B,A) \Rightarrow C = B)$$

Using a Σ_4 definition of $\mathtt{IsIn}$ (cf. Theorem 37), the following formula is Π_5

$$\forall C \; (\mathtt{IsIn}(C,Z) \Rightarrow \exists A,B \; (\mathtt{IsIn}(A,X) \wedge \mathtt{IsIn}(B,Y) \wedge \theta(A,B,C)))$$
$$\wedge \; \forall A,B,C \; (\mathtt{IsIn}(A,X) \wedge \mathtt{IsIn}(B,Y) \wedge \theta(A,B,C) \Rightarrow \mathtt{IsIn}(C,Z))$$

and defines the predicate $X \downarrow Y = Z$.

6.2   Defining the Uparrow Operation with the Order

Proposition 39. *The* $\uparrow$ *operation is* Π_1 *definable in* $\langle \mathcal{P}(L); \preceq \rangle$.

Proof. Proposition 14 insures that $\uparrow$ is the join operation in $\langle \mathcal{P}(L); \preceq \rangle$. Thus, the
Π_1 formula

$$\forall U \; ((X \preceq U \; \wedge \; Y \preceq U) \iff Z \preceq U)$$

is a definition of the predicate $X \uparrow Y = Z$ in $\langle \mathcal{P}(L); \preceq \rangle$. □

6.3   Equivalent First-Order Structures

With the notion of equivalence of structure defined in paragraph 2.2, we may state the main result. We also give, at no cost, an easy extension by considering not only the $(x, y) \mapsto \max\{x, y\}$ function lifted to sets but also the $(x, y) \mapsto \min\{x, y\}$ function lifted to sets.

Theorem 40. *For a given linear ordering L the three structures*

$$\mathcal{S}_1 = \langle \mathcal{P}(L); =, \uparrow \rangle \qquad \mathcal{S}_2 = \langle \mathcal{P}(L); =, \downarrow \rangle \qquad \mathcal{S}_3 = \langle \mathcal{P}(L); =, \preceq \rangle$$

are first-order interpretable one from each other and, in each of them, one can define a structure isomorphic to

$$\mathcal{S}_4 = \langle L, \mathcal{P}(L); =_L, <, \in \rangle$$

for the isomorphism mapping a subset of L to itself and an element $a \in L$ to the singleton set $\{a\}$.

Proof. Theorem 37 and Lemma 27 show that the map $x \mapsto \{x\}$ and $X \mapsto X$ defines an isomorphism between the multisorted structure $\mathcal{S}_4$ and a multisorted structure $\mathcal{S}_1'$ expressible in $\mathcal{S}_1$:

$$\mathcal{S}_1' = \langle U, \mathcal{P}(L); \mathrm{Eq}, \mathrm{Leq}, \mathrm{IsIn} \rangle$$

where $\begin{cases} U = \{X \mid X \subseteq L, \mathtt{Single}(X)\} \\ \mathrm{Eq} = \{(X, Y) \mid \mathtt{Single}(X) \wedge \mathtt{Single}(Y) \wedge X = Y\} \\ \mathrm{Leq} = \{(X, Y) \mid \mathtt{Single}(X) \wedge \mathtt{Single}(Y) \wedge X \prec Y\} \\ \mathrm{IsIn} = \{(X, Y) \mid \mathtt{Single}(X) \wedge \mathtt{IsIn}(X, Y)\} \end{cases}$.

Proposition 14 (and the fact that $\preceq$ is defined with $\uparrow$) shows that the operation of $\mathcal{S}_1$ is interpretable in $\mathcal{S}_3$ and vice-versa. Thus, $\mathcal{S}_1$ and $\mathcal{S}_3$ are equivalent.

Proposition 38 shows that the operation of $\mathcal{S}_2$ is interpretable in $\mathcal{S}_1$. Observing that $\uparrow$ and $\downarrow$ considered in the reverse linear order $(L, \geq)$ are respectively $\downarrow$ and $\uparrow$ in $(L, \leq)$, we see that the operation of $\mathcal{S}_1$ is interpretable in $\mathcal{S}_2$. Thus, $\mathcal{S}_1$ and $\mathcal{S}_2$ are equivalent. $\blacksquare$

References

1. Büchi, J.R.: On a decision problem in restricted second-order arithmetic. In: Proceedings of the 1960 International Congress for Logic, Methodology and Philosophy, pp. 1–11. Stanford Univ. Press (1962)
2. Büchi, J.R.: The Monadic Second-Order Theory of All Countable Ordinals. Lecture Notes in Math., vol. 328. Springer, Heidelberg (1973)
3. Büchi, J.R., Zaiontz, C.: Deterministic automata and the monadic theory of ordinals ω_2. Zeitschrift für math. Logik und Grundlagen der Mat. **29**, 313–336 (1983)
4. Choffrut, C., Grigorieff, S.: Logical theory of the additive monoid of subsets of natural integers. In: Adamatzky, A. (ed.) Automata, Universality, Computation. ECC, vol. 12, pp. 39–74. Springer, Heidelberg (2015)

5. Choffrut, C., Grigorieff, S.: Logical theory of the monoid of languages over a non-tally alphabet. Fundamenta Informaticae **138**(1–2), 159–177 (2015)
6. Gurevich, Y.: Elementary properties of ordered abelian groups. Algebra Logic **3**(1), 5–39 (1964). English version in AMS Translations **46**, 165–192 (1965)
7. Gurevich, Y., Magidor, M., Shelah, S.: The monadic theory of ω_2. J. Symbolic Logic **48**(2), 387–398 (1983)
8. Gurevich, Y., Shelah, S.: Modest theory of short chains II. J. Symbolic Logic **44**, 491–502 (1979)
9. Gurevich, Y., Shelah, S.: Monadic theory of order and topology in ZFC. Ann. Math. Logic **23**, 179–198 (1982)
10. Gurevich, Y., Shelah, S.: Interpreting second-order logic in the monadic theory of order. J. Symbolic Logic **48**, 816–828 (1983)
11. Gurevich, Y., Shelah, S.: The monadic theory and the 'next world'. Israel J. Math. **49**, 55–68 (1984)
12. Lifsches, S., Shelah, S.: The monadic theory of ω_2 may be complicated. Arch. Math. Logic **31**, 207–213 (1992)
13. Rosenstein, J.G.: Linear Orderings. Academic Press, New York (1982)
14. Shelah, S.: The monadic theory of order. Ann. Math. **102**, 379–419 (1975)

Regularity Equals Monadic Second-Order Definability for Quasi-trees

Bruno Courcelle[(⊠)]

LaBRI, CNRS, 351 Cours de la Libération, 33405 Talence, France
`courcell@labri.fr`

Abstract. *Quasi-trees* generalize trees in that the unique "path" between two nodes may be infinite and have any finite or countable order type, in particular that of rational numbers. They are used to define the rank-width of a countable graph in such a way that it is the least upper-bound of the rank-widths of its finite induced subgraphs. *Join-trees* are the corresponding directed "trees" and they are also useful to define the modular decomposition of a countable graph. We define algebras with finitely many operations that generate (via infinite terms) these generalized trees. We prove that the associated regular objects (those defined by regular terms) are exactly the ones definable by (i.e., are the unique models of) monadic second-order sentences. These results use and generalize a similar result by W. Thomas for countable linear orders.

1 Introduction

We define and study countable *quasi-trees* that generalize trees in that the unique "path" between two nodes may be infinite and have any order type, in particular that of rational numbers. Our motivation comes from the notion of *rank-width*, a complexity measure of finite graphs investigated first in [12,13]. Rank-width is based on graph decompositions formalized with finite subcubic trees. In order to extend rank-width to countable graphs in such a way that *the compactness property* holds, i.e., that the rank-width of a countable graph is the least upper-bound of those of its finite induced subgraphs, we base decompositions on subcubic quasi-trees [5]. For a comparison, the natural extension of tree-width to countable graphs has the compactness property [11] and does not need quasi-trees.

Our objective is to obtain finitary descriptions (usable in algorithms) of certain quasi-trees. For this purpose we define in [6] an algebra of quasi-trees with finitely many operations such that the finite and infinite terms over these operations define all quasi-trees. The *regular quasi-trees* are those defined by regular terms. We prove in [6] that a quasi-tree is regular if and only if it is *monadic second-order definable*, i.e., is the unique model (up to isomorphism) of a monadic second-order sentence.

This definition uses another notion of generelized tree for the following reason. An algebra that generates all finite (unrooted) trees must also include the finite rooted trees and have an operation that build trees by gluing two rooted

© Springer International Publishing Switzerland 2015
L.D. Beklemishev et al. (Eds.): Gurevich Festschrift II 2015, LNCS 9300, pp. 129–141, 2015.
DOI: 10.1007/978-3-319-23534-9_7

trees at their roots. Trees are then obtained from rooted trees by an operation that makes the root into an ordinary node. In a similar way, we define quasi-trees from the corresponding directed structures that we call *join-trees*. A join-tree is a partial order $(N, \leq)$ such that every two elements have a least upper-bound (called their *join*) and each set $\{y \mid y \geq x\}$ (denoted by $[x, +\infty[)$ is linearly ordered. The modular decomposition of a countable graph is a (labelled) join-tree [7].

In this introductory article, we mainly consider *binary join-trees*: they can be seen as directed subcubic quasi-trees. In [6], we define algebras of rooted trees, of ordered rooted trees, of join-trees, of ordered join-trees and of quasi-trees. Binary join-trees and subcubic quasi-trees form subalgebras of two of them. In all cases, an object is regular if and only if it is monadic second-order definable.

A linear order whose elements are labelled by letters from an alphabet is called an *arrangement*. Regular arrangements are studied in [2,10], and their monadic second-order definability is proved in [14]. We use the result of [14] in order to generalize it to join-trees and quasi-trees.

2 Definitions, Notation and Basic Facts

All ordered sets, trees and logical structures are finite or countably infinite.

We denote by ω the first infinite ordinal and also the linear order $(\mathbb{N}, \leq)$.

Let $(V, \leq)$ be a partial order. The least upper bound of x and y is denoted by $x \sqcup y$ if it exists and is called their *join*. A *line* is a subset Y that is linearly ordered and satisfies the following *convexity property*: if $x, z \in Y$, $y \in V$ and $x \leq y \leq z$, then $y \in Y$. Particular notations for convex sets (not necessarily linearly ordered) are $[x, y]$ denoting $\{z \mid x \leq z \leq y\}$, $]x, y]$ denoting $\{z \mid x < z \leq y\}$, $]-\infty, x]$ denoting $\{y \mid y \leq x\}$ (even if V is finite), $]x, +\infty[$ denoting $\{y \mid x < y\}$ etc.

2.1 Finite and Infinite Terms

Let F be a finite set of operations, each given with a fixed arity. We call such a set a *signature*. We denote by $T(F)$ (resp. $T^\infty(F)$) the set of finite (resp. finite and infinite) terms written with the symbols of F. A typical example (easily describable linearly) is, with f binary and a and b nullary, the term $t_\infty = f(a, f(b, f(a, f(b, f(....))))))$ that is the unique solution in $T^\infty(F)$ of the equation $t = f(a, f(b, t))$. (We do not accept "terms" of the form $...g(g(a))...$ with countably many occurrences of function symbol g to the left of the nullary symbol a). Positions in a term are designated by Dewey words (i.e., by sequences of positive integers that encode branchings; an example is given below). The set $Pos(t)$ of positions of a term t is ordered by $\leq_t$, the reversal of the prefix order.

We have a structure of F-algebra on $T^\infty(F)$ of which $T(F)$ is a subalgebra. If $\mathbb{M} = \langle M, (f_\mathbb{M})_{f \in F} \rangle$ is an F-algebra, a *value mapping* is a homomorphism $h : T^\infty(F) \to \mathbb{M}$. Its restriction to finite terms is uniquely defined.

Regular terms

A term $t \in T^\infty(F)$ as *regular* if there is a mapping h from $Pos(t)$ into a finite set Q and a mapping $\tau : Q \to F \times Seq(Q)$ such that:

if u is an occurrence of a symbol f of arity k, then $\tau(h(u)) = (f, (h(u_1), ..., h(u_k)))$ where $(u_1, ..., u_k)$ is the sequence of sons of u. $(Seq(Q)$ is the set of finite sequences of elements of Q).

Intuitively, $\tau : Q \to F \times Seq(Q)$ is the transition function of a top-down deterministic automaton with set of states Q, $h(\varepsilon)$ is the initial (root) state and h defines its unique run. This is equivalent to requiring that t has finitely many different subterms, or is a component of a finite system of equations that has a unique solution in $T^\infty(F)$. (The set of unknowns of such a system is in bijection with Q). The above term t_∞ is regular.

A term t can be represented by the relational structure $\lfloor t \rfloor := (Pos(t), \leq_t, (br_i)_{1 \leq i \leq \rho(F)}, (lab_f)_{f \in F})$ where $br_i(u)$ is true if and only if u is the i-th son of his father and $lab_f(u)$ is true if and only if f occurs at position u. ($\rho(F)$ is the maximal arity of a symbol in F). It is regular if and only if $\lfloor t \rfloor$ is *monadic second-order definable* (in short, *MS-definable*), i.e., is, up to isomorphism, the unique model of a monadic second-order (MS) sentence, see [15].

2.2 Arrangements

We review a notion introduced in [2] and further studied in [10,14]. Let X be a set (say of letters). A linear order $(V, \leq)$ equipped with a labelling mapping $lab : V \to X$ is called an *arrangement* over X. It is *simple* if lab is injective. We denote by $\mathcal{A}(X)$ the set of arrangements over X. Every linear order $(V, \leq)$ is identified with the simple arrangement $(V, \leq, lab)$ such that $lab(v) := v$ for each v. If $w = (V, \leq, lab) \in \mathcal{A}(X)$ and $h : X \to Y$, then, $h(w) := (V, \leq, h \circ lab) \in \mathcal{A}(Y)$.

An arrangement can be considered as a generalized word. The concatenation of linear orders yield a concatenation of arrangements denoted by $\bullet$. We denote by Ω the empty arrangement and by a the one reduced to a single occurrence of $a \in X$. Clearly, $w \bullet \Omega = \Omega \bullet w = w$ for every w. The infinite word $w = a^\omega$ is the arrangement over $\{a\}$ with underlying order ω; it is a solution of the equation $w = a \bullet w$, and even its *initial* solution, a canonical one, unique up to isomorphism. This notion is defined in [2]. Similarly, the arrangement $w = a^\eta$ over $\{a\}$ with underlying linear order $(\mathbb{Q}, \leq)$ (that of rational numbers) is the initial solution of the equation $w = w \bullet (a \bullet w)$. We will generalize arrangements to tree structures.

Let X be a set of nullary symbols and $t \in T^\infty(\{\bullet, \Omega\} \cup X)$. Hence, $Pos(t) \subseteq \{1, 2\}^*$. The *value* of t is the arrangement $val(t) := (Occ(t, X), \leq_{lex}, lab)$ where $Occ(t, X)$ is the set of positions of elements of X and $lab(u)$ is the symbol of X occurring at position u. We say that t *denotes* w if w is isomorphic to $val(t)$.

For an example, $t_\bullet = \bullet(a, \bullet(b, \bullet(a, \bullet(b, \bullet(..........))))))$ denotes the infinite word $abab...$. Its value is defined from $Occ(t_\bullet, \{a, b\}) = 2^*1$, lexicographically ordered by $1 < 21 < 221 < ...$, by $lab(2^i1) = a$ if i is even and $lab(2^i1) = b$ if i is odd. The arrangements a^ω and a^η are denoted by the terms that are respectively the unique solutions in $T^\infty(\{\bullet, \Omega, a\})$ of the equations $w = a \bullet w$ and $w = w \bullet (a \bullet w)$.

An arrangement is *regular* if it is denoted by a regular term. (The term $t_\bullet$ is regular). The arrangement a^η is also regular. An arrangement is regular if and only if it is a component of the initial solution of a regular system of equations over F [2] or the value of a *regular expression* in the sense of [10].

We will use the result of [14] that an arrangement over a finite alphabet is regular if and only if is MS-definable. For this result, we represent an arrangement w over X by the relational structure $\lfloor w \rfloor := (V, \leq, (lab_a)_{a \in X})$ where $lab_a(u)$ is true if and only if $lab(u) = a$.

2.3   Trees and Rooted Trees

A *tree* is a finite or countable, undirected, acyclic and connected graph. (Being acyclic, it has no loop and no parallel edges.) The set of nodes of a tree T is N_T.

A *rooted tree* is a tree equipped with a distinguished node called its *root*. Its edges are directed towards the root. The *level* of a node x is the number of edges of the path from it to the root. The father of a node x (its immediate ancestor) is denoted by $p_T(x)$ and its set of sons by $Sons(x)$. The set of nodes N_T is partially ordered by $\leq_T$ such that $x \leq_T y$ if and only if y is on the unique path from x to the root. Then $x \sqcup_T y$ defined as the least upper bound of $\{x, y\}$, the *join* of x and y, is their least common ancestor. We will specify a rooted tree T by $(N_T, \leq_T)$ and we will omit the index T when T is clear. If x is a node of T, then T/x is the *subtree issued from* x, defined as $(N_{T/x}, \leq_T \restriction N_{T/x})$ where $N_{T/x} :=]-\infty, x]$.

A partial order $(N, \leq)$ is $(N_T, \leq_T)$ for some rooted tree T if and only if it has a greatest element max and, for each $x \in N$, the set $[x, max]$ is finite and linearly ordered. These conditions imply that any two elements have a join.

2.4   Join-Trees

We have used join-trees in [7] for defining modular decomposition of countable graphs. Quasi-trees, that are the corresponding undirected structures will be defined in Sect. 4.

(2.1) *Definition*: *Join-trees*.

A *join-tree* is a pair $J = (N, \leq)$ such that:

(1) N is a finite or countable set called the set of *nodes*,
(2) $\leq$ is a partial order on N such that, for every node x, the set $[x, +\infty[$ (the set of nodes $y \geq x$) is linearly ordered,
(3) every two nodes x and y have a join $x \sqcup y$.

A minimal node is a *leaf*. The set of strict upper-bounds of a nonempty set $X \subseteq N$ is a line L. If L has a smallest element, we denote it by $\widehat{X}$ and we say that $\widehat{X}$ is *the top* of X.

(2.2) *Definitions*: *Directions and degrees*.

Let $J = (N, \leq)$ be a join-tree and x one of its nodes. Let $\sim$ be the equivalence relation on $]-\infty, x[$ such that $z \sim y$ if and only if $z \sqcup y < x$. Each equivalence class C is called a *direction of J relative to x*. The set of directions relative to x is denoted by $Dir(x)$ and the *degree* of x is the number of its directions. The leaves are the nodes of degree 0. A join-tree is *binary* if its nodes have degree at most 2. We call it a BJ-tree.

(2.3) *Definition: Structured binary join-tree.*

Let $J = (N, \leq)$ be a BJ-tree. For each set $X \subseteq N$, we denote by $\downarrow X$ the union of the convex sets $]-\infty, x]$ for $x \in X$. A *structuring* of J is a set $\mathcal{U}$ of nonempty lines forming a partition of N that satisfies some conditions, stated with the following notation : if $x \in N$, then $U(x)$ denotes the line of $\mathcal{U}$ containing x, $U_-(x) := U(x) \cap]-\infty, x[$ and $U_+(x) := U(x) \cap [x, +\infty[$. (The set $[x, +\infty[$ has no top but can have a greatest element that we do not specify). The conditions are:

(1) exactly one line of $\mathcal{U}$ has no strict upper-bound, hence, no top; we call it the *axis*, denoted by A; we also require that if A has a smallest element, then its degree is 0 or 1,
(2) each other line U has a top $\widehat{U}$,
(3) for each x in N, the sequence $y_0 = x, y_1, y_2, \ldots$ such that $y_{i+1} = \widehat{U(y_i)}$ is finite. Its last element is $y_k \in A$ (hence y_{k+1} is undefined). We call k the *depth* of x.

The nodes on the axis are those at depth 0. The lines $[y_i, y_{i+1}[$ for $i = 0, \ldots, k-1$ and $[y_k, +\infty[$ (as in 3) above) are convex subsets of pairwise distinct lines of $\mathcal{U}$. We have $[x, +\infty[= [y_0, y_1[\cup [y_1, y_2[\cup \ldots \cup [y_k, +\infty[$, $[y_i, y_{i+1}[= U_+(y_i)$ for each $i < k$, $[y_k, +\infty[= U_+(y_k) \subseteq A$ and the depth of y_i is $k - i$.

We call such a triple $(N, \leq, \mathcal{U})$ a *structured binary join-tree*, an *SBJ-tree* for short. Every linear order is an SBJ-tree whose elements are all of depth 0.

(2.4) *Example:* Fig. 1 shows a structuring of a BJ-tree, where $\mathcal{U} = \{U_0, \ldots, U_5\}$, $A = U_0$. The directions relative to x_2 are $U_-(x_2) \cup U_1$ and $U_2 \cup U_3$. The maximal depth of a node is 2.

(2.5) *Definition: SBJ-trees as relational structures.*

Let $J = (N, \leq, \mathcal{U})$ be an SBJ-tree. Let $S(J)$ be the relational structure $(N, \leq, N_0, N_1)$ such that N_0 is the set of nodes at even depth and $N_1 = N - N_0$ is the set of those at odd depth. (N_0 and N_1 are sets but we consider them also as unary relations).

If $X \subseteq N$ then $G(X) := (X, \rightarrow)$ is the directed graph such that $x \rightarrow y$ if and only if $x < y$ and $[x, y] \subseteq X$. We say that X is *laminar* if the connected components of $G(X)$ are lines, so that X is the union of pairwise disjoint lines of J, that we call the *components* of X.

(2.6) **Proposition**: For J and $S(J)$ as above, the following properties hold:

(1) the sets N_0 and N_1 are laminar, $\mathcal{U}$ is the set of their components and the axis A is a component of N_0,
(2) there is an MS formula $\varphi(N_0, N_1)$ expressing that a structure $(N, \leq, N_0, N_1)$ is $S(J)$ for some SBJ-tree $J = (N, \leq, \mathcal{U})$,

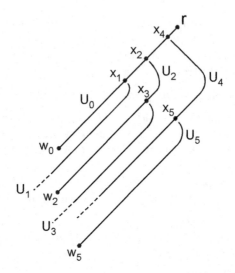

Fig. 1. A structured join-tree.

(3) there exist MS formulas $\theta_{Ax}(X, N_0, N_1)$ and $\theta(u, U, N_0, N_1)$ express-ing, respectively, in a structure $(N, \leq, N_0, N_1) = S(N, \leq, \mathcal{U})$, that X is the axis and that $U \in \mathcal{U} \wedge u = \hat{U}$.

The proof is easy from the definitions. The construction of φ uses the fact that the finiteness of a linearly ordered set is MS-expressible.

(2.7) **Proposition**: Every join-tree has a structuring.

Proof sketch: Let $J = (N, \leq)$ be a join-tree. Let us choose an enumeration of N and a maximal line B_0 ; it contains each line $[x, +\infty[$ for $x \in B_0$. For each $i > 0$, we choose a maximal line B_i containing the first node not in $B_{i-1} \cup ... \cup B_0$. We define $U_0 := B_0$ and, for $i > 0$, $U_i := B_i - (U_{i-1} \cup ... \cup U_0) = B_i - (B_{i-1} \cup ... \cup B_0)$. We define $\mathcal{U}$ as the set of lines U_i. $\square$

Each line is the linearly ordered set of leaves of an ordered, finite or countable, binary rooted tree. By combining the trees of the lines of $\mathcal{U}$, we can build a binary tree that represents (is a precise MS-definable way) a BJ-tree. This type of construction has first been defined and used in [7]. Proposition 3.6 below and the proofs in [6] give it an algebraic meaning.

2.5   The Rank-Width of a Countable Graph

Rank-width and modular decomposition (cf. [7]) motivate the study of quasi-trees and join-trees. Rank-width is a width measure on finite graphs investigated first in [12,13]. Here is its generalization to countable graphs. We let $\mathcal{G}$ be the class of finite or countable, undirected graphs without loops or parallel edges.

(2.8) *Definition* : *Rank-width.*

(a) Let $G \in \mathcal{G}$, let X and Y be pairwise disjoint sets of vertices. The associated *adjacency matrix* is $M : X \times Y \to \{0,1\}$ with $M[x,y] = 1$ if and only if x and y are adjacent. If $U \subseteq X$ and $W \subseteq Y$, we denote by $M[U,W]$ the matrix that is the restriction of M to $U \times W$. Ranks are over $GF(2)$. The *rank* of M, defined as the maximum cardinality of an independent set of rows (equivalently, of columns) is denoted by $rk(M)$; it belongs to $\mathbb{N} \cup \{\omega\}$. It is convenient to take $rk(M[\emptyset, W]) = rk(M[U, \emptyset]) = 0$.

(2.8.1) *Fact*: If $X \cup Y$ is infinite, then $rk(M) = \sup\{rk(M[U,W]) \mid U \subseteq X, W \subseteq Y, U$ and W are finite$\}$.

(b) Let T be a binary join-tree with set of leaves V_G. We call it a *layout of G*. The *rank* of T is the least upper-bound of the ranks $rk(M[X \cap V_G, X^c \cap V_G])$ where $X \subseteq N_T$ is directed and downwards closed. The *rank-width* of G, denoted by $rwd(G)$, is the smallest rank of a layout. *Discrete rank-width*, denoted by $rwd^{dis}(G)$ is similar except that layouts are binary (countable) trees. Hence, $rwd(G) \leq rwd^{dis}(G)$. For finite graphs, we get the rank-width of [12].

The notation $G \subseteq_i H$ means that G is an induced subgraph of H [9].

(2.9) **Theorem** [5]: (1) If $G \subseteq_i H$, then $rwd(G) \leq rwd(H)$ and $rwd^{dis}(G) \leq rwd^{dis}(H)$,

(2) *Compactness* : $rwd(G) = \mathrm{Sup}\{rwd(H) \mid H \subseteq_i G$ and H is finite$\}$,

(3) *Compactness with gap* : $rwd^{dis}(G) \leq 2.\mathrm{Sup}\{rwd(H) \mid H \subseteq_i G$ and H is finite$\}$.

The *gap function* in (3) is $n \mapsto 2n$, showing a weak form of compactness. A similar gap occurs for the clique-width of countable graphs [4].

Proof sketch: (1) is clear from the definitions. (2) is proved by Koenig's Lemma. (3) is based on the fact that a countable linear order is the ordered set of leaves of a binary tree; this construction is adapted from [7].   □

We now leave rank-width and we consider binary join-trees.

3   The Algebra of Binary Join-Trees

We define three operations on structured binary join-trees (*SBJ-trees*). The finite and infinite terms over these operations define all SBJ-trees.

(*3.1*) *Definition* : *Operations on structured binary join-trees.*

Concatenation along axes.

Let $J = (N, \leq, \mathcal{U})$ and $J' = (N', \leq', \mathcal{U}')$ be disjoint SBJ-trees, with respective axes A and A'. We define:

$J \bullet J' := (N \cup N', \leq'', \mathcal{U}'')$ where :
$x \leq'' y :\Longleftrightarrow x \leq y \vee x \leq' y \vee (x \in N \wedge y \in A')$,
$\mathcal{U}'' := \{A \cup A'\} \cup (\mathcal{U} - \{A\}) \cup (\mathcal{U}' - \{A'\})$.

$J \bullet J'$ is an SBJ-tree with axis $A \cup A'$; its depth is the maximum of those of J and J'.

This operation generalizes the concatenation of linear orders: if $(N, \leq)$ and $(N', \leq')$ are disjoint linear orders, then the SBJ-tree $(N, \leq, \{N\}) \bullet (N', \leq', \{N'\})$ corresponds to the concatenation of $(N, \leq)$ and $(N', \leq')$ usually denoted by $(N, \leq) + (N', \leq')$.

The empty SBJ-tree:
The nullary symbol Ω denotes the empty SBJ-tree.

Extension:
Let $J = (N, \leq, \mathcal{U})$ be an SBJ-tree, and $u \notin N$. Then:

$ext_u(J) := (N \cup \{u\}, \leq', \{u\} \cup \mathcal{U})$ where :
$x \leq' y :\Longleftrightarrow x \leq y \vee y = u$,
the axis is $\{u\}$.

Then $ext_u(J)$ is an SBJ-tree. The depth of $v \in N$ is its depth in J plus 1. When handling SBJ-trees up to isomorphism, we use the notation $ext(J)$ instead of $ext_u(J)$.

Forgetting structuring:
If J is an SBJ-tree as above, $fgs(J) := (N, \leq)$ is the underlying BJ-tree (binary join-tree).

Anticipating the sequel, we observe that a linear order $a_1 < ... < a_n$, identified with the SBJ-tree $(\{a_1, ..., a_n\}, \leq, \{\{a_1, ..., a_n\}\})$ is defined by the term $t = ext_{a_1}(\Omega) \bullet ext_{a_2}(\Omega) \bullet ... \bullet ext_{a_n}(\Omega)$. The binary (actually unary) join-tree $(\{a_1, ..., a_n\}, \leq)$ is defined by the term $fgs(t)$ and also by the term $fgs(ext_{a_n}(ext_{a_{n-1}}(...(ext_{a_1}(\Omega))..)))$.

(3.2) *The algebra* $\mathbb{SBJT}$

We let F be the signature $\{\bullet, ext, \Omega\}$. We obtain an algebra $\mathbb{SBJT}$ whose domain is the set of isomorphism classes of SBJ-trees. Concatenation is associative with neutral element Ω. We denote by $T^\infty(F)$ and $T(F)$ the sets of terms and finite terms over F.

(3.3) *Definitions* : *The value of a term.*

Let $t \in T^\infty(F)$.
    (a) We compare positions of t as follows: $u \approx v$ if and only if every position w such that $u <_t w \leq_t u \sqcup v$ or $v <_t w \leq_t u \sqcup v$ is an occurrence of $\bullet$. This relation is an equivalence.
    We will also use the lexicographic order $\leq_{lex}$.
    (b) We define the *value* $val(t) := (N, \leq, \mathcal{U})$ of t as follows:

$N := Occ(t, ext)$, the set of occurences of the symbol ext (or of the symbols ext_a if nodes are designated) in t,
$u \leq v :\Longleftrightarrow u \leq_t w \leq_{lex} v$ for some $w \in N$ such that $w \approx v$,
$\mathcal{U}$ is the set of equivalence classes of $\approx$.

(3.3.1) *Claim*: The mapping *val* is a value mapping into $\mathbb{SBJT}$.

We say that t *denotes* J if J is isomorphic to $val(t)$, and, in this case, we also say that $fgs(t)$ denotes the BJ-tree $fgs(J)$.

(3.4) *Examples and remarks.*

(1) The term t that is the unique solution of the equation $t = t \bullet t$ denotes the empty SBJ-tree Ω.

(2) Let t_1 be the solution in $T^\infty(F)$ of the equation $t = ext(ext(\Omega)) \bullet t$. We can write this term linearly by naming $a, b, c, d, e, f, \ldots$ the nodes created by the operations ext :

$$t_1 = ext_a(ext_b(\Omega)) \bullet (ext_c(ext_d(\Omega)) \bullet (ext_e(ext_f(\Omega)) \bullet \ldots))).$$

Its value is shown in Fig. 2. The bold edges link nodes in the axis.

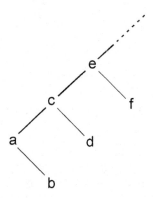

Fig. 2. The SBJ-tree $val(t_1)$.

(3.5) *Definition: Flat terms*

(a) A term $t \in T^\infty(F)$ is *flat* if no occurrence of ext is below any other occurrence of ext. (Any two occurrences of ext are equivalent with respect to $\approx$). The value of a flat term is a simple arrangement over $Occ(t, ext)$.

(b) Let $t \in T^\infty(F)$ and $u \in Pos(t)$. We denote by $\mathrm{Max}(t, u)$ the set of maximal occurrences of ext in t that are below or equal to u. We define $t\{u\}$ as the flat term obtained from t/u by replacing by $ext_w(\Omega)$ each of its subterms t/w, for all $w \in \mathrm{Max}(t, u)$. In $t\{u\}$ the operations ext are indexed by positions from $Pos(t)$. It follows that $t\{\varepsilon\} = ext_\varepsilon(\Omega)$ if $t = ext(t')$. The value of $t\{u\}$ is a simple arrangement over $\mathrm{Max}(t, u)$.

For t_1 as in the previous example, $t_1\{\varepsilon\} = ext_a(\Omega) \bullet (ext_c(\Omega) \bullet (ext_e(\Omega) \bullet \ldots))$; it denotes the arrangement *ace...* (here we keep the original naming of positions). If $t_2 = ext(ext(\Omega)) \bullet (ext(ext(\Omega)) \bullet ext(ext(\Omega)))$ then $t_2\{\varepsilon\} = ext_1(\Omega) \bullet (ext_{21}(\Omega) \bullet ext_{22}(\Omega))$.

(3.5.1) *Claim*: Let $J = (N, \leq, \mathcal{U}) = val(t)$, cf. Definition 3.3. Then $val(t\{\varepsilon\})$ $= (A, \leq)$ (the axis) and, if $U \in \mathcal{U}$ and $\widehat{U} = p_t(u)$, we have $val(t\{u\}) = (U, \leq)$.

(3.6) **Proposition**: Every SBJ-tree is the value of a term.

Proof sketch: Let $S = (N, \leq, \mathcal{U})$ be an SBJ-tree. For each U in $\mathcal{U}$, we define a flat term that denotes $(U, \leq)$. We combine these terms in order to get a term denoting S.   □

For the example of Fig. 1, if t_i is a flat term denoting U_i, then we obtain the term $t_0[t_1, t_2[t_3], t_4[t_5]]$ where [...] denotes appropriate substitutions to occurrences of Ω.

(3.7) *Definition: Description schemes for SBJ-trees.*

An *SBJ-scheme* is a triple $S = (Q, w_{Ax}, (w_q)_{q \in Q})$ such that Q is a set, $w_{Ax} \in \mathcal{A}(Q)$ (is an arrangement over Q), and for each q, $w_q \in \mathcal{A}(Q)$. It is *regular* if Q is finite and the arrangements w_{Ax} and w_q are regular.

An SBJ-scheme S *describes* an SBJ-tree $J = (N_J, \leq, \mathcal{U})$ if there exists a mapping $r : N_J \to Q$ such that $r(A_J, \leq) = w_{Ax}$ and for every $x \in N_J, w_{r(x)} = r(U, \leq)$ if $U \in \mathcal{U}$ and $\widehat{U} = x$, and $w_{r(x)} = \Omega$ if $x = \widehat{U}$ for no $U \in \mathcal{U}$. As $(U, \leq)$ is considered as the arrangement $(U, \leq, Id_U)$, its image under r is an arrangement over Q. We also say that S *describes* the BJ-tree $fgs(J)$.

(3.8) **Proposition**: Every SBJ-scheme S describes an SBJ-tree $J(S)$ that is unique up to isomorphism.

Proof sketch: Given $S = (Q, w_{Ax}, (w_q)_{q \in Q})$, we construct $J(S)$ by defining first its axis so as to be isomorphic to w_{Ax}, by a mapping r_{Ax}. Then we add the nodes at depth 1 by adding nonempty lines U isomorphic to $w_q \neq \Omega$ such that $\widehat{U} = x$ for each x in the axis such that $r_{Ax}(x) = q$. The isomorphism between such a line U and w_q is r_x. We proceed in a similar way with the nodes of depth 2,3.... We obtain an SBJ-tree. The mapping r is the union of the mappings r_{Ax} and r_x for all relevant x. Unicity holds because each step is forced, up to isomorphism. □

(3.9) *Definition: Regular objects.*

A BJ-tree (resp. an SBJ-tree) T is *regular* if it is denoted by $fgs(t)$ (resp. by t) where t is a regular term in $T^\infty(F)$.

(3.10) **Theorem:** The following properties of a BJ-tree J are equivalent:
   (1) J is regular,
   (2) J is described by a regular scheme,
   (3) J is MS-definable.

Proof sketch: (1)$\Longrightarrow$(2) Let $J = fgs(J')$ with J' denoted by a regular term t in $T^\infty(F)$. Let $h : Pos(t) \to Q$ and τ be as in Sect. 2.1. If x is an occurrence of *ext* with son u, the flat term $t\{u\}$ is regular. It defines the simple arrangement $(U, \leq)$ where $\widehat{U} = x$. Its image $h(U, \leq)$ is a regular arrangement over Q.

Furthermore, if $h(x) = h(x') = q$, then the corresponding terms $t\{u\}$ and $t\{u'\}$ are isomorphic and $h(U, \leq)$ and $h(U', \leq)$ are also isomorphic (with $x' = p_t(u')$

and $\widehat{U'} = x'$). We can denote them by w_q. We let w_{Ax} be $h(val(t\{\varepsilon\}))$. These definitions give us a regular scheme describing J', hence, also J.

$(2) \Longrightarrow (3)$ Let $J = (N, \leq)$ be a BJ-tree. (This property of $(N, \leq)$ is MS-expressible). Assume $J = fgs(J')$ where $J' = (N, \leq, \mathcal{U})$ is described by a regular SBJ-scheme R with $Q = \{1, ..., m\}$ and regular arrangements over $Q : w_{Ax}$ and w_i for $i \in Q$. Let r be the corresponding mapping. For each $i \in Q$, let ψ_i be an MS sentence that characterizes w_i up to isomorphism by the main result of [14]. Similarly, ψ_{Ax} characterizes w_{Ax}. We claim that a relational structure $(N, \leq)$ is isomorphic to J if and only if :

there exist subsets $N_0, N_1, M_1, ..., M_m$ of N such that:

(i) $(N, \leq, N_0, N_1) = S(J'')$ for some SBJ-tree $J'' = (N, \leq, \mathcal{U})$,
(ii) $(M_1, ..., M_m)$ is a partition of N; we let r' map each $w \in N$ to the unique i such that $w \in N_i$,
(iii) for every i and node u in M_i, the arrangement $r'(U)$ over Q such that $U \in \mathcal{U}$ and $u = \widehat{U}$ is isomorphic to w_i,
(iv) the arrangement $r'(A)$ over Q such that A is the axis of J'' is isomorphic to w_{Ax}.

Conditions (ii)-(iv) express that R describes J'', and hence that J'' is isomorphic to J', and so, that $(N, \leq) = fgs(J') = J$.

By Proposition 2.6, Condition (i) is MS-expressible by $\varphi(N_0, N_1)$, and the property $U \in \mathcal{U} \wedge u = \widehat{U}$ is also MS-expressible in terms of N_0, N_1 by $\theta(u, U, U_0, N_1)$. Conditions (iii) and (iv) are MS-expressible by means of the sentences w_{Ax} and w_i suitably adapted to take $N_0, N_1, M_1, ..., M_m$ as arguments. Hence, J is the unique model of an MS sentence of the form:

$\exists N_0, N_1(\varphi(N_0, N_1) \wedge \exists M_1, ..., M_m. \varphi'(N_0, N_1, M_1, ..., M_m)))$.

$(3) \Longrightarrow (1)$ By Definition 3.3, the mapping α that transforms the relational structure $\lfloor t \rfloor$ for t in $T^\infty(F)$ into the BJ-tree $J = (N, \leq) = fgs(val(t))$ is an MS-transduction: an MS formula can identify the nodes of J among the positions of t and another one can define $\leq$.

Let $J = (N, \leq)$ be an MS-definable BJ-tree. It is, up to isomorphism, the unique model of an MS sentence β. It follows by a standard argument (called the Backwards Translation Theorem, Theorem 7.10 in [8]) that the set $L(\beta)$ of terms t in $T^\infty(F)$ such that $\alpha(\lfloor t \rfloor) \models \beta$ is MS-definable and thus, contains a regular term (a result by Rabin, see [15]). This term denotes J, hence J is regular. □

(3.11) **Corollary:** Whether two regular BJ-trees are isomorphic is decidable.

Proof: A regular BJ-tree can be given either by a regular term, a regular scheme or an MS sentence. The proof of Theorem (3.10) is effective: algorithms can convert a specification into another one. Two regular BJ-trees can be given, one by an MS sentence β, the other by a regular term t. They are isomorphic if and only if $\alpha(\lfloor t \rfloor) \models \varphi$ (cf. the above proof of $(3) \Longrightarrow (1)$) if and only if $t \in L(\beta)$, which is decidable. □

We have defined regular BJ-trees from regular terms, that have finitary descriptions. There are other infinite terms having finitary descriptions: the algebraic ones and more generally, those of Caucal's hierarchy [1,3]. Such terms yield effective notions of BJ-trees.

4   Quasi-trees

Quasi-trees can be seen informally as undirected join-trees. We now define them independently.

(4.1) *Definition: Betweenness.*

If T is a tree, $x, y \in N_T$, its *betweenness relation* is the ternary relation B_T such that $B_T(x, y, z)$ holds if and only if x, y, z are pairwise distinct and y is on the unique path between x and z. If R is a rooted tree and $T = Und(R)$ is the tree obtained from T by forgetting its root and edge directions, then :

$$B_T(x, y, z) \iff x, y, z \text{ are pairwise distinct and } x <_R y \leq_R x \sqcup_R z \text{ or } z <_R y \leq_R x \sqcup_T z.$$

(4.2) **Proposition**: The betweenness relation $B = B_T$ of a tree T satisfies the following first-order properties for all u, x, y, z in N_T :

A1 : $B(x, y, z) \Rightarrow x \neq y \neq z \neq x$.
A2 : $B(x, y, z) \Rightarrow B(z, y, x)$.
A3 : $B(x, y, z) \Rightarrow \neg B(x, z, y)$.
A4 : $B(x, y, z) \wedge B(y, z, u) \Rightarrow B(x, y, u) \wedge B(x, z, u)$.
A5 : $B(x, y, z) \wedge B(x, u, y) \Rightarrow B(x, u, z) \wedge B(u, y, z)$.
A6 : $B(x, y, z) \wedge B(x, u, z) \Rightarrow$
$y = u \vee (B(x, u, y) \wedge B(u, y, z)) \vee (B(x, y, u) \wedge B(y, u, z))$.
A7 : $x \neq y \neq z \neq x \Rightarrow$
$B(x, y, z) \vee B(x, z, y) \vee B(y, x, z) \vee (\exists u. B(x, u, y) \wedge B(y, u, z) \wedge B(x, u, z))$.

(4.3) *Definition: Quasi-trees.*

A *quasi-tree* is a structure $S = (N, B)$ such that B is a ternary relation on N that satisfies conditions A1-A7.

   In a quasi-tree, the four cases of the conclusion of A7 are exclusive and in the fourth one, there is at most one u satisfying $B(x, u, y) \wedge B(y, u, z) \wedge B(x, u, z)$. A *leaf* of (N, B) is a node z such that $B(x, z, y)$ holds for no x, y. Directions and degrees of nodes can be defined and we get the notion of subcubic quasi-tree.

   From a join-tree $J = (N, \leq)$ we define a ternary relation B_J on N by:

$$B_J(x, y, z) :\iff x, y, z \text{ are pairwise distinct and } x < y \leq x \sqcup z \text{ or } z < y \leq x \sqcup z.$$

Conversely, by selecting a suitable line in a subcubic quasi-tree and two nodes that fix its direction, we can make a quasi-tree into a BJ-tree. This construction is MS-definable. This indicates how Theorem (3.10) (in particular (2)$\Longrightarrow$(3)) extends to subcubic quasi-trees in Theorem (4.5) below.

(4.4) **Proposition:** For every join-tree (resp. BJ-tree) $J = (N, \leq)$, the structure (N, B_J) is a quasi-tree (resp. a subcubic quasi-tree) denoted by $qt(J)$. Each quasi-tree (resp. subcubic quasi-tree) is of this form.

The algebra of quasi-trees is the algebra of join-trees augmented with the *forgetting operation qt* (similar to *fgs*).

(4.5) **Theorem:** A subcubic quasi-tree is regular if and only if it is MS-definable.

This algebraic approach and Theorems (3.10) and (4.5) extend to rooted trees, to ordered rooted trees, to join-trees and to ordered join-trees of finite or countable degree [6].

References

1. Blumensath, A., Colcombet, T., Löding, C.: Logical theories and compatible operations. In: Flum, J., et al. (eds.) Logic and Automata: History and perspectives, pp. 73–106. Amsterdam University Press, Amsterdam (2008)
2. Courcelle, B.: Frontiers of infinite trees. ITA **12**(4), 319–337 (1978). (former name of the journal: RAIRO Informatique théorique)
3. Courcelle, B.: Fundamental properties of infinite trees. Theor. Comput. Sci. **25**, 95–169 (1983)
4. Courcelle, B.: Clique-width of countable graphs: a compactness property. Discrete Math. **276**, 127–148 (2004)
5. Courcelle, B.: Several notions of rank-width for countable graphs (2014). (submitted)
6. Courcelle, B.: Algebras of quasi-trees (2015). (in preparation)
7. Courcelle, B., Delhommé, C.: The modular decomposition of countable graphs. Definition and construction in monadic second-order logic. Theor. Comput. Sci. **394**, 1–38 (2008)
8. Courcelle, B., Engelfriet, J.: Graph structure and monadic second-order logic, a language theoretic approach. Cambridge University Press, Cambridge (2012)
9. Diestel, R.: Graph Theory, 4th edn. Springer-Verlag, Heidelberg (2010)
10. Heilbrunner, S.: An algorithm for the solution of fixed-point equations for infinite words. ITA **14**, 131–141 (1980)
11. Kriz, I., Thomas, R.: Clique-sums, tree-decompositions and compactness. Discrete Math. **81**, 177–185 (1990)
12. Oum, S.: Rank-width and vertex-minors. J. Comb. Theory, Ser. B **95**, 79–100 (2005)
13. Oum, S., Seymour, P.: Approximating clique-width and branch-width. J. Comb. Theory Ser. B **96**, 514–528 (2006)
14. Thomas, W.: On frontiers of regular trees. ITA **20**, 371–381 (1986)
15. Thomas, W.: Automata on infinite objects, in Handbook of Theoretical Computer Science, vol. B. Elsevier, Amsterdam (1990)

Capturing MSO with One Quantifier

Anuj Dawar[1]([⊠]) and Luc Segoufin[2]

[1] University of Cambridge Computer Laboratory, Cambridge, UK
anuj.dawar@cl.cam.ac.uk
[2] INRIA and ENS Cachan, Cachan, France

Abstract. We construct a single Lindström quantifier Q such that FO(Q), the extension of first-order logic with Q has the same expressive power as monadic second-order logic on the class of binary trees (with distinct left and right successors) and also on unranked trees with a sibling order. This resolves a conjecture by ten Cate and Segoufin. The quantifier Q is a variation of a quantifier expressing the Boolean satisfiability problem.

1 Introduction

Trees as data structures are ubiquitous, serving as a means of representing and structuring data in almost all fields of computer science. In the last two decades there has been a significant amount of research devoted to investigating the power of languages for querying tree-structured data. In this context monadic second-order logic (MSO) has emerged as a standard against which the expressive power of other languages is compared. On the one hand, satisfiability of MSO formulas is decidable on trees, and model-checking is tractable. On the other hand, the language is expressive enough to subsume most practical query languages for tree-structured data. To be precise, the classes of trees definable in MSO are exactly the regular languages and this close correspondence between the logic and tree automata is one of its most attractive features.

In [9], ten Cate and Segoufin consider a logic for querying trees that is intermediate in expressive power between first-order logic (FO) and MSO, that is FO(MTC), the extension of first-order logic with an operator for defining the transitive closure of a definable binary relation (here MTC stands for *monadic transitive closure*, to distinguish from the general transitive closure operator which would allow us to define the transitive closure of any definable $2k$-ary relation). They show that the expressive power of this logic corresponds to a natural extension of the widely studied XML path language XPath, and also characterise it in terms of an automaton model—that of nested tree-walking automata. Among the results they establish is that the expressive power of FO(MTC) is strictly weaker than that of MSO on trees (whether finite or infinite, ranked or unranked).

The research reported here was carried out while the first author was a visitor at ENS Cachan, funded by a Leverhulme Trust Study Abroad Fellowship.

L.D. Beklemishev et al. (Eds.): Gurevich Festschrift II 2015, LNCS 9300, pp. 142–152, 2015.
DOI: 10.1007/978-3-319-23534-9_8

FO(MTC) can naturally be seen as an extension of FO with a single generalized quantifier in the sense of Lindström [7]. Such quantifiers are a standard means in abstract model theory (see [1]) of defining a minimal extension of a logic adding the ability to define a particular property. Note, in contrast, that FO(TC)—the extension of first-order logic with the general transitive closure operator, well studied in descriptive complexity theory (see [5])—does not extend FO with a single quantifier but with an infinite family of *vectorized* quantifiers generated from a single one (as in [3]). In the conclusions of [9], ten Cate and Segoufin ask the question whether there is any finite set of Lindström quantifiers $Q_1, \ldots, Q_n$ such that the extension of FO with these quantifiers would have exactly the expressive power of MSO on trees[1]. In this paper, we answer this question by constructing a single Lindström quantifier Q such that FO(Q) has exactly the same expressive power as MSO on finite trees. We first establish this for binary trees (with distinguished left and right successors) and then, in Sect. 5 consider the case of (sibling-ordered) unranked trees. The quantifier that we construct, which we call qSAT, is a version of a Boolean satisfiability quantifier. It is obtained by modifying a representation of satisifiability as a class of finite relational structures originally given by Lovász and Gács [8]. The precise definition is given in Sect. 3.

2   Preliminaries

We write $\mathbb{N}$ for the natural numbers, and we fix an arbitrary finite alphabet Σ for the remainder of this paper. We work with finite trees, either binary or unranked, over Σ. A *binary tree* t over Σ is a finite set $T \subseteq \{0,1\}^*$ of strings that is prefix closed and such that for any string w, $w0 \in T$ iff $w1 \in T$, along with a labelling function $\lambda : T \to \Sigma$. An *unranked tree* t over Σ is a finite set $T \subseteq \mathbb{N}^*$, which is prefix closed and such that if $wj \in T$ for some $w \in \mathbb{N}^*$ and $j \in \mathbb{N}$ then $wi \in T$ for all $i < j$, along with a labelling function $\lambda : T \to \Sigma$. In either case, we refer to the elements of T as nodes, to the empty sequence ε as the *root* of the tree t and any maximal sequence in the set T as a *leaf* of t. A subtree s of a binary tree $t = (T, \lambda)$ is the substructure induced by a set of nodes $S \subseteq T$ such that for some $x \in T$ and some set of tree nodes $W \subseteq \{0,1\}^*$, $S = \{xw \mid w \in W\}$.

In order to define queries over trees in logic, such as first-order or second-order logic, we consider two vocabularies of relations—one for binary trees and one for unranked trees. In the former case, we have two binary relations lsucc (for left successor) and rsucc (for right successor) which are interpreted in a tree t by lsucc(x,y) if, and only if, $y = x0$ and rsucc(x,y) if, and only if, $y = x1$. In addition, for each $\sigma \in \Sigma$, we have a unary relation (which we also write σ) so that $\sigma(x)$ holds just in case $\lambda(x) = \sigma$.

---

[1] As written in [9], the question asks for a set of such quantifiers with expressive power equivalent to FO(MTC). This is clearly a typographical error and MSO is what is meant.

In the case of unranked trees, in addition to the unary relations Σ, we have two binary relations succ (the parent relation) and $\prec$ (the sibling order) which are defined by $\mathrm{succ}(x, y)$ just in case $y = xz$ for some $z \in \mathbb{N}$ and $x \prec y$ just in case $x = zi$ and $y = zj$ for some $z \in \mathbb{N}^*$ and some $i, j \in \mathbb{N}$ with $i < j$.

The formulas of first-order logic (FO) and monadic second-order logic (MSO) are defined as usual, starting with atomic formulas using the predicate symbols $\Sigma \cup \{\mathrm{lsucc}, \mathrm{rsucc}\}$ (in the case of binary trees) and $\Sigma \cup \{\mathrm{succ}, \prec\}$ in the case of unranked trees and closing under Boolean operations and quantification over elements for FO and over *sets* of elements for MSO. We always assume that the equality predicate is available. For a tree t and a sentence ϕ of any logic, we write $t \models \phi$ to denote that t makes ϕ true in the usual way. In general, for a relational signature τ, we write $\mathrm{Str}(\tau)$ for the collection of finite τ-structures. For a τ-structure $\mathbf{A}$, we write A for its universe, and if ϕ is a formula with free first-order variables, we write $\phi^{\mathbf{A}}$ for the relation defined by the formula ϕ when interpreted in $\mathbf{A}$.

We also sometimes write $x < y$ for nodes x and y in a tree t to denote that $y = xz$ for a non-empty string z, i.e. x is an *ancestor* of y. Note that this relation is definable in MSO as it is the transitive closure of succ (or $\mathrm{lsucc} \cup \mathrm{rsucc}$, in the case of binary trees). This relation is not, in general, definable in FO. Thus, the absence of the ancestor relation from our vocabulary makes the main result adjoining a single quantifier to FO to achieve the expressive power of MSO stronger. We do, however, need the sibling order $\prec$.

A tree automaton is a tuple $A = (Q, s, F, \delta)$ where Q is a finite set of *states*, $s \in Q$ is the *initial state*, $F \subseteq Q$ is the set of *accepting states* and $\delta \subseteq Q \times \Sigma \times Q \times Q$ is the *transition relation*. A *run* of an automaton A on a binary tree $t = (T, \lambda)$ starting with state q is a map $\rho : T \to Q$ such that: $\rho(\varepsilon) = q$; and if $x, y, z \in T$ are such that y is the left successor of x and z is the right successor of x, $\rho(x) = q_1$, $\rho(y) = q_2$, $\rho(z) = q_3$ and $\lambda(x) = \sigma$ then $(q_1, \sigma, q_2, q_3) \in \delta$. We say ρ is an *accepting run* starting with state q if for all leaves x of t, $\rho(x) \in F$. We simply say ρ is *accepting* if it is an accepting run starting from s. We say that A *accepts* t if there is some accepting run of A on t. We also use the term *partial run* of A to depth i from node x to mean a run on the subtree of t rooted at x and including all descendants of x at distance at most i. Note that our automata are top-down in the sense that it is the root that is labelled by the initial state and the leaves by final states in an accepting run. The bottom-up automaton model where leaves are labelled by initial states and the root by a final state yields is known to be equivalent.

It is known since the work Thatcher and Wright [10] and Doner [4] that the class of tree languages accepted by automata is exactly the same as those definable by sentences of MSO (see [11] for an exposition). We formally state one direction of this equivalence for future use.

Theorem 2.1 ([4,10]). *For any sentence ϕ of MSO there is a tree automaton A such that for any binary tree t, $t \models \phi$ if, and only if, A accepts t.*

Let τ and $\tau' = \{R_1, \ldots, R_m\}$ be relational signatures, where R_i is a relation symbol of arity r_i. A sequence $\Psi = \psi_1(\bar{x}_1, \bar{y}), \ldots, \psi_m(\bar{x}_m, \bar{y})$ of formulas of signature τ, where ψ_i has free variables among $x_1, \ldots, x_{r_i}$ and $\bar{y}$ defines an interpretation Ψ that takes a pair $(\mathbf{A}, \bar{a})$ consisting of a τ structure $\mathbf{A}$ and a tuple $\bar{a}$ from its universe A interpreting the variables $\bar{y}$ to a τ'-structure $\Psi(\mathbf{A}, \bar{a}) = (A, \psi_1^{\mathbf{A}, \bar{a}}, \ldots, \psi_m^{\mathbf{A}, \bar{a}})$. When $\bar{y}$ is empty, we say that Ψ is an interpretation without parameters.

The following definition of a generalized quantifier is essentially due to Lindström [7].

Definition 2.2. *Let K be a collection of structures of some fixed signature τ, which is closed under isomorphisms, i.e. if $\mathbf{A} \in K$ and $\mathbf{A} \cong \mathbf{B}$ then $\mathbf{B} \in K$. With K we associate the* quantifier Q_K, *which can be adjoined to first-order logic to form an extension* $\mathrm{FO}(Q_K)$, *which is defined by closing* FO *under the following rule for building formulas:*

If $\Psi = (\psi_1, \ldots, \psi_k)$ is an interpretation from τ to τ' then $Q_K \bar{x} \Psi$ is a formula of $\mathrm{FO}(Q_K)$ of signature τ whose free variables are the parameters of Ψ.

The semantics of is given by the following rule: for a τ-structure $\mathbf{A}$ and a valuation $\bar{a}$ for $\bar{y}$,

$$(\mathbf{A}, \bar{a}) \models Q_K \bar{x} \Psi \iff \Psi(\mathbf{A}, \bar{a}) \in K.$$

Where it causes no confusion, we write K both for the quantifier Q_K and the class of structures that defines it.

It should be noted that there are definitions of first-order interpretation in the literature that are more general than what we define. In particular, in our definition, the universe of the interpreted structure $\Psi \mathbf{A}$ is always the same as the universe of $\mathbf{A}$. We do not allow relativization (which restricts the universe to a definable subset), quotienting (where the universe is obtained by taking the quotient of $\mathbf{A}$ under a definable congruence) or vectorizations (where the universe of the interpreted structure is a set of tuples from $\mathbf{A}$). One reason for restricting ourselves in this way is that the simple notion is sufficient for our purpose. Another is that, while relativization and quotienting are harmless, MSO definability is not closed under vectorized interpretations. There are other general notions of interpretation that preserve MSO definability (such as the MSO transductions of Courcelle (see [2]), but we do not need this generality here.

With our definition, MSO definability is closed under first-order interpretations in the sense that if K is definable by an MSO sentence and Ψ is an interpretation, then the class $\{\mathbf{A} \mid \Psi\mathbf{A} \in K\}$ is also MSO-definable. An immediate consequence is the following lemma, which we state for future reference.

Lemma 2.3. *If K is definable by an* MSO *sentence, then every formula of $\mathrm{FO}(Q_K)$ is equivalent to a formula of* MSO.

3   Satisfiability Quantifier

The quantifier we define is based on a representation of the Boolean satisfiability problem as a class of relational structures. We first consider a classical representation due to Lovász and Gács [8], who showed that this class of structures is NP-complete under (vectorized) first-order interpretations.

Definition 3.1. *Let τ_{SAT} denote the vocabulary (V, C, P, N) where V and C are unary relation symbols and P and N are binary relation symbols. We denote by SAT the class of τ_{SAT}-structures $\mathbf{A}$ in which:*

1. *$V^{\mathbf{A}}$ and $C^{\mathbf{A}}$ partition the universe A;*
2. *$P^{\mathbf{A}}, N^{\mathbf{A}} \subseteq V^{\mathbf{A}} \times C^{\mathbf{A}}$.*
3. *there is a set $S \subseteq V^{\mathbf{A}}$ such that for each $c \in C^{\mathbf{A}}$ there is a $v \in V^{\mathbf{A}}$ such that: either $v \in S$ and $P(v, c)$ or $v \notin S$ and $N(v, c)$.*

The idea is that a structure in SAT represents a propositional formula in CNF. V is the set of variables and C the set of clauses. $P(v, c)$ holds if the variable v appears positively in the clause c and $N(v, c)$ holds if v appears negatively in c. The third condition in the definition ensures that $\mathbf{A} \in$ SAT only if it represents a *satisfiable* formula. It is immediate from the definition that SAT is definable by a sentence of MSO, since each of the three conditions is easily expressed as an MSO formula.

While SAT is a natural quantifier, expressing a well-known problem, we find it convenient to consider a modification of it, which makes our proof considerably easier. Let τ_{qSAT} be the vocabulary (Cl, Pos, Neg) where Cl is a binary relation and Pos and Neg are ternary relations. For a τ_{qSAT}-structure $\mathbf{A} = (A, Cl, Pos, Neg)$, write flat($\mathbf{A}$) for the τ_{SAT}-structure whose universe is $A \uplus Cl$ (i.e. the disjoint union of A and Cl), which interprets the unary relations V and C by A and Cl respectively, where P is interpreted as the set of pairs (a, c) such that if $c = (a_1, a_2) \in Cl$, then $Pos(a, a_1, a_2)$ holds and similarly N is interpreted as the set of pairs (a, c) such that if $c = (a_1, a_2) \in Cl$, then $Neg(a, a_1, a_2)$ holds.

Definition 3.2. *We define qSAT to be the class of τ_{qSAT}-structures $\mathbf{A}$ such that* flat($\mathbf{A}$) $\in$ *SAT.*

In other words, while in the τ_{SAT} representation of Boolean formulas, we explicitly have elements for each variable and clause, in the τ_{qSAT} Representation, the universe consists just of the set of variables and the clauses are coded by pairs of variables. This limits us to Boolean formulas where the number of clauses is at most n^2 (where n is the number of variables) but this suffices for our purpose. The reason for considering this more convoluted definition is that in defining an interpretation of τ_{SAT} in a tree t, we are limited to constructing instances where the number of variables *and* clauses is at most the number of nodes in the tree. On the other hand, in interpreting τ_{qSAT}, we can effectively construct instances of quadratic size. This simplifies our argument.

Again, it is quite easy to see that the class of structures qSAT is definable in MSO. Indeed, the definition is obtained as a conjunction of the wellformedness condition:

$$\forall x, y, z (Pos(x, y, z) \vee Neg(x, y, z)) \Rightarrow Cl(y, z)$$

with the satisfiability condition:

$$\exists S \forall x, y (Cl(x, y) \Rightarrow \exists s (S(s) \wedge Pos(s, x, y)) \vee (\neg S(s) \wedge Neg(s, x, y))).$$

Thus, by Lemma 2.3 we immediately have the following lemma.

Lemma 3.3. *Every formula of* FO(*qSAT*) *is equivalent to a formula of* MSO.

Note that this holds in general, not just on trees.

4   Capturing MSO

In this section, we begin by showing that FO(qSAT) has the same expressive power as MSO on binary trees. Lemma 3.3 established one direction of this equivalence. For the other, we aim to show that for any MSO sentence ϕ, the class of binary trees t such that $t \models \phi$ is reducible, by a first-order interpretation, to the class qSAT. The basic idea of the construction is similar to the proof that any MSO sentence is equivalent, on the class of binary trees, to an *existential* MSO sentence with exactly one second-order quantifier (see [11]).

Fix an MSO sentence ϕ and let $A = (Q, q_1, F, \delta)$ be a tree automaton accepting the set of trees $\{t \mid t \models \phi\}$. Without loss of generality we assume that A is complete: that is, for any state q and any $\sigma \in \Sigma$, there are states s and t with $(q, \sigma, s, t) \in \delta$. Also, we assume $Q = \{q_1, \ldots, q_k\}$ with q_1 being the initial state.

Let t be a tree and let ρ be a run of A on t. Let S_ρ be the set of nodes defined inductively as follows. The root of t is in S_ρ. If x is a node of t with x in S_ρ and $\rho(x) = q_i$ then all descendants of x at distance i are in S_ρ. No other nodes are in S_ρ.

Now, given a binary tree $t = (T, \lambda)$ and a set $S \subseteq T$, we can say that $S = S_\rho$ for some *accepting* run ρ of A if, and only if, the following conditions are satisfied:

1. The root is in S. The left and right successors of the root are in S.
2. For any node x in S, other than root, there is an ancestor of x at distance less than k from x that is in S. We call the ancestor of x that is closest to x and in S the *S-predecessor of x*.
3. If x is in S and y, the S-predecessor of x, is at distance i from x then all descendants of y at distance i are in S and no descendant of y at distance less than i is in S. In this case we say that y is an *i-node*.
4. For every i-node x in S, if $y_1, \ldots, y_n$ are the descendants of x at distance i from x then there is a run of A starting in x in state q_i and reaching y_j in state q_{α_j} such that for all $j \leq n$:
   (a) if the subtree of t rooted at y_j has depth less than α_j then there is an accepting run of A starting from y_j in state q_{α_j}; and
   (b) if the subtree rooted at y_j has depth at least α_j then y_j is a α_j-node.
   Moreover, if y is a leaf of t at distance less than i from x then the run reaches an accepting state in y.

Note that each of the conditions above can be expressed by a first-order formula with a unary relation for S. This is because each of the conditions is only about the local neighbourhood (to distance at most k) of a node x. This shows, in particular, that the class of trees accepted by A is defined by a formula $\exists S \theta$ where θ is first-order. Our aim here is slightly different. We want to use this construction to obtain from a tree t, a *propositional* formula θ_t which is satisfiable if, and only if, there is an accepting run of A on t. The variables of θ_t are exactly the nodes T so any subset S of T determines a truth assignment to the variables making the variables in S true and all other variables false. Then, each of the conditions above translates into a set of clauses on the variables T. We now show that this translation can be achieved by means of a first-order interpretation.

Lemma 4.1. *For any tree automaton A, there is a first-order interpretation Θ such that for any binary tree t, $\Theta t \in$ qSAT if, and only if, A accepts t.*

Proof. The instance Θt of qSAT that we construct has as its universe (and therefore the set of variables), the nodes T of t. The clauses are indexed, as required by the definition of qSAT, by pairs of variables. The number of clauses is bounded by $c|T|$ for some constant c (depending on A) and we find it convenient to index the clauses by pairs $(x, y) \in T^2$ where y is an ancestor of x at distance at most c. The distance of y from x effectively serves as an integer index. For any positive integer i, we write $y = \mathrm{anc}_i(x)$ to denote that y is the ancestor of x at distance i. Note that for fixed i this is expressible as a first-order formula with free variables x and y. We also fix an injective mapping of tuples of natural numbers as natural numbers and write, for instance, $\langle l, m, n \rangle$ for the number that codes the triple (l, m, n).

To represent condition 1, for each $x \in \{\varepsilon, 0, 1\}$ we have a clause indexed by (x, x) which is just x (i.e. a single positive occurrence of the variable x).

To represent condition 2 we have, for each node x that is not in $\{\varepsilon, 0, 1\}$, a clause indexed by (x, x) that is $x \rightarrow (y_1 \vee \cdots y_k)$ where $y_i = \mathrm{anc}_i(x)$.

To represent condition 3 for any node x, and any i with $1 \leq i \leq k$, let $w_1, \ldots, w_l$ be the descendants of x at distance exactly i from x and $z_1, \ldots, z_m$ be the descendants of x at distance less than i from x. Note that $l, m \leq 2^k$. Then, for each such i, and each j and j' with $1 \leq j, j' \leq l$ we have the clause $x \wedge w_j \rightarrow w_{j'}$, indexed by (x, y) for $y = \mathrm{anc}_{\langle 1, i, j, j' \rangle}(x)$. Also for each j and j' with $1 \leq j \leq l$ and $1 \leq j' \leq m$ we have the clause $x \wedge w_j \rightarrow \neg z_{j'}$, indexed by (x, y) for $y = \mathrm{anc}_{\langle 2, i, j, j' \rangle}(x)$.

To represent condition 4, for each node x and each $1 \leq i \leq k$, let z be the lexicographically smallest descendant of x at distance i if there is one and let $w_1, \ldots, w_n$ enumerate all the descendants of x at distance i. Consider any run ρ of the automaton A on the subtree rooted at x starting in state q_i, and let $\rho(w_j) = q_l$. We write α_{ρ, w_j} for the propositional formula that is:

- **true** if w_j has no descendants at distance l and there is a run of A starting in q_l on the subtree rooted at w_j which ends in a final state on all leaves; and
- z', where z' is a descendant of w_j at distance l from w_j otherwise.

We now construct the propositional formula:

$$x \wedge z \rightarrow \bigvee_\rho \bigwedge_w \alpha_{\rho, w} \tag{1}$$

where ρ ranges over all partial runs of A on the subtree rooted at x starting in state q_i, and up to depth i such that for any descendant u of x that is at distance less than i from x and is a leaf $\rho(u) \in F$; and w ranges over $\{w_1, \ldots, w_n\}$.

Let $d_1, \ldots, d_r$ be the clauses when the formula (1) is converted to CNF. Note that r is bounded by a function of k. Then, we include the clause d_l indexed by the pair (x, y) where $y = \text{anc}_{\langle i, l \rangle}(x)$.

Note that in the above, clauses are indexed by pairs (x, y) with y an ancestor of x at distance at most c, where c is a function of k. The interpretation Θ takes the tree t to an instance (T, Cl, Pos, Neg) of qSAT where Cl is the set of indices defined above. It is easy to see that Cl is definable by a first-order formula because the distance between x and y is bounded. The only variables that appear in a clause indexed by (x, y) are at distance at most $2k$ from x. Since the number of such nodes is bounded (by a function of k) and a total order on this set is definable in first-order logic, any relation on these is first-order definable. Moreover, whether or not a variable is included in the clause and if so, positively or negatively also depends only on the neighbourhood of x to a bounded distance. In particular, this means that the relations Pos and Neg are easily defined by first-order formulas. The construction above really defines clauses only for nodes x that are far enough away from the root. In particular, if x is at distance less than c from the root, it may not have enough ancestors to code the number of clauses required. However, there are only a bounded number of such nodes and we can deal with them exhaustively inside a first-order formula.

It is easily checked that the instance of qSAT so defined is satisfiable if, and only if, t is accepted by A.

Theorem 4.2. FO(qSAT) *has the same expressive power as* MSO *on binary trees.*

Proof. Immediate from Lemmas 3.3 and 4.1.

It should be noted that the interpretation constructed in the proof of Lemma 4.1 is one *without parameters*. Thus, the proof also establishes a normal form for the logic FO(qSAT) on binary trees, in which each formula is of the form qSATΨ for a first-order interpretation Ψ.

5   Unranked Trees

In this section, we sketch an argument to show that, even on unranked trees, the expressive power of FO(qSAT) is the same as that of MSO. One direction of this is immediate by Lemma 3.3. For the other direction, we reduce the question to that of binary trees through the standard encoding of unranked trees as binary trees (see, for instance, [6]). Below, we describe the encoding and briefly sketch the reduction.

We define a *partial binary tree* $t = (T, \lambda)$ where $T \subseteq \{0, 1\}^*$ is a finite prefix-closed set of strings and $\lambda : T \to \Sigma$ is a labelling function. In other words, we do not require that every node has either 0 or 2 successors—a node may also have just a left or just a right successor. We treat such trees, in the natural way, as structures over the signature $\Sigma \cup \{\text{lsucc}, \text{rsucc}\}$.

For an unranked tree $t = (T, \lambda)$ its binary encoding is the unique partial binary tree $s = (S, \mu)$ for which there is a bijection $h : T \to S$ such that for any $x, y \in T$: if y is the $\prec$-first successor of x then $h(y)$ is the left successor of $h(x)$; and if y is the $\prec$-successor of x then $h(y)$ is the right successor of x.

Now, it is easily seen that there is an MSO interpretation that takes a structure $\mathbf{A}$ that is the binary encoding of an unranked tree t to a structure isomorphic to t. Indeed, we can define the $x \prec y$ as the transitive closure of $\text{rsucc}^{\mathbf{A}}$ and $\text{succ}(x, y)$ by $\exists z \text{lsucc}(x, z) \wedge (z = y \vee z \prec y)$. Both of these are MSO definable. This immediately gives us a translation of MSO formulas on unranked trees into corresponding formulas on their binary encodings as stated in the following proposition.

Proposition 5.1. *For any MSO formula ϕ there is an MSO formula ψ such that an unranked t satisfies ϕ if, and only if, its binary encoding satisfies ψ.*

We next define the *completion* of a partial binary tree $t = (T, \lambda)$ as the binary tree over the alphabet $\Sigma \cup \{\bot\}$ over the set of strings T' which is the minimal set that includes T and also includes $x0$ iff it includes $x1$, for any $x \in \{0, 1\}^*$ and such that the label of any $x \in T$ is $\lambda(x)$, while the label of any $x \notin T$ is $\bot$. While it is not possible to construct an interpretation (in the sense we have defined it) from partial binary trees to their completions because the universes of the structures are different, it is still possible to translate MSO formulas. More specifically, the standard translation of MSO formulas on binary trees to automata easily yields, for any MSO sentence ϕ a tree automaton A such that ϕ is satisfied on a partial binary tree t if, and only if, A accepts the completion of t. It is then an easy exercise to modify the construction in the proof of Lemma 4.1 to obtain, from A an interpretation that takes the partial binary tree t to an instance of qSAT that is satisfiable if, and only if, A accepts the completion of t.

Finally, we note that there is an FO interpretation that takes an unranked tree t and yields (a structure isomorphic to) the binary encoding of t. This is obtained by defining $\text{lsucc}(x, y)$ by the formula $\text{succ}(x, y) \wedge \forall z \neg z \prec x$ and $\text{rsucc}(x, y)$ by $x \prec y \wedge \forall z(y \prec z \Rightarrow (z = y \vee y \prec z))$. This means that for any FO(qSAT) formula ϕ there is an FO(qSAT) formula ψ such that ψ is satisfied in an unranked tree t if, and only if, ϕ is satisfied in the binary encoding of t. This completes the cycle of translations and establishes the following.

Theorem 5.2. *FO(qSAT) has the same expressive power as MSO on unranked trees.*

Proof. One direction is immediate from Lemma 3.3. In the other direction, if we have a sentence ϕ of MSO, this translates to a sentence of MSO interpreted on the binary encodings of unranked trees. In turn, this can be turned into an automaton on the completion of the binary encoding, whose acceptance condition is expressed as a FO(qSAT) sentence on binary encodings. This then translates into an FO(qSAT) sentence on unranked trees.

6   Conclusion

We have shown that we can construct a single Lindström quantifier Q such that adding it to first-order logic yields a logic that is able to express all regular tree languages (on either binary or unranked trees). There is one sense in which this is a *completeness* result. It shows that all regular tree languages can be reduced to Q by rather simple first-order reductions, without vectorizations—reductions which MSO is closed under—and at the same time Q is itself definable in MSO. What prevents us from saying that Q is complete for regular tree languages under simple first-order reductions is that Q is not itself a tree language. It might be interesting to find a quantifier that is a tree language that has this property. In other words, is there a tree language that is MSO-complete under simple first-order reductions? One may also ask if similar results hold for natural classes of structures other than trees.

Our quantifier qSAT is a variation of a natural quantifier coding the satisfiability of CNF formulas. As we noted, SAT is perhaps a more natural quantifier coding this problem. Our reasons for using qSAT instead of SAT were technical: the number of clauses in the CNF formulas we construct is potentially greater than (though by no more than a constant factor) the number of nodes in the tree. Perhaps a more sophisticated construction could circumvent this and show that even the quantifier SAT has the property we formulated. It should be noted that qSAT is reducible to SAT by a *vectorized* first-order reduction, indeed one of dimension 2. If this could be achieved by a simple reduction instead, it would indeed establish that FO(SAT) was as expressive as MSO on trees.

Finally, it is interesting to ask if a similar result holds for the full infinite binary tree. That is, is there a quantifier Q so that FO(Q) has the same expressive power as MSO. In this case, the expressive power of MSO is strictly greater than that of weak MSO, where set quantification is restricted to finite sets. It seems plausible that one could show that at least the expressive power of weak MSO is captured by a single quantifier.

References

1. Barwise, J., Feferman, S.: Model-Theoretic Logics. Springer, New York (1985)
2. Courcelle, B., Engelfriet, J.: Graph Structure and Monadic Second-Order Logic, a Language Theoretic Approach. Cambridge University Press, New York (2012)
3. Dawar, A.: Generalized quantifiers and logical reducibilities. J. Logic Comput. **5**(2), 213–226 (1995)
4. Doner, J.: Tree acceptors and some of their applications. J. Comput. Syst. Sci. **4**, 406–451 (1970)
5. Immerman, N.: Descriptive Complexity. Springer, New York (1999)
6. Libkin, L.: Logics for unranked trees: an overview. Log. Methods Comput. Sci. **2**, (2006)
7. Lindström, P.: First order predicate logic with generalized quantifiers. Theoria **32**, 186–195 (1966)
8. Lovász, L., Gács, P.: Some remarks on generalized spectra. Zeitschrift für Mathematische Logik und Grundlagen der Mathematik **23**, 27–144 (1977)

9. Cate, B.T., Segoufin, L.: Transitive closure logic, nested tree walking automata, and XPath. J. ACM **57**(3), 18:1–18:41 (2010)
10. Thatcher, J.W., Wright, J.B.: Generalized finite automata theory with an application to a decision problem of second-order logic. Math. Syst. Theory **2**, 57–81 (1968)
11. Thomas, W.: Languages, automata and logic. In: Rozenberg, G., Salomaa, A. (eds.) Handbook of Formal Languages, vol. 3, pp. 389–455. Springer, Heidelberg (1997)

Logics for Weighted Timed Pushdown Automata

Manfred Droste and Vitaly Perevoshchikov$^{(\boxtimes)}$

Institut für Informatik, Universität Leipzig, 04109 Leipzig, Germany
{droste,perev}@informatik.uni-leipzig.de

Abstract. Weighted dense-timed pushdown automata with a timed stack were introduced by Abdulla, Atig and Stenman to model the behavior of real-time recursive systems. Motivated by the decidability of the optimal reachability problem for weighted timed pushdown automata and weighted logic of Droste and Gastin, we introduce a weighted MSO logic on timed words which is expressively equivalent to weighted timed pushdown automata. To show the expressive equivalence result, we prove a decomposition theorem which establishes a connection between weighted timed pushdown languages and visibly pushdown languages of Alur and Mudhusudan; then we apply their result about the logical characterization of visibly pushdown languages.

Keywords: Timed automata · Weighted automata · Monadic second-order logic · Weighted logic · Formal power series · Pushdown automata · Timed stack

1 Introduction

Timed automata introduced by Alur and Dill [3] are a prominent model for the specification and analysis of real-time systems. Timed pushdown automata (TPDA) with a stack were studied in [7,10,16] in the context of the verification of real-time recursive systems. Recently, Abdulla, Atig and Stenman [1] proposed TPDA with a timed stack which keeps track of the age of its elements. In [2], they introduced weighted timed pushdown automata (WTPDA) as a model for quantitative properties of timed recursive systems and showed that the optimal reachability problem for WTPDA is decidable.

Since the seminal Büchi-Elgot-Trakhtenbrot theorem [9,15,22] about the expressive equivalence of finite automata and monadic second-order logic, a significant field of research investigates logical characterizations of language classes appearing from practically relevant automata models. The goal of this paper is to provide a logical characterization for weighted timed pushdown automata, i.e., to design a weighted logic on timed words which is expressively equivalent to WTPDA.

On the one hand, logic provides an intuitive way to describe the properties of systems. On the other hand, logical formulas can be translated into automata

V. Perevoshchikov—Supported by DFG Research Training Group 1763 (QuantLA).

L.D. Beklemishev et al. (Eds.): Gurevich Festschrift II 2015, LNCS 9300, pp. 153–173, 2015.
DOI: 10.1007/978-3-319-23534-9_9

which may have interesting algorithmic properties. Furthermore, logic provides good insights into the understanding of the automata behaviors.

Related work. A logical characterization of unweighted TPDA was given in [14] where a *timed matching logic* is introduced. As in the logic of Lautemann, Schwentick and Thérien [18], we handle the stack functionality by means of a binary *matching* predicate. As in the logic of Wilke [23], we use *relative distance formulas* to handle the functionality of clocks. Moreover, to handle the ages of stack elements, we lift the binary matchings to the timed setting, i.e., we can compare the time distance between matched positions with a constant.

On the other side, Droste and Gastin [11] introduced and investigated weighted MSO logic over semirings; this logic permits to describe quantitative properties of systems. In [11] it was shown that syntactically restricted weighted MSO logic is expressively equivalent to weighted automata over semirings (cf. [12] for surveys). In [13, 21] this result was extended to the setting of weighted timed automata. In [19] a logical characterization of algebraic formal power series was given.

Contribution of this paper. In this paper, we extend our result for unweighted TPDA to the setting of semiring-weighted TPDA. We introduce a *weighted timed matching logic* (wTML) and study its relation to WTPDA. As in [11], unrestricted weighted timed matching logic is more expressive than WTPDA. We study which formulas lead to unrecognizable weighted timed languages and introduce a reasonable syntactically restricted fragment of wTML which is expressively equivalent to WTPDA.

For the proof of our expressive equivalence result, we use the idea of [13] for weighted timed automata to separate weights from timed automata. In contrast to timed automata, TPDA as extensions of pushdown automata are not closed under intersection. Moreover, the storing weights in a timed stack are closely connected to the inner components of TPDA. Therefore, we have to modify the approach of [13]. We introduce a technique which establishes a connection between *weighted timed* pushdown automata and *visibly pushdown languages* of Alur and Madhusudan [4], a subclass of the classical context-free languages. In other words, our method permits to simultaneously separate weights and time from the discrete part of the model.

We show our expressive equivalence result as follows.

- We prove a Nivat-like decomposition theorem for WTPDA (cf. [5, 20]) which may be of independent interest; this theorem establishes a connection between weighted timed pushdown languages and unweighted untimed visibly pushdown languages of [4] by means of operations like renamings and intersections with simple weighted timed pushdown languages. This result extends our decomposition result for unweighted TPDA presented in [14].
- In a similar way, we separate the weighted timed part of wTML from the boolean part described by MSO logic with matchings over a visibly pushdown alphabet [4].
- Then we deduce our result from the logical characterization result of [4] for visibly pushdown languages.

Since our proof is constructive and the optimal reachability for WTPDA is decidable [2], we obtain the corresponding decidability result for restricted wTML.

Outline. For the clarity of presentation and convenience of the reader, we will concentrate on the simplified model of WTPDA without global clocks. In Sect. 2 we define WTPDA over timed semirings. In Sect. 3 we introduce our weighted timed matching logic and state our main result, namely Theorem 3.8. The proof of Theorem 3.8 will be given in Sect. 6. As a preparation for this proof, in Sect. 4 we recall some basic definitions about visibly pushdown languages and in Sect. 5 we prove our Nivat-like decomposition theorem. In Sect. 7 we explain how global clocks can be added to our main result. Our proof technique can easily recover this case.

2   Weighted Timed Pushdown Automata

Timed pushdown automata (TPDA) with a timed stack are introduced and investigated in [1]. These machines are nondeterministic automata equipped with *global clocks* (like timed automata [3]) and a stack (like pushdown automata). In contrast to untimed pushdown automata, in timed pushdown automata we push together with a letter a *local clock* which will measure the age of this letter in the stack. Then, we can pop this letter only if its age satisfies a given constraint. *Weighted timed pushdown automata* (WTPDA) of [2] extend TPDA by adding time-independent costs to the transitions of TPDA (like in the classical weighted automata [12]) and costs for storing a letter in the stack which depend on the age of this letter in the stack.

In this section, we introduce an algebraic model for WTPDA which is based on the classical model of *semiring-weighted* automata [12]. Moreover, we follow the idea of Quaas [21] to model time-dependent costs by means of functions of a real argument. Recall from the introduction that the goal of this paper is to give a logical characterization of WTPDA. Weighted timed automata with global clocks and without stack were studied in [13,21] with respect to their logical characterization. The new feature of WTPDA is the quantitative timed stack, i.e., the timed stack equipped with time-dependent costs for storing stack letters. In order to concentrate on the significant details and for the clarity of presentation, we will omit global clocks in our considerations. However, in Sect. 7 we discuss how they can be added to our definitions and proofs.

An *alphabet* is a non-empty finite set. Let Σ be a non-empty set (possibly infinite). A *finite word* over Σ is a finite sequence $a_1...a_n$ where $n \geq 0$ and $a_1,...,a_n \in \Sigma$. If $n = 0$, then w is *empty* and we denote it by ε. Otherwise, we call w *non-empty*. Let Σ^* denote the set of all words and Σ^+ the set of all non-empty words over Σ. Let $\mathbb{R}_{\geq 0}$ be the set of all non-negative real numbers. A *timed word* over Σ is a sequence $(a_1,t_1)(a_2,t_2)...(a_n,t_n) \in (\Sigma \times \mathbb{R}_{\geq 0})^*$ such that $t_1 \leq t_2 \leq ... \leq t_n$. Let $\mathbb{T}\Sigma^*$ denote the set of all timed words over Σ and $\mathbb{T}\Sigma^+$ the set of all non-empty timed words over Σ. Any set $\mathcal{L} \subseteq \mathbb{T}\Sigma^+$ of non-empty timed words is called a *timed language*. Let $\mathcal{I}$ denote the class of all intervals of the form $[a, b], (a, b], [a, b), (a, b), [a, \infty)$ or (a, ∞) where $a, b \in \mathbb{N}$. If Γ is an alphabet, $u = (g_1, t_1)...(g_n, t_n) \in \mathbb{T}\Gamma^*$ and $t \in \mathbb{R}_{\geq 0}$, then let $u + t = (g_1, t_1 + t)...(g_n, t_n + t) \in \mathbb{T}\Gamma^*$.

A *timed semiring* is a tuple $\mathbb{S} = (S, \mathcal{F}, +, \cdot, 0, 1)$ such that $(S, +, \cdot, 0, 1)$ is a semiring and $\mathcal{F} \subseteq S^{\mathbb{R}_{\geq 0}}$ is a collection of functions containing the function $\overline{1} \in S^{\mathbb{R}_{\geq 0}}$ defined for all $t \in \mathbb{R}_{\geq 0}$ by $\overline{1}(t) = 1$.

Example 2.1. (a) The tropical semiring $(\mathbb{R}_{\geq 0} \cup \{\infty\}, \min, +, \infty, 0)$ together with the collection of linear functions $\mathbb{L} = \{t \mapsto c \cdot t \mid c \in \mathbb{R}_{\geq 0}\}$ forms a timed semiring which we denote by $\mathbb{L}\text{TROP}$. The model of [2] can be considered as WTPDA over $\mathbb{L}\text{TROP}$.

(b) The boolean semiring $(\{0, 1\}, \vee, \wedge, 0, 1)$ together with $\mathcal{F} = \{\overline{1}\}$ form a timed semiring which we denote by 1BOOL. Unweighted TPDA of [1] can be considered as WTPDA over 1BOOL.

(c) It could be also interesting to consider the case where the storing costs in the timed stack grow exponentially in time (cf., e.g., [8]). We augment the tropical semiring $(\mathbb{R}_{\geq 0} \cup \{\infty\}, \min, +, \infty, 0)$ with the collection of exponential functions $\mathcal{F} = \{t \mapsto e^{c \cdot t} \mid c \in \mathbb{R}_{\geq 0}\}$ and obtain a timed semiring which we denote by EXPTROP.

Let $\mathcal{S}(\Gamma) = \{\text{push}(\gamma) \mid \gamma \in \Gamma\} \cup \{\#\} \cup \{\text{pop}(\gamma, I) \mid \gamma \in \Gamma, I \in \mathcal{I}\}$ be the set of *stack commands* over Γ.

Definition 2.2. *Let Σ be an alphabet and $\mathbb{S} = (S, \mathcal{F}, +, \cdot, 0, 1)$ a timed semiring. A* weighted timed pushdown automaton *(WTPDA) over Σ and $\mathbb{S}$ is a tuple $\mathcal{A} = (L, \Gamma, L_0, E, L_f, \text{wt})$ where L is a finite set of locations, Γ is a finite stack alphabet, $L_0, L_f \subseteq L$ are sets of initial resp. final locations, $E \subseteq L \times \Sigma \times \mathcal{S}(\Gamma) \times L$ is a finite set of edges, and $\text{wt} : E \cup \Gamma \to S \cup \mathcal{F}$ is a weight function with $\text{wt}(E) \subseteq S$ and $\text{wt}(\Gamma) \subseteq \mathcal{F}$.*

A stack command $\text{push}(\gamma)$ means that we push the letter γ into the timed stack with the initial age 0. The stack command $\#$ means that we do not perform any operations with the timed stack. A stack command $\text{pop}(\gamma, I)$ means that we pop from the stack the letter γ with the age lying in the interval I. The weights of the stack letters in WTPDA have the following meaning. Whenever we pop a letter γ with the age τ from the stack, the storing cost $\text{wt}(\gamma)(\tau)$ arises.

We will denote an edge $e = (\ell, a, \text{st}, \ell') \in E$ by $\ell \xrightarrow{a, \text{st}} \ell'$. We say that a is the *label* of e and denote in by $\text{label}(e)$. We also let $\text{stack}(e) = \text{st}$, the stack command of e. Let $E^{\text{push}} \subseteq E$ denote the set of all *push* edges e with $\text{stack}(e) = \text{push}(\gamma)$ for some $\gamma \in \Gamma$. Similarly, let $E^{\#} = \{e \in E \mid \text{stack}(e) = \#\}$ be the set of *local* edges and $E^{\text{pop}} = \{e \in E \mid \text{stack}(e) = \text{pop}(\gamma, I) \text{ for some } \gamma \in \Gamma \text{ and } I \in \mathcal{I}\}$ the set of *pop* edges. Then, we have $E = E^{\text{push}} \cup E^{\#} \cup E^{\text{pop}}$.

A *configuration* c of $\mathcal{A}$ is described by the present location and the stack which is a timed word over Γ. That is, c is a pair $\langle \ell, u \rangle$ where $\ell \in L$ and $u \in \mathbb{T}\Gamma^*$. We say that c is *initial* if $\ell \in L_0$ and $u = \varepsilon$. We say that c is *final* if $\ell \in L_f$ and $u = \varepsilon$. Let $\mathcal{C}_{\mathcal{A}}$ denote the set of all configurations of $\mathcal{A}$, $\mathcal{C}_{\mathcal{A}}^0 \subseteq \mathcal{C}_{\mathcal{A}}$ the set of all initial configurations, and $\mathcal{C}_{\mathcal{A}}^f \subseteq \mathcal{C}_{\mathcal{A}}$ the set of all final configurations.

Consider configurations $c = \langle \ell, u \rangle$ and $c' = \langle \ell', u' \rangle$ with $u = (\gamma_1, t_1)...(\gamma_k, t_k)$ and let $e = \left(q \xrightarrow{a, \text{st}} q' \right) \in E$ be an edge. We say that $c \vdash_e c'$ is a *switch transition* if $\ell = q$, $\ell' = q'$, and

- if st $= \text{push}(\gamma)$ for some $\gamma \in \Gamma$, then $u' = (\gamma, 0)u$;
- if st $= \#$, then $u' = u$;
- if st $= \text{pop}(\gamma, I)$ with $\gamma \in \Gamma$ and $I \in \mathcal{I}$, then $k \geq 1$, $\gamma = \gamma_1$, $t_1 \in I$ and $u' = (\gamma_2, t_2)...(\gamma_k, t_k)$.

The weight of this switch transition is defined as follows. If st $= \text{push}(\gamma)$ or st $= \#$, then we let $\text{wt}(c \vdash_e c') = \text{wt}(e)$. If st $= \text{pop}(\gamma, I)$, then we let $\text{wt}(c \vdash_e c') = \text{wt}(e) \cdot \text{wt}(\gamma)(t_1)$.

For $t \in \mathbb{R}_{\geq 0}$, we say that $c \vdash_t c'$ is a *delay transition* if $\ell = \ell'$ and $u' = u + t$. For $t \in \mathbb{R}_{\geq 0}$ and $e \in E$, we write $c \vdash_{t,e} c'$ if there exists $c'' \in \mathcal{C}_\mathcal{A}$ with $c \vdash_t c''$ and $c'' \vdash_e c'$. Note that, for every $c \in \mathcal{C}_\mathcal{A}$ and $t \in \mathbb{R}_{\geq 0}$, there exists at most one $c'' \in \mathcal{C}_\mathcal{A}$ with $c \vdash_t c''$. Then, we let $\text{wt}(c \vdash_{t,e} c') = \text{wt}(c'' \vdash_e c')$. A *run* ρ of $\mathcal{A}$ is an alternating sequence of delay and switch transitions which starts in an initial configuration and ends in a final configuration, formally, $\rho = c_0 \vdash_{t_1, e_1} c_1 \vdash_{t_2, e_2} ... \vdash_{t_n, e_n} c_n$ where $n \geq 1$, $c_0 \in \mathcal{C}_\mathcal{A}^0$ and $c_n \in \mathcal{C}_\mathcal{A}^f$. The *label* of ρ is the timed word $\text{label}(\rho) = (\text{label}(e_1), t_1)(\text{label}(e_2), t_1 + t_2)...(\text{label}(e_n), \sum_{i=1}^n t_i) \in \mathbb{T}\Sigma^+$. The *weight* of ρ is defined as $\text{wt}(\rho) = \prod_{i=1}^n \text{wt}(c_{i-1} \vdash_{t_i, e_i} c_i)$.

For each timed word $w \in \mathbb{T}\Sigma^+$, let $\text{Run}_\mathcal{A}(w)$ denote the set of all runs ρ of $\mathcal{A}$ such that $\text{label}(\rho) = w$. The *behavior* of $\mathcal{A}$ is the mapping $[\![\mathcal{A}]\!] : \mathbb{T}\Sigma^+ \to \mathbb{S}$ defined for every timed word $w \in \mathbb{T}\Sigma^+$ as $[\![\mathcal{A}]\!](w) = \sum \left(\text{wt}(\rho) \mid \rho \in \text{Run}_\mathcal{A}(w) \right)$. A mapping $\mathbb{L} : \mathbb{T}\Sigma^+ \to \mathbb{S}$ is called a *weighted timed language* (WTL). We say $\mathbb{L}$ is *pushdown recognizable* over $\mathbb{S}$ if there exists a WTPDA $\mathcal{A}$ over Σ and $\mathbb{S}$ such that $[\![\mathcal{A}]\!] = \mathbb{L}$.

Remark 2.3. Note that in our model of WTPDA without global clocks the first time stamp of a timed word is irrelevant for the behavior of a WTPDA. However, this is not the case if we add global clocks to this model.

Example 2.4. Let $\Sigma = \{[,]\}$ be the set of brackets. Let $b = [$, $\bar{b} =]$ and $I \in \mathcal{I}$ be an interval. We consider the timed language $\mathcal{D} \subseteq \mathbb{T}\Sigma^+$ of timed words $w = (a_1, t_1)...(a_n, t_n)$ where $a_1...a_n$ is a sequence of correctly nested brackets and, for all $i < j$ such that $a_i = b$ and $a_j = \bar{b}$ are two matching brackets, the time distance $t_j - t_i$ is in the interval I. Consider the weighted timed language $\mathbb{W}_\mathcal{D} : \mathbb{T}\Sigma^+ \to \mathbb{R}_{\geq 0} \cup \{\infty\}$ such that $\mathbb{W}_\mathcal{D}(w) = \infty$ for all $w \notin \mathcal{D}$ and, for every $w \in \mathcal{D}$, $\mathbb{W}_\mathcal{D}(w)$ is the minimal time distance between matching brackets in w. Let $\mathbb{L}\text{TROP}$ be the timed semiring of Example 2.1 (a). We show that $\mathbb{W}_\mathcal{D}$ is pushdown recognizable over $\mathbb{L}\text{TROP}$. Let $\text{id} : \mathbb{R}_{\geq 0} \to \mathbb{R}_{\geq 0}$ with $\text{id}(t) = t$ for all t. Consider the WTPDA $\mathcal{A}$ over Σ and $\mathbb{L}\text{TROP}$ depicted in Fig. 1 with the stack alphabet $\Gamma = \{\gamma, \delta\}$, $\text{wt}(\gamma) = \bar{1}$, $\text{wt}(\delta) = \text{id}$, and $\text{wt}(e) = 0$ for all edges e of $\mathcal{A}$. Then $[\![\mathcal{A}]\!] = \mathbb{W}_\mathcal{D}$. For instance, let $I = [0, 3]$ and $w = (b, 0)(b, 1)(\bar{b}, 2)(\bar{b}, 3) \in \mathcal{D}$. Then there are two runs of $\mathcal{A}$ on w: the run ρ

$$\langle 1, \varepsilon \rangle \vdash_{0, \text{push}(\gamma)} \langle 1, (\gamma, 0) \rangle \vdash_{1, \text{push}(\delta)} \langle 2, (\delta, 0)(\gamma, 1) \rangle \vdash_{1, \text{pop}(\delta, I)} \langle 3, (\gamma, 2) \rangle \vdash_{1, \text{pop}(\gamma, I)} \langle 3, \varepsilon \rangle$$

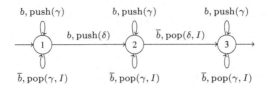

Fig. 1. The WTPDA $\mathcal{A}$ of example 2.4

with $\mathrm{wt}(\rho) = \mathrm{id}(1) = 1$ and the run ρ'

$$\langle 1,\varepsilon \rangle \vdash_{0,\mathrm{push}(\delta)} \langle 2,(\delta,0)\rangle \vdash_{1,\mathrm{push}(\gamma)} \langle 2,(\gamma,0)(\delta,1)\rangle \vdash_{1,\mathrm{pop}(\gamma,I)} \langle 2,(\delta,2)\rangle \vdash_{1,\mathrm{pop}(\delta,I)} \langle 3,\varepsilon\rangle$$

with $\mathrm{wt}(\rho') = \mathrm{id}(3) = 3$. Here, for simplicity, we write in $\vdash_{t,\mathrm{st}}$ a stack command st instead of an edge e. Then $[\![\mathcal{A}]\!](w) = \min\{\mathrm{wt}(\rho), \mathrm{wt}(\rho')\} = 1 = \mathsf{W}_\mathcal{D}(w)$.

3   Weighted Timed Matching Logic

The goal of this section is to develop a logical formalism which is expressively equivalent to WTPDA defined before. Our logic will use binary *matchings* introduced by Lautemann, Schwentick and Thérien [18] for context-free languages as well as the approach of Droste and Gastin [11] to weighted logic over semirings. Moreover, we augment our logic with the possibility to measure the time distance between matched positions:

- we will be able to check whether this time distance belongs to a given interval (in order to model the timed stack);
- we will also be able to apply a function from a timed semiring to the time distance between matched positions (in order to model the storing costs in the timed stack).

As in [6], in order to describe easily boolean properties, we introduce two levels of formulas: boolean and weighted. We operate with the boolean formulas as in the usual logic. On the weighted level, we add weights and extend the logical operations by computations in a semiring.

Let V_1 and V_2 be countable pairwise disjoint sets of first-order and second-order variables. We also fix a *matching variable* $\mu \notin V_1 \cup V_2$. Let $V = V_1 \cup V_2 \cup \{\mu\}$.

Let Σ be an alphabet and $\mathbb{S} = (S, \mathcal{F}, +, \cdot, 0, \mathbb{1})$ a timed semiring. The set **wTML**$(\Sigma, \mathbb{S})$ of *weighted timed matching formulas* is the set of all formulas of the form $\bigoplus \mu.\varphi$ where φ is produced by the grammar

$$\beta ::= P_a(x) \mid x \leq y \mid x \in X \mid \mu(x,y) \in I \mid \beta \vee \beta \mid \neg\beta \mid \exists x.\beta \mid \exists X.\beta$$
$$\varphi ::= \beta \mid s \mid f(\mu - x) \mid \varphi \oplus \varphi \mid \varphi \otimes \varphi \mid \bigoplus x.\varphi \mid \bigoplus X.\varphi \mid \bigotimes x.\varphi$$

with $a \in \Sigma$, $s \in S$, $f \in \mathcal{F}$, $I \in \mathcal{I}$, $x,y \in V_1$ and $X \in V_2$. The formulas β are called *boolean-valued* (or, simply, *boolean*) over Σ. Let **BOOL**(Σ) denote the set of all boolean formulas over Σ. The formulas of the form $\mu(x,y) \in I$ are called *distance matchings.* For a formula $\mu(x, y) \in [0, \infty)$ we will simply write $\mu(x, y)$. Using boolean formulas, we define the formulas $x < y$, $x = y$, $\beta_1 \wedge \beta_2$, $\forall x.\beta$, $\forall X.\beta$, $\beta_1 \to \beta_2$ and $\beta_1 \leftrightarrow \beta_2$ as usual.

The $\mathbf{wTML}(\Sigma, \mathbb{S})$-formulas are interpreted over timed words over Σ and assignments of variables. Let $w \in \mathbb{T}\Sigma^+$ be a timed word and $\mathrm{dom}(w) = \{1, ..., |w|\}$, the *domain* of w. We say that a binary relation $M \subseteq \mathrm{dom}(w) \times \mathrm{dom}(w)$ is a *matching* on w (cf. [18]) if:

- M is compatible with $<$, i.e., whenever $(i, j) \in M$, we have $i < j$;
- each element $i \in \mathrm{dom}(w)$ belongs to at most one pair in M;
- M is *noncrossing*, i.e., whenever $(i, j), (u, v) \in M$ with $i < u < j$, we have $i < v < j$.

Let $\mathrm{Match}(w)$ denote the set of all matchings on w.

A *w-assignment* is a mapping $\sigma : V \to \mathrm{dom}(w) \cup 2^{\mathrm{dom}(w)} \cup \mathrm{Match}(w)$ such that $\sigma(V_1) \subseteq \mathrm{dom}(w)$, $\sigma(V_2) \subseteq 2^{\mathrm{dom}(w)}$ and $\sigma(\mu) \in \mathrm{Match}(w)$. Let $\mathbb{T}\Sigma_V^+$ denote the set of all pairs (w, σ) where $w \in \mathbb{T}\Sigma^+$ and σ is a w-assignment.

Let σ be a w-assignment. For $x \in V_1$ and $j \in \mathrm{dom}(w)$, the *update* $\sigma[x/j]$ is the w-assignment defined by $\sigma[x/j](x) = j$ and $\sigma[x/j](y) = \sigma(y)$ for all $y \in V \setminus \{x\}$. Similarly, for $X \in V_2$ and $J \subseteq \mathrm{dom}(w)$, we define the update $\sigma[X/J]$ and, for $M \in \mathrm{Match}(w)$, the update $\sigma[\mu/M]$.

For a formula $\beta \in \mathbf{BOOL}(\Sigma)$, a timed word $w = (a_1, t_1)...(a_n, t_n) \in \mathbb{T}\Sigma^+$ and a w-assignment σ, we define the *satisfaction relation* $(w, \sigma) \models \beta$ inductively on the structure of β as shown in Table 1. Now let $\psi \in \mathbf{wTML}(\Sigma, \mathbb{S})$. The *semantics* of ψ is the mapping $[\![\psi]\!] : \mathbb{T}\Sigma^+ \to S$ defined inductively on the structure of ψ as shown in Table 2.

Given a formula $\psi \in \mathbf{wTML}(\Sigma, \mathbb{S})$, the set $\mathrm{Free}(\psi)$ of *free variables* of ψ is defined as usual. We say that ψ is a *sentence* if $\mathrm{Free}(\psi) = \emptyset$. Clearly, the semantics of a sentence ψ does not depend on a variable assignment. Then, we may consider the semantics of ψ as the weighted timed language $[\![\psi]\!] : \mathbb{T}\Sigma^+ \to S$.

Remark 3.1. (a) Let $\mathbb{1}\mathrm{BOOL}$ be the timed semiring of Example 2.1 (b). If in the definition of $\mathbf{wTML}(\Sigma, \mathbb{1}\mathrm{BOOL})$ we replace the quantitative formulas $\mu(x, y) \in I$ by the qualitative formulas $\mu(x, y)$, then the timed part of the timed words will be irrelevant and we obtain the matching logic of [18] for context-free languages.

Table 1. The satisfaction relation for boolean formulas

$(w, \sigma) \models P_a(x)$	$\Leftrightarrow a_{\sigma(x)} = a$
$(w, \sigma) \models x \leq y$	$\Leftrightarrow \sigma(x) \leq \sigma(y)$
$(w, \sigma) \models x \in X$	$\Leftrightarrow \sigma(x) \in \sigma(X)$
$(w, \sigma) \models \mu(x, y) \in I$	$\Leftrightarrow (\sigma(x), \sigma(y)) \in \sigma(\mu)$ and $t_{\sigma(y)} - t_{\sigma(x)} \in I$
$(w, \sigma) \models \varphi_1 \vee \varphi_2$	$\Leftrightarrow (w, \sigma) \models \varphi_1$ or $(w, \sigma) \models \varphi_2$
$(w, \sigma) \models \neg\varphi$	$\Leftrightarrow (w, \sigma) \models \varphi$ does not hold
$(w, \sigma) \models \exists x.\varphi$	$\Leftrightarrow \exists j \in \mathrm{dom}(w) : (w, \sigma[x/j]) \models \varphi$
$(w, \sigma) \models \exists X.\varphi$	$\Leftrightarrow \exists J \subseteq \mathrm{dom}(w) : (w, \sigma[X/J]) \models \varphi$

Table 2. The semantics of weighted timed matching formulas

$$[\beta](w,\sigma) \quad = \begin{cases} 1, & \text{if } (w,\sigma) \models \beta, \\ 0, & \text{otherwise} \end{cases}$$

$$[s](w,\sigma) \quad = s$$

$$[f(\mu - x)](w,\sigma) = \begin{cases} f(t_j - t_{\sigma(x)}), & \text{if } (\sigma(x), j) \in \sigma(\mu) \text{ for some } j, \\ 1, & \text{otherwise} \end{cases}$$

$$[\varphi_1 \oplus \varphi_2](w,\sigma) \quad = [\varphi_1](w,\sigma) + [\varphi_2](w,\sigma)$$

$$[\varphi_1 \otimes \varphi_2](w,\sigma) \quad = [\varphi_1](w,\sigma) \cdot [\varphi_2](w,\sigma)$$

$$[\bigoplus x.\varphi](w,\sigma) \quad = \sum \left([\varphi](w,\sigma[x/i]) \mid i \in \mathrm{dom}(w)\right)$$

$$[\bigoplus X.\varphi](w,\sigma) \quad = \sum \left([\varphi](w,\sigma[X/I]) \mid I \subseteq \mathrm{dom}(w)\right)$$

$$[\bigotimes x.\varphi](w,\sigma) \quad = \prod \left([\varphi](w,\sigma[x/i]) \mid i \in \mathrm{dom}(w)\right)$$

$$[\bigoplus \mu.\varphi](w,\sigma) \quad = \sum \left([\varphi](w,\sigma[\mu/M]) \mid M \in \mathrm{Match}(w)\right)$$

(b) If we exclude the formulas $\mu(x,y) \in I$ and $f(\mu - x)$ from the definition of φ and β in $\mathbf{wTML}(\Sigma, \mathbb{S})$, then the formulas of the form $\bigoplus \mu.(\neg \exists x. \exists y. \mu(x,y) \otimes \varphi)$ correspond to the weighted MSO logic of Droste and Gastin [11].

Example 3.2. Let $\mathbb{W}_D : \mathbb{T}\Sigma^+ \to \mathbb{R}_{\geq 0}$ be the WTL of Example 2.4. Recall that $b = [$ and $\overline{b} =]$. Consider the $\mathbf{BOOL}(\Sigma)$-formula

$$\beta(\mu) = \forall x.([P_b(x) \to \exists y.\mu(x,y)] \wedge [P_{\overline{b}}(x) \to \exists y.\mu(y,x)])$$

which demands that for every opening bracket there is a matched closing bracket and vice versa. Then the WTL $\mathbb{W}_D$ can be described by the following $\mathbf{wTML}(\Sigma, \mathbb{L}\mathrm{Trop})$-sentence:

$$\psi = \bigoplus \mu.([\beta(\mu) \wedge \forall x. \forall y.(\mu(x,y) \to \mu(x,y) \in I)] \otimes \bigoplus x.(\exists y.\mu(x,y) \otimes \mathrm{id}(\mu - x)))$$

where id is defined as in Example 2.4. Note that the boolean subformula of ψ in the square brackets checks whether a timed word belongs to $\mathcal{D}$ (cf. Example 2.4). Then, the formula $\bigoplus x.(\exists y.\mu(x,y) \otimes \mathrm{id}(\mu - x))$ computes the minimal time distance between matching brackets.

Next we show that, as in [11], the logical $\otimes$- and $\bigotimes x.$-operators of $\mathbf{wTML}$ in general are not stable with respect to recognizability by WTPDA.

Example 3.3. Here we show that the use of a formula $f(\mu - x)$ in the scope of a quantifier $\bigotimes y$ with $y \neq x$ can lead to unrecognizability by WTPDA.

Let $\Sigma = \{a\}$ be a singleton alphabet and $\mathbb{L}\mathrm{Trop}$ the timed semiring of Example 2.1 (a). Let $\beta(\mu) \in \mathbf{BOOL}(\Sigma)$ denote the formula $\forall x. \forall y.(\mu(x,y) \leftrightarrow \forall z.(x \leq z \leq y))$. Consider the $\mathbf{wTML}(\Sigma, \mathbb{L}\mathrm{Trop})$-sentence

$$\psi = \bigoplus \mu.(\beta(\mu) \otimes \bigoplus x. \bigotimes y.[(x \leq y) \otimes \mathrm{id}(\mu - x)]).$$

For $n \in \mathbb{N} \setminus \{0,1\}$, let $w_n = (a,0)^{n-1}(a,n) \in \mathbb{T}\Sigma^+$. Then $[\psi](w_n) = n^2$.

Suppose that there exists a WTPDA $\mathcal{A}$ over Σ and $\mathbb{L}\text{TROP}$ with $[\![\mathcal{A}]\!] = [\![\psi]\!]$. We may assume that $\mathcal{A}$ does not contain edges of the infinite weight. Let $M \in \mathbb{R}_{\geq 0}$ be the maximal value of all m which are either weights of edges of $\mathcal{A}$ or appear in functions $t \mapsto m \cdot t$ which are the weights of the stack letters. Let $n \in \mathbb{N}\setminus\{0,1\}$ and $\rho \in \text{Run}_{\mathcal{A}}(w_n)$. Then $\text{wt}(\rho) \leq 2Mn$. Since $[\![\mathcal{A}]\!](w_n) = n^2 \neq \infty$, we have $n^2 = [\![\mathcal{A}]\!](w_n) \leq 2Mn$ which is false for big enough n. A contradiction. Hence the WTL $[\![\psi]\!]$ is not pushdown recognizable over $\mathbb{L}\text{TROP}$.

Example 3.4. Here we show that the nested use of quantifiers $\bigotimes y$ can lead to unrecognizability by WTPDA. Consider the **wTML**$(\Sigma, \mathbb{L}\text{TROP})$-sentence

$$\psi' = \bigoplus\mu.(\beta(\mu) \otimes \bigotimes x.\bigotimes y.[(\exists z.z < x) \oplus ((\forall z.x \leq z) \otimes \text{id}(\mu - x))])$$

where $\beta(\mu)$ is defined as in the previous example. Then $[\![\psi']\!] = [\![\psi]\!]$ where ψ is defined as in the previous example. Hence the WTL $[\![\psi']\!]$ is not pushdown recognizable over $\mathbb{L}\text{TROP}$.

Example 3.5. Here we show that the use of formulas $f(\mu-x)\otimes g(\mu-x)$ with $f, g \in \mathcal{F}$ can lead to the unrecognizability. Consider the timed semiring EXP TROP of Example 2.1 (c). Let $f_1 : t \mapsto e^t$ and $f_2 : t \mapsto e^{2t}$. Let $\Sigma = \{a\}$ be a singleton alphabet. Consider the **wTML**$(\Sigma, \text{EXP TROP})$-sentence

$$\psi = \bigoplus\mu.(\beta(\mu) \otimes \bigotimes x.(f_1(\mu - x) \otimes f_2(\mu - x))$$

where $\beta(\mu) = \exists x.\exists y.(x < y \wedge \forall z.(z = x \vee z = y) \wedge \mu(x,y))$. For $t \in \mathbb{R}_{\geq 0}$, let $w_t = (a,0)(a,t) \in \mathbb{T}\Sigma^+$. Then $[\![\psi]\!](w_t) = e^t + e^{2t}$. Suppose that there exists a WTPDA $\mathcal{A}$ over Σ and EXP TROP with $[\![\mathcal{A}]\!] = [\![\psi]\!]$. Then, for every $t \in \mathbb{R}_{\geq 0}$, there exist $s(t), c(t) \in \mathbb{R}_{\geq 0}$ with $[\![\mathcal{A}]\!](w_t) = s(t) + e^{c(t)\cdot t}$. Moreover, the sets $\{s(t) \mid t \in \mathbb{R}_{\geq 0}\}$ and $\{c(t) \mid t \in \mathbb{R}_{\geq 0}\}$ are finite. Then for a big enough value $t_0 \in \mathbb{R}_{\geq 0}$ and all $t \geq t_0$ we have $c(t) = \frac{\ln(e^t + e^{2t} - s(t))}{t}$. So $c(t)$ has infinitely many values. A contradiction.

Motivated by these examples, we introduce a syntactically restricted fragment of **wTML** as follows. As in [11], we restrict the use of the $\bigotimes x$-quantifier to the *almost boolean formulas*. In contrast to [11], we have new formulas of the form $f(\mu - x)$ for which we have to take into account the situations described in Examples 3.3 and 3.4.

For $x \in V_1$, the set **aBOOL**$(\Sigma, \mathbb{S}, x)$ of *almost boolean formulas* over $\Sigma, \mathbb{S}$ and x is generated by the grammar

$$\gamma ::= \beta \mid s \otimes f(\mu - x) \mid \gamma \oplus \gamma \mid \beta \otimes \gamma$$

where $s \in \mathbb{S}$, $f \in \mathcal{F}$ and $\beta \in \textbf{BOOL}(\Sigma)$.

Definition 3.6. Restricted weighted timed matching logic **wTML**$^{\text{res}}(\Sigma, \mathbb{S}) \subseteq$ **wTML**$(\Sigma, \mathbb{S})$ is defined to be the set of all formulas of the form $\bigoplus\mu.\varphi$ where φ is produced by the grammar

$$\varphi ::= \beta \mid s \otimes f(\mu - x) \mid \varphi \oplus \varphi \mid \beta \otimes \varphi \mid \bigoplus x.\varphi \mid \bigoplus X.\varphi \mid \bigotimes x.\gamma$$

with $\beta \in \textbf{BOOL}(\Sigma, \mathbb{S})$, $s \in \mathbb{S}$, $f \in \mathcal{F}$, $x \in V_1$, $X \in V_2$ *and* $\gamma \in$ **aBOOL**$(\Sigma, \mathbb{S}, x)$.

Remark 3.7. Note that, in the logical fragments **aBOOL**$(\Sigma, \mathbb{S}, x)$ and **wTML**$^{\text{res}}(\Sigma, \mathbb{S})$, a constant $s \in S$ can be expressed by means of the formula $s \otimes \bar{\mathbb{1}}(\mu - x)$. Moreover, a formula $f(\mu - x)$ can be expressed by means of the formula $\mathbb{1} \otimes f(\mu - x)$.

Our main result is the following theorem.

Theorem 3.8. *Let Σ be an alphabet, $\mathbb{S} = (S, \mathcal{F}, +, \cdot, \mathbb{0}, \mathbb{1})$ a timed semiring and $\mathbb{W} : \mathbb{T}\Sigma^+ \to S$ a WTL. Then $\mathbb{W}$ is pushdown recognizable over $\mathbb{S}$ iff $\mathbb{W}$ is* **wTML**$^{\text{res}}(\Sigma, \mathbb{S})$-*definable.*

We will prove this theorem in Sect. 6.

4   Visibly Pushdown Languages

For the rest of the paper, we fix a special stack symbol $\perp$.

A *pushdown alphabet* is a triple $\tilde{\Sigma} = \langle \Sigma^{\text{push}}, \Sigma^{\#}, \Sigma^{\text{pop}} \rangle$ with pairwise disjoint sets Σ^{push}, $\Sigma^{\#}$ and Σ^{pop} of *push*, *local* and *pop* letters, respectively. Let $\Sigma = \Sigma^{\text{push}} \cup \Sigma^{\#} \cup \Sigma^{\text{pop}}$. A *visibly pushdown automaton (VPA)* over $\tilde{\Sigma}$ is a tuple $\mathcal{A} = (Q, \Gamma, Q_0, T, Q_f)$ where Q is a finite set of states, $Q_0, Q_f \subseteq Q$ are sets of initial resp. final states, Γ is a stack alphabet with $\perp \notin \Gamma$, and $T = T^{\text{push}} \cup T^{\#} \cup T^{\text{pop}}$ is a set of transitions where $T^{\text{push}} \subseteq Q \times \Sigma^{\text{push}} \times \Gamma \times Q$ is a set of push transitions, $T^{\#} \subseteq Q \times \Sigma^{\#} \times Q$ is a set of local transitions and $T^{\text{pop}} \subseteq Q \times \Sigma^{\text{pop}} \times (\Gamma \cup \{\perp\}) \times Q$ is a set of pop transitions.

We define the label of a transition $\tau \in T$ depending on its sort as follows. If $\tau = (p, c, \gamma, p') \in T^{\text{push}} \cup T^{\text{pop}}$ or $\tau = (p, c, p') \in T^{\#}$, we let $\text{label}(\tau) = c$, so $c \in \Sigma^{\text{push}} \cup \Sigma^{\text{pop}}$ resp. $c \in \Sigma^{\#}$.

A *configuration* of $\mathcal{A}$ is a pair $\langle q, u \rangle$ where $q \in Q$ and $u \in \Gamma^*$. Let $\tau \in T$ be a transition. Then, we define the transition relation $\vdash_\tau$ on configurations of $\mathcal{A}$ as follows. Let $c = \langle q, u \rangle$ and $c' = \langle q', u' \rangle$ be configurations of $\mathcal{A}$.

- If $\tau = (p, a, \gamma, p') \in T^{\text{push}}$, then we put $c \vdash_\tau c'$ iff $p = q$, $p' = q'$ and $u' = \gamma u$.
- If $\tau = (p, a, p') \in T^{\#}$, then we put $c \vdash_\tau c'$ iff $p = q$, $p' = q'$ and $u' = u$,
- If $\tau = (p, a, \gamma, p') \in T^{\text{pop}}$ with $\gamma \in \Gamma \cup \{\perp\}$, then we put $c \vdash_\tau c'$ iff $p = q$, $p' = q'$ and either $\gamma \neq \perp$ and $u = \gamma u'$, or $\gamma = \perp$ and $u' = u = \varepsilon$.

We say that $c = \langle q, u \rangle$ is an *initial* configuration if $q \in Q_0$ and $u = \varepsilon$. We call c a *final* configuration if $q \in Q_f$. A *run* of $\mathcal{A}$ is a sequence $\rho = c_0 \vdash_{\tau_1} c_1 \vdash_{\tau_2} ... \vdash_{\tau_n} c_n$ where $c_0, c_1, ..., c_n$ are configurations of $\mathcal{A}$ such that c_0 is initial, c_n is final and $\tau_1, ..., \tau_n \in T$. Let $\text{label}(\rho) = \text{label}(\tau_1) ... \text{label}(\tau_n) \in \Sigma^+$, the *label* of ρ. Let $\mathcal{L}(\mathcal{A}) = \{w \in \Sigma^+ \mid \text{there exists a run } \rho \text{ of } \mathcal{A} \text{ with } \text{label}(\rho) = w\}$. We say that a language $\mathcal{L} \subseteq \Sigma^+$ is a *visibly pushdown language* over $\tilde{\Sigma}$ if there exists a VPA $\mathcal{A}$ over Σ with $\mathcal{L}(\mathcal{A}) = \mathcal{L}$.

Remark 4.1. Note that we do not demand for final configurations that $u = \varepsilon$ and we can read a pop letter even if the stack is empty (using the special stack symbol $\perp$). This permits to consider the situations where some pop letters are not balanced by push letters and vice versa.

We say that a VPA $\mathcal{A} = (Q, \Gamma, Q_0, T, Q_f)$ is *deterministic* [4] if $|Q_0| = 1$ and for every $q \in Q$:

- for every $a \in \Sigma^{\text{push}}$, there is at most one transition of the form $(q, a, \gamma, q') \in T$,
- for every $a \in \Sigma^{\#}$, there is at most one transition of the form $(q, a, q') \in T$, and
- for every $a \in \Sigma^{\text{pop}}$ and $\gamma \in \Gamma$, there is at most one transition of the form $(q, a, \gamma, q') \in T$.

Note that in a deterministic VPA $\mathcal{A}$ for every word $w \in \Sigma^+$ there exists at most one run with label w.

Theorem 4.2. (Alur, Madhusudan [4]). *Let $\tilde{\Sigma}$ be a pushdown alphabet and $\mathcal{A}$ a VPA over $\tilde{\Sigma}$. Then there exists a deterministic VPA $\mathcal{A}'$ over $\tilde{\Sigma}$ with $\mathcal{L}(\mathcal{A}') = \mathcal{L}(\mathcal{A})$.*

We note that the visibly pushdown languages over $\tilde{\Sigma}$ form a proper subclass of the context-free languages over Σ, cf. [4] for further properties.

For any word $w = a_1...a_n \in \Sigma^+$, let $\text{MASK}(w) = b_1...b_n \in \{-1, 0, 1\}^+$ such that, for all $1 \le i \le n$, $b_i = 1$ if $a_i \in \Sigma^{\text{push}}$, $b_i = 0$ if $a_i \in \Sigma^{\#}$, and $b_i = -1$ otherwise. Let $\mathbb{L}(\tilde{\Sigma}) \subseteq \{-1, 0, 1\}^*$ be the language which contains ε and all words $b_1...b_n \in \{-1, 0, 1\}^+$ such that $\sum_{j=1}^{n} b_j = 0$ and $\sum_{j=1}^{i} b_j \ge 0$ for all $i \in \{1, ..., n\}$. Here, we interpret 1 as the left parenthesis, -1 as the right parenthesis and 0 as an irrelevant symbol. Then, $\mathbb{L}(\tilde{\Sigma})$ is the set of all sequences with correctly nested parentheses.

Next, we turn to the logic $\mathbf{MSO_L}(\tilde{\Sigma})$ over the pushdown alphabet $\tilde{\Sigma}$ which extends the classical MSO logic on finite words by the binary relation which checks whether a push letter and a pop letter are matching. This logic was shown in [4] to be equivalent to visibly pushdown automata. The logic $\mathbf{MSO_L}(\tilde{\Sigma})$ is defined by the grammar

$$\varphi ::= P_a(x) \mid x \le y \mid X(x) \mid \mathbb{L}(x, y) \mid \varphi \vee \varphi \mid \neg\varphi \mid \exists x.\varphi \mid \exists X.\varphi$$

where $a \in \Sigma$, $x, y \in V_1$ and $X \in V_2$. The formulas in $\mathbf{MSO_L}(\tilde{\Sigma})$ are interpreted over a word $w = a_1...a_n \in \Sigma^+$ and a variable assignment $\sigma : V_1 \cup V_2 \to \text{dom}(w) \cup 2^{\text{dom}(w)}$. We will write $(w, \sigma) \models \mathbb{L}(x, y)$ iff $\sigma(x) < \sigma(y)$, $a_{\sigma(x)} \in \Sigma^{\text{push}}$, $a_{\sigma(y)} \in \Sigma^{\text{pop}}$ and $\text{MASK}(a_{\sigma(x)+1}...a_{\sigma(y)-1}) \in \mathbb{L}(\tilde{\Sigma})$. For other formulas, the satisfaction relation is defined as usual. If φ is a sentence, then the satisfaction relation does not depend on a variable assignment and we can simply write $w \models \varphi$. For a sentence $\varphi \in \mathbf{MSO_L}(\tilde{\Sigma})$, let $\mathcal{L}(\varphi) = \{w \in \Sigma^+ \mid w \models \varphi\}$. We say that a language $\mathcal{L} \subseteq \Sigma^+$ is $\mathbf{MSO_L}(\tilde{\Sigma})$-*definable* if there exists a sentence $\varphi \in \mathbf{MSO_L}(\tilde{\Sigma})$ such that $\mathcal{L}(\varphi) = \mathcal{L}$.

The following result states the expressive equivalence of visibly pushdown automata and $\mathbf{MSO_L}$-logic.

Theorem 4.3. (Alur, Madhusudan [4]). *Let $\tilde{\Sigma} = \langle \Sigma^{\text{push}}, \Sigma^{\#}, \Sigma^{\text{pop}} \rangle$ be a pushdown alphabet, $\Sigma = \Sigma^{\text{push}} \cup \Sigma^{\#} \cup \Sigma^{\text{pop}}$, and $\mathcal{L} \subseteq \Sigma^+$ a language. Then, $\mathcal{L}$ is a visibly pushdown language over $\tilde{\Sigma}$ iff $\mathcal{L}$ is $\mathbf{MSO_L}(\tilde{\Sigma})$-definable.*

5   Decomposition of Weighted Timed Pushdown Automata

In this section we prove a Nivat-like (cf. [5,20]) decomposition theorem for WTPDA. This result establishes a connection between pushdown recognizable WTL and visibly pushdown languages of Alur and Madhusudan [4]. We will use this theorem for the proof of our Theorem 3.8. However, our result could be also of independent interest.

The key idea of our decomposition result is to consider a pushdown recognizable WTL as a renaming of a pushdown recognizable WTL over an extended alphabet which encodes the information about weights and a timed stack; on the level of this extended alphabet we can separate the setting of visibly pushdown languages from the weighted timed setting. Our separation technique appeals to the partitioning of $\mathbb{R}_{\geq 0}$ into finitely many intervals; this finite partition will be used for the construction of the desired extended alphabet.

A Nivat-like theorem for weighted timed automata without stack was given in [13] where a connection between recognizable weighted timed languages and unambiguously recognizable unweighted timed languages was established. This approach is not suitable for WTPDA since pushdown languages are not closed under intersection and the weights of the timed stack depend on the inner components of unweighted TPDA.

Let Σ be an alphabet and $\mathbb{S} = (S, \mathcal{F}, +, \cdot, \mathbb{0}, \mathbb{1})$ a timed semiring.

Let $k \in \mathbb{N}$ and $\hat{S} \subseteq S$, $\hat{\mathcal{F}} \subseteq \mathcal{F}$ be finite non-empty sets. Let $\mathbb{P}(k) = \{[0,0], (0,1), [1,1], (1,2), ..., [k,k], (k,\infty)\} \subseteq 2^{\mathcal{I}}$, the k-interval partition of $\mathbb{R}_{\geq 0}$. Let $\Delta = \{\text{push}, \#, \text{pop}\}$ and Ω be an alphabet. For each $\delta \in \Delta$, let $\mathcal{R}^{\delta} = \Omega \times \mathbb{P}(k) \times \hat{S} \times \hat{\mathcal{F}} \times \{\delta\}$. For our decomposition result, we will use the extended alphabet $\mathcal{R} = \mathcal{R}^{\text{push}} \cup \mathcal{R}^{\#} \cup \mathcal{R}^{\text{pop}}$ and the extended pushdown alphabet $\tilde{\mathcal{R}} = \langle \mathcal{R}^{\text{push}}, \mathcal{R}^{\#}, \mathcal{R}^{\text{pop}} \rangle$. Note that $\mathcal{R}$ and $\tilde{\mathcal{R}}$ depend on the variables k, $\hat{S}$, $\hat{\mathcal{F}}$ and Ω. However, we will not explicitly designate this dependence.

Let $\mathcal{T} \subseteq \mathbb{T}\mathcal{R}^+$ be the timed language defined as follows. Consider the timed word $w = (r_1, t_1)...(r_n, t_n) \in \mathbb{T}\mathcal{R}^+$ with $r_i = (\omega_i, I_i, s_i, f_i, \delta_i) \in \mathcal{R}$. Then we let $w \in \mathcal{T}$ iff the following hold:

- $\text{MASK}(r_1...r_n) \in \mathbb{L}(\tilde{\mathcal{R}})$;
- for all $i, i' \in \{1, ..., n\}$ with $i < i'$, $\delta_i = \text{push}$, $\delta_{i'} = \text{pop}$ and $\text{MASK}(r_{i+1}...r_{i'-1}) \in \mathbb{L}(\tilde{\mathcal{R}})$, we have $t_{i'} - t_i \in I_{i'}$.

Note that in the definition of $\mathcal{T}$ there are no restrictions on the components $\hat{S}$ and $\hat{\mathcal{F}}$ and that $\mathcal{T}$ is captured by a "simple" TPDA with a single state and a single stack letter; this TPDA processes the timed stack according to the information encoded in the additional components $\mathbb{P}(k)$ and Δ of the extended alphabet $\tilde{\mathcal{R}}$.

Let $\text{val}(\mathcal{T}) : \mathbb{T}\mathcal{R}^+ \to S$ denote the WTL defined as follows. For all $w \in \mathbb{T}\mathcal{R}^+ \setminus \mathcal{T}$, we let $\text{val}(\mathcal{T})(w) = \mathbb{0}$. For all $w = (r_1, t_1)...(r_n, t_n) \in \mathcal{T}$ with $r_j = (\omega_j, I_j, s_j, f_j, \delta_j)$, we let $\text{val}(\mathcal{T})(w) = \prod_{j=1}^{n}(s_j \cdot \phi_j)$ where $\phi_j = \mathbb{1}$ whenever $\delta_j \neq \text{pop}$ and $\phi_j = f_i(t_j - t_i)$ otherwise where $i < j$ and $\text{MASK}(r_i...r_j) \in \mathbb{L}(\tilde{\mathcal{R}})$.

We introduce the following operations.

– Let $\mathbb{W} : \mathbb{T}\mathcal{R}^+ \to S$ be a WTL and $\mathcal{L} \subseteq \mathcal{R}^+$ a language. Let $(\mathbb{W} \cap \mathcal{L}) : \mathbb{T}\mathcal{R}^+ \to S$ be the "restriction"of $\mathbb{W}$ to $\mathcal{L}$, i.e., for all $w = (r_1, t_1)...(r_n, t_n) \in \mathbb{T}\mathcal{R}^+$, we have: $(\mathbb{W} \cap \mathcal{L})(w) = \mathbb{W}(w)$ if $r_1...r_n \in \mathcal{L}$ and $(\mathbb{W} \cap \mathcal{L})(w) = 0$ otherwise.

– Let $\pi : \Omega \to \Sigma$ be a mapping called henceforth a *renaming*. For a letter $r = (\omega, I, s, f, \delta)$, let $h(r) = (h(\omega), I, s, f, \delta)$. For a word $w = (r_1, t_1)...(r_n, t_n) \in \mathbb{T}\mathcal{R}^+$, let $\pi(w) = (\pi(r_1), t_1)...(\pi(r_n), t_n) \in \mathbb{T}\Sigma^+$. For a WTL $\mathbb{W} : \mathbb{T}\mathcal{R}^+ \to S$, let $\pi(\mathbb{W}) : \mathbb{T}\Sigma^+ \to S$ be defined for all $w \in \mathbb{T}\Sigma^+$ as $\pi(\mathbb{W})(w) = \sum \big(\mathbb{W}(u) \mid u \in \mathbb{T}\mathcal{R}^+ \text{ and } \pi(u) = w \big)$.

Now we formulate our decomposition theorem.

Theorem 5.1. *Let Σ be an alphabet, $\mathbb{S} = (S, \mathcal{F}, +, \cdot, 0, 1)$ a timed semiring and $\mathbb{W} : \mathbb{T}\Sigma^+ \to S$ a WTL. Then the following are equivalent.*

(a) $\mathbb{W}$ is pushdown recognizable over $\mathbb{S}$.
(b) There exist $k \in \mathbb{N}$, alphabets $\hat{S} \subseteq S$, $\hat{\mathcal{F}} \subseteq \mathcal{F}$ and Ω, a visibly pushdown language $\mathcal{L} \subseteq \mathcal{R}^+$ over the pushdown alphabet $\tilde{\mathcal{R}}$, and a renaming $\pi : \Omega \to \Sigma$ such that $\mathbb{W} = \pi(\mathrm{val}(\mathcal{T}) \cap \mathcal{L})$.

First we show that (a) implies (b).

Lemma 5.2. *Let $\mathcal{A}$ be a WTPDA over Σ and $\mathbb{S}$. Then there exist $k \in \mathbb{N}$, finite non-empty sets $\hat{S} \subseteq S$ and $\hat{\mathcal{F}} \subseteq \mathcal{F}$, a visibly pushdown language $\mathcal{L} \subseteq \mathcal{R}^+$ over the pushdown alphabet $\tilde{\mathcal{R}}$, and a renaming $\pi : \Omega \to \Sigma$ such that $[\![\mathcal{A}]\!] = \pi(\mathrm{val}(\mathcal{T}) \cap \mathcal{L})$.*

Proof. Let $\mathcal{A} = (L, \Gamma, L_0, E, L_f, \mathrm{wt})$. If $E^{\mathrm{pop}} = \emptyset$, then let $k = 0$. Otherwise, let $k \in \mathbb{N}$ be the maximal natural number which appears in E (in the $\mathcal{S}(\Gamma)$-component of some edge in E^{pop}). Let $\hat{S} = \mathrm{wt}(E)$, $\hat{\mathcal{F}} = \mathrm{wt}(\Gamma)$ and $\Omega = E$. Consider the visibly pushdown automaton $\mathcal{A}' = (L, \Gamma, L_0, T, L_f)$ over the pushdown alphabet $\tilde{\mathcal{R}}$ where the set $T = T^{\mathrm{push}} \cup T^\# \cup T^{\mathrm{pop}}$ is defined as follows. We simulate every edge $e = (\ell \xrightarrow{a, \mathrm{st}} \ell') \in E$ with $\mathrm{wt}(e) = s$ by (possibly multiple) transitions in T depending on the sort of e as follows.

– Let $e \in E^{\mathrm{push}}$. Then we let $(\ell, r, \gamma, \ell') \in T^{\mathrm{push}}$ where $r = (e, [0, 0], s, \bar{1}, \mathrm{push})$.
– Let $e \in E^\#$. Then we let $(\ell, r, \ell') \in T^\#$ where $r = (e, [0, 0], s, \bar{1}, \#)$.
– Let $e \in E^{\mathrm{pop}}$ and $\mathrm{st} = (\mathrm{pop}, \gamma, I)$. Let $\mathrm{wt}(\gamma) = f$. Then we let $(\ell, r, \gamma, \ell') \in T^{\mathrm{pop}}$ for all $r = (a, \sigma, s, f, \mathrm{pop})$ with $\sigma \in \mathbb{P}(k)$ such that $\sigma \subseteq I$. Note that we do not have transitions in T^{pop} whose stack letter is $\bot$.

Note that although the emptiness of the stack at the end of run is not required by visibly pushdown automata, it is checked by intersection with the WTL $\mathrm{val}(\mathcal{T})$.

Let $\pi : \Omega \to \Sigma$ be defined as $\pi(e) = \mathrm{label}(e)$ for all $e \in \Omega$. Then $[\![\mathcal{A}]\!] = \pi(\mathrm{val}(\mathcal{T}) \cap \mathcal{L}(\mathcal{A}'))$. This can be shown using the intuition that the WTL $\mathrm{val}(\mathcal{T}) \cap \mathcal{L}(\mathcal{A}')$ checks whether a timed word over the extended alphabet $\mathcal{R}$ encodes a run of $\mathcal{A}$ and, if this is the case, computes the weight of this run; then the renaming π removes the auxiliary components of the extended alphabet and computes the sum of the weights of all runs over a given timed word. $\square$

Now we turn to the converse direction of Theorem 5.1.

Lemma 5.3. *Let $k \in \mathbb{N}$, $\hat{S} \subseteq S$, $\hat{\mathcal{F}} \subseteq \mathcal{F}$ and Ω be alphabets, and $\mathcal{L} \subseteq \mathcal{R}^{+}$ a visibly pushdown language over the pushdown alphabet $\tilde{\mathcal{R}}$. Then there exists a WTPDA $\mathcal{A}'$ over $\mathcal{R}$ and S such that $[\![\mathcal{A}']\!] = \mathrm{val}(T) \cap \mathcal{L}$.*

Proof. The main difficulty of the proof is to assign weights to the stack letters; note that they are encoded in the $\hat{\mathcal{F}}$-component of the extended alphabet $\mathcal{R}$. We proceed as follows. We take a deterministic VPA for $\mathcal{L}$. We mark the stack letters of $\mathcal{A}$ with a function from $\hat{\mathcal{F}}$ which will be the weight of this compound stack letter. Whenever we have to push a letter γ into the stack of $\mathcal{A}$, we nondeterministically push into the stack of $\mathcal{A}'$ all letters (γ, f) with $f \in \hat{\mathcal{F}}$. Whenever we pop a letter γ from the stack of $\mathcal{A}$, in $\mathcal{A}'$ we can pop only the pair (γ, f) where f is the $\hat{\mathcal{F}}$-component of the input $\mathcal{R}^{\mathrm{pop}}$-letter. Note that this construction is unambiguous, i.e., for every input word w there exists at most one run labeled by w.

By Theorem 4.2 there exists a deterministic visibly pushdown automaton $\mathcal{A} = (L, \Gamma, L_0, T, L_f)$ over the pushdown alphabet $\tilde{\mathcal{R}}$ such that $\mathcal{L}(\mathcal{A}) = \mathcal{L}$. Then we put $\mathcal{A}' = (L, \Gamma \times \hat{\mathcal{F}}, L_0, E, L_f, \mathrm{wt})$ where $E = E^{\mathrm{push}} \cup E^{\#} \cup E^{\mathrm{pop}}$ is defined as follows.

– For every push transition $t = (\ell, r, \gamma, \ell') \in T^{\mathrm{push}}$ with $r = (\omega, I, s, f, \mathrm{push})$ we let $e = (\ell \xrightarrow{r, (\mathrm{push}, (\gamma, \varphi))} \ell') \in E^{\mathrm{push}}$ for all $\varphi \in \hat{\mathcal{F}}$. Moreover, we put $\mathrm{wt}(e) = s$.
– For every local transition $t = (\ell, r, \ell') \in T^{\#}$ with $r = (\omega, I, s, f, \#)$ we let $e = (\ell \xrightarrow{r, \#} \ell') \in E^{\#}$. Moreover, we put $\mathrm{wt}(e) = s$.
– For every pop transition $t = (\ell, r, \gamma, \ell') \in T^{\mathrm{pop}}$ with $r = (\omega, I, s, f, \mathrm{pop})$ we let $e = (\ell \xrightarrow{r, (\mathrm{pop}, (\gamma, f), I)} \ell') \in E^{\mathrm{pop}}$. Moreover, we put $\mathrm{wt}(e) = s$.

For every stack letter $(\gamma, f) \in \Gamma \times \hat{\mathcal{F}}$, we let $\mathrm{wt}(\gamma, f) = f$. Then $[\![\mathcal{A}']\!] = \mathrm{val}(T) \cap \mathcal{L}$. □

Lemma 5.4. *Let $k \in \mathbb{N}$, $\hat{S} \subseteq S$, $\hat{\mathcal{F}} \subseteq \mathcal{F}$ and Ω be alphabets, $\mathbb{W} : \mathbb{T}\mathcal{R}^{+} \to S$ be a WTL which is pushdown recognizable over S, and $\pi : \Omega \to \Sigma$ a renaming. Then the WTL $\pi(\mathbb{W})$ is also pushdown recognizable over S.*

Proof. Our construction is a slight modification of the standard renaming construction for semiring-weighted automata [12].

Let $\mathcal{A} = (L, \Gamma, L_0, E, L_f, \mathrm{wt})$ be a WTPDA over $\mathcal{R}$ and S with $[\![\mathcal{A}]\!] = \mathbb{W}$. We consider the WTPDA $\mathcal{A}' = (L, \Gamma, L_0, E', L_f, \mathrm{wt}')$ over $\mathcal{R}$ and S where E' and wt' are defined as follows. For every edge $e = (\ell \xrightarrow{r, \mathrm{st}} \ell') \in E$ with $r \in \mathcal{R}$, let $\pi(e) = (\ell \xrightarrow{\pi(r), \mathrm{st}} \ell')$. Then we let $E' = \bigcup \{\pi(e) \mid e \in E\}$, $\mathrm{wt}'(e') = \sum (\mathrm{wt}(e) \mid e \in E$ and $\pi(e) = e')$ for all $e' \in E'$, and $\mathrm{wt}'(\gamma) = \mathrm{wt}(\gamma)$ for all $\gamma \in \Gamma$. Then $[\![\mathcal{A}']\!] = \pi([\![\mathcal{A}]\!])$. □

Now Theorem 5.1 (b) implies (a) is immediate by Lemmas 5.3 and 5.4.

6 Definability Equals Recognizability

In this section, we give a proof of Theorem 3.8.

First we show that definability by $\mathbf{wTML}^{\text{res}}(\Sigma, \mathbb{S})$-sentences implies recognizability by WTPDA. We follow a similar approach as in Theorem 6.6 of [13]. First, we transform a $\mathbf{wTML}^{\text{res}}(\Sigma, \mathbb{S})$-formula ψ into a canonical formula of the simpler form. Then, using Theorem 4.3, we establish for a canonical formula a decomposition of the form $\pi(\text{val}(\mathcal{T}) \cap \mathcal{L})$ as stated in Theorem 5.1. Then, by Theorem 5.1, the WTL $\llbracket \psi \rrbracket$ is pushdown recognizable over $\mathbb{S}$.

For $\varphi \in \mathbf{wTML}(\Sigma, \mathbb{S})$ and a finite set $\mathcal{V} = \{\mathcal{X}_1, ..., \mathcal{X}_k\} \subseteq V_1 \cup V_2$ of pairwise distinct variables $\mathcal{X}_1, ..., \mathcal{X}_k$, let $\bigoplus \mathcal{V}.\varphi$ denote the formula $\bigoplus \mathcal{X}_1...\bigoplus \mathcal{X}_k.\varphi$. In particular, we let $\bigoplus \emptyset.\varphi = \varphi$. We say that a sentence $\psi \in \mathbf{wTML}^{\text{res}}(\Sigma, \mathbb{S})$ is *canonical* if it is of the form $\psi = \bigoplus \mu.\bigoplus \mathcal{V}.\bigotimes x.\bigoplus_{i=1}^{l}(\beta_i \otimes s_i \otimes f_i(\mu - x))$ where $\mathcal{V} \subseteq V_1 \cup V_2$ is a finite set, $x \in V_1$, $l \geq 1$, $s_i \in S$, $f_i \in \mathcal{F}$ and $\beta_i \in \mathbf{BOOL}(\Sigma)$ such that, for every $(w, \sigma) \in \mathbb{T}\Sigma_V^+$, there exists exactly one $i \in \{1, ..., l\}$ with $(w, \sigma) \models \beta_i$. Let $\mathbf{wTML}^{\text{can}}(\Sigma, \mathbb{S})$ denote the set of all canonical sentences. Clearly, $\mathbf{wTML}^{\text{can}}(\Sigma, \mathbb{S}) \subseteq \mathbf{wTML}^{\text{res}}(\Sigma, \mathbb{S})$.

Lemma 6.1. *The logical fragments* $\mathbf{wTML}^{\text{can}}(\Sigma, \mathbb{S})$ *and* $\mathbf{wTML}^{\text{res}}(\Sigma, \mathbb{S})$ *are expressively equivalent.*

Proof. Let $\psi \in \mathbf{wTML}^{\text{res}}(\Sigma, \mathbb{S})$. We show that there exists a canonical sentence $\chi \in \mathbf{wTML}^{\text{can}}(\Sigma, \mathbb{S})$ with $\llbracket \chi \rrbracket = \llbracket \psi \rrbracket$. Let $\psi = \bigoplus \mu.\psi'$.

We say that a formula ζ is *semi-canonical* if it is of the form $\bigoplus \mathcal{V}.\bigotimes x.\gamma$ with $\gamma \in \mathbf{aBOOL}(\Sigma, \mathbb{S}, x)$. Note that here we do not quantify over the matching variable μ. First, we show by induction on the structure of a subformula ξ of ψ' that there exists a semi-canonical formula $\zeta(\xi)$ with $\text{Free}(\zeta(\xi)) = \text{Free}(\xi)$ and $\llbracket \zeta(\xi) \rrbracket = \llbracket \xi \rrbracket$.

- Let $x \in V_1$ and ξ be a maximal $\mathbf{aBOOL}(\Sigma, \mathbb{S}, x)$-subformula of ψ'. Let $y \in V_1$ be a fresh variable. First, assume that $x \in \text{Free}(\xi)$. Let $\xi[x/y] \in \mathbf{aBOOL}(\Sigma, \mathbb{S}, y)$ be obtained from ξ by replacing x by y. Then, we let $\zeta(\xi) = \bigoplus \emptyset.\bigotimes y.((x \neq y) \oplus (x = y) \otimes \xi[x/y])$.
  Now assume that $x \notin \text{Free}(\xi)$. Let $\min(y)$ denote the formula $\forall z.(y \leq z)$. Then, we let $\zeta(\xi) = \bigoplus \emptyset.\bigotimes y.((\neg \min(y)) \oplus (\min(y) \otimes \xi))$.
- Let $\xi = \xi_1 \oplus \xi_2$ be not almost boolean. By simple manipulations with formulas such as renamings of variables and assignments of concrete values to useless variables (e.g., V_1-variables are assigned to the first position of a word and V_2-variables to the empty set), we may assume that $\zeta(\xi_1) = \bigoplus \mathcal{V}.\bigotimes x.\gamma_1$ and $\zeta(\xi_2) = \bigoplus \mathcal{V}.\bigotimes x.\gamma_2$ with $\gamma_1, \gamma_2 \in \mathbf{aBOOL}(\Sigma, \mathbb{S}, x)$. Let $X \in V_2$ be a fresh variable. Then, we let $\zeta(\xi) = \bigoplus(\mathcal{V} \cup \{X\}).\bigotimes x.((\Psi_1 \otimes \gamma_1) \oplus (\Psi_2 \otimes \gamma_2))$ where $\Psi_1, \Psi_2 \in \mathbf{BOOL}(\Sigma)$ determine two distinct concrete values for X, e.g., $\Psi_1 = \neg \exists z.X(z)$ and $\Psi_2 = \forall z.X(z)$.
- Let $\xi = \beta \otimes \xi'$ with $\beta \in \mathbf{BOOL}(\Sigma)$. Let $\zeta(\xi') = \bigoplus \mathcal{V}.\bigotimes x.\gamma$. We may assume that the variables from $\mathcal{V} \cup \{x\}$ do not appear in β. Then we let $\zeta(\xi) = \bigoplus \mathcal{V}.\bigotimes x.(\beta \otimes \gamma)$.

- Let $\xi = \bigoplus \mathcal{X}.\xi'$ where $\mathcal{X} \in V_1 \cup V_2$. Let $\zeta(\xi') = \bigoplus \mathcal{V}.\bigotimes x.\gamma$. We may assume that $\mathcal{X} \notin \mathcal{V}$. Then we let $\zeta(\xi) = \bigoplus (\mathcal{V} \cup \{\mathcal{X}\}).\bigotimes x.\gamma$.
- Let $\xi = \bigotimes x.\gamma$ with $\gamma \in \mathbf{aBOOL}(\Sigma, \mathbb{S}, x)$. Then we let $\zeta(\xi) = \bigoplus \emptyset.\bigotimes x.\gamma$.

Next we show that every formula $\gamma \in \mathbf{aBOOL}(\Sigma, \mathbb{S}, x)$ can be transformed into a formula of the form $\pi(\gamma) = \bigoplus_{i=1}^{l}(\beta_i \otimes [\bigoplus_{j=1}^{r} s_{i,j} \otimes f_{i,j}(\mu - x)])$ where $l, r \geq 1$, $b_i \in \mathbf{BOOL}(\Sigma)$, $s_{i,j} \in S$, $f_{i,j} \in \mathcal{F}$ and, for every $(w, \sigma) \in \mathbb{T}\Sigma_V^+$, there exists exactly one $i \in \{1, ..., l\}$ with $(w, \sigma) \models \beta_i$. In other words, we show that $\mathrm{Free}(\pi(\gamma)) = \mathrm{Free}(\gamma)$ and $[\![\pi(\gamma)]\!] = [\![\gamma]\!]$. Again we proceed by induction on the structure of γ.

- Let $\gamma = \beta \in \mathbf{BOOL}(\Sigma)$. Then we define the formula $\pi(\gamma)$ as $\pi(\gamma) = (\beta \otimes [\mathbb{1} \otimes \bar{\mathbb{1}}(\mu - x)]) \oplus (\neg\beta \otimes [\mathbb{0} \otimes \bar{\mathbb{1}}(\mu - x)])$.
- Let $\gamma = s \otimes f(\mu - x)$. Then we let $\pi(\gamma) = \mathrm{TRUE} \otimes [s \otimes f(\mu - x)]$ where $\mathrm{TRUE} \in \mathbf{BOOL}(\Sigma)$ is a boolean sentence with $(w, \sigma) \models \mathrm{TRUE}$ for all $(w, \sigma) \in \mathbb{T}\Sigma_V^+$, e.g., $\mathrm{TRUE} = \forall x.(x \leq x)$.
- Let $\gamma = \gamma_1 \oplus \gamma_2$. Assume that $\pi(\gamma_1) = \bigoplus_{i=1}^{l}(\beta_i \otimes \kappa_i)$ such that $\kappa_i = \bigoplus_{j=1}^{r}[s_{i,j} \otimes f_{i,j}(\mu - x)]$. We assume also that $\pi(\gamma_2) = \bigoplus_{i'=1}^{l'}(\beta'_{i'} \otimes \kappa'_{i'})$ with $\kappa_{i'} = \bigoplus_{j'=1}^{r'}[s'_{i',j'} \otimes f'_{i',j'}(\mu - x)]$. Then we let

$$\pi(\gamma) = \bigoplus_{i=1}^{l}\bigoplus_{i'=1}^{l'}([\beta_i \wedge \beta'_{i'}] \otimes [\kappa_i \oplus \kappa'_{i'}]).$$

- Let $\gamma = \beta \otimes \gamma'$. Assume that $\pi(\gamma') = \bigoplus_{i=1}^{l}(\beta_i \otimes \kappa_i)$ such that $\kappa_i = \bigoplus_{j=1}^{r}[s_{i,j} \otimes f_{i,j}(\mu - x)]$. Then, we let $\pi(\gamma) = \bigoplus_{i=1}^{l}([\beta_i \wedge \beta] \otimes \kappa_i) \oplus (\neg\beta \otimes \kappa')$ with $\kappa' = \mathbb{0} \otimes \bar{\mathbb{1}}(\mu - x)$.

Our final goal is to resolve the sums $\bigoplus_{j=1}^{r} s_{i,j} \otimes f_{i,j}(\mu - x)$. They can be resolved using the fact that the formula $\bigotimes x.(\varphi_1 \oplus \varphi_2)$ is equivalent to the formula $\bigoplus X.\bigotimes x.([X(x) \otimes \varphi_1] \oplus [\neg X(x) \otimes \varphi_2])$.

By these transformations we obtain a canonical sentence $\chi \in \mathbf{wTML}^{\mathrm{can}}(\Sigma, \mathbb{S})$ with $[\![\chi]\!] = [\![\psi]\!]$. □

Lemma 6.2. *Let $\psi \in \mathbf{wTML}^{\mathrm{can}}(\Sigma, \mathbb{S})$. Then there exist a natural number k, alphabets $\hat{S} \subseteq S$ and $\hat{\mathcal{F}} \subseteq \mathcal{F}$ and Ω, a sentence $\varphi \in \mathbf{MSO}_{\mathbb{L}}(\tilde{\mathcal{R}})$, and a renaming $\pi : \Omega \to \Sigma$ such that $[\![\psi]\!] = \pi(\mathrm{val}(\mathcal{T}) \cap \mathcal{L}(\varphi))$.*

Proof. Here we use a similar idea as in the proof of Theorem 6.6 of [13].

Let $\psi = \bigoplus \mu.\bigoplus \mathcal{V}.\bigotimes x.\bigoplus_{i=1}^{l}(\beta_i \otimes s_i \otimes f_i(\mu - x))$ be a canonical formula. Assume that $\mathcal{V} = \{\mathcal{X}_1, ..., \mathcal{X}_p\}$ where $\mathcal{X}_1, ..., \mathcal{X}_p \in V_1 \cup V_2$ are pairwise distinct variables. If ψ does not contain any subformula of the form $\mu^I(x, y)$, then we let $k = 0$. Otherwise, let $k \in \mathbb{N}$ be the maximal natural number appearing as a lower or upper bound of some interval $I \in \mathcal{I}$ appearing in some subformula $\mu^I(x, y)$ of ψ. Let $\hat{S} = \{s_i \mid 1 \leq i \leq l\}$ and $\hat{\mathcal{F}} = \{f_i \mid 1 \leq i \leq l\}$. Let $\Omega = \Sigma \times 2^{\mathcal{V}}$. Let $\pi : \Omega \to \Sigma$ be the projection to the Σ-component. It remains to construct a sentence $\varphi \in \mathbf{MSO}_{\mathbb{L}}(\tilde{\mathcal{R}})$. For any formula $\beta \in \mathbf{BOOL}(\Sigma)$, let $\beta^* \in \mathbf{MSO}_{\mathbb{L}}(\tilde{\mathcal{R}})$ be obtained from β by the following substitutions.

– If $P_a(x)$ with $a \in \Sigma$ is a subformula of β, then $P_a(x)$ is replaced by the formula $\bigvee \left(P_{(a,\kappa)}(x) \mid \kappa \in 2^{\mathcal{V}} \times \mathbb{P}(k) \times \hat{S} \times \hat{\mathcal{F}} \times \Delta \right)$.

– If $\mu^I(x,y)$ is a subformula of β with $I \in \mathcal{I}$ such that either $I \subseteq [0,k]$ or $I = [k, \infty)$ or $I = (k, \infty)$, then $\mu^I(x,y)$ is replaced by the formula $\mathbb{L}(x,y) \wedge \bigvee \left(P_{(\omega, J, \kappa)}(y) \mid \omega \in \Omega, J \in \mathbb{P}(k) \text{ with } J \subseteq I, \kappa \in \hat{S} \times \hat{\mathcal{F}} \times \{\text{pop}\} \right)$.

For a variable $\mathcal{Z} \in \mathcal{V}$ and $x \in V_1$, let $G_{\mathcal{Z}}(x)$ denote an $\mathbf{MSO_L}(\tilde{\mathcal{R}})$-formula which demands that $\mathcal{Z}$ belongs to the $2^{\mathcal{V}}$-component of the letter at the position x. Using the standard Büchi encoding technique we construct the formula $\phi \in \mathbf{MSO_L}(\tilde{\mathcal{R}})$ which encodes the values of $\mathcal{V}$-variables in the $2^{\mathcal{V}}$-component of a timed word. We let $\phi = \forall x.\left(\bigwedge_{z \in \mathcal{V} \cap V_1} (G_z(y) \leftrightarrow (x = z)) \wedge \bigwedge_{Z \in \mathcal{V} \cap V_2} (G_Z(x) \leftrightarrow (x \in Z)) \right)$. For $s \in \hat{S}$ and $f \in \hat{\mathcal{F}}$ and $x \in V_1$, let $Q_{s,f}(x)$ denote the $\mathbf{MSO_L}(\tilde{\mathcal{R}})$-formula $\bigvee \left(P_{(\kappa, s, f, \delta)}(x) \mid \kappa \in \Omega \times \mathbb{P}(k), \delta \in \Delta \right)$.

In addition, we need a formula to "fix" the $\mathbb{P}(k)$-component of the letters in $\mathcal{R}^{\text{push}} \cup \mathcal{R}^{\#}$: $\zeta = \forall x. \left[\bigvee (P_r(x) \mid r \in \Omega \times \mathbb{P}(k) \times \hat{S} \times \hat{\mathcal{F}} \times \{\text{push}, \#\}) \rightarrow \bigvee (P_{(\omega, [0,0], \kappa)}(x) \mid \omega \in \Omega, \kappa \in \hat{S} \times \hat{\mathcal{F}} \times \Delta) \right]$. Then the sentence φ is defined as

$$\varphi = \exists \mathcal{X}_1 ... \exists \mathcal{X}_p. \left(\phi \wedge \zeta \wedge \forall x. \bigvee_{i=1}^{l} (\beta_i^* \wedge Q_{s_i, f_i}(x)) \right).$$

Note that the $\mathbf{MSO_L}(\tilde{\mathcal{R}})$-formulas $\beta_1^*, ..., \beta_l^*$ define a partition on the set of pairs (w, σ) where $w \in \mathbb{T}\mathcal{R}^+$ and σ is a variable assignment. Then, the $\hat{S}$- and $\hat{\mathcal{F}}$- components of the words satisfying φ are uniquely determined by this partition. Then $[\![\psi]\!] = \pi(\text{val}(\mathcal{T}) \cap \mathcal{L}(\varphi))$. □

As a corollary from Lemmas 6.1 and 6.2 and Theorems 4.3 and 5.1 we obtain:

Corollary 6.3. *Let $\psi \in \mathbf{wTML}^{\text{res}}(\Sigma, \mathbb{S})$ be a sentence. Then the WTL $[\![\psi]\!]$ is pushdown recognizable over $\mathbb{S}$.*

Now we turn to the converse direction of Theorem 3.8.

Lemma 6.4. *Let $\mathcal{A}$ be a WTPDA over Σ and $\mathbb{S}$. Then there exists a sentence $\psi \in \mathbf{wTML}^{\text{res}}(\Sigma, \mathbb{S})$ with $[\![\psi]\!] = [\![\mathcal{A}]\!]$.*

Proof. We prove this theorem by a direct translation. Let $\mathcal{A} = (L, \Gamma, L_0, E, L_f, \text{wt})$. Let $(e_i)_{1 \le i \le m}$ be an enumeration of E. We associate with every edge e_i a fresh second-order variable X_i which keeps track of positions where e_i is taken along a run of $\mathcal{A}$. Let $\overline{X} = (X_1, ..., X_m)$. Let $\beta(\overline{X}) \in \mathbf{BOOL}(\Sigma)$ denote the formula which demands that values of the variables $X_1, ..., X_m$ form a partition of the domain of an input timed word, the successive edges of a run are connected via the same location, the labels of edges are compatible with the label of a run, a run starts in L_0 and ends in L_f.

Whenever $e_i \in E^{\text{push}}$ assume that $e_i = \left(\ell_i \xrightarrow{a_i, \text{push}(\gamma_i)} \ell_i' \right)$. Whenever $e_i \in E^{\text{pop}}$ assume that $e_i = \left(\ell_i \xrightarrow{a_i, \text{pop}(\gamma_i, I_i)} \ell_i' \right)$. For $e_i \in E^{\text{pop}}$, let $\Phi_i = \text{wt}(\gamma_i) \in \mathcal{F}$.

For $e_i \in E^{\text{push}} \cup E^{\#}$, let $\Phi_i = \bar{1}$. Consider the **BOOL**(Σ)-formula

$$\text{STACK}(\overline{X}, \mu) = \forall x. \forall y. \left(\mu(x, y) \rightarrow \bigvee_{\substack{1 \leq i,j \leq m, \\ e_i \in E^{\text{push}}, \\ e_j \in E^{\text{pop}}, \\ \gamma_i = \gamma_j}} (X_i(x) \wedge X_j(y) \wedge \mu^{I_j}(x, y)) \right) \wedge$$

$$\forall x. \left(\exists y. (\mu(x, y) \vee \mu(y, x)) \vee \bigvee_{\substack{1 \leq i \leq m, \\ e_i \in E^{\#}}} X_i(x) \right)$$

which describes the functionality of the timed stack. Finally, we construct a formula which takes care of the weights:

$$\text{WEIGHTED}(\overline{X}, \mu) = \bigotimes x. \bigoplus_{i=1}^{m} (X_i(x) \otimes \text{wt}(e_i) \otimes \Phi_i(\mu - x)).$$

We let $\psi = \bigoplus \mu. \bigoplus X_1 ... \bigoplus X_m. ((\beta(\overline{X}) \wedge \text{STACK}(\overline{X}, \mu)) \otimes \text{WEIGHTED}(\overline{X}, \mu))$. Then $\psi \in \mathbf{wTML}^{\text{res}}(\Sigma, \mathbb{S})$ and $[\![\psi]\!] = [\![\mathcal{A}]\!]$. □

Proof of Theorem 3.8. Immediate by Corollary 6.3 and Lemma 6.4.

7   Weighted Timed Pushdown Automata with Global Clocks

Let Σ be an alphabet and $\mathbb{S} = (S, \mathcal{F}, +, \cdot, 0, 1)$ a timed semiring. In this section, we augment the model of WTPDA of Sect. 2 with a finite set of global clocks as in the classical timed automata [3]. Note that this extended model was considered in [2].

A *weighted timed pushdown automaton with global clocks* (GWTPDA) over Σ and $\mathbb{S}$ is a tuple $\mathcal{A} = (L, \Gamma, C, L_0, E, L_f, \text{wt})$ where $L, \Gamma, L_0, L_f, \text{wt}$ are defined as for WTPDA, C is a finite set of global clocks, and every edge $e : \ell \xrightarrow[\phi, \Lambda]{a, \text{st}} \ell'$ of E is augmented with two additional components: a constraint $\phi : C \rightarrow \mathcal{I}$ on global clocks (i.e., the edge e can be taken only if the value of every global clock $c \in C$ is in the interval $\phi(c)$) and a subset $\Lambda \subseteq C$ of global clocks to be reset after taking e. Then, every configuration of $\mathcal{A}$ is a triple $c = (\ell, u, \nu)$ where $\ell \in L$ is a location, $u \in \mathbb{T}\Gamma^*$ is a timed stack and $\nu : C \rightarrow \mathbb{R}_{\geq 0}$ is a global clock valuation. In all other respects, the behavior of $\mathcal{A}$ is defined as in Sect. 2.

As it was shown in [23], the performance of a global clock $c \in C$ can be described by means of the so-called *relative distance formula* $\overleftarrow{d}(D_c, x) \in I$ where $D_c \in V_2$, $x \in V_1$ and $I \in \mathcal{I}$. Here, the variable D_c keeps track of all positions where the clock c is reset. The relative distance $\overleftarrow{d}(D_c, x)$ measures the time between the last reset of c before the current position x, i.e., models the current value of the clock c. If such a second-order variable D_c is allowed to be quantified only in the existential prefix of a logical formula, then we obtain a logical fragment which is expressively equivalent to timed automata [23].

In order to give a logical characterization of GWTPDA, we modify the fragment $\mathbf{wTML}^{\mathrm{res}}(\Sigma, \mathbb{S})$ as follows. On the level of $\mathbf{BOOL}(\Sigma)$ we add relative distance predicates of the form $\overleftarrow{\mathrm{d}}(D_c, x) \in I$ and, for such a variable D_c, allow only the existential quantification $\bigoplus D_c$ in the prefix of φ (cf. Definition 3.6). So we obtain logic $\mathbf{wTML}^{\mathrm{res}}_{\mathrm{rd}}(\Sigma, \mathbb{S})$ (where rd stays for "relative distance").

Theorem 7.1. *Let Σ be an alphabet, $\mathbb{S} = (S, \mathcal{F}, +, \cdot, 0, 1)$ a timed semiring and $\mathbb{W} : \mathbb{T}\Sigma^+ \to S$ a WTL. Then, $\mathbb{W}$ is recognizable by a GWTPDA iff $\mathbb{W}$ is $\mathbf{wTML}^{\mathrm{res}}_{\mathrm{rd}}(\Sigma, \mathbb{S})$-definable.*

The proof of this theorem follows the same lines as the proof of Theorem 3.8 with several changes. The main difference is that we have to reflect the global clocks in the extended alphabet $\mathcal{R}$ and the extended pushdown alphabet $\tilde{\mathcal{R}}$. For every global clock c, we add the component $\mathbb{P}(k) \times \{0, 1\}$ where the k-interval partition $\mathbb{P}(k)$ takes care of the clock constraints and the $\{0, 1\}$-component indicates whether the clock was reset or not. Then, we correspondingly modify the definition of the timed language $\mathcal{T} \subseteq \mathbb{T}\mathcal{R}^+$.

Since the proof of Theorem 7.1 is constructive, as a corollary from our Theorem 7.1 and Theorem 1 of [2], we obtain:

Corollary 7.2. *Let $\mathbb{L}\mathrm{TROP}$ be the timed semiring of Example 2.1 (a). Then, it is decidable, given an alphabet Σ, a sentence $\psi \in \mathbf{wTML}^{\mathrm{res}}_{\mathrm{rd}}(\Sigma, \mathbb{S})$ and a threshold $\theta \in \mathbb{R}_{\geq 0}$, whether there exists a timed word $w \in \mathbb{T}\Sigma^+$ with $[\![\psi]\!](w) < \theta$.*

If we apply Theorem 7.1 to the timed semiring $1\mathrm{BOOL}$ of Example 2.1 (b) and exclude redundant formulas, then we obtain a logical characterization result for unweighted TPDA stated in [14].

8 Conclusion

We introduced a weighted logic on timed words which is expressively equivalent to WTPDA. Since the proof of our expressive equivalence result is constructive, decidability results for WTPDA can be transferred into corresponding decidability results for our new logic.

For the proof of the main result we proved a decomposition theorem for WTPDA establishing a connection between WTPDA and visibly pushdown languages. We believe that this result can be helpful for the further study of WTPDA. In addition, our proof technique is robust against adding new components of the model (e.g., global clocks as in Sect. 7) and could be applied in different contexts.

It would be also interesting to investigate the model of WTPDA with time-dependent costs for staying in locations (as in the model of weighted timed automata without stack, cf. [21]) and its logical characterization.

Acknowledgement. Yuri Gurevich' survey article [17] was a source of inspiration for the first named author when he got interested in monadic second-order logic. Due to stimulating friendly contact since 1981, the authors would like to dedicate their paper to Yuri Gurevich.

References

1. Abdulla, P.A., Atig, M.F., Stenman, J.: Dense-timed pushdown automata. In: LICS 2012, pp. 35–44. IEEE Computer Society (2012)
2. Abdulla, P.A., Atig, M.F., Stenman, J.: Computing optimal reachability costs in priced dense-timed pushdown automata. In: Dediu, A.-H., Martín-Vide, C., Sierra-Rodríguez, J.-L., Truthe, B. (eds.) LATA 2014. LNCS, vol. 8370, pp. 62–75. Springer, Heidelberg (2014)
3. Alur, R., Dill, D.L.: A theory of timed automata. Theoret. Comput. Sci. **126**(2), 183–235 (1994)
4. Alur, R., Madhusudan, P.: Visibly pushdown languages. In: STOC 2004, pp. 202–211. ACM (2004)
5. Berstel, J.: Transductions and Context-Free Languages. Teubner Studienbücher: Informatik. Teubner, Stuttgart (1979)
6. Bollig, B., Gastin, P.: Weighted versus probabilistic logics. In: Diekert, V., Nowotka, D. (eds.) DLT 2009. LNCS, vol. 5583, pp. 18–38. Springer, Heidelberg (2009)
7. Bouajjani, A., Echahed, R., Robbana, R.: On the automatic verification of systems with continuous variables and unbounded discrete data structures. In: Antsaklis, P.J., Kohn, W., Nerode, A., Sastry, S. (eds.) HS 1994. LNCS, vol. 999, pp. 64–85. Springer, Heidelberg (1995)
8. Bouyer, P., Fahrenberg, U., Larsen, K.G., Markey, N.: Timed automata with observers under energy constraints. In: HSCC 2010, pp. 61–70. ACM (2010)
9. Büchi, J.R.: Weak second order arithmetic and finite automata. Z. Math. Logik Grundlagen Informatik **6**, 66–92 (1960)
10. Dang, Z.: Pushdown timed automata: a binary reachability characterization and safety verification. Theoret. Comput. Sci. **302**, 93–121 (2003)
11. Droste, M., Gastin, P.: Weighted automata and weighted logics. Theoret. Comp. Sci. **380**(1–2), 69–86 (2007)
12. Droste, M., Kuich, W., Vogler, H. (eds.): Handbook of Weighted Automata. EATCS Monographs on Theoretical Computer Science. Springer, Heidelberg (2009)
13. Droste, M., Perevoshchikov, V.: A Nivat theorem for weighted timed automata and weighted relative distance logic. In: Esparza, J., Fraigniaud, P., Husfeldt, T., Koutsoupias, E. (eds.) ICALP 2014, Part II. LNCS, vol. 8573, pp. 171–182. Springer, Heidelberg (2014)
14. Droste, M., Perevoshchikov, V.: A logical characterization of timed pushdown languages. In: Beklemishev, L.D. (ed.) CSR 2015. LNCS, vol. 9139, pp. 189–203. Springer, Heidelberg (2015)
15. Elgot, C.C.: Decision problems of finite automata design and related arithmetics. Trans. Amer. Math. Soc. **98**, 21–51 (1961)
16. Emmi, M., Majumdar, R.: Decision problems for the verification of real-time software. In: Hespanha, J.P., Tiwari, A. (eds.) HSCC 2006. LNCS, vol. 3927, pp. 200–211. Springer, Heidelberg (2006)
17. Gurevich, Y.: Monadic theories. In: Barwise, J., Feferman, S. (eds.) Model-Theoretic Logics, pp. 479–506. Springer, Heidelberg (1985)
18. Lautemann, C., Schwentick, T., Thérien, D.: Logics for context-free languages. In: Pacholski, L., Tiuryn, J. (eds.) CSL 1994. LNCS, vol. 933. Springer, Heidelberg (1995)

19. Mathissen, C.: Weighted logics for nested words and algebraic formal power series. Log. Methods Comput. Sci. 6(1:5), 1–34 (2010)
20. Nivat, M.: Transductions des langages de Chomsky. Ann. de l'Inst. Fourier 18, 339–456 (1968)
21. Quaas, K.: MSO logics for weighted timed automata. Form. Methods Syst. Des. 38(3), 193–222 (2011)
22. Trakhtenbrot, B.A.: Finite automata and logic of monadic predicates. Doklady Akademii Nauk SSSR 140, 326–329 (1961). In Russian
23. Wilke, T.: Specifying timed state sequences in powerful decidable logics and timed automata. In: Langmaack, H., de Roever, W.-P., Vytopil, J. (eds.) FTRTFT 1994 and ProCoS 1994. LNCS, vol. 863, pp. 694–715. Springer, Heidelberg (1994)

Inherent Vacuity in Lattice Automata

Hila Gonen and Orna Kupferman[(⊠)]

School of Computer Science and Engineering, The Hebrew University,
Jerusalem, Israel
orna@cs.huji.ac.il

Abstract. *Vacuity checking* is traditionally performed after model checking has terminated successfully. It ensures that all the elements of the specification have played a role in its satisfaction by the system. The need to check the quality of specifications is even more acute in *property-based design*, where the specification is the only input, serving as a basis to the development of the system. *Inherent vacuity* adapts the theory of vacuity in model checking to the setting of property-based design. Essentially, a specification is inherently vacuous if it can be mutated into a simpler equivalent specification, which is known, in the case of specifications in linear temporal logic, to coincide with the fact the specification is satisfied vacuously in all systems.

A recent development in formal methods is an extension of the Boolean setting to a *multi-valued* one. In particular, instead of Boolean automata, which either accept or reject their input, there is a growing interest in weighted automata, which map an input word to a value from a semiring over a large domain. A distributive finite lattice is a special case of a semiring, and *lattice automata* are used in several methods for reasoning about multi-valued objects. We study inherent vacuity in the setting of lattice automata, namely the ability to mutate the value of a transition in the automaton without changing its language. We define the concept of inherent vacuity in lattice automata, study the complexity of deciding different types of vacuity, and relate the setting to the one known for linear temporal logics.

1 Introduction

In recent years, we see a growing awareness to the importance of assessing the quality of (formal) specifications. In the context of model checking, the quality of the specification is assessed by analyzing the effect of applying mutations to the formulas. If the system satisfies the mutated specification, we know that some elements of the specification do not play a role in its satisfaction, thus the specification is satisfied in some *vacuous* way [5,28]. Vacuity is successfully used

The research leading to these results has received funding from the European Research Council under the European Union's Seventh Framework Programme (FP7/2007–2013) / ERC grant agreement no 278410, and from The Israel Science Foundation (grant no 1229/10).

L.D. Beklemishev et al. (Eds.): Gurevich Festschrift II 2015, LNCS 9300, pp. 174–192, 2015.
DOI: 10.1007/978-3-319-23534-9_10

in order to improve specifications and detect design errors [26] and has been a subject of extensive research [4, 5, 10, 18, 28, 31].

Property assurance is the activity of eliciting specifications that faithfully capture designer intent [7,33]. Obvious quality checks one may perform for a given specification are *non-validity* and *satisfiability* [34]. More involved quality checks are studied in the PROSYD project [32]. As discussed in [33], checking vacuity of the specifications in the context of property assurance would be of great importance. While early work on vacuity was done in the context of model checking, researchers have also developed the concept of "vacuity without design" [13], which is formalized for linear temporal logic (LTL) formulas in [17], by means of *inherent vacuity*.

Consider a system S and a formula φ. We say that a subformula ψ of φ *does not affect the satisfaction of φ in S* if S also satisfies the formula $\forall x.\varphi[\psi \leftarrow x]$, in which ψ is replaced by a universally quantified proposition. Then, a formula φ is *vacuously satisfied* in S if φ has a subformula that does not affect its satisfaction in S [4]. Now, as defined in [17], the formula φ is inherently vacuous if there exists a subformula ψ of φ such that $\varphi \equiv \forall x.\varphi[\psi \leftarrow x]$ or, equivalently, if for every system S, if $S \models \varphi$, then S satisfies φ vacuously.

The framework in [17] studies specifications given by LTL formulas. A recent development in formal methods is an extension of the Boolean setting to a multivalued one. In particular, instead of Boolean automata, which either accept or reject their input, there is a growing interest in weighted automata, which map an input word to a value from a semiring over a large domain [15,30]. Focusing on applications in formal verification, the multi-valued setting arises directly in *quantitative verification* [21] and in reasoning about quality of systems [1], and indirectly in applications like *abstraction methods*, in which it is useful to allow the abstract system to have unknown assignments to atomic propositions and transitions [35], *query checking* [11], which can be reduced to model checking over multi-valued systems, and verification of systems from *inconsistent viewpoints* [23], in which the value of the atomic propositions is the composition of their values in the different viewpoints.

As mentioned above, in the multi-valued setting, the automata map words to a value from a semiring over a large domain. A *distributive finite lattice* is a special case of a semiring. A lattice $\langle A, \leq \rangle$ is a partially ordered set in which every two elements $a, b \in A$ have a least upper bound (a *join* b) and a greatest lower bound (a *meet* b). Finite lattices are useful in many of the applications of the multi-valued setting described above. For example (see Fig. 1), in the abstraction application, researchers use the lattice $\mathcal{L}_3$ of three fully ordered values [8], as well as its generalization to $\mathcal{L}_n$ [12]. In query checking, the lattice elements are sets of formulas, ordered by the inclusion order [9]. When reasoning about inconsistent viewpoints, each viewpoint is Boolean, and their composition gives rise to products of the Boolean lattice, as in $\mathcal{L}_{2,2}$ [16]. Finally, when specifying prioritized properties of system, one uses lattices in order to specify the priorities [3].

In a *nondeterministic lattice automaton* on finite words (LNFW, for short) [27], each transition is associated with a *transition value*, which is a lattice element. Intuitively, the value indicates the truth of the statement "the transition exists". Each state in the LNFW is associated with an *initial value* and an *acceptance value*, indicating the truth of the statements "the state is initial/accepting", respectively. The value of a run r of an LNFW $\mathcal{A}$ is the *meet* of the values of all the components of r: the initial value of the first state, the transition values of all the transitions taken along r, and the acceptance value of the last state. The value of a word w is then the *join* of the values of all the runs of $\mathcal{A}$ on w. Accordingly, an LNFW over an alphabet Σ and lattice $\mathcal{L}$ induces an $\mathcal{L}$-language $L : \Sigma^* \to \mathcal{L}$. Note that traditional finite automata (NFWs) correspond to LNFWs over the lattice $\mathcal{L}_2$. In a *deterministic lattice automaton on finite words* (LDFW, for short), exactly one state has an initial value that is not $\bot$ (the least lattice element), and for every state q and letter σ, at most one state q' is such that the value of the transition from q to q' with σ is not $\bot$. Thus, an LDFW $\mathcal{A}$ has at most one run whose value is not $\bot$ on each input word, and the value of this run is the value of the word in the language of $\mathcal{A}$.

Since being introduced in [27], lattice automata have been used in different contexts. Fully-ordered lattices are sometimes useful as is (for example, when modeling priorities [3]), and sometimes thanks to the fact that real values can often be abstracted to finitely many linearly ordered classes. The power-set lattice models a wide range of partially-ordered values. For example, as mentioned above, in a setting with inconsistent viewpoints, we have a set of agents, each with a different viewpoint of the system, and the truth value of an atomic proposition or a formula indicates the set of agents according to whose viewpoint the atomic proposition or the formula are true. As another example, in [2] the authors study a model of incomplete information in the multi-valued setting using lattice automata. Researchers have also studied theoretical properties of lattice automata, like their minimization and approximation [19,20], and a bisimulation relation for them [14].

We study vacuity and inherent vacuity in lattice automata. Essentially, the goal is to formalize the ability to mutate the value of a transition in the automaton without changing its language. Consider a transition τ in an LNFW. We say that τ is *v-tolerant*, for a value v of the lattice, if changing the value of τ to v does not change the language of $\mathcal{A}$. We say that a transition τ is *universally flexible* ($\forall$-flexible, for short) if τ is v-tolerant for every value v in $\mathcal{L}$. Likewise, τ is *existentially flexible* ($\exists$-flexible, for short) if τ is v-tolerant for some value v in $\mathcal{L}$ that is different from the value of τ.

Natural decision problems arise from the above definitions. Specifically, the $\forall$-FLEXIBILITY problem is to decide, given an LNFW and a transition τ in it, whether τ is $\forall$-flexible, and dually for the $\exists$-FLEXIBILITY problem. Solving the flexibility decision problems, we distinguish between four classes of LNFWs, induced by the branching structure of the LNFW (that is, whether it is deterministic or non-deterministic), and the lattice with respect to which it is defined (that is, whether the lattice is fully or partially ordered). Note that our definition of $\forall$-flexible is similar to the definition of "does not affect the satisfaction" for LTL formulas, in the sense that the mutated component is universally quantified.

In the case of LTL, checking whether a sub formula ψ affect the the satisfaction of a specification φ, it is possible to check only the "most challenging" mutation – one that replaces ψ by *true* or by *false*, according to the polarity of ψ in φ [28]. Given a transition τ, in $\mathcal{A}$, deciding whether τ is universally or existentially flexible can be done by checking all the mutations of the value of τ. An intermediate question we study is whether it is sufficient to check a single "most challenging" mutation. We show that both universal and existential flexibility are NLOGSPACE-complete for LDFWs and PSPACE-complete for LNFWs, regardless of the type of the lattice. The difference between full-order LNFWs and partial-order LNFWs is reflected, however, in the time complexity of the problems.

As done in [17] for LTL formulas, we introduce and compare two definitions of inherent vacuity for lattice automata. Given two LNFWs $\mathcal{A}$ and $\mathcal{A}'$, we say that the language of $\mathcal{A}'$ is contained in the language of $\mathcal{A}$, denoted $L(\mathcal{A}') \leq L(\mathcal{A})$, if for every word $w \in \Sigma^*$, we have $L(\mathcal{A}')(w) \leq L(\mathcal{A})(w)$. For two LNFWs $\mathcal{A}$ and $\mathcal{A}'$ such that $L(\mathcal{A}') \leq L(\mathcal{A})$, we say that a transition τ in $\mathcal{A}$ *does not affect the containment of $L(\mathcal{A}')$ in $L(\mathcal{A})$*, if for every $v \in \mathcal{L}$, the inequality $L(\mathcal{A}') \leq L(\mathcal{A})$ holds also when changing the value of τ in $\mathcal{A}$ to v. Also, $\mathcal{A}'$ is *vacuously contained* in $\mathcal{A}$ if there is a transition τ in $\mathcal{A}$ that does not affect the containment of $L(\mathcal{A}')$ in $L(\mathcal{A})$. Now, an LNFW $\mathcal{A}$ is *inherently vacuous* if there exists a $\forall$-flexible transition in $\mathcal{A}$, which we show to be equivalent to a definition according to which $\mathcal{A}$ is inherently vacuous if for every LNFW $\mathcal{A}'$, if $L(\mathcal{A}') \leq L(\mathcal{A})$, then $\mathcal{A}'$ is vacuously contained in $\mathcal{A}$. Thus, as in the case of LTL formulas, the two definitions coincide.

Due to the lack of space, some proofs are missing and can be found in a full version, in the authors' URLs.

2   Preliminaries

2.1   Lattices

Let $\langle A, \leq \rangle$ be a partially ordered set, and let P be a subset of A. An element $a \in A$ is an *upper bound* on P if $a \geq b$ for all $b \in P$. Dually, a is a *lower bound* on P if $a \leq b$ for all $b \in P$. An element $a \in A$ is the *least element of P* if $a \in P$ and a is a lower bound on P. Dually, $a \in A$ is the *greatest element of P* if $a \in P$ and a is an upper bound on P. A partially ordered set $\langle A, \leq \rangle$ is a *lattice* if for every two elements $a, b \in A$ both the least upper bound and the greatest lower bound of $\{a, b\}$ exist, in which case they are denoted $a \vee b$ (*a join b*) and $a \wedge b$ (*a meet b*), respectively. A lattice is *fully ordered* if every two elements in it are comparable. Note that w.l.o.g. every fully-ordered lattice corresponds to the lattice $\langle \{0, \ldots, n\}, \leq \rangle$ for some n. For ease of presentation, from now on we assume that every fully-ordered lattice is the lattice $\langle \{0, \ldots, n\}, \leq \rangle$ for some n. We use $a < b$ to indicate that $a \leq b$ and $a \neq b$. We say that a is a *child* of b, denoted $a \prec b$, if $a < b$ and there is no c such that $a < c < b$. A lattice is *complete* if for every subset $P \subseteq A$ both the least upper bound and the greatest lower bound of P exist, in which case they are denoted $\bigvee P$

and $\bigwedge P$, respectively. In particular, $\bigvee A$ and $\bigwedge A$ are denoted $\top$ (*top*) and $\bot$ (*bottom*), respectively. A lattice $\langle A, \leq \rangle$ is finite if A is finite. Note that every finite lattice is complete. A lattice $\langle A, \leq \rangle$ is *distributive* if for every $a, b, c \in A$, we have $a \wedge (b \vee c) = (a \wedge b) \vee (a \wedge c)$ and $a \vee (b \wedge c) = (a \vee b) \wedge (a \vee c)$.

Consider a lattice $\mathcal{L} = \langle A, \leq \rangle$. We sometimes abuse notation and refer to $\mathcal{L}$ also as a set of elements, and thus talk about elements $l \in \mathcal{L}$ (rather than $l \in A$). A *join irreducible element* $l \in \mathcal{L}$ is a value, other than $\bot$, such that for all $a, b \in \mathcal{L}$, if $a \vee b \geq l$ then either $a \geq l$ or $b \geq l$. We denote the set of join irreducible elements of $\mathcal{L}$ by $JI(\mathcal{L})$. By Birkhoff's representation theorem for finite distributive lattices, in order to prove that $a = b$ it is sufficient to prove that for every join irreducible element l, it holds that $a \geq l$ iff $b \geq l$.

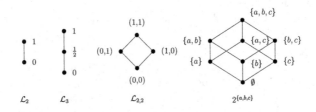

Fig. 1. Some lattices.

In Fig. 1 we describe some finite lattices. The elements of the lattice $\mathcal{L}_2$ are the usual truth values 1 (*true*) and 0 (*false*) with the order $0 \leq 1$. The lattice $\mathcal{L}_n$ contains the values $0, 1, \ldots, n - 1$, with the order $0 \leq 1 \leq, \ldots, \leq n - 1$. The lattice $\mathcal{L}_{2,2}$ is the Cartesian product of two $\mathcal{L}_2$ lattices, thus $(a, b) \leq (a', b')$ if both $a \leq a'$ and $b \leq b'$. Finally, the lattice $2^{\{a,b,c\}}$ is the power set of $\{a, b, c\}$ with the set-inclusion order. In this lattice, for example, $\{a\} \vee \{b\} = \{a, b\}$, $\{a\} \wedge \{b\} = \bot$, $\{a, c\} \vee \{b\} = \top$, and $\{a, c\} \wedge \{b\} = \bot$. Note that the join irreducible elements of the lattice $\mathcal{L}_n$ are all the elements in the lattice except for $\bot$. In the case of the lattice $2^{\{a,b,c\}}$, the join irreducible elements are all the singletons, that is, $JI(\mathcal{L}) = \{\{a\}, \{b\}, \{c\}\}$.

We define the *graph of* $\mathcal{L}$ as the undirected graph $\langle A, E_{\prec} \rangle$ in which $E_{\prec}(v, v')$ iff $v \prec v'$ or $v' \prec v$. The *distance* between two elements $a, b \in \mathcal{L}$, denoted $dist(a, b)$, is the shortest path from a to b in the graph of $\mathcal{L}$. For example, in the fully-ordered lattice $\mathcal{L}$, we have $dist(i, j) = |i - j|$, and in the power-set lattice, the distance coincides with the Hamming distance, thus $dist(X_1, X_2) = |(X_1 \setminus X_2) \cup (X_2 \setminus X_1)|$. When $dist(a, b) = 1$, we say that a and b are neighbors. Note that a and b are neighbors iff $a \prec b$ or $b \prec a$. For two elements i and j in a fully-ordered lattice, we define $i + j$ as $min\{\top, i + j\}$ and $i - j$ as $max\{\bot, i - j\}$.

For a set X of elements, an $\mathcal{L}$-*set over* X is a function $S : X \to \mathcal{L}$ assigning to each element of X a value in $\mathcal{L}$. It is convenient to think about $S(x)$ as the truth value of the statement "x is in S". We say that an $\mathcal{L}$-set S is *Boolean* if $S(x) \in \{\top, \bot\}$ for all $x \in X$.

Consider a lattice $\mathcal{L}$ and an alphabet Σ. An $\mathcal{L}$-*language* over Σ is an $\mathcal{L}$-set over Σ^*. Thus, an $\mathcal{L}$-language $L : \Sigma^* \to \mathcal{L}$ assigns a value in $\mathcal{L}$ to each word over Σ. For two $\mathcal{L}$-languages L_1 and L_2, we say that L_1 is *contained* in L_2, denoted $L_1 \leq L_2$, if for every word $w \in \Sigma^*$ it holds that $L_1(w) \leq L_2(w)$. The meet of two languages L_1 and L_2, denoted $L_1 \wedge L_2$, is the language that maps each word $w \in \Sigma^*$ to the meet of the values of w in L_1 and in L_2; that is, for all w, we have that $(L_1 \wedge L_2)(w) = L_1(w) \wedge L_2(w)$. The join of L_1 and L_2, denoted $L_1 \vee L_2$, is defined dually, thus, for every w, we have $(L_1 \vee L_2)(w) = L_1(w) \vee L_2(w)$.

Below is a useful extension of Birkhoff's representation theorem [6] from equality to inequality.

Proposition 1. *Consider a lattice $\mathcal{L}$ and two elements $a, b \in \mathcal{L}$. If for every join irreducible element $l \in \mathcal{L}$ it holds that $a \geq l$ implies $b \geq l$, then $b \geq a$.*

2.2 Lattice Automata

A *nondeterministic lattice automaton* on finite words (LNFW, for short) [27] is a six-tuple $\mathcal{A} = \langle \mathcal{L}, \Sigma, Q, Q_0, \delta, F \rangle$, where $\mathcal{L}$ is a finite lattice, Σ is an alphabet, Q is a finite set of states, $Q_0 \in \mathcal{L}^Q$ is an $\mathcal{L}$-set of initial states, $\delta \in \mathcal{L}^{Q \times \Sigma \times Q}$ is an $\mathcal{L}$-set of transitions, and $F \in \mathcal{L}^Q$ is an $\mathcal{L}$-set of accepting states. An LNFW is a full-order LNFW if $\mathcal{L}$ is a fully-ordered lattice. Otherwise, it is called a partial-order LNFW to emphasize that the lattice is not fully-ordered. We use $|\mathcal{A}|$ to refer to the size of $\mathcal{A}$, that is, $|\mathcal{A}| = |Q \times \Sigma \times Q|$.

A *run* of $\mathcal{A}$ on a word $w = \sigma_1 \cdot \sigma_2 \cdots \sigma_n$ is a sequence $r = \tau_1, \ldots, \tau_n$ of n successive transitions, where $\tau_i \in Q \times \Sigma \times Q$. Let $q_0, \ldots, q_n$ be such that $\tau_i = \langle q_{i-1}, \sigma_i, q_i \rangle$ for every $1 \leq i \leq n$. In particular, q_0 is the first state of the run, and q_n is the last state of the run. The *value* of r is $val(r) = Q_0(q_0) \wedge \bigwedge_{i=1}^{n} \delta(\tau_i) \wedge F(q_n)$. Intuitively, $Q_0(q_0)$ is the value of q_0 being initial, $\delta(\tau_i)$ is the value of taking the transition τ_i, namely, the value of q_i being a successor of q_{i-1} when σ_i is the input letter, $F(q_n)$ is the value of q_n being accepting, and the value of r is the meet of all these values.

We refer to $Q_0(q_0) \wedge \bigwedge_{i=1}^{n} \delta(\tau_i)$ as the *traversal value* of r and refer to $F(q_n)$ as its *acceptance value*. For a word w, the value of $\mathcal{A}$ on w, denoted $\mathcal{A}(w)$, is the join of the values of all the possible runs of $\mathcal{A}$ on w. That is, $val(\mathcal{A}, w) = \bigvee \{val(r) : r \text{ is a run of } \mathcal{A} \text{ on } w\}$. The $\mathcal{L}$-language of $\mathcal{A}$, denoted $L(\mathcal{A})$, maps each word w to its value in $\mathcal{A}$. That is, $L(\mathcal{A})(w) = val(\mathcal{A}, w)$.

Let $\mathcal{A}$ be an LNFW, and δ_1, δ_2 be $\mathcal{L}$-sets of transitions of $\mathcal{A}$. We say that $\delta_1 \leq \delta_2$ if for every transition $\tau \in Q \times \Sigma \times Q$, it holds that $\delta_1(\tau) \leq \delta_2(\tau)$.

An LNFW is *deterministic* (LDFW, for short) if there is exactly one state $q \in Q$, called the *initial state* of $\mathcal{A}$, such that $Q_0(q) \neq \bot$, and for every state $q \in Q$ and letter $\sigma \in \Sigma$, there is at most one state $q' \in Q$, called the σ-*successor* of q, such that $\delta(q, \sigma, q') \neq \bot$. Note that if $\mathcal{A}$ is deterministic, then it has at most one run on w whose value is not $\bot$.

Traditional nondeterministic automata over finite words (NFW, for short) correspond to LNFW over the lattice $\mathcal{L}_2$. Indeed, over $\mathcal{L}_2$, the value of a run r is either $\top$, in case the run uses only transitions with value $\top$ and its final state has value $\top$, or $\bot$ otherwise. Also, the value of $\mathcal{A}$ on w is $\top$ iff the value of some run on it is $\top$. This reflects the fact that a word w is accepted by an NFW if some legal run on w is accepting. Similarly, traditional deterministic automata over finite words (DFW, for short) correspond to LDFW over the lattice $\mathcal{L}_2$.

Below is a simple yet useful proposition about the relation between two LNFWs.

Proposition 2. *Let* $\mathcal{A}_1 = \langle \mathcal{L}, \Sigma, Q, Q_0, \delta_1, F \rangle$ *and* $\mathcal{A}_2 = \langle \mathcal{L}, \Sigma, Q, Q_0, \delta_2, F \rangle$ *be LNFWs such that* $\delta_1 \leq \delta_2$. *Then, for every word* $w \in \Sigma^*$, *it holds that* $L(\mathcal{A}_1)(w) \leq L(\mathcal{A}_2)(w)$.

3 Vacuity in Lattice Automata

The essence of vacuity is detection of components of the specification that play no role in its satisfaction. In this section we formalize and study this intuition in the setting of lattice automata. That is, we formalize and study the influence that the value of a single transition has or may not have on the language of a lattice automaton.

We start by defining tolerance and flexibility of transitions, which formalize and quantify the ability to mutate the value of transitions without changing the language of the automaton. We first need some definitions regarding runs of lattice automata.

Consider an LNFW $\mathcal{A} = \langle \mathcal{L}, \Sigma, Q, Q_0, \delta, F \rangle$. We say that a run r on a word w is a *critical run* in $\mathcal{A}$ if removing it from the set of runs of $\mathcal{A}$ on w changes the value of w in $\mathcal{A}$. Formally, $L(\mathcal{A})(w) \neq \bigvee \{ val(r') : r' \neq r$ is a run of $\mathcal{A}$ on $w \}$. Note that for the case of a full-order LNFW, a run r on a word w is critical iff $L(\mathcal{A})(w) = val(r)$ and there is no run $r' \neq r$ on w such that $L(\mathcal{A})(w) = val(r')$.

Consider a run r, and let q_0 and q_n be the first and last states of r, respectively. For a transition τ taken in r, the value of r without τ, denoted $val_{-\tau}(r)$, is $Q_0(q_0) \wedge \bigwedge_{\tau' \in \{r \setminus \tau\}} \delta(\tau') \wedge F(q_n)$. We say that τ is a *bottleneck in r* if $val(r) \neq val_{-\tau}(r)$. That is, removing the effect of τ from the value of r changes it. Note that since the value of a run r on w is the meet of the values of all its components (transitions, initial state and accepting state), for the case of a fully-ordered lattice, the value of a run is actually determined by the minimal value throughout the run. Thus, in a full-order LNFW, a transition τ is a bottleneck in a run r iff $\delta(\tau)$ is the minimal value in r, and there is no other value v throughout the run r such that $\delta(\tau) = v$.

For a transition τ in $\mathcal{A}$, we use $\mathcal{A}_{\tau \leftarrow v}$ to denote $\mathcal{A}$ with the value $\delta(\tau)$ being changed to v. We say that τ is *v-tolerant* if changing $\delta(\tau)$ to v does not change the language of $\mathcal{A}$; that is, if $L(\mathcal{A}) = L(\mathcal{A}_{\tau \leftarrow v})$.

We say that a transition τ is *universally flexible with respect to δ* ($\forall$-*flexible*, for short, when δ is clear from the context) if τ is v-tolerant for every value v in $\mathcal{L}$. Likewise, τ is *existentially flexible with respect to δ* ($\exists$-*flexible*, for short) if τ is v-tolerant for some value $v \neq \delta(\tau)$ in $\mathcal{L}$.

Remark 1. Recall that an LNFW over the lattice $\mathcal{L}_2$ is a standard NFW. In this case, we get that a transition τ is $\forall$-flexible iff τ is $\exists$-flexible. Consider an NFW $\mathcal{A}' = \langle \Sigma, Q, Q_0, \delta, F \rangle$. For every $q, q' \in Q$ and $\sigma \in \Sigma$, the transition $\tau = \langle q, \sigma, q' \rangle$ is *flexible* if it exists in $\mathcal{A}'$, and removing it does not change the language of $\mathcal{A}'$, or if it does not exist in $\mathcal{A}'$, and adding it as a transition does not change the language of $\mathcal{A}'$. Note that a transition in an NFW is flexible iff its corresponding transition in the matching LNFW over the lattice $\mathcal{L}_2$ is $\forall$-flexible, or, equivalently, $\exists$-flexible.   □

Two basic questions we would like to study consider the universal and existential flexibility of transitions, as formally specified below.

– $\forall$-FLEXIBILITY: Given an LNFW and a transition τ in it, decide whether τ is $\forall$-flexible.
– $\exists$-FLEXIBILITY: Given an LNFW and a transition τ in it, decide whether τ is $\exists$-flexible.

Remark 2. The definitions above refer to a single transition. That is, our study examines the influence of the value of a single transition on the language of the automaton. In the full version, we consider also sets of transitions. There, we define $\forall$-*uniform-flexibility*, which indicates that we can mutate the vector of values of the transitions in the set to any uniform vector of values without changing the language, and $\forall$-*mixed-flexibility*, which indicates that we can mutate the vector of values to any vector without changing the language of the automaton. We prove equivalence between these two definitions, study also the dual $\exists$-*uniform-flexibility* and $\exists$-*mixed-flexibility* notions, and study the complexity of the corresponding decision problems.   □

4   Useful Observations on Tolerance and Flexibility

In this section we provide some useful observations towards the solution of the flexibility decision problems. We distinguish between four classes of LNFWs, induced by the branching structure of the LNFW (that is, whether it is deterministic or non-deterministic), and the lattice with respect to which it is defined (that is, whether the lattice is fully or partially ordered). Note that the four classes are partially ordered according to their generalization, with the deterministic linear class being a special case of the nondeterministic linear and the deterministic partially ordered classes. The latter two classes are not ordered, and are special cases of the most general class, namely the one of nondeterministic and partial-order LNFWs. Accordingly, we are going to present positive results on the most general class for which they apply, and present negative results on the most restricted ones. Throughout the section we refer to a lattice automaton $\mathcal{A} = \langle \mathcal{L}, \Sigma, Q, Q_0, \delta, F \rangle$.

In the context of vacuity in LTL, we say that a subformula ψ of a specification φ does not affect the satisfaction of φ in a system $\mathcal{S}$ that satisfies φ if $\mathcal{S}$ also satisfies the specification obtained from φ by replacing ψ by a universally quantified atomic proposition. Thus, the approach taken there is the universal one – all mutations of ψ should result in a formula that is satisfied in $\mathcal{S}$. It is shown in [28] that rather than checking φ with ψ being replaced by a universally quantified atomic proposition, it is sufficient to check a single "most challenging" mutation – one that replaces ψ by *true* or by *false*, according to the polarity of ψ in φ. Given a transition τ in $\mathcal{A}$, deciding whether τ is $\forall$-flexible or $\exists$-flexible can be done by checking all the replacements to $\delta(\tau)$. One of the questions we would like to answer is whether it is sufficient to change $\delta(\tau)$ to $\bot$, $\top$, or perhaps to another single value in order to answer the flexibility questions.

We first show that there is no single value $v \in \mathcal{L}$ such that for every transition τ in $\mathcal{A}$, the transition τ is $\forall$-flexible iff τ is v-tolerant. This holds already for full-order LDFWs.

Example 1. Consider the LDFW $\mathcal{A}$ with $\mathcal{L} = \{1, 2, 3\}$, described in Fig. 2.

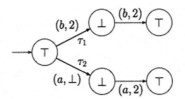

Fig. 2. No single value to check.

It is easy to see that $L(\mathcal{A})(bb) = 2$ and $L(\mathcal{A})(aa) = \bot$. The transitions τ_1 and τ_2 are not $\forall$-flexible. Indeed, if we change $\delta(\tau_1)$ to $\bot$, we get $L(\mathcal{A})(bb) = \bot$, and if we change $\delta(\tau_2)$ to $\top$ we get $L(\mathcal{A})(aa) = 2$. Assume by way of contradiction that there is a value $v \in \mathcal{L}$ that satisfies the requirement in the claim. If $v \geq 2$, then changing $\delta(\tau_1)$ to v does not change the language of $\mathcal{A}$. Thus, we get that τ_1 is not $\forall$-flexible, but is v-tolerant. Otherwise, $v < 2$ and changing $\delta(\tau_2)$ to v does not change the language of $\mathcal{A}$. Thus, we get that τ_2 is not $\forall$-flexible, but is v-tolerant. Hence, there is no single value that enables us to determine the $\forall$-flexibility of all the transitions in $\mathcal{A}$.   □

Thus, we can not expect to check flexibility of all the transitions in a lattice automaton using a single value, in particular the values $\bot$ and $\top$ do not serve as a single replacement. In the following sections we check the situation for a single transition, and we consider universal and existential flexibility in the four classes of lattice automata.

4.1   Full-Order LDFW

Universal flexibility Recall that a transition τ of $\mathcal{A}$ is $\forall$-flexible if τ is v-tolerant for every value v in $\mathcal{L}$. Since $\mathcal{L}$ is fully ordered, it is tempting to believe that we can check the tolerance of τ with respect to a single "most challenging" value.

The transition τ_1 in the LDFA in Example 1 demonstrates that $\top$-tolerance does not imply $\forall$ flexibility. Indeed, τ_1 is $\top$-tolerant but is not $\forall$-flexible, as changing $\delta(\tau_1)$ to $\bot$ changes $L(\mathcal{A})(bb)$ to $\bot$. As we now show, however, a unique check is sufficient for checking universal flexibility. This is similar to the case of subformulas in LTL, where a unique (either *true* or *false*) mutation is sufficient, and depends on the polarity of the mutated subformula. Here, the original value plays the role of the polarity.

Proposition 3. *Consider a transition τ in a full-order LDFW $\mathcal{A}$. If $\delta(\tau) \neq \bot$, then τ is $\forall$-flexible iff τ is $\bot$-tolerant. If $\delta(\tau) = \bot$, then τ is $\forall$-flexible iff τ is $\top$-tolerant.*

Proof. We start with the case $\delta(\tau) \neq \bot$. First, if τ is $\forall$-flexible, then, by definition, τ is $\bot$-tolerant. Now, since $\mathcal{A}$ is deterministic, if changing $\delta(\tau)$ to $\bot$ does not change the language of $\mathcal{A}$, then the value of every run that traverses τ was $\bot$ before the change. Since $\mathcal{L}$ is fully ordered, this means that every run that traverses τ had value $\bot$ in it, either in a transition or in an initial or an accepting state. Thus, the value of every run that traverses this transition is $\bot$ regardless what $\delta(\tau)$ is, or in other words, τ is $\forall$-flexible.

We continue to the case $\delta(\tau) = \bot$. First, if τ is $\forall$-flexible, then, by definition, τ is $\top$-tolerant. Now, if τ is $\top$-tolerant, then we have $L(\mathcal{A}) = L(\mathcal{A}_{\tau \leftarrow \top})$. Let v be a value in $\mathcal{L}$. By Proposition 2, since $\bot \leq v \leq \top$ we have that $L(\mathcal{A}) \leq L(\mathcal{A}_{\tau \leftarrow v}) \leq L(\mathcal{A}_{\tau \leftarrow \top})$. Thus, we get that $L(\mathcal{A}) = L(\mathcal{A}_{\tau \leftarrow v})$ for every $v \in \mathcal{L}$, namely, τ is $\forall$-flexible, and we are done.

Existential Flexibility. Recall that a transition τ of $\mathcal{A}$ is $\exists$-flexible if τ is v-tolerant for some value $v \neq \delta(\tau)$ in $\mathcal{L}$. The transition τ_1 in the LDFA in Example 1 demonstrates that $\exists$-flexibility does not imply $\bot$-tolerance. Indeed, while changing $\delta(\tau_1)$ to $\bot$ changes $L(\mathcal{A})(bb)$ to $\bot$, the transition τ_1 is $\top$-tolerant. As in the case of universal flexibility, however, a unique check is sufficient.

Lemma 1. *Consider a transition τ in an LDFW $\mathcal{A}$. If τ is a bottleneck in some run, then it is not $\exists$-flexible.*

Proof. Since $\mathcal{A}$ is over a fully ordered lattice, then τ being a bottleneck in some run implies that $\delta(\tau)$ is the meet of all the values throughout that run, and there is no value throughout that run that equals $\delta(\tau)$. Thus, since $\mathcal{A}$ is deterministic, changing $\delta(\tau)$ to a lower value decreases the value of some word in the language of $\mathcal{A}$, and changing $\delta(\tau)$ to a greater value increases the value of some word in the language of $\mathcal{A}$. Thus, the transition τ is not $\exists$-flexible.

Proposition 4. *Consider a transition τ in an LDFW $\mathcal{A}$. If $\delta(\tau) \neq \top$, then τ is $\exists$-flexible iff τ is $\top$-tolerant. If $\delta(\tau) = \top$, then τ is $\exists$-flexible iff τ is $(\top - 1)$-tolerant.*

Proof. We start with the case $\delta(\tau) \neq \top$. First, if τ is $\top$-tolerant, then, by definition, τ is $\exists$-flexible. Now, if τ is $\exists$-flexible, then by Lemma 1 we get that τ

is not a bottleneck in any run. Thus, we can increase $\delta(\tau)$ without changing the language and τ is $\top$-tolerant.

We continue to the case $\delta(\tau) = \top$. First, if τ is $(\top - 1)$-tolerant, then, by definition, τ is $\exists$-flexible. Now, if τ is $\exists$-flexible, then τ is v-tolerant for some value $v \neq \top$ in $\mathcal{L}$. Thus, we have $L(\mathcal{A}_{\tau \leftarrow v}) = L(\mathcal{A})$. Since $v \leq (\top - 1) \leq \tau$, we get by Proposition 2 that $L(\mathcal{A}_{\tau \leftarrow v}) \leq L(\mathcal{A}_{\tau \leftarrow (\top - 1)}) \leq L(\mathcal{A})$, and so $L(\mathcal{A}_{\tau \leftarrow (\top - 1)}) = L(\mathcal{A})$. Namely, the transition τ is $(\top - 1)$-tolerant.

4.2   Full-Order LNFW

In Propositions 3 and 4 we showed that in the case of full-order LDFW, if $\delta(\tau) \neq \bot$ then τ is $\forall$-flexible iff τ is $\bot$-tolerant, and that if $\delta(\tau) \neq \top$ then τ is $\exists$-flexible iff τ is $\top$-tolerant. As we now show in Example 2 below, This does not hold for LNFWs.

Example 2. with Let $\mathcal{L} = \{1, 2, 3\}$. Consider the LNFW $\mathcal{A}_1$ described in the left of Fig. 3.

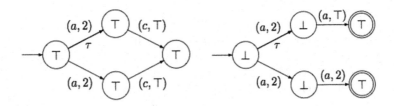

Fig. 3. Propositions 3 and 4 do not hold for partial-order LDFWs.

It is easy to see that $L(\mathcal{A}_1)(a) = L(\mathcal{A}_1)(ac) = 2$. Consider the upper-left transition τ. If we change $\delta(\tau)$ to $\bot$ we get an equivalent LNFW. However, τ is not $\forall$-flexible. Indeed, changing $\delta(\tau)$ to $\top$ changes $L(\mathcal{A}_1)(a)$ and $L(\mathcal{A}_1)(ac)$ to $\top$.

Consider now the LNFW $\mathcal{A}_2$ described in the right of the figure. It is easy to see that $L(\mathcal{A}_2)(aa) = 2$. Consider the upper-left transition τ. If we change $\delta(\tau)$ to $\bot$ we get an equivalent LNFW. However, τ is not $\top$-tolerant. Indeed, changing $\delta(\tau)$ to $\top$ changes $L(\mathcal{A}_2)(aa)$ to $\top$.   □

Example 2 is a negative result for the class of full-order LNFWs. In Propositions 5 and 6 we will show a positive result for the more general partial-order LNFW.

4.3   Partial-Order LDFW

In Example 2 we showed that Propositions 3 and 4, which apply to full-order LDFWs, do not hold for full-order LNFWs. Below we show that they do not hold for partial-order LDFWs either. Thus, we conclude that Propositions 3 and 4 are tight for full-order LDFWs and do not hold for partial-order LDFWs or for LNFWs.

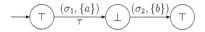

Fig. 4. Propositions 3 and 4 do not hold for full-order LNFWs.

Example 3. Let $\mathcal{L} = 2^{\{a,b\}}$. Consider the LDFW $\mathcal{A}$ described in Fig. 4.

It is easy to see that $L(\mathcal{A})(\sigma_1 \cdot \sigma_2) = \emptyset$. Consider the left transition τ. If we change $\delta(\tau)$ to $\bot$ we get an equivalent LDFW. However, τ is not $\forall$-flexible. Indeed, changing $\delta(\tau)$ to $\{a,b\}$ changes $L(\mathcal{A})(\sigma_1 \cdot \sigma_2)$ to $\{b\}$. Thus, there exists a partial-order LDFW with a transition τ in it, such that $\delta(\tau) \neq \bot$ and τ is $\bot$-tolerance but is not $\forall$-flexible.

Further observe that τ, which is $\bot$-tolerance and hence $\exists$-flexible, is not $\top$-tolerant. Indeed, changing $\delta(\tau)$ to $\top$ changes $L(\mathcal{A}_2)(\sigma_1 \cdot \sigma_2)$ to $\{b\}$. Thus, there exists a partial-order LDFW with a transition τ in it, such that $\delta(\tau) \neq \top$ and τ is $\exists$-flexible but is not $\top$-tolerant. In particular, $\exists$-flexibility does not imply $\top$-tolerance.   □

Example 3 is a negative result for the class of partial-order LDFWs. In Propositions 5 we will show a positive result for the more general partial-order LNFW. The last negative result we are going to show concerns existential flexibility and shows that there, checking even both extreme values $\top$ and $\bot$ may not be of help. In Example 4 below we formalize this intuition.

Example 4. Consider the LDFW $\mathcal{A}$ with $\mathcal{L} = 2^{\{a,b,c\}}$, described in Fig. 5.

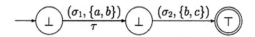

Fig. 5. τ is $\exists$-flexible, but is neither $\bot$-tolerant nor $\top$-tolerant.

It is easy to see that $L(\mathcal{A})(\sigma_1 \cdot \sigma_2) = \{b\}$. Consider the left transition τ. If we change $\delta(\tau)$ to $\{b\}$ we get an equivalent LDFW, thus, τ is $\exists$-flexible. However, changing $\delta(\tau)$ to $\bot$ changes $L(\mathcal{A})(\sigma_1 \cdot \sigma_2)$ to $\bot$, and changing $\delta(\tau)$ to $\top$ changes $L(\mathcal{A})(\sigma_1 \cdot \sigma_2)$ to $\{b,c\}$, thus, τ is neither $\bot$-tolerant nor $\top$-tolerant.   □

4.4   Partial-Order LNFW

Universal Flexibility. As shown in Examples 2 and 3, checking only $\bot$-tolerance or $\top$-tolerance is not sufficient in order to determine $\forall$-flexibility. As we show, however, in Proposition 5 below, checking both is sufficient, even in the most general model.

Proposition 5. *A transition τ in an LNFW $\mathcal{A}$ is $\forall$-flexible iff τ is both $\bot$-tolerant and $\top$-tolerant.*

Proof. If τ is $\forall$-flexible, then, by definition, τ is $\bot$-tolerant and $\top$-tolerant. Now, if τ is $\bot$-tolerant and $\top$-tolerant, we have $L(\mathcal{A}_{\tau\leftarrow\bot}) = L(\mathcal{A}) = L(\mathcal{A}_{\tau\leftarrow\top})$. Let v be a value in $\mathcal{L}$. By Proposition 2, since $\bot \leq v \leq \top$, we have that $L(\mathcal{A}_{\tau\leftarrow\bot}) \leq L(\mathcal{A}_{\tau\leftarrow v}) \leq L(\mathcal{A}_{\tau\leftarrow\top})$. Since $L(\mathcal{A}_{\tau\leftarrow\bot}) = L(\mathcal{A}_{\tau\leftarrow\top})$, it must be that $L(\mathcal{A}_{\tau\leftarrow\bot}) = L(\mathcal{A}_{\tau\leftarrow v}) = L(\mathcal{A}_{\tau\leftarrow\top})$. This holds for every $v \in \mathcal{L}$, thus, we get that τ is v-tolerant for every $v \in \mathcal{L}$, that is, τ is $\forall$-flexible, and we are done.

By Proposition 2, since $\bot \leq \delta(\tau) \leq \top$, we have $L(\mathcal{A}_{\tau\leftarrow\bot}) \leq L(\mathcal{A}) \leq L(\mathcal{A}_{\tau\leftarrow\top})$. Hence, the two tolerance checks from Proposition 5 can be performed in a single language-containment check:

Lemma 2. *Consider an LNFW $\mathcal{A}$. A transition τ in $\mathcal{A}$ is $\forall$-flexible iff $L(\mathcal{A}_{\tau\leftarrow\top}) \leq L(\mathcal{A}_{\tau\leftarrow\bot})$.*

Existential flexibility. Unlike the case of $\forall$-flexibility, which amounts to tolerance of the two extreme values, namely $\top$-tolerance and $\bot$-tolerance, Example 4 shows that this is not true for $\exists$-flexibility, even in LDFW. As we prove below, we can still avoid checking all possible values and restrict attention to the neighbors of the original value of the mutated transition.

Lemma 3. *Let τ be a transition in an LNFW $\mathcal{A}$. If τ is v'-tolerant for some $v' \in \mathcal{L}$, then τ is v''-tolerant for every value $v'' \in \mathcal{L}$ such that $(\delta(\tau) \wedge v') \leq v'' \leq v'$, $v' \leq v'' \leq (\delta(\tau) \vee v')$, $(\delta(\tau) \wedge v') \leq v'' \leq \delta(\tau)$, or $\delta(\tau) \leq v'' \leq (\delta(\tau) \vee v')$.*

Lemma 3 implies that the search for a value with respect to which a transition is tolerant can consider only the neighbors of the current value. Formally, we have the following. The proof, which appears in the full version, analyzes all possible relations between the value of $\delta(\tau)$ and a value that witnesses its $\exists$-flexibility.

Proposition 6. *Consider an LNFW $\mathcal{A}$ and a transition τ in $\mathcal{A}$. The transition τ is $\exists$-flexible iff τ is v'-tolerant for some neighbor v' of $\delta(\tau)$ in the graph of the lattice $\mathcal{L}$.*

Remark 3. In order to justify the need to check all the neighbors of $\delta(\tau)$, consider the LDFW $\mathcal{A}$ with $\mathcal{L} = 2^{\{a,b,c,d\}}$, described in Fig. 6.

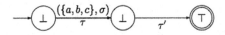

Fig. 6. Checking tolerance for neighbors.

Consider the right transition τ'. If $\delta(\tau') = \{a, b, d\}$, then the only value v for which τ is v-tolerant is $\{a, b\}$. If $\delta(\tau') = \{a, c, d\}$, then the only value v for which τ is v-tolerant is $\{a, c\}$. If $\delta(\tau') = \{b, c, d\}$, then the only value v for which τ is v-tolerant is $\{b, c\}$. If $\delta(\tau') = \{a, b, c\}$, then the only value v for which τ is v-tolerant is $\{a, b, c, d\}$. It is easy to see that in each case, the only value that can give an indication for the $\exists$-flexibility of τ is a neighbor of $\delta(\tau)$. Also, note that every neighbor of $\delta(\tau)$ is useful in one of the cases. Thus, it is required to check at least all the neighbors of $\delta(\tau)$ in order to determine $\exists$-flexibility.   □

5   Complexity of the Decision Problems

In this section we use the observations from Sect. 4 in order to find the complexity of the flexibility decision problems.

We first prove a lower bound for the flexibility problem in DFWs and NFWs. As discussed in Remark 1, an NFW corresponds to an LNFW over the lattice $\mathcal{L}_2$, and similarly, a DFW corresponds to an LDFW over this lattice. Then, universal and existential flexibility coincide, and a transition in an NFW is flexible iff the corresponding transition in the matching LNFW over the lattice $\mathcal{L}_2$ is $\forall$-flexible and $\exists$-flexible. Accordingly, the FLEXIBILITY problem for NFW is to decide, given an NFW and a transition τ in it, whether τ is flexible.

Theorem 1. *The FLEXIBILITY problem is NLOGSPACE-hard for DFWs and is PSPACE-hard for NFWs.*

Proof. We start with DFWs and describe a reduction from the non-reachability problem, proven to be NLOGSPACE-hard in [24,25]. Given a graph $G = \langle V, E \rangle$ and two vertices u, v, we construct a DFW $\mathcal{A} = \langle \Sigma, Q, q_0, \delta, F \rangle$ with a transition τ such that τ is flexible iff v is not reachable from u. The DFW $\mathcal{A}$ is similar to G, with an additional transition τ from v to a new state. We define $\mathcal{A}$ so that this new transition is flexible iff v is not reachable from u. Intuitively, v is not reachable from u off τ is not reachable from an initial state, which determines τ's flexibility.

Formally, $\mathcal{A} = \langle E \cup \{e_{new}\}, V \cup \{q\}, u, \delta, \{q\} \rangle$. For every edge $e \in E$ such that $e = (w, w')$, we add to $\mathcal{A}$ a transition $\tau' = \langle w, e, w' \rangle$. That is, all the edges of the graph are transitions in the automaton with different letters. We also add to $\mathcal{A}$ the transition $\tau = \langle v, e_{new}, q \rangle$, where $e_{new} \notin E$, and $q \notin V$. Note that $\mathcal{A}$ is a DFW, as required, and that this reduction is computable using logarithmic space. In the full version we prove that indeed τ is flexible iff v is not reachable from u.

For the nondeterministic setting, we show a reduction from the universality problem for NFWs, namely, the problem of deciding, given an NFW $\mathcal{A}$, whether $L(\mathcal{A}) = \Sigma^*$. The reduction is to the flexibility problem for NFWs. Since the universality problem is PSPACE-hard [29], hardness in PSPACE follows.

Given an NFW $\mathcal{A} = \langle \Sigma, Q, Q_0, \delta, F \rangle$, we define $\mathcal{A}' = \langle \Sigma', Q', Q_0', \delta', F' \rangle$ to be similar to $\mathcal{A}$, with an additional component that includes, among others, a transition τ that is going to be flexible iff $L(\mathcal{A}) = \Sigma^*$. Intuitively, if $L(\mathcal{A}) = \Sigma^*$, then the additional component does not contribute to the language of $\mathcal{A}$, and τ is flexible. If, however, $L(\mathcal{A}) \neq \Sigma^*$, there are words that are accepted only using the new component, so τ is not flexible. We assume that if there is a word $w \notin L(\mathcal{A})$, then w is of length at least 1. This assumption does not affect the hardness of the universality problem.

Formally, $\mathcal{A}' = \langle \Sigma \cup \{\sigma_{new}\}, Q \cup \{s_0, s_f\}, Q_0 \cup \{s_0\}, \delta', F \cup \{s_f\} \rangle$. We obtain $\mathcal{A}'$ from $\mathcal{A}$ by adding to $\mathcal{A}$ a transition $\tau = \langle q, \sigma_{new}, q \rangle$, for every accepting state $q \in F$. Next, we add to $\mathcal{A}'$ an additional component with two states: s_0 and s_f (see Fig. 7). The state s_0 is added to the set of initial states, and the state s_f is added to the set of accepting states. For each $\sigma \in \Sigma$, we add a transition $\langle s_0, \sigma, s_0 \rangle$, and a transition $\langle s_0, \sigma, s_f \rangle$. Finally, we add a transition $\tau = \langle s_f, \sigma_{new}, s_f \rangle$. Note that the reduction is computable using logarithmic space. In the full version we prove that indeed $\tau = \langle s_f, \sigma_{new}, s_f \rangle$ is flexible iff $L(\mathcal{A}) = \Sigma^*$.

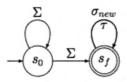

Fig. 7. The new component added to $\mathcal{A}'$.

Theorem 2. *The $\forall$-FLEXIBILITY problem is NLOGSPACE-complete for LDFWs and is PSPACE-complete for LNFWs.*

Proof. We start with the upper bounds. As shown in Lemma 2, in order to check whether a transition τ is $\forall$-flexible, it is sufficient to perform a single containment check: $L(\mathcal{A}_{\tau \leftarrow \top}) \leq L(\mathcal{A}_{\tau \leftarrow \bot})$. The language-containment problem is in NLOGSPACE and PSPACE, for LDFWs and LNFWs, respectively [27], implying the required upper bounds.

Now, since flexibility in DFWs and NFWs corresponds to universal flexibility in LDFWs and LNFWs, respectively, the lower bounds follow from Theorem 1.

Theorem 3. *The $\exists$-FLEXIBILITY problem is NLOGSPACE-complete for LDFWs and is PSPACE-complete for LNFWs.*

Proof. For the upper bounds, consider an LNFW $\mathcal{A} = \langle \mathcal{L}, \Sigma, Q, Q_0, \delta, F \rangle$, and let τ be a transition in $\mathcal{A}$ with $\delta(\tau) = v$. By Proposition 6, the transition τ is $\exists$-flexible iff τ is v'-tolerant for some neighbor v' of v in the graph of the lattice $\mathcal{L}$; that is, $L(\mathcal{A}) = L(\mathcal{A}_{\tau \leftarrow v'})$. By Proposition 2, for a value $v' \in \mathcal{L}$ such that $v' > v$ we have $L(\mathcal{A}) \leq L(\mathcal{A}_{\tau \leftarrow v'})$, and for a value $v' \in \mathcal{L}$ such that $v' < v$, we have $L(\mathcal{A}_{\tau \leftarrow v'}) \leq L(\mathcal{A})$. Hence, it is sufficient to check for every neighbor v' of v such that $v' > v$, if $L(\mathcal{A}_{\tau \leftarrow v'}) \leq L(\mathcal{A})$ holds, and for every neighbor v' of v such that $v' < v$ or if $L(\mathcal{A}) \leq L(\mathcal{A}_{\tau \leftarrow v'})$ holds. We get that τ is $\exists$-flexible iff there exists a neighbor of v for which the corresponding inequality holds. The upper bound now follows from the known NLOGSPACE and PSPACE complexities of the language-containment problem, for LDFWs and LNFWs, respectively.

Finally, since flexibility in DFWs and NFWs corresponds to existential flexibility in LDFWs and LNFWs, respectively, the lower bounds follow from Theorem 1.

By Theorems 2 and 3, the complexity of the flexibility problems coincide for full-order and partial-order lattice automata. The difference between the two settings is reflected in the time-complexity analysis of the algorithms we described. Given an LNFW $\mathcal{A}$ over a lattice $\mathcal{L}$, let $n = |\mathcal{A}|$, $m = |\mathcal{L}|$, and $k = |JI|$. Precisely, we have the following.

Theorem 4. *The $\forall$-FLEXIBILITY problem can be decided in time $O(n(m+n))$ for full-order LDFWs, in time $O(kn(m + n))$ for partial-order LDFWs, and in time $O(k(nm + 2^{O(n)}))$ for LNFWs.*

Theorem 5. *The $\exists$-FLEXIBILITY problem can be decided in time $O(n(m+n))$ for full-order LDFWs, in time $O(rkn(m+n))$ for partial-order LDFWs, in time $O(k(nm + 2^{O(n)}))$ for full-order LNFWs, and in time $O(rk(nm + 2^{O(n)}))$ for partial-order LNFWs, where r is the number of the neighbors of $\delta(\tau)$ in the graph of $\mathcal{L}$.*

Remark 4. In practice, systems and specifications are sometimes underspecified as the designer intentionally does not care about some values in some configurations [22]. Our algorithms can be easily changed to handle settings in which a transition can get the value $\varnothing$ (?don?t care?) or get a set of possible values. In this case, flexibility gets additional significance, as we can assume that the value of transitions for which the designer did bother to specify a value is important. For example, if a transition has a value different than $\varnothing$, and it turns out to be $\forall$-flexible, we can assume that there is an error in the modeling of the specification, since this transition could have also gotten the value $\varnothing$.   □

6 Inherent Vacuity with Analogy to Temporal Logic

In [17], the authors introduce two different definitions of inherent vacuity for LTL formulas and prove that they coincide. Consider an LTL formula φ. We say that a subformula ψ of φ does not affect the satisfaction of φ in $\mathcal{S}$ if $\mathcal{S}$ also satisfies the formula $\forall x.\varphi[\psi \leftarrow x]$. We refer to the formula $\forall x.\varphi[\psi \leftarrow x]$ as the ψ-strengthening of φ. Also, we say that a formula φ is vacuously satisfied in $\mathcal{S}$ if φ has a subformula that does not affect its satisfaction in $\mathcal{S}$ [4].

We can now describe the two different definitions of inherent vacuity for LTL formulas from [17]. According to the first definition, an LTL formula φ is inherently vacuous (by mutation) if there exists a subformula ψ of φ such that $\varphi \equiv \forall x.\varphi[\psi \leftarrow x]$. That is, φ is equivalent to its ψ-strengthening. As opposed to the first definition, the second one does not restrict attention to a single subformula. According to the second definition, an LTL formula φ is inherently vacuous (by reference) if for every system $\mathcal{S}$, if $\mathcal{S} \models \varphi$, then $\mathcal{S}$ satisfies φ vacuously. In this section we introduce two different definitions of inherent vacuity for lattice automata, analogous to the definitions in [17], and show that they coincide as well.

Given two LNFWs $\mathcal{A}$ and $\mathcal{A}'$ such that $L(\mathcal{A}') \leq L(\mathcal{A})$, we say that a transition τ in $\mathcal{A}$ *does not affect the containment* of $L(\mathcal{A}')$ in $L(\mathcal{A})$, if for every $v \in \mathcal{L}$ it holds that $L(\mathcal{A}') \leq L(\mathcal{A}_{\tau \leftarrow v})$. Note that this requirement applies to every value in $\mathcal{L}$. Also, $\mathcal{A}'$ is *vacuously contained* in $\mathcal{A}$ if there is a transition τ in $\mathcal{A}$ that does not affect the containment of $L(\mathcal{A}')$ in $L(\mathcal{A})$.

Definition 1. An LNFW $\mathcal{A}$ is *inherently vacuous by mutation* if there exist a transition τ in $\mathcal{A}$ that is $\forall$-flexible. We then say that $\mathcal{A}$ is inherently vacuous by mutation with witness τ.

Definition 2. An LNFW $\mathcal{A}$ is *inherently vacuous by reference* if for every LNFW $\mathcal{A}'$, if $L(\mathcal{A}') \leq L(\mathcal{A})$, then $\mathcal{A}'$ is vacuously contained in $\mathcal{A}$.

Theorem 6. *An LNFW $\mathcal{A}$ is inherently vacuous by mutation iff $\mathcal{A}$ is inherently vacuous by reference.*

Proof. For the first direction, assume that $\mathcal{A} = \langle \mathcal{L}, \Sigma, Q, Q_0, \delta, F \rangle$ is inherently vacuous by mutation. Then, there is a transition τ in $\mathcal{A}$ that is $\forall$-flexible, that is, for every $v \in \mathcal{L}$ it holds that $L(\mathcal{A}) = L(\mathcal{A}_{\tau \leftarrow v})$. Accordingly, for every LNFW $\mathcal{A}'$, if $L(\mathcal{A}') \leq L(\mathcal{A})$, then for every $v \in \mathcal{L}$ we have that $L(\mathcal{A}') \leq L(\mathcal{A}_{\tau \leftarrow v})$, and so $\mathcal{A}'$ is vacuously contained in $\mathcal{A}$. Thus, $\mathcal{A}$ is inherently vacuous by reference.

For the second direction, assume that $\mathcal{A}$ is inherently vacuous by reference, and assume, by way of contradiction, that $\mathcal{A}$ is not inherently vacuous by mutation. Then, there exist no transition τ in $\mathcal{A}$ that is $\forall$-flexible. It is not hard to prove that then, there is no transition τ in $\mathcal{A}$ such that for all LNFWs $\mathcal{A}'$ with $L(\mathcal{A}') \leq L(\mathcal{A})$, the transition τ does not affect the containment of $L(\mathcal{A}')$ in $L(\mathcal{A})$. Indeed, since $L(\mathcal{A}) \leq L(\mathcal{A})$, the existence of such a transition would have implied universal flexibility of τ.

Let k be the number of transitions in $\mathcal{A}$. By the assumption, for every candidate transition τ_i, with $1 \leq i \leq k$, there is an LNFW $\mathcal{A}_i = \langle \mathcal{L}, \Sigma, Q_i, Q_i^0, \delta_i, F_i \rangle$ such that $L(\mathcal{A}_i) \leq L(\mathcal{A})$ but there is a value $v \in \mathcal{L}$ such that $L(\mathcal{A}_i) \not\leq L(\mathcal{A}_{\tau_i \leftarrow v})$. Without loss of generality, we assume that the state spaces Q_i are pairwise disjoint. Let $\mathcal{A}'$ be the LNFW obtained by "putting all the LNFWs $\mathcal{A}_i$ next to each other". Formally, $\mathcal{A}' = \langle \mathcal{L}, \Sigma, \bigcup \{Q_i\}_{1 \leq i \leq k}, \bigcup \{Q_i^0\}_{1 \leq i \leq k}, \bigcup \{\delta_i\}_{1 \leq i \leq k}, \bigcup \{F_i\}_{1 \leq i \leq k} \rangle$. Note that, naturally, $L(\mathcal{A}') = \bigvee_{1 \leq i \leq k} L(\mathcal{A}_i)$. Since $L(\mathcal{A}_i) \leq L(\mathcal{A})$ for every $1 \leq i \leq k$ we get that $\bigvee_{1 \leq i \leq k} L(\mathcal{A}_i) \leq L(\mathcal{A})$ and thus $L(\mathcal{A}') \leq L(\mathcal{A})$. Now, since $\mathcal{A}$ is inherently vacuous by reference, then $\mathcal{A}'$ is vacuously contained in $\mathcal{A}$. Let τ_i be a transition that does not affect the containment of $L(\mathcal{A}')$ in $L(\mathcal{A})$. Then, for every $v \in \mathcal{L}$ it holds that $L(\mathcal{A}') \leq L(\mathcal{A}_{\tau_i \leftarrow v})$. Since $L(\mathcal{A}_i) \leq L(\mathcal{A}')$, we get that for every $v \in \mathcal{L}$ it holds that $L(\mathcal{A}_i) \leq L(\mathcal{A}_{\tau_i \leftarrow v})$, and so τ_i does not affect the containment of $L(\mathcal{A}_i)$ in $L(\mathcal{A})$, and we have reached a contradiction.

Thus, as in the case of LTL formulas, the two definitions of inherent vacuity coincide.

Remark 5. As discussed in Sect. 1, lattices and lattice automata have practical applications in formal methods. Some of the applications use the specification formalism *latticed LTL* (LLTL, for short), which extends LTL by mapping computations in which atomic propositions have values from a lattice into lattice values [12]. The translation of LTL into automata [36] has been extended to a translation of LLTL into latticed automata [27]. When applied to the lattice automata obtained from LLTL formulas, vacuity in the automata correspond to vacuity in the formulas. Since changes in subformulas induce changes in transitions from all states of the automaton that are associated with these subformulas, the relevant type of vacuity is the one discussed in Remark 2, namely when the value of a set of transitions is mutated. □

References

1. Almagor, S., Boker, U., Kupferman, O.: Formalizing and reasoning about quality. In: Fomin, F.V., Freivalds, R., Kwiatkowska, M., Peleg, D. (eds.) ICALP 2013, Part II. LNCS, vol. 7966, pp. 15–27. Springer, Heidelberg (2013)
2. Almagor, S., Kupferman, O.: Latticed-LTL synthesis in the presence of noisy inputs. In: Muscholl, A. (ed.) FOSSACS 2014 (ETAPS). LNCS, vol. 8412, pp. 226–241. Springer, Heidelberg (2014)
3. Alur, R., Kanade, A., Weiss, G.: Ranking automata and games for prioritized requirements. In: Gupta, A., Malik, S. (eds.) CAV 2008. LNCS, vol. 5123, pp. 240–253. Springer, Heidelberg (2008)
4. Armoni, R., Fix, L., Flaisher, A., Grumberg, O., Piterman, N., Tiemeyer, A., Vardi, M.Y.: Enhanced vacuity detection in linear temporal logic. In: Hunt Jr., W.A., Somenzi, F. (eds.) CAV 2003. LNCS, vol. 2725, pp. 368–380. Springer, Heidelberg (2003)
5. Beer, I., Ben-David, S., Eisner, C., Rodeh, Y.: Efficient detection of vacuity in ACTL formulas. Formal Methods Syst. Des. **18**(2), 141–162 (2001)
6. Birkhoff, G.: Rings of sets. Duke Math. J. **3**(3), 443–454 (1937)
7. Bloem, R., Cavada, R., Pill, I., Roveri, M., Tchaltsev, A.: RAT: a tool for the formal analysis of requirements. In: Damm, W., Hermanns, H. (eds.) CAV 2007. LNCS, vol. 4590, pp. 263–267. Springer, Heidelberg (2007)
8. Bruns, G., Godefroid, P.: Model checking partial state spaces with 3-valued temporal logics. In: Halbwachs, N., Peled, D.A. (eds.) CAV 1999. LNCS, vol. 1633, pp. 274–287. Springer, Heidelberg (1999)
9. Bruns, G., Godefroid, P.: Temporal logic query checking. In: Proceedings of 16th IEEE Symposium on Logic in Computer Science, pp. 409–420. IEEE Computer Society (2001)
10. Bustan, D., Flaisher, A., Grumberg, O., Kupferman, O., Vardi, M.Y.: Regular vacuity. In: Borrione, D., Paul, W. (eds.) CHARME 2005. LNCS, vol. 3725, pp. 191–206. Springer, Heidelberg (2005)
11. Chan, W.: Temporal-logic queries. In: Emerson, E.A., Sistla, A.P. (eds.) CAV 2000. LNCS, vol. 1855, pp. 450–463. Springer, Heidelberg (2000)
12. Chechik, M., Devereux, B., Gurfinkel, A.: Model-checking infinite state-space systems with fine-grained abstractions using SPIN. In: Dwyer, M.B. (ed.) SPIN 2001. LNCS, vol. 2057, pp. 16–36. Springer, Heidelberg (2001)
13. Chockler, H., Strichman, O.: Easier and more informative vacuity checks. In: Proceedings of 5th International Conference on Formal Methods and Models for Co-Design, pp. 189–198 (2007)
14. Ciric, M., Ignjatovic, J., Damljanovic, N., Basic, M.: Bisimulations for fuzzy automata. Fuzzy Sets Syst. **186**(1), 100–139 (2012)
15. Droste, M., Kuich, W., Vogler, H. (eds.): Handbook of Weighted Automata. Springer, Heidelberg (2009)
16. Easterbrook, S., Chechik, M.: A framework for multi-valued reasoning over inconsistent viewpoints. In: Proceedings 23rd Internatioanl Conference on Software Engineering, pp. 411–420. IEEE Computer Society Press (2001)
17. Fisman, D., Kupferman, O., Sheinvald-Faragy, S., Vardi, M.Y.: A framework for inherent vacuity. In: Chockler, H., Hu, A.J. (eds.) HVC 2008. LNCS, vol. 5394, pp. 7–22. Springer, Heidelberg (2009)
18. Gurfinkel, A., Chechik, M.: Extending extended vacuity. In: Hu, A.J., Martin, A.K. (eds.) FMCAD 2004. LNCS, vol. 3312, pp. 306–321. Springer, Heidelberg (2004)

19. Halamish, S., Kupferman, O.: Approximating deterministic lattice automata. In: Chakraborty, S., Mukund, M. (eds.) ATVA 2012. LNCS, vol. 7561, pp. 27–41. Springer, Heidelberg (2012)
20. Halamish, S., Kupferman, O.: Minimizing deterministic lattice automata. ACM Trans. Computat. Logic 16(1), 1–21 (2015)
21. Henzinger, T.A.: From Boolean to quantitative notions of correctness. In: Proceedings of 37th ACM Symposium on Principles of Programming Languages, pp. 157–158 (2010)
22. Hoskote, Y., Kam, T., Ho, P.-H., Zhao, X.: Coverage estimation for symbolic model checking. In: Proceedings of 36th Design Automation Conference, pp. 300–305 (1999)
23. Hussain, A., Huth,M.: On model checking multiple hybrid views. Technical report TR-2004-6, University of Cyprus (2004)
24. Immerman, N.: Nondeterministic space is closed under complement. Inf. Comput. 17, 935–938 (1988)
25. Jones, N.D.: Space-bounded reducibility among combinatorial problems. J. Comput. Syst. Sci. 11, 68–75 (1975)
26. Kupferman, O.: Sanity checks in formal verification. In: Baier, C., Hermanns, H. (eds.) CONCUR 2006. LNCS, vol. 4137, pp. 37–51. Springer, Heidelberg (2006)
27. Kupferman, O., Lustig, Y.: Lattice automata. In: Cook, B., Podelski, A. (eds.) VMCAI 2007. LNCS, vol. 4349, pp. 199–213. Springer, Heidelberg (2007)
28. Kupferman, O., Vardi, M.Y.: Vacuity detection in temporal model checking. Softw. Tools Technol. Transfer 4(2), 224–233 (2003)
29. Meyer, A.R., Stockmeyer, L.J.: The equivalence problem for regular expressions with squaring requires exponential time. In: Proceedings of 13th IEEE Symposium on Switching and Automata Theory, pp. 125–129 (1972)
30. Mohri, M.: Finite-state transducers in language and speech processing. Comput. Linguist. 23(2), 269–311 (1997)
31. Namjoshi, K.S.: An efficiently checkable, proof-based formulation of vacuity in model checking. In: Alur, R., Peled, D.A. (eds.) CAV 2004. LNCS, vol. 3114, pp. 57–69. Springer, Heidelberg (2004)
32. PROSYD.: The Prosyd project on property-based system design (2007). http://www.prosyd.org
33. Roveri, M.: Novel techniques for property assurance. Technical report, PROSYD FP6-IST-507219 (2007)
34. Rozier, K.Y., Vardi, M.Y.: LTL satisfiability checking. In: Bošnački, D., Edelkamp, S. (eds.) SPIN 2007. LNCS, vol. 4595, pp. 149–167. Springer, Heidelberg (2007)
35. Graf, S., Saidi, H.: Construction of abstract state graphs with PVS. In: Grumberg, O. (ed.) CAV 1997. LNCS, vol. 1254, pp. 72–83. Springer, Heidelberg (1997)
36. Vardi, M.Y., Wolper, P.: Reasoning about infinite computations. Inf. Comput. 115(1), 1–37 (1994)

Is Polynomial Time Choiceless?

Erich Grädel[✉] and Martin Grohe

RWTH Aachen University, Aachen, Germany
graedel@logic.rwth-aachen.de, grohe@informatik.rwth-aachen.de

For Yuri Gurevich on the occasion of his 75th birthday

Abstract. A long time ago, Yuri Gurevich made precise the problem
of whether there is a logic capturing polynomial-time on arbitrary finite
structures, and conjectured that no such logic exists. This conjecture
is still open. Nevertheless, together with Andreas Blass and Saharon
Shelah, he has also proposed what still seems to be the most promising
candidate for a logic for polynomial time, namely Choiceless Polynomial
Time (with counting). We survey some recent results on this logic.

1 Introduction

Is there a logic for PTIME? More than thirty years after this problem has first
been posed by Chandra and Harel (in somewhat different form) in the context of
database theory, and after Yuri Gurevich has reformulated the question in logical
terms, we still do not know the answer. The quest for a logic for PTIME, or for a
proof that no such logic exists, still remains the perhaps most fundamental and
challenging open problem of finite model theory.

Yuri Gurevich has made many important contributions to this problem,
including numerous studies on the expressive power, structure, and complexity of a number of different logics that arise in this context. Let us focus here on
two main achievements.

The precise formulation of what would really constitute a logic for PTIME has
been extremely influential, and is of course an indispensable prerequisite for all
attempts to prove that such a logic cannot exist. Gurevich's first requirement is
that a *logic* should have a decidable syntax, that is, a decidable set of *sentences*.
Each sentence *defines* a *property* of finite[1] structures, that is, an isomorphism
closed class of structures of the same vocabulary. For the logic to *capture* polynomial time we want every polynomial-time decidable property of structures to be
definable by some sentence of the logic. This is Gurevich's second requirement
for a logic capturing PTIME. Conversely, we want every property definable in the
logic to be decidable in polynomial time. However, this is not sufficient to exclude
pathological examples. For example, we could take an (arbitrary, not necessarily
computable) enumeration $P_0, P_1, P_2, \ldots$ of all polynomial-time decidable properties of structures and define a logic whose sentences are the natural numbers

---

[1] Structures are always assumed to be finite in this paper, with the exception of the
herditarily finite expansions introduced in Sect. 2.

© Springer International Publishing Switzerland 2015
L.D. Beklemishev et al. (Eds.): Gurevich Festschrift II 2015, LNCS 9300, pp. 193–209, 2015.
DOI: 10.1007/978-3-319-23534-9_11

and where sentence i defines the property P_i. What we are still missing is an effective link between sentences and the properties they define. Therefore, the third requirement for a logic capturing PTIME is the existence of a "compiler" that translates a sentence into a polynomial time evaluation algorithm, that is, an algorithm that computes for each sentence φ of the logic a polynomial time algorithm A_φ deciding the property P_φ defined by φ.

Despite his conjecture that there is no logic capturing PTIME, Yuri Gurevich has, together with Andreas Blass and Saharon Shelah [6], also proposed *Choiceless Polynomial Time*, a logical formalism that, arguably, is still the most promising candidate for a logic that might actually capture PTIME. This paper is a survey of recent results on Choiceless Polynomial Time.

2   Choiceless Polynomial Time

There are several different presentations of Choiceless Polynomial Time (CPT). The original intention was to explore a model for efficient computations on abstract finite structures (and not on presentations of these via finite strings) which preserve symmetries at every step in the computation. This prohibits the explicit introduction of an ordering or, equivalently, arbitrary choices between indistinguishable elements of the input structure (or of the current state). Notice that such choices appear in many algorithms of fundamental importance, including depth-first search, Gaussian elimination, the augmenting-path algorithm for bipartite matching and many more.

Thus, Blass, Gurevich, and Shelah set out to define a computation model that avoids symmetry breaking choices, but allows essentially everything else, including parallelism and "fancy data structures", as long as all operations can be carried out in polynomial time. For a precise definition, they proposed a model based on abstract state machines, which, given a finite input structure, works on its extension by all hereditarily finite sets over it, which may be seen as a powerful higher-order data structure.

Inspired by Rossman [27], we give a more "logical" definition of CPT.

2.1   BGS-Logic

We need to review a few set theoretic notions first. For a finite set A, the set $\mathrm{HF}(A)$ of *hereditarily finite sets* over A is defined as follows: we let $H_0 := A \cup \{\emptyset\}$ and $H_{i+1} := H_i \cup 2^{H_i}$ for all $i \geq 0$ and $\mathrm{HF}(A) := \bigcup_{i \geq 0} H_i$. For every $x \in \mathrm{HF}(A)$, we define the *rank* of x to be the least i such that $x \in H_i$. We call the elements $a \in A \subseteq \mathrm{HF}(A)$ the *atoms*; all other elements of $\mathrm{HF}(A)$ are *sets*. With every natural number $n \in \mathbb{N}$ we associate the corresponding *van Neumann ordinal* n, inductively by $0 := \emptyset$ and $n+1 := n \cup \{n\}$.

Suppose now that we have a finite structure $\mathfrak{A}$ with universe A over some vocabulary τ consisting of relation, function, and constant symbols. We let τ^{HF} be the extension of τ by a binary relation symbol $\in$, a binary function symbol Pair, unary function symbols Union, TheUnique, Card, and constant symbols $\emptyset$ and Atoms (of course we assume that none of these symbols appears in τ).

We define the *hereditarily finite expansion of* A to be the τ^{HF}-structure $\mathrm{HF}(\mathfrak{A})$ with universe $\mathrm{HF}(A)$, all symbols from τ interpreted as in $\mathfrak{A}$, with the convention that functions take all arguments not from A to $\emptyset$, and the new symbols in $\tau^{\mathrm{HF}} \setminus \tau$ are interpreted in the natural way: $\in$ is the binary "element"-relation, Pair maps x, y to the set $\{x, y\}$, Union maps x to the union of all sets in x, TheUnique maps singleton sets $\{x\}$ to their unique element x and all other sets to the empty set, Card maps a set to its cardinality (represented as a von Neumann ordinal), $\emptyset$ is the empty set, and Atoms is the set A, viewed as an element of $\mathrm{HF}(A)$ of rank 1.

The next step towards the definition of CPT is the definition of a more general logic called *BGS-logic*. The syntactic objects of BGS-logic are *terms* and *formulae*. There are three different types of terms, or rather, term constructions: *ordinary terms, comprehension terms,* and *iteration terms*. The *ordinary terms* of BGS-logic of vocabulary τ are τ^{HF}-terms defined in the usual way. The *formulae* of BGS-logic are Boolean combinations of *atomic formulae* of the form $t = u$, $t \in u$, and $R(t_1, \ldots, t_k)$ for every k-ary relation symbol $R \in \sigma$, where $t, u, t_1, \ldots, t_k$ are terms. Thus all formulae are quantifier-free. (Example 2 below gives an indication on how quantifiers can be simulated.) Besides the ordinary terms, BGS-logic has *comprehension terms* of the form

$$\{t : v \in u : \varphi\}, \tag{1}$$

where t, u are terms, v is a variable that is not free in u, and φ is a formula. More suggestively, we may write $\{t(v) : v \in u : \varphi(v)\}$ to indicate that this term defines the set of all values $t(x)$, where x is an element of the set defined by the term u that satisfies the formula φ. Note that t, u, and v may have other free variables besides v.

Finally, for every term t with just one free variable we have an *iteration term* t^*. More suggestively, we may write $t(v)^*$, where v is the free variable of t. Intuitively, the value of the term t^* is the first fixed point of the sequence $t(\emptyset), t(t(\emptyset)), t(t(t(\emptyset))), \ldots$, if such a fixed point exists, or $\emptyset$ if no fixed point exists.

We define the *free variables* of terms and formulae in the natural way, stipulating that the variable v in a comprehension term of the form (1) and in an iteration term $t(v)^*$ be bound. Thus iteration terms t^* can never have free variables.

Terms and formulae of vocabulary τ are interpreted in the hereditarily finite expansion of τ-structures in the natural way. Formally, the denotation of a term $t = t(v_1, \ldots, v_k)$ of vocabulary τ and with free variables $v_1, \ldots, v_k$ in a τ-structure $\mathfrak{A}$ is the function $[\![t]\!]^{\mathfrak{A}} : \mathrm{HF}(A)^k \to \mathrm{HF}(A)$ that maps $(x_1, \ldots, x_k) \in \mathrm{HF}(A)^k$ to the value of the term if $v_1, \ldots, v_k$ are interpreted by $x_1, \ldots, x_k$, repectively. If a term t has no free variables, then $[\![t]\!]^{\mathfrak{A}}$ is a nullary function, which we interpret as a constant. Similarly, we define the denotation $[\![\varphi]\!]^{\mathfrak{A}}$ of a formula $\varphi = \varphi(v_1, \ldots, v_k)$ in $\mathfrak{A}$ to be the set of all $(x_1, \ldots, x_k) \in \mathrm{HF}(A)^k$ satisfying φ. Note that if φ is a *sentence*, that is, a formula without free variables, then either $[\![\varphi]\!]^{\mathfrak{A}} = \{\emptyset\} =:$ True or $[\![\varphi]\!]^{\mathfrak{A}} = \emptyset =:$ False. In these and similar notations, we omit the superscript $^{\mathfrak{A}}$ if $\mathfrak{A}$ is clear from the context. The definition is straightforward for ordinary terms and formulae. For a comprevension term

$s := \{t : v \in u : \varphi\}$, where for simplicity we assume that t and φ have the same free variables $v, v_1, \ldots, v_k$ and u has free variables $v_1, \ldots, v_k$, we define

$$[\![s]\!](x_1, \ldots, x_k) := \{[\![t]\!](x, x_1, \ldots, x_k) \mid x \in [\![u]\!](x_1, \ldots, x_k)$$
$$\text{such that } (x, x_1, \ldots, x_k) \in [\![\varphi]\!]\},$$

for all $(x_1, \ldots, x_k) \in \mathrm{HF}(A)^k$. For an iteration term t^* we define a sequence $(x_i)_{i \geq 0}$ by $x_0 := \emptyset$ and $x_{i+1} := [\![t]\!](x_i)$, and we let

$$[\![t^*]\!] := \begin{cases} x_\ell & \text{for the least } \ell \text{ such that } x_\ell = x_{\ell+1} \text{ if such an } \ell \text{ exists,} \\ \emptyset & \text{otherwise.} \end{cases}$$

If there is no ℓ such that $x_\ell = x_{\ell+1}$, we say that t^* *diverges* in $\mathfrak{A}$. We define the *length of the iteration* $\mathrm{len}(t^*, \mathfrak{A})$ of t^* in $\mathfrak{A}$ to be the least ℓ such that $x_\ell = x_{\ell+1}$, or ∞ if t^* diverges.

Remark 1. Instead of defining $[\![t^*]\!]$ to be the emptyset if t^* diverges, we could also leave it undefined and work with a three valued logic. This would be closer to Blass, Gurevich and Shelah's original approach, but complicate things unnecessarily. For the fragment CPT of BGS-logic that we are mainly interested in, this makes no difference, because all terms in this fragment will be required to converge anyway.

The iteration terms play the role of the *programs* in Rossman's version of BGS-logic. It is easy to see that programs can be simulated by iteration terms and, conversely, iteration terms can be simulated by programs. However, as opposed to Rossman, we allow iteration terms to appear inside of other terms and formulae, whereas Rossman does not allow nested programs. But again, for the fragment CPT this makes no difference.

Example 2 (Triangles in a Graph). Let $\tau = \{E\}$ with one binary relation symbol E; we view τ-structures as directed, or if E is symmetric undirected, graphs. We shall construct a BGS-term that defines the set of all triangles (viewed as 3-element sets) in an undirected graph.

We let $\varphi(v_1, v_3, v_3) := E(v_1, v_2) \wedge E(v_2, v_3) \wedge E(v_3, v_1)$ and

$$t_1(v_2, v_3) := \{\mathsf{Union}(\mathsf{Pair}(\mathsf{Pair}(v_1, v_1), \mathsf{Pair}(v_2, v_3))) : v_1 \in \mathsf{Atoms} : \varphi(v_1, v_3, v_3)\},$$
$$t_2(v_3) := \{t_1(v_2, v_3) : v_2 \in \mathsf{Atoms} : v_2 = v_2\},$$
$$t_3 := \{t_2(v_3) : v_3 \in \mathsf{Atoms} : v_3 = v_3\}.$$

Then $[\![t_3]\!]^{\mathfrak{G}}$ is the set of all triangles of an undirected graph $\mathfrak{G}$.

We can now define a formula $\psi(v)$ expressing that v is contained in a triangle: we simply let $\psi(v) := v \in \mathsf{Union}(t_3)$.

Using ideas similar to those in the example, it is not difficult to express bounded quantifiers $\exists v \in t$ and $\forall v \in t$ in BGS-logic. Thus all formulae of bounded first-order logic (called Δ_0-formulae in set theory) over the hereditarily finite sets can be expressed by equivalent BGS-formulae (without using iteration).

Example 3 (Power Set). We shall construct a BGS-term that defines the power set of the set of atoms.

We observe that we can express the union of two sets s and t as

$$s \cup t := \mathsf{Union}(\mathsf{Pair}(s, t)).$$

We define an auxiliary term

$$s(w) := \{w \cup \mathsf{Pair}(w', w') \colon w' \in \mathsf{Atoms} \colon w' = w'\},$$

which defines the collection of sets obtained by adding an atom to w, and let

$$t(v) := \mathsf{Pair}(\emptyset, \emptyset) \cup \mathsf{Union}(\{s(w) \colon w \in v \colon w = w\}).$$

Then $\overbrace{t(t(\cdots t(\emptyset)\cdots))}^{i \text{ times}}$ defines the set of sets of at most $i - 1$ atoms. Thus for every structure $\mathfrak{A}$ we have $[\![t^*]\!] = 2^A$.

We can use the previous example to show that BGS-logic can simulate monadic second-order logic, and by iterating the construction, higher order logic. Thus the logic is far too powerful to stay within the realm of polynomial time computations.

2.2   Definition of Choiceless Polynomial Time

Intuitively, *Choiceless Polynomial Time* (CPT) is the polynomial-time fragment of BGS-logic. To define CPT we first restrict the length of iterations to be polynomial in the size of the input. However, this alone is not sufficient, as can be seen by Example 3. In addition, it is necessary to restrict also the number of elements that are being used, or *active*, in any step of the computation.

We inductively define for every term $s = s(v_1, \ldots, v_k)$, every structure $\mathfrak{A}$, and every tuple $\bar{x} = (x_1, \ldots, x_k) \in \mathsf{HF}(A)^k$ the set $\mathrm{act}(s, \mathfrak{A}, \bar{x})$ of *active elements* as follows.

- If $s = v$ is a variable then $\mathrm{act}(s, \mathfrak{A}, x) = \{x\}$, and if $s = c$ is a constant then $\mathrm{act}(s, \mathfrak{A}) = \{[\![c]\!]\}$.
- If $s = f(t_1, \ldots, t_\ell)$ then

$$\mathrm{act}(s, \mathfrak{A}, \bar{x}) = \{[\![s]\!](\bar{x})\} \cup \bigcup_{i=1}^{\ell} \mathrm{act}(t_i, \mathfrak{A}, \bar{x}_i),$$

   where $\bar{x}_i$ is the subtuple of $\bar{x}$ corresponding the free variables of t_i.
- If $s = \{t \colon v \in u \colon \varphi(v)\}$, then

$$\mathrm{act}(s, \mathfrak{A}, \bar{x}) = \{[\![s]\!](\bar{x})\} \cup \mathrm{act}(u, \mathfrak{A}, \bar{x}) \cup \bigcup_{x \in [\![u]\!](\bar{x})} \left(\mathrm{act}(t, \mathfrak{A}, x\bar{x}) \cup \mathrm{act}(\varphi, \mathfrak{A}, x\bar{x}) \right),$$

   where $x\bar{x}$ denotes the tuple $(x, x_1, \ldots, x_k)$ and for simplicity we assume that the free variables of t and φ are $v, v_1, \ldots, v_k$ and the free variables of u are $v_1, \ldots, v_k$.

- If $s = t^*$ we define the sequence $(x_i)_{i \geq 0}$ as in the definition of $[\![t^*]\!]$ and let

$$\mathrm{act}(s, \mathfrak{A}) = \bigcup_{i \geq 0} \mathrm{act}(t, \mathfrak{A}, x_i).$$

Note that if s converges then $\mathrm{act}(s, \mathfrak{A}) = \bigcup_{i=0}^{\mathrm{len}(t^*, \mathfrak{A})} \mathrm{act}(t, \mathfrak{A}, x_i)$, and thus $\mathrm{act}(s, \mathfrak{A}) \in \mathrm{HF}(A)$. This is not necessarily the case if t diverges.

For a formula φ, we define $\mathrm{act}(\varphi, \mathfrak{A}, \overline{x})$ to be the union of the sets $\mathrm{act}(t, \mathfrak{A}, \overline{x}_t)$ for the terms t that are used to built φ.

We are now ready to define *Choiceless Polynomial Time (CPT)* as the fragment of BGS-logic consisting of all sentences φ for which there is a polynomial $p(x)$ such that for all structures $\mathfrak{A}$ of order $|A| = n$ we have

$$|\mathrm{act}(\varphi, \mathfrak{A})| \leq p(n).$$

Observe that this implies that for all iteration terms t^* appearing in φ (also as subterms of other terms) we have $\mathrm{len}(t^*, \mathfrak{A}) \leq p(n)$, because all values appearing in the steps of the iteration are active elements.

Remark 4. Defined this way, CPT is not a logic in the strict sense because it does not have a decidable syntax. However, it is easy to define a syntactic fragment that does have a decidable syntax, but still has the same expressive power. The key idea is to include explicit counters and cardinality tests in iteration terms. The next example illustrates how this can be done.

Example 5 (Counter). In this example, we show how to modify an iteration term s^* in such a way that the iteration is aborted if no fixed-point is reached after n (= order of the structure) steps.

It is not hard to define a binary term $\langle \cdot, \cdot \rangle$ that combines its two arguments into an ordered pair and projection terms π_1, π_2 that map an ordered pair to its entries. Moreover, the term $\mathrm{succ}(v) := v \cup \mathrm{Pair}(v)$ maps a von-Neumann ordinal n to ist successor n+1. Note that m < n $\Leftrightarrow$ m $\in$ n for all $n, m \in \mathbb{N}$.

Now consider an iteration term s^*. We let

$$t(v) := \langle 0, \emptyset \rangle \cup \{\langle \mathrm{succ}(\pi_1(w)), s(\pi_2(w)) \rangle : w \in v : \pi_1(w) \in \mathrm{Card}(\mathrm{Atoms})\}.$$

Then for all structure $\mathfrak{A}$ of order $n := |A| = [\![\mathrm{Card}(\mathrm{Atoms})]\!]$ we have $[\![t^*]\!] = \{(\mathrm{i}, x_i) \mid 0 \leq i \leq n\}$, where the sequences $(x_i)_{i \geq 0}$ is defined by $x_0 := \emptyset$ and $x_{i+1} := [\![s]\!](x_i)$. Obsserve that if s^* converges then $x_n = s^*$ if and only if $x_n = x_{n+1}$. Let

$$u := \mathsf{TheUnique}\Big(\{\pi_2(w) : w \in t^* : \pi_1(w) = \mathrm{Card}(\mathrm{Atoms}) \wedge \pi_2(w) = s(\pi_2(w))\} \Big).$$

Then $[\![u]\!] = [\![s^*]\!]$ if $\mathrm{len}(s, \mathfrak{A}) \leq n$ and $[\![u]\!] = \emptyset$ otherwise.

2.3 Defining Properties of Small Substructures

To illustrate the power of CPT, we consider specific structures that we call padded graphs. The vocabulary τ consist of a unary relation symbol V and a binary relation symbol E. A *padded graph* is a τ-structure $\mathfrak{A}$ where $E^{\mathfrak{A}} \subseteq V^{\mathfrak{A}} \times V^{\mathfrak{A}}$ and $E^{\mathfrak{A}}$ is symmetric and irreflexive. The *underlying graph* of a padded graph $\mathfrak{A}$ is the graph $\mathfrak{G}_{\mathfrak{A}}$ with vertex set $V^{\mathfrak{A}}$ and edge relation $E^{\mathfrak{A}}$. In the following, we always use n to denote the order $|A|$ of a padded graph $\mathfrak{A}$ and ℓ to denote the order $|V^{\mathfrak{A}}|$ of its underlying graph. We usually assume that $\ell \ll n$.

Example 6 (3-Colourability of Padded Graphs). In this example, we consider padded graphs $\mathfrak{A}$ where $\ell \leq \log n$. Using the construction of Example 3, we obtain a term t that defines the powerset of V, that is, $[\![t]\!] = 2^{V^{\mathfrak{A}}}$. The assumption $\ell \leq \log n$ guarantees that this works within the polynomial bounds imposed by CPT. Using this term, we can easily write a CPT-sentence of the form $\exists v_1 \in t \, \exists v_2 \in t \, \exists v_3 \in t \, (\cdots)$ stating that the underlying graph of $\mathfrak{A}$ is 3-colourable.

The following example is due to Blass, Gurevich, and Shelah.

Example 7 (Linear Orders). We consider padded graphs where $\ell! \leq n$. Then, using a similar idea as in Examples 3 and 6, we construct a term t that defines the set of all linear orders of V. As there are $\ell!$ linear orders of V, the assumption $\ell! \leq n$ guarantees that we stay within the polynomial bounds imposed by CPT.

Now, exploiting the facts that least fixed-point logic LFP captures polynomial time on ordered graphs and that CPT is at least as expressive as LFP, it is easy to show that CPT can express all polnomial time properties of the underlying graph of the given padded graph.

It is not hard to show that there are polynomial time properties of the underlying graph that cannot be expressed in LFP, not even in fixed-point logic with counting FPC (see Sect. 3), because the padding does not help these logics very much. This is the easiest way to show that CPT is strictly more expressive than FPC.

Laubner [25], in his PhD-thesis, slightly strengthened the result of the previous example and proved the following theorem, which intuitively says that CPT expresses all polynomial time properties of definable subgraphs of logarithmic size.

Theorem 8. *For every property P of graphs that is decidable in polynomial time there is a CPT-sentence φ such that for all padded graphs $\mathfrak{A}$ with $\ell \leq \log n$, the following are equivalent.*

1. $\mathfrak{A}$ *satisfies φ.*
2. *The underlying graph $\mathfrak{G}_{\mathfrak{A}}$ has property P.*

The crucial step in the proof of this theorem is the implementation of a combinatorial graph canonization algorithm due to Corneil and Goldberg [11], running in time $2^{O(\ell)}$ on graphs of order ℓ, in CPT.

2.4   Choiceless Polynomial Time Without Counting

To be a serious candidate for being a logic for polynomial time, CPT has (and needs) the cardinality operator Card. Blass, Gurevich and Shelah also considered a variant of CPT without the Card-operator, which we denote by CPT$^-$.

Not surprisingly, CPT$^-$ is unable to determine whether a structure has an even or odd number of elements, but this is much more difficult to prove than for, say, least fixed-point logic. The proof requires a sophisticated analysis of the support of hereditarily finite sets used in CPT-computations (see [27]). Nevertheless CPT$^-$ is quite a powerful language; for instance it has been in shown in [14] that CPT$^-$ can express (a variant of) the CFI-query that separates fixed-point logic with counting (FPC) from PTIME and is therefore incomparable with FPC. An interesting result on CPT$^-$ is the zero-one law established by Shelah (see [5] for details) saying that for every CPT$^-$-definable property P of relational τ-structures the probability $\mu_n(P)$ that a random τ-structure of cardinality n satisfies property P tends either to 0 or 1 as n goes to infinity.

3   Fixed-Point Logic with Counting

The logic of reference, or yardstick, in the search for a logic for PTIME is fixed-point logic with counting, denoted FPC. This logic was introduced, somewhat informally, by Immerman [23], a more formal definition, based on two-sorted structures, inflationary fixed-points, and counting terms was given in [17]. For a recent survey on FPC, see [12].

Fixed-point logic with counting comes actually rather close to being a logic for polynomial time. It is strong enough to express most of the fundamental algorithmic techniques leading to polynomial-time procedures and it captures PTIME on many interesting classes of finite structures, including trees, planar graphs, structures of bounded tree width, and actually all classes of graphs with an excluded minor [20]. Indeed, these classes even admit FPC-*definable canonisation* which means that FPC can define, given an input structure, an isomorphic copy of that structure over a linearly ordered universe. Clearly, if a class of structures admits FPC-definable canonisations, then FPC captures PTIME on this class, since by the Immerman-Vardi Theorem (see e.g. [19]) fixed-point logic can define every polynomial-time query on ordered structures.

Although it has been known for more than twenty years that FPC fails to capture PTIME in general, by the fundamental CFI-construction due to Cai, Fürer, and Immerman [10], we still know only relatively few properties of finite structures that provably separate FPC from PTIME.

Roughly we have, at this time, two main sources for such problems. The first one includes tractable cases of the isomorphism problem for finite structures, in particular for graphs. It is, in general still open, whether the general graph isomorphism problem is solvable in polynomial time, but efficient isomorphism tests are known in many special cases, including all classes of graphs of bounded degree *or* bounded colour class size. However, the CFI-construction shows that FPC cannot define the isomorphism problem even on graphs with bounded degree *and* bounded colour class size.

Multipedes. An interesting instance of such a problem is the isomorphism problem for *multipedes*. Multipedes[2] have been introduced in [7] and studied also in [21]. Informally, a multipede is a finite two-sorted structure, consisting of an ordered set of segments, and a set of feet, such that exactly two feet are attached to each segment. Further there is a collection of hyperedges H of size 3 on the segments, and a corresponding collection of hyperedges P of feet, also of size 3, called positive triples, such that each positive triple of feet is attached to a hyperedge H of segments, and out of the eight triples of feet attached to H, exactly four are positive. Further if P and P' are two positive triples of feet attached to the same hyperedge H, then $|P - P'|$ is even. Finally, exactly one of the two feet attached to the first segment carries a shoe.

Blass, Gurevich, and Shelah [7] proved that the isomorphism problem for multipedes can be solved in polynomial time, but that it is not expressible in fixed-point logic with counting. They asked the question whether it is definable in CPT.

Linear Algebra. The second class of hard problems for FPC includes queries from linear algebra. In general, the definability of central problems of linear algebra provides an interesting challenge in the study of the expressive power of logical systems and for the quest for a logic for PTIME. On one side, it has turned out that a fair amount of linear algebra, in particular for fields of characteristic zero, is expressible in fixed-point logic with counting, including arithmetic operations on matrices, singularity of matrices, determinants, characteristic polynomials, and matrix rank over $\mathbb{Q}$ (but not over fields of prime characteristic). On the other side, Atserias, Bulatov and Dawar [3] proved that FPC cannot express the solvability of linear equation systems over any finite Abelian group, and it then follows that also a number of other problems from linear algebra are not definable in FPC either. This motivated the introduction of *rank logic*, which extends FPC by operators for the rank of definable matrices over prime fields $\mathbb{F}_p$, and which permits to express the solvability of linear equation systems over finite fields [13]. Interestingly, also the CFI-query can be formulated as linear equation system over $\mathbb{F}_2$ and is thus expressible in rank logic. There are different variants of rank logic. For the most powerful of them, with a rank operator where the prime over which the rank is computed is not fixed, but part of the input, it is still open whether it captures PTIME [18].

4   Structures of Bounded Colour Class Size

Recall a that a preorder of width q is a reflexive, transitive, and total binary relation $\preceq$ such that the induced equivalence relation $a \sim b := (a \preceq b \preceq a)$ only has equivalence classes of size $\leq q$. A *q-bounded structure* is a structure that is

---

[2] Actually, Gurevich and Shelah introduced a number of different variants of multipedes. What we use here are called 3-multipedes with shoes in [7].

equipped with a pre-order $\preceq$ of width q. The equivalence classes induced by $\preceq$ are also called colour classes.

It is still open whether Choiceless Polynomial Time captures PTIME on all classes of finite structures with bounded colour class size. A partial positive answer was given in [1], for any class of *q-bounded structures with Abelian colours*, which means that the automorphism groups of all substructures induced by the colour classes are commutative.

An important ingredient in the CPT-canonization procedure for such classes is a choiceless algorithm for solving a special class of linear equation systems. Clearly linear equation systems over an *ordered* set of variables can be solved in fixed-point logic with counting. However, classical solution algorithms for linear equation systems require choice, and for *unordered* sets of variables they cannot be carried out in FPC. An intermediate class are *cyclic linear equation systems* (CES) over finite rings $\mathbb{Z}_{p^k}$, equipped with a pre-order $\preceq$ on the set of variables, such that every pair of $\preceq$-equivalent variables x, y is related by an equation $x + a = y$ for some constant a. This means that fixing the value of one variable in a solution of the CES fixes also the values for all other variables in the same $\preceq$-class. Cyclic equation systems arise for instance in Cai-Fürer-Immerman (CFI) constructions. The original CFI-query (over ordered input graphs) can be formulated as cyclic equation systems over $\mathbb{Z}_2$ where the cyclic constraint on pairs x_0, x_1 of $\preceq$-equivalent variables simply has the form $x_0 + x_1 = 1$. In Holm's PhD-thesis [22] and also in [18] a generalized CFI-construction over rings $\mathbb{Z}_q$ has been exhibited which is, for instance, relevant for the study of rank logic. Again, the isomorphism problem for generalized CFI-structures, which can be formulated as a CES over $\mathbb{Z}_q$, separates PTIME from FPC, but it also gives rise to a number of further separation results, concerning for instance different variants of rank logics [18].

Theorem 9. *The solvability problem for cyclic linear equation systems can be defined in Choiceless Polynomial Time.*

Any $\preceq$-class of variables in a CES has a cyclic structure, and we can order each such class by fixing one variable. However, in Choiceless Polynomial Time it is not possible to simultaneously fix one variable in each class, since this would require to take into account also all symmetric choices of which there may be exponentially many. One can circumvent this problem by means of so-called *hyperterms* which avoid this exponential blow-up by identifying equivalent choices and encoding equivalence classes as hereditarily finite sets over the universe of variables. Choiceless Polynomial Time is powerful enough to perform arithmetic operation on hyperterms, and to translate any cyclic linear equation system into an *ordered system of hyperequations*. Finally the solvability of such systems can then be determined in CPT by a variant of Gaussian elimination for finite rings.

Cyclic linear equation systems are an essential ingredient in the canonization procedure for q-bounded structures with Abelian colours. For details, we refer to [1] and the forthcoming PhD thesis of Wied Pakusa.

Theorem 10. *CPT captures* PTIME *on every class of q-bounded structures with Abelian colours.*

Notice that 2-bounded structures trivially have Abelian colours, since the automorphism group of every colour class is either trivial or $\mathbb{Z}_2$. Hence CPT capture polynomial-time on 2-bounded structures. Further, since also multipedes are 2-bounded structures, this resolves the above-mentioned problem posed by Blass, Gurevich, and Shelah (cf. [7, Question 5.12, p. 1115]).

Corollary 11. *The isomorphism problem for multipedes is CPT-definable.*

5 Symmetric Circuits

Any property of finite τ-structures can be considered as a sequence of Boolean functions $(f_n)_{n\in\mathbb{N}}$ where f_n takes as inputs the truth values of the atomic τ-formulae on a given structure $\mathfrak{A}$ with universe $[n] = \{0, \ldots, n-1\}$, and returns either 0 or 1, depending on whether or not $\mathfrak{A}$ satisfies the given property. To represent really a property of structures of size n, and not of ordered presentations of these, the function f_n must be invariant under any permutation of the universe $[n]$.

Clearly every property of finite structures that is decidable in polynomial time is also decidable by a p-uniform sequence $(C_n)_{n\in\mathbb{N}}$ of polynomial-size Boolean circuits that are invariant in the semantic sense just described. More precisely, every permutation $\pi \in S_n$ of the universe $[n]$ induces a permutation of the input gates of C_n, and the value computed by the circuit C_n does not change if the values $\bar{a}$ of the input gates (representing a structure $\mathfrak{A}$ with universe $[n]$) are changed to $\pi\bar{a}$ (representing the structure $\pi\mathfrak{A} \cong \mathfrak{A}$). Such circuits, and circuit families, are called *invariant*.

On the other side, if we translate a formula from a simple logical language, say, first-order logic or fixed-point logic, into a sequence of circuits, such that circuit C_n simulates the evaluation of the formula on input structures with universe $[n]$, then these circuits are of course invariant, of polynomial size, and in fact p-uniform in the sense that the circuit C_n is computable in polynomial time in n. But moreover such circuits satisfy the stronger property that every permutation of the input universe induces in fact an *automorphism* of the circuit. Circuits with this property are called *symmetric*. Obviously, symmetric circuits are invariant, and it is easy to see that the converse is not true. However, it is *a priori* not clear whether polynomial size symmetric circuits (over a given basis) define a weaker computation model than invariant ones.

For logics with counting, such as FPC, it is natural to consider circuits with threshold or majority gates. Notice that the extension of the standard Boolean basis by majority gates does not change the power of polynomial-size circuit families, but it can make a difference for specific classes of circuits, such as bounded-depth circuits or symmetric ones. It is a simple observation that every sentence of FPC is equivalent to a p-uniform sequence of symmetric circuits with majority gates.

Can also Choiceless Polynomial Time be translated into such circuits families? If this were the case, then one might use methods from circuit complexity theory to study the power of CPT and understanding its connection with PTIME. With this question in mind, Anderson and Dawar [2] set out to study the power of polynomial-size families of symmetric circuits, both over the standard Boolean basis, and the extension by majority or threshold gates. However, their main results show that symmetric circuits (of polynomial size) are too weak for CPT. In fact, in the version with threshold gates, they are equivalent to FPC and thus cannot define, say, the CFI-query.

Theorem 12. *A class of finite structures is decided by a p-uniform sequence of symmetric threshold circuits if, and only if, it is definable in fixed-point logic with counting. Similarly, a class of finite structures $\mathfrak{A}$ is decided by a p-uniform sequence of Boolean circuits if, and only if, it is definable in least fixed-point logic over their two-sorted expansions $\mathfrak{A}^* = \mathfrak{A} \cup \langle n, < \rangle$.*

This theorem has interesting consequences for the study of Choiceless Polynomial Time. It shows that a translation of CPT programs into equivalent sequences of symmetric threshold circuits cannot be done in a p-uniform way. To put it differently, any p-uniform translation from CPT into equivalent sequences of threshold circuits has to break symmetry in some way.

6   Interpretation Logic

While the common presentations of Choiceless Polynomial Time via the manipulation of hereditarily finite sets, by abstract state machines or terms in BGS-logic is convenient and powerful for the design of abstract computations on structures, it makes the analysis of the expressive power of CPT rather difficult. Standard techniques for the analysis of logical systems as used in finite model theory, for instance those based on Ehrenfeucht-Fraïssé methods, are not directly available. In particular, applications of comprehension terms increase the rank of objects and are difficult to handle by the common logical tools, which are usually restricted to 'flat' objects.

However, as recently shown in [16], one can provide alternative presentations of CPT (with and without counting) that are based on classical model-theoretic techniques. In particular, the 'fancy data structures' of the hereditarily finite sets and the manipulation of comprehension terms can be replaced by traditional first-order interpretations. In this context, counting can then be handled by Härtig quantifiers which are classical quantifiers for cardinality comparison. Thus choiceless computations on finite structures can be captured by *iterations of interpretations*. A run is a sequence of states, each of which is now a *finite* structure of a fixed vocabulary. There is an initial interpretation that produces the initial state as a structure interpreted in the input structure, and a second interpretation $\mathcal{I}_{\text{step}}$ that always maps the current state to its successor state. Since interpretations need not be one-dimensional they can increase the size of the states. Although one application of an interpretation increases the size only polynomially, without imposing restrictions, the iterated application through a polynomial number of steps could produce states of exponential size.

Polynomial-Time Interpretation Logic, denoted PIL, is obtained by imposing polynomial bounds on the length of such computations and the size of the states. It turns out that PIL has precisely the same expressive power as Choiceless Polynomial Time.

Theorem 13. PIL ≡ CPT.

The equivalence survives also in the absence of counting: Polynomial-Time Interpretation Logic without the Härtig quantifier PIL⁻ is equivalent to CPT⁻.

Further, the presentation of CPT in terms of first-order interpretations leads to natural fragments and stratifications of this logic along familiar syntactic parameters. For instance, one can consider the natural restrictions of PIL to k-dimensional interpretations, and/or to interpretations where the domain or equivalence formulae are trivial. It turns out that the iteration of one-dimensional interpretations is in fact equivalent to the familiar relational iteration appearing in the partial fixed-point logic PFP, or equivalently, in the database language while. Thus, without the Härtig quantifier, one-dimensional Polynomial-Time Interpretation Logic turns out to be equivalent to the polynomial-time restriction of PFP, which by means of a classical result due to Abiteboul and Vianu implies that one-dimensional PIL⁻ is equivalent to LFP if, and only if, PTIME = PSPACE. On the other hand, it is known (see e.g. [26]) that the polynomial-time restriction of PFP with counting is actually equivalent to FPC. It follows that one-dimensional PIL, when evaluated on the expansions of finite structures by an ordered numerical sort, has precisely the expressive power of FPC. One can thus view FPC as a one-dimensional fragment of PIL and CPT. This confirms the intuition that the additional power of Choiceless Polynomial Time over FPC comes from the generalization of relational iteration in a fixed arity (as in fixed-point logics) to iterations of relations of changing arities. Already two-dimensional interpretations give us this additional flexibility of relational iteration and, indeed, two-dimensional PIL turns out to be equivalent to full PIL.

Another interesting aspect is the representation of equality by congruence relations and the passage to quotient structures. One may ask whether these are really necessary for obtaining the full expressive power of PIL. The answer is yes.

In the absence of counting, PIL⁻ without congruences is equivalent to a previously studied extension of the database language while, called while$_{\text{new}}$ |PTIME which is known to be strictly weaker than CPT. In the presence of counting, the situation is even more intriguing. On any class of structures of bounded colour class size, PIL without congruences can be simulated by CPT-programs that access only hereditarily finite sets of bounded rank. In particular this holds for the class of CFI-graphs. Since Dawar, Richerby, and Rossman prove in [14] that the CFI-query is definable in CPT, but not by programs of bounded rank, this separates also congruence-free PIL from full PIL. Hence with or without counting, congruences are really essential for reaching the full power of PIL.

7   Challenges for Future Research

Of course the main open problem concerning Choiceless Polynomial Time remains the question whether it captures all of PTIME. But no matter whether or not this is the case, there are a number of interesting open problems that seem to be within the reach of current techniques.

7.1   A Characterization Without Explicit Polynomial Bounds

An unsatisfactory point in the definition of both CPT and PIL is the requirement for explicit polynomial bounds on the running time, the number of active elements or the size of the interpreted structures appearing in a run. It would be desirable to have a characterization of CPT that does not depend on such explicit bounds, but guarantees polynomial-time evaluation implicitly, by construction, as in classical logical approaches such as fixed-point logics.

7.2   Polynomial-Time Properties of Small Definable Subgraphs

Recall Theorem 8, intuitively stating that CPT expresses all polynomial time properties of definable substructures of logarithmic size. It is quite possible that this theorem can further be strengthened, say, to definable substructures of poly-logarithmic size.

Is there a function f with $f(n) = \omega(\log n)$ such that the theorem can be strengthened to hold for all $\ell \leq f(n)$? Or is this even the case for all f with polylogarithmic growth rate?

7.3   Isomorphism of CFI-Graphs and Graphs of Bounded Colour Class Size

We have already mentioned the question of whether isomorphism of graphs of bounded colour class size is in CPT; this is basically only known for graphs with Abelian colours (see Sect. 4). The CFI-graphs are usually presented as a special case. These are graphs of colour class size four (or more general structures of colour class size two) with Abelian colours, provided that the input graphs are coloured in a certain way. This is not inherent in the construction, but just a convenience of the presentation.

It is an open problem whether the isomorphism of uncoloured CFI-graphs (which is still in polynomial time) is in CPT. Actually, this might be a candidate for separating CPT from PTIME.

7.4   Constraint Satisfaction Problems

Constraint satisfaction problems (CSPs), defined in terms of their constraint language, form a rich family of problems in NP that contains many practically important problems, but is still relatively well behaved and excludes pathological examples of problems such as Ladner's [24] NP-problems that are neither in PTIME nor NP-complete. Indeed, Feder and Vardi's [15] well known Dichotomy Conjecture states that all CSPs are either in PTIME or NP-complete. Bulatov, Jeavons, and Krokhin [9] made a refined conjecture characterising the CSPs in PTIME algebraically.

We may ask which CSPs are *solvable* in CPT. If this class coincides with the class of CSPs conjectured to be PTIME-solvable by Bulatov, Jeavons, and Krokhin, this could be seen as evidence that CPT captures polynomial time, or at least does so on the class of all CSPs.

Atserias, Bulatov, and Dawar [3] characterised the CSPs solvable in FPC as precisely those with a property called *bounded width*. It is known that CPT can solve CSPs of unbounded width; cyclic equation systems are examples. These equations systems are CSPs that belong to a polynomial time solvable class of CSPs known as CSPs with *Mal'tsev polymorphisms* [8]. As a first step towards the general question, we ask whether all CSPs with Mal'tsev constraints are solvable in CPT. We remark that an affirmative answer to this question would imply that isomorphism of graphs of bounded colour class size is in CPT (via a reduction described in [4]).

7.5   A Notion of Symmetric Circuits for CPT

We mentioned in Sect. 5 the result by Anderson and Dawar that p-uniform symmetric circuits are too weak for CFP, and that therefore any p-uniform translation of CPT into equivalent sequences of threshold circuits has to break symmetry in some way. It is an interesting challenge to see how, and to come up with a circuit model capturing CPT. Anderson and Dawar suggest to consider weaker notions of symmetry, requiring induced automorphisms of the circuit only for certain subgroups of the symmetric group on the input universe.

7.6   Choiceless Polynomial Time versus Rank Logic

Besides Choiceless Polynomial Time, one may consider rank logic to be the most prominent candidate for a logic for PTIME. The relationship between these two logics is, at this point unclear.

Theorem 9 about the solvability of cyclic linear equation systems might provide a handle to separate the two logics. Indeed, while the solvability of (arbitrary) linear equation systems over finite fields can clearly be expressed in rank logic, we see no way how rank logic would be able to deal with solvability problems for CES over rings $\mathbb{Z}_{p^k}$ for $k > 1$. Indeed we conjecture that the solvability of CES over $\mathbb{Z}_4$ might be problem that is definable in CPT but not in rank logic.

References

1. Abu Zaid, F., Grädel, E., Grohe, M., Pakusa, W.: Choiceless polynomial time on structures with small abelian colour classes. In: Csuhaj-Varjú, E., Dietzfelbinger, M., Ésik, Z. (eds.) MFCS 2014, Part I. LNCS, vol. 8634, pp. 50–62. Springer, Heidelberg (2014)

2. Anderson, M., Dawar, A.: On symmetric circuits and fixed-point logics. In: STACS, pp. 41–52 (2014)
3. Atserias, A., Bulatov, A., Dawar, A.: Affine systems of equations and counting infinitary logic. Theor. Comput. Sci. **410**, 1666–1683 (2009)
4. Berkholz, C., Grohe, M.: Limitations of algebraic approaches to graph isomorphism testing (2015). arXiv: arXiv:1502.05912 [cs.CC]
5. Blass, A., Gurevich, Y.: Strong extension axioms and shelah's zero-one law for choiceless polynomial time. J. Symb. Logic **68**(1), 65–131 (2003)
6. Blass, A., Gurevich, Y., Shelah, S.: Choiceless polynomial time. Ann. Pure Appl. Logic **100**, 141–187 (1999)
7. Blass, A., Gurevich, Y., Shelah, S.: On polynomial time computation over undered structures. J. Symb. Logic **67**, 1093–1125 (2002)
8. Bulatov, A., Dalmau, V.: A simple algorithm for Mal'tsev constraints. SIAM J. Comput. **36**(1), 16–27 (2006)
9. Bulatov, A., Jeavons, P., Krokhin, A.: Classifying the complexity of constraints using finite algebras. SIAM J. Comput. **34**, 720–742 (2005)
10. Cai, J., Fürer, M., Immerman, N.: An optimal lower bound on the number of variables for graph identification. Combinatorica **12**, 389–410 (1992)
11. Corneil, D.G., Goldberg, M.K.: A non-factorial algorithm for canonical numbering of a graph. J. Algorithms **5**(3), 345–362 (1984)
12. Dawar, A.: The nature and power of fixed-point logic with counting. ACM SIGLOG News **2**(1), 8–21 (2015)
13. Dawar, A., Grohe, M., Holm, B., Laubner, B.: Logics with rank operators. In: Proceedings of 24th IEEE Symposium on Logic in Computer Science (LICS 2009), pp. 113–122 (2009)
14. Dawar, A., Richerby, D., Rossman, B.: Choiceless polynomial time, counting and the Cai-Fürer-Immerman graphs. Ann. Pure Appl. Logic **152**, 31–50 (2009)
15. Féder, T., Vardi, M.Y.: The computational structure of monotone monadic SNP and constraint satisfaction: a study through datalog and group theory. SIAM J. Comput. **28**, 57–104 (1998)
16. E., Grädel, Ł., Kaiser, W.P., Schalthöfer, S.: Characterising choiceless polynomial time with first-order interpretations. In: LICS (2015)
17. Grädel, E., Otto, M.: Inductive definability with counting on finite structures. In: Börger, E., Jäger, G., Büning, H.K., Martini, S., Richter, M.M. (eds.) CSL 1992. LNCS, vol. 702, pp. 231–247. Springer, Heidelberg (1992)
18. Grädel, E., Pakusa, W.: Rank logic is dead, long live rank logic! (2015). http://arxiv.org/abs/1503.05423
19. Grädel, E., et al.: Finite Model Theory and Its Applications. Springer, New York (2007)
20. Grohe, M.: Fixed-point definability and polynomial time on graph with excluded minors. J. ACM **59**(5), 27:1–27:64 (2012)
21. Gurevich, Y., Shelah, S.: On finite rigid structures. J. Symb. Logic **61**, 549–562 (1996)
22. Holm, B.: Descriptive Complexity of Linear Algebra. Ph.D. thesis, University of Cambridge (2010)
23. Immerman, N.: Expresibility as a complexity measure: results and directions. In: Structure in Complexity Theory, pp. 194–202 (1987)
24. Ladner, R.E.: On the structure of polynomial time reducibility. J. ACM **22**, 155–171 (1975)

25. Laubner, B.: The Structure of Graphs and New Logics for the Characterization of Polynomial Time. Ph.D. thesis, Humboldt-Universitätt zu Berlin (2011)
26. Otto, M.: Bounded Variable Logics and Counting. Springer, Heidelberg (1997)
27. Rossman, B.: Choiceless computation and symmetry. In: Blass, A., Dershowitz, N., Reisig, W. (eds.) Fields of logic and computation. LNCS, vol. 6300, pp. 565–580. Springer, Heidelberg (2010)

Arithmetical Congruence Preservation: From Finite to Infinite

Patrick Cégielski[1], Serge Grigorieff[2], and Irène Guessarian[2]([⊠])

[1] LACL, EA 4219, Université Paris-Est Créteil,
IUT Fontainebleau-Sénart, Fontainebleau, France
[2] LIAFA, CNRS UMR 7089, Université Paris 7 Denis Diderot, Paris, France
ig@liafa.univ-paris-diderot.fr

To Yuri, on his 75th birthday, with thanks for many stimulating discussions on Logic and Computation.

Abstract. Various problems on integers lead to the class of functions defined on a ring of numbers (or a subset of such a ring) and verifying $a - b$ divides $f(a) - f(b)$ for all a, b. We say that such functions are "congruence preserving". In previous works, we characterized these classes of functions for the cases $\mathbb{N} \to \mathbb{Z}$, $\mathbb{Z} \to \mathbb{Z}$ and $\mathbb{Z}/n\mathbb{Z} \to \mathbb{Z}/m\mathbb{Z}$ in terms of sums series of rational polynomials (taking only integral values) and the function giving the least common multiple of $1, 2, \ldots, k$. In this paper we relate the finite and infinite cases via a notion of "lifting": if $\pi \colon X \to Y$ is a surjective morphism and f is a function $Y \to Y$ a lifting of f is a function $F : X \to X$ such that $\pi \circ F = f \circ \pi$. We prove that the finite case $\mathbb{Z}/n\mathbb{Z} \to \mathbb{Z}/n\mathbb{Z}$ can be so lifted to the infinite cases $\mathbb{N} \to \mathbb{N}$ and $\mathbb{Z} \to \mathbb{Z}$. We also use such liftings to extend the characterization to the rings of p-adic and profinite integers, using Mahler representation of continuous functions on these rings.

1 Introduction

A function f (on $\mathbb{N}$ or $\mathbb{Z}$) is said to be congruence preserving if $a - b$ divides $f(a) - f(b)$. Polynomial functions are obvious examples of congruence preserving functions. In [2,3] we characterized such functions $\mathbb{N} \to \mathbb{Z}$ and $\mathbb{Z} \to \mathbb{Z}$ (which we named "functions having the integral difference ratio property"). In [4] we extended the characterization to functions $\mathbb{Z}/n\mathbb{Z} \to \mathbb{Z}/m\mathbb{Z}$ with $n, m \geq 1$ (for the suitable notion of congruence preservation).

In the present paper, we prove in Sect. 2 that every congruence preserving function $\mathbb{Z}/n\mathbb{Z} \to \mathbb{Z}/m\mathbb{Z}$ (with m dividing n) can be lifted to congruence preserving functions $\mathbb{N} \to \mathbb{N}$ and $\mathbb{Z} \to \mathbb{Z}$ (i.e. it is the modular projection of such a function). As a corollary (i) we show that such a lift also works replacing $\mathbb{N}$ with $\mathbb{Z}/qn\mathbb{Z}$ and (ii) we give an alternative proof of a representation (obtained in [4]) of congruence preserving functions $\mathbb{Z}/n\mathbb{Z} \to \mathbb{Z}/m\mathbb{Z}$ as linear sums of "rational" polynomials.

Partially supported by TARMAC ANR agreement 12 BS02 007 01.
I. Guessarian—Emeritus at UPMC Université Paris 6.

L.D. Beklemishev et al. (Eds.): Gurevich Festschrift II 2015, LNCS 9300, pp. 210–225, 2015.
DOI: 10.1007/978-3-319-23534-9_12

In Sect. 3 we consider the rings of p-adic integers (resp. profinite integers) and prove that congruence preserving functions on these rings are inverse limits of congruence preserving functions on the $\mathbb{Z}/p^k\mathbb{Z}$ (resp. on the $\mathbb{Z}/n\mathbb{Z}$). Considering the Mahler representation of continuous functions by series, we prove that congruence preserving functions correspond to those series for which the linear coefficient with rank k is divisible by the least common multiple of $1, \ldots, k$.

2 Switching Between Finite and Infinite

In order to characterize congruence preserving functions on $\mathbb{Z}/n\mathbb{Z}$, we first lift each such function into a congruence preserving function $\mathbb{N} \to \mathbb{N}$. In a second step, we use our characterization of congruence preserving functions $\mathbb{N} \to \mathbb{Z}$ to characterize the congruence preserving functions $\mathbb{Z}/n\mathbb{Z} \to \mathbb{Z}/n\mathbb{Z}$.

2.1 Lifting Functions $\mathbb{Z}/n\mathbb{Z} \to \mathbb{Z}/m\mathbb{Z}$ to $\mathbb{N} \to \mathbb{N}$ and $\mathbb{Z} \to \mathbb{Z}$

Definition 1. *Let X be a subset of a commutative ring $(R, +, \times)$. A function $f \colon X \to R$ is said to be congruence preserving if*

$$\forall x, y \in X \quad \exists d \in R \quad f(x) - f(y) = d(x - y), \quad \text{i.e. } x - y \text{ divides } f(x) - f(y).$$

Definition 2 (Lifting). *Let $\sigma \colon X \to N$ and $\rho \colon Y \to M$ be surjective maps. A function $F \colon X \to Y$ is said to be a (σ, ρ)-lifting of a function $f \colon N \to M$ (or simply lifting if σ, ρ are clear from the context) if the following diagram commutes:*

$$
\begin{array}{ccc}
X & \xrightarrow{\ F\ } & Y \\
\sigma \downarrow & & \downarrow \rho \\
N & \xrightarrow{\ f\ } & M
\end{array}
\qquad \text{i.e.} \qquad \rho \circ F = f \circ \sigma.
$$

We will consider elements of $\mathbb{Z}/k\mathbb{Z}$ as integers and vice versa via the following modular projection maps.

Notation 3. *1. Let $\pi_k \colon \mathbb{Z} \to \mathbb{Z}/k\mathbb{Z}$ be the canonical surjective homomorphism associating to an integer its class in $\mathbb{Z}/k\mathbb{Z}$.*
2. Let $\iota_k \colon \mathbb{Z}/k\mathbb{Z} \to \mathbb{N}$ be the injective map associating to an element $x \in \mathbb{Z}/k\mathbb{Z}$ its representative in $\{0, \ldots, k-1\}$.
3. Let $\pi_{n,m} \colon \mathbb{Z}/n\mathbb{Z} \to \mathbb{Z}/m\mathbb{Z}$ be the map $\pi_{n,m} = \pi_m \circ \iota_n$.
If $m \leq n$ let $\iota_{m,n} \colon \mathbb{Z}/m\mathbb{Z} \to \mathbb{Z}/n\mathbb{Z}$ be the injective map $\iota_{m,n} = \pi_n \circ \iota_m$.

Lemma 4. *If m divides n then $\pi_m = \pi_{n,m} \circ \pi_n$ and $\pi_{n,m}$ is a surjective homomorphism.*

The next theorem insures that congruence preserving functions $\mathbb{Z}/n\mathbb{Z} \to \mathbb{Z}/n\mathbb{Z}$ can be lifted to congruence preserving functions $\mathbb{N} \to \mathbb{N}$ and $\mathbb{N} \to \mathbb{Z}$.

Theorem 5 (Lifting Functions $\mathbb{Z}/n\mathbb{Z} \to \mathbb{Z}/n\mathbb{Z}$ to $\mathbb{N} \to \mathbb{N}$). *Let $f \colon \mathbb{Z}/n\mathbb{Z} \to \mathbb{Z}/n\mathbb{Z}$ with $m \geq 2$. The following conditions are equivalent:*

(1) f is congruence preserving.
(2) f can be (π_n, π_n)-lifted to a congruence preserving function $F : \mathbb{N} \to \mathbb{N}$.
(3) f can be (π_n, π_n)-lifted to a congruence preserving function $F : \mathbb{N} \to \mathbb{Z}$.

In view of applications in the context of p-adic and profinite integers, we state and prove a slightly more general version. As $\mathbb{Z}/n\mathbb{Z}$ and $\mathbb{Z}/m\mathbb{Z}$ are different rings we use an extension of the notion of congruence preservation introduced in Chen [5] and studied in Bhargava [1]) which we recall below.

Definition 6. *A function $f : \mathbb{Z}/n\mathbb{Z} \to \mathbb{Z}/m\mathbb{Z}$ is congruence preserving if*

$$\text{for all } x, y \in \mathbb{Z}/n\mathbb{Z}, \quad \pi_{n,m}(x - y) \text{ divides } f(x) - f(y) \text{ in } \mathbb{Z}/m\mathbb{Z}. \tag{1}$$

Theorem 7 (Lifting Functions $\mathbb{Z}/n\mathbb{Z} \to \mathbb{Z}/m\mathbb{Z}$ to $\mathbb{N} \to \mathbb{N}$). *Let $f \colon \mathbb{Z}/n\mathbb{Z} \to \mathbb{Z}/m\mathbb{Z}$ with m divides n and $m \geq 2$. The following conditions are equivalent:*

(1) f is congruence preserving.
(2) f can be (π_n, π_m)-lifted to a congruence preserving function $F : \mathbb{N} \to \mathbb{N}$.
(3) f can be (π_n, π_m)-lifted to a congruence preserving function $F : \mathbb{N} \to \mathbb{Z}$.

Proof. $(2) \Rightarrow (3)$ is trivial.

$(3) \Rightarrow (1)$. Assume f lifts to the congruence preserving function $F : \mathbb{N} \to \mathbb{Z}$, i.e. $f \circ \pi_n = \pi_m \circ F$. Since $\pi_n \circ \iota_n$ is the identity we get $f = i_m \circ F \circ \iota_n$. The following diagrams are thus commutative:

Let $x, y \in \mathbb{Z}/n\mathbb{Z}$. As F is congruence preserving, $\iota_n(x) - \iota_n(y)$ divides $F(\iota_n(x)) - F(\iota_n(y))$, hence $F(\iota_n(x)) - F(\iota_n(y)) = (\iota_n(x) - \iota_n(y)) \delta$. Since π_m is a morphism and $\pi_m \circ \iota_n = \pi_{n,m}$, we get $\pi_m(F(\iota_n(x))) - \pi_m(F(\iota_n(x))) = \pi_{n,m}(x - y) \pi_m(\delta)$. As F lifts f we have $\pi_m(F(\iota_n(x))) - \pi_m(F(\iota_n(y))) = f(x) - f(y)$ whence (1).

$(1) \Rightarrow (2)$. By induction on $t \in \mathbb{N}$ we define a sequence of functions $\varphi_t \colon \{0, \dots, t\} \to \mathbb{N}$ for $t \in \mathbb{N}$ such that φ_{t+1} extends φ_t and (*) and (**) below hold.

(*) φ_t is congruence preserving,
(**) $\pi_m(\varphi_t(u)) = f(\pi_n(u))$, for all $u \in \{0, \dots, t\}$,

i.e. the following diagram commutes:

Basis. We choose $\varphi_0(0) \in \mathbb{N}$ such that $\pi_m(\varphi_0(0)) = f(\pi_n(0))$. Properties (*) and (**) clearly hold for φ_0.

Induction: From φ_t to φ_{t+1}. Since the wanted φ_{t+1} has to extend φ_t to the domain $\{0, \ldots, t, t+1\}$, we only have to find a convenient value for $\varphi_{t+1}(t+1)$. By the induction hypothesis, (*) and (**) hold for φ_t; in order for φ_{t+1} to satisfy (*) and (**), we have to find $\varphi_{t+1}(t+1)$ such that $t+1-i$ divides $\varphi_{t+1}(t+1) - \varphi_t(i)$, for $i = 0, \ldots, t$, and $\pi_m(\varphi_{t+1}(t+1)) = f(\pi_n(t+1))$. Rewritten in terms of congruences, these conditions amount to say that $\varphi_{t+1}(t+1)$ is a solution of the following system of congruence equations:

$$
\left.
\begin{array}{lll}
\star(0) & \left| \varphi_{t+1}(t+1) \equiv \varphi_t(0) \right. & (\mathrm{mod}\ t+1) \\
& \qquad\qquad \vdots & \\
\star(i) & \left| \varphi_{t+1}(t+1) \equiv \varphi_t(i) \right. & (\mathrm{mod}\ t+1-i) \\
& \qquad\qquad \vdots & \\
\star(t\text{-}1) & \left| \varphi_{t+1}(t+1) \equiv \varphi_t(t-1) \right. & (\mathrm{mod}\ 2) \\
\star\star & \left| \varphi_{t+1}(t+1) \equiv \iota_m(f(\pi_n(t+1))) \right. & (\mathrm{mod}\ m)
\end{array}
\right\} \quad (2)
$$

Recall the Generalized Chinese Remainder Theorem (cf. Sect. 3.3, exercice 9 p. 114, in Rosen's textbook [12]): a system of congruence equations

$$
\bigwedge_{i=0,\ldots,t} x \equiv a_i \quad (\mathrm{mod}\ n_i)
$$

has a solution if and only if $a_i \equiv a_j \mod \gcd(n_i, n_j)$ for all $0 \leq i < j \leq t$.

Let us show that the conditions of application of the Generalized Chinese Remainder Theorem are satisfied for system (2).

- Lines $\star(i)$ and $\star(j)$ of system (2) (with $0 \leq i < j \leq t-1$).
  Every common divisor to $t+1-i$ and $t+1-j$ divides their difference $j-i$ hence $\gcd(t+1-i, t+1-j)$ divides $j-i$. Since φ_t satisfies (*), $j-i$ divides $\varphi_t(j) - \varphi_t(i)$ and a fortiori $\gcd(t+1-i, t+1-j)$ divides $\varphi_t(j) - \varphi_t(i)$.
- Lines $\star(i)$ and $\star\star$ of system (2) (with $0 \leq i \leq t-1$).
  Let $d = \gcd(t+1-i, m)$. We have to show that d divides $\iota_m(f(\pi_n(t+1))) - \varphi_t(i)$. Since f is congruence preserving, $\pi_{n,m}(\pi_n(t+1) - \pi_n(i))$ divides $f(\pi_n(t+1)) - f(\pi_n(i))$. As m divides n, by Lemma 4, $\pi_{n,m}(\pi_n(t+1) - \pi_n(i)) = \pi_m(t+1) - \pi_m(i) = \pi_m(t+1-i)$ and $f(\pi_n(t+1)) - f(\pi_n(i)) = k\pi_m(t+1-i)$ for some $k \in \mathbb{Z}/m\mathbb{Z}$. Applying ι_m, there exists $\lambda \in \mathbb{Z}$ such that

$$
\iota_m(f(\pi_n(t+1))) - \iota_m(f(\pi_n(i))) = \iota_m(k)\iota_m(\pi_m(t+1-i)) + \lambda m
$$

as $\iota_m(\pi_m(u)) \equiv u \pmod{m}$ for every $u \in \mathbb{Z}$, there exists $\mu \in \mathbb{Z}$ such that

$$
\iota_m(f(\pi_n(t+1))) - \iota_m(f(\pi_n(i))) = \iota_m(k)(t+1-i) + \mu m + \lambda m. \quad (3)
$$

Since φ_t satisfies (**), we have $\pi_m(\varphi_t(i)) = f(\pi_n(i))$ hence $\varphi_t(i) \equiv \iota_m(f(\pi_n(i))) \pmod{m}$. Thus Eq. (3) can be rewritten

$$
\iota_m(f(\pi_n(t+1))) - \varphi_t(i) = (t+1-i)\iota_m(k) + \nu m \quad \text{for some } \nu. \quad (4)
$$

As $d = \gcd(t + 1 - i, m)$ divides m and $t + 1 - i$, (4) shows that d divides $\iota_n(f(\pi_n(t + 1))) - \varphi_t(i)$ as wanted.

Thus, we can apply the Generalized Chinese Theorem and get the wanted value of $\varphi_{t+1}(t + 1)$, concluding the induction step.

Finally, taking the union of the φ_t's, $t \in \mathbb{N}$, we get a function $F : \mathbb{N} \to \mathbb{N}$ which is congruence preserving and lifts f.   □

Example 8 (Counterexample to Theorem 7). Lemma 4 and Theorem 7 do not hold if m does not divide n. Consider $f : \mathbb{Z}/6\mathbb{Z} \to \mathbb{Z}/8\mathbb{Z}$ defined by $f(0) = 0$, $f(1) = 3$, $f(2) = 4$, $f(3) = 1$, $f(4) = 4$, $f(5) = 7$. Note first that, in $\mathbb{Z}/8\mathbb{Z}$, 1, 3 and 5 are invertible, hence f is congruence preserving iff for $k \in \{2, 4\}$, for all $x \in \mathbb{Z}/6\mathbb{Z}$, k divides $f(x + k) - f(x)$ which is easily checked; nevertheless, f has no congruence preserving lift $F : \mathbb{Z} \to \mathbb{Z}$. If such a lift F existed, we should have

(1) because F lifts f, $\pi_8(F(0)) = f(\pi_6(0)) = 0$ and $\pi_8(F(8)) = f(\pi_6(8)) = f(2) = 4$;
(2) as F is congruence preserving, 8 must divide $F(8) - F(0)$; we already noted that 8 divides $F(0)$, hence 8 divides $F(8)$ and $\pi_8(F(8)) = 0$, contradicting $\pi_8(F(8)) = 4$.

Note that $\pi_{6,8}$ is neither a homomorphism nor surjective and $0 = \pi_8(8) \neq \pi_{6,8} \circ \pi_6(8) = 2$.   □

We can also lift congruence preserving functions from $\mathbb{Z}/n\mathbb{Z} \to \mathbb{Z}/m\mathbb{Z}$ to $\mathbb{Z} \to \mathbb{Z}$ instead of $\mathbb{N} \to \mathbb{N}$.

Theorem 9 (Lifting Functions $\mathbb{Z}/n\mathbb{Z} \to \mathbb{Z}/m\mathbb{Z}$ to $\mathbb{Z} \to \mathbb{Z}$). *Let $f : \mathbb{Z}/n\mathbb{Z} \to \mathbb{Z}/m\mathbb{Z}$ with m divides n and $m \geq 2$. The following conditions are equivalent:*

(1) f is congruence preserving.
(2) f can be (π_n, π_m)-lifted to a congruence preserving function $F : \mathbb{Z} \to \mathbb{Z}$.

Proof. (2) $\Rightarrow$ (1). The proof is the same as that of (3) $\Rightarrow$ (1) in Theorem 7.
(1) $\Rightarrow$ (2). The argument is a slight modification of that for the same implication in Theorem 7. We define the lift $F : \mathbb{Z} \to \mathbb{Z}$ of $f : \mathbb{Z}/n\mathbb{Z} \to \mathbb{Z}/m\mathbb{Z}$ as the union of a series of functions φ_t, $t \in \mathbb{N}$ such that

- φ_{2t} has domain $\{-t, \ldots, t\}$ and φ_{2t+1} has domain $\{-t, \ldots, t + 1\}$,
- φ_{t+1} extends φ_t,
- φ_t is congruence preserving. The induction step is done exactly as in Theorem 7 via a system of congruence equations and an application of the Generalized Chinese Remainder Theorem.   □

2.2 Representation of Congruence Preserving Functions $\mathbb{Z}/n\mathbb{Z} \to \mathbb{Z}/m\mathbb{Z}$

As a first corollary of Theorem 7 we get a new proof of the representations of congruence preserving functions $\mathbb{Z}/n\mathbb{Z} \to \mathbb{Z}/m\mathbb{Z}$ as finite linear sums of polynomials with rational coefficients (cf. [4]). Let us recall the so-called binomial polynomials.

Definition 10. *For $k \in \mathbb{N}$, let $P_k(x) = \binom{x}{k} = \frac{1}{k!} \prod_{\ell=0}^{\ell=k-1}(x - \ell)$.*

Though P_k has rational coefficients, it maps $\mathbb{N}$ into $\mathbb{Z}$. Also, observe that $P_k(x)$ takes value 0 for all $k > x$. This implies that for any sequence of integers $(a_k)_{k \in \mathbb{N}}$, the infinite sum $\sum_{k \in \mathbb{N}} a_k P_k(x)$ reduces to a finite sum for any $x \in \mathbb{N}$ hence defines a function $\mathbb{N} \to \mathbb{Z}$.

Definition 11. *We denote by $lcm(k)$ the least common multiple of integers $1, \ldots, k$ (with the convention $lcm(0) = 1$).*

Definition 12. *To each binomial polynomial P_k, $k \in \mathbb{N}$, we associate a function $P_k^{n,m} \colon \mathbb{Z}/n\mathbb{Z} \to \mathbb{Z}/m\mathbb{Z}$ which sends an element $x \in \mathbb{Z}/n\mathbb{Z}$ to $(\pi_m \circ P_k \circ \iota_n)(x) \in \mathbb{Z}/m\mathbb{Z}$.*

In other words, consider the representative t of x lying in $\{0, \ldots, n-1\}$, evaluate $P_k(t)$ in $\mathbb{N}$ and then take the class of the result in $\mathbb{Z}/m\mathbb{Z}$. Hence, the following diagram commutes:

$$
\begin{array}{ccc}
\mathbb{N} & \xrightarrow{\quad P_k \quad} & \mathbb{Z} \\
\iota_n \uparrow & & \downarrow \pi_m \\
\mathbb{Z}/n\mathbb{Z} & \xrightarrow{\quad P_k^{n,m} \quad} & \mathbb{Z}/m\mathbb{Z}
\end{array}
$$

Lemma 13. *If $lcm(k)$ divides a_k in $\mathbb{Z}$, then the function $\pi_m(a_k)P_k^{n,m} \colon \mathbb{Z}/n\mathbb{Z} \to \mathbb{Z}/m\mathbb{Z}$ (represented by $a_k P_k$) is congruence preserving.*

Proof. In [2] we proved that if $lcm(k)$ divides a_k then $a_k P_k$ is a congruence preserving function on $\mathbb{N}$. Let us now show that $\pi_m(a_k)P_k^{n,m} \colon \mathbb{Z}/n\mathbb{Z} \to \mathbb{Z}/m\mathbb{Z}$ is also congruence preserving. Let $x, y \in \mathbb{Z}/n\mathbb{Z}$: as $a_k P_k$ is congruence preserving, $\iota_n(x) - \iota_n(y)$ divides $a_k P_k(\iota_n(x)) - a_k P_k(\iota_n(y))$. As π_m is a morphism $\pi_m(\iota_n(x)) - \pi_m(\iota_n(y))$ divides $\pi_m(a_k)\pi_m(P_k(\iota_n(x))) - \pi_m(a_k)\pi_m(P_k(\iota_n(y))) = \pi_m(a_k)P_k^{n,m}(x) - \pi_m(a_k)P_k^{n,m}(x)$. As $\pi_m \circ \iota_n = \pi_{n,m}$ we have $\pi_m(\iota_n(x)) - \pi_m(\iota_n(y)) = \pi_{n,m}(x) - \pi_{n,m}(y)$ and we conclude that $\pi_m(a_k)P_k^{n,m}$ is congruence preserving. $\square$

Corollary 14 ([4]). *Let $1 \leq m = p_1^{\alpha_1} \cdots p_\ell^{\alpha_\ell}$, p_i prime. Suppose m divides n and let $\nu(m) = \max_{i=1,\ldots,\ell} p_i^{\alpha_i}$. A function $f \colon \mathbb{Z}/n\mathbb{Z} \to \mathbb{Z}/m\mathbb{Z}$ is congruence preserving if and only if it is represented by a finite $\mathbb{Z}$-linear sum $f = \sum_{k=0}^{\nu(m)-1} \pi_m(a_k)P_k^{n,m}$ such that $lcm(k)$ divides a_k (in $\mathbb{Z}$) for all $k < \nu(m)$. Moreover, such a representation is unique.*

Proof. Assume $f \colon \mathbb{Z}/n\mathbb{Z} \to \mathbb{Z}/m\mathbb{Z}$ is congruence preserving. Applying Theorem 7, lift f to $F \colon \mathbb{N} \to \mathbb{N}$ which is congruence preserving.

$$
\begin{array}{ccc}
\mathbb{N} & \xrightarrow{\quad F = \sum_{k=0}^{\nu(m)-1} a_k P_k \quad} & \mathbb{Z} \\
\pi_n \downarrow & & \downarrow \pi_m \qquad f \circ \pi_n = \pi_m \circ F \\
\mathbb{Z}/n\mathbb{Z} & \xrightarrow{\quad f \quad} & \mathbb{Z}/m\mathbb{Z}
\end{array}
$$

We proved in [4] that every congruence preserving function $F\colon \mathbb{N} \to \mathbb{N}$ is of the form $F = \sum_{k=0}^{\infty} a_k P_k$ where $lcm(k)$ divides a_k for all k. As π_m is a morphism (because m divides n) and F lifts f, we have, for $u \in \mathbb{Z}$

$$f(\pi_n(u)) = \pi_m(F(u)) = \pi_m\left(\sum_{k=0}^{\infty} a_k\, P_k(u)\right)$$

$$= \sum_{k=0}^{\infty} \pi_m(a_k)\, \pi_m(P_k(u)) = \sum_{k=0}^{k=\nu(m)-1} \pi_m(a_k)\, \pi_m(P_k(u)) \quad (5)$$

The last equality is obtained by noting that for $k \geq \nu(m)$, m divides $lcm(k)$ hence as a_k is a multiple of $lcm(k)$, $\pi_m(a_k) = 0$. From (5) we get $f(\pi_n(u)) = \sum_{k=0}^{k=\nu(m)-1} \pi_m(a_k)\, \pi_m(P_k(u)) = \pi_m(\sum_{k=0}^{k=\nu(m)-1} a_k\, P_k(u))$. This proves that f is lifted to the rational polynomial function $\sum_{k=0}^{k=\nu(m)-1} a_k\, P_k$. Since $P_k(k) = 1$ for all $k \in \mathbb{N}$, and $P_k(i) = 0$ for $k > i$, we easily check the unicity of the representation.

The converse follows from Lemma 13 and the fact that any finite sum of congruence preserving functions is congruence preserving. $\qquad\square$

2.3   Lifting Functions $\mathbb{Z}/n\mathbb{Z} \to \mathbb{Z}/m\mathbb{Z}$ to $\mathbb{Z}/r\mathbb{Z} \to \mathbb{Z}/s\mathbb{Z}$

As a second corollary of Theorem 7 we can lift congruence preserving functions $\mathbb{Z}/n\mathbb{Z} \to \mathbb{Z}/n\mathbb{Z}$ to congruence preserving functions $\mathbb{Z}/qn\mathbb{Z} \to \mathbb{Z}/qn\mathbb{Z}$.

We state a slightly more general result.

Corollary 15. *Assume $m, n, s, r \geq 1$, m divides both n and s, and n, s both divide r. If $f\colon \mathbb{Z}/n\mathbb{Z} \to \mathbb{Z}/m\mathbb{Z}$ is congruence preserving then it can be $(\pi_{r,n}, \pi_{s,m})$-lifted to $g\colon \mathbb{Z}/r\mathbb{Z} \to \mathbb{Z}/s\mathbb{Z}$ which is also congruence preserving.*

Proof. As m divides n, using Theorem 7, we lift f to a congruence preserving $F\colon \mathbb{N} \to \mathbb{N}$ and set $g = \pi_s \circ F \circ \iota_r$.

We first show that the rectangular subdiagram around f, g commutes:

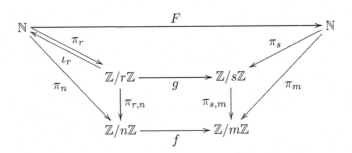

$$\pi_{s,m} \circ g = \pi_{s,m} \circ (\pi_s \circ F \circ \iota_r)$$
$$= (\pi_m \circ F) \circ \iota_r \qquad m \text{ divides } s \text{ yields } \pi_m = \pi_{s,m} \circ \pi_s \text{ (Lemma 4)}$$
$$= (f \circ \pi_n) \circ \iota_r \qquad \text{since } F \text{ lifts } f$$
$$= f \circ \pi_{r,n} \qquad \text{since } \pi_n \circ \iota_r = \pi_{r,n}$$

Thus, $\pi_{s,m} \circ g = f \circ \pi_{r,n}$, i.e. g lifts f.

Finally, if $x, y \in \mathbb{Z}/r\mathbb{Z}$ then $\iota_r(x) - \iota_r(y)$ divides $F(\iota_r(x)) - F(\iota_r(y))$ (by congruence preservation of F). As π_s is a morphism, and $\pi_s = \pi_{r,s} \circ \pi_r$ (because s divides r), and $\pi_r \circ \iota_r$ is the identity on $\mathbb{Z}/r\mathbb{Z}$, we deduce that $\pi_s(\iota_r(x)) - \pi_s(\iota_r(y)) = (\pi_{r,s} \circ \pi_r \circ \iota_r)(x) - (\pi_{r,s} \circ \pi_r \circ \iota_r)(y) = \pi_{r,s}(x - y)$ divides $\pi_s(F(\iota_r(x))) - \pi_s(F(\iota_r(y))) = g(x) - g(y)$ (by definition of g). We thus conclude that g is congruence preserving.   □

Remark 16. Let us check that the previous diagram is completely commutative. The large trapezoid around F, f commutes because F lifts f. The upper trapezoid F, g, ι_r, π_s commutes by definition of g. The upper trapezoid F, g, π_r, π_s commutes since $g \circ \pi_r = (\pi_s \circ F \circ \iota_r) \circ \pi_r = \pi_s \circ F$ (as $\iota_r \circ \pi_r$ is the identity). The left and right triangles $\pi_n, \pi_r, \pi_{r,n}$ and $\pi_m, \pi_s, \pi_{s,m}$ commute by Lemma 4 as n divides r and m divides s. Finally, the triangle $\pi_n, \iota_r, \pi_{r,n}$ commutes by definition of $\pi_{r,n}$ (cf. Notation 3).

3   Congruence Preservation on p-adic/profinite Integers

All along this section, p is a prime number; we study congruence preserving functions on the rings $\mathbb{Z}_p$ of p-adic integers and $\widehat{\mathbb{Z}}$ of profinite integers. $\mathbb{Z}_p$ is the projective limit $\varprojlim \mathbb{Z}/p^n\mathbb{Z}$ relative to the projections π_{p^n, p^m}. Usually, $\widehat{\mathbb{Z}}$ is defined as the projective limit $\varprojlim \mathbb{Z}/n\mathbb{Z}$ of the finite rings $\mathbb{Z}/n\mathbb{Z}$ relative to the projections $\pi_{n,m}$, for m dividing n. We here use the following equivalent definition which allows to get completely similar proofs for $\mathbb{Z}_p$ and $\widehat{\mathbb{Z}}$.

$$\widehat{\mathbb{Z}} = \varprojlim \mathbb{Z}/n!\mathbb{Z} = \{\hat{x} = (x_n)_{n=1}^{\infty} \in \textstyle\prod_{n=1}^{\infty} \mathbb{Z}/n!\mathbb{Z} \mid \forall m < n,\ x_m \equiv x_n \pmod{m!}\}$$

Recall that $\mathbb{Z}_p$ (resp. $\widehat{\mathbb{Z}}$) contains the ring $\mathbb{Z}$ and is a compact topological ring for the topology given by the ultrametric d such that $d(x, y) = 2^{-n}$ where n is largest such that p^n (resp. $n!$) divides $x - y$, i.e. x and y have the same first n digits in their base p (resp. base factorial) representation. We refer to the Appendix for some basic definitions, representations and facts that we use about the compact topological rings $\mathbb{Z}_p$ and $\widehat{\mathbb{Z}}$.

We first prove that on $\mathbb{Z}_p$ and $\widehat{\mathbb{Z}}$ every congruence preserving function is continuous (Proposition 18).

3.1   Congruence Preserving Functions Are Continuous

Definition 17. *1. Let $\mu : \mathbb{N} \to \mathbb{N}$ be increasing. A function $\Psi : \mathbb{Z}_p \to \mathbb{Z}_p$ admits μ as modulus of uniform continuity if and only if $d(x, y) \leq 2^{-\mu(n)}$ implies $d(\Psi(x), \Psi(y)) \leq 2^{-n}$.*

2. Φ is 1-Lipschitz if it admits the identity as modulus of uniform continuity.

Since the rings $\mathbb{Z}_p$ and $\widehat{\mathbb{Z}}$ are compact, every continuous function admits a modulus of uniform continuity. For congruence preserving function, we get a tight bound on the modulus.

Proposition 18. *Every congruence preserving function* $\Psi : \mathbb{Z}_p \to \mathbb{Z}_p$ *is 1-Lipschitz (hence continuous). Idem with* $\widehat{\mathbb{Z}}$ *in place of* $\mathbb{Z}_p$.

Proof. If $d(x,y) \leq 2^{-n}$ then p^n divides $x-y$ hence (by congruence preservation) p^n also divides $\Psi(x) - \Psi(y)$ which yields $d(\Psi(x), \Psi(y)) \leq 2^{-n}$. □

The converse of Proposition 18 is false: a 1-Lipschitz function is not necessarily congruence preserving as will be seen in Example 31.

Note the following quite expectable result.

Corollary 19. *There are functions* $\mathbb{Z}_p \to \mathbb{Z}_p$ *(resp.* $\widehat{\mathbb{Z}} \to \widehat{\mathbb{Z}}$*) which are not continuous hence not congruence preserving.*

Proof. As $\mathbb{Z}_p$ has cardinality $2^{\aleph_0}$ there are $2^{2^{\aleph_0}}$ functions $\mathbb{Z}_p \to \mathbb{Z}_p$. Since $\mathbb{N}$ is dense in $\mathbb{Z}_p$, $\mathbb{Z}_p$ is a separable space, hence there are at most $2^{\aleph_0}$ continuous functions. □

3.2   Congruence Preserving Functions and Inverse Limits

In general an arbitrary continuous function on $\mathbb{Z}_p$ is not the inverse limit of a sequence of functions $\mathbb{Z}/p^n\mathbb{Z} \to \mathbb{Z}/p^n\mathbb{Z}$'s. However, this is true for congruence preserving functions. We first recall how any continuous function $\Psi \colon \mathbb{Z}_p \to \mathbb{Z}_p$ is the inverse limit of an inverse system of continuous functions $\psi_n \colon \mathbb{Z}/p^{\mu(n)}\mathbb{Z} \to \mathbb{Z}/p^n\mathbb{Z}$, $n \in \mathbb{N}$, i.e. the diagram of Fig. 1 commutes for any $m \leq n$. For legibility, we use notations adapted to $\mathbb{Z}_p$.

Notation 20. *We write* $\widehat{\pi_n}$ *for the canonical surjection* $\mathbb{Z}_p \to \mathbb{Z}/p^n\mathbb{Z}$ *mapping a p-adic integer with representation* $(a_k)_{k \in \mathbb{N}}$ *to the integer* $\sum_{k=0}^{k=n-1} a_k p^k \in \mathbb{Z}/p^n\mathbb{Z}$, *and* $\widehat{\iota_n}$ *for the canonical injection* $\mathbb{Z}/p^n\mathbb{Z} \to \mathbb{Z}_p$ *(which maps* $\sum_{k=0}^{k=n-1} a_k p^k$ *to* $(a_0, \ldots, a_{k-1}, 0, 0, \ldots)$*).*

Lemma 4 has an avatar in the profinite framework.

Lemma 21. $\widehat{\pi_n} \circ \widehat{\iota_n}$ *is the identity on* $\mathbb{Z}/p^n\mathbb{Z}$. *If* $m \leq n$ *then* $\widehat{\pi_m} = \pi_{p^n, p^m} \circ \widehat{\pi_n}$.

Proposition 22. *Consider* $\Psi : \mathbb{Z}_p \to \mathbb{Z}_p$ *and a strictly increasing* $\mu : \mathbb{N} \to \mathbb{N}$. *Define* $\psi_n : \mathbb{Z}/p^{\mu(n)}\mathbb{Z} \to \mathbb{Z}/p^n\mathbb{Z}$ *as* $\psi_n = \widehat{\pi_n} \circ \Psi \circ \widehat{\iota_{\mu(n)}}$ *for all* $n \in \mathbb{N}$. *Then the following conditions are equivalent :*

(1) Ψ *is uniformly continuous and admits* μ *as a modulus of uniform continuity.*
(2) The sequence $(\psi_n)_{n \in \mathbb{N}}$ *is an inverse system with* Ψ *as inverse limit (in other words, for all* $1 \leq m \leq n$, *the diagrams of Fig. 1 commute)*
(3) For all $n \geq 1$, *the upper half (dealing with* Ψ *and* ψ_n*) of the diagram of Fig. 1 commutes.*

Idem with $\widehat{\mathbb{Z}}$ *in place of* $\mathbb{Z}_p$.

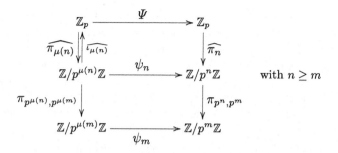

Fig. 1. The inverse system $(\psi_n)_{n\in\mathbb{N}}$ and its inverse limit Ψ.

Proof. $(1) \Rightarrow (2)$. We first show $\widehat{\pi_n}\circ\Psi = \psi_n\circ\widehat{\pi_{\mu(n)}}$. Let $u \in \mathbb{Z}_p$. Since $\widehat{\pi_{\mu(n)}}\circ\widehat{\iota_{\mu(n)}}$ is the identity on $\mathbb{Z}/p^{\mu(n)}\mathbb{Z}$, we have $\widehat{\pi_{\mu(n)}}(u) = \widehat{\pi_{\mu(n)}}(\widehat{\iota_{\mu(n)}}(\widehat{\pi_{\mu(n)}}(u)))$ hence $p^{\mu(n)}$ (considered as an element of $\mathbb{Z}_p$) divides the difference $u - \widehat{\iota_{\mu(n)}}(\widehat{\pi_{\mu(n)}}(u))$, i.e. the distance between these two elements is at most $2^{-\mu(n)}$. As μ is a modulus of uniform continuity for Ψ, the distance between their images under Ψ is at most 2^{-n}, i.e. p^n divides their difference, hence $\widehat{\pi_n}(\Psi(u)) = \widehat{\pi_n}(\Psi(\widehat{\iota_{\mu(n)}}(\widehat{\pi_{\mu(n)}}(u))))$. By definition, $\psi_n = \widehat{\pi_n}\circ\Psi\circ\widehat{\iota_{\mu(n)}}$. Thus, $\widehat{\pi_n}(\Psi(u)) = \psi_n(\widehat{\pi_{\mu(n)}}(u))$, which proves that Ψ lifts ψ_n.

We now show $\pi_{p^n,p^m} \circ \psi_n = \psi_m \circ \pi_{p^{\mu(n)},p^{\mu(m)}}$. Observe that, since $n \geq m$ and μ is increasing, p^m divides p^n and $p^{\mu(m)}$ divides $p^{\mu(n)}$. We just proved above equality $\widehat{\pi_m} \circ \Psi = \psi_m \circ \widehat{\pi_{\mu(m)}}$. Applying three times Lemma 21, we get

$$\widehat{\pi_m} \circ \Psi \circ \widehat{\iota_{\mu(n)}} = \psi_m \circ \widehat{\pi_{\mu(m)}} \circ \widehat{\iota_{\mu(n)}}$$
$$(\pi_{p^n,p^m} \circ \widehat{\pi_n}) \circ \Psi \circ \widehat{\iota_{\mu(n)}} = \psi_m \circ (\pi_{p^{\mu(n)},p^{\mu(m)}} \circ \widehat{\pi_{\mu(n)}}) \circ \widehat{\iota_{\mu(n)}}$$
$$\pi_{p^n,p^m} \circ \psi_n = \psi_m \circ \pi_{p^{\mu(n)},p^{\mu(m)}} \quad \text{as } \widehat{\pi_{\mu(n)}} \circ \widehat{\iota_{\mu(n)}} \text{ is the identity.}$$

The last equality means that ψ_n lifts ψ_m.

$(2) \Rightarrow (3)$. Trivial

$(3) \Rightarrow (1)$. The fact that Ψ lifts ψ_n shows that two elements of $\mathbb{Z}_p$ with the same first $\mu(n)$ digits (in the p-adic representation) have images with the same first n digits. This proves that μ is a modulus of uniform continuity for Ψ.   □

For congruence preserving functions $\Phi : \mathbb{Z}_p \to \mathbb{Z}_p$, the representation of Proposition 22 as an inverse limit gets smoother since then $\mu(n) = n$.

Theorem 23. *For a function* $\Phi : \mathbb{Z}_p \to \mathbb{Z}_p$, *letting* $\varphi_n : \mathbb{Z}/p^n\mathbb{Z} \to \mathbb{Z}/p^n\mathbb{Z}$ *be defined as* $\varphi_n = \widehat{\pi_n} \circ \Phi \circ \widehat{\iota_n}$, *the following conditions are equivalent.*

(1) Φ *is congruence preserving.*

(2) *All* φ_n's *are congruence preserving function and the sequence* $(\varphi_n)_{n\geq 1}$ *is an inverse system with* Φ *as inverse limit (in other words, for all* $1 \leq m \leq n$, *the diagrams of Fig. 2 commute).*

A similar equivalence also holds for functions $\Phi : \widehat{\mathbb{Z}} \to \widehat{\mathbb{Z}}$.

Proof. (1) $\Rightarrow$ (2). Proposition 18 insures that Φ is 1-Lipschitz. The implication (1) $\Rightarrow$ (2) in Proposition 22, applied with the identity as μ, insures that the sequence $(\varphi_n)_{n \geq 1}$ is an inverse system with Φ as inverse limit. It remains to show that φ_n is congruence preserving. Since Φ is congruence preserving, if $x, y \in \mathbb{Z}/p^n\mathbb{Z}$ then $\widehat{\iota_n}(x) - \widehat{\iota_n}(y)$ divides $\Phi(\widehat{\iota_n}(x)) - \Phi(\widehat{\iota_n}(y))$. Now, the canonical projection $\widehat{\pi_n}$ is a morphism hence $\widehat{\pi_n}(\widehat{\iota_n}(x)) - \widehat{\pi_n}(\widehat{\iota_n}(y))$ divides $\widehat{\pi_n}(\Phi(\widehat{\iota_n}(x))) - \widehat{\pi_n}(\Phi(\widehat{\iota_n}(y)))$. As $\widehat{\pi_n} \circ \widehat{\iota_n}$ is the identity on $\mathbb{Z}/p^n\mathbb{Z}$, $x - y$ divides $\widehat{\pi_n}(\Phi(\widehat{\iota_n}(x))) - \widehat{\pi_n}(\Phi(\widehat{\iota_n}(y))) = \varphi_n(x) - \varphi_n(y)$ as wanted.

(2) $\Rightarrow$ (1). Let $x, y \in \mathbb{Z}_p$. Since φ_n is congruence preserving $\widehat{\pi_n}(x) - \widehat{\pi_n}(y)$ divides $\varphi_n(\widehat{\pi_n}(x)) - \varphi_n(\widehat{\pi_n}(y))$. Let

$$U_n^{x,y} = \left\{ u \in \mathbb{Z}/p^n\mathbb{Z} \mid \varphi_n(\widehat{\pi_n}(x)) - \varphi_n(\widehat{\pi_n}(y)) = (\widehat{\pi_n}(x) - \widehat{\pi_n}(y))\, u \right\}.$$

If $m \leq n$ and $u \in U_n^{x,y}$ then, applying π_{p^n, p^m} to the equality defining $U_n^{x,y}$, using the commutative diagrams of Fig. 2 and letting $v = \pi_{p^n, p^m}(u)$, we get

$$\varphi_n(\widehat{\pi_n}(x)) - \varphi_n(\widehat{\pi_n}(y)) = (\widehat{\pi_n}(x) - \widehat{\pi_n}(y))\, u$$
$$\pi_{p^n,p^m}(\varphi_n(\widehat{\pi_n}(x))) - \pi_{p^n,p^m}(\varphi_n(\widehat{\pi_n}(y))) = (\pi_{p^n,p^m}(\widehat{\pi_n}(x)) - \pi_{p^n,p^m}(\widehat{\pi_n}(y)))\, v$$
$$\varphi_m(\pi_{p^n,p^m}(\widehat{\pi_n}(x))) - \varphi_m(\pi_{p^n,p^m}(\widehat{\pi_n}(y))) = (\widehat{\pi_m}(x) - \widehat{\pi_m}(y))\, v$$
$$\varphi_m(\widehat{\pi_m}(x)) - \varphi_m(\widehat{\pi_m}(y)) = (\widehat{\pi_m}(x) - \widehat{\pi_m}(y))\, v$$

Thus, if $u \in U_n^{x,y}$ then $v = \pi_{p^n, p^m}(u) \in U_m^{x,y}$.

Consider the tree $\mathcal{T}$ of finite sequences $(u_0, \ldots, u_n)$ such that $u_i \in U_i^{x,y}$ and $u_i = \pi_{p^n, p^i}(u_n)$ for all $i = 0, \ldots, n$. Since each $U_n^{x,y}$ is nonempty, the tree $\mathcal{T}$ is infinite. Since it is at most p-branching, using König's Lemma, we can pick an infinite branch $(u_n)_{n \in \mathbb{N}}$ in $\mathcal{T}$. This branch defines an element $z \in \mathbb{Z}_p$. The commutative diagrams of Fig. 2 show that the sequences $(\widehat{\pi_n}(x) - \widehat{\pi_n}(y))_{n \in \mathbb{N}}$ and $\varphi_n(\widehat{\pi_n}(x)) - \varphi_n(\widehat{\pi_n}(y))$ represent $x - y$ and $\Phi(x) - \Phi(y)$ in $\mathbb{Z}_p$. Equality $\varphi_m(\widehat{\pi_m}(x)) - \varphi_m(\widehat{\pi_m}(y)) = (\widehat{\pi_m}(x) - \widehat{\pi_m}(y))\, \pi_{p^n, p^m}(u)$ shows that (going to the projective limits) $\Phi(x) - \Phi(y) = (x - y)\, z$. This proves that Φ is congruence preserving. $\qquad\square$

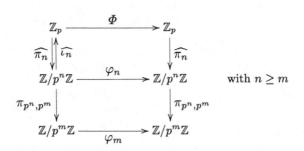

Fig. 2. Φ as the inverse limit of the φ_n's, $n \in \mathbb{N}$.

3.3 Extension of Congruence Preserving Functions $\mathbb{N} \to \mathbb{N}$

Congruence preserving functions $\mathbb{Z}_p \to \mathbb{Z}_p$ (resp. $\widehat{\mathbb{Z}} \to \widehat{\mathbb{Z}}$) are determined by their restrictions to $\mathbb{N}$ since $\mathbb{N}$ is dense in $\mathbb{Z}_p$ (resp. $\widehat{\mathbb{Z}}$). Let us state a (partial) converse result.

Theorem 24. *Every congruence preserving function $F : \mathbb{N} \to \mathbb{Z}$ has a unique extension to a congruence preserving function $\Phi : \mathbb{Z}_p \to \mathbb{Z}_p$ (resp. $\widehat{\mathbb{Z}} \to \widehat{\mathbb{Z}}$).*

Proof. Let us denote by $\widetilde{\mathbb{N}}$ and $\widetilde{\mathbb{Z}}$ the canonical copies of $\mathbb{N}$ and $\mathbb{Z}$ in $\mathbb{Z}_p$ and by $\widetilde{F} :$ $\widetilde{\mathbb{N}} \to \widetilde{\mathbb{Z}}$ the copy of F as a partial function on $\mathbb{Z}_p$. As F is congruence preserving so is $\widetilde{F}$, which is thus also uniformly continuous (as a partial function on $\mathbb{Z}_p$). Since $\widetilde{\mathbb{N}}$ is dense in $\mathbb{Z}_p$, $\widetilde{F}$ has a unique uniformly continuous extension $\Phi : \mathbb{Z}_p \to \mathbb{Z}_p$. To show that this extension Φ is congruence preserving, observe that Φ, being uniformly continuous, is the inverse limit of the $\varphi_n = \widehat{\pi_n} \circ \Phi \circ \widehat{\iota_n}$. Now, since $\widehat{\iota_n}$ has range exactly $\widetilde{\mathbb{N}}$ we see that $\varphi_n = \widehat{\pi_n} \circ \widetilde{F} \circ \widehat{\iota_n}$; as $\widetilde{F}$ is congruence preserving so is φ_n. Finally, Theorem 23 insures that Φ is also congruence preserving. $\square$

Polynomials in $\mathbb{Z}_p[X]$ obviously define congruence preserving functions $\mathbb{Z}_p \to \mathbb{Z}_p$. But non polynomial functions can also be congruence preserving.

Consequence 25. *The extensions to $\mathbb{Z}_p$ and $\widehat{\mathbb{Z}}$ of the $\mathbb{N} \to \mathbb{Z}$ functions [2, 3]*

$$x \mapsto \lfloor e^{1/a} a^x x! \rfloor \quad (\text{for } a \in \mathbb{Z} \setminus \{0, 1\}) \quad , \quad x \mapsto \text{if } x = 0 \text{ then } 1 \text{ else } \lfloor e\, x! \rfloor$$

and the Bessel like function $f(n) = \sqrt{\dfrac{e}{\pi}} \times \dfrac{\Gamma(1/2)}{2 \times 4^n \times n!} \displaystyle\int_1^\infty e^{-t/2}(t^2 - 1)^n dt$ *are congruence preserving.*

3.4 Representation of Congruence Preserving Functions $\mathbb{Z}_p \to \mathbb{Z}_p$

We now characterize congruence preserving functions via their representation as infinite linear sums of the P_k's (suitably extended to $\mathbb{Z}_p$). This representation is a refinement of Mahler's characterization of continuous functions (Theorem 28). First recall the notion of valuation.

Definition 26. *The p-valuation (resp. the factorial valuation) $Val(x)$ of $x \in \mathbb{Z}_p$, or $x \in \mathbb{Z}/p^n\mathbb{Z}$ (resp. $x \in \widehat{\mathbb{Z}}$) is the largest s such that p^s (resp. $s!$) divides x or is $+\infty$ in case $x = 0$. It is also the length of the initial block of zeros in the p-adic (resp. factorial) representation of x.*

Note that for any polynomial P_k (or more generally any polynomial), the below diagram commutes for any $m \leq n$ (recall that $P_k^{p^n, p^n} = \pi_{p^n} \circ P_k \circ \iota_{p^n}$, cf. Definition 12):

$$
\begin{array}{ccc}
\mathbb{Z}/p^n\mathbb{Z} & \xrightarrow{\ P_k^{p^n,p^n}\ } & \mathbb{Z}/p^n\mathbb{Z} \\[2pt]
{\scriptstyle \pi_{p^n,p^m}}\Big\downarrow & & \Big\downarrow{\scriptstyle \pi_{p^n,p^m}} \\[2pt]
\mathbb{Z}/p^m\mathbb{Z} & \xrightarrow{\ P_k^{p^m,p^m}\ } & \mathbb{Z}/p^m\mathbb{Z}
\end{array}
\qquad \text{i.e. } \pi_{p^n,p^m} \circ P_k^{p^n,p^n} = P_k^{p^m,p^m} \circ \pi_{p^n,p^m}.
$$

This allows to define the interpretation $\widehat{P_k}$ of P_k in $\mathbb{Z}_p$ (resp. $\widehat{\mathbb{Z}}$) as an inverse limit.

Definition 27. $\widehat{P_k}\colon \mathbb{Z}_p \to \mathbb{Z}_p$ *is the inverse limit of the inverse system* $(P_k^{p^n,p^n})_{n\geq 1}$. *Otherwise stated, for* $x \in \mathbb{Z}_p$ *such that* $x = \varprojlim_{n\in\mathbb{N}} x_n$, *we have*

$$\widehat{P_k}(x) = \varprojlim_{n\in\mathbb{N}} P_k^{p^n,p^n}(x_n) = \varprojlim_{n\in\mathbb{N}} \pi_{p^n}(P_k(\iota_{p^n}(x_n)))$$

Thus, the following diagram commutes for all n :

$$
\begin{array}{ccc}
\mathbb{Z}_p & \xrightarrow{\widehat{P_k}} & \mathbb{Z}_p \\
\widehat{\pi_n}\downarrow & & \downarrow\widehat{\pi_n} \\
\mathbb{Z}/p^n\mathbb{Z} & \xrightarrow{P_k^{p^n,p^n}} & \mathbb{Z}/p^n\mathbb{Z} \\
\iota_{p^n}\downarrow & & \downarrow\iota_{p^n} \\
\mathbb{N} & \xrightarrow{P_k} & \mathbb{N}
\end{array}
$$

Recall Mahler's characterization of continuous functions on $\mathbb{Z}_p$ (resp. $\widehat{\mathbb{Z}}$).

Theorem 28 (Mahler, 1956 [9]**).** *1. A series* $\sum_{k\in\mathbb{N}} a_k \widehat{P_k}(x)$, $a_k \in \mathbb{Z}_p$, *is convergent in* $\mathbb{Z}_p$ *if and only if* $\lim_{k\to\infty} a_k = 0$, *i.e. the corresponding sequence of valuations* $(Val(a_k))_{k\in\mathbb{N}}$ *tends to* $+\infty$.
2. A function $\mathbb{Z}_p \to \mathbb{Z}_p$ *is represented by a convergent series if and only if it is continuous. Moreover, such a representation is unique.*
Idem with $\widehat{\mathbb{Z}}$.

Theorem 29 refines Mahler's characterization to congruence preserving functions.

Theorem 29. *A function* $\Phi : \mathbb{Z}_p \to \mathbb{Z}_p$ *represented by a series* $\Phi = \sum_{k\in\mathbb{N}} a_k \widehat{P_k}$ *is congruence preserving if and only if* $lcm(k)$ *divides* a_k *for all* k.

Note. The condition "$lcm(k)$ divides a_k for all k" is stronger than $\lim_{k\to\infty} a_k = 0$.

Proof. Suppose Φ is congruence preserving and let $\varphi_n = \widehat{\pi_n} \circ \Phi \circ \widehat{\iota_n}$. Theorem 23 insures that $\Phi = \varprojlim_{n\in\mathbb{N}} \varphi_n$ and the φ_n's are congruence preserving on $\mathbb{Z}/p^n\mathbb{Z}$. Using Corollary 14, we get $\varphi_n = \sum_{k=0}^{\nu(n)-1} b_k^n P_k^{p^n,p^n}$ with $lcm(k)$ dividing b_k^n for all $k \leq \nu(n)-1$. By Proposition 18, Φ is uniformly continuous hence by Mahler's Theorem 28, $\Phi = \sum_{k\in\mathbb{N}} a_k \widehat{P_k}$ with $a_k \in \mathbb{Z}_p$ such that $\lim_{k\to\infty} a_k = 0$. Equation $\varphi_n = \widehat{\pi_n} \circ \Phi \circ \widehat{\iota_n}$ then yields

$$\varphi_n = \widehat{\pi_n} \circ (\sum_{k\in\mathbb{N}} a_k \widehat{P_k}) \circ \widehat{\iota_n} = \sum_{k\in\mathbb{N}} \widehat{\pi_n}(a_k)\,\widehat{\pi_n} \circ \widehat{P_k} \circ \widehat{\iota_n} = \sum_{k\in\mathbb{N}} \widehat{\pi_n}(a_k)\, P_k^{p^n,p^n} .$$

The unicity of the representation of φ_n (cf. Corollary 14) insures that $b_k^n = \widehat{\pi_n}(a_k)$. Similarly, $b_k^m = \widehat{\pi_m}(a_k)$; as for $m \leq n$, $\widehat{\pi_m} = \pi_{p^n,p^m} \circ \widehat{\pi_n}$ (Lemma 21), we obtain $b_k^m = \pi_{p^n, p^m}(b_k^n)$. Thus, $(b_k^n)_{n \in \mathbb{N}}$ is an inverse system such that $a_k = \varprojlim_{n \in \mathbb{N}} b_k^n$. Since φ_n is congruence preserving Corollary 14 insures that $lcm(k)$ divides b_k^n; applying Lemma 30, we see that for all n, $\nu_p(k) \leq Val(b_k^n)$. Noting that $Val(a_k) = Val(b_k^n)$, we deduce that $\nu_p(k) \leq Val(a_k)$, hence $p^{\nu_p(k)}$ and thus also $lcm(k)$ divide a_k. In particular, this implies that $d(a_k, 0) \leq 2^{-\nu_p(k)}$ and $\lim_{k \to \infty} a_k = 0$.

Conversely, if $\Phi = \sum_{k \in \mathbb{N}} a_k \widehat{P_k}$ and $lcm(k)$ divides a_k for all k then $lcm(k)$ divides $\widehat{\pi_n}(a_k)$ for all n, k. Thus, the associated φ_n are congruence preserving which implies that so is Φ by Theorem 23. $\qquad\square$

Lemma 30. *Let $\nu_p(k)$ be the largest i such that $p^i \leq k < p^{i+1}$. In $\mathbb{Z}/p^n\mathbb{Z}$, $lcm(k)$ divides a number x iff $\nu_p(k) \leq Val(x)$.*

Proof. In $\mathbb{Z}/p^n\mathbb{Z}$ all numbers are invertible except multiples of p. Hence $lcm(k)$ divides x iff $p^{\nu_p(k)}$ divides x. $\qquad\square$

Example 31. Let $\Phi = \sum_{k \in \mathbb{N}} a_k P_k$ with $a_k = p^{\nu_p(k)-1}$, with $\nu_p(k)$ as in Lemma 30. Φ is uniformly continuous by Theorem 28. By Lemma 30, $lcm(k)$ does not divide a_k; hence by Theorem 29, Φ is *not* congruence preserving.

4   Conclusion

We here studied functions having congruence preserving properties. These functions appeared as uniformly continuous functions in a variety of finite groups (see [10]).

The contribution of the present paper is to *characterize congruence preserving functions* on various sets derived from $\mathbb{Z}$ such as $\mathbb{Z}/n\mathbb{Z}$, (resp. $\mathbb{Z}_p, \widehat{\mathbb{Z}}$) via polynomials (resp. series) with *rational coefficients* which share the following common property: $lcm(k)$ divides the k-th coefficient. Examples of *non polynomial* (Bessel like) congruence preserving functions can be found in [3].

Acknowledgments. We thank the anonymous referee for careful reading and valuable comments.

Appendix

Appendix 1: Basics on p-adic and profinite Integers

Recall some classical equivalent approaches to the topological rings of p-adic integers and profinite integers, cf. Lenstra [7,8], Lang [6] and Robert [11].

Proposition 32. *Let p be prime. The three following approaches lead to isomorphic structures, called the topological ring $\mathbb{Z}_p$ of p-adic integers.*

– *The ring $\mathbb{Z}_p$ is the inverse limit of the following inverse system:*

- *the family of rings $\mathbb{Z}/p^n\mathbb{Z}$ for $n \in \mathbb{N}$, endowed with the discrete topology,*
- *the family of surjective morphisms $\pi_{p^n,p^m} : \mathbb{Z}/p^n\mathbb{Z} \to \mathbb{Z}/p^m\mathbb{Z}$ for $0 \leq n \geq m$.*
- *The ring $\mathbb{Z}_p$ is the set of infinite sequences $\{0,\ldots,p-1\}^{\mathbb{N}}$ endowed with the Cantor topology and addition and multiplication which extend the usual way to perform addition and multiplication on base p representations of natural integers.*
- *The ring $\mathbb{Z}_p$ is the Cauchy completion of the metric topological ring $(\mathbb{N}, +, \times)$ relative to the following ultrametric: $d(x,x) = 0$ and for $x \neq y$, $d(x,y) = 2^{-n}$ where n is the p-valuation of $|x-y|$, i.e. the maximum k such that p^k divides $x - y$.*

Recall the factorial representation of integers.

Lemma 33. *Every positive integer n has a unique representation as*

$$n = c_k k! + c_{k-1}(k-1)! + \ldots + c_2 2! + c_1 1!$$

where $c_k \neq 0$ and $0 \leq c_i \leq i$ for all $i = 1, \ldots, k$.

Proposition 34. *The four following approaches lead to isomorphic structures, called the topological ring $\widehat{\mathbb{Z}}$ of profinite integers.*

- *The ring $\widehat{\mathbb{Z}}$ is the inverse limit of the following inverse system:*
  - *the family of rings $\mathbb{Z}/k\mathbb{Z}$ for $k \geq 1$, endowed with the discrete topology,*
  - *the family of surjective morphisms $\pi_{n,m} : \mathbb{Z}/n\mathbb{Z} \to \mathbb{Z}/m\mathbb{Z}$ for $m \mid n$.*
- *The ring $\widehat{\mathbb{Z}}$ is the inverse limit of the following inverse system:*
  - *the family of rings $\mathbb{Z}/k!\mathbb{Z}$ for $k \geq 1$, endowed with the discrete topology,*
  - *the family of surjective morphisms $\pi_{(n+1)!,n!} : \mathbb{Z}/n!\mathbb{Z} \to \mathbb{Z}/m!\mathbb{Z}$ for $n \geq m$.*
- *The ring $\widehat{\mathbb{Z}}$ is the set of infinite sequences $\prod_{n \geq 1}\{0,\ldots,n\}$ endowed with the product topology and addition and multiplication which extend the obvious way to perform addition and multiplication on factorial representations of natural integers.*
- *The ring $\widehat{\mathbb{Z}}$ is the Cauchy completion of the metric topological ring $(\mathbb{N}, +, \times)$ relative to the following ultrametric: for $x \neq y \in \mathbb{N}$, $d(x,x) = 0$ and $d(x,y) = 2^{-n}$ where n is the maximum k such that $k!$ divides $x - y$.*
- *The ring $\widehat{\mathbb{Z}}$ is the product ring $\prod_{p \ prime} \mathbb{Z}_p$ endowed with the product topology.*

Proposition 35. *The topological rings $\mathbb{Z}_p$ and $\widehat{\mathbb{Z}}$ are compact and zero dimensional (i.e. they have a basis of closed open sets).*

Appendix 2: $\mathbb{N}$ and $\mathbb{Z}$ in $\mathbb{Z}_p$ and $\widehat{\mathbb{Z}}$

Proposition 36. *Let $\lambda : \mathbb{N} \to \mathbb{Z}_p$ (resp. $\lambda : \mathbb{N} \to \widehat{\mathbb{Z}}$) be the function which maps $n \in \mathbb{N}$ to the element of $\mathbb{Z}_p$ (resp. $\widehat{\mathbb{Z}}$) with base p (resp. factorial) representation obtained by suffixing an infinite tail of zeros to the base p (resp. factorial) representation of n.*
The function λ is an embedding of the semiring $\mathbb{N}$ onto a topologically dense semiring in the ring $\mathbb{Z}_p$ (resp. $\widehat{\mathbb{Z}}$).

Remark 37. In the base p representation, the opposite of an element $f \in \mathbb{Z}_p$ is the element $-f$ such that, for all $m \in \mathbb{N}$,

$$(-f)(i) = \begin{cases} 0 & \text{if } \forall s \leq i \ f(s) = 0, \\ p - f(i) & \text{if } i \text{ is least such that } f(i) \neq 0, \\ p - 1 - f(i) & \text{if } \exists s < i \ f(s) \neq 0. \end{cases}$$

In particular,
- Integers in $\mathbb{N}$ correspond in $\mathbb{Z}_p$ to infinite base p representations with a tail of 0's.
- Integers in $\mathbb{Z} \setminus \mathbb{N}$ correspond in $\mathbb{Z}_p$ to infinite base p representations with a tail of digits $p - 1$.

Similar results hold for the infinite factorial representation of profinite integers.

References

1. Bhargava, M.: Congruence preservation and polynomial functions from $\mathbb{Z}_n$ to $\mathbb{Z}_m$. Discrete Math. **173**, 15–21 (1997)
2. Cégielski, P., Grigorieff, S., Guessarian, I.: Newton representation of functions over natural integers having integral difference ratios. To be published in Int. J. Number Theor. Preliminary version on arXiv, **11** (2015). doi:10.1142/S179304211550092X
3. Cégielski, P., Grigorieff, S., Guessarian, I.: Integral difference ratio functions on integers. In: Calude, C.S., Freivalds, R., Kazuo, I. (eds.) Computing with New Resources. LNCS, vol. 8808, pp. 277–291. Springer, Heidelberg (2014)
4. Cégielski, P., Grigorieff, S., Guessarian, I.: Characterizing congruence preserving functions $\mathbb{Z}/n\mathbb{Z} \rightarrow \mathbb{Z}/m\mathbb{Z}$ via rational polynomials (2015), Submitted
5. Chen, Z.: On polynomial functions from $\mathbb{Z}_n$ to $\mathbb{Z}_m$. Discrete Math. **137**, 137–145 (1995)
6. Lang, S.: Algebra, 3rd edn. Springer, Heidelberg (2002)
7. Lenstra, H.W.: Profinite Fibonacci numbers. Nieuw Arch. Wiskd., (5) **6**(4), 297–300 (2005)
8. Lenstra, H.W.: Profinite groups. Lecture notes available on the web
9. Mahler, K.: An interpolation series for continuous functions of a p-adic variable. J. für die reine und Angew. Math. **199**, 23–34 (1956)
10. Pin, J.É., Silva, P.V.: On profinite uniform structures defined by varieties of finite monoids. Int. J. Algebra Comput. **21**, 295–314 (2011)
11. Robert, A.: A Course in *p*-adic Analysis. Springer, New York (2000)
12. Rosen, K.: Elementary Number Theory and its Applications. Addison-Wesley, Reading (1984)

An Extension of the Ehrenfeucht-Fraïssé Game for First Order Logics Augmented with Lindström Quantifiers

Simi Haber[1]([✉]) and Saharon Shelah[2,3]

[1] Bar-Ilan University, 5290002 Ramat-Gan, Israel
habber@gmail.com
[2] The Hebrew University of Jerusalem, 91904 Jerusalem, Israel
[3] Rutgers, Piscataway, NJ 08854-8019, USA

Dedicated to Yuri Gurevich on the occasion of his 75th birthday.

Abstract. We propose an extension of the Ehrenfeucht-Fraïssé game able to deal with logics augmented with Lindström quantifiers. We describe three different games with varying balance between simplicity and ease of use.

1 Introduction

The Ehrenfeucht-Fraïssé game [7–10] is an important tool in contemporary model theory, allowing to determine whether two structures are elementarily equivalent up to some quantifier depth. It is one of the few model theoretic machineries that survive the transition from general model theory to the finite realm.

There are quite a few known extensions of the Ehrenfeucht-Fraïssé game and in the following we mention a few (this is far from bring a comprehensive list). In [12] Immerman describes how to adapt the Ehrenfeucht-Fraïssé game in order to deal with finite variable logic, first dealt with in Poizat's article [20]. Infinitary logic has a precise characterization by a similar game [2,11]. An extension for fixpoint logic and stratified fixpoint logic was provided by Bosse [3].

Lindström quantifiers were first introduced and studied by Lindström in the sixties [16–19] and may be seen as precursors to his theorem. There are several extensions and modifications of the Ehrenfeucht-Fraïssé game for logics augmented with Lindström quantifiers. We give a partial description of the history of the subject. Perhaps the first treatment of this subject was provided by Krawczyk and Krynicki, [15], who introduced a game capturing $\mathcal{L}_{\omega\omega}(Q)$ equivalence for monotone simple unary quantifier Q. A back-and-forth technique was given by Caicedo in [5], who considered also fragments of bounded quantifier degree. Weese, in [21], gave a sufficient condition for equivalence relative to first-order logic with Lindström quantifiers in the form of a game. This condition is also necessary in the case of monotone quantifiers.

Research partially supported by National Science Foundation grant no. DMS 1101597. Research partially supported by European Research Council grant 338821. Number 1059 on author's list.

L.D. Beklemishev et al. (Eds.): Gurevich Festschrift II 2015, LNCS 9300, pp. 226–236, 2015.
DOI: 10.1007/978-3-319-23534-9_13

Games dealing with the special case of *counting quantifiers* were also investigated [4, 13].

Probably the most relevant for our work is the work of Kolaitis and Väänänen, [14]. In their paper the authors describe four similar games, all for unary Lindström quantifiers. Of the four variants, one game is similar, but not identical, to the first game we propose here – the *definable (k, Q)-Pebble game*. This game captures $\mathcal{L}^k_{\infty\omega}(Q)$-equivalence, and also $\mathcal{L}^k_{\omega\omega}(Q)$-equivalence for finite models. However, as the authors mention, describing a winning strategy for this game may be difficult in practice since this requires an analysis of definability on the structures forming the game-board. Hence the authors go on to describe two more games: the *invariant (k, Q)-Pebble game* and the *monotone (k, Q)-Pebble game*. While all games are equivalent for monotone quantifiers, this is not the case in general. This leaves the task of finding a game avoiding definability requirements but capturing extensions by general Lindström quantifiers as an open problem.

The main aim of this paper is to present several related extensions of the Ehrenfeucht-Fraïssé game adapted to logics augmented with Lindström quantifiers. Our main contribution is a description of an Ehrenfeucht-Fraïssé like game capturing general Lindström quantifiers without forcing the players to chose definable structures by the game rules.

2   The Game

Notation 1. 1. Let τ denote a vocabulary. We assume τ has no function symbols, but that is purely for the sake of clearer presentation. τ may have constant symbols.

2. First order logic will be denoted by $\mathcal{L}_{\mathcal{FO}}$. In the course of this paper we will consider extensions of first order logic; therefore the logic under discussion will change according to our needs. Of course, we always assume closure under substitution. We shall denote the logic currently under discussion by $\mathcal{L}$, and we will explicitly redefine $\mathcal{L}$ whenever needed.

3. Given a vocabulary τ, we use $\mathcal{L}(\tau)$ to denote the *language* with logic $\mathcal{L}$ and vocabulary τ. We will use this notation only when clarity demands, so in fact we may abuse notation and use $\mathcal{L}$ also for the unspecified language under discussion.

4. For even further transparency, all the examples in this work (in particular, all cases of pairs of models to be proved equivalent) will be dealing with simple[1] graphs. Hence (only in examples) we further assume that τ is the vocabulary of graphs denoted henceforth by τ_{GRA}. Explicitly, $\tau_{\text{GRA}} = \{\sim\}$ where $\sim$ is a binary, anti-reflexive and symmetric relation. For the Lindström quantifiers given in examples, we may use vocabularies other than τ_{GRA}.

A few basic graph theoretic notions will be used in the examples and are defined here (with the standard notation): In the context of graphs we will

---

[1] An undirected graph with no loops and no double edges is called *a simple graph*.

refer to the relation $\sim$ as *adjacency*. Given a graph $G = (V, E)$ we will denote the *neighborhood* of a vertex x in G by $N_G(x)$, defined as the set $N_G(x) = \{y \in V \mid x \sim y\}$. The *degree* of x will be denoted by $d_G(x) = |N_G(x)|$. We may omit the subscript G when it is clear which is the graph under discussion. We shall denote the *graph induced on* U by $G[U] = (U, \{e \in E \mid e \subset U\})$ where $U \subseteq V$ is a set of vertices. Finally, we will denote the *complement graph of* G by $\overline{G} = (V, \binom{V}{2} \setminus E)$, where $\binom{V}{2}$ is the set of all subsets of V of size two.

5. Let $\mathbf{A}_1, \mathbf{A}_2, \ldots, \mathbf{A}_n$ be classes of models, each closed under isomorphism. The models in $\mathbf{A}_i$ are all τ_i-structures in some relational vocabulary $\tau_i = \{P_{i,1}^{a_{i,1}}, \ldots, P_{i,t_i}^{a_{i,t_i}}\}$, where $P_{i,j}$ is the jth relation in τ_i and $a_{i,j}$ is the arity of $P_{i,j}$. We assume $\mathbf{A}_0$ represents the existential quantifier and is always defined.

6. For simplicity, we will assume that each τ_i has an additional relation, $P_{i,0}^1$. This will serve for the formula defining the universe of the model. Formally, our models may have any set as their domain (perhaps some set used as the entire universe for the discussion), and the first relation will define a subset serving as the domain de facto. See also Remark 6 where we mention other flavors of Lindström quantifiers.

7. We set $a_{i,0} = 1$ for every i.

8. For each i, the class $\mathbf{A}_i$ corresponds to a Lindström quantifier Q_i, binding $a_i = \sum_{j=0}^{t_i} a_{i,j}$ variables.

Remark 2. The games and the claims associating them with logics remain valid even with the absence of the existential quantifier. Still, it seems that the main interesting case is when first order logic is properly *extended*, and so we focus on this case.

Example 3. 1. $\mathbf{A}_1$ may be the class of commutative groups, in which case τ_1 consists of a constant symbol encoding zero[2] and a ternary relation encoding the group operation.

2. Another example may be finite Hamiltonian graphs, in which case the vocabulary is the vocabulary of graphs and the class $\mathbf{A}_1$ will be the class of all finite Hamiltonian graphs.

Notation 4. Given a vector $\bar{x}$, we denote the number of elements in the vector by $\text{len}(\bar{x})$.

Definition 5. *We define the quantifier Q_i corresponding to the class $\mathbf{A}_i$ as follows: Let G be a τ-structure with domain V. For any sequence of formulae $\varphi_0(x_0, \bar{y}), \varphi_1(\bar{x}_1, \bar{y}), \ldots, \varphi_{t_i}(\bar{x}_{t_i}, \bar{y})$ such that $\text{len}(\bar{x}_j) = a_{i,j}$ and denoting the elements of $\bar{x}_j$ are by subscript l (i.e., $x_{j,l}$), we determine the satisfaction of the sentence $Q_i\, x_0, \bar{x}_1, \ldots, \bar{x}_{t_i}(\varphi_0(x_0, \bar{b}), \varphi_1(\bar{x}_1, \bar{b}), \ldots, \varphi_{t_i}(\bar{x}_{t_i}, \bar{b}))$ according to the satisfaction of*

---

[2] Of course, one may encode zero using the relation.

$$G \models Q_i \quad x_0, \bar{x}_1, \ldots, \bar{x}_{t_i}(\varphi_0(x_0, \bar{b}), \varphi_1(\bar{x}_1, \bar{b}), \ldots, \varphi_{t_i}(\bar{x}_{t_i}, \bar{b})) \Longleftrightarrow$$
$$(\{x_0 \in V \mid G \models \varphi_0(x_0, \bar{b})\},$$
$$\{\bar{x}_1 \in V^{a_{i,1}} \mid \bigwedge_{l=1}^{a_{i,1}} G \models \varphi_0(x_{1,l}, \bar{b}) \wedge G \models \varphi_1(\bar{x}_1, \bar{b})\}, \ldots,$$
$$\{\bar{x}_{t_i} \in V^{a_{i,t_i}} \mid \bigwedge_{l=1}^{a_{i,t_i}} G \models \varphi_0(x_{t_i,l}, \bar{b}) \wedge G \models \varphi_{t_i}(\bar{x}_{t_i}, \bar{b})\}) \in \mathbf{A}_i,$$

where $\bar{b}$ are parameters.

Remark 6. Definition 5 requires φ_0 to have exactly one free variable, x_0 (excluding $\bar{y}$, saved for parameters). However there is no real reason to avoid sets of vectors of any fixed length from serving as the domain of the model defined in the quantifier. We will not discuss this here, but the generalization of the proposed games to this case are straightforward. Sometime Lindström quantifiers are defined over *equivalence classes* of such vectors. See, e.g., [6]. Again, we will not discuss this generalization here.

Definition 7. *Let φ be a formula in $\mathcal{L}$. The* quantifier depth *of φ, denoted* $QD(\varphi)$, *is defined as follows:*

1. *If φ is an atomic formula, in our examples this means φ is of the form $x = y$ or $x \sim y$, then we define $QD(\varphi) = 0$.*
2. *If $\varphi = \neg\psi$ then $QD(\varphi) = QD(\psi)$.*
3. *If $\varphi = \psi_1 \vee \psi_2$ or $\varphi = \psi_1 \wedge \psi_2$, then $\varphi = \max(QD(\psi_1), QD(\psi_2))$.*
4. *If[3]*

$$\varphi = Q_i \, x_0, \bar{x}_1, \ldots, \bar{x}_{t_i}(\psi_0(x_0, \bar{b}), \psi_1(\bar{x}_1, \bar{b}), \ldots, \psi_{t_i}(\bar{x}_{t_i}, \bar{b})),$$

then

$$\varphi = 1 + \max(QD(\psi_1), QD(\psi_2), \ldots, QD(\psi_{t_i})).$$

Definition 8. *An important role in the following is played by the notion of* k-equivalency:

1. *Let τ be a vocabulary and $\mathcal{L} = \mathcal{L}(\tau)$ be a language. Given two τ-structures G_1, G_2 (not necessarily with distinct universe sets) and two sequences of elements $\bar{x}_1 \in G_1$, $\bar{x}_2 \in G_2$ of equal length a, we say that $(G_1, \bar{x}_1)$ and $(G_2, \bar{x}_2)$ are k-equivalent with respect to $\mathcal{L}$ if for any formula $\varphi(\bar{x}) \in \mathcal{L}$ of quantifier depth at most k one has*

$$G_1 \models \varphi(\bar{x}_1) \Longleftrightarrow G_2 \models \varphi(\bar{x}_2).$$

2. *When considering only one model, that is, when we take $G = G_1 = G_2$, we refer to the equivalence classes of this relation in the domain of G simply by the (a, k, G) -equivalence classes where a is the length of tuples in the equivalence class. As usual, when the parameters are clear enough from the context we shall simple use "equivalence classes" for (a, k, G)-equivalence classes.*

---

[3] Notice that by our definition in 1. item (5) above, Q_0 is always the existential quantifier, and so our definition coincides with the standard definition when relevant.

Remark 9. Notice that unions of (a, k, G)-equivalence classes are exactly the definable sets of a-tuples of elements in $\dm(G)$ using $\mathcal{L}$-formulas of quantifier depth at most k.

Example 10. Let $\mathcal{L}$ be the first order language of graphs, $\mathcal{L} = \mathcal{L}_{\mathcal{FO}}(\tau_{\mathrm{GRA}})$, and let $G = (V, E)$ be a graph. If G is simple then the $(1, 0, G)$-equivalence classes are V and $\emptyset$. If $|V| > 1$ then the $(1, 1, G)$-equivalence classes are[4] the set of isolated vertices in G, the set of vertices adjacent to all other vertices and the set of vertices having at least one neighbor and one non-neighbor (some of which may be empty of course).

Notation 11. We denote the logic obtained by augmenting the first order logic with the quantifiers $Q_1, Q_2, \ldots, Q_n$ by $\mathcal{L} = \mathcal{L}[Q_1, Q_2, \ldots, Q_n]$.

Example 12. Consider the language $\mathcal{L} = \mathcal{L}[Q_{\mathrm{HAM}}](\tau_{\mathrm{GRA}})$, where Q_{HAM} stands for the "Hamiltonicity quantifier" (corresponding to the class of graphs containing a Hamiltonian cycle — a cycle visiting each vertex precisely once). Let G be a graph. Then the set of all vertices x for which all of the graphs $G[N_G(x)], \overline{G}[N_G(x)], G[N_{\overline{G}}(x)], \overline{G}[N_{\overline{G}}(x)]$ are Hamiltonian is an example of a $(1, 1, G)$-equivalence class with respect to $\mathcal{L}[Q_{\mathrm{HAM}}]$. The set of vertices with degree exactly two is a union of $(1, 1, G)$-equivalence classes, as can be seen by[5]

$$\varphi(x) = Q_{\mathrm{HAM}} x_0, x_1, x_2(\, x_0 \sim x, x_1 \neq x_2).$$

2.1   Description of the First Game

Before describing the game, we need the following definition:

Definition 13. *Let τ be a vocabulary, $\mathcal{L} = \mathcal{L}(\tau)$ a language over that vocabulary (not necessarily first order) and G a structure of vocabulary τ. Additionally, let $M = (S', R'_1, \ldots, R'_t)$ be a structure of another vocabulary τ'. A copy of M in G is a tuple $(S, R_1, \ldots, R_t)$ such that*

1. *S is a subset of $\dm(G)$ with the same cardinality as $\dm(M) = S'$ (where $\dm(G)$ is the universe or underlying set of G).*
2. *$R_1, \ldots, R_t$ are relations over S, such that each R_j has the same arity as R'_j.*
3. *$(S, R_1, \ldots, R_t)$ is isomorphic to $(S', R'_1, \ldots, R'_t)$.*

For our first (and simplest) game we will need a more restrictive notion, defined below:

Definition 14. *In the setting of Definition 13, if in addition to requirements (1) – (3) of Definition 13 the following holds*

4. *S is a union of $(1, k, G)$-equivalence classes, and each relation R_j of arity a_j is a union of (a_j, k, G)-equivalence classes,*

---

[4] The atomic sentences appearing in $\varphi(x)$ are $x = y$ and $x \sim y$.

[5] φ expresses: "the complete graph $K_{d(x)}$ is Hamiltonian" which is true when $d(x) > 2$ and false when $d(x) = 2$ (we may treat K_0 and K_1 separately, if needed).

we say that a copy of M in G is k-induced by $\mathcal{L}$. When k or $\mathcal{L}$ can be clearly determined by the context, we may omit mentioning it.

We are now ready to define the first game.

Definition 15. *Consider Lindström quantifiers $Q_1, Q_2, \ldots, Q_n$ and define $\mathcal{L} = \mathcal{L}[Q_1, Q_2, \ldots, Q_n](\tau)$ to be a language over some relational vocabulary τ defined as in definition 5 above. Let G_1 and G_2 be two τ-structures with domains V_1 and V_2 respectively. Let $k \geq 0$ an integer and $\bar{c}_\ell = (c_\ell^1, \ldots, c_\ell^r) \in V_\ell^r$ for $\ell \in \{1, 2\}$ two finite sequences. We define the game[6] $\mathrm{EFL}_1[G_1, G_2, \bar{c}_1, \bar{c}_2 \, ; \, k]$. There are two players, named by the (by now) traditional names Duplicator and Spoiler, as suggested by Spencer. The game board is the models G_1 and G_2 plus the sequences $\bar{c}_\ell$ and there are k rounds. Each round is divided into two parts, and each part consists of two sub-rounds. The game is defined recursively. If $k = 0$, then if the mapping $c_1^i \to c_2^i$ is a partial isomorphism, then Duplicator wins, otherwise Spoiler wins.*

When $k > 0$ then first Spoiler plays. He picks one of the models G_1 or G_2 (denoted henceforth by G_ℓ) and a quantifier Q_i (or the existential quantifier[7]). Next Spoiler picks a model $M \in \mathbf{A}_i$, and embeds it into G_ℓ in a manner that preserves $(k - 1, G_\ell)$-equivalence classes. That is, Spoiler picks a tuple $(S_\ell, R_{\ell,1}, \ldots, R_{\ell,t_i})$ that is a copy of M in G which is $(k - 1)$-induced by $\mathcal{L}$ enriched with r constants having values $\bar{c}_\ell$. If Spoiler can not find such an embedding, he loses[8]. Implicitly Spoiler claims that Duplicator can not find a matching induced copy of a model from $\mathbf{A}_i$.

Second, Duplicator responds by choosing a model M' from $\mathbf{A}_i$ (M' may not necessarily be the same as M), and then picking an induced copy of M' in $G_{3-\ell}$ which we naturally denote by $(S_{3-\ell}, R_{3-\ell,1}, \ldots, R_{3-\ell,t_i})$. She is implicitly claiming that her choices match the picks of Spoiler, that is, each $R_{3-\ell,j}$ (or $S_{3-\ell,j}$) is a union of $(a_{i,j}, k - 1, G_{3-\ell})$-equivalence classes defined by the same formulas as the formulas defining the $(a_{i,j}, k - 1, G_\ell)$-equivalence classes of which $R_{\ell,j}$ is made. If Duplicator can not complete this part she loses. This ends the first part of the round.

In the second part of the round Spoiler chooses $m \in \{1, 2\}$ and $0 \leq j \leq t_i$. He then picks $(c_m^{r+1}, \ldots, c_m^{r+a_{i,j}}) \in R_{m,j}$ (implicitly challenging Duplicator to do the same). Finally Duplicator picks $(c_{3-m}^{r+1}, \ldots, c_{3-m}^{r+a_{i,j}}) \in R_{3-m,j}$ and they move on to play

$$\mathrm{EFL}_1[G_1, G_2, \quad (c_1^1, \ldots, c_1^r, c_1^{r+1}, \ldots, c_1^{r+a_{i,j}}),$$
$$(c_2^1, \ldots, c_2^r, c_2^{r+1}, \ldots, c_2^{r+a_{i,j}}); k - 1].$$

This ends the second part and the round. Since k goes down every round, the game ends when $k = 0$, as described above.

---

[6] We will describe a few variants, hence the subscript.

[7] In this case, $\mathbf{A}_\exists = P(V) \setminus \{\emptyset\}$, so Spoiler may choose any non-empty subset S_ℓ of V_ℓ.

[8] We will consider only logics stronger than first-order, hence the existential quantifier is always assumed to be at Spoiler' disposal and he will never lose in this manner.

Given the description above, the following should be self-evident:

Lemma 16. *Let $\mathcal{L} = \mathcal{L}[Q_1, Q_2, \ldots](\tau)$ be a language over some vocabulary τ where $Q_1, Q_2, \ldots$ are Lindström quantifiers, and let G_1, G_2 be two structures with vocabulary τ. Then,* Duplicator *has a winning strategy for* $\mathrm{EFL}_1[G_1, G_2, \emptyset, \emptyset\,;\,k]$ *if and only if for any sentence $\varphi \in \mathcal{L}$ of quantifier depth at most k*

$$G_1 \models \varphi \Longleftrightarrow G_2 \models \varphi.$$

2.2   A Game Where Definability is Not Forced

While the claim of Lemma 16 may seem satisfying, in practice it may be hard to put this lemma into use since it takes finding unions of $(a, k-1, G)$-equivalence classes for granted, being a rule of the game. This might hinder strategy development and we would like to describe another game with looser rules, denoted EFL_2.

In this version the players are not bound to choosing unions of $(a, k-1, G)$-equivalence classes when picking a copy of the chosen model (hence we call their action "picking a copy of M in G_ℓ", omitting the "induced" part). That is, we omit requirement 4 in Definition 13. It falls to the other player to challenge the claim that indeed every relation is a union of the relevant equivalence classes.

Definition 17. *Our definition of the game* $\mathrm{EFL}_2[G_1, G_2, \bar{c}_1, \bar{c}_2\,;\,k]$ *is based on the definition of* $\mathrm{EFL}_1[G_1, G_2, \bar{c}_1, \bar{c}_2\,;\,k]$. *The setting is the same, but now a round goes as follows:*

Spoiler *picks a structure $G_\ell \in \{G_1, G_2\}$ and a quantifier Q_i (or, as before, the existential quantifier). Next* Spoiler *picks a model $M \in \mathbf{A}_i$ and picks a copy of M in G_ℓ. His implicit claim now includes the claim that each of the relations he chose is a union of $(a_{i,j}, k-1, G_\ell)$-equivalence classes with respect to $\mathcal{L}$ enriched with r constants having values $\bar{c}_\ell$.*

Duplicator *can respond in two different ways — she can "accept the challenge" (as she did in* EFL_1*), or attack the second part of the claim of* Spoiler. *That is, she can do one of the following:*

1. Duplicator *accepts the challenge. In this case she chooses $M' \in \mathbf{A}_i$ and picks a copy of M' in $G_{3-\ell}$. Implicitly she is claiming that her choices match the choices of* Spoiler. *That is, the set of vertices $S_{3-\ell}$ and each of the relations defined on it are a union of the $(a_{i,j}, k-1, G_{3-\ell})$-equivalence classes corresponding[9] to the ones that* Spoiler *picked. This ends the first part of the round.*

   Spoiler *may continue in a two different ways.*

---

[9] We say that E_1, an (a, k, G_1)-equivalence class of a-tuples in G_1 corresponds to E_2 — a set of a-tuples in G_2 if for any $\bar{x}_1 \in E_1$ and $\bar{x}_2 \in E_2$ one has

$$G_1 \models \varphi(\bar{x}_1) \Leftrightarrow G_2 \models \varphi(\bar{x}_2)$$

for any $\varphi \in \mathcal{L}$ of quantifier depth at most k.

(a) Spoiler *rejects the fact that the set* $S_{3-\ell}$ *or one of the relations picked by* Duplicator *is a union of equivalence classes. In order to settle this, we recursively use* EFL_2:

This part of the round begins with Spoiler *picking* $j \in \{0, \ldots, t\}$, *presumably according to the relation that is not a union of equivalence classes. Again, we let* $a = a_{i,j}$ *be the arity of the allegedly invalid relation* $R_{3-\ell,j}$. *Next,* Spoiler *picks two a-tuples of elements from the same structure,*

$$(c^{r+1}, \ldots, c^{r+a}) \in R_{3-\ell,j} \quad and \quad (c'^{r+1}, \ldots, c'^{r+a}) \in V_{3-\ell}^a \setminus R_{3-\ell,j},$$

and they move on to play

$$\mathrm{EFL}_2[G_{3-\ell}, G_{3-\ell}, \quad (c_{3-\ell}^1, \ldots, c_{3-\ell}^r, c^{r+1}, \ldots, c^{r+a}),$$
$$(c_{3-\ell}^1, \ldots, c_{3-\ell}^r, c'^{r+1}, \ldots, c'^{r+a}); k-1].$$

with exchanged roles (since this time Spoiler *claims the two tuples are actually* $(a, k-1, G_{3-\ell})$-*equivalent).*

(b) Spoiler *rejects the fact that* Duplicator's *choice matches his choice (as he did in* EFL_1). *In this case* Spoiler *picks a relation* $P_j \in \tau_i$ *and an* $a_{i,j}$-*tuple of elements from* S_ℓ *(or one element if he challenges* Duplicator's *choice of* $S_{3-\ell}$). *Denote the choices of* Spoiler *by* $(c_\ell^{r+1}, \ldots, c_\ell^{r+a_{i,j}}) \in S_\ell$. Duplicator *responds by picking another a-tuple* $(c_{3-\ell}^{r+1}, \ldots, c_{3-\ell}^{r+a_{i,j}}) \in S_{3-\ell}$, *and they move on to play*

$$\mathrm{EFL}_2[G_1, G_2, \quad (c_1^1, \ldots, c_1^r, c_1^{r+1}, \ldots, c_1^{r+a_{i,j}}),$$
$$(c_2^1, \ldots, c_2^r, c_2^{r+1}, \ldots, c_2^{r+a_{i,j}}); k-1].$$

2. Duplicator *rejects* Spoiler's *claim. In this case* Duplicator *wants to prove that* S_ℓ *or one of the relations picked by* Spoiler *is not a union of equivalence classes. We continue similarly to case 1.(b):*

As before, we begin this move with Duplicator *picking* $j \in \{0, \ldots, t\}$, *presumably according to the relation that is not a union of equivalence classes. Again, we let* $a = a_{i,j}$ *be the arity of the allegedly invalid relation* $R_{\ell,j}$ *splitting an equivalence class. Next,* Duplicator *picks two a-tuples of elements from the same structure,*

$$(c^{r+1}, \ldots, c^{r+a}) \in R_{\ell,j} \quad and \quad (c'^{r+1}, \ldots, c'^{r+a}) \in V_\ell^a \setminus R_{3-\ell,j},$$

and they move to play

$$\mathrm{EFL}_2[G_\ell, G_\ell, \quad (c_\ell^1, \ldots, c_\ell^r, c^{r+1}, \ldots, c^{r+a}),$$
$$(c_\ell^1, \ldots, c_\ell^r, c'^{r+1}, \ldots, c'^{r+a}); k-1].$$

this time keeping their original roles.

For any two models G_1 and G_2, constants $\bar{c}_1, \bar{c}_2$ of elements from the domains of G_1 and G_2 respectively, and $k \in \mathbb{N}$, whoever has a winning strategy for

$\mathrm{EFL}_1[G_1, G_2, \bar{c}_1, \bar{c}_2; k]$ has a winning strategy for $\mathrm{EFL}_2[G_1, G_2, \bar{c}_1, \bar{c}_2; k]$. Hence the parallel of Lemma 16 is true for EFL_2 as well.

While we got the benefit of in-game validation of the equivalence classes integrity claims, EFL_2 is not easy to analyze in applications because the game-board and players' role change over time. We amend this in the last suggested version of the game.

2.3 A Game with Fixed Game-Board and Fixed Roles

The last version, denoted EFL_3, forks from EFL_2 in two places.

Definition 18. *We define* EFL_3 *like* EFL_2 *except that:*

1. *First, assume the game reaches step 2., where* Duplicator *wants to prove that* Spoiler *has chose a relation* $R_{\ell,j}$ *splitting an equivalence class. In this case the first part of the round ends immediately and the second part goes as follows:*

   Duplicator *picks* $j \in \{0, \ldots, t\}$, *as before. Next,* Duplicator *chooses two* $a_{i,j}$-*tuples,* $\bar{c}_{\ell,1}$ *from* $R_{\ell,j}$ *and* $\bar{c}_{\ell,2}$ *from the complement of* $R_{\ell,j}$. *She then picks another* $a_{i,j}$-*tuple from the universe set of* $G_{3-\ell}$, *denoted* $\bar{c}_{3-\ell}$. Spoiler *than picks one of* $\bar{c}_{\ell,1}$ *or* $\bar{c}_{\ell,2}$ *and they move on to play* EFL_3 *with* $\bar{c}_{3-\ell}$ *concatenated to the constants of* $G_{3-\ell}$ *and* Spoiler*'s choice concatenated to the constants of* G_ℓ, *and* $k - 1$ *moves. They keep their roles and the game-board remains* G_1 *and* G_2.

   If Duplicator *cannot find a matching tuple in* $G_{3-\ell}$, *she cannot disprove the integrity claim of* Spoiler, *but it does not matter as* G_1 *and* G_2 *are not* k-*equivalent and she is bound to lose anyway.*

   Notice that in this case the first part of the round had only Spoiler *playing, and in the second part* Duplicator *played first.*

2. *The second (and last) change from* EFL_2 *happens when the game is in step 1a. In this case* Spoiler *wants to prove that* Duplicator*'s choice of at least one relation* $R_{3-\ell,j}$ *is splitting an equivalence relation. As always, here also the move begins with* Spoiler *choosing* j. *Then* Spoiler *picks a tuple* $\bar{c}_{3-\ell}$ *(from the suspicious equivalence class) in* $G_{3-\ell}$ *that is not in* $R_{3-\ell,j}$ *and challenges* Duplicator *to find a matching tuple* $\bar{c}_\ell$ *in* $G_{3-\ell}$ *that is not in* $R_{\ell,j}$. *They move on to play* EFL_3 *with these choices and* $k - 1$ *moves. Again both roles and game-board remain as they were. Notice that the game flow in this case is actually the same as the game flow in 1b.*

As before, it is easy to convince oneself that the claim of Lemma 16 is still valid. We repeat it here:

Lemma 19. Duplicator *has a winning strategy for* $\mathrm{EFL}_3[G_1, G_2, \emptyset, \emptyset; k]$ *if and only if for any sentence* $\varphi \in \mathcal{L}$ *of quantifier depth at most* k

$$G_1 \models \varphi \Longleftrightarrow G_2 \models \varphi.$$

3 Summary

We have presented three equivalent variants of the celebrated Ehrenfeucht-Fraïssé game adapted to deal with logics extended by Lindström quantifiers. We believe EFL$_3$ may be easier to analyse than direct quantifier elimination and it is our hope that it will find applications.

Acknowledgements. We would like to thanks the anonymous referees whose comments helped significantly in improving the presentation of this paper and in putting it in the right frame.

References

1. Arruda, A.I., Chuaqui, R., Da Costa, N.C.A. (eds.): Mathematical Logic in Latin America, Studies in Logic and the Foundations of Mathematics, vol. 99. North-Holland Publishing Company, Amsterdam (1980). Proceedings of the IV Latin American Symposium on Mathematical Logic held in Santiago, December 1978
2. Barwise, J.: On moschovakis closure ordinals. J. Symbolic Log. **42**(2), 292–296 (1977)
3. Bosse, U.: An "Ehrenfeucht-Fraïssé game" for fixpoint logic and stratified fixpoint logic. In: Martini, S., Börger, E., Kleine Büning, H., Jäger, G., Richter, M.M. (eds.) CSL 1992. LNCS, vol. 702, pp. 100–114. Springer, Heidelberg (1993)
4. Cai, J.Y., Fürer, M., Immerman, N.: An optimal lower bound on the number of variables for graph identification. Combinatorica **12**(4), 389–419 (1992)
5. Caicedo, X.: Back-and-forth systems for arbitrary quantifiers. In: Arruda et al. [1], Proceedings of the IV Latin American Symposium on Mathematical Logic held in Santiago, pp. 88–102, December 1978
6. Ebbinghaus, H.D., Flum, J.: Finite Model Theory. Springer Monographs in Mathematics, 2nd edn. Springer, Heidelberg (2006)
7. Ehrenfeucht, A.: An application of games to the completeness problem for formalized theories. Fundamenta Mathematicae **49**, 129–141 (1961)
8. Fraïssé, R.: Sur une nouvelle classification des systèmes de relations. Comptes rendus hebdomadaires des séances de l'Académie des sciences **230**, 1022–1024 (1950). French
9. Fraïssé, R.: Sur quelques classifications des systèmes de relations. Ph.D. thesis, University of Paris (1953), published in [10]. (French)
10. Fraïssé, R.: Sur quelques classifications des systèmes de relations. Publications Scientifiques de l'Université d'Alger, Série A, Alger-mathématiques, vol. 1, pp. 35–182 (1954). (French)
11. Immerman, N.: Upper and lower bounds for first order expressibility. J. Comput. Syst. Sci. **25**(1), 76–98 (1982)
12. Immerman, N.: Descriptive Complexity. Graduate Texts in Computer Science. Springer, New York (1998)
13. Immerman, N., Lander, E.: Describing graphs: a first-order approach to graph canonization. In: Selman, A.L. (ed.) Complexity Theory Retrospective, pp. 59–81. Springer, New York (1990). Chapter 4
14. Kolaitis, P.G., Väänänen, J.A.: Generalized quantifiers and pebble games on finite structures. Ann. Pure Appl. Log. **74**(1), 23–75 (1995)

15. Krawczyk, A., Krynicki, M.: Ehrenfeucht games for generalized quantifiers. In: Marek, W., Srebrny, M., Zarach, A. (eds.) Set Theory and Hierarchy Theory. Lecture Notes in Mathematics, vol. 537, pp. 145–152. Springer-Verlag, Berlin (Mar (1976)

16. Lindström, P.: First order predicate logic with generalized quantifiers. Theoria **32**(3), 186–195 (1966). http://onlinelibrary.wiley.com/doi/10.1111/j.1755-2567.1966.tb00600.x/abstract

17. Lindström, P.: On characterizability in $L_{\omega_1\omega_0}$. Theoria **32**(3), 165–171 (1966). http://onlinelibrary.wiley.com/doi/10.1111/j.1755-2567.1966.tb00598.x/abstract

18. Lindström, P.: On relations between structures. Theoria **32**(3), 172–185 (1966)

19. Lindström, P.: On extensions of elementary logic. Theoria **35**(1), 1–11 (1969). http://onlinelibrary.wiley.com/doi/10.1111/j.1755-2567.1969.tb00356.x/pdf

20. Poizat, B.: Deux ou trois choses que je sais de l_n. J. Symbolic Log. **47**(3), 641–658 (1982). http://projecteuclid.org/euclid.jsl/1183741092

21. Weese, M.: Generalized ehrenfeucht games. Fundamenta Mathematicae **109**(2), 103–112 (1980). http://eudml.org/doc/211151

Logics of Finite Hankel Rank

Nadia Labai[1,2]([⊠]) and Johann A. Makowsky[1]

[1] Department of Computer Science,
Technion - Israel Institute of Technology, Haifa, Israel
`janos@cs.technion.ac.il`
[2] Department of Informatics, Vienna University of Technology, Vienna, Austria
`labai@forsyte.tuwien.ac.at`

Abstract. We discuss the Feferman-Vaught Theorem in the setting of abstract model theory for finite structures. We look at sum-like and product-like binary operations on finite structures and their Hankel matrices. We show the connection between Hankel matrices and the Feferman-Vaught Theorem. The largest logic known to satisfy a Feferman-Vaught Theorem for product-like operations is CFOL, first order logic with modular counting quantifiers. For sum-like operations it is CMSOL, the corresponding monadic second order logic. We discuss whether there are maximal logics satisfying Feferman-Vaught Theorems for finite structures.

1 Introduction

1.1 Yuri's Quest for Logics for Computer Science

The second author (JAM) first met Yuri Gurevich in spring 1976, while being a Lady Davis fellow at the Hebrew University, on leave from the Free University, Berlin. Yuri had just recently emigrated to Israel. Yuri was puzzled by the supposed leftist views of JAM, perceiving them as antagonizing. This lead to heated political discussions. In the following time, JAM spent more visiting periods in Israel, culminating in the Logic Year of 1980/81 at the Einstein Institute of the Hebrew University, after which he finally joined the Computer Science Department at the Technion in Haifa.

At this time both Yuri and JAM worked on chapters to be published in [1], Yuri on Monadic Second Order Logic, and JAM on abstract model theory. Abstract model theory deals with meta-mathematical characterizations of logic. Pioneered by P. Lindström, G. Kreisel and J. Barwise, in [1,2,26,30,31], First Order Logic and admissible fragments of infinitary logic were characterized. Inspired by H. Scholz's problem, [10], R. Fagin initiated similar characterizations when models are restricted to finite models, connecting finite model theory to complexity theory.

Partially supported by a grant of the graduate school of the Technion, the National Research Network RiSE (S114), and the LogiCS doctoral program (W1255) funded by the Austrian Science Fund (FWF).
Partially supported by a grant of Technion Research Authority.

L.D. Beklemishev et al. (Eds.): Gurevich Festschrift II 2015, LNCS 9300, pp. 237–252, 2015.
DOI: 10.1007/978-3-319-23534-9_14

At about the same time Yuri and JAM both underwent a transition in research orientation, slowly refocusing on questions in theoretical Computer Science. Two papers document their evolving views at the time, [23,37]. Yuri was vividly interested in [37] and frequent discussions between Yuri and JAM between 1980 and 1982 shaped both papers. In [37] the use for theoretical computer science of classical model theoretic methods, in particular, the role of the classical preservation theorems (see below), was explored, see also [34,36]. Yuri grasped early on that these preservation theorems do not hold when one restricts First Order Logic to finite models.

Under the influence of JAM's work in abstract model theory, the foundations of database theory and logic programming, [5,6,34,36,38,43], and the work of N. Immerman and M. Vardi, [24,47], Yuri stressed the difference between classical model theory and finite model theory. In [23], he formulated what he calls the Fundamental Problem of finite model theory. This problem is, even after 30 years, still open ([23]): Is there a logic $\mathcal{L}$ such that any class Φ of finite structures is definable in $\mathcal{L}$ iff Φ is recognizable in polynomial time. For *ordered* finite structures there are several such logics, [21,24,39,41,42,47]. We give a precise statement of the Fundamental Problem in Sect. 2, Problem 1.

1.2   Preservation Theorems

Let $\mathcal{F}_1, \mathcal{F}_2$ be two syntactically defined fragments of a logic $\mathcal{L}$, and let R be a binary relation between structures. *Preservation theorems* are of the form:

> Let $\phi \in \mathcal{F}_1$. The following are equivalent:
> (i) For all structures $\mathfrak{A}, \mathfrak{B}$ with $R(\mathfrak{A}, \mathfrak{B})$, we have that if $\mathfrak{A}$ satisfies $\phi_1 \in \mathcal{F}_1$, then also $\mathfrak{B}$ satisfies ϕ_1.
> (ii) There is $\phi_2 \in \mathcal{F}_2$ which is logically equivalent to ϕ_1.

A typical example is Tarski's Theorem for first order logic, with $\mathcal{F}_1$ all of first order logic, $\mathcal{F}_2$ its universal formulas, and $R(\mathfrak{A}, \mathfrak{B})$ holds if $\mathfrak{B}$ is a substructure of $\mathfrak{A}$. Many other preservation theorems can be found in [7]. In response to [37,43], Yuri pointed out in [23] that most of the preservation theorems for first order logic fail when one restricts models to be finite.

1.3   Reduction Theorems

Let $(\mathcal{F}_2)^*$ denote the finite sequences of formulas in $\mathcal{F}_2$, and let $\square$ be a binary operation on finite structures. *Reduction theorems* are of the form:

> There is a function $p : \mathcal{F}_1 \to (\mathcal{F}_2)^*$ with $p(\phi) = (\psi_1, \ldots, \psi_{2 \cdot k(\phi)})$ and a Boolean function B_ϕ such that for all structures $\mathfrak{A} = \mathfrak{B}_1 \square \mathfrak{B}_2$ and all $\phi \in \mathcal{F}_1$, the structure $\mathfrak{A}$ satisfies $\phi \in \mathcal{F}_1$ iff

$$B(\psi_1^{B_1}, \ldots, \psi_{k(\phi)}^{B_1}, \psi_1^{B_2}, \ldots, \psi_{k(\phi)}^{B_2}) = 1 \qquad (1)$$

where for $1 \leq j \leq k$ we have $\psi_j^{B_1} = 1$ iff $\mathfrak{B}_1 \models \psi_j$ and $\psi_j^{B_2} = 1$ iff $\mathfrak{B}_2 \models \psi_j$. There are also versions for (n)-ary operations $\square$.

The most famous examples of such reduction theorems are the Feferman-Vaught-type theorems, [12–15,22,40]. A simple case is Monadic Second Order Logic (MSOL), where $\mathcal{F}_1 = \mathcal{F}_2 = $ MSOL and $\mathfrak{A}$ is the disjoint union $\sqcup$ of $\mathfrak{B}_1$ and $\mathfrak{B}_2$. Additionally it is required that the quantifier ranks of the formulas in $p(\phi)$ do not exceed the quantifier rank of ϕ. In [38, Chapter 4] such reduction theorems are discussed in the context of abstract model theory. However, in [38, Chapter 4] the quantifier rank has no role.

In contrast to preservation theorems, reduction theorems still hold when restricted to finite structures.

1.4 Purpose of This Paper

In [40] JAM discussed Feferman-Vaught-type theorems in finite model theory and their algorithmic uses. In Sect. 7 of that paper, it was asked whether one can characterize logics over finite structures which satisfy the Feferman-Vaught Theorem for the disjoint union $\sqcup$. The purpose of this paper is to outline new directions to attack this problem. The novelty in our approach is in relating the Feferman-Vaught Theorem to Hankel matrices of sum-like and connection-like operations on finite structures. Hankel matrices for connection-like operations, aka connection matrices, have many algorithmic applications, cf. [28,33].

In Sect. 2 we set up the necessary background on Lindström logics, quantifier rank, translation schemes, and sum-like operations. A Hankel matrix $H(\Phi, \square)$ involves a binary operation $\square$ on finite σ-structures which results in a τ-structure, and a class of τ-structures Φ closed under isomorphisms (aka a τ-property). In Sect. 3 we give the necessary definitions of Hankel matrices and their rank. We then study τ-properties Φ where $H(\Phi, \square)$ has finite rank. We show that there are uncountably many such properties and state that the class of all properties that have finite rank for every sum-like operation $\square$ forms a Lindström logic, Theorems 5 and 8. In Sect. 4 we define various forms of Feferman-Vaught-type properties of Lindström logics equipped with a quantifier rank, and discuss their connection to Hankel matrices. Theorem 16 describes their exact relationship. A logic has finite S-rank, if all its definable τ-properties have Hankel matrices of finite rank for every sum-like operation. In Sect. 5 we sketch how to construct a logic satisfying the Feferman-Vaught Theorem for sum-like operations from a logic which has finite S-rank. Finally, in Sect. 6, we discuss our conclusions and state open problems. A full version of this paper is in preparation, [27].

2   Background

2.1   Logics with Quantifier Rank

We assume the reader is familiar with the basic definitions of generalized logics, see [1,11]. We denote by τ finite relational vocabularies, possibly with constant symbols for named elements. τ-structures are always *finite* unless otherwise stated. A finite structure of size n is always assumed to have as its universe the set $[n] = \{1, \ldots, n\}$. A class of finite τ-structures Φ closed under τ-isomorphisms is called a τ-*property*.

A *Lindström Logic* $\mathcal{L}$ is a triple

$$\langle \mathcal{L}(\tau), \mathrm{Str}(\tau), \models_{\mathcal{L}}, \rangle$$

where $\mathcal{L}(\tau)$ is the set of τ-sentences of $\mathcal{L}$, $\mathrm{Str}(\tau)$ are the *finite* τ-structures, $\models_{\mathcal{L}}$ is the satisfaction relation. The satisfaction relation is a ternary relation between τ-structures, assignments and formulas. An *assignment* for variables in a τ-structure $\mathfrak{A}$ is a function which assigns to each variable an element of the universe of $\mathfrak{A}$. We always assume that the logic contains all the atomic formulas with free variables, and is closed under Boolean operations and first order quantifications. A logic $\mathcal{L}_0$ is a *sublogic* of a logic $\mathcal{L}$ iff $\mathcal{L}_0(\tau) \subseteq \mathcal{L}(\tau)$ for all τ and the satisfaction relation of $\mathcal{L}_0$ is the satisfaction relation induced by $\mathcal{L}$.

A *Gurevich logic* $\mathcal{L}$ is a Lindström logic where additionally the sets $\mathcal{L}(\tau)$ are uniformly computable.

A *Lindström logic* $\mathcal{L}$ *with a quantifier rank* is a quadruple

$$\langle \mathcal{L}(\tau), \mathrm{Str}(\tau), \models_{\mathcal{L}}, \rho \rangle$$

where additionally ρ is a *quantifier rank function*. A quantifier rank (q-rank) ρ is a function $\rho : \mathcal{L}(\tau) \to \mathbb{N}$ such that

(i) For atomic formulas ϕ the q-rank $\rho(\phi) = 0$.
(ii) Boolean operations and translations induced by translation schemes (see Subsect. 2.2) with formulas of q-rank 0 preserve maximal q-rank.

A quantifier rank ρ is *nice* if additionally it satisfies the following:

(iii) For finite τ, there are, up to logical equivalence, only finitely many $\mathcal{L}(\tau)$-formulas of fixed q-rank with a fixed set of free variables.

In the presence of (iii) we define *Hintikka formulas* as maximally consistent $\mathcal{L}(\tau)$-formulas of fixed q-rank. A *nice logic* $\mathcal{L}$ is Lindström logic with a nice quantifier rank ρ. We note that in a nice logic, the only formulas ϕ of q-rank $\rho(\phi) = 0$ are Boolean combinations of atomic formulas.

We denote by FOL, MSOL, SOL, first order, monadic second order, and full second order logic, respectively. All these logics are nice Gurevich logics with their natural quantifier rank, and they are sublogics of SOL.

We denote by CFOL, CMSOL, first order and monadic second order logic augmented by the modular counting quantifiers $D_{k,m} x. \phi(x)$ which say that there are modulo m, exactly k many elements satisfying ϕ. In the presence of the quantifier $D_{k,m}$ there are two definitions of the quantifier rank: $\rho_1(D_{k,m} x. \phi(x)) = 1 + \rho_1(\phi)$ and $\rho_2(D_{k,m} x. \phi(x)) = m + \rho_2(\phi)$. Given any finite set of variables, for ρ_1 we have, up to logical equivalence, infinitely many formulas ϕ with $\rho_1(\phi) = 1$, whereas for ρ_2 there are only finitely many such formulas. CFOL and CMSOL with the quantifier rank ρ_2 are nice Gurevich logics. In the sequel we always use ρ_2 as the quantifier rank for CFOL and CMSOL.

FPL, fixed point logic, is also a Gurevich logic and a sublogic of SOL. However, *order invariant FPL* is a sublogic of SOL which is not a Lindström logic. The definable τ-properties in order invariant FPL are exactly the τ-properties recognizable in polynomial time. For FPL and order invariant FPL see [21,24,39,41,42,47].

Problem 1 (Y. Gurevich, [23]). *Is there a Gurevich logic $\mathcal{L}$ such that the $\mathcal{L}$-definable τ-properties are exactly the τ-properties recognizable in polynomial time.*

2.2   Sum-Like and Product-Like Operations on τ-structures

The following definitions are taken from [40]. Let τ, σ be two relational vocabularies with $\tau = \langle R_1, \ldots, R_m \rangle$, and denote by $r(i)$ the arity of R_i. A $(\sigma - \tau)$ *translation scheme* T is a sequence of $\mathcal{L}(\sigma)$-formulas $(\phi; \phi_1, \ldots, \phi_m)$ where ϕ has k free variables, and each ϕ_i has $k \cdot r(i)$ free variables. In this paper we do not allow redefining equality, nor do we allow name changing of constants.

We associate with T two mappings $T^* : \mathrm{Str}(\sigma) \to \mathrm{Str}(\tau)$ and $T^\sharp : \mathcal{L}(\tau) \to \mathcal{L}(\sigma)$, the *transduction and translation induced by* T. The transduction of a σ-structure $\mathfrak{A}$ is the τ-structure $T^*(\mathfrak{A})$ where the vocabulary is interpreted by the formulas given in the translation scheme. The translation of a τ-formula is obtained by substituting atomic τ-formulas with their definition through σ-formulas given by the translation scheme. A translation scheme (induced transduction, induced translation) is *scalar* if $k = 1$, otherwise it is k-*vectorized*. It is *quantifier-free* if so are the formulas $\phi; \phi_1, \ldots, \phi_m$.

If τ has no constant symbols, the disjoint union $\mathfrak{A} \sqcup \mathfrak{B}$ of two τ-structures $\mathfrak{A}, \mathfrak{B}$ is the τ-structure obtained by taking the disjoint union of the universes and of the corresponding relation interpretations in $\mathfrak{A}$ and $\mathfrak{B}$. On the other hand, if τ has finitely many constant symbols $a_1, \ldots, a_k$ the disjoint union of two τ-structures is a τ'-structure with twice as many constant symbols, $\tau' = \tau \cup \{a'_1, \ldots, a'_k\}$. *Connection operations* are similar to disjoint unions with constants, where equally named elements are identified. We call the disjoint union followed by the pairwise identification of k constant pairs the k-sum, cf. [33].

A binary operation $\square : \mathrm{Str}(\sigma) \times \mathrm{Str}(\sigma) \to \mathrm{Str}(\tau)$ is *sum-like (product-like)* if it is obtained from the disjoint union of σ-structures by applying a quantifier-free scalar (vectorized) $(\sigma - \tau)$-transduction. A binary operation $\square : \mathrm{Str}(\sigma) \times \mathrm{Str}(\sigma) \to \mathrm{Str}(\tau)$ is *connection-like* if it is obtained from a connection operation on σ-structures by applying a quantifier-free scalar $(\sigma - \tau)$-transduction. If $\sigma = \tau$, we say $\square$ is an operation on τ-structures.

Connection-like operations are not sum-like according to the definitions in this paper[1]. Although connection operations are frequently used in the literature, cf. [33,40], we do not deal with them in this paper. Most of our results here can

---

[1] They are nevertheless called sum-like in [40].

be carried over to connection-like operations, but the formalism required to deal with the identification of constants is tedious and needs more place than available here.

Proposition 1. *Let τ be a fixed finite relational vocabulary.*

(i) *There are only finitely many sum-like binary operations on τ-structures.*
(ii) *There is a function $\alpha : \mathbb{N} \to \mathbb{N}$ such that for each $k \in \mathbb{N}$ there are only $\alpha(k)$ many k-vectorized product-like binary operations on τ-structures.*

2.3   Abstract Lindström Logics

In [31] a syntax-free definition of a logic is given. An *abstract Lindström logic* $\mathcal{L}$ consists of a family $\mathrm{Mod}(\tau)$ of τ-properties closed under certain operations between properties of possibly different vocabularies. One thinks of $\mathrm{Mod}(\tau)$ as the family of $\mathcal{L}$-definable τ-properties. We do not need all the details here, the reader may consult [1,30,31]. The main point we need is that every abstract Lindström logic $\mathcal{L}$ can be given a canonical syntax $\mathcal{L}(\tau)$ using generalized quantifiers.

3   Hankel Matrices of τ-properties

3.1   Hankel Matrices

In linear algebra, a *Hankel matrix*, named after Hermann Hankel, is a real or complex square matrix with constant skew-diagonals. In automata theory, a *Hankel matrix* $H(f, \circ)$ is an infinite matrix where the rows and columns are labeled with words w over a fixed alphabet Σ, and the entry $H(f, \circ)_{u,v}$ is given by $f(u \circ v)$. Here $f : \Sigma^\star \to \mathbb{R}$ is a real-valued word function and $\circ$ denotes concatenation. A classical result of G.W. Carlyle and A. Paz [4] in automata theory characterizes real-valued word functions f recognizable by weighted (aka multiplicity) automata in algebraic terms.

Hankel matrices for graph parameters (aka connection matrices) were introduced by L. Lovász [32] and used in [18,33] to study real-valued partition functions of graphs. In [18,33] the role of concatenation is played by k-connections of k-graphs, i.e., graphs with k distinguished vertices $v_1, \ldots, v_k$.

In this paper we study $(0, 1)$-matrices which are Hankel matrices of properties of general relational τ-structures and the role of k-connections is played by more general binary operations, the sum-like and product-like operations introduced in [44] and further studied in [40].

Definition 2. *Let $\square : \mathrm{Str}(\sigma) \times \mathrm{Str}(\sigma) \to \mathrm{Str}(\tau)$ be a binary operation on finite σ-structures returning a τ-structure, and let Φ be a τ-property.*

(i) *The Boolean Hankel matrix $H(\Phi, \square)$ is the infinite $(0, 1)$-matrix where the rows and columns are labeled by all the finite σ-structures, and $H(\Phi, \square)_{\mathfrak{A}, \mathfrak{B}} = 1$ iff $\mathfrak{A} \square \mathfrak{B} \in \Phi$.*

(ii) *The rank of $H(\Phi, \square)$ over $\mathbb{Z}_2$ is denoted by $r(\Phi, \square)$, and is referred to as the Boolean rank.*

(iii) *We say that Φ has finite $\square$-rank iff $r(\Phi, \square)$ is finite.*

(iv) *Two σ-structures are $(\Phi, \square)$-equivalent, $\mathfrak{A} \equiv_{\Phi, \square} \mathfrak{B}$, if for all finite σ-structures $\mathfrak{C}$ we have*

$$\mathfrak{A} \square \mathfrak{C} \in \Phi \quad \text{iff} \quad \mathfrak{B} \square \mathfrak{C} \in \Phi \tag{2}$$

(v) *For a σ-structure $\mathfrak{A}$, we denote by $[\mathfrak{A}]_{\Phi, \square}$ the $(\Phi, \square)$-equivalence class of $\mathfrak{A}$.*

(vi) *We say that Φ has finite $\square$-index[2] iff there are only finitely many $(\Phi, \square)$-equivalence classes.*

Proposition 3. *Let Φ be a τ-property.*
Φ has finite $\square$-rank iff Φ has finite $\square$-index.

Proof (Sketch of proof). We first note that two σ-structures $\mathfrak{A}, \mathfrak{B}$ are in the same equivalence class of $\equiv_{\Phi, \square}$ iff they have identical rows in $H(\Phi, \square)$. As the rank is over $\mathbb{Z}_2$, finite rank implies there are only finitely many different rows in $H(\Phi, \square)$. The converse is obvious.   Q.E.D.

3.2 τ-Properties of Finite $\square$-rank

We next show that there are uncountably many τ-properties of finite $\sqcup$-rank. We also study the relationship between the $\square_1$-rank and $\square_2$-rank of τ-properties for different operations $\square_1$ and $\square_2$.

We first need a lemma.

Lemma 4. *Let $A \subseteq \mathbb{N}$ and let M_A be the infinite $(0,1)$-matrix whose columns and rows are labeled by the natural numbers $\mathbb{N}$, and $(M_A)_{i,j} = 1$ iff $i + j \in A$. Then M_A has finite rank over $\mathbb{Z}_2$ iff A is ultimately periodic.*

Theorem 5. *Let τ_{graphs} be the vocabulary with one binary edge-relation, and τ_1 be τ_{graphs} augmented by one vertex label. Let $C_A, \overline{C_A}$ and P_A be the graph properties defined by $C_A = \{K_n : n \in A\}$, $\overline{C_A} = \{E_n : n \in A\}$, and $P_A = \{P_n : n \in A\}$, where E_n is the complement graph of the clique K_n of size n, and P_n is a path graph of size n.*

(i) *$H(C_A, \sqcup)$ has finite rank for all $A \subseteq \mathbb{N}$.*

(ii) *For two graphs G_1, G_2, let $G_1 \sqcup^c G_2$ be the sum-like operation defined as the loopless complement graph of $G_1 \sqcup G_2$.*
$H(C_A, \sqcup^c)$ has infinite rank for all $A \subseteq \mathbb{N}$ which are not ultimately periodic. Equivalently, for the τ_{graphs}-property $\overline{C_A}$, the Hankel matrix $H(\overline{C_A}, \sqcup)$ has infinite rank for all $A \subseteq \mathbb{N}$ which are not ultimately periodic.

---

[2]   K. Compton and I. Gessel, [8,19], already considered τ-properties of finite $\sqcup$-index for the disjoint union of τ-structures. In [17] this is called *Gessel index*. C. Blatter and E. Specker, in [3,46], consider a substitution operation on pointed τ-structures, $Subst(\mathfrak{A}, a, \mathfrak{B})$, where the structure $\mathfrak{B}$ is inserted into $\mathfrak{A}$ at a point a. $Subst(\mathfrak{A}, a, \mathfrak{B})$ is sum-like, and the $Subst$-index is called in [17] *Specker index*.

(iii) $H(P_A, \square)$ has finite rank for all sum-like operations $\square$ on τ_{graphs}-structures and all $A \subseteq \mathbb{N}$.

(iv) For two graphs G_1, G_2 with one vertex label, i.e. τ_1-structures, let $G_1 \sqcup^1 G_2$ be the sum-like operation defined as the graph resulting from $G_1 \sqcup G_2$ by adding an edge between the two labeled vertices and then removing the labels. $H(P_A, \sqcup^1)$ has infinite rank for all $A \subseteq \mathbb{N}$ which are not ultimately periodic.

(v) $H(C_A, \sqcup_k)$ has finite rank for all $A \subseteq \mathbb{N}$.

Theorem 5 needs an interpretation: (i) says that there is a specific sum-like operation $\square$ such that there uncountably many classes of τ-structures with finite $\square$-rank[3]. (ii) says that if a class has finite $\square$-rank for one sum-like operation, it does not have to hold for all sum-like operations[4]. (iii) produces uncountably many classes of τ-structures which have finite $\square$-rank for all sum-like operations on τ-structures. (iv) finally shows that such classes can still have infinite $\square$-rank for sum-like operations which take as inputs σ-structures (labeled paths) and output a τ-structure (unlabeled paths). This leads us to the following definition:

Definition 6. *Let τ be a vocabulary and Φ be a τ-property.*

(i) *Φ has finite S-rank (P-rank, C-rank) if for every sum-like (product-like, connection-like) operation $\square : \mathrm{Str}(\sigma) \times \mathrm{Str}(\sigma) \to \mathrm{Str}(\tau)$ the Boolean rank of $H(\Phi, \square)$ is finite.*

(ii) *A nice logic $\mathcal{L}$ has finite S-rank (P-rank, C-rank) iff all its definable properties have finite S-rank (P-rank, C-rank).*

Examples 7.

(i) *([20]): FOL and CFOL have finite S-rank, C-rank and P-rank.*

(ii) *([20]): MSOL and CMSOL have finite S-rank and C-rank.*

(iii) *The examples C_A, P_A above do not have finite S-rank.*

3.3   Proof of Theorem 5

Proof. (i) The disjoint union of two graphs is never connected. Therefore all the entries of $H(C_A \sqcup)$ are zero, unless we consider the empty graph to be structure. In this case we have exactly one row and one column representing C_A. In any case, the rank is ≤ 2.

(ii) Consider the submatrix of $H(C_A, \sqcup)$ consisting of rows and columns labeled with the edgeless graphs E_n and use Lemma 4.

(iii) We first observe that

(*) for any sum-like operation $\square$ on τ_{graphs}-structures (i.e., graphs), G and H, if $G \square H = P_n$ for $n \geq 3$, either G or H must be the empty graph.

---

[3] A similar construction was first suggested by E. Specker in conversations with the second author in 2000, cf. [40, Section 7].

[4] This observation was suggested by T. Kotek in conversations with the second author in summer 2014.

This is due to the fact that τ_{graphs} has no constant symbols. Therefore, a row or column containing non-zero entries must be labeled by the empty graph.

(iv) Here we consider (σ, τ)-translation schemes for sum-like operations, with $\sigma = \tau_{graphs} \cup \{a\}$. Hence (*) from the proof of (iii) is not true anymore because now P_{m+n+1} can be obtained from P_n and P_m with the a being an end vertex, using $\sqcup^1$. So we apply Lemma 4.

(v) Connection operations of two large enough cliques still produce connected graphs, but never form a clique.   Q.E.D.

3.4   Properties of Finite S-rank and Finite P-rank

Let $\mathcal{S}(\tau)$ and $\mathcal{P}(\tau)$ denote the collection of all τ-properties of finite S-rank and finite P-rank respectively, and let $\mathcal{S} = \bigcup_\tau \mathcal{S}(\tau)$ and $\mathcal{P} = \bigcup_\tau \mathcal{P}(\tau)$.

Theorem 8. *$\mathcal{S}$ and $\mathcal{P}$ and are abstract Lindström logics which have finite S-rank and finite P-rank, respectively.*

Proof (Sketch of proof:). One first gives $\mathcal{S}$ and $\mathcal{P}$ a canonical syntax as described in [31, 35]. The proof then is a tedious induction which will be published elsewhere.

It is unclear whether the abstract Lindström logic $\mathcal{S}$ goes beyond CMSOL. As of now, we were unable to find a τ-property which has finite S-rank, but is not definable in CMSOL.

Problem 2.

(i) Is every τ-property with finite S-rank definable in $CMSOL(\tau)$?

(ii) Is every τ-property with finite P-rank definable in $CFOL(\tau)$?

It seems to us that the same can be shown for connection-like operations, but we have not yet checked the details.

4   Hankel Matrices and the Feferman-Vaught Theorem

4.1   The FV-property

In this section we look at nice Lindström logics with a fixed quantifier rank. We use it to derive from the classical Feferman-Vaught theorem an abstract version involving the quantifier rank. This differs from the treatment in [1, Chapter xviii]. Our purpose is to investigate the connection between Hankel matrices of finite rank and the Feferman-Vaught Theorem on finite structures in an abstract setting.

Definition 9. *Let $\mathcal{L}$ be a nice logic with quantifier rank ρ.*

(i) We denote by $\mathcal{L}(\tau)^q$ the set of $\mathcal{L}(\tau)$-sentences ϕ (without free variables) with $\rho(\phi) = q$.

(ii) *Two τ-structures $\mathfrak{A}, \mathfrak{B}$ are $\mathcal{L}^q$ equivalent, $\mathfrak{A} \sim_{\mathcal{L}}^q \mathfrak{B}$, if for every $\phi \in \mathcal{L}(\tau)^q$ we have $\mathfrak{A} \models \phi$ iff $\mathfrak{B} \models \phi$.*

(iii) *$\mathcal{L}$ has the FV-property for $\square$ with respect to ρ if for every $\phi \in \mathcal{L}(\tau)^q$ there are $k = k(\phi) \in \mathbb{N}$, $\psi_1, \ldots, \psi_k \in \mathcal{L}(\tau)^q$ and $B_\phi \in 2^{2k}$ such that for all τ-structures $\mathfrak{A}, \mathfrak{B}$ we have that*

$$\mathfrak{A} \square \mathfrak{B} \models \phi$$

iff

$$B_\phi(\psi_1^A, \ldots \psi_k^A, \psi_1^B, \ldots \psi_k^B) = 1$$

where for $1 \le j \le k$ we have $\psi_j^A = 1$ iff $\mathfrak{A} \models \psi_j$ and $\psi_j^B = 1$ iff $\mathfrak{B} \models \psi_j$.

(iv) *$\square$ is $\mathcal{L}$-smooth with respect to ρ if for every two pairs of τ-structures $\mathfrak{A}_1, \mathfrak{A}_2, \mathfrak{B}_1, \mathfrak{B}_2$ with $\mathfrak{A}_1 \sim_{\mathcal{L}}^q \mathfrak{A}_2$ and $\mathfrak{B}_1 \sim_{\mathcal{L}}^q \mathfrak{B}_2$ we also have $\mathfrak{A}_1 \square \mathfrak{B}_1 \sim_{\mathcal{L}}^q \mathfrak{A}_2 \square \mathfrak{B}_2$.*

If ρ is clear from the context we omit it.

A close inspection of the classical proofs shows that the requirements concerning the quantifier rank are satisfied in the following cases.

Examples 10.

- ([16]): FOL has the FV-property for all product-like and connection-like operations $\square$.
- ([25]): CFOL with quantifier rank ρ_2 has the FV-property for all product-like and connection-like operations $\square$.
- ([22,29,45]): MSOL has the FV-property for all sum-like and connection-like operations $\square$.
- ([9]): CMSOL with quantifier rank ρ_2 has the FV-property for all sum-like and connection-like operations $\square$.

4.2   The FV-property and Finite Rank

Definition 11. *Let $\mathcal{L}$ be a nice logic.*

(i) *Let $\square$ be a binary operation on τ-structures. $\mathcal{L}$ is $\square$-closed if all the equivalence classes of $\equiv_{\phi,\square}$ are definable in $\mathcal{L}(\tau)$.*

(ii) *$\mathcal{L}$ is S-closed (P-closed, C-closed) if for every sum-like (product-like, connection-like) binary operation $\square$ the logic $\mathcal{L}$ is $\square$-closed.*

Proposition 12. *Let $\mathcal{L}$ have the FV-property for $\square$.*

(i) *$\square$ is $\mathcal{L}$-smooth.*

(ii) *Let Φ be a τ-property definable by a formula $\phi \in \mathcal{L}(\tau)^q$. Then each equivalence class $[\mathfrak{A}]_{\Phi,\square}$ of $\equiv_{\Phi,\square}$ is definable by a formula $\psi(\mathfrak{A}) \in \mathcal{L}(\tau)^q$.*

(iii) *If $\mathcal{L}$ has the FV-property for all sum-like (product-like) operations then $\mathcal{L}$ is S-closed (P-closed).*

Proof (Sketch of proof). (i) Follows because for $i = 1, 2$, the truth value of $\mathfrak{A}_i \square \mathfrak{B}_i \models \phi \in \mathcal{L}(\tau)^q$ depends only on B_ϕ, the Boolean function associated with the FV-property.

(ii) Fix a τ-structure $\mathfrak{A}$. We want to show that $[\mathfrak{A}]_{\Phi, \square}$ is definable by some formula $\psi(\mathfrak{A}) \in \mathcal{L}(\tau)^q$.

$\mathfrak{B} \in [\mathfrak{A}]_{\square, \Phi}$ iff for all $\mathfrak{C}$, $\mathfrak{A} \square \mathfrak{C} \in \Phi$ iff $\mathfrak{B} \square \mathfrak{C} \in \Phi$.
We have, using B_ϕ, that

$$\mathfrak{A} \equiv_{\Phi, \square} \mathfrak{B}$$

iff for all $\mathfrak{C}$,

$$B_\phi(\psi_1^A, \ldots, \psi_k^A, \psi_1^C, \ldots, \psi_k^C) = B_\phi(\psi_1^B, \ldots, \psi_k^B, \psi_1^C, \ldots, \psi_k^C) \tag{3}$$

iff $\forall X_1, \ldots, X_k \in \{0, 1\}$,

$$B_\phi(\psi_1^A, \ldots, \psi_k^A, X_1, \ldots, X_k) = B_\phi(\psi_1^B, \ldots, \psi_k^B, X_1, \ldots, X_k) \tag{4}$$

where ψ_i^A, ψ_i^B and ψ_i^C are as in Definition 9(iii). Equation (4) can be expressed by a formula $\psi(\mathfrak{A}) \in \mathcal{L}(\tau)^q$.

(iii) Follows from (ii).   Q.E.D.

By analyzing the proof in [20], one can prove:

Theorem 13. *Let $\mathcal{L}$ be a nice Lindström logic with quantifier rank ρ and $\square$ be a binary operation on τ-structures. If $\square$ is $\mathcal{L}$-smooth with respect to ρ, then every $\mathcal{L}$-definable τ-property Φ has finite $\square$-rank.*

Proof (Sketch of proof). Let Φ be definable by ϕ with quantifier rank $\rho(\phi) = q$. Now let $\phi_i : i \leq \alpha \in \mathbb{N}$ be an enumeration of maximally consistent $\mathcal{L}(\tau)^q$-sentences (aka Hintikka sentences). By our assumption ρ is nice, so this is a finite set. Furthermore ϕ is logically equivalent to a disjunction $\bigvee_{i \in I} \phi_i$ with $I \subseteq [\alpha]$, any every τ-structure satisfies exactly one ϕ_i.
Now we use the smoothness of $\square$. If $\mathfrak{A}, \mathfrak{B}$ are two τ-structures satisfying the same ϕ_i, then their rows (columns) in $H(\Phi, \square)$ are identical. Hence the rank of $H(\Phi, \square)$ is at most α, or $\alpha + 1$ when empty τ-structures are allowed.   Q.E.D.

Combining Theorem 13 with Proposition 12(i) we get:

Corollary 14. *Let $\mathcal{L}$ be a nice Lindström logic which has the FV-property for the binary operation $\square$, and let Φ be definable in $\mathcal{L}$. Then $r(\Phi, \square)$ is finite.*

Proposition 15. *Let $\mathcal{L}$ be a nice logic with quantifier rank ρ and $\square$ be a fixed operation on τ-structure, which is associative. Assume further that for every $\phi \in \mathcal{L}(\tau)$,*

(i) The rank of $H(\phi, \square)$ is finite, and
(ii) All equivalence classes of $\equiv_{\phi, \square}$ are definable with formulas of $\mathcal{L}$ with quantifier rank $\leq qr(\phi)$.

Then $\mathcal{L}$ has the FV-property for $\square$.

We have now shown that $\mathcal{L}$ having the FV-property for $\square$ implies that $\square$ is $\mathcal{L}$-smooth, and that smoothness implies finite rank, or equivalently, finite index.

In fact we have:

Theorem 16. *Let $\mathcal{L}$ be a nice S-closed logic and let $\square_1$ be a sum-like operation. Then the following are equivalent:*

(i) $\mathcal{L}$ has the FV-property for every sum-like operation $\square$.
(ii) $\square_1$ is $\mathcal{L}$-smooth.
(iii) For all $\phi \in \mathcal{L}(\tau)$ and every sum-like $\square$, the $\square$-rank of ϕ is finite.
(iv) For all $\phi \in \mathcal{L}(\tau)$ and every sum-like $\square$, the index of $\equiv_{\phi,\square}$ is finite.

The same holds if we replace S-closed and sum-like by P-closed and product-like.

Proof. (i) implies (ii) is Proposition 12.
(ii) implies (iii) is Theorem 13.
(iii) is equivalent to (iv) by Proposition 3.
Finally, (iii) implies (i) is Proposition 15.   Q.E.D.

5   The S-Closure of a Nice Logic

Let $\mathcal{L}$ be a nice logic of finite S-rank with quantifier rank ρ. We define $Cl_S(\mathcal{L})$ to be the smallest Lindström logic such that for all sum-like

$$\square : \mathrm{Str}(\sigma) \times \mathrm{Str}(\sigma) \to \mathrm{Str}(\tau)$$

and all $Cl_S(\mathcal{L})$-definable τ-properties Φ, all the equivalence classes of $\equiv_{\Phi,\square}$ are also definable in $Cl_S(\mathcal{L})$. This gives us a Lindström logic which is S-closed. However, in order to be a nice logic, we have to extend ρ to ρ' in such a way that ensures it is still nice.

We proceed inductively. Recall that there are only finitely many sum-like operations $\square$ for fixed σ and τ. Let $\ell(\sigma) = \sum_{R \in \sigma} r(R) + 1$ where R is a relation symbol of arity $r(R)$ or a constant symbol of arity 0. Two vocabularies are *similar* if they have the same number of symbols of the same arity. The effect of a sum-like operation only depends on the similarity type of σ and τ. Hence for fixed $\ell(\sigma)$ and $\ell(\tau)$, there are only finitely many sum-like operations.

A typical step in the induction is as follows.

Given $\mathcal{L}$ and $\phi \in \mathcal{L}(\tau)^{\rho(\phi)}$ and a sum-like $\square : \mathrm{Str}(\sigma) \times \mathrm{Str}(\sigma) \to \mathrm{Str}(\tau)$, there are only finitely many equivalence classes of $\equiv_{\phi,\square}$. Let $E_i = E(\phi,\square)_i$ with $i \leq \alpha = \alpha(\phi,\square)$ be a list of these equivalence classes.

We form $\mathcal{L}'$ with quantifier rank ρ' as follows: If E_i is not definable in $\mathcal{L}(\sigma)$ then we add it to $\mathcal{L}$ using a Lindström quantifier with quantifier rank $\rho'(E_i) = \rho(\phi) + \ell(\sigma) + \ell(\tau)$.

$\mathcal{L}'$ is a Lindström logic. We have to show that ρ' is nice, i.e., for fixed q and fixed number of free variables, $\mathcal{L}'(\tau)^q$ is finite up to logical equivalence. This follows from the fact that we only added finitely many Lindström quantifiers and that for all $\phi \in \mathcal{L}$ we have that $\rho'(\phi) = \rho(\phi)$.

For our induction we start with $\mathcal{L}_0 = \mathcal{L}$. $\mathcal{L}_1$ is obtained by doing the typical step for each $\phi \in \mathcal{L}_0$ and each sum-like $\square$. ρ_1 is the union of all quantifier rank functions of the previous steps. We still have iterate this process by defining $\mathcal{L}_j$ and ρ_j and take the limit.

We finally get:

Theorem 17. *Let $\mathcal{L}$ be nice with quantifier rank ρ and of finite S-rank. Then $Cl_S(\mathcal{L})$ with quantifier rank ρ' is nice and has the FV-property for all sum-like operations.*

The details will be published in [27].

6   Conclusions and Open Problems

At the beginning of this paper we asked whether one can characterize logics over finite structures which satisfy the Feferman-Vaught Theorem for the disjoint union, or more generally, for sum-like and product-like operations on τ-structures. The purpose of this paper was to investigate new directions to attack this problem, specifically by relating the Feferman-Vaught Theorem to Hankel matrices of finite rank. Theorem 16 describes their exact relationship.

We also investigated under which conditions one can construct logics satisfying the Feferman-Vaught Theorem. Theorem 5 shows that there are uncountably many τ-properties which have finite rank Hankel matrices for specific sum-like operations. Theorem 8 shows the existence of maximal Lindström logics $\mathcal{S}$ and $\mathcal{P}$ where all their definable τ-properties have finite rank for all sum-like, respectively product-like, operations. However, we have no explicit description of these maximal logics.

Problem 3.

(i) Is every τ-property with finite P-rank (or both finite P-rank and finite C-rank) definable in CFOL?

(ii) Is every τ-property with finite S-rank (finite C-rank) definable in CMSOL?

In case the answers to the above are negative, we can ask:

Problem 4.

(i) How many τ-properties are there with finite S-rank (P-rank, C-rank)?

(ii) Is there a nice Gurevich logic where all the τ-properties in $\mathcal{S}$ are definable?

In [40, Section 7, Conjecture 2] it is conjectured that there are continuum many nice Gurevich logics with the FV-property for the disjoint union. Adding C_A or P_A from Theorem 5 for fixed $A \subseteq \mathbb{N}$ as Lindström quantifiers to FOL together with all the equivalence classes of $\equiv_{C_A, \sqcup}$ or $\equiv_{P_A, \sqcup}$ gives us a nice Lindström logic. However, the definable τ_{graph}-property that the complement of a graph G is in C_A has infinite $\sqcup$-rank, see Theorem 5(ii).

Problem 5. *How many different nice Gurevich logics with the FV-property for the disjoint union are there?*

A similar analysis for connection-like operations will be developed in [27].

Acknowledgments. We would like to thank T. Kotek for letting us use his example, and for valuable discussions.

References

1. Barwise, J., Feferman, S.: Model-Theoretic Logics. Perspectives in Mathematical Logic. Springer, Heidelberg (1985)
2. Barwise, K.J.: Axioms for abstract model theory. Ann. Math. Logic **7**(2), 221–265 (1974)
3. Blatter, C., Specker, E.: Le nombre de structures finies d'une th'eorie à charactère fin, pp. 41–44. Sciences Mathématiques, Fonds Nationale de la recherche Scientifique, Bruxelles (1981)
4. Carlyle, J.W., Paz, A.: Realizations by stochastic finite automata. J. Comput. Syst. Sci. **5**, 26–40 (1971)
5. Chandra, A., Lewis, H., Makowsky, J.A.: Embedded implicational dependencies and their implication problem. In: (1981) ACM Symposium on the Theory of Computing, pp. 342–354. ACM (1981)
6. Chandra, A.K., Lewis, H.R., Makowsky, J.A.: Embedded implicational dependencies and their inference problem. In: XP1 Workshop on Database Theory (1980)
7. Chang, C.C., Keisler, H.J.: Model Theory. Studies in Logic, vol. 73, 3rd edn. Elsevier, Haarlem, North-Holland (1990)
8. Compton, K.J.: Some useful preservation theorems. J. Symb. Log. **48**(2), 427–440 (1983)
9. Courcelle, B.: The monadic second-order logic of graphs I: recognizable sets of finite graphs. Inf. Comput. **85**, 12–75 (1990)
10. Durand, A., Jones, N.D., Makowsky, J.A., More, M.: Fifty years of the spectrum problem: survey and new results. Bull. Symb. Logic **18**(04), 505–553 (2012)
11. Ebbinghaus, H.-D., Flum, J., Thomas, W.: Mathematical Logic. Undergraduate Texts in Mathematics, 2nd edn. Springer, Heidelberg (1994)
12. Feferman, S.: Persistent and invariant formulas for outer extensions. Compos. Math. **20**, 29–52 (1968)
13. Feferman, S.: Two notes on abstract model theory, I: properties invariant on the range of definable relations between strcutures. Fundam. Math. **82**, 153–165 (1974)
14. Feferman, S., Kreisel, G.: Persistent and invariant formulas relative to theories of higher order. Bull. Am. Math. Soc. **72**, 480–485 (1966)
15. Feferman, S., Vaught, R.: The first order properties of algebraic systems. Fundam. Math. **47**, 57–103 (1959)
16. Feferman, S., Vaught, R.: The first order properties of products of algebraic systems. Fundam. Math. **47**, 57–103 (1959)
17. Fischer, E., Kotek, T., Makowsky, J.A.: Application of logic to combinatorial sequences and their recurrence relations. In: Grohe, M., Makowsky, J.A. (eds.) Model Theoretic Methods in Finite Combinatorics, Contemporary Mathematics, vol. 558, pp. 1–42. American Mathematical Society (2011)

18. Freedman, M., Lovász, L., Schrijver, A.: Reflection positivity, rank connectivity, and homomorphisms of graphs. J. AMS **20**, 37–51 (2007)
19. Gessel, I.: Combinatorial proofs of congruences. In: Jackson, D.M., Vanstone, S.A. (eds.) Enumeration and Design, pp. 157–197. Academic Press (1984)
20. Godlin, B., Kotek, T., Makowsky, J.A.: Evaluations of graph polynomials. In: Broersma, H., Erlebach, T., Friedetzky, T., Paulusma, D. (eds.) WG 2008. LNCS, vol. 5344, pp. 183–194. Springer, Heidelberg (2008)
21. Grädel, E.: The expressive power of second order horn logic. In: Jantzen, M., Choffrut, C. (eds.) STACS 1991. LNCS, vol. 480, pp. 466–477. Springer, Heidelberg (1991)
22. Gurevich, Y.: Modest theory of short chains I. J. Symb. Logic **44**, 481–490 (1979)
23. Gurevich, Y.: Logic and the challenge of computer science. In: Börger, E. (ed) Trends in Theoretical Computer Science, Principles of Computer Science Series, Chap. 1. Computer Science Press (1988)
24. Immerman, N.: Languages that capture complexity classes. SIAM J. Comput. **16**(4), 760–778 (1987)
25. Kotek, T., Makowsky, J.A.: Connection matrices and the definability of graph parameters. Log. Methods Comput. Sci. 10(4) (2014)
26. Kreisel, G.: Choice of infinitary languages by means of definability criteria; generalized recursion theory. In: Barwise, J. (ed.) The Syntax and Semantics of Infinitary Languages. LNM, vol. 72, pp. 139–151. Springer, Heidelberg (1968)
27. Labai, N., Makowsky, J.A.: The Feferman-Vaught theorem and finite Hankel rank. In preparation (2015)
28. Labai, N., Makowsky, J.: Tropical graph parameters. In: DMTCS Proceedings of 26th International Conference on Formal Power Series and Algebraic Combinatorics (FPSAC), vol. 1, pp. 357–368 (2014)
29. Läuchli, H.: A decision procedure for the weak second order theory of linear order. In: Logic Colloquium 1966, pp. 189–197, North Holland (1968)
30. Lindström, P.: First order predicate logic with generalized quantifiers. Theoria **32**, 186–195 (1966)
31. Lindström, P.: On extensions of elementary logic. Theoria **35**, 1–11 (1969)
32. Lovász, L.: Connection matrics. In: Grimmet, G., McDiarmid, C. (eds.) Combinatorics, Complexity and Chance, A Tribute to Dominic Welsh, pp. 179–190. Oxford University Press (2007)
33. Lovász, L.: Large Networks and Graph Limits, vol. 60. Colloquium Publications, AMS, Providence (2012)
34. Mahr, B., Makowsky, J.A.: Characterizing specification languages which admit initial semantics. Theor. Comput. Sci. **31**, 49–60 (1984)
35. Makowsky, J.A.: Δ-logics and generalized quantifiers. Ph.D. thesis, Department of Mathematics, ETH-Zurich, Switzerland (1974)
36. Makowsky, J.A.: Why horn formulas matter for computer science: initial structures and generic examples. J. Comput. Syst. Sci. **34**(2/3), 266–292 (1987)
37. Makowsky, J.A.: Model theoretic issues in theoretical computer science, part I: relational databases and abstract data types. In: Lolli, G. et al. (eds.) Logic Colloquium 1982, Studies in Logic, pp. 303–343, North Holland (1984)
38. Makowsky, J.A.: Compactness, embeddings and definability. In: Barwise, J., Feferman, S. (eds.) Model-Theoretic Logics, Perspectives in Mathematical Logic, Chap. 18. Springer, Heidelberg (1985)
39. Makowsky, J.A.: Invariant definability. In: Gottlob, G., Leitsch, A., Mundici, D. (eds.) KGC 1997. LNCS, vol. 1289, pp. 186–202. Springer, Heidelberg (1997)

40. Makowsky, J.A.: Algorithmic uses of the Feferman-Vaught theorem. Ann. Pure Appl. Logic **126**(1–3), 159–213 (2004)
41. Makowský, J.A., Pnueli, Y.: Logics capturing oracle complexity classes uniformly. In: Leivant, D. (ed.) LCC 1994. LNCS, vol. 960. Springer, Heidelberg (1995)
42. Makowsky, J.A., Pnueli, Y.B.: Oracles and quantifiers. In: Meinke, K., Börger, E., Gurevich, Y. (eds.) CSL 1993. LNCS, vol. 832. Springer, Heidelberg (1994)
43. Makowsky, J.A., Vardi, M.: On the expressive power of data dependencies. Acta Inform. **23**(3), 231–244 (1986)
44. Ravve, E.: Model checking for various notions of products. Master's thesis, Thesis, Department of Computer Science, Technion-Israel Institute of Technology (1995)
45. Shelah, S.: The monadic theory of order. Ann. Math. **102**, 379–419 (1975)
46. Specker, E.: Application of logic and combinatorics to enumeration problems. In: Börger, E. (ed.) Trends in Theoretical Computer Science, pp. 141–169. Computer Science Press (1988). (Reprinted In: Specker, E., Selecta, B., pp. 324–350 (1990))
47. Vardi, M.: The complexity of relational query languages. In: STOC 1982, pp. 137–146. ACM (1982)

The Strategy of Campaigning

Rohit Parikh[1,2]([✉]) and Çağıl Taşdemir[2]

[1] Brooklyn College of the City University of New York, New York, USA
{rparikh,ctasdemir}@gc.cuny.edu
[2] Graduate Center of the City University of New York, New York, USA

Abstract. We prove an abstract theorem which shows that under certain circumstances, a candidate running for political office should be as explicit as possible in order to improve her impression among the voters. But this result conflicts with the perceived reality that candidates are often cagey and reluctant to take stances except when absolutely necessary. Why this hesitation on the part of the candidates? We offer some explanations.

1 Introduction

In [3] Dean and Parikh considered a political candidate campaigning to be elected. The candidate's chances of being elected depend on how various groups of voters perceive her, and how they perceive her depends on what she has said. Different groups of voters may have different preferences and a statement preferred by one group of voters may be disliked by another.

They consider three types of voters: Optimistic (those who are willing to think the best of the candidate), pessimistic (those who are inclined to expect the worse), and expected value voters, who average over various possibilities which may come about if the candidate is elected. They show that if the voters are expected value voters, then the candidate is best off being as explicit as possible.

While interesting, this result is counter intuitive in that politicians are often cagey and avoid committing themselves on issues. What explains this?

In this paper, we extend the previous work by Dean and Parikh in two ways.

We use the Fubini theorem to provide a very general, abstract version of their *(best to be explicit)* result which applies to the case where we consider a single candidate who merely wants to improve her status among the voters.

Later we introduce a belief set for the candidate and impose the condition that she would not make any statements against her honest beliefs. We also take into account the scenarios where there may be optimistic voters, or where other problems, like voters staying at home, enter. Such scenarios offer a possible explanation for the cageyness of some candidates.

2 A General Theorem

This section presumes that the candidate has made some statements in the past and as a consequence the voters can assume that if she is elected then the state

© Springer International Publishing Switzerland 2015
L.D. Beklemishev et al. (Eds.): Gurevich Festschrift II 2015, LNCS 9300, pp. 253–260, 2015.
DOI: 10.1007/978-3-319-23534-9_15

of the world (or nation) will belong to a certain set Z of (possible) states, those which agree with the statements she has made.[1]

A voter may have different views about the different states in Z, finding some good and others not so good. Also, different voters may have different views about the same state.

If the candidate reveals more of her views on some issues, then the set of states compatible with her views will shrink. Some voters may be displeased, finding that their favorite states are no longer compatible with her new stance. Other voters may be pleased seeing that some states they feared are no longer in the running.

How should the candidate speak so as to improve her overall position given these forces pulling in different directions?

Let V denote the set of voters, and Ω the set of the states of the world.[2] Both V, Ω are assumed to be compact (i.e., closed and bounded) subsets of some Euclidean space $\mathbb{R}^n$. Let the satisfaction function $s : V \times \Omega \mapsto \mathbb{R}$ represent the extent to which voter $v \in V$ *likes* the state $\omega \in \Omega$. What is the candidate's current average degree of satisfaction among all voters? It is given by the following (Lebesgue) integral over all voters and all states in Z.

$$\alpha = \frac{\int_{\omega \in Z} \int_{v \in V} s(v, \omega) \mathrm{d}v \mathrm{d}\omega}{\mu(Z)} \tag{1}$$

Namely the average value of $s(v, \omega)$ over all voters v and all states ω in Z. [3] Here $\int_{v \in V} s(v, \omega) \mathrm{d}v$ is the extent to which a particular state ω is liked by the average voter. Alternately $\int_{\omega \in Z} s(v, \omega) \mathrm{d}\omega$ is the extent to which a particular voter v likes the set Z. α is the average over all voters in V and states in Z.

The candidate is now wondering whether she should make a statement A or its negation $\neg A$. At the moment we are assuming that she has no restrictions as to what she can say with popularity being her only concern, so she is free to say A or its negation. Later on we will consider *restrictions* on what she can say. Whatever she says will have the effect of changing the set Z.[4]

Let X and Y be the two disjoint subsets of Z where X is the set of states where A is true and Y the set where A is false, i.e., where $\neg A$ is true. Z is $X \cup Y$.

---

[1] If the statements which she has already made constitute a set T, then Z is the set of those states ω which satisfy T.

[2] Note that we are not making assumptions like single peak preference. The model we use allows for a candidate who is a social conservative and an economic liberal (e.g. Carter), or a socially liberal candidate who is hawkish on foreign policy (Johnson).

[3] We assume that the measure of the set of voters is normalized to be 1.

[4] Note that the set V is fixed but Z depends on what the candidate has said so far and may say in the future. However, fights between Democrats and Republicans over "illegal voters" or "voter suppression" are over the precise makeup of the set V. A candidate may well seek to increase her average satisfaction by seeking to include in V some members who like her present positions or to exclude those who dislike these positions.

Then the average satisfaction on $X \cup Y$ could be rewritten as

$$\alpha = \frac{\int_{\omega \in X \cup Y} \int_{v \in V} s(v, \omega) dv d\omega}{\mu(X \cup Y)} \tag{2}$$

where $\mu(X \cup Y)$ is the measure of the set $X \cup Y$.

We could rewrite (2) as

$$\alpha = \frac{\beta_x + \beta_y}{\mu_x + \mu_y} \tag{3}$$

where

$\beta_x = \int_{\omega \in X} \int_{v \in V} s(v, \omega) dv d\omega,$
$\beta_y = \int_{\omega \in Y} \int_{v \in V} s(v, \omega) dv d\omega,$
μ_x is the measure of X, and
μ_y is the measure of Y.

Then either $\dfrac{\beta_x}{\mu_x} = \dfrac{\beta_y}{\mu_y} = \dfrac{\beta_x + \beta_y}{\mu_x + \mu_y}$, or one of $\dfrac{\beta_x}{\mu_x}$ and $\dfrac{\beta_y}{\mu_y}$ is greater than $\dfrac{\beta_x + \beta_y}{\mu_x + \mu_y}$.

To see this, note that

$$\frac{\beta_x + \beta_y}{\mu_x + \mu_y} = \alpha \tag{4}$$

Now suppose that

$$\frac{\beta_x}{\mu_x} = \alpha_1 \leq \alpha \tag{5}$$

$$\frac{\beta_y}{\mu_y} = \alpha_2 < \alpha \tag{6}$$

Then, $\beta_x + \beta_y = \alpha * \mu_x + \alpha * \mu_y$ by (4), and
$\beta_x + \beta_y = \alpha_1 * \mu_x + \alpha_2 * \mu_y$ by (5) and (6),
but $\alpha_1 \leq \alpha$ and $\alpha_2 < \alpha$, so we have a contradiction. So at least one of the ratios is greater than or equal to α, her current level of satisfaction.

Say $\alpha_1 = \dfrac{\beta_x}{\mu_x}$ is greater than α. then by uttering the statement A she will move from α to α_1 and benefit overall. Some voters may dislike A but they will be outweighed by those who like it.

Thus at least one of the statements A and $\neg A$ will either benefit her (raise her level of satisfaction) or at least leave her level the same. □

Corollary: A candidate is best off being as explicit as she can.

Proof: Consider all possible theories (sets of statements) which she could utter. And let T be the best theory she could utter. If T is not complete, i.e. leaves some question A open, then there is an extension of T which includes either A or its negation and is no worse than T. It follows that among her best theories there is one which is complete, i.e., as explicit as possible. □

3   Ambiguity and Pessimism

Pessimistic voters are voters who assume the worst of all the states which are currently possible. Thus if Z is the current set of possible states of the world then a pessimistic voter will value Z as $v(Z) = min\{s(v, \omega) : \omega \in Z\}$. It is obvious that being more explicit with pessimistic voters can only help a candidate, for it might well eliminate states which the voter dislikes and at worst it will leave things the same way.

What if the voters are a mixture of expected value voters and pessimistic voters? Then given the choice of saying A and $\neg A$, at least one of the two, say A will help her with the expected value voters and can do no harm with the pessimists. Now it could be that saying $\neg A$ will help her more with the pessimists than it hurts with the expected value voters, but at least one of A and $\neg A$ is safe for her to say.

Thus *one* possible reason for a candidate to be cagey is the presence of a large number of optimists. Optimistic voters will put $v(Z) = max\{s(v, \omega) : \omega \in Z\}$. If a voter strongly prefers ω and another strongly prefers ω' and both are optimists then the candidate may prefer to remain ambiguous between ω and ω'.

A second reason may be that a strong candidate who expects to win may refrain from committing herself on issues in order to leave freedom of action open if and when she takes office.

Yet another reason could be that the candidate does not want to say something contrary to her beliefs even if that would help her with voters.

Later, we consider another reason - stay-at-home voters - to explain why a candidate may prefer to be cagey.

4   The Logical Formalism of Dean and Parikh

The last section gave an abstract presentation of the scenario without saying what the states of the world were and where the satisfaction function s came from. Now we will proceed to be more explicit.

- The candidate's views are formulated in a propositional language L containing finitely many atomic propositions $At = \{P_1, ..., P_n\}$
- Propositional valuations and states are conflated. $\omega \in 2^{At}$
- Propositional valuations are defined as follows in order to make the arithmetic simpler: $\omega[i] = 1$ if $\omega \models P_i$, and $\omega[i] = -1$ if $\omega \not\models P_i$
- Voters are characterized by their preference for a set of ideal states. This is formalized via two functions p_v and x_v.
  - $p_v(i) = 1$ if v would prefer P_i to be true,
    $p_v(i) = 0$ if v is neutral about P_i,
    $p_v(i) = -1$ if v would prefer P_i to be false.

  - $x_v(i) : At \rightarrow [0, 1]$ the weight which voter v assigns to P_i such that $\sum x_v(i) \leq 1$

- The utility of a state ω for voter v is defined as

$$s(v, \omega) = \sum_{1 \leq i \leq n} p_v(i) \times x_v(i) \times \omega[i]$$

- We will first consider expected value voters. Their utility for a given (current) theory T of a candidate is calculated as follows:

$$ut_v(T) = \frac{\sum_{\omega \models T} s(v, \omega)}{|\{\omega : \omega \models T\}|}$$

- The value of a statement A for a given theory T is

$$val(A, T) = ut(T + A) - ut(T)$$

where $ut(T + A)$ is the utility when a candidate's theory T is updated by statement A.

- In Dean and Parikh, a candidate chooses what to say next by calculating the *best statement* for a given theory T (this is what she has said so far) as follows:

$$best(T, X) = argmax_A val(A, T) : A \in X$$

where X is the set of formulas from which the candidate chooses what to say. X could be defined differently depending on the type of the candidate. (i.e. depending on the restrictions that are imposed on the candidate as to what she can say.)

5   Extension of the Framework

Dean and Parikh showed that (given expected value voters) it is always to a candidate's benefit to say something on a certain issue than to remain silent and we gave a generalization of their result in Sect. 2. We find that this is not the case in practical cases. Here is a well known quote from the satirical newspaper *The Onion*.

> NEW YORK After Sen. Barack Obama's comments last week about what he typically eats for dinner were criticized by Sen. Hillary Clinton as being offensive to both herself and the American voters, the number of acceptable phrases presidential candidates can now say are officially down to four. At the beginning of 2007 there were 38 things candidates could mention in public that wouldn't be considered damaging to their campaigns, but now they are mostly limited to 'Thank you all for coming,' and 'God bless America,' ABC News chief Washington correspondent George Stephanopoulos said on Sunday's episode of This Week.
> *The Onion*, May 8, 2008

For a more scholarly source consider [5]

> Modern U.S. candidates have proven just as willing to use ambiguity as a campaign strategy. Jimmy Carter and George H.W. Bush were renowned for taking fuzzy positions at crucial points during their successful runs for the presidency (Bartels 1988, 101), and Barack Obama captured the White House in 2008 while remaining vague on key issues.

Candidate Beliefs

We extend the framework of Dean and Parikh by considering a belief set B for the candidate to represent her honest beliefs (this set need not be complete, allowing the candidate to form her opinions on certain issues later on), and a theory T to represent the statements she has uttered so far. We will impose the requirement that the candidate will not make statements that are against her beliefs. This requires B and T to be consistent with each other, and every possible statement A for this candidate to be consistent with $B \cup T$. We could call this type of candidate *tactically honest*. In this case it is easy to see that sometimes such a candidate might want to remain silent.

Remaining Silent

Example 1. We consider a single candidate c whose belief set B_c and theory T_c are given below:

$$B_c = \{\neg P, Q, \neg R\}$$
$$T_c = \{\neg R\}$$

There are four assignments satisfying T_c that the voters will take into account. The assignments are given in the form of $\langle p_v(P), p_v(Q), p_v(R) \rangle$

$\omega_1 = \langle -1, -1, -1 \rangle$, $\omega_2 = \langle -1, 1, -1 \rangle$, $\omega_3 = \langle 1, -1, -1 \rangle$, and $\omega_4 = \langle 1, 1, -1 \rangle$

We will consider two groups of voters v_1 and v_2 of the same size:

v_1's preferences:

$p_1(P) = 1$, $p_1(Q) = 1$, $p_1(R) = -1$
$x_1(P) = 0.4$, $x_1(Q) = 0.2$, $x_1(R) = 0.2$

v_2's preferences:

$p_2(P) = 1$, $p_2(Q) = -1$, $p_2(R) = -1$
$x_2(P) = 0.3$, $x_2(Q) = 0.1$, $x_2(R) = 0.4$

What should c say about P?

In this initial situation, v_1 has 0.2 points for c and v_2 has 0.4 points. $v_1(T_c) = 0.2$ and $v_2(T_c) = 0.4$. c would like to say $\neg P$ since it is in her belief set. However the popular opinion among the voters is P, so if she were to say $\neg P$ her points would go down among both groups of voters. $v_1(T_c + \neg P) = -0.2$ and $v_2(T_c + \neg P) = 0.1$. She also cannot say P as it contradicts her opinions i.e. her belief set. So she might choose to remain silent in regard to P.

Revealing Partial Truths

Example 2. In Example 1 we showed that remaining silent about P would be a reasonable option for the candidate if she doesn't want to lie about her honest beliefs. Another option is that she could say $(P \vee Q)$ which allows her not to directly contradict her belief set, but also to increase her points at the same time by revealing only a partial truth. In this case the voters will remove the possible state $\omega_1 = \langle -1, -1, -1 \rangle$ from their calculations, and her points will go up among both groups of voters. $v_1(T_c + (P \vee Q)) = 0.4$ and $v_2(T_c + (P \vee Q)) = 0.47$.

This example shows that a candidate who does not want her statements and her beliefs to conflict can achieve more by remaining silent on a certain issue than by voicing her opinion. However she may occasionally achieve even more by making a vague statement (i.e. by revealing partial truth (and not lying)) than by remaining silent.

Dishonest Candidates. If we allow a candidate to be dishonest (i.e. to make statements that can contradict her belief set), then we can ignore the candidate's belief set altogether. This candidate will choose to be as explicit as possible given that the voters are expected-value voters as per Dean and Parikh's result. It is easily seen that the candidate will then have more leeway against the candidates who choose to be honest. Moreover, even a candidate who is honest, but has some leeway is better off by being less explicit at the start of a campaign. For let T_1 and T_2 be two positions to which she could commit at the start of the campaign. Assume moreover that $T_1 \subset T_2$. Then the number of permissible extensions of T_2 is less than the number of permissible extensions of T_1. So the best she could gain by starting only with T_1 is higher than the best she could gain by starting with T_2.

One could ask, but if T_2 was something she was going to say anyway, then why not say it at the start of the campaign? The answer is that the function $s(v, \omega)$, the extent to which voter v likes the state ω is not constant and may vary as time passes. The tastes and preferences of voters do change. So it may be wiser to wait. But when further changes in s are unlikely then being explicit can be helpful.

5.2 Stay-At-Home Voters

For another explanation as to why a candidate might want to remain silent, we will introduce a threshold value t for voters. We will stipulate that a voter's utility for a candidate c must be greater than t for that voter to vote for c.

Example 3. Consider a candidate c with the following belief set and theory.

$B_c = \{P, \neg Q, \neg R\}$
$T_c = \{(P \vee Q), \neg R\}$

Assume two groups of voters v_1 and v_2 of the same size with the following preferences.

v_1's preferences:

$p_1(P) = 1, p_1(Q) = -1, p_1(R) = -1$
$x_1(P) = 0.4, x_1(Q) = 0.1, x_1(R) = 0.4$

Table 1. How stating P affects the candidate's scores

	Initial scores	Updated scores if c says P
v_1	0.5	0.8
v_2	0.6	0.4

v_2's preferences:

$p_2(P) = -1,\ p_2(Q) = 1,\ p_2(R) = -1$
$x_2(P) = 0.1,\ x_2(Q) = 0.4,\ x_2(R) = 0.5$

If we assume a threshold value of $t = 0.5$, in this initial situation both groups of voters would vote for c as shown in the left column of Table 1.

If c wanted to say P, which is in her belief set, the sum of her points would go up (from 1.1 to 1.2). However in this case v_2 becomes a stay-at-home voter and c is actually hurt by saying P. Considering this, she might want to remain silent regarding P.

Note that even if the candidate was dishonest and wanted to say $\neg P$, this time she would lose v_1's votes as shown in Table 2.

Table 2. How stating not P affects the candidate's scores

	Initial scores	Updated scores if c says $\neg P$
v_1	0.5	-0.1
v_2	0.6	1

6   Conclusions and Future Work

We have developed a model which explains why a candidate might wish to become explicit about issues, as well as situations where a candidate may prefer to remain silent on some issues. Our model differs in significant ways from the models developed by [1,4,5] in that we are including a semantics for the language in which candidates speak and raising questions about when they would speak and when they would remain quiet. See also [2] for a comprehensive discussion of elections.

References

1. Alesina, A.F., Cukierman, A.: 'The politics of ambiguity. Q. J. Econ. **105**(4), 829–850 (1987)
2. Brams, S.: The Presidential Election Game. Yale University Press, New Haven (1978). Revised edn., 2008 (A K Peters)
3. Dean, W., Parikh, R.: The logic of campaigning. In: Banerjee, M., Seth, A. (eds.) Logic and Its Applications. LNCS, vol. 6521, pp. 38–49. Springer, Heidelberg (2011)
4. Shepsle, K.A.: The strategy of ambiguity: uncertainty and electoral competition. Am. Polit. Sci. Rev. **66**(02), 555–568 (1972)
5. Tomz, M., Van Houweling, R.P.: The electoral implications of candidate ambiguity. Am. Polit. Sci. Rev. **103**(01), 83–98 (2009)

On Almost Future Temporal Logics

Alexander Rabinovich[(⊠)]

The Blavatnik School of Computer Science, Tel Aviv University, Tel Aviv, Israel
rabinoa@post.tau.ac.il

Dedicated to Yuri Gurevich on the occasion of his 75th birthday.

Abstract. Kamp's theorem established the expressive completeness of the temporal modalities Until and Since for the First-Order Monadic Logic of Order (*FOMLO*) over real and natural time flows. Over natural time, a single future modality (Until) is sufficient to express all future *FOMLO* formulas. These are formulas whose truth value at any moment is determined by what happens from that moment on. Yet this fails to extend to real time domains: here no finite basis of future modalities can express all future *FOMLO* formulas. Almost future formulas extend future formulas; they depend just on the very near past, and are independent of the rest of the past. For almost future formulas finiteness is recovered over Dedekind complete time flows. In this paper we show that there is no temporal logic with finitely many modalities which is expressively complete for the almost future fragment of *FOMLO* over all linear flows.

1 Introduction

Temporal Logic (*TL*) introduced to Computer Science by Pnueli in [7] is a convenient framework for reasoning about "reactive" systems. This made temporal logics a popular subject in the Computer Science community, enjoying extensive research in the past 30 yrs. In *TL* we describe basic system properties by *atomic propositions* that hold at some points in time, but not at others. More complex properties are expressed by formulas built from the atoms using Boolean connectives and *Modalities* (temporal connectives): A k-place modality M transforms statements $\varphi_1 \ldots \varphi_k$ possibly on 'past' or 'future' points to a statement $M(\varphi_1 \ldots \varphi_k)$ on the 'present' point t_0. The rule to determine the truth of a statement $M(\varphi_1 \ldots \varphi_k)$ at t_0 is called a *Truth Table*. The choice of particular modalities with their truth tables yields different temporal logics. A temporal logic with modalities $M_1, \ldots, M_k$ is denoted by $TL(M_1, \ldots, M_k)$.

The simplest example is the one place modality $\mathsf{F}X$ saying: "X holds some time in the future". Its truth table is formalized by $\varphi_{\mathsf{F}}(t_0, X) \equiv (\exists t > t_0)X(t)$. This is a formula of the First-Order Monadic Logic of Order (*FOMLO*) - a fundamental formalism in Mathematical Logic where formulas are built using atomic propositions $P(t)$, atomic relations between elements $t_1 = t_2$, $t_1 < t_2$, Boolean connectives and first-order quantifiers $\exists t$ and $\forall t$. Most modalities used in the literature are defined by such *FOMLO* truth tables, and as a result every

© Springer International Publishing Switzerland 2015
L.D. Beklemishev et al. (Eds.): Gurevich Festschrift II 2015, LNCS 9300, pp. 261–272, 2015.
DOI: 10.1007/978-3-319-23534-9_16

temporal formula translates directly into an equivalent *FOMLO* formula. Thus, the different temporal logics may be considered a convenient way to use fragments of *FOMLO*. *FOMLO* can also serve as a yardstick by which to check the strength of temporal logics: A temporal logic is *expressively complete* for a fragment L of *FOMLO* if every formula of L with a single free variable is equivalent to a temporal formula.

Actually, the notion of expressive completeness is with respect to the type of the underlying model since the question whether two formulas are equivalent depends on the domain over which they are evaluated. Any (partially) ordered set with monadic predicates is a model for *TL* and *FOMLO*, but the main, *canonical*, linear time intended models are the naturals $\langle \mathbb{N}, < \rangle$ for discrete time and the reals $\langle \mathbb{R}, < \rangle$ for continuous time.

A major result concerning *TL* is Kamp's theorem [2,6], which states that the pair of modalities "X *until* Y" and "X *since* Y" is expressively complete for *FOMLO* over the above two linear time canonical models.

Many temporal formalisms studied in computer science concern only future formulas - whose truth value at any moment is determined by what happens from that moment on. For example the formula X *until* Y says that X will hold from now (at least) until a point in the future when Y will hold. The truth value of this formula at a point t_0 does not depend on the question whether $X(t)$ or $Y(t)$ hold at earlier points $t < t_0$.

Over the discrete model $\langle \mathbb{N}, < \rangle$ Kamp's theorem holds also for *future formulas* of *FOMLO*: The future fragment of *FOMLO* has the same expressive power as *TL*(Until) [2,4]. The situation is radically different for the continuous time model $\langle \mathbb{R}, < \rangle$. In [5] it was shown that *TL*(Until) is not expressively complete for the future fragment of *FOMLO* and there is no easy way to remedy it. In fact it was shown in [5] that there is no temporal logic with a finite set of modalities which is expressively equivalent to the future fragment of *FOMLO* over the reals.

It was proved in [2] that all future formulas are expressible over the reals in a temporal language based on the future modality Until plus the modality K^-. The formula $\mathsf{K}^-(P)$ holds at a time point t_0 if given any 'earlier' t, no matter how close, we can always come up with a t' in between ($t < t' < t_0$) where P holds. This is of course not a future modality - the formula $\mathsf{K}^-(P)$ is past-dependent. This future-past mixture of Until and K^- is somewhat better than the standard Until - Since basis in the following sense: Although K^- is (like Since) a past modality, it does not depend on much of the past: The formula $\mathsf{K}^-(P)$ depends just on an arbitrarily short 'near past', and is actually independent of most of the past. In this sense we may say that it is an "almost future" formula (see Sect. 3 for precise definitions).

In [8] it was proved that *TL*(Until, K^-) is expressively equivalent over the reals (and over all Dedekind complete time domains) to the almost future fragment of *FOMLO*.

Kamp's theorem was generalized by Stavi who introduced two new modalities Until$'$ and Since$'$ and proved that *TL*(Until, Since, Until$'$, Since$'$) and *FOMLO* have the same expressive power over all linear time flows [2,4].

Our main theorem shows that Stavi's theorem cannot be generalized to almost future fragments. We show that there is no temporal logic with a finite set of modalities which is expressively equivalent to the almost future fragment of *FOMLO* over all linear time flows.

The rest of the paper is organized as follows: In Sect. 2 we recall the definitions of the monadic logic, the temporal logics and Kamp's and Stavi's theorems. In Sect. 3 we define "future" and "almost future" fragments of *FOMLO* and state expressive completeness results for these fragments. In Sect. 4 we prove that over the class of all linear orders there is no finite basis for a temporal logic which is expressively complete for almost future formulas. The ideas and techniques are similar to those in [5]. We will define a sequence of future formulas ψ_i such that given any (finite or infinite) set B of modalities definable in the almost future fragment of *FOMLO* by formulas of quantifier depth at most n, there is k such that ψ_k is not expressible in $TL(B)$. Thus, in particular, no logic with finitely many almost future modalities can express all ψ_i.

2 Preliminaries

We start with the basic definitions of First-Order Monadic Logic of Order (*FOMLO*) and Temporal Logic (*TL*), and some well known results concerning their expressive power.

Fix a **signature** (finite or infinite) S of **atoms**. We use $P, Q, R, S \ldots$ to denote members of S. Syntax and semantics of both logics are defined below with respect to such a fixed signature.

2.1 First-Order Monadic Logic of Order

Syntax: In the context of *FOMLO*, the atoms of S are referred to (and used) as **unary predicate symbols**. Formulas are built using these symbols, plus two binary relation symbols, $<$ and $=$, and a finite set of **first-order variables** (denoted by $x, y, z, \ldots$). Formulas are defined by the grammar:

$$atomic ::= \quad x < y \mid x = y \mid P(x) \qquad (\text{where } P \in S)$$

$$\varphi ::= \quad atomic \mid \neg\varphi_1 \mid \varphi_1 \vee \varphi_2 \mid \varphi_1 \wedge \varphi_2 \mid \exists x \varphi_1 \mid \forall x \varphi_1$$

The notation $\varphi(x_1, \ldots, x_n)$ implies that φ is a formula where the x_i's are the only variables that may occur free; writing $\varphi(x_1, \ldots, x_n, P_1, \ldots, P_k)$ additionally implies that the P_i's are the only predicate symbols that may occur in φ. We will also use the standard abbreviated notation for **bounded quantifiers**, e.g.: $(\exists x)_{>z}(\ldots)$ denotes $\exists x((x > z) \wedge (\ldots))$, $(\forall x)^{\leq z}(\ldots)$ denotes $\forall x((x \leq z) \rightarrow (\ldots))$, $(\forall x)_{>l}^{\leq u}(\ldots)$ denotes $\forall x((l < x < u) \rightarrow (\ldots))$, etc. Finally, as usual, **True(x)** denotes $P(x) \vee \neg P(x)$ and **False(x)** denotes $P(x) \wedge \neg P(x)$.

Semantics: Formulas are interpreted over *structures*. A **structure** over S is a triplet $\mathcal{M} = (\mathcal{T}, <, \mathcal{I})$ where $\mathcal{T}$ is a set - the **domain** of the structure, $<$ is an irreflexive partial order relation on $\mathcal{T}$, and $\mathcal{I} : \mathcal{S} \to \mathcal{P}(\mathcal{T})$ is the **interpretation** of the structure (where $\mathcal{P}$ is the powerset notation). We use the standard notation $\mathcal{M}, t_1, t_2, \ldots t_n \models \varphi(x_1, x_2, \ldots x_n)$. The semantics is defined in the standard way. Notice that for **formulas with at most one free first-order variable**, this reduces to:

$$\mathcal{M}, t \models \varphi(x).$$

We will often abuse terminology, and shortly refer to such formulas as **monadic** formulas (or to the corresponding syntactical fragment - as **FOMLO**).

2.2   Propositional Temporal Logics

Syntax: In the context of TL, the atoms of $\mathcal{S}$ are used as **atomic propositions** (also called **propositional atoms**). Formulas are built using these atoms, and a set (finite or infinite) B of **modality names**, where a non-negative integer **arity** is associated with each $\mathsf{M} \in B$. The syntax of TL with the **basis** B over the signature $\mathcal{S}$, denoted by **TL(B)**, is defined by the grammar:

$$F ::= \quad P \mid \neg F_1 \mid F_1 \vee F_2 \mid F_1 \wedge F_2 \mid \mathsf{M}(F_1, F_2, \ldots, F_n)$$

where $P \in \mathcal{S}$ and $\mathsf{M} \in B$ an n-place modality (that is, with arity n). As usual **True** denotes $P \vee \neg P$ and **False** denotes $P \wedge \neg P$.

Semantics: Formulas are interpreted at **time-points** (or **moments**) in structures (elements of the domain). The domain $\mathcal{T}$ of $\mathcal{M} = (\mathcal{T}, <, \mathcal{I})$ is called the **time domain**, and $(\mathcal{T}, <)$ - the **time flow** of the structure. The semantics of each n-place modality $\mathsf{M} \in B$ is defined by a 'rule' specifying how the set of moments where $\mathsf{M}(F_1, \ldots, F_n)$ holds (in a given structure) is determined by the n sets of moments where each of the formulas F_i holds. Such a 'rule' for M is formally specified by an operator $\mathcal{O}_\mathsf{M}$ on time flows, where given a time flow $\mathcal{F} = (\mathcal{T}, <)$, $\mathcal{O}_\mathsf{M}(\mathcal{F})$ is an operator in $(\mathcal{P}(\mathcal{T}))^n \longrightarrow \mathcal{P}(\mathcal{T})$.

The semantics of $TL(B)$ formulas is then defined inductively: Given a structure $\mathcal{M} = (\mathcal{T}, <, \mathcal{I})$ and a moment $t \in \mathcal{M}$ (read $t \in \mathcal{M}$ as $t \in \mathcal{T}$), define when a formula F **holds** in $\mathcal{M}$ at t - notation: $\mathcal{M}, t \models F$ - as follows:

- $\mathcal{M}, t \models P$ iff $t \in \mathcal{I}(P)$, for any propositional atom P.
- $\mathcal{M}, t \models F \vee G$ iff $\mathcal{M}, t \models F$ or $\mathcal{M}, t \models G$; similarly ("pointwise") for $\wedge$, $\neg$.
- $\mathcal{M}, t \models \mathsf{M}(F_1, \ldots, F_n)$ iff $t \in [\mathcal{O}_\mathsf{M}(\mathcal{T}, <)](T_1, \ldots, T_n)$ where $\mathsf{M} \in B$ is an n-place modality, $F_1, \ldots, F_n$ are formulas and $T_i =_{def} \{s \in \mathcal{T} : \mathcal{M}, s \models F_i\}$.

Truth Tables: Practically most standard modalities studied in the literature can be specified in **FOMLO**: A **FOMLO** formula $\varphi(x, P_1, \ldots, P_n)$ with a single free first-order variable x and with n predicate symbols P_i is called an n-**place first-order truth table**. Such a truth table φ **defines** an n-ary modality M (whose semantics is given by an operator $\mathcal{O}_\mathsf{M}$) iff for any time flow $(\mathcal{T}, <)$, for any $T_1, \ldots, T_n \subseteq \mathcal{T}$ and for any structure $\mathcal{M} = (\mathcal{T}, <, \mathcal{I})$ where $\mathcal{I}(P_i) = T_i$:

$$[\mathcal{O}_\mathsf{M}(\mathcal{T}, <)](T_1, \ldots, T_n) = \{t \in \mathcal{T} : \mathcal{M}, t \models \varphi(x, P_1, \ldots, P_n)\}$$

Example 2.1. Below are truth-table definitions for the well known "*Eventually*" and "*Globally*", the (binary) *strict*-**Until** and *strict*-**Since** of [6] and for **K**$^+$ and **K**$^-$ of [2]:

- $\diamond$ ("***Eventually***") defined by: $\varphi_\diamond(x, P) =_{def} (\exists x')_{>x} P(x')$
- $\square$ ("***Globally***") defined by: $\varphi_\square(x, P) =_{def} (\forall x')_{>x} P(x')$
- **Until** defined by: $\varphi_{\mathsf{Until}}(x, Q, P) =_{def} (\exists x')_{>x}(Q(x') \wedge (\forall y)^{<x'}_{>x} P(y))$
- **Since** defined by: $\varphi_{\mathsf{Since}}(x, Q, P) =_{def} (\exists x')^{<x}(Q(x') \wedge (\forall y)^{<x}_{>x'} P(y))$
- **K**$^+$ defined by: $\varphi_{\mathsf{K+}}(x, P) =_{def} (\forall x')_{>x}(\exists y)^{<x'}_{>x} P(y)$
- **K**$^-$ defined by: $\varphi_{\mathsf{K-}}(x, P) =_{def} (\forall x')^{<x}(\exists y)^{<x}_{>x'} P(y)$

We will use infix notation for the binary modalities Until and Since: P Until Q denotes $\mathsf{Until}(Q, P)$, meaning "there is some future moment where Q holds, and P holds all along till then". The ***non-strict*** version Until^{ns} is defined as $P \wedge (P$ Until $Q)$, requiring that P should hold at the "present moment" as well.

The formula $\mathsf{K}^-(P)$ holds at the "present moment" t_0 iff given any earlier $t < t_0$ - no matter how close - there is a moment t' in between $(t < t' < t_0)$ where the formula P holds. Notice that K^+ and K^- are definable in terms of Until and Since:

$$\mathsf{K}^+(P) \equiv \neg(\neg P \text{ Until } \mathit{True})$$

$$\mathsf{K}^-(P) \equiv \neg(\neg P \text{ Since } \mathit{True})$$

2.3 Kamp's and Stavi's Theorems

We are interested in the relative expressive power of *TL* (compared to *FOMLO*) over the class of **linear structures**. Major results in this area are with respect to the subclass of **Dedekind complete structures** - where the order is Dedekind complete, that is, where every non empty subset (of the domain) which has an upper bound has a least upper bound.

Equivalence between temporal and monadic formulas is naturally defined: $F \equiv \varphi(x)$ iff for any $\mathcal{M}$ and $t \in \mathcal{M}$: $\mathcal{M}, t \models F \Leftrightarrow \mathcal{M}, t \models \varphi(x)$. We will occasionally write $\equiv_\mathcal{L} / \equiv_{\mathcal{DC}} / \equiv_\mathcal{C}$ to distinguish equivalence over linear / Dedekind complete / any class $\mathcal{C}$ of structures.

Definability: A temporal modality is definable in *FOMLO* iff it has a *FOMLO* truth table; a temporal formula F is definable in *FOMLO* over a class $\mathcal{C}$ of structures iff there is a monadic formula $\varphi(z)$ such that $F \equiv_c \varphi(z)$. In this case we say that φ ***defines*** F over $\mathcal{C}$. Similarly, a monadic formula $\varphi(z)$ may be definable in *TL(B)* over $\mathcal{C}$.

Expressive Completeness / Equivalence: A temporal language *TL(B)* (as well as the basis B) is expressively complete for (a fragment of) *FOMLO* over a class $\mathcal{C}$ of structures iff all monadic formulas (of that fragment) $\varphi(z)$ are definable over $\mathcal{C}$ in *TL(B)*. Similarly, one may speak of expressive completeness of *FOMLO* for some temporal language. If we have expressive completeness in both directions between two languages - they are ***expressively equivalent***.

As Until and Since are definable in $FOMLO$, it follows that $FOMLO$ is expressively complete for $TL(\text{Until}, \text{Since})$. The fundamental theorem of Kamp shows that for Dedekind complete structures the opposite direction holds as well:

Theorem 2.2 (Kamp [2,6,9]). $TL(\text{Until}, \text{Since})$ *is expressively equivalent to* $FOMLO$ *over Dedekind complete structures.*

This was further generalized by Stavi who introduced two new modalities Until$'$ and Since$'$ and proved

Theorem 2.3 (Stavi [2,4]). $TL(\text{Until}, \text{Since}, \text{Until}', \text{Since}')$ *is expressively equivalent to* $FOMLO$ *over all linear time structures.*

The definitions of Stavi's modalities are not needed for the proofs of our main result. However, for the sake of completeness, they are described below.

A *gap* of a linearly ordered set $(T, <)$ is a downward closed non-empty set $C \subseteq T$ which has an upper bound in $(T, <)$, yet has no least upper bound. Informally, we can think of a gap as a hole in the Dedekind-incomplete order.

$P\text{Until}'Q$ holds at t if there is a gap C such that:

- $t \in C$, i.e., C is in the future of t,
- P is true on $(t, \infty) \cap C$, i.e., P holds from t until the gap,
- for every $t_1 \notin C$ there is $t_2 \in (-\infty, t_1) \setminus C$ such that $\neg P(t_2)$, i.e., in the future of the gap, P is false arbitrary close to the gap, and
- there is $t' \notin C$ such that Q is true on $(-\infty, t') \setminus C$, i.e., Q is true from the gap into the future for some uninterrupted stretch of time.

Note that a natural formalization of the above definition of Until$'$ uses a second-order quantifier - "there is a gap"; however, Until$'$ has a first-order truth table [2].

Since$'$ is the mirror image of Until$'$.

3   Future and Almost Future Formulas

We use standard ***interval*** notations and terminology for subsets of the domain of a structure $\mathcal{M} = (T, <, \mathcal{I})$, e.g.: $(t, \infty) =_{def} \{t' \in T | t' > t\}$; similarly we define $(t, t'), [t, t'), (t, \infty), [t, \infty)$, etc., where $t < t'$ are the ***endpoints*** of the interval. The ***sub-structure*** of $\mathcal{M}$ restricted to an interval is defined naturally. In particular: $\mathcal{M}|_{>t_0}$ denotes the sub-structure of $\mathcal{M}$ restricted to (t_0, ∞): Its domain is (t_0, ∞) and its order relation and interpretation are those of $\mathcal{M}$, restricted to this interval. $\mathcal{M}|_{\geq t_0}$ is defined similarly with respect to $[t_0, \infty)$. Notice that if $\mathcal{M}$ is Dedekind complete then so is any sub-structure of $\mathcal{M}$. If structures $\mathcal{M}, \mathcal{M}'$ have domains T, T', and if I is an interval of $\mathcal{M}$, with endpoints $t_1 < t_2$ in $\mathcal{M}$, such that $I \cup \{t_1, t_2\} \subseteq T \cap T'$ and the order relations of both structures coincide on $I \cup \{t_1, t_2\}$ - we will say that I is a ***common interval*** of both structures. This is defined similarly for intervals with ∞ or $-\infty$ as either endpoint. Two structures ***coincide*** on a common interval iff the interpretations coincide there. Two structures ***agree*** on a formula at a given common time-point (or along a common interval) iff the formula has the same truth value at that point (or along that interval) in both structures.

Definition 3.1 (Future and Almost Future Formulas and Modalities).
*A formula (temporal, or monadic with at most one free variable) F is (**semantically**):*

- *A **future** formula iff whenever two linear structures coincide on a common interval $[t, \infty)$ they agree on F at t; equivalently, whenever two linear structures coincide on a common interval $[t, \infty)$ they agree on F all along $[t, \infty)$.*
- *A **pure future** formula iff whenever two linear structures coincide on a common interval (t, ∞) they agree on F at t; equivalently, whenever two linear structures coincide on a common interval (t, ∞) they agree on F all along $[t, \infty)$.*
- *An **almost future** formula iff whenever two linear structures coincide on a common interval (t, ∞) they agree on F all along (t, ∞).*

***Past** and **pure past** formulas are defined similarly. A temporal modality is a first-order **future (almost future) modality** iff it is definable in FOMLO by a future (almost future) truth table.*

Looking at their truth tables, it is easy to verify that Until is a (pure) future modality and Since is a past modality and K^- is almost future modality. The pair $\{\mathsf{Until}, \mathsf{Since}\}$ forms an expressively complete (finite) basis in the sense of Kamp's theorem. Do we have a finite basis of future modalities which is expressively complete for all future formulas? Here are some answers:

Theorem 3.2 ([4]). *TL(Until) is expressively equivalent to the future fragment of FOMLO over discrete time flows (naturals, integers, finite).*

Theorem 3.3 ([5]). *There is no temporal logic with a finite basis which is expressively equivalent to the future fragment of FOMLO over real time flows.*

However, for the almost future fragment there is a finite base over Dedekind complete time flows.

Theorem 3.4 ([8]). *TL(Until, K^-) is expressively equivalent to the almost future fragment of FOMLO over Dedekind complete time flows.*

The situation is radically different for the class of all linear flows. Our main result shows that there is no finite base for the almost future fragment over all linear flows.

Theorem 3.5 (Main). *There is no temporal logic with a finite basis which is expressively equivalent to the almost future fragment of FOMLO over all linear time flows.*

4   No Finite Base for Almost Future Formulas

Observe that if a temporal logic is expressively equivalent to the almost future fragment of *FOMLO*, then all its modalities are almost future and are definable by *FOMLO* truth tables. The main theorem is a consequence of the next proposition:

Proposition 4.1. *Assume that B is a set of almost future modalities defin-able by FOMLO truth tables of quantifier depth at most n. Then, $TL(B)$ is not expressively complete for the future fragment of FOMLO over all linear time flows.*

Note that Proposition 4.1 is much stronger than Theorem 3.5.

First, it allows for a temporal logic to have infinitely many almost future modalities and only requires that the quantifier depth of their truth table is bounded. Second, it concludes that such a temporal logic cannot express not only all almost future formulas, but even all future formulas.

We are going to define a sequence of future formulas ψ_i such that for any (finite or infinite) set B of modalities definable in the almost future fragment of FOMLO by formulas of quantifier depth at most n, there is a k such that ψ_k is not expressible in $TL(B)$.

For our proof of Proposition 4.1 we need some rudimentary facts on the ordinal numbers. Not much set theory is needed for our purpose; it suffices to say that every ordinal is a chain. We use the following ordinals which we define directly:

– The ordinal ω is the set of natural numbers with its natural order.
– The ordinal ω^2 is an ω-sequence of blocks, each isomorphic to ω. We also declare each point to be bigger than every point in a previous block.
– More generally, ω^{n+1} is an ω-sequence of blocks, each isomorphic to ω^n. Each point is declared larger than all points in previous blocks.

An alternative definition of the ordered set ω^n is the set of n-tuples of natural numbers ordered lexicographically. The element which corresponds to a tuple $\langle m_{n-1}, m_{n-2}, \ldots, m_0 \rangle$ is denoted by $\omega^{n-1} m_{n-1} + \omega^{n-2} m_{n-2} + \cdots + m_0$.

An easy induction proves the following useful feature of these ordinals:

Lemma 4.2. *Every suffix of the ordinal ω^k is isomorphic to ω^k.*

We are going to define linear orders and chains which are very homogeneous with respect to almost future formulas:

Define the following linear orders:

$$(\mathcal{A}^k, <) := \big((0,1) \cup (1,2) \big) \times \omega^k,$$

where $(0,1)$ and $(1,2)$ are subintervals of the reals and for $\langle a, \alpha \rangle, \langle b, \beta \rangle \in \mathcal{A}^k$, $\langle a, \alpha \rangle < \langle b, \beta \rangle$ if $\alpha < \beta$ or $\alpha = \beta$ and $a < b$.

Note that $(\mathcal{A}^k, <)$ are Dedekind-incomplete. For every $\beta \in \omega^k$, the sets $C_\beta^1 := \{\langle a, \alpha \rangle \mid a < 1 \wedge \alpha \leq \beta\}$ and $C_\beta^2 := \{\langle a, \alpha \rangle \mid a < 2 \wedge \alpha \leq \beta\}$ are bounded and downward closed, yet none has a least upper bound.

Define a unary predicate $P^k := (0,1) \times \omega^k$ on $\mathcal{A}^k$ and define the following chains inthe signature $\{<, P\}$:

$$\mathcal{C}^k := (\mathcal{A}^k, <, P^k).$$

A unary predicate is said to be trivial on a chain in the signature $\{<, P\}$ if it is equal to P, $\neg P$, $True$ or $False$.

Proposition 4.1 immediately follows from the next two lemmas.

Lemma 4.3. *For every k there is a FOMLO future formula ψ_k such that for every $m > k$, ψ_k is equivalent to $True$ in $\mathcal{C}^m$ and ψ_k is equivalent to $False$ in $\mathcal{C}^k$.*

Lemma 4.4. *Assume that B is any (finite or infinite) set of almost future modalities definable by FOMLO truth tables of quantifier depth at most n, then there is an infinite subset $J \subseteq \mathbb{N}$ such that for every formula $\varphi \in TL(B)$, and all $m, i \in J$ one of the following holds:*

1. *φ is equivalent to $P(x)$ in $\mathcal{C}^m$ and in $\mathcal{C}^i$.*
2. *φ is equivalent to $\neg P(x)$ in $\mathcal{C}^m$ and in $\mathcal{C}^i$.*
3. *φ is equivalent to $True$ in $\mathcal{C}^m$ and in $\mathcal{C}^i$.*
4. *φ is equivalent to $False$ in $\mathcal{C}^m$ and in $\mathcal{C}^i$.*

Proof (of Proposition 4.1). Take two numbers $i < m$ in J. By Lemma 4.3, ψ_i is equivalent to $False$ in $\mathcal{C}^i$ and is equivalent to $True$ in $\mathcal{C}^m$. Hence, by Lemma 4.4 it is not equivalent to any formula $\varphi \in TL(B)$.   □

Lemmas 4.3 and 4.4 are proved in the next two subsections. Subsection 4.3 states a generalization of Proposition 4.1.

4.1   Proof of Lemma 4.3

Let $\mathcal{C}$ be a chain, $\varphi(x)$ be a formula, and $a < b$ be elements of $\mathcal{C}$. We say that a, b are in the same φ interval if either all elements in $[a, b]$ satisfy φ or none of them satisfies φ. We say that a, b are φ-equivalent if they are in the same φ-interval. Clearly, φ-equivalence is first-order definable and the φ equivalence classes are subintervals of $\mathcal{C}$. The set of φ-equivalence classes are naturally ordered: an equivalence class I_1 precedes a class I_2 if all elements of I_1 precede all elements of I_2. A φ-equivalence class I is (left) limit if for every φ-equivalence class $I_1 < I$ there is a φ-equivalence class I_2 such that $I_1 < I_2 < I$. Note that according to this definition the minimal φ-equivalence class is limit.

Define $\varphi_0(x) := P(x)$ and $\varphi_{i+1}(x) :=$"x is in a limit φ_i-equivalence class".

In $\mathcal{C}^n$ only the points of the form $\langle a, \omega^{n-1}m_{n-1} + \omega^{n-2}m_{n-2} + \cdots + \omega m_1 + 0 \rangle$ where $a \in (0, 1)$ satisfy φ_1; only the points of the form $\langle a, \omega^{n-1}m_{n-1} + \omega^{n-2}m_{n-2} + \cdots + \omega^2 m_2 + \omega 0 + 0 \rangle$ where $a \in (0, 1)$ satisfy φ_2 and only the points of the form $\langle a, \omega^{n-1}m_{n-1} + \omega^{n-2}m_{n-2} + \cdots + \omega^l m_l + \omega^{l-1}0 + \cdots + \omega 0 + 0 \rangle$ where $a \in (0, 1)$ satisfy φ_l.

Note that φ_k is not an almost future formula, but if we define $\psi_k(x_0)$ to be $(\exists x > x_0)\varphi_k(x) \wedge$ "x is not $\varphi_k - $ equivalent to x_0", then ψ_k is a future formula. Moreover, if $m \leq k$ then ψ_k is unsatisfiable in $\mathcal{C}^m$ and if $m > k$ then ψ_k holds at all elements in $\mathcal{C}^m$.

4.2   Proof of Lemma 4.4

We start from the following observation about chains $\mathcal{C}^k$ which shows that they are very homogeneous with respect to almost future formulas. Let $a \in P^k$ then there is $b < a$ and an isomorphism from $\mathcal{C}^k$ to the subchains of $\mathcal{C}^k$ over the interval (b, ∞) which maps $\langle 1/2, 0, 0, \ldots, 0 \rangle$ to a. Similarly, if $a \notin P^k$ then there is $b < a$ and an isomorphism from $\mathcal{C}^k$ to the subchains of $\mathcal{C}^k$ over the interval (b, ∞) which maps $\langle 3/2, 0, 0, \ldots, 0 \rangle$ to a.

This observation and the definition of almost future formulas immediately imply the following Lemma.

Lemma 4.5. *Let $\varphi(x)$ be an almost future formula. The predicate definable by φ in $\mathcal{C}^k$ is trivial.*

Proof. Let $a_0 := \langle 1/2, 0, 0, \ldots, 0 \rangle$ and $a_1 := \langle 3/2, 0, 0, \ldots, 0 \rangle$. The above observation, invariance of formulas under isomorphisms, and the definition of almost future formulas imply that for every almost future formula $\varphi(x)$:

if $\mathcal{C}^k, a_0 \models \varphi$ and $\mathcal{C}^k, a_1 \models \varphi$, then φ is equivalent to $True$ in $\mathcal{C}^k$.
if $\mathcal{C}^k, a_0 \models \varphi$ and $\mathcal{C}^k, a_1 \models \neg\varphi$, then φ is equivalent to $P(x)$ in $\mathcal{C}^k$.
if $\mathcal{C}^k, a_0 \models \neg\varphi$ and $\mathcal{C}^k, a_1 \models \varphi$, then φ is equivalent to $\neg P(x)$ in $\mathcal{C}^k$.
if $\mathcal{C}^k, a_0 \models \neg\varphi$ and $\mathcal{C}^k, a_1 \models \neg\varphi$, then φ is equivalent to $False$ in $\mathcal{C}^k$.   □

We introduce the notation $\equiv_n$ to say that two models cannot be distinguished by a first order sentence of quantifier depth n. More precisely, let M and M' be two structures of the same signature. We write $M \equiv_n M'$ if and only if for any sentence φ with $\mathrm{qd}(\varphi) \leq n$ we have $M \models \varphi$ iff $M' \models \varphi$. There are only finitely many semantically different sentences of quantifier depth n in the signature $\{<, P\}$ (see e.g., [3]). Therefore, for every n there are finitely many $\equiv_n$-classes. Hence, by pigeon-hole principle we have[1]:

Lemma 4.6. *For every n there is an infinite subset $J(n) \subseteq \mathbb{N}$ such that $\mathcal{C}^j \equiv_n \mathcal{C}^i$ for every $j, i \in J(n)$.*

Lemma 4.7. *Let $\varphi(x)$ be an almost future FOMLO formula of quantifier depth at most n. If $\mathcal{C}^m \equiv_{n+1} \mathcal{C}^k$ then one of the following holds:*

1. *φ is equivalent to $P(x)$ in $\mathcal{C}^m$ and in $\mathcal{C}^k$.*
2. *φ is equivalent to $\neg P(x)$ in $\mathcal{C}^m$ and in $\mathcal{C}^k$.*
3. *φ is equivalent to $True$ in $\mathcal{C}^m$ and in $\mathcal{C}^k$.*
4. *φ is equivalent to $False$ in $\mathcal{C}^m$ and in $\mathcal{C}^k$.*

If one of the conditions (1)-(4) holds for a formula φ, we say that φ defines the same trivial predicate in $\mathcal{C}^m$ and in $\mathcal{C}^k$.

Proof. By Lemma 4.5, φ defines a trivial predicate in every $\mathcal{C}^m$. Hence, in every $\mathcal{C}^m$ exactly one of the following sentences holds: $\forall x (P(x) \leftrightarrow \varphi(x))$, $\forall x (\neg P(x) \leftrightarrow \varphi(x))$, $\forall x \varphi(x)$ or $\forall x \neg\varphi(x)$. These sentences have quantifier depth $n + 1$. Since $\mathcal{C}^m \equiv_{n+1} \mathcal{C}^k$ we obtain that one of (1)-(4) holds.   □

---

[1] A more detailed analysis which relies on Ehrenfeucht-Fraïssé games shows that $\mathcal{C}^i \equiv_n \mathcal{C}^n$ for every $i \geq n$.

Lemma 4.8. *Assume that B is a set of almost future modalities definable by FOMLO truth tables of quantifier depth at most n. If $C^m \equiv_{n+1} C^k$ then for every formula $\varphi \in TL(B)$, one of the following holds:*

1. *φ is equivalent to $P(x)$ in C^m and in C^k.*
2. *φ is equivalent to $\neg P(x)$ in C^m and in C^k.*
3. *φ is equivalent to $True$ in C^m and in C^k.*
4. *φ is equivalent to $False$ in C^m and in C^k.*

Proof. We proceed by induction.

For the atomic formulas P, $True$ and $False$ the claim is obvious.

For Boolean combinations the result follows immediately from the induction assumption.

It remains to deal with the case where $\varphi = M(\varphi_1, \cdots, \varphi_l)$ where M is an l place modality with almost future truth table $\Psi(x, P_1, \cdots, P_l)$ of quantifier depth n. By the inductive assumption φ_i defines the same trivial predicate T_i in C^m and in C^k. Let ψ be obtained from Ψ when P_i are replaced by the corresponding trivial predicate. Note that (1) ψ defines the same predicate as φ in C^m and in C^k. (2) the quantifier depth of ψ is at most n and it is an almost future formula, therefore by Lemma 4.7, ψ defines the same trivial predicate in C^m and in C^k. Finally, (1) and (2) imply that φ defines the same trivial predicate in C^m and in C^k. □

Proof. (of Lemma 4.4). Define J as $J(n+1)$. By Lemma 4.6 and 4.8 this J satisfies the conclusion of Lemma 4.4. □

4.3   A Generalization

Proposition 4.1 holds even when modalities are definable in the monadic second-order logic of order. Monadic second-order logic of order (MLO) extends first-order monadic logic of order with second-order monadic variables $X, Y, Z, \ldots$ that range over subsets of the domain, and allows quantification over them. It is much more expressive than *FOMLO* and plays a fundamental role in Mathematics and Computer Science (see Gurevich's survey [3]). An MLOformula $\varphi(x, P_1, \ldots, P_n)$ with a single free first-order variable x and with n predicate symbols P_i is called an n-place MLOtruth table. Similar to a FOMLO truth table, such an MLOtruth table φ defines an n-ary modality M. The definition of MLO future and almost future formulas is exactly like the definition of *FOMLO* future and almost future formulas (Definition 3.1). Proposition 4.1 can be strengthened as follows:

Proposition 4.9. *Assume that B is a set of almost future modalities definable by MLO truth tables of quantifier depth at most n. Then, $TL(B)$ is not expressively complete for the future fragment of FOMLO.*

The proof of Proposition 4.9 is almost identical to the proof of Proposition 4.1. The only change is replace "$\equiv_n$" by "$\equiv_n^{MLO}$", where two structures are $\equiv_n^{MLO}$-equivalent iff they satisfy the same MLO sentences of the quantifier depth n.

Acknowledgments. I am very grateful to Dorit Pardo for numerous insightful discussions and to the anonymous referee for his helpful suggestions.

References

1. Ehrenfeucht, A.: An application of games to the completeness problem for formalized theories. Fundam. Math. **49**, 129–141 (1961)
2. Gabbay, D., Hodkinson, I., Reynolds, M.: Temporal logic: Mathematical Foundations and Computational Aspects. Oxford University Press, Cary (1994)
3. Gurevich, Y.: Monadic second order theories. In: Barwise, J., Feferman, S. (eds.) Model Theoretic Logics, pp. 479–506. Springer, Heidelberg (1985)
4. Gabbay, D., Pnueli, A., Shelah, S., Stavi, J.: On the temporal analysis of fairness. In: POPL 1980, pp. 163–173 (1980)
5. Hirshfeld, Y., Rabinovich, A.: Future temporal logic needs infinitely many modalities. Inf. Comput. **187**, 196–208 (2003)
6. Kamp, H.W.: Tense logic and the theory of linear order. Ph.D. thesis. University of California, Los Angeles (1968)
7. Pnueli, A.: The temporal logic of programs. In: Proceeding of IEEE 18th Annual Symposium on Foundations Computer Science, pp. 46–57, New York (1977)
8. Pardo (Ordentlich), D., Rabinovich, A.: A finite basis for 'almost future' temporal logic over the reals. In: Rovan, B., Sassone, V., Widmayer, P. (eds.) MFCS 2012. LNCS, vol. 7464, pp. 740–751. Springer, Heidelberg (2012)
9. Rabinovich, A.: A Proof of Kamp's Theorem. Log. Methods Comput. Sci. 10(1) (2014)

Minsky Machines and Algorithmic Problems

Mark Sapir[✉]

Department of Mathematics, Vanderbilt University, Nashville, U.S.A
m.sapir@vanderbilt.edu

To Yuri Gurevich, in honor of his 75th birthday.
С Днём Рождения, Юрий Шлёмович!

Abstract. This is a survey of using Minsky machines to study algorithmic problems in semigroups, groups and other algebraic systems.

Keywords: Minsky machines · Word problem · Uniform word problem · Semigroup · Group · Identity · Variety

1 Introduction

In 1966, Yuri Gurevich [11] proved that the universal theory of finite semigroups is undecidable. One can interpret that result in several ways. For example, it means that given a finite number of semigroup relations $u_i = v_i$ and another relation $u = v$, we cannot algorithmically decide if the equality $u = v$ holds in every finite semigroup satisfying all the relations $u_i = v_i$. In that sense the universal theory of finite semigroups can be called the *uniform word problem* of finite semigroups. Note that individually every finite semigroup has, of course, decidable word problem. Gurevich's result means that there is no uniform algorithm that works for all finite semigroups. That result turned out to be influential for two reasons. First, it opened the area of studying the uniform word problem in several classes of algebras, including semigroups and groups. Second, it was one of the first applications of Minsky (register) machines in proving undecidability of an algorithmic problem in algebra (the first result was the proof of undecidability of exponential diophantine equations from [7]). The goal of this paper is to survey some applications of Minsky machines to various algorithmic problems in semigroups, groups and other types of algebras. Note that there is some intersection of this paper with the (250-page) survey paper [18] about algorithmic problems in varieties. But most results surveyed here are not about varieties and are more recent than [18].

The research was supported in part by the NSF grants DMS 1418506 and DMS 1318716, and a BSF grant.

L.D. Beklemishev et al. (Eds.): Gurevich Festschrift II 2015, LNCS 9300, pp. 273–292, 2015.
DOI: 10.1007/978-3-319-23534-9_17

2   Turing Machines and Minsky Machines

2.1   Turing Machines

In this paper, we shall consider several types of machines. A machine M in general has an alphabet and a set of words in that alphabet called configurations (by "words" we may also mean "numbers written in binary or unary" or "tuples of numbers"). It also has a finite set of commands. Each command is a partial injective transformation of the set of configurations. A machine is called *deterministic* if the domains of its commands are disjoint. A machine usually has a distinguished *stop* configuration, and a set $I = I(M)$ of *input* configurations.

A *computation* of M is a finite or infinite sequence of configurations and commands from P:

$$w_1 \xrightarrow{\theta_1} w_2 \xrightarrow{\theta_2} \dots \xrightarrow{\theta_l} w_{l+1}, \dots$$

such that $\theta_i(w_i) = w_{i+1}$ for every $i = 1, \dots, l, \dots$.

If the computation is finite and w_{l+1} is the last configuration, then l is called the *length* of the computation. A configuration is called *accepted* by M if there exists a computation connecting that configuration with the stop configuration. The *time function* $T_M(n)$ of M is the minimal function such that every accepted word of length $\leq n$ has an accepting computation of length $\leq T_M(n)$.

The machine $\mathrm{Sym}(M)$ is made from M by adding the inverses of all commands of M. Two configurations w, w' are called *equivalent*, written $w \equiv_M w'$, if there exists a computation of $\mathrm{Sym}(M)$ connecting these configurations. Clearly, $\equiv_M$ is an equivalence relation.

The following general lemma is an easy exercise but it is very useful.

Lemma 1. *Suppose that M is deterministic. Then two configurations w, w' of M are equivalent if and only if there exist two computations of M connecting w, w' with the same configuration w'' of M.*

We say that a set X of natural numbers is *enumerated* by a machine M if there exists a recursive encoding μ of natural numbers by input configurations of M such that a number u belongs to X if and only if $\mu(u)$ is accepted by M. The set X is *recognized* by M if M enumerates X and, for every input configuration, every computation starting with that configuration eventually halts (arrives at a configuration to which no command of M is applicable).

We say that machine M' *polynomially reduces* to a machine M if there exists a deterministic polynomial time algorithm A checking equivalence of configurations of M' which uses an oracle checking equivalence of configurations of M.

We say that M and M' are *polynomially equivalent* if there are polynomial reductions of M to M' and vice versa.

For example, a Turing machine M with K tapes consists of hardware (the tape alphabet $A = \sqcup_{i=1}^{k} A_i$, and the state alphabet $Q = \sqcup_{i=1}^{K} Q_i{}^1$) and program

---

[1] $\sqcup$ denotes disjoint union.

P (the list of commands, defined below). A *configuration* of a Turing machine M is a word

$$\alpha_1 u_1 q_1 v_1 \omega_1 \ \alpha_2 u_2 q_2 v_2 \omega_2 \ \ldots \ \alpha_K u_K q_K v_K \omega_K$$

we included spaces to make the word more readable) where u_i, v_i are words in A_i, $q_i \in Q_i$ and α_i, ω_i are special symbols (not from $A \cup Q$). A tape of the machine is a part of the configuration, it is a subword from α_i to ω_i.

A command simultaneously replaces subwords $a_i q_i b_i$ by words $a_i' q_i' b_i'$ where a_i, a_i', are either letters from $A_i \cup \{\alpha_i\}$ or empty, b_i, b_i' are either letters from $A_i \cup \{\omega_i\}$ or empty. A command cannot insert or erase α_i or ω_i, so if, say, $a_i = \alpha_i$, then $a_i' = \alpha_i$. Note that with every command θ one can consider the *inverse* command θ^{-1} which undoes what θ does.

For the Turing machine we choose *stop states* q_i^0 in each Q_i. Then a configuration w is accepted if there exists a computation starting with w and ending with a configuration where all state symbols are q_i^0 and all tapes are empty (which is the stop configuration for the Turing machine). Also we choose *start states* q_i^1 in each Q_i. Then an input configuration corresponding to a word u over A_1 is a configuration inp(u) of the form

$$\alpha_1 u q_1^1 \omega_1 \ \alpha_2 q_2^1 \omega_2 \ \ldots \ \alpha_K q_K^1 \omega_K.$$

We say that a word u over A_1 is accepted by M if the configuration inp(u) is accepted. The set of all words accepted by M is called the *language accepted by M*.

2.2 Minsky Machines

The hardware of a K-glass Minsky machine, $K \geq 2$, consists of K glasses containing coins. We assume that these glasses are of infinite height. The machine can add a coin to a glass, and remove a coin from a glass (provided the glass is not empty). The number of coins in the glass $\#k$ is denoted by ϵ_k.

In the *program* of every Minsky machine, the commands are numbered, command $\#1$ is the *start command*, command $\#0$ is the *stop command*. A *configuration* of a 2-glass Minsky machine is a triple of numbers $(i; m, n)$ where i is the number of command being executed, m is the number of coins in the first glass, n is the number of coins in the second glass. The start configurations have the form $(1; m, n)$ and the stop configurations have the form $(0; m, n)$.

A *command* $\#i$, $i \geq 1$, has one of the following forms:

– Put a coin in the glass $\#k$ and go to command $\#j$. We shall encode this command by

$$\mathrm{Add}(k); j;$$

– If the glass $\#k$ is not empty then take a coin from it and go to command $\#j$. This command is encoded by

$$\epsilon_k > 0 \rightarrow \mathrm{Sub}(k); j;$$

– If the glass #k is empty, then go to instruction #j. This command is encoded by

$$\epsilon_k = 0 \rightarrow j;$$

Note that here j may be equal to 0, but there is no instruction associated with command #0.

Remark 2. This defines deterministic Minsky machines. We will also need non-deterministic Minsky machines. Those will have two or more commands with the same number.

The proof of Part (a) of the following theorem can be found in Minsky [26] (see also Malcev [24]). The proof of Part (b) can be extracted from the proof in [24, 26].

Theorem 3. *Let X be a recursively enumerable set of natural numbers. Then the following holds:*

(a) *there exists a 2-glass deterministic Minsky machine M which satisfy the following property: For every $m \in \mathbb{N}$, M begins its work in configuration $(1; 2^m, 0)$ and halts in configuration $(0; 0, 0)$ if and only if $m \in X$, and it works forever if $m \notin X$.*

(b) *Every computation of M starting with a configuration c empties each glass after at most $O(|c|)$ steps.*

3 The Three Main Semigroups Simulating Minsky Machines

There are three basic ways to interpret 2-glass Minsky machines in semigroups. They correspond to the three ways to put two glasses and the machine head (the one that counts the commands and puts coins in the glasses) on the line: the head can be between two glasses, to the left of the glasses and to the right of the glasses. If we imagine the head to have a short hand used to put the coins in glasses, then in the last two cases we should be able to permute the two glasses: if the counter wants to put a coin in, say, glass #2, and glass #1 is between the head and glass #2, then first the two glasses are permuted.

The three semigroups corresponding to a 2-glass Minsky machine M are $S_1(M)$, $\overrightarrow{S_2}(M)$ and $\overleftarrow{S_2}(M)$. The last two semigroups are anti-isomorphic, so we only define $S_1(M)$ and $\overrightarrow{S_2}(M)$. Each of the three semigroups has zero 0.

Let M be a Minsky machine with 2 glasses and commands #$#1, 2, ..., N, 0$. Then both semigroups $S_1(M)$ and $\overrightarrow{S_2}(M)$ are generated by the elements $q_0, q_1,$ $..., q_N$ and $\{a_i, A_i, i = 1, 2\}$. Here a_i play the role of coins in glass #i, q_i play the role of numbers of commands (i.e., the states of the head), and A_i play the role of the bottoms of glasses (these are needed in order to be able to check if a glass is empty). The set of defining relations of $S_1(M)$ and $\overrightarrow{S_2}(M)$ contains the following relations corresponding to the commands of M.

Command # i of $M, i \geq 1$	Relation of $S_1(M)$	Relation of $\overrightarrow{S_2}(M)$
Add(1); j	$q_i = a_1 q_j$	$q_i = q_j a_1$
Add(2); j	$q_i = q_j a_2$	$q_i = q_j a_2$
$\epsilon_1 > 0 \to \text{Sub}(1); j$	$a_1 q_i = q_j$	$q_i a_1 = q_j$
$\epsilon_2 > 0 \to \text{Sub}(2); j$	$q_i a_2 = q_j$	$q_i a_2 = q_j$
$\epsilon_1 = 0 \to j$	$A_1 q_i = A_1 q_j$	$q_i A_1 = q_j A_1$
$\epsilon_2 = 0 \to j$	$q_i A_2 = q_j A_2$	$q_i A_2 = q_i A_2$

These will be called the *Minsky relations*. The semigroups $S_1(M)$, $\overrightarrow{S_2}(M)$ also have the following *auxiliary relation*.

The Auxiliary Relations of $S_1(M)$:

- All 2-letter words in the generators of $S_1(M)$ that are not subwords of the words $A_1 a_1^m q_i a_2^n A_2$, $m, n \in \mathbb{N}$, $i = 1, ..., N$, are equal to 0;
- $q_0 = 0$.

The Auxiliary Relations of $\overrightarrow{S_2}(M)$:

- (Glass permuting relations) each letter in $\{a_1, A_1\}$ commutes with each letter in $\{a_2, A_2\}$;
- All 2-letter words in generators of $\overrightarrow{S_2}(M)$ that are not subwords of the words that are equal to $q_i a_1^m A_1 a_2^n A_2$ modulo the glass permuting relations are equal to 0;
- $q_0 = 0$.

A configuration $(i; m, n)$ of the Minsky machine M corresponds to the element $w_1(i; m, n) = A_1 a_1^m q_i a_2^n A_2$ in $S_1(M)$ and to the element $w_2(i; m, n) = q_i a_1^m A_1 a_2^n A_2$ in $\overrightarrow{S_2}(M)$.

Remark 4. The auxiliary relations ensure that every word in the generators of $S_1(M)$ (resp. $S_2(M)$) that is not equal to 0 is a subword of a word of the form $w_1(i; m, n)$ (resp. a subword of a word that is equal to one of the words $w_2(i; m, n)$ modulo the glass permuting relations).

Remark 5. Thus the semigroups $S_1(M)$, $\overrightarrow{S_2}(M)$, $\overleftarrow{S_2}(M)$ basically consist of the subwords of the words corresponding to the configurations of M. This is a crucial property of Minsky machines which makes them much better suited for semigroup simulation than the general Turing machines.

4   Varieties of Semigroups and the Word Problem

The proof of the following statement is straightforward, it is discussed in [18].

Theorem 6 (See [18]). *Let M be a Minsky machine. For every two configurations $(i; m, n)$ and $(i'; m', n')$ the words $w_s(i; m, n)$ and $w_s(i', m', n')$, $s = 1, 2, 3$ are equal in $S_1(M)$ (resp. $\overrightarrow{S_2}(M)$ or $\overleftarrow{S_2}(M)$) if and only if the configurations are equivalent. In particular, if M has undecidable halting problem, then the word problem in each of the three semigroups associated with M is undecidable. Moreover, the equality to 0 is undecidable in these semigroups.*

Of course constructing a finitely presented semigroup with undecidable word problem (first done by Markov and Post, see [24]) is easy enough using the ordinary Turing machines. The advantage of Minsky machines is that the semigroups $S_1(M), \overrightarrow{S}_2(M), \overleftarrow{S}_2(M)$ are in some sense "small".

For example while examples corresponding to the ordinary Turing machines usually contain non-commutative free subsemigroups, and hence do not satisfy non-trivial identities (laws), it is easy to see that each of the three semigroups $S_1(M), \overrightarrow{S}_2(M), \overleftarrow{S}_2(M)$ satisfies a non-trivial identity. For example, each of them satisfies $x^2 y^2 = y^2 x^2$. This follows immediately from Remark 4 and the auxiliary defining relations of these semigroups. In fact, one can describe all identities satisfied by these semigroups [29].

In particular, the following theorem holds. Let e_{ij} denote the 2×2-matrix unit with (i, j)-entry 1 and all other entries 0. Let $\overrightarrow{P}$ denote the three element semigroup $\{e_{11}, e_{12}, 0\}$, $\overleftarrow{P}$ denote the three-element semigroup $\{e_{11}, e_{21}, 0\}$ and T denote the four element semigroup $\{e_{11}, e_{12}, e_{22}, 0\}$. For every semigroup S let S^1 be the semigroup S with an identity element formally adjoined. For example P^1 is the four element semigroup $\{1, e_{11}, e_{12}, 0\}$. Let $\mathbb{N}$ be the additive semigroup of natural numbers. It is well-known and trivial that an identity $u = v$ is true in $\mathbb{N}$ if and only if it is *balanced*, that is if every letter occurs the same number of times in u and in v.

Theorem 7 (Sapir, [29]). *For every Minsky machine M the variety generated by $S_1(M)$, i.e., the smallest class of semigroups containing $S_1(M)$ and given by identities coincides with the variety $\mathcal{M}_1$ generated by the direct product $T \times \mathbb{N}$. The variety generated by $\overrightarrow{S}_2(M)$ coincides with the variety $\overrightarrow{\mathcal{M}}_2$ generated by $\overrightarrow{P} \times \overleftarrow{P}{}^1 \times \mathbb{N}$, and the variety generated by $\overleftarrow{S}_2(M)$ coincides with the variety $\overleftarrow{\mathcal{M}}_2$ generated by $\overleftarrow{P}{}^1 \times \overrightarrow{P} \times \mathbb{N}$ (thus these varieties do not depend on M).*

Moreover Minsky machines and the easy construction above proved to be the universal tool in dealing with the word problem in semigroups satisfying identities. In particular, one can completely describe non-periodic varieties containing finitely presented semigroups with undecidable word problem.

We say that a finitely generated semigroup S is finitely presented inside a variety $\mathcal{V}$ if it is defined by the identities of $\mathcal{V}$ plus a finite number of relations. We shall need the following sequence of *Zimin words*:

$$Z_1 = x_1, ..., Z_{n+1} = Z_n x_{n+1} Z_n.$$

This sequence of words plays an important role in combinatorial algebra (see [18], [33]). We say that a word W is *not* an isoterm for an identity $u = v$ if for some substitution ϕ of words for letters of u, v we have that $\phi(u) \neq \phi(v)$ but W contains either $\phi(u)$ or $\phi(v)$ as a subword. For example, the word $ababbab$ is not an isoterm for the identity $x^2 = x^3$ because the word contains a subword $abab$ which is equal to $\phi(x^2)$ under the substitution $x \to ab$, and $\phi(x^2) \neq \phi(x^3)$. But it is an isoterm for the identity $x^3 = x^4$ because it does not contain any subword of the form u^3 or u^4.

Theorem 8 (Sapir, [29]). *Let V be a variety of semigroups defined by identities $u_i = v_i$ in at most n variables and non-periodic (i.e., containing the semigroup $\mathbb{N}$, or, equivalently, every identity $u_i = v_i$ is balanced). Then the following conditions are equivalent.*

(1) Every semigroup that is finitely presented inside V has decidable word problem.
(2) Every semigroup that is finitely presented inside V has decidable elementary theory.
(3) Every semigroup that is finitely presented inside V is faithfully representable by matrices over a field.
(4) The variety does not contain varieties $\mathcal{M}_1, \overrightarrow{\mathcal{M}_2}, \overleftarrow{\mathcal{M}_2}$ and the word Z_{n+1} is an isoterm for every identity $u_i = v_i$.

As mentioned in [29], Property (4) of Theorem 8 is algorithmically verifiable given a finite number of identities $u_i = v_i$.

5   Gurevich's Theorem. The Uniform Word Problem for Finite Semigroups

Let L be a finite conjunction of equalities $u = v$, where u, v are words in some alphabet X. Let U, V be two words in X. Then the universal formula $L \to U = V$ is called a *quasi-identity*. We say that the *uniform word problem* is solvable in a class of semigroups V if there exists algorithm that, given a quasi-identity θ, decides whether θ holds in V. Clearly, the uniform word problem is solvable if V consists of finitely many finite semigroups. For every variety V of semigroups V_{fin} denotes the set of finite semigroups from V. Yu. Gurevich proved [11] that if V is the variety of all semigroups, then the uniform word problem is not decidable in V_{fin}. Generalizing that result, we completely described in [29,30] all finitely based varieties V such that the uniform word problem is decidable in V_{fin}.

Theorem 9 (Sapir, [30]). *For every finite set of identities Σ in n variables defining a variety V, the following conditions are equivalent:*

(1) The uniform word problem is decidable in V_{fin}.
(2) The word Z_{n+1} is not an isoterm for Σ and either V is periodic (i.e., does not contain $\mathbb{N}$, or, equivalently Σ contains a non-balanced identity), or does not contain any of the semigroups T, $\overrightarrow{P}^1 \times \overleftarrow{P}$ and $\overrightarrow{P} \times \overleftarrow{P}^1$.

The proof of Theorem 9 proceeds as follows. (1) $\to$ (2). Suppose that the uniform word problem is decidable in V_{fin}.

First suppose that V contains one of the varieties $\mathcal{M}_1, \overrightarrow{\mathcal{M}_2}, \overleftarrow{\mathcal{M}_2}$. In order to get a contradiction, consider the following modification of semigroups $S_1(M)$, $\overrightarrow{S}_2(M)$, $\overleftarrow{S}_2(M)$. We add three letters c, c', e, C to the generating set of each semigroup. The construction below uses ideas from [11] and is somewhat easier than a construction from [29]. The Minsky relations of the semigroups $S_1'(M)$, $\overrightarrow{S}_2'(M)$, $\overleftarrow{S}_2'(M)$ are defined as follows.

Command # i of $M, i \geq 1$	Relation of $S_1'(M)$	Relation of $\overrightarrow{S}_2'(M)$
Add(1); j	$q_i = a_1 q_j$	$q_i = q_j a_1$
Add(2); j	$q_i = q_j a_2$	$q_i = q_j a_2$
$\epsilon_1 = 1 \to \mathrm{Sub}(1); j$	$A_1 a_1 w_1 = c A_1 q_1$	$q_1 a_1 A_1 = q_1 A_1 c$
$\epsilon_1 \geq 2 \to \mathrm{Sub}(1); j$	$a_1 q_i = q_j$	$q_i a_1 = q_j$
$\epsilon_2 > 0 \to \mathrm{Sub}(2); j$	$q_i a_2 = q_j$	$q_i a_2 = q_j$
$\epsilon_1 = 0 \to j$	$A_1 q_i = A_1 q_j$	$q_i A_1 = q_j A_1$
$\epsilon_2 = 0 \to j$	$q_i A_2 = q_j A_2$	$q_i A_2 = q_i A_2$

One can also view this modification as a modification of the machine M: we add a new *counter* glass which "counts" how many times during a computation the first glass becomes empty: every time we remove the only remaining coin from the first glass, we add a coin in the new glass.

The Auxiliary Relations of $S_1'(M)$ are

- (Counter relations) $cc' = c'c = e, ec = c = ce, ec' = c'e = c'$, that is the subsemigroup generated by c, c' is a subgroup isomorphic to the group $\mathbb{Z}$ with identity element e.
- Every 2-letter word in the generators of $S_1'(M)$ which is not a subword of a word that is equal to a word of the form $Cc^k A_1 a_1^m q_i a_2^n A_2$ modulo the counter relations is equal to 0.
- $CeA_1 q_i = 0$ for every i.

The Auxiliary Relations of $\overrightarrow{S}_2'(M)$ are

- (Counter relation) $cc' = c'c = e, ec = c = ce, ec' = c'e = c'$, that is the subsemigroup generated by c, c' is a subgroup isomorphic to $\mathbb{Z}$.
- (Glass permuting relations) Every letter from $\{a_1, A_1\}$ commutes with every letter from $\{a_2, A_2\}$, every letter from $\{a_1, a_2, A_1, A_2\}$ commutes with every letter from $\{c, c', e, C\}$
- Every 2-letter word in the generators of $S_1'(M)$ which is not a subword of a word that is equal to a word of the form $q_i a_1^m A_1 a_2^n A_2 c^k C$ modulo the Counter and Glass permuting relations is equal to 0.

Now it is proved in [29] that $S_1 = S_1'(M)$ belongs to the variety $\mathcal{M}_1$, and $S_2 = \overrightarrow{S}_2'(M)$ belongs to the variety $\mathcal{M}_2 = \overrightarrow{\mathcal{M}}_2$ generated by $\overleftarrow{P} \times \overrightarrow{P}^1 \times \mathbb{N}$. Let L_i, $i = 1, 2$, be the conjunction of the defining relations of S_i. For every input configuration $(1; m, n)$ of M let $W_1(1; m, n)$ be the word $CA_1 a_1^m q_1 a_2^n A_2$ and $W_2(1; m, n) = q_1 a_1^m A_1 a_2^n A_2 C$. Consider the quasi-identity $L_i \to W_i = 0$. Suppose that a configuration $(1; 2^m, 0)$ is accepted by M. Then it is proved in [30] that there are only finitely many elements in S_i that divide the element $W_i(1; 2^m, 0)$ (recall that we say that an element b *divides* element a if for some

x_1, x_2 we have $a = x_1 b x_2$). Consider the set of all elements of S_i that do not divide $W_i = W_i(1; 2^m, 0)$. This set is an ideal J_i of S_i, not containing W_i. Consider the Rees quotient $F_i = S_i/J$. It is a finite semigroup and it belongs to $\mathcal{M}_i$ as a quotient of S_i. We can assume that F_i is generated by the same generating set as S_i. Therefore F_i satisfies L_i. But $W_i \neq 0$ in F_i because $W_i \notin J$. Thus a finite semigroup in $\mathcal{M}_i$ does not satisfy the quasi-identity

$$L_i \to W_i(1; 2^m, 0) = 0.$$

On the other hand, suppose that M works indefinitely long starting with the configuration $(1; 2^m, 0)$. Then by Part (b) of Theorem 3 the word $W_i(1; 2^m, 0)$ is equal in S_i to words of the form $Cc^s A_1 q_t a_2^n A_2$ for arbitrary s. Let R_i be a periodic semigroup satisfying the formula L_i for some interpretation of its variables in R_i. In other words, let R_i be a quotient of S_i generated by the same generating set as S_i. Then R_i satisfies the relations of the form $W_i(1; 2^m, 0) = Cc^s A_1 q_t a_2^n A_2$ for every s. Since R_i is periodic, $c^s = c^{2s}$ for some s. Since the subsemigroup generated by c, c' in S_i is a group (isomorphic to $\mathbb{Z}$) with identity element e, the subsemigroup generated by c in R_i is a finite cyclic group, and so $c^s = e$ for some s. But $CeA_1 q_t = 0$ in S_1, and hence in R_i. Therefore we can conclude that the quasi-identity $L_i \to W_i(1; 2^m, 0) = 0$ holds in every periodic semigroup.

Since there exists a Minsky machine satisfying the conditions of Theorem 3 for which the language of accepted input configurations is not recursive, there is no algorithm separating the quasi-identities that fail in some finite semigroup of $\mathcal{V}$ from the set of quasi-identities that hold in all periodic semigroups. Thus the uniform word problem in $\mathcal{V}$ is undecidable, a contradiction.

Now suppose that Z_{n+1} is an isoterm for identities from Σ. Then it is proved in [28] (see also [33]) that there exist a finite alphabet $x_1, ..., x_k$ and a substitution $\phi: x_i \mapsto \phi(x_i)$ where $\phi(x_i)$ is a word in $\{x_1, ..., x_k\}$, such that $\phi^s(x_1)$ is an isoterm for every identity from Σ for every s. In that case, we construct in [30] another semigroup $S(M)$ simulating arbitrary 2-glass Minsky machine. In that semigroup the number s of coins in glass #j is simulated not by the power a_j^s (as in the constructions above) but by the word $\phi^s(x_1)$. As a result the words corresponding to configurations of M are isoterms of the identities of Σ, and the situation is similar to the situation with the variety of all semigroups (since the identities of the variety cannot "mix up" the words corresponding to configurations of the Minsky machine). Of course replacing a_i^s by $\phi^s(x_1)$ costs us something. For example, to simulate one command of M, we need several relations of $S(M)$, but it can be done, see [30]. This proves that in the case when Z_{n+1} is not an isoterm for Σ, the uniform word problem in $\mathcal{V}$ is also undecidable, which concludes the proof of implication (1) $\to$ (2) in Theorem 9.

(2) $\to$ (1). Suppose that the conditions of (2) hold. Then either $\mathcal{V}$ is periodic or it contains $\mathbb{N}$. If it is periodic, then we proved in [31] that the *restricted Burnside* property holds in $\mathcal{V}$. This means that for every natural number $k \geq 1$ there are only finitely many (effectively computable) finite semigroups in $\mathcal{V}$ with at most k generators. To prove that, we were using the celebrated positive solution of the restricted Burnside problem for groups by Zelmanov [35,36], and

our results on Burnside problems in semigroup varieties [28]. This property easily implies solvability of the uniform word problem in $\mathcal{V}_{\mathrm{fin}}$.

If $\mathcal{V}$ is not periodic and contains none of the three semigroups listed in Part (2) of the theorem, then by Theorem 8 every semigroup that is finitely presented in $\mathcal{V}$ is faithfully represented by matrices over a field, hence residually finite [25]. This also implies solvability of the uniform word problem in $\mathcal{V}_{\mathrm{fin}}$. Indeed, in order to check if a quasi-identity $L \to W = W'$ holds in $\mathcal{V}_{\mathrm{fin}}$, consider the semigroup E defined by the relations from L in $\mathcal{V}$. If $W \neq W'$ in that semigroup, then $W \neq W'$ in some finite quotient E' of E. Thus E' does not satisfy $L \to W = W'$. Hence $L \to W = W'$ does not hold in $\mathcal{V}_{\mathrm{fin}}$. On the other hand, if $W = W'$ holds in E, then this equality holds in every homomorphic image of E, hence $L \to W = W'$ holds in $\mathcal{V}_{\mathrm{fin}}$. Since the word problem is decidable in E by Theorem 8, we can decide whether or not $W = W'$ in E, and hence whether or not $L \to W = W'$ holds in $\mathcal{V}_{\mathrm{fin}}$.

6   The Uniform Word Problem for Finite Groups

6.1   Slobodskoi's Theorem

The first simulation of Minsky machines in groups was done by Slobodskoi [34]. This is not as easy as in the case of semigroups. The main problem is that we cannot simulate a command of a Minsky machine, say,

$$i : \mathrm{Add}(1); j$$

by a substitution $q_i = q_j a_1$ because then the group would collapse. For example, if $i = j$, then we would have $q_i = q_i a_1$ and $a_1 = 1$. Thus the idea is to abandon the product operation in the group and use some other *derived* operation, say, commutator. Thus if $*$ is the new binary operation, we can simulate the command of a Minsky machine by $q_i = q_j * a_i$ and since $*$ does not necessarily satisfy the cancellation property, we avoid at least immediate collapse of the group. But then several new problems occur. For example $*$ will not be associative, and so we would have to interpret a configuration $(i; m, n)$ of a Minsky machine by a nested word like $(...(q_i * a_1)...) * a_1) * A_1)....$ In this case, it may be difficult to simulate permutation of glasses. These difficulties and ways to resolve them are described in details in [18]. Slobodskoi proved

Theorem 10 (Slobodskoi, [34]). *The uniform word problem is undecidable in the class of finite groups.*

Several generalizations of Theorem 10 were then proved by Kharlampovich (see [16,17]); each time Minsky machines were used. Finally in [19], we proved the following result, again using Minsky machines.

Theorem 11. *Let $\mathcal{G}_1$ be the set of finite groups G which have a normal series $N_1 \trianglelefteq N_2 \trianglelefteq G$ such that N_1 and N_2 are Abelian groups of the same prime exponent p, and G/N_2 is Abelian. Let $\mathcal{G}_2$ be the set of finite groups G with normal series*

$N_1 \trianglelefteq N_2 \trianglelefteq G$ such that N_1 is contained in the center of G, N_2/N_1 is nilpotent of class at most 5, and G/N_2 is Abelian. Let $\mathcal{G} = \mathcal{G}_1 \cap \mathcal{G}_2$. Then the uniform word problem is undecidable in any set of finite groups containing $\mathcal{G}$.

6.2   Some Applications of Slobodskoi's Theorem

Embeddings of Finite Semigroups into Simple Semigroups. A semigroup with 0 is called *0-simple* if it does not have any ideals except 0 and itself (i.e., every two non-zero elements divide each other). These semigroups play very important role in the theory of semigroups being the building blocks from which all other semigroups are constructed. Finite 0-simple semigroups have very explicit structure (proved by Sushkevich and Rees independently [4]). For every such semigroup S there exist a (finite) group G and an $m \times n$-matrix P where every entry is an element of G or 0. The elements of S are 0 and all triples (i, g, j) where $1 \leq i \leq m, 1 \leq j \leq n, g \in G$. The product $(i, g, j)(i', g', j')$ is defined as 0 if $P(i', j) = 0$ and $(i, gP(i', j)g', j')$ if $P(i', j) \neq 0$. Since finite 0-simple semigroups are so easy, it would be natural to guess that the set of their subsemigroups is also easy. That was proved not to be the case by Kublanovsky (first published in [12]). For every finite partial group G, that is a finite set with a partial operation $\cdot$, he constructed a finite effectively computable set of 4-nilpotent finite semigroups $N_i(G)$. This set satisfies the property that G embeds into a group if and only if one of the $N_i(G)$ embeds into a finite 0-simple semigroup. The semigroups $N_i(G)$ are constructed as follows. We can assume G contains the identity element, every element of G has an inverse, and for every $a, b, c \in G$ we have $(a \cdot b) \cdot c = a \cdot (b \cdot c)$ provided each of the products involved in that equality is defined. Indeed, otherwise G cannot be embeddable into a group. Consider all (finitely many) partial groups G_i such that

- $G \leq G_i$;
- $G_i = G \cdot G \cdot G$.

Then $N_i(G) = N(G_i)$ is the semigroup defined on the set

$$(\{1\} \times G \times \{2\}) \cup (\{2\} \times G \times \{3\}) \cup (\{3\} \times G \times \{4\})$$
$$\cup(\{1\} \times (G \cdot G) \times \{3\}) \cup (\{2\} \times (G \cdot G) \times \{4\}) \cup \{1\} \times G_i \times \{4\} \cup \{0\}$$

with the operation $(i, u, j)(j, v, k) = (i, u \cdot v, k)$ if the right hand side is in $N_i(G) \setminus \{0\}$ or 0 otherwise (that construction uses the idea of *split systems* from my undergraduate diploma thesis [27]).

It is well known [8] that the problem whether a finite partial group embeds into a finite group is decidable if and only if the uniform word problem for finite groups is decidable. Thus Slobodskoi's Theorem 10 implies

Theorem 12 (Kublanovsky [12]). *The set of (4-nipotent) subsemigroups of finite 0-simple semigroups is not recursive.*

Equations over Finite Semigroups, the Rhodes' Problem. Let S be a finite semigroup, $X = \{x_1, ..., x_n\}$ be a set of variables. Let u_i, v_i be words in $S \cup X$. Then the set of equalities $u_i = v_i$ is called a *system of equations over S*. We say that a system of equations over S is *solvable* if there exists a finite semigroup $T \geq S$ and a map $X \to T$ which makes all equalities $u_i = v_i$ true in T.

For example, solvability of the equation $a = x_1 b x_2$ $(a, b \in S)$ means that b divides a in a finite semigroup containing S. The problem of eventual solvability of that equation was known as the *Rhodes problem* since the 60s. Similar problems were known to be decidable (Lyapin [22]). Rhodes' problem was believed to be decidable also, and some partial results in that direction were proved. For example, Hall and Putcha [13] proved that the solvability of that equation over S is decidable provided a and b are regular elements. Nevertheless, using Slobodskoi's result and split systems, we proved

Theorem 13 (Kublanovsky, Sapir [20]). *(i) There is no algorithm to decide, given a finite 4-nilpotent semigroup S and two elements a, b in S, whether there exists a bigger finite semigroup $T > S$ such that $a = x_1 b x_2$ for some $x_1, x_2 \in T$.*

(ii) There is no algorithm to decide, given a finite 4-nilpotent semigroup S and two elements a, b in S, whether there exists a bigger finite semigroup $T > S$ such that $a = x_1 b x_2$ and $b = x_1' a x_2'$ for some $x_1, x_1', x_2, x_2' \in T$.

Similar problems turned out to be undecidable for finite associative rings as well.

Profinite Groups and the Restricted Burnside Problem for General Algebras. Recently Theorem 10 found several interesting and unexpected applications in the theory of profinite groups. In particular, Bridson and Wilton proved.

Theorem 14 (Bridson, Wilton [2]). *There are recursive sequences of finite presentations for residually finite groups G_n and Γ_n with explicit monomorphisms $u_n : G_n \hookrightarrow \Gamma_n$ such that (1) the profinite completions $\hat{G}_n$ and $\hat{\Gamma}_n$ are isomorphic if and only if the induced map $\hat{u}_n$ is an isomorphism; (2) $\hat{u}_n$ is an isomorphism if and only if u_n is surjective; and (3) the set $\{n \in \mathbb{N} \mid \hat{G}_n$ is not isomorphic to $\hat{\Gamma}_n\}$ is recursively enumerable but not recursive.*

They also applied Slobodskoi's theorem to prove

Theorem 15 (Bridson, Wilton [3]). *There is no algorithm which, given a finite presentation of a group G decides if G has only finitely many finite quotients.*

That result, in turn, was used in [33] to prove that there is no algorithm which, given a finite set of identities of general algebras, decides whether the restricted Burnside property is true in the variety defined by these identities. More precisely we proved

Theorem 16 (Sapir, [33]). *There is no algorithm to decide, given a finite set of identities of some type, whether for every n there are only finitely many finite n-generated algebras satisfying these identities.*

7   Other Algorithmic Applications of Minsky Machines

Historically the first application of Minsky (register) machines was the result by Davis, Putnam and Robinson [7] of unsolvability exponential diophantine equations: they associated an exponential diophantine equation $D(M)$ to every Minsky machine and its configuration $(1; m, 0)$, and then proved that M accepts the configuration $(1; m, 0)$ if and only if $D(M)$ has an integer solution. This result turned out to be the first major step in solving Hilbert's 10th problem.

7.1   Collatz Type Problems

A probably lesser known application of Minsky machines is the John Conway's version of Collatz problem [5]. Recall that Collatz problem concerns with the function $\kappa \colon \mathbb{N} \to \mathbb{N}$ that takes every even number n to $n/2$ and every odd number n to $3n + 1$. The problem is whether for every number n, $\kappa^s(n) = 1$ for some s. Conway generalised this problem as follows. Let κ be a piece-wise linear function $\mathbb{N} \to \mathbb{N}$ with finitely many pieces. Can we decide, given $n \in \mathbb{N}$, whether $\kappa^s(n) = 1$ for some s?

Conway [5] showed that the answer is negative even if we assume that the linear functions are just dilations (i.e., linear functions without the translation part). A simulation of Minsky machines is in that case not difficult. Let M be a 2-glass Minsky machine with commands $\#\#1, 2, ..., N, 0$. We encode every configuration $(i; m, n)$ of M by the number $p_i 2^m 3^n$ where p_i is the $i + 3$'d prime (that is $p_0 = 5, p_1 = 7$, etc.). Commands of M are then encoded as pieces of the piece-wise dilation function κ:

Command # i of M	value of $\kappa(n)$	condition on n
Add$(1); j$	$\frac{2p_j}{p_i} n$	p_i divides n
Add$(2); j$	$\frac{3p_j}{p_i} n$	p_i divides n
$\epsilon_1 > 0 \to$ Sub$(1); j$	$\frac{p_j}{2p_i} n$	$2p_i$ divides n
$\epsilon_2 > 0 \to$ Sub$(2); j$	$\frac{p_j}{3p_i}$	$3p_i$ divides n
$\epsilon_1 = 0 \to j$	$\frac{p_j}{p_i} n$	p_i divides n but 2 does not divide n
$\epsilon_2 = 0 \to j$	$\frac{p_j}{p_i} n$	p_i divides n but 3 does not divide n
Stop $(i = 0)$	$\frac{1}{5} n$	$n = 5$

In all other cases (say, when none of p_i divides n), we set $\kappa(n) = n$. Then it is easy to show that for $n = 7 \cdot 2^m$ there exists s such that $\kappa^s(n) = 1$ if and only if the configuration $(1; m, 0)$ is accepted by M, and Conway's statement follows from Theorem 3.

7.2   Amalgams of Finite Semigroups

Let D and E be two semigroups generated by sets X and Y respectively. Let $U = X \cap Y$, and the subsemigroups generated by U in D and in E coincide.

Then we say that $D \cup_{\langle U \rangle} E$ is an amalgam of the semigroups D and E with amalamated subsemigroup $\langle U \rangle$. The corresponding amalgamated free product is the semigroup defined by the generating set $X \cup Y$ and all relations of D and E.

It is well known that any amalgam of two finite groups is embeddable into a group [23]. Moreover the free product with amalgamation of two finite groups and in general the fundamental group of any graph of finite groups has a free subgroup of finite index (Karras, Pietrowski, Solitar, [15]) so it is residually finite. Hence it has solvable word problem and any amalgam of finite groups is embeddable into a finite group. The situation with semigroup amalgams is quite different, and there are many papers that tried to clarify the situation (see the introduction of [32]). In some sense these efforts were finalized by two results from [32] (very similar proofs of Parts (b), and (c) were obtained independently and almost simultaneously by Jackson [14]):

Theorem 17 (Sapir, [32]). *(a) There exists an amalgam of two finite semigroups such that the word problem is undecidable in the corresponding free product with amalgamation and the amalgam embeds in the amalgamated free product.*

(b) The problem of whether an amalgam of two finite semigroups is embeddable into a semigroup is undecidable.

(c) The problem of whether an amalgam of two finite semigroups is embeddable into a finite semigroup is undecidable.

The proofs of Parts (b), (c) uses Slobodskoi's Theorem 10 (and hence, implicitly, Minsky machines). The proof of Part (a) of Theorem 17 provides a simulation of a Minsky machine M with $N + 1$ commands $\#\#1, ..., N, 0$ in an amalgamated product of two finite (even nilpotent) semigroups $D(M)$ and $E(M)$ described as follows.

First let us describe the generating sets of $D(M)$ and $E(M)$. The intersection of these generating sets is the set $U(M)$ which consists of $0, q_0, q_1, u_{i,j}$, $i = 0, ..., N$, $j = 1, 2$. The generator 0 acts as zero in both $D(M)$ and $E(M)$. The semigroup $D(M)$ is generated by the union of the set $\{a, \bar{b}, q_i, p_i \mid i = 0, ..., N\}$ and the set U; $E(M)$ is generated by the union of the set $\{A, b, \bar{a}, B\}$ and U.

We shall see that the set $U(M)$ is in fact a subsemigroup with zero product: the product of every two elements in $U(M)$ is equal to 0. The other relations of $D(M)$ and $E(M)$ are not as transparent and are much less transparent than in the cases considered above, so we start with explaining how these relations simulate the Minsky machine.

The word in the amalgamated free product $D(M) *_{U(M)} E(M)$ that corresponds to a configuration $(i; m, n)$ of the machine M is

$$W(i; m, n) = A(ab)^m q_i (\bar{a}\bar{b})^n B.$$

Thus A, B correspond to the bottoms of the two glasses, $(ab)^m$ simulates the coins in the first glass, $(\bar{a}\bar{b})^n$ simulates the coins in the second glass.

Suppose that the ith command of M adds a coin in the first glass. Then first we replace q_i by $au_{i,1}p_i$ using a relation of $D(M)$. Then using a relation of $E(M)$ we replace $u_{i,1}$ by $bu_{i,2}$. As a result the word $A(ab)^m q_i (\bar{a}\bar{b})^n B$ transforms into

$A(ab)^{m+1}u_{i,2}p_i(\bar{a}\bar{b})^n B$. Finally using a relation of $D(M)$ we replace $u_{i,2}p_i$ by q_j, and we produce the word $W(j; m+1, n)$ as desired. Other commands of M are simulated in a similar manner.

Here is the list of Minsky relations of semigroups $D(M), E(M)$:

Command # i of M	relation in $D(M)$	relation in $E(M)$
Add(1); j	$q_i = au_{i,1}p_i,$ $u_{i,2}p_i = q_j$	$u_{i,1} = bu_{i,2}$
Add(2); j	$q_i = p_iu_{i,1}\bar{a}$ $p_iu_{i,2} = q_j$	$u_{i,1} = u_{i,2}b$
$\epsilon_1 > 0 \rightarrow$ Sub(1); j	$q_i = u_{i,1}p_i$ $au_{i,2}p_i = q_j$	$bu_{i,1} = u_{i,2}$
$\epsilon_2 > 0 \rightarrow$ Sub(2); j	$q_i = p_iu_{i,1}$ $p_iu_{i,2}\bar{b} = q_j$	$u_{i,1}\bar{a} = u_{i,2}$
$\epsilon_1 = 0 \rightarrow j$	$q_i = u_{i,1}p_i$ $u_{1,2}p_i = q_j$	$Au_{i,1} = Au_{1,2}$
$\epsilon_2 = 0 \rightarrow j$	$q_i = p_iu_{i,1}$ $p_iu_{i,2} = q_j$	$u_{i,1}B = u_{i,2}B$

We also add to $D(M)$ (resp. $E(M)$) all relations of the form $w = 0$ where w is any word in generators of $D(M)$ (resp. $E(M)$) which is not a subword of any word participating in the Minsky relations, or the words Aq_1B and Aq_0B. For example, $a\bar{a} = aq_i = q_i\bar{a} = 0$ in $D(M)$, $Ab = AB = 0$ in $E(M)$. Thus, in particular, $U(M)$ is indeed the semigroup with zero product, and both semigroups $D(M)$ and $E(M)$ are 4-nilpotent and finite.

The proof that the amalgamated product R of $D(M)$ and $E(M)$ simulates M proceeds as follow. First we prove that if two configurations $(i; m, n)$ and $(i'; m', n')$ of M are equivalent, then the corresponding words $W(i; m, n)$ and $W(i'; m', n')$ are equal in R. Then we notice that the presentation of R is confluent [33]. Hence if two words W, W' are equal in R, then there exist two sequences of applications of relations of R from left to right, one starting at W, another starting at W' which end at the same word W''. This implies that if $W(i; m, n) = W(i'; m', n')$ in R, then the configurations $(i; m, n)$ and $(i'; m', n')$ of the Minsky machine M are equivalent.

7.3 Complicated Residually Finite Semigroups

paginationIt is well known that finitely presented residually finite algebras (of finite signature) are much simpler algorithmically than arbitrary finitely presented algebras. For example, the word problem in every such algebra is decidable (see McKinsey's algorithm in [25]). Moreover the most "common" residually finite algebras, say, the linear groups over fields, are algorithmically "tame": the word problem in any linear group is decidable in polynomial time and even log-space [21]. Surprisingly till [19] not much was known about possible complexity of arbitrary finitely presented residually finite algebras, even in the cases of semigroups and groups.

Recall that the McKinsey's algorithm for solving the word problem in a finitely presented algebra A consists of two competing parts running in parallel. The first part enumerates all finite homomorphic factors of A and checks if the images of two elements a, b are different in one of these factors. The second part enumerates all consequences of the defining relations of A. If $a \neq b$ in A, then the first part will eventually "win", if $a = b$, then the second part "wins". In either case we will eventually know whether or not $a = b$ in A.

Thus there are three ways to estimate the complexity of a residually finite algebra:

(1) The computational complexity of the word problem.
(2) The *depth function* $\rho_A(n)$ which is the smallest function $\mathbb{N} \to \mathbb{N}$ such that given two words u, v [2] of size $\leq n$ in generators of A, such that $u \neq v$ in A, there exists a homomorphism from A onto a finite algebra of size at most $\rho_A(n)$ which separates u and v.
(3) The *Dehn function* $d_A(n)$ which is the smallest function $\mathbb{N} \to \mathbb{N}$ such that, given two words u, v of size $\leq n$ in generators of A, such that $u = v$ in A one needs at most $d_A(n)$ applications of relations of A to deduce the equality $u = v$.

Note that the Dehn function and the depth function are two of the most important asymptotic characterics of an algebra. Both functions are recursive for every finitely presented residually finite algebra (of finite signature). Gersten [9,10] asked for a bound of the Dehn function of a finitely presented linear group. The answer is still not known. The depth function of groups was first studied by Bou-Rabee [1]. It is known (and easy) that for linear groups, it is at most polynomial. In fact till [19], no finitely presented group or semigroup with Dehn function or depth function greater than an exponent was known.

The next result from [19] shows that there are finitely presented residually finite semigroups and groups with arbitrary high complexity in each of the three ways to measure the complexity, and also semigroups and groups with word problem in P but arbitrary large (recursive) Dehn and depth functions.

Theorem 18. *Let* $f \colon \mathbb{N} \to \mathbb{N}$ *be any recursive function. Then*

(i) there is a residually finite finitely presented group that is solvable of class 3 with Dehn function d_G *such that* $d_G \succcurlyeq f$. *In addition, one can make the group* G *such that the time complexity of the word problem in* G *is at least as large as any given recursive function or one can make* G *such that the word problem is in polynomial time.*

(ii) there is a residually finite finitely presented solvable of class 3 group G *with depth function greater than* f. *In addition, one can make the group* G *such that the word problem in* G *is at least as hard as the membership problem in a*

---

[2] By a "word" I understand any term involving operations of A. It is an ordinary word in the case of semigroups, a word possibly containing inverses of generators in the case of groups, a non-commutative polynomial in the case of rings, etc. The size of a word is the number of symbols needed to write it.

given recursive set of natural numbers $\mathbb{Z}$ or one can make G such that the word problem is in polynomial time.

Here for two functions $f, g \colon \mathbb{N} \to \mathbb{N}$ we write $f \succcurlyeq g$ if for some constants $c_1, c_2, c_3 \geq 0$, we have $f(n) \geq c_1 g(c_2 n) - c_3$ for all n.

To illustrate the proof of Theorem 18, we will present a construction of complicated residually finite semigroups. In the case of groups, the construction is based on a similar idea but is technically much more complicated.

We start with a deterministic Turing machine TM that recognizes a recursive set Z of natural numbers. By [6], we can assume that TM is universally halting. This means that TM has only finite number of computations starting from any given configuration. We modify TM to obtain a Sym-universally halting machine TM'. That means that the (non-deterministic) Turing machine $\mathrm{Sym}(TM')$ is universally halting. The construction from [24] (used to prove Theorem 3 above) produces then a Sym-universally halting 3-glass Minsky machine M_3 that recognizes the set Z. One can easily modify the construction of the semigroup $\overrightarrow{S_2}$ above to produce a finitely presented semigroup $\overrightarrow{S_3}$ that simulates the 3-glass Minsky machine M_3. As above every word in the generators of $\overrightarrow{S_3}$ which is non-zero in $\overrightarrow{S_3}$ is a subword of a word $W_3(i; m, n, k)$ corresponding to a configuration $(i; m, n, k)$ of M_3 modulo the glass permuting relations. The semigroup $\overrightarrow{S_3}$ is residually finite. Indeed, take any two words u, v in the generators of $\overrightarrow{S_3}$, such that $u \neq v$ in $\overrightarrow{S_3}$. We can assume that $u \neq 0$ in $\overrightarrow{S_3}$. Then since M_3 is Sym-universally halting, there are only finitely many elements of $\overrightarrow{S_3}$ that divide u. It is not difficult to prove that if v divides u, then $v \neq 0$ in $\overrightarrow{S_3}$ and u does not divide v. Thus in that case we can interchange u and v. So we can assume that v does not divide u in $\overrightarrow{S_3}$. As above take the ideal J of all elements in $\overrightarrow{S_3}$ that do not divide u. Then the Rees quotient $\overrightarrow{S_3}/J$ is finite and $u \neq v$ in the quotient which proves residual finiteness.

Now the word problem in $\overrightarrow{S_3}$ polynomially reduces to the configuration equivalence problem for M_3. It is at least as hard as the membership problem for Z, and in fact by carefully choosing TM', we can make that problem polynomially equivalent to the membership problem for Z. Therefore we can make the complexity of the word problem in $\overrightarrow{S_3}$ as hard or as easy (i.e., at most polynomial time) as we want. The Dehn function of $\overrightarrow{S_3}$ is at least as large as the time function of TM' (in fact much larger). Even in the case when Z is in P, we can construct a Turing machine recognizing Z and with arbitrary large (recursive) time function. Say, after the machine wants to stop, we make it compute something really complicated, and only then stop. This way we construct a finitely presented residually finite semigroup with polynomial time complexity of the word problem and arbitrary high recursive Dehn function.

To make the depth function high, we add two more glasses to the Minsky machine M_3 and modify the commands to obtain a 5-glass non-deterministic Minsky machine M_5. We modify the commands of M_3 as follows. First to every command of M_3, we add the instruction to add a coin to glass #4 provided glass

#5 is empty. Also assuming M_3 had $N+1$ commands, for every $i = 1, ..., N$ we add two commands #i:

$$i; (\text{Add}(4), \text{Add}(5)), i. \tag{1}$$

and

$$i; (\epsilon_4 = 0, \epsilon_5 = 0) \to 0 \tag{2}$$

That is executing command i the machine can add as many coins (equal amounts) to glasses #4, #5 and if both these glasses are empty, then the machine can stop. It is not difficult to prove, as above, that the semigroup $\overrightarrow{S_5}$ simulating M_5 is residually finite and its word problem is polynomially equivalent to the membership problem for Z. Let a_4 and a_5 be the generators of $\overrightarrow{S_5}$ simulating coins in glasses 4 and 5. In order to ensure that the depth function of $\overrightarrow{S_5}$ is high we take a word $W_5 = W_5(1; z, 0, 0, 0, 0)$ of length n, corresponding to the input configuration such that $z \notin Z$ and there exists a very long computation, say of length $L \gg n$ of M_5 starting at W_5 and not using commands (1) (we can always assume modify the Turing machine TM' to make this happen). Note that since $z \notin Z$, $W_5 \neq 0$ in $\overrightarrow{S_5}$. Suppose that there exists a homomorphism from $\overrightarrow{S_5}$ to a finite semigroup E of order l, and, say, with $l! < L$, which separates W_5 from 0. Then for every element x in E we will have $x^m = x^{2m}$ for $m = l!$. Consider a very long computation of M_5 starting with the configuration $(1; z, 0, 0, 0, 0)$. In that computation, we must get a configuration δ where the glass #4 contains m coins and glass #5 is empty. The corresponding word $W_5(\delta)$ will contain the subword $a_4^m A_4 A_5$. Applying now relations corresponding to the command (1), we can change this subword (without touching the rest of the word) to $a_4^{2m} A_4 a_5^m A_5 = a_4^m A_4 a_5^m A_5$ in E. Applying the relations corresponding to (1) again (this time from right to left), we obtain a word that is equal to W_5 in E and has subword $A_3 A_4 A_5$ (it corresponds to a configuration with empty glasses ##4, 5). Applying now the relations corresponding to (2), and then the relation $q_0 = 0$, we deduce that $W_5 = 0$ in E, a contradiction. This contradiction shows that the factorial of the order $|E|$ cannot be smaller than L. Thus the depth function of $\overrightarrow{S_5}$ can be as large as we want.

Acknowledgement. I am grateful to the anonymous referees for numerous helpful comments.

References

1. Bou-Rabee, K.: Quantifying residual finiteness. J. Algebra **323**, 729–737 (2010)
2. Bridson, M.R., Wilton, H.: The isomorphism problem for profinite completions of finitely presented, residually finite groups. (English Summary) Groups Geom. Dyn. **8**(3), 733–745 (2014)

3. Bridson, M.R., Wilton, H.: The triviality problem for profinite completions. arXiv:1401.2273
4. Clifford, A.H., Preston, G.B.: The Algebraic Theory of Semigroups, Math. Surveys 7, Vol. 1, 2, Amer. Math. Soc, Providence, RI (1961) (1967)
5. Conway, J.H.: Unpredictable iterations. In: Proceedings of the Number Theory Conference (Univ. Colorado, Boulder, Colo., 1972), pp. 49–52. Univ. Colorado, Boulder, Colo. (1972)
6. Davis, M.: A note on universal Turing machines. Automata studies. Annals of mathematics studies, no. 34, pp. 167–175. Princeton University Press, Princeton, N. J. (1956)
7. Davis, M., Putnam, H., Robinson, J.: The decision problem for exponential diophantine equations. Ann. Math. **74**(2), 425–436 (1961)
8. Evans, T.: Some connections between residual finiteness, finite embeddability and the word problem. J. London Math. Soc. **1**(2), 399–403 (1969)
9. Gersten, S.M.: Isoperimetric and isodiametric functions of finite presentations. Geometric group theory, Vol. 1 (Sussex, 1991), 79–96, London Math. Soc. Lecture Note Ser., 181, Cambridge Univ. Press, Cambridge (1993)
10. Gersten, S.M., Riley, T.R.: Some duality conjectures for finite graphs and their group theoretic consequences. Proc. Edin. Math. Soc. **48**(2), 389–421 (2005)
11. Gurevich, JuSh: The problem of equality of words for certain classes of semigroups. Algebra i Logika **5**(5), 25–35 (1966)
12. Hall, T.E., Kublanovskii, S., Margolis, S., Sapir, M., Trotter, P.G.: Algorithmic problems for finite groups and finite 0-simple semigroups. J. Pure Appl. Algebra **119**(1), 75–96 (1997)
13. Hall, T.E., Putcha, M.S.: The potential *J*-relation and amalgamation bases for finite semigroups. Proc. AMS **3**, 361–364 (1985)
14. Jackson, M.: The embeddability of ring and semigroup amalgams is undecidable. J. Austral. Math. Soc. Ser. A **69**(2), 272–286 (2000)
15. Karrass, A., Pietrowski, A., Solitar, D.: Finite and infinite cyclic extensions of free groups. J. Austr. Math. Soc. **16**, 458–466 (1973)
16. Kharlampovich, O.: The universal theory of the class of finite nilpotent groups is undecidable. Mat. Zametki **33**(4), 499–516 (1983)
17. Kharlampovich, O.: The word problem for groups and Lie algebras, Doctor's Thesis (Russian), Moscow Steklov Mathematical Institute (1990)
18. Kharlampovich, O., Sapir, M.: Algorithmic problem in varieties. Int. J. Algebra Comput. **5**(4–5), 379–602 (1995)
19. Kharlampovich, O., Myasnikov, A., Sapir, M.: Residually finite finitely presented solvable groups. arXiv:1204.6506
20. Kublanovsky, S., Sapir, M.: Potential divisibility in finite semigroups is undecidable. Internat. J. Algebra Comput. **8**(6), 671–679 (1998)
21. Lipton, R.J., Zalcstein, Y.: Word problems solvable in logspace. J. Assoc. Comput. Mach. **24**, 522–526 (1977)
22. Lyapin, E.S.: Semigroups. Gos. Izd. Fiz.-Mat. Lit, Moscow (1960)
23. Lyndon, R.C., Schupp, P.E.: Combinatorial Group Theory. Springer-Verlag, Berlin (1977)
24. Malcev, A.I.: Algorithms and Recursive Functions. Nauka, Moscow (1965)
25. Malcev, A.I.: On homomorphisms onto finite groups. Uchen. Zap. Ivanovskogo Gos. Ped. Inst. **18**, 49–60 (1958). English translation. In: Amer. Math. Soc. Transl. Ser. **2**(119), 67–79 (1983)
26. Minsky, M.L.: Recursive unsolvability of post's problem of "Tag" and other topics in theory of turing machines. Annals Math. Second Ser. **74**(3), 437–455 (1961)

27. Sapir, M.: Residually finite semigroups, Diploma Thesis, Ural State University, Russian (1978)
28. Sapir, M.: Problems of Burnside type and the finite basis property in varieties of semigroups. Izv. Akad. Nauk. SSSR. Ser. Mat. **51**(2), 319–340 (1987). transl. in Math USSR-Izv, 30(2):295–314: (1988)
29. Sapir, M.: Algorithmic problems in varieties of semigroups. Algebra i Logika **27**(4), 440–463 (1988)
30. Sapir, M.: Weak word problem for finite semigroups. Monoids and semigroups with applications (Berkeley, CA, : 206–219. World Sci. Publ, River Edge, NJ (1989) (1991)
31. Sapir, M.: The restricted Burnside problem for varieties of semigroups. Izv. Akad. Nauk SSSR Ser. Mat. **55**(3), 670–679 (1991). translation in Math. USSR-Izv. **38**(3), 659–667 (1992)
32. Sapir, M.: Algorithmic problems for amalgams of finite semigroups. J. Algebra **229**(2), 514–531 (2000)
33. Sapir, M.: Combinatorial algebra: syntax and semantics, Springer Monographs in Mathematics (2014)
34. Slobodskoi, A.: Undecidability of the universal theory of finite groups. Algebra Logic **20**(2), 207–230 (1981)
35. Zel'manov, E.: The solution of the restricted Burnside problem for groups of odd exponent. Izv. Akad. Nauk. SSSR. Ser. Mat. **54**(1), 42–59 (1990). transl. in Math. USSR-Izv. 36 (1991), no.1, 41–60
36. Zel'manov, E.: The solution of the restricted Burnside problem for 2-groups. Mat. Sb. **182**(4), 568–592 (1991)

On Failure of 0-1 Laws

Saharon Shelah[1,2]([⊠])

[1] Einstein Institute of Mathematics, Edmond J. Safra Campus,
Givat Ram, The Hebrew University of Jerusalem,
91904 Jerusalem, Israel
[2] Department of Mathematics, Hill Center - Busch Campus Rutgers,
The State University of New Jersey,
110 Frelinghuysen Road, Piscataway, NJ 08854-8019, USA
shelah@math.huji.ac.i
http://shelah.logic.at

Dedicated to Yuri Gurevich on the occasion of his 75th birthday.

Abstract. Let $\alpha \in (0,1)_{\mathbb{R}}$ be irrational and $G_n = G_{n,1/n^\alpha}$ be the random graph with edge probability $1/n^\alpha$; we know that it satisfies the 0-1 law for first order logic. We deal with the failure of the 0-1 law for stronger logics: $\mathbb{L}_{\infty,\mathbf{k}}$, $\mathbf{k}$ a large enough natural number and the inductive logic.

Keywords: Finite model theory · Zero-one laws · Random graphs · Inductive logic · Infinitary logic on finite structures

Let $G_{n,p}$ be the random graph with set of nodes $[n] = \{1, \ldots, n\}$, each edge of probability $p \in [0,1]_{\mathbb{R}}$, the edges being drawn independently, (see $⊞_1$ below). On 0-1 laws (and random graphs) see the book of Spencer [6] or Alon-Spencer [1], in particular on the behaviour of the random graph $G_{n,1/n^\alpha}$ for $\alpha \in (0,1)_{\mathbb{R}}$ irrational. On finite model theory see Flum-Ebbinghaus [2], e.g. on the logic $\mathbb{L}_{\infty,\mathbf{k}}$ and on inductive logic, also called LFP logic (i.e. least fix point logic). A characteristic example of what can be expressed in this logic is "in the graph G there is a path from the node x to the node y", this is closed to what we shall use. We know that $G_{n,p}$ (i.e. the case the probability p is constant), satisfies the 0-1 law for first order logic (proved independently by Fagin [3] and Glebskii-et-al [4]). This holds also for many stronger logics like $\mathbb{L}_{\infty,\mathbf{k}}$ and the inductive logic. If $\alpha \in (0,1)_{\mathbb{R}}$ is irrational, the 0-1 law holds for $G_{n,(1/n^\alpha)}$ and first order logic.

The question we address is whether this holds also for stronger logics as above. Though our real aim is to address the problem for the case of graphs, the proof seems more transparent when we have two random graph relations (with appropriate probabilities; we make them directed graphs just for simplicity). So

This work was partially supported by European Research Council grant 338821. Publication 1061 on Shelah's list. The author thanks Alice Leonhardt for the beautiful typing.

L.D. Beklemishev et al. (Eds.): Gurevich Festschrift II 2015, LNCS 9300, pp. 293–296, 2015.
DOI: 10.1007/978-3-319-23534-9_18

we shall deal with two cases A and B. In Case A, the usual graph, we have to show that there are (just first order) formulas $\varphi_\ell(x,y)$ for $\ell = 1,2$ with some special properties, (actually we have also $\varphi_0(x,y)$). For Case B, those formulas are $R_\ell(x,y), \ell = 1,2$, the two directed graph relations. Note that (for Case B), the satisfaction of the cases of the R_ℓ are decided directly by the drawing and so are independent, whereas for Case A there are (small) dependencies for different pairs, so the probability estimates are more complicated.

Recall

$\boxplus_1$ a 0-1 context consists of:

(a) a vocabulary τ, here just the one of graphs or double directed graphs,
(b) for each n, K_n is a set of τ-models with set of elements $=$ nods $[n]$, in our case graphs or double directed graphs,
(c) a distribution μ_n on K_n, i.e. $\mu_n : K \to [0,1]_\mathbb{R}$ satisfying $\Sigma\{\mu_n(G) : G \in K_n\} = 1$
(d) the random structure is called $G_n = G_{\mu_n}$ and we tend to speak on G_{μ_n} or G_n rather than on the context.

Note that in this work "for every random enough G_n ..." is a central notion, where:

$\boxplus_2$ for a given 0-1 context, let "for every random enough G_n we have $G_n \models \psi$, i.e. G satisfies ψ" <u>means</u> that the sequence $\langle \mathrm{Prob}(G_n \models \psi) : n \in \mathbb{N}\rangle$ converge to 1; of course, $\mathrm{Prob}(G_n \models \psi) = \Sigma\{\mu_n(G) : G \in K_n$ and $G \models \psi\}$.

But

$\boxplus_3$ $G_{n,p}$ is the case $K_n = $ graph on $[n]$ and we draw the edges independently,

(a) with probability p when p is constant, e.g. $\frac{1}{2}$, and
(b) with probability $p(n)$ or probability p_n when p is a function from $\mathbb{N}$ to $[0,1]_\mathbb{R}$.

In the constant p case, the 0-1 law is strong: it is done by proving elimination of quantifiers and it works also for stronger logics: $\mathbb{L}_{\infty,\mathbf{k}}$ and so also for inductive logic $\mathbb{L}_{\mathrm{ind}}$. Another worthwhile case is:

$\boxplus_4$ $G_{n,1/n^\alpha}$ where $\alpha \in (0,1)_\mathbb{R}$; so $p_n = 1/n^\alpha$.

Again the edges are drawn independently but the probability depends on n.

  · The 0-1 law holds if α is irrational, but we have elimination of quantifiers only up to (Boolean combination of) existential formulas. Do we have 0-1 law also for those stronger logics? We shall <u>show that not</u> by proving that for some so called scheme $\bar{\varphi}$ of interpretation, for any random enough G_n, $\bar{\varphi}$ interpret an initial segment of number theory, say up to $m(G_n)$ where $m(G_n)$ is not too small; e.g. at least $\log_2(\log_2(n))$.

For the probabilistic argument we use estimates; they are as in the first order case (see [1], so we do not repeat them).

For the full version see the author website or the mathematical arXive. The statements for which we need more estimates will probably be further delayed; those are the ones proving that:

⊞₅ • using n^ε instead of $\log_2(\log_2(n))$ in the proof for Case 1 so the value of "$\mathrm{Prob}(G_{n,1/n^\alpha}) = \psi$" may change more quickly,

• we can define "n even" (i.e. $\mathrm{Lim}(\mathrm{Prob}(G_{n,1/n^\alpha} \models \psi$ iff n is even) exists and is one; this is done by defining a linear order on $G_{n,\bar\alpha}$.

• we may formalize the quantification on paths, so getting a weak logic failing the 0-1 law, but its naturality is not so clear.

A somewhat related problem asks whether for some logic the 0-1 law holds for $G_{n,p}$ (for constant $p \in (0,1)_{\mathbb{R}}$, e.g. $p = \frac{1}{2}$) but does not have the elimination of quantifier, see [5].

We now try to informally describe the proof, naturally concentrating on case B.

Fix reals $\alpha_1 < \alpha_2$ from $(0,\frac{1}{4})_{\mathbb{R}}$, so $\bar\alpha = (\alpha_1, \alpha_2)$ letting $\alpha(\ell) = \alpha_\ell$;

⊞₆ let the random digraph $G_{n,\bar\alpha} = ([n], R_1, R_2) = ([n], R_1^{G_{n,\bar\alpha}}, R_2^{G_{n,\bar\alpha}})$ with R_1, R_2 irreflexive relations drawn as follows:

(a) for each $a \neq b$, we draw a truth value for $R_2(a,b)$ with probability $\frac{1}{n^{1-\alpha_2}}$ for yes

(b) for each $a \neq b$, we draw a truth value for $R_1(a,b)$ with probability $\frac{1}{n^{1+\alpha_1}}$ for yes

(c) those drawings are independent.

Now for random enough digraph $G = G_n = G_{n,\bar\alpha} = ([n], R_1, R_2)$ and node $a \in G$ we try to define the set $S_k = S_{G,a,k}$ of nodes of G not from $\cup\{S_m : m < k\}$ by induction on k as follows:

For $k = 0$ let $S_k = \{a\}$. Assume $S_0, \ldots, S_k$ has been chosen, and we shall choose S_{k+1}.

⊞₇ For $\iota = 1,2$ we ask: is there an R_ι-edge (a,b) with $a \in S_k$ and b not from $\cup\{S_m : m \leq k\}$?

If the answer is no for both $\iota = 1,2$ we stop and let $\mathrm{height}(a,G) = k$. If the answer is yes for $\iota = 1$, we let S_{k+1} be the set of b such that for some a the pair (a,b) is as above for $\iota = 1.$, If the answer is no for $\iota = 1$ but yes for $\iota = 2$ we define S_{k+1} similarly using $\iota = 2$.

Let the height of G be $\max\{\mathrm{height}(a,G) : a \in G\}$. Now we can prove that for every random enough G_n, for $a \in G_n$ or easier- for most $a \in G_n$, for not too large k we have:

$\boxplus_8$ $S_{G_n,a,k}$ is on the one hand not empty and on the other hand with $\leq n^{2\alpha_2}$ members.

This is proved by drawing the edges not all at once but in k stages. In stage $m \leq k$ we already can compute $S_{G_n,a,0}, \ldots S_{G_n,a,m}$ and we have already drawn all the R_1-edges and R_2-edges having at least one node in $S_{G_n,a,0} \cup \cdots \cup S_{G_n,a,m-1}$; that is for every such pair (a,b) we draw the truth values of $R_1(a,b), R_2(a,b)$. So arriving to m we can draw the edges having a nod in S_m and not dealt with earlier, and hence can compute S_{m+1}.

The point is that in the question $\boxplus_7$ above, if the answer is yes for $\iota = 1$ then the number of nodes in S_{m+1} will be small, essentially smaller than in S_m. Further, if the answer for $\iota = 1$ the answer is no but for $\iota = 2$ the answer is yes then necessarily S_m is smaller than say $n^{(\alpha_1+\alpha_2)/2}$ but it is known that the R_2-valency of any nod of G_n is near n^{α_2}. So the desired inequality holds.

By a similar argument, if we stop at k then in $S_0 \cup \cdots \cup S_k$ there are many nodes- e.g. at least near n^{α_2} by a crud argument. As each S_m is not too large necessarily the height of G_n is large.

The next step is to express in our logic the relation $\{(a_1, b_1, a_2, b_2) :$ for some k_1, k_2 we have $b_1 \in S_{G_n,a_1,k_1}, b_2 \in S_{G_n,a_2,k_2}, k_1 \leq k_2\}$.

By this we can interpret a linear order with height(G_n) members. Again using the relevant logic this suffice to interpret number theory up to this height. Working more we can define a linear order with n elements, so can essentially find a formula "saying" n is even (or odd).

For random graphs we have to work harder: instead of having two relations we have two formulas; one of the complications is that their satisfaction for the relevant pairs are not fully independent.

References

1. Alon, N., Spencer, J.H.: The Probabilistic Method. Wiley-Interscience Series in Discrete Mathematics and Optimization, 3rd edn. Wiley, Hoboken (2008). With an appendix on the life and work of Paul Erdős
2. Ebbinghaus, H.-D., Flum, J.: Finite Model Theory. SMM, enlarged edn. Springer, Berlin (2006)
3. Fagin, R.: Probabilities in finite models. J. Symb. Logic **45**, 129–141 (1976)
4. Glebskii, Y.V., Kogan, D.I., Liagonkii, M.I., Talanov, V.A.: Range and degree of reliability of formulas in restricted predicate calculus. Kibernetica **5**, 17–27 (1969). Translation of Cybernetics, vol. 5, pp. 142–154
5. Shelah, S.: Random graphs: stronger logic but with the 0–1 law. In preparation
6. Spencer, J.: The Strange Logic of Random Graphs. Algorithms and Combinatorics, vol. 22. Springer, Berlin (2001)

Composition Over the Natural Number Ordering with an Extra Binary Relation

Wolfgang Thomas$^{(\boxtimes)}$

RWTH Aachen University, Aachen, Germany
thomas@informatik.rwth-aachen.de

Abstract. The composition method was developed in the 1970's and 1980's by Shelah and Gurevich as a powerful tool in the study of monadic second-order theories of labelled orderings and trees. In this paper, we use a variant of the technique for first-order theories of structures $(\mathbb{N}, <, R)$ where R is binary. For the case that R is of "finite valency" (where each element has only finitely many neighbors in the symmetric closure of R), we show results on (non-) definability, on decidability, and on the recursion theoretic complexity of such theories.

1 Introduction

The composition method combines two rather diverse features. It opens a way to study theories of labelled orderings (and labelled trees) by considering these structures as sums of substructures, such that from properties of the substrutures and the way they are concatenated one derives properties of the full structure. This is a natural, simple, and intuitively appealing view. On the other hand, the technical details of this attractive idea are somewhat involved, and the landmark papers of Shelah and Gurevich in the 1970's and 1980's ([Sh75, Gu79, Gu82, Gu85, GS79, GS83, GS85]) that developed the theory are demanding. Thus – at least in theoretical computer science – not many researchers invested the effort to go deeper into the subject, although it is a key to many decidability results in monadic second-order logic (MSO-logic), complementing and extending results that had earlier been shown by a reduction of MSO-logic to finite automata (Büchi [Bü62], Rabin [Ra69]).

The core idea is best explained for infinite labelled linear orderings, for example structures $\mathcal{A} = (A, <, P)$ with infinite A and unary predicate P. One considers a finite fragment of the MSO-theory of $\mathcal{A}$, in which only sentences of some fixed quantifier-depth m are taken into account, called "m-theory" of $\mathcal{A}$ (sometimes the quantifier alternation rank is used instead), aiming at the decision whether a sentence up to quantifier-depth m belongs to this m-theory. One composes this m-theory from the m-theories of intervals. Invoking a combinatorial argument (e.g., Ramsey's Theorem [Ra29]) it may turn out that such a decomposition can be guaranteed which is "homogeneous": For example, for a structure $(\mathbb{N}, <, P)$, this is a decomposition into finite segments where – excepting the first – all have the same m-theory. This can be exploited to infer (non-) definability and decidability results concerning MSO-logic over the given structure.

© Springer International Publishing Switzerland 2015
L.D. Beklemishev et al. (Eds.): Gurevich Festschrift II 2015, LNCS 9300, pp. 297–306, 2015.
DOI: 10.1007/978-3-319-23534-9_19

In the present paper, it is shown how to apply the composition method over the ordering $(\mathbb{N}, <)$ of the natural numbers where the labelling (given by a predicate $P \subseteq \mathbb{N}$) is replaced by a binary relation R. We consider relations that are of "finite valency", i.e., where for each a there are only finitely many b such that $R(a, b)$ or $R(b, a)$. Also we restrict the logical framework to first-order logic FO. As it turns out, one can then again decompose, for any given quantifier-depth m, the structure $(\mathbb{N}, <, R)$ into a sequence of appropriately defined "segments" where (excepting the first) all segments have the same m-theory. As a consequence, we obtain results on first-order definability in such structures $(\mathbb{N}, <, R)$ – in particular, that addition and multiplication are not FO-definable – and on the recursion theoretic complexity of the FO-theory of such structures. Also examples R are exhibited where the first-order theory of $(\mathbb{N}, <, R)$ is decidable, namely graphs of recursive functions $f : \mathbb{N} \to \mathbb{N}$ where the distance function $f(n+1) - f(n)$ is strictly increasing.[1]

The exposition will not be very formal; for details we refer to [Th80].

2 $(\mathbb{N}, <, P)$ with Monadic P

Let us first recall the composition method for structures $(\mathbb{N}, <, P)$ with monadic P. We identify this labelled ordering with an infinite 0-1-word α such that $\alpha(i) = 1$ iff $i \in P$. Finite segments of the structure are then finite words over $\{0, 1\}$ (denoted by $u, v, w, \ldots$). We restrict here to first-order logic FO although the results of the present section can as well be obtained for monadic second-order logic MSO.

The quantifier-depth of a formula φ is the depth of nesting of quantifiers in φ. Two labelled orderings u and v are called m-equivalent (written $u \equiv_m v$) if for all FO-sentences φ of quantifier-depth m we have $u \models \varphi$ iff $v \models \varphi$. It is well-known that a convenient method to verify $\equiv_m$-equivalence is the Ehrenfeucht-Fraïssé game. We extend the relation also to infinite words. Then, for example, $1 \equiv_1 1111\ldots$ but $1 \not\equiv_2 1111\ldots$; in the latter case, the sentence $\forall x \exists y\ x < y$ shows the $\equiv_2$-inequivalence.

Let us list some basic facts (see. e.g., [EF95]).

Lemma 1.

1. $\equiv_m$ is an equivalence relation of finite index. (The equivalence classes are called m-types.)

---

[1] When the present author took his first steps in the study of the composition method, he met Yuri Gurevich and gained a lot by discussions with him, also by his kind encouragement. The results mentioned above were then included in the author's habilitation thesis [Th80], which however was not published due to the author's move to computer science. Now, 35 years later, at Yuri's 75th birthday, it seems fitting to come back to this outgrowth of the author's first contact with Yuri and to explain these results.

2. An m-type τ is definable by a sentence φ_τ of quantifier-depth m.
3. Each sentence of quantifier-depth m is equivalent to a disjunction of sentences φ_τ. (If φ_τ implies φ, we say that τ induces φ.)

"Composition" refers to the fact that the m-types of two words u, v determine the m-type of their concatenation uv.

Lemma 2.

1. From the m-types of u and v one can compute the m-type of uv, and from the m-types of a segment u and an infinite word α one can compute the m-type of $u\alpha$.
2. Given a word $\alpha = v_1 v_2 v_3 \ldots$ where all v_i have the same m-type τ, the m-type ϱ of α is computable from τ.

Given the types σ and τ of u, v (or α), respectively, we write $\sigma + \tau$ for the m-type of uv (or $u\alpha$), similarly for a word $\alpha = v_1 v_2 v_3 \ldots$ where all v_i have m-type τ, we write $\sum_\omega \tau$ for the m-type of α.

Over a model $\alpha = (\mathbb{N}, <, P)$ the m-types induce a finite coloring on pairs (i, j) of natural numbers; we define the color of (i, j) (for $i < j$) to be the m-type of the substructure over the interval $[i, j)$. Invoking Ramsey's Theorem (for infinite sets), one obtains an infinite "homogeneous set" $H = \{h_0 < h_1 < h_2 \ldots\}$ such that all the colors of intervals $[h_k, h_{k+1})$ and even of all intervals $[h_k, h_\ell)$ with $\ell < k$ coincide.

Thus, taking m-types as colors, for arbitrary α a decomposition of α in the form $uv_1 v_2 v_3 \ldots$ exists such that all v_i share the same m-type τ, and – writing σ for the m-type of u – the m-type of α is obtained as $\sigma + \sum_\omega \tau$. In this sense, truth of a sentence φ of quantifier-depth m in a model α can be reduced to the question whether α is decomposable in this way such that $\sigma + \sum_\omega \tau$ induces φ. So a sentence φ of quantifier-depth m is equivalent to a finite disjunction of MSO-statements $\chi_{\sigma,\tau}$ saying that there is a homogeneous set for the colors σ and τ, taken for all σ, τ such that $\sigma + \sum_\omega \tau$ induces φ. More precisely, $\chi_{\sigma,\tau}$ expresses that a homogeneous set $H = \{h_0 < h_1 < h_2 \ldots\}$ exists where the m-type of the interval $[0, h_0)$ is σ and for all $i < j$, the m-ype of the interval $[h_i, h_j)$ is τ.

Our next aim is to derive from this ultimately periodic structure of an infinite model α a *normal form* of FO-sentences. Here we follow [Th81]. Assume we have a coloring C of pairs (i, j) with $i < j$ by colors in a finite set Col, and that this coloring is *additive*, i.e. that the colors c_1 of (i, j) and c_2 of (j, k) determine the color d of (i, k). (So an example is given by associating with (i, j) the m-type of the interval $[i, j)$.) As mentioned, the statement that a decomposition according to Ramsey's Theorem with the two colors c, d exists is an MSO-formula (here in the signature with the binary relations $x < y$ and $C(x, y) = c$ for $c \in$ Col):

(∗) there is an infinite set $H = \{h_0 < h_1 < h_2 \ldots\}$ such that $(0, h_0)$ has color c and for all $i < j$, (h_i, h_j) has color d.

An analysis of Ramsey's Theorem (see [Th81]) shows that (∗) can be written as a *first-order* formula in the mentioned signature:

Theorem 1. *Over* $(\mathbb{N}, <, C)$ *with additive finite coloring C of the number pairs (i, j) with $i < j$, the condition $(*)$ can be expressed by a finite disjunction of first-order formulas of the form*

$$\forall x \exists y > x \; \psi(y) \quad \wedge \quad \exists x \forall y > x \; \psi'(y)$$

where $\psi(y), \psi'(y)$ are bounded in y, i.e. all quantifiers $\exists z, \forall z$ are relativized to $z \leq y$.

This result also holds for MSO-logic, with the same proof strategy. It is then a logical version of McNaughton's Theorem on the determinization of Büchi automata. In that context, one starts with a condition $(*)$ where the $\equiv_m$-relation is replaced by an automata theoretic equivalence between finite words. In the logical context, one obtains the remarkable consequence that over ω-words MSO has the same expressive power as weak MSO (where set quantification is restricted to finite sets). As stated, Theorem 1 amounts to a first-order version of McNaughton's Theorem.

3 $(\mathbb{N}, <, R)$ with Binary R of Finite Valency

Now we consider structures $(\mathbb{N}, <, R)$ with binary R. Then a problem arises in the attempt to compose the m-type of an interval $[i, k)$ from the m-types of subintervals $[i, j)$ and $[j, k)$: There may be elements $a \in [i, j), b \in [j, k)$ with $R(a, b)$; this connection is present in the full interval $[i, k)$ but not detectable from the (m-types of the) two subintervals. Moreover, there may be elements $a < i, b \geq k$ with $R(a, b)$; also in this case the "R-link" between a and b is not visible in the interval $[i, j)$ which lies in between.

On the other hand, one knows from first-order model theory, in particular from a result of Hanf [Ha65], that a formula of quantifier-depth m can only establish a connection between a and b via R if they are not too far in terms of their "R-distance" – more precisely, if b belongs to the 2^m-sphere around a (which contains all elements connected to a via a path of length 2^m of edges of the symmetric closure of R). This motivates to work with long enough segments in a decomposition (for given quantifier-depth m), where we try to ensure that R-connections between elements a, b can be established by formulas of quantifier-depth m only if a, b belong to the same or two successive segments of the decomposition. More concretely, one can try to reach a situation where we use a segment $[i, j)$ with $[h, i)$ in front and $[j, k)$ afterwards if the 2^m-spheres of elements in $[i, j)$ do not extend below h, say only down to $i^* \geq h$, and that the 2^m-spheres of elements in $[j, \infty)$ do not extend below i, say only down to $j^* \geq i$. It will turn out that for relations R of finite valency, this approach will work. It leads to decompositions where the participating segments overlap (namely, rather than $[i, j)$ we shall consider $[i^*, j)$). With these overlappings a composition result on appropriately defined m-types still holds. This will allow us to obtain results in good analogy to the above mentioned case of structures $(\mathbb{N}, <, P)$ with monadic P. Since we are dealing with overlapping intervals, we refer to intervals $[i, j]$ rather than $[i, j)$.

Recall that a binary relation $R \subseteq M \times M$ is of *finite valency* if for any $a \in M$ there are only finitely many $b \in M$ such that $R(a, b)$ or $R(b, a)$. Call $[a, b]$ an R-segment if $R(a, b)$ or $R(b, a)$.

We begin by noting a key property of relations of finite valency when the underlying ordering is $(\mathbb{N}, <)$: For any b there are only finitely many elements $d > b$ such that d is R-connected to some element $\leq b$.

So, given any $[a, b]$, two elements $c \leq a$ and $d \geq b$ can be found such that no R-connection exists between elements $< c$ and $> d$. We iterate this process of separation, following the idea of building "spheres" as mentioned above. Our eventual aim is to work with intervals $[a, b]$ such that R-connections from above b will only reach elements downward to some element $b^* > a$.

Definition 1. *Define for each b a sequence $b(0) \geq b(1) \geq \ldots$ as follows:*

- *$b(0) = b$*
- *$b(i+1) = $ maximal c which is below all R-segments $[k, \ell]$ intersecting $[b(i), \infty)$, if such c exists, otherwise 0*

We call the segment $[a, b]$ m-admissible if $b(2^m) > a$, and we write b^* for $b(2^m)$ if m is clear.

Let us denote by $\widetilde{b}$ the sequence $(b(0), \ldots, b(2^m))$. Invoking the remark above we see that for any k there exist admissible segments $[a, b]$ above k.

We now define generalized m-types of intervals $[a, b]$ in which an element b^* is designated as explained above. In order to allow inductive proofs, we define the m-types for expansions of intervals by additional elements $a_0, \ldots, a_{r-1} \in [a, b]$.

Definition 2. *Let $[a, b]$ be an m-admissible interval in $(\mathbb{N}, <, R)$, $a_0, \ldots, a_{r-1} \in [a, b]$.*

- *$T_R^m[a, b](a_0, \ldots, a_{r-1})$ is the m-type of the restriction of $(\mathbb{N}, <, R)$ to $[a, b]$.*
- *$D_R^m[a, b](a_0, \ldots, a_{r-1})$ is the m-type $T_R^m[a^*, b](\widetilde{a}, \widetilde{b}, a_0, \ldots, a_{r-1})$*

So $D_R^m[a, b]$ refers also to elements $< a$, namely those down to a^*; note that the parameter a occurs in $\widetilde{a}$ and thus is not lost.

Lemma 3 (Composition Lemma).

1. *Given m-admissible segments $[a, b]$ and $[b, c]$ of $(\mathbb{N}, <, R)$ with R of finite valency, $D_R^m[a, b]$ and $D_R^m[b, c]$ determine effectively the type $D_R^m[a, c]$.*
2. *Given a sequence $a_0, a_1, \ldots$ such that $[a_i, a_{i+1}]$ is m-admissible and such that $D_R^m[a_i, a_{i+1}] = \tau$ for some m-type τ, $D_R^m[a_0, \infty)$ is determined effectively from τ.*

Remark 1. In the inductive proof of the Composition Lemma, segment types $D_R^m[a, b](\overline{a})$ with parameters $\overline{a}$ have to be considered. It is then relevant whether an element a_i occurs below or above the element $b^* \in [a, b]$. This distinction is not needed in a situation where a composition of m-admissible segments

$[k_0, k_1], [k_1, k_2], [k_2, k_3]$ is treated such that no parameters occur in the middle segment $[k_1, k_2]$. For example, if $a_0 \in [k_0, k_1]$ and $b, c \in [k_2, k_3]$, then the m-type $D_R^m[k_0, k_3](a, b, c)$ is determined as a sum

$$D_R^m[k_0, k_1](a) + D_R^m[k_1, k_2] + D_R^m[k_2, k_3](b, c).$$

Now we proceed in analogy to the case of structures $(\mathbb{N}, <, P)$ with unary P. For any structure $(\mathbb{N}, <, R)$ with R of finite valency and for given m we can pick a sequence $\{n_0, n_1, n_2, \ldots\}$ forming an infinite set N such that each $[n_i, n_j]$ is m-admissible. Over N we obtain an additive coloring and can apply Ramsey's Theorem. We get a homogeneous subset H of N, $H = \{h_0 < h_1 < h_2 \ldots\}$, whence the m-type of $(\mathbb{N}, <, R)$ can be obtained as a sum $\sigma + \sum_\omega \tau$ where $\sigma = D_R^m[0, h_0]$ and $\tau = D_R^m[h_0, h_1](= D_R^m[h_i, h_j]$ for all $i < j)$. Applying further Theorem 1, we conclude:

Theorem 2 (Normal Form Theorem). *Over a structure $(\mathbb{N}, <, R)$ with R of finite valency, a sentence of quantifier-depth m can (effectively) be written as a disjunction of sentences*

$$\forall x \exists y > x \; \psi(y) \quad \wedge \quad \exists x \forall y > x \; \psi'(y)$$

where $\psi(y), \psi'(y)$ are bounded in y, with atomic formulas of the form $x < y$ and $D_R^m[x, y] = \tau$.

4   Applications

Theorem 3. *In a structure $(\mathbb{N}, <, R)$ with R of finite valency, neither addition nor multiplication is FO-definable.*

We derive this result from the following:

Proposition 1. *Let $f : \mathbb{N}^2 \to \mathbb{N}$ be FO-definable in $(\mathbb{N}, <, R)$ where R is of finite valency. Then one of the following two sets is finite:*

$$X_f := \{x \in \mathbb{N} \mid \lambda y f(x, y) \text{ is injective}\}, Y_f := \{y \in \mathbb{N} \mid \lambda x f(x, y) \text{ is injective}\}$$

It is clear that this proposition implies the theorem above since $X_+, Y_+, X_\cdot, Y_\cdot$ are all infinite. For example, X_+ contains all x such that the function $y \mapsto x + y$ is injective; hence $X_+ = \mathbb{N}$.

Proof. Assume f is FO-definable by $\varphi(x, y, z)$ of quantifier-depth m. Consider the coloring D_R^{m+1} and a corresponding homogeneous set $H = \{h_0 < h_1 < \ldots\}$.

Assume for contradiction that X_f, Y_f are both infinite. Then we can pick $a_0 \in X_f$, $b_0 \in Y_f$ in two different H-segments beyond h_0, say $a_0 \in [h_{i+1}, h_{i+2}]$ and $b_0 \in [h_{j+1}, h_{j+2}]$ such that, moreover, $a_0 < b_0$ and $[h_i, h_{i+4}] \cap [h_j, h_{j+4}] = \emptyset$. Since $D_R^{m+1}[h_{i+1}, h_{i+2}] = D_R^{m+1}[h_{i+2}, h_{h+3}]$, we can choose $a' \in [h_{i+2}, h_{i+3}]$ such that $D_R^m[h_{i+1}, h_{i+2}](a_0) = D_R^m[h_{i+2}, h_{i+3}](a')$, similarly $b' \in [h_{j+2}, h_{j+3}]$ such that $D_R^m[h_{j+1}, h_{j+2}](b_0) = D_R^m[h_{j+2}, h_{j+3}](b')$. Since the m-types $D_R^m[h_k, h_\ell]$ are for all $k < \ell$ equal to a fixed type τ (in particular, we have $\tau + \tau = \tau$), we have, by Remark 1,

$$D_R^m[h_i, h_{i+4}](a_0) = D_R^m[h_i, h_{i+4}](a'), \quad D_R^m[h_j, h_{j+4}](b_0) = D_R^m[h_j, h_{j+4}](b');$$

note that in all cases the segment with a designated element is preceded and succeeded by a segment of type τ.

Let $c_0 = f(a_0, b_0)$. If $c_0 \notin [h_i, h_{i+4}]$, say $c_0 > h_{i+4}$, then we apply Remark 1 and obtain

$$D_R^m[0, h_i] + D_R^m[h_i, h_{i+4}](a_0) + D_R^m[h_{i+4}, \infty)(b_0, c_0)$$
$$= D_R^m[0, h_i] + D_R^m[h_i, h_{i+4}](a') + D_R^m[h_{i+4}, \infty)(b_0, c_0)$$

which implies that the types $T_R^m[0, \infty)(a_0, b_0, c_0)$ and $T_R^m[0, \infty)(a', b_0, c_0)$ coincide. So, by the definition of f using a formula $\varphi(x, y, z)$ of quantifier-depth m, we see that $f(a_0, b_0) = f(a', b_0)$, a contradiction to $b_0 \in Y_f$. If $c_0 \in [h_i, h_{i+1}]$ we have that $c_0 \notin [h_j, h_{j+4}]$ and proceed analogously with the change from b_0 to b'.

In a next step we analyze Theorem 2 in terms of quantifier complexity.

Proposition 2. *Over $(\mathbb{N}, <, R)$ each FO-sentence φ is equivalent to a disjunction of sentences*

$$\forall x \exists y \forall z \; \varphi_i(x, y, z) \land \exists x \forall y \exists z \; \psi_i(x, y, z)$$

where the φ_i, ψ_i are bounded in z.

Proof. We analyze the atomic formulas $D_R^m[x, y] = \tau$ in the formula of Theorem 2, in order to reach a sentence in the signature with $<, R$ alone. We can define $D_R^m[x, y] = \tau$ relative to a bound z by a formula $D_R^m[x, y] \restriction z = \tau$ bounded in z. The D_R^m-type of $[x, y]$ may change when referring to submodels over domains $[0, z]$ for larger and larger z since more and more R-segments may become visible. However, due to the condition of finite valency, there is a z_0 above which no change occurs and where the type $\tau = D_R^m[x, y]$ is reached. This is equivalent to the requirement that τ occurs for infinitely many z. So we have

$$D_R^m[x, y] = \tau \; \Leftrightarrow \; \exists z \forall z' > z \, D_R^m[x, y] \restriction z' = \tau \; \Leftrightarrow \; \forall z \exists z' > z \, D_R^m[x, y] \restriction z' = \tau$$

Hence we can rewrite the formula of the Normal Form Theorem 2 in the signature with $<, R$, while increasing the alternation of unbounded quantifiers by 1. We arrive at a Boolean combination of Σ_3-sentences.

From this proposition we can conclude a statement on the recursion theoretic degree of the first-order theory of $(\mathbb{N}, <, R)$ when R is of finite valency and recursive. (We use here and in the sequel basic facts from recursion theory; see, e.g., [Ro67, Od89]).

Theorem 4. *If $R \subseteq \mathbb{N}^2$ is recursive and of finite valency, then the first-order theory of $(\mathbb{N}, <, R)$ belongs to level $\Sigma_4 \cap \Pi_4$ of the arithmetical hierarchy.*

Proof. It was shown above that each first-order sentence over $(\mathbb{N}, <, R)$, given the assumptions on R, is equivalent to a Boolean combination of Σ_3-sentences. Thus the first-order theory of $(\mathbb{N}, <, R)$ is Turing-reducible to a complete Σ_3-set. By the theorem of Kleene and Post on Turing-reducibility this means membership in $\Sigma_4 \cap \Pi_4$.

If R is not recursive, then one can establish a relativized version of the above theorem, obtaining that for a relation R of finite valency, the first-order theory of $(\mathbb{N}, <, R)$ is Turing-reducible to R''', the third jump of R. This gives another perspective on non-definability of addition and multiplication (together): If R is arithmetical, then the FO-theory of $(\mathbb{N}, <, R)$ is arithmetical as well and hence cannot be full first-order arithmetic.

From the results of Sect. 2 we know that for structures $(\mathbb{N}, <, P)$ with unary P, one obtains analogous results but with the levels of recursion theoretic complexity decreased by 1. Let us show that allowing binary R (of finite valency) really leads to a higher complexity.

Theorem 5. *There is a Π_3-complete set that is Turing-reducible to the first-order theory of $(\mathbb{N}, <, R)$ with a suitable recursive relation R of finite valency.*

Proof. Consider the following Π_3-complete set (where W_n is the n-th recursively enumerable set in some effective enumeration):

$$V_3 := \{m \mid \forall k \exists \ell > k (\ell \in W_m \wedge W_\ell = \emptyset)\}$$

So we have $m \in V_3$ iff W_m contains infinitely many indices of the empty set. We build a recursive relation R of finite valency. Let (ℓ_i, m_i) the i-th pair in an enumeration of all (ℓ, m) with $\ell \in W_m$.

We construct R in stages: At stage i

1. include $(i, i + m_i + 1)$ in R,
2. include (i, j) in R for all $j \leq i$ with $\ell_j = m_i$, but only if there is no i' with $j < i' < i$ and (i', j) already included in R,
3. (i, i) if $\ell_i = m_j$ for some $j \leq i$.

The relation R is recursive since for deciding $R(a, b)$ it suffices to run the procedure up to stage $\max(a, b)$. Also R is of finite valency since for any a there are at most three b with $R(a, b)$ or $R(b, a)$. By 1., a pair (i, k) is in R with $i < k$ codes an element of W_{m_i}. By 2. and 3., we have a pair (i', i) in R with $i' \geq i$ iff $W_{\ell_i} \neq \emptyset$. Hence $m \in V_3$ iff there are infinitely many $\ell \in W_m$ such that $W_\ell = \emptyset$ iff

$$(\mathbb{N}, <, R) \models \forall y \exists x > y \, (R(x, x + m + 1) \wedge \forall z \, \neg R(z, x))$$

However, one can sharpen the bound on the level of the arithmetical hierarchy where the FO-theory of $(\mathbb{N}, <, R)$ occurs when working with special relations R: Let us call R *effectively of finite valency* if the finite sets $N_a = \{b \mid R(a, b)\}$ and $N_b = \{a \mid R(a, b)\}$ are computable from a, b, respectively. It is easy to see that in this case the preceding theorems now hold in precise analogy to the case of unary predicates: The first-order theory of $(\mathbb{N}, <, R)$ is Turing-reducible to a complete Σ_2-set, and this bound is optimal.

As a last application we mention (without giving the tedious proof) a decidability result. For a monotone function $f : \mathbb{N} \to \mathbb{N}$ define Δ_f by $\Delta_f(n) = f(n + 1) - f(n)$. Call f *strongly monotone* if Δ_f is strictly monotone (in the sense that $x < y$ implies $\Delta_f(x) < \Delta_f(y)$). Note that in this case f itself is monotone (and even strictly monotone from the argument 1 onwards). Examples of strongly monotone functions are the natural enumerations of the set of squares, the set of powers of 2, the set of factorial numbers, etc. Each strongly monotone function is injective over the positive natural numbers, hence its graph is of finite valency. A closer analysis (not given here) of Theorem 2 in this context shows the following result:

Theorem 6. *If f is strongly monotone and recursive, the first-order theory of $(\mathbb{N}, <, f)$ is decidable.*

This result is in an interesting contrast to the case of the MSO-theories of structures $(\mathbb{N}, <, f)$. As Robinson showed in [Ro58], the MSO-theory of $(\mathbb{N}, <, d)$ is undecidable when d is the double function with $d(n) = 2n$. More generally, if we adjoin a unary function f with $f(n) \geq n$ which deviates from the identity in the sense that $\lambda n(f(n) - n)$ is monotone and unbounded, then the MSO-theory of $(\mathbb{N}, <, f)$ is undecidable ([Th75]). So a condition on the growth of unary functions f has opposite effects in FO-logic and MSO-logic.

For the function $f_\mathbb{P}$ given by $f_\mathbb{P}(i) = i$-th prime, $\Delta_{f_\mathbb{P}}$ is not strictly monotone. Indeed, it is open whether the first-order theory of $(\mathbb{N}, <, f_\mathbb{P})$ is decidable. Note that the twin-prime hypothesis holds iff the sentence

$$\forall x \exists y (x < y \wedge f_\mathbb{P}(y) + 2 = f_\mathbb{P}(y + 1))$$

is true in $(\mathbb{N}, <, f_\mathbb{P})$ (and where successor is defined in terms of $<$).

5   Conclusion

We have outlined a way to approach the first-order theory of a structure $(\mathbb{N}, <, R)$ using the idea of composition when R is of finite valency. It turns out that in the context of first-order logic these structures can be given an "ultimately periodic shape" when considering their m-types only. So, perhaps surprisingly, relations of finite valency show here a similarity to unary predicates.

With more technical work, one obtains analogous results when replacing a single relation R of finite valency by a tuple $(R_1, \ldots, R_n)$ of such relations. On the other hand, it is essential to work with an ordering that is of type ω or ω^*. For example, there is a relation R of finite valency over the ordinal ω^2 such that in the FO-theory of $(\omega^2, <, R)$ addition and multiplication over the first copy of ω are definable.

Let us finally mention an open question. As shown in Theorem 5, one can construct recursive relations R of finite valency such that the first-order theory of $(\mathbb{N}, <, R)$ is undecidable. However, these relations are built for the purpose and are based on recursion theoretic concepts. Are there "natural" relations R of finite valency, defined in a way not involving recursion theory, such that the first-order theory of $(\mathbb{N}, <, R)$ is undecidable?

Finally, it should be mentioned that in computer science the study of non-terminating behavior of systems may lead to ω-words equipped with binary relations, induced by connections between separated points of time (e.g. the call and the termination of procedures, or the occurrence of requests and their acknowledgments). It would be interesting to see whether the present work can be applied in such settings.

References

[Bü62] Büchi, J.R.: On a decision method in restricted second order arithmetic. In: Nagel, E., et al. (eds.) Proceedings of the 1960 International Congress for Logic, Methodology and Philosophy of Science, pp. 1–11. Stanford Univ. Press (1962)

[EF95] Ebbinghaus, H.-D., Flum, J.: Finite Model Theory. Springer, New York (1995)

[Gu79] Gurevich, Y.: Modest theory of short chains I. J. Symb. Logic **44**, 481–490 (1979)

[Gu82] Gurevich, Y.: Crumbly spaces. In: Sixth International Congress for Logic, Methodology, and Philosophy of Science (1979), pp. 179–191. North-Holland, Amsterdam (1982)

[Gu85] Gurevich, Y.: Monadic second-order theories. In: Barwise, J., Feferman, S. (eds.) Model-Theoretic Logics, pp. 479–506. Springer, Heidelberg (1985)

[GS79] Gurevich, Y., Shelah, S.: Modest theory of short chains II. J. Symb. Logic **44**, 491–502 (1979)

[GS83] Gurevich, Y., Shelah, S.: Rabin's uniformization problem. J. Symb. Logic **48**, 1105–1119 (1983)

[GS85] Gurevich, Y., Shelah, S.: The decision problem for branching time logic. J. Symb. Logic **50**, 668–681 (1985)

[Ha65] Hanf, W.: Model-theoretic methods in the study of first-order logic. In: Addison, J., et al. (eds.) The Theory of Models, pp. 132–145. North-Holland, Amsterdam (1965)

[Od89] Odifreddi, P.: Classical Recursion Theory. North-Holland, Amsterdam (1989)

[Ra69] Rabin, M.O.: Decidability of second-order theories and automata on infinite trees. Trans. Amer. Math. Soc. **141**, 1–35 (1969)

[Ra29] Ramsey, F.P.: On a problem of formal logic. Proc. London Math. Soc. **30**, 264–286 (1929)

[Ro58] Robinson, R.M.: Restricted set-theoretical definitions in arithmetic. Proc. Amer. Math. Soc. **9**, 238–242 (1958)

[Ro67] Rogers, H.: Theory of Recursive Functions and Effective Computability. McGraw-Hill, New York (1967)

[Sh75] Shelah, S.: The monadic theory of order. Ann. Math. **102**, 379–419 (1975)

[Th75] Thomas, W.: A note on undecidable extensions of monadic second-order arithmetic. Arch. Math. Logik Grundl. Math. **17**, 43–44 (1975)

[Th80] Thomas, W.: Relationen endlicher Valenz über der Ordnung der natürlichen Zahlen, Habilitationsschrift, Universität Freiburg (1980)

[Th81] Thomas, W.: A combinatorial approach to the theory of ω-automata. Inform. Contr. **48**, 261–283 (1979)

The Fundamental Nature of the Log Loss Function

Vladimir Vovk$^{(\boxtimes)}$

Department of Computer Science, Royal Holloway,
University of London, Egham, Surrey, UK
`v.vovk@rhul.ac.uk`

Abstract. The standard loss functions used in the literature on probabilistic prediction are the log loss function, the Brier loss function, and the spherical loss function; however, any computable proper loss function can be used for comparison of prediction algorithms. This note shows that the log loss function is most selective in that any prediction algorithm that is optimal for a given data sequence (in the sense of the algorithmic theory of randomness) under the log loss function will be optimal under any computable proper mixable loss function; on the other hand, there is a data sequence and a prediction algorithm that is optimal for that sequence under either of the two other standard loss functions but not under the log loss function.

Keywords: Algorithmic theory of randomness · Mixability · Predictive complexity · Predictive randomness · Probabilistic prediction · Proper loss functions

1 Introduction

In his work Yuri Gurevich has emphasized practical aspects of algorithmic randomness. In particular, he called for creating a formal framework allowing us to judge whether observed events can be regarded as random or point to something dubious going on (see, e.g., the discussion of the lottery organizer's wife winning the main prize in [5]). The beautiful classical theory of randomness started by Andrey Kolmogorov and Per Martin-Löf has to be restricted in order to achieve this goal and avoid its inherent incomputabilities and asymptotics.

This note tackles another practically-motivated question: what are the best loss functions for evaluating probabilistic prediction algorithms? Answering this question, however, requires extending rather than restricting the classical theory of algorithmic randomness.

In the empirical work on probabilistic prediction in machine learning (see, e.g., [2]) the most standard loss functions are log loss and Brier loss, and spherical loss is a viable alternative; all these loss functions will be defined later in this note. It is important to understand which of these three loss functions is likely to lead to better prediction algorithms. We formalize this question using

© Springer International Publishing Switzerland 2015
L.D. Beklemishev et al. (Eds.): Gurevich Festschrift II 2015, LNCS 9300, pp. 307–318, 2015.
DOI: 10.1007/978-3-319-23534-9_20

a generalization of the notion of Kolmogorov complexity called predictive complexity (see, e.g., [7]; it is defined in Sect. 3). Our answer is that the log loss function is likely to lead to better prediction algorithms as it is more selective: if a prediction algorithm is optimal under the log loss function, it will be optimal under the Brier and spherical loss functions, but the opposite implications are not true in general.

As we discuss at the end of Sect. 3, the log loss function corresponds to the classical theory of randomness. Therefore, our findings confirm once again the importance of the classical theory and are not surprising at all from the point of view of that theory. But from the point of view of experimental machine learning, our recommendation to use the log loss function rather than Brier or spherical is less trivial.

This note is, of course, not the first to argue that the log loss function is fundamental. For example, David Dowe has argued for it since at least 2008 ([3], footnote 175; see [4], Sect. 4.1, for further references). Another paper supporting the use of the log loss function is Bickel's [1].

2   Loss Functions

We are interested in the problem of binary probabilistic prediction: the task is to predict a binary label $y \in \{0, 1\}$ with a number $p \in [0, 1]$; intuitively, p is the predicted probability that $y = 1$. The quality of the prediction p is measured by a *loss function* $\lambda : [0, 1] \times \{0, 1\} \to \mathbb{R} \cup \{+\infty\}$. Intuitively, $\lambda(p, y)$ is the loss suffered by a prediction algorithm that outputs a prediction p while the actual label is y; the value $+\infty$ (from now on abbreviated to ∞) is allowed. Following [10], we will write $\lambda_y(p)$ in place of $\lambda(p, y)$, and so identify λ with the pair of functions (λ_0, λ_1) where $\lambda_0 : [0, 1] \to \mathbb{R} \cup \{+\infty\}$ and $\lambda_1 : [0, 1] \to \mathbb{R} \cup \{+\infty\}$. We will assume that $\lambda_0(0) = \lambda_1(1) = 0$, that the function λ_0 is increasing, that the function λ_1 is decreasing, and that $\lambda_y(p) < \infty$ unless $p \in \{0, 1\}$.

A loss function λ is called η-*mixable* for $\eta \in (0, \infty)$ if the set

$$\left\{ (u, v) \in [0, 1]^2 \mid \exists p \in [0, 1] : u \le e^{-\eta\lambda(p,0)} \text{ and } v \le e^{-\eta\lambda(p,1)} \right\}$$

is convex; we say that λ is *mixable* if it is η-mixable for some η.

A loss function λ is called *proper* if, for all $p, q \in [0, 1]$,

$$\mathbb{E}_p \lambda(p, \cdot) \le \mathbb{E}_p \lambda(q, \cdot), \tag{1}$$

where $\mathbb{E}_p f := pf(1) + (1 - p)f(0)$ for $f : \{0, 1\} \to \mathbb{R}$. It is *strictly proper* if the inequality in (1) is strict whenever $q \ne p$.

We will be only interested in computable loss functions (the notion of computability is not defined formally in this note; see, e.g., [7]). We will refer to the loss functions satisfying the properties listed above as *CPM* (computable proper mixable) loss functions.

Besides, we will sometimes make the following *smoothness assumptions*:

- λ_0 is infinitely differentiable over the interval $[0, 1)$ (the derivatives at 0 being one-sided);
- λ_1 is infinitely differentiable over the interval $(0, 1]$ (the derivatives at 1 being one-sided);
- for all $p \in (0, 1)$, $(\lambda_0'(p), \lambda_1'(p)) \neq 0$.

We will refer to the loss functions satisfying all the properties listed above as *CPMS* (computable proper mixable smooth) loss functions.

Examples

The most popular loss functions in machine learning are the *log loss function*

$$\lambda_1(p) := -\ln p, \quad \lambda_0(p) := -\ln(1 - p)$$

and the *Brier loss function*

$$\lambda(p, y) := (y - p)^2.$$

Somewhat less popular is the *spherical loss function*

$$\lambda_1(p) := 1 - \frac{p}{\sqrt{p^2 + (1 - p)^2}}, \quad \lambda_0(p) := 1 - \frac{1 - p}{\sqrt{p^2 + (1 - p)^2}}.$$

All three loss functions are mixable, as we will see later. They are also computable (obviously), strictly proper (this can be checked by differentiation), and satisfy the smoothness conditions (obviously). Being computable and strictly proper, these loss functions can be used to measure the quality of probabilistic predictions.

Mixability and Propriety

Intuitively, propriety can be regarded as a way of parameterizing loss functions, and we get it almost for free for mixable loss functions. The essence of a loss function is its *prediction set*

$$\{(\lambda_0(p), \lambda_1(p)) \mid p \in [0, 1]\}. \tag{2}$$

When given a prediction set, we can parameterize it by defining $(\lambda_0(p), \lambda_1(p))$ to be the point (x, y) of the prediction set at which $\inf_{(x,y)}(py + (1-p)x)$ is attained. This will give us a proper loss function. And if the original loss function satisfies the smoothness conditions (and so, intuitively, the prediction set does not have corners), the new loss function will be strictly proper.

3   Repetitive Predictions

Starting from this section we consider the situation, typical in machine learning, where we repeatedly observe data $z_1, z_2, \ldots$ and each observation $z_t = (x_t, y_t) \in$

$\mathbf{Z} = \mathbf{X} \times \{0, 1\}$ consists of an *object* $x_t \in \mathbf{X}$ and its *label* $y_t \in \{0, 1\}$. Let us assume, for simplicity, that $\mathbf{X}$ is a finite set, say a set of natural numbers.

A *prediction algorithm* is a computable function $F : \mathbf{Z}^* \times \mathbf{X} \to [0, 1]$; intuitively, given a data sequence $\sigma = (z_1, \ldots, z_T)$ and a new object x, F outputs a prediction $F(\sigma, x)$ for the label of x. For any data sequence $\sigma = (z_1, \ldots, z_T)$ and loss function λ, we define the cumulative loss that F suffers on σ as

$$\text{Loss}_F^\lambda(\sigma) := \sum_{t=1}^{T} \lambda(F(z_1, \ldots, z_{t-1}, x_t), y_t)$$

(where $z_t = (x_t, y_t)$ and $\infty + a$ is defined to be ∞ for any $a \in \mathbb{R} \cup \{\infty\}$). Functions $\text{Loss}_F^\lambda : \mathbf{Z}^* \to \mathbb{R}$ that can be defined this way for a given λ are called *loss processes under* λ. In other words, $L : \mathbf{Z}^* \to \mathbb{R}$ is a loss process under λ if and only if $L(\square) = 0$ (where $\square$ is the empty sequence) and

$$\forall \sigma \in \mathbf{Z}^* \, \forall x \in \mathbf{X} \, \exists p \in [0, 1] \, \forall y \in \{0, 1\} : L(\sigma, x, y) = L(\sigma) + \lambda(p, y). \quad (3)$$

A function $L : \mathbf{Z}^* \to \mathbb{R}$ is said to be a *superloss process under* λ if (3) holds with $\geq$ in place of $=$. If λ is computable and mixable, there exists a smallest, to within an additive constant, upper semicomputable superloss process:

$$\exists L_1 \, \forall L_2 \, \exists c \in \mathbb{R} \, \forall \sigma \in \mathbf{Z}^* : L_1(\sigma) \leq L_2(\sigma) + c,$$

where L_1 and L_2 range over upper semicomputable superloss processes under λ. (For a precise statement and proof, see [7], Theorem 1, Lemma 6, and Corollary 3; [7] only considers the case of a trivial one-element $\mathbf{X}$, but the extension to the case of general $\mathbf{X}$ is easy.) For each computable mixable λ (including the log, Brier, and spherical loss functions), fix such a smallest upper semicomputable superloss process; it will be denoted $\mathcal{K}^\lambda$, and $\mathcal{K}^\lambda(\sigma)$ will be called the *predictive complexity* of $\sigma \in \mathbf{Z}^*$ under λ. The intuition behind $\mathcal{K}^\lambda(\sigma)$ is that this is the loss of the ideal prediction strategy whose computation is allowed to take an infinite amount of time.

In this note we consider infinite data sequences $\zeta \in \mathbf{Z}^\infty$, which are idealizations of long finite data sequences. If $\zeta = (z_1, z_2, \ldots) \in \mathbf{Z}^\infty$ and T is a nonnegative integer, we let ζ^T to stand for the prefix $z_1 \ldots z_T$ of ζ of length T.

The *randomness deficiency* of $\sigma \in \mathbf{Z}^*$ with respect to a prediction algorithm F under a computable mixable loss function λ is defined to be

$$D_F^\lambda(\sigma) := \text{Loss}_F^\lambda(\sigma) - \mathcal{K}^\lambda(\sigma); \quad (4)$$

since Loss_F^λ is upper semicomputable ([7], Sect. 3.1), the function $D_F^\lambda : \mathbf{Z}^* \to \mathbb{R}$ is bounded below. Notice that the indeterminacy $\infty - \infty$ never arises in (4) as $\mathcal{K}^\lambda < \infty$. We will sometimes replace the upper index λ in any of the three terms of (4) by "ln" in the case where λ is the log loss function.

Let us say that $\zeta \in \mathbf{Z}^\infty$ is *random with respect to F under* λ if

$$\sup_T D_F^\lambda(\zeta^T) < \infty.$$

The intuition is that in this case F is an optimal prediction algorithm for ζ under λ.

Log Randomness

In the case where λ is the log loss function and $\mathbf{X}$ is a one-element set, the predictive complexity of a finite data sequence σ (which is now a binary sequence if we ignore the uninformative objects) is equal, to within an additive constant, to $-\ln M(\sigma)$, where M is Levin's *a priori* semimeasure. (In terms of this note, a *semimeasure* can be defined as a process of the form e^{-L} for some superloss process L under the log loss function; *Levin's* a priori *semimeasure* is a largest, to within a constant factor, lower semicomputable semimeasure.) The randomness deficiency $D_F^{\ln}(\sigma)$ of σ with respect to a prediction algorithm F is then, to within an additive constant, $\ln(M(\sigma)/P(\sigma))$, where P is the probability measure corresponding to F,

$$P(y_1, \ldots, y_T) := \bar{p}_1 \cdots \bar{p}_T, \quad \bar{p}_t := \begin{cases} F(y_1, \ldots, y_{t-1}) & \text{if } y_t = 1 \\ 1 - F(y_1, \ldots, y_{t-1}) & \text{if } y_t = 0 \end{cases}$$

(we continue to ignore the objects, which are not informative). Therefore, $D_F^{\ln}(\sigma)$ is a version of the classical randomness deficiency of σ, and $\zeta \in \{0, 1\}^\infty$ is random with respect to F under the log loss function if and only if ζ is random with respect to P in the sense of Martin Löf.

4   A Simple Statement of Fundamentality

In this section, we consider computable proper mixable loss functions.

Theorem 1. *Let λ be a CPM loss function. If a data sequence $\zeta \in \mathbf{Z}^\infty$ is random under the log loss function with respect to a prediction algorithm F, it is random under λ with respect to F.*

A special case of this theorem is stated as Proposition 16 in [13].

Let us say that a CPM loss function λ is *fundamental* if it can be used in place of the log loss function in Theorem 1. The proof of the theorem will in fact demonstrate its following quantitative form: for any computable $\eta > 0$ and any computable proper η-mixable λ there exists a constant c_λ such that, for any prediction algorithm F,

$$D_F^{\ln} \geq \eta D_F^\lambda - c_\lambda. \tag{5}$$

Let us define the *mixability constant* η_λ of a loss function λ as the supremum of η such that λ is η-mixable. It is known that a mixable loss function λ is η_λ-mixable ([12], Lemmas 10 and 12); therefore, (5) holds for $\eta = \eta_\lambda$, provided η_λ is computable.

If $\mathbf{X}$ is a one-element set (and so the objects do not play any role and can be ignored), the notion of randomness under the log loss function coincides with the standard Martin-Löf randomness, as discussed in the previous section. Theorem 1 shows that other notions of randomness are either equivalent or weaker.

A *superprediction* is a point in the plane that lies Northeast of the prediction set (2) (i.e., a point $(x, y) \in \mathbb{R}^2$ such that $\lambda_0(p) \leq x$ and $\lambda_1(p) \leq y$ for some $p \in [0, 1]$).

Proof (of Theorem 1). We will prove (5) for a fixed $\eta \in (0, \infty)$ such that η is computable and λ is η-mixable. Let L be a superloss process under λ and F be a prediction algorithm. Fix temporarily $(\sigma, x) \in \mathbf{Z}^* \times \mathbf{X}$ and set $p := F(\sigma, x) \in [0, 1]$; notice that $(a, b) := (L(\sigma, x, 0) - L(\sigma), L(\sigma, x, 1) - L(\sigma))$ is a λ-superprediction. By the definition of η-mixability there exists a parallel translation of the curve $e^{-\eta x} + e^{-\eta y} = 1$ that passes through the point $\lambda^p := (\lambda_0(p), \lambda_1(p))$ and lies Southeast of the prediction set of λ. Let h be the affine transformation of the plane mapping that translation onto the curve $e^{-x} + e^{-y} = 1$; notice that h is the composition of the scaling $(x, y) \mapsto \eta(x, y)$ by η and then parallel translation moving the point $\eta\lambda^p$ to the point $(-\ln(1 - p), -\ln p)$. The λ-superprediction (a, b) is mapped by h to the ln-superprediction

$$(\eta a + (-\ln(1 - p)) - \eta\lambda_0(p), \eta b + (-\ln p) - \eta\lambda_1(p)).$$

We can see that $\eta L + \operatorname{Loss}_F^{\ln} - \eta \operatorname{Loss}_F^{\lambda}$ is a superloss process under $\ln$. It is clear that this ln-superloss process is upper semicomputable if L is. Therefore, for some constant c_λ,

$$\mathcal{K}^{\ln} \leq \eta \mathcal{K}^{\lambda} + \operatorname{Loss}_F^{\ln} - \eta \operatorname{Loss}_F^{\lambda} + c_\lambda,$$

which is equivalent to (5). □

5   A Criterion of Fundamentality

In this section, we only consider computable proper mixable loss functions that satisfy, additionally, the smoothness conditions. The main result of this section is the following elaboration of Theorem 1 for CPMS loss functions.

Theorem 2. *A CPMS loss function λ is fundamental if and only if*

$$\inf_p (1 - p)\lambda_0'(p) > 0. \tag{6}$$

Equivalently, it is fundamental if and only if

$$\inf_p (-p)\lambda_1'(p) > 0. \tag{7}$$

We can classify CPMS loss functions λ by their *degree*

$$\deg(\lambda) := \inf \left\{ k : \lambda_0^{(k)}(0) \neq 0 \text{ and } \lambda_1^{(k)}(1) \neq 0 \right\},$$

where (k) stands for the kth derivative and, as usual, $\inf \emptyset := \infty$. We will see later in this section that Theorem 2 can be restated to say that the fundamental loss functions are exactly those of degree 1. Furthermore, we will see that for a CPMS loss function λ of degree $1 < k < \infty$ there exist a data sequence $\zeta \in \mathbf{Z}^\infty$ and a prediction algorithm F such that ζ is random with respect to F under λ while the randomness deficiency $D_F^{\ln}(\zeta^T)$ of ζ^T with respect to F under the log loss function grows almost as fast as $T^{1-1/k}$ as $T \to \infty$.

Straightforward calculations show that the log loss function has degree 1 and the Brier and spherical loss functions have degree 2.

In the proof of Theorem 2 we will need the notion of the *signed curvature* of the *prediction curve* $(\lambda_0(p), \lambda_1(p))$ at a point $p \in (0, 1)$, which can be defined as

$$k_\lambda(p) := \frac{\lambda_0'(p)\lambda_1''(p) - \lambda_1'(p)\lambda_0''(p)}{(\lambda_0'(p)^2 + \lambda_1'(p)^2)^{3/2}}. \tag{8}$$

The mixability constant η_λ (i.e., the largest η for which λ is η-mixable) is

$$\eta_\lambda = \inf_p \frac{k_\lambda(p)}{k_{\ln}(p)}.$$

Therefore, λ is mixable if and only if

$$\inf_p \frac{k_\lambda(p)}{k_{\ln}(p)} > 0. \tag{9}$$

Lemma 1. *A CPMS loss function λ is fundamental if and only if*

$$\sup_p \frac{k_\lambda(p)}{k_{\ln}(p)} < \infty$$

(cf. (9)).

The proof the part "if" of Lemma 1 goes along the same lines as the proof of Theorem 1, and also shows that, if λ and Λ are CPMS loss functions such that

$$\eta_\lambda := \inf_p \frac{k_\lambda(p)}{k_{\ln}(p)} > 0 \quad \text{and} \quad H_\Lambda := \sup_p \frac{k_\Lambda(p)}{k_{\ln}(p)} < \infty$$

are computable numbers, then there exists $c_{\lambda,\Lambda} \in \mathbb{R}$ such that, for any prediction algorithm F,

$$H_\Lambda D_F^\Lambda \geq \eta_\lambda D_F^\lambda - c_{\lambda,\Lambda}.$$

We will call H_Λ the *fundamentality constant* of Λ (analogously to η_λ being called the mixability constant of λ).

Notice that the log loss function (perhaps scaled by multiplying by a positive constant) is the only loss function for which the mixability and fundamentality constants coincide, $\eta_{\ln} = H_{\ln}$. Therefore, fundamental CPMS loss functions can be regarded as log-loss-like.

The part "only if" of Lemma 1 will be proved below, in the proof of Theorem 2.

The computation of k_λ for the three basic loss functions using (8) gives:

– For the log loss function, the result is

$$k_{\ln}(p) = \frac{p(1-p)}{(p^2 + (1-p)^2)^{3/2}}. \tag{10}$$

– For the Brier loss function, the result is

$$k_{\text{Brier}}(p) = \frac{1}{2} \frac{1}{(p^2 + (1-p)^2)^{3/2}}.$$

– For the spherical loss function, the result is

$$k_{\text{spher}}(p) = 1.$$

We can plug the expression (10) for the signed curvature of the log loss function into Lemma 1 to obtain a more explicit statement. Because of the propriety of λ, this statement can be simplified, which gives the following corollary.

Corollary 1. *A CPMS loss function λ is fundamental if and only if*

$$\sup_p \frac{\lambda_0'(p)\lambda_1''(p) - \lambda_1'(p)\lambda_0''(p)}{\lambda_0'(p)\lambda_1'(p)(\lambda_1'(p) - \lambda_0'(p))} < \infty. \tag{11}$$

Proof. In view of the expressions (8) and (10), the condition in Lemma 1 can be written as

$$\sup_p \frac{\lambda_0'(p)\lambda_1''(p) - \lambda_1'(p)\lambda_0''(p)}{(\lambda_0'(p)^2 + \lambda_1'(p)^2)^{3/2}} \frac{(p^2 + (1-p)^2)^{3/2}}{p(1-p)} < \infty.$$

Therefore, it suffices to check that

$$\frac{(\lambda_0'(p)^2 + \lambda_1'(p)^2)^{3/2}}{\lambda_0'(p)\lambda_1'(p)(\lambda_1'(p) - \lambda_0'(p))} = \frac{(p^2 + (1-p)^2)^{3/2}}{p(1-p)}.$$

The last equality follows from

$$\frac{\lambda_1'(p)}{\lambda_0'(p)} = \frac{p-1}{p}, \tag{12}$$

which in turn follows from the propriety of λ. $\qquad\square$

It is instructive to compare the criterion (11) with the well-known criterion

$$\inf_p \frac{\lambda_0'(p)\lambda_1''(p) - \lambda_1'(p)\lambda_0''(p)}{\lambda_0'(p)\lambda_1'(p)(\lambda_1'(p) - \lambda_0'(p))} > 0 \tag{13}$$

for λ being mixable (see, e.g., [6] or [8], Theorem 2; it goes back to [11], Lemma 1). The criterion (13) can be derived from (9) as in the proof of Corollary 1.

Proof (of Theorem 2). Differentiating (12) we obtain

$$\frac{\lambda_1''(p)\lambda_0'(p) - \lambda_1'(p)\lambda_0''(p)}{\lambda_0'(p)^2} = p^{-2},$$

and the fundamentality constant (11) of λ is

$$\sup_p \frac{p^{-2}\lambda_0'(p)^2}{\lambda_0'(p)\lambda_1'(p)(\lambda_1'(p)-\lambda_0'(p))} = \sup_p \frac{p^{-2}}{\lambda_0'(p)(\lambda_1'(p)/\lambda_0'(p))(\lambda_1'(p)/\lambda_0'(p)-1)}$$

$$= \sup_p \frac{p^{-2}}{\lambda_0'(p)(1-1/p)(-1/p)} = \sup_p \frac{1}{\lambda_0'(p)(1-p)},$$

where we have used (12). This gives us (6); in combination with (12) we get (7).

Let us now prove the part "only if" of Theorem 2 (partly following the argument given after Proposition 16 of [13]). According to (6), (7) and (12) are equivalent. Suppose that

$$\inf_p (1-p)\lambda_0'(p) = 0,$$

and let us check that λ is not fundamental. By the smoothness assumptions, we have $(1-p)\lambda_0'(p) = 0$ either for $p = 0$ or for $p = 1$. Suppose, for concreteness, that $(1-p)\lambda_0'(p) = 0$ for $p = 0$ (if $(1-p)\lambda_0'(p) = 0$ for $p = 1$, we will have $(-p)\lambda_1'(p) = 0$ for $p = 1$, and we can apply the same argument as below for $p = 1$ in place of $p = 0$). Let k be such that $\lambda_0^{(k)}(0) > 0$ but $\lambda_0^{(i)}(0) = 0$ for all $i < k$; we know that $k \geq 2$ (the easy case where $\lambda_0^{(i)}(0) = 0$ for all i should be considered separately). Consider any data sequence $\zeta = (x_1, y_1, x_2, y_2, \ldots) \in \mathbf{Z}^\infty$ in which all labels are 0: $y_1 = y_2 = \cdots = 0$. We then have $\sup_T K^{\ln}(\zeta^T) < \infty$ and $\sup_T K^\lambda(\zeta^T) < \infty$. Let F be the prediction algorithm that outputs $p_t := t^{-1/k-\epsilon}$ at step t, where $\epsilon \in (0, 1-1/k)$. Then ζ is random with respect to F under λ since the loss of this prediction algorithm over the first T steps is

$$\sum_{t=1}^{T} \lambda_0(p_t) \leq 2 \sum_{t=1}^{T} \frac{\lambda_0^{(k)}(0)}{k!} p_t^k + O(1)$$

(we have used Taylor's approximation for λ_0) and the series $\sum_t p_t^k$ is convergent. On the other hand, the randomness deficiency of ζ^T with respect to F under the log loss function grows as

$$-\sum_{t=1}^{T} \ln(1-p_t) \sim \sum_{t=1}^{T} p_t \sim \frac{k}{k-1-k\epsilon} T^{1-1/k-\epsilon}.$$

$\square$

Notice that the criterion of mixability (13) can be simplified when we use (12): it becomes

$$\sup_p (1-p)\lambda_0'(p) < \infty$$

or, equivalently,

$$\sup_p (-p)\lambda_1'(p) < \infty.$$

The function $(1-p)\lambda_0'(p) = (-p)\lambda_1'(p)$ can be computed as

– 1 in the case of the log loss function;
– $2p(1 - p)$ in the case of the Brier loss function;
– $p(1 - p)(p^2 + (1 - p)^2)^{-3/2}$ in the case of the spherical loss function.

Therefore, all three loss functions are mixable, but only the log loss function is fundamental.

It is common in experimental machine learning to truncate allowed probabilistic predictions to the interval $[\epsilon, 1 - \epsilon]$ for a small constant $\epsilon > 0$ (this boils down to cutting off the ends of the prediction sets corresponding to the slopes below ϵ and above $1 - \epsilon$). It is easy to check that in this case all CPMS loss functions lead to the same notion of randomness.

Corollary 2. *CPMS loss functions λ and Λ restricted to $p \in [\epsilon, 1 - \epsilon]$, where $\epsilon > 0$, lead to the same notion of randomness.*

We can make the corollary more precise as follows: for prediction algorithms F restricted to $[\epsilon, 1 - \epsilon]$, D_F^{λ} and D_F^{Λ} coincide to within a factor of

$$\max \left(\sup_{p \in [\epsilon, 1-\epsilon]} \frac{k_{\lambda}(p)}{k_{\Lambda}(p)}, \sup_{p \in [\epsilon, 1-\epsilon]} \frac{k_{\Lambda}(p)}{k_{\lambda}(p)} \right)$$

and an additive constant.

6   Frequently Asked Questions

This section is more discursive than the previous ones; "frequently" in its title means "at least once" (but with a reasonable expectation that a typical reader might well ask similar questions).

What is the role of the requirement of propriety in Theorem 1?

The theorem says that the log loss function leads to the most restrictive notion of randomness: if a sequence is random with respect to some prediction algorithm under the log loss function, then it is random with respect to the "same" prediction algorithm under an arbitrary CPM loss function. One should explain, however, what is meant by the same prediction algorithm, because of the freedom in parameterization (say, we can replace each prediction p by p^2). The requirement of propriety imposes a canonical parameterization.

What is the role of the requirement of mixability in Theorem 1?

The requirement of mixability ensures the existence of predictive complexity, which is used in the definition of predictive randomness.

Mixability is sufficient for the existence of predictive complexity (for computable loss functions). Is it also necessary?

Yes, it is: see Theorem 1 in [9].

What is the geometric intuition behind the notions of propriety and mixability?

The intuitions behind the two notions overlap; both involve requirements of convexity of the "superprediction set" (the area Northeast of the prediction set (2)). Let us suppose that the loss function λ is continuous in the prediction p, so that the prediction set is a curve. Propriety then means that the superprediction set is strictly convex (in particular, the prediction set has no straight segments) and that the points on the prediction set are indexed in a canonical way (namely, each such point is indexed by $1/(1 - s)$ where $s < 0$ is the slope of the tangent line to the prediction set at that point: cf. (12)). Mixability means that the superprediction set is convex in a stronger sense: it stays convex after being transformed by the mapping $(x, y) \in [0, \infty]^2 \mapsto (e^{-\eta x}, e^{-\eta y})$ for some $\eta > 0$.

Why should we consider not only the log loss function (which nicely corresponds to probability distributions) but also other loss functions? You say "the log loss function, being most selective, should be preferred to the alternatives such as Brier or spherical loss". But this does not explain why these other loss functions were interesting in the first place.

Loss functions different from the log loss function are widely used in practice; in particular, the Brier loss function is at least as popular as (and perhaps even more popular than) the log loss function in machine learning: see, e.g., the extensive empirical study [2]. An important reason for the popularity of Brier loss is that the log loss function often leads to infinite average losses on large test sets for state-of-the-art prediction algorithms, which is considered to be "unfair", and some researchers even believe that any reasonable loss function should be bounded.

7   Conclusion

This note offers an answer to the problem of choosing a loss function for evaluating probabilistic prediction algorithms in experimental machine learning. Our answer is that the log loss function, being most selective, should be preferred to the alternatives such as Brier or spherical loss. This answer, however, remains asymptotic (involving unspecified constants) and raises further questions. To make it really practical, we need to restrict our generalized theory of algorithmic randomness, as Yuri did in a different context.

Acknowledgments. I am grateful to Mitya Adamskiy, Yuri Kalnishkan, Ilia Nouretdinov, Ivan Petej, and Vladimir V'yugin for useful discussions. Thanks to an anonymous reviewer whose remarks prompted me to add Sect. 6 (and were used in both questions and answers). This work has been supported by EPSRC (grant EP/K033344/1) and the Air Force Office of Scientific Research (grant "Semantic Completions").

References

1. Bickel, J.E.: Some comparisons among quadratic, spherical, and logarithmic scoring rules. Decis. Anal. **4**, 49–65 (2007)
2. Caruana, R., Niculescu-Mizil, A.: An empirical comparison of supervised learning algorithms. In: Proceedings of the Twenty Third International Conference on Machine Learning, pp. 161–168. ACM, New York (2006)
3. Dowe, D.L., Wallace, C.S.: Foreword re C. Comput. J. **51**, 523–560 (2008)
4. Dowe, D.L.: Introduction to Ray Solomonoff 85th memorial conference. In: Dowe, D.L. (ed.) Algorithmic Probability and Friends. LNCS, vol. 7070, pp. 1–36. Springer, Heidelberg (2013)
5. Gurevich, Y., Passmore, G.O.: Impugning randomness, convincingly. Stud. Logica. **82**, 1–31 (2012)
6. Haussler, D., Kivinen, J., Warmuth, M.K.: Sequential prediction of individual sequences under general loss functions. IEEE Trans. Inf. Theory **44**, 1906–1925 (1998)
7. Kalnishkan, Y.: Predictive complexity for games with finite outcome spaces. In: Vovk, V., Papadopoulos, H., Gammerman, A. (eds.) Measures of Complexity: Festschrift for Alexey Chervonenkis, pp. 119–141. Springer, Berlin (2015)
8. Kalnishkan, Y., Vovk, V.: The existence of predictive complexity and the Legendre transformation.Technical report. CLRC-TR-00-04, Computer Learning Research Centre, Royal Holloway, University of London (March 2000)
9. Kalnishkan, Y., Vovk, V., Vyugin, M.V.: A criterion for the existence of predictive complexity for binary games. In: Ben-David, S., Case, J., Maruoka, A. (eds.) ALT 2004. LNCS (LNAI), vol. 3244, pp. 249–263. Springer, Heidelberg (2004)
10. Reid, M.D., Frongillo, R.M., Williamson, R.C., Mehta, N.: Generalized mixability via entropic duality. In: Proceedings of the 28th Conference on Learning Theory, pp. 1501–1522 (2015)
11. Vovk, V.: Aggregating strategies. In: Fulk, M., Case, J. (eds.) Proceedings of the Third Annual Workshop on Computational Learning Theory, pp. 371–383. Morgan Kaufmann, San Mateo (1990)
12. Vovk, V.: A game of prediction with expert advice. J. Comput. Syst. Sci. **56**, 153–173 (1998)
13. Vovk, V.: Probability theory for the Brier game. Theoret. Comput. Sci. **261**, 57–79 (2001)

Author Index

Printed in the United States
By Bookmasters